GMAT® 2016

STRATEGIES, PRACTICE, AND REVIEW

PUBLISHING

New York

© 2015 by Kaplan, Inc.

Published by Kaplan Publishing, a division of Kaplan, Inc.
395 Hudson Street
New York, NY 10014

Printed in the United States of America

10 9 8 7 6 5 4 3 2 1

ISBN: 978-1-62523-136-9

Kaplan Publishing print books are available at special quantity discounts to use for sales promotions, employee premiums, or educational purposes. For more information or to purchase books, please call the Simon & Schuster special sales department at 866-506-1949.

CONTENTS

How to Use This Book vii

PART ONE: THE GMAT

Chapter 1: Introduction to the GMAT 3

    GMAT Format 3

    GMAT Scoring 4

    GMAT Attitude 7

    GMAT Checklist 9

Chapter 2: Understanding the CAT 13

    The CAT Explained 13

    Are the First Questions More Important? 15

    The Importance of Pacing 16

    Other CAT Strategies 17

PART TWO: PRETEST

Chapter 3: GMAT Pretest 21

    How to Take This Test 21

    GMAT Pretest Answer Sheet 23

Chapter 4: Pretest Answers and Explanations 61

    How to Review This Test 61

    Answer Key 63

    Pretest Scoring Tool 64

    Quantitative Section Explanations 65

    Verbal Section Explanations 83

PART THREE: VERBAL SECTION AND STRATEGIES

Chapter 5: Verbal Section Overview **105**

Composition of the Verbal Section 105

Pacing on the Verbal Section 106

How the Verbal Section Is Scored 108

Core Competencies on the Verbal Section 108

Introduction to Strategic Reading 113

Chapter 6: Critical Reasoning **117**

Previewing Critical Reasoning 118

Question Format and Structure 119

The Basic Principles of Critical Reasoning 120

The Kaplan Method for Critical Reasoning 125

Critical Reasoning Question Types 128

Advanced Strategies: Three Special Cases 166

Critical Reasoning Quiz 180

Answers and Explanations 186

GMAT by the Numbers: Critical Reasoning 231

Chapter 7: Reading Comprehension **233**

Previewing Reading Comprehension 234

Question Format and Structure 236

The Basic Principles of Reading Comprehension 236

The Kaplan Method for Reading Comprehension 246

Reading Comprehension Question Types 254

Reading Comprehension Quiz 268

Answers and Explanations 284

GMAT by the Numbers: Reading Comprehension 335

Chapter 8: Sentence Correction **341**

Previewing Sentence Correction 342

Question Format and Structure 343

The Kaplan Method for Sentence Correction 343

Commonly Tested Grammar on the GMAT 348

Answers and Explanations 400

GMAT by the Numbers: Sentence Correction 467

PART FOUR: QUANTITATIVE SECTION AND STRATEGIES

Chapter 9: Quantitative Section Overview 471

    Composition of the Quantitative Section 471

    What the Quantitative Section Tests.. 472

    Pacing on the Quantitative Section 473

    How the Quantitative Section Is Scored.................................... 474

    Core Competencies on the Quantitative Section 475

Chapter 10: Problem Solving.. 481

    Previewing Problem Solving 482

    Question Format and Structure.. 484

    The Kaplan Method for Problem Solving 485

    The Basic Principles of Problem Solving.................................... 489

    Problem Solving Strategy... 495

    Answers and Explanations 523

    GMAT by the Numbers: Problem Solving 547

Chapter 11: Data Sufficiency.. 549

    Previewing Data Sufficiency 550

    Question Format and Structure.. 551

    The Kaplan Method for Data Sufficiency 552

    The Basic Principles of Data Sufficiency.................................... 558

    Data Sufficiency Strategy... 568

    Answers and Explanations 577

    GMAT by the Numbers: Data Sufficiency 597

Chapter 12: GMAT Math Fundamentals 599

    Arithmetic.. 599

    Number Properties.. 604

    Proportions and Math Formulas 614

    Algebra 636

    Statistics... 648

    Geometry 653

    Other Topics 676

PART FIVE: ANALYTICAL WRITING AND INTEGRATED REASONING SECTIONS

Chapter 13: Analytical Writing Assessment................................... **685**

    Essay Format and Structure..686

    The Basic Principles of Analytical Writing................................686

    How the AWA Is Scored...689

    The Kaplan Method for Analytical Writing 691

    Breakdown: Analysis of an Argument....................................693

    GMAT Style Checklist 698

    Practice Essays...700

Chapter 14: Integrated Reasoning **707**

    Section Format and Structure...707

    The Integrated Reasoning Question Types.................................709

    Conclusion 749

PART SIX: TEST DAY AND BUSINESS SCHOOL

Chapter 15: Take Control of Test Day **753**

    Mental Conditioning 753

    Stress Management...755

    Stress Management Quiz 757

    The Week Before Test Day 761

    On Test Day..761

    Cancellation and Multiple Scores Policy 763

**Chapter 16: Business School Admissions Myths Destroyed
             (Before They Destroy You!)** **765**

    Myth #1: The Admissions Committee Wants a Specific Type 766

    Myth #2: My High GMAT Score Will Get Me In 767

    Myth #3: My Supervisor Graduated from HBS—He Knows 767

    Myth #4: If I Did Not Go to an Ivy, I'm Not Getting In.........................768

    Myth #5: If I Have a Gap in My History, I'm Not Getting In 768

    Myth #6: If I Have No Managerial Experience, I'm Not Getting In.................769

    Myth #7: I Must Submit in Round 1 770

    Myth #8: Writing My Own Recommendation Puts Me in the Driver's Seat.........771

    Myth #9: HBS Is for Everyone 771

    Myth #10: If My Application Has a Typo, I'm Not Getting In 772

How to Use This Book

WELCOME TO KAPLAN'S GMAT 2016 STRATEGIES, PRACTICE, AND REVIEW

Congratulations on your decision to pursue an MBA or other graduate management degree, and thank you for choosing Kaplan for your GMAT preparation.

You've made the right choice in acquiring this book—you're now armed with a convenient and efficient GMAT program that is the result of decades of researching the GMAT and teaching many thousands of students the skills they need to succeed. You have what you need to score higher; the next step is to commit to a study plan that will help you to achieve your goals.

Let's start by walking you through everything you need to know to take advantage of this book and your Online Center.

YOUR BOOK

There are two main components to your *GMAT Strategies, Practice, and Review* study package: your book and your Online Center. This book contains the following:

- Detailed instruction covering the essential verbal, math, and writing concepts

- Time-tested and effective Kaplan Methods and strategies for every question type

- A pretest (Chapter 3) featuring full-length Quantitative and Verbal sections, designed to help you diagnose your strengths and weaknesses

- Over 250 practice questions, followed by detailed answer explanations

YOUR ONLINE CENTER

Your Kaplan Online Center gives you access to a full-length computer-adaptive practice test (CAT) and analysis of your performance, including detailed answer explanations. Don't forget to take advantage of this valuable resource.

You will also find practice sets for the Integrated Reasoning section in your Online Center, since these interactive question formats are better presented in the computer-based test interface than in a printed book.

GETTING STARTED

Studying for the GMAT can be daunting, and it may not be clear where to begin. Don't worry; we'll break it down one step at a time, just the way we'll break down the GMAT questions that you will soon be on your way to mastering.

GETTING STARTED

1. Register your Online Center.

2. Sign up for a free Classroom Anywhere event.

3. Take a GMAT practice test to identify your strengths and weaknesses.

4. Create a study plan.

5. Learn and practice using this book.

6. Take another practice test to gauge your progress.

STEP 1: REGISTER YOUR ONLINE CENTER

Register your Online Center using these simple steps:

1. Go to **kaptest.com/booksonline.**

2. Follow the on-screen instructions. Please have a copy of your book available.

Access to the Online Center is limited to the original owner of this book and is nontransferable. Kaplan is not responsible for providing access to the Online Center to customers who purchase or borrow used copies of this book. Access to the Online Center expires one year after you register.

STEP 2: SIGN UP FOR A FREE CLASSROOM ANYWHERE EVENT

Kaplan's GMAT Classroom Anywhere events are interactive, instructor-led GMAT training sessions that you can join from anywhere you can access the Internet.

Classroom Anywhere events are held in a state-of-the-art virtual classroom in real time, just like a physical classroom experience. You'll interact with your teacher and other classmates using audio, instant chat, whiteboard, polling, and screen-sharing functionality. And just like in-person courses, a GMAT Classroom Anywhere event is led by an experienced Kaplan instructor.

To register for a free GMAT Classroom Anywhere event, go to your Online Center or to **KaplanGMAT.com** and search for a free event. (You may be asked for a U.S. or Canadian ZIP code; Classroom Anywhere events are available for all locations.)

STEP 3: TAKE A GMAT PRACTICE TEST

It's essential to take a practice test early on. Doing so will give you the initial feedback and diagnostic information that you will need to achieve your maximum score. Taking a full-length test right at the start can be intimidating. Place enough importance on your practice test to turn off your cell phone, give the test your full attention, and learn from your performance. But also remember: Your practice test score does not count.

We highly recommend you start by taking the full-length test found in your Online Center. This test is a computer-adaptive test in the same format as the actual GMAT. However, for your convenience, we've also included a paper-based pretest in Chapter 3 of this book. The pretest includes full-length Quantitative and Verbal sections and will give you a chance to familiarize yourself with the various question types. It also allows you to accurately gauge the content you know and identify areas for practice and review.

Review the detailed answer explanations to better understand your performance. Our explanations label each question according to its question type and topic; these labels align with the material covered throughout this book. Look for patterns in the questions you answered correctly and incorrectly. Were you stronger in some areas than others? This analysis will help you target your practice time to specific concepts.

STEP 4: CREATE A STUDY PLAN

Use what you've learned from your initial practice test to identify areas for closer study and practice. Take time to familiarize yourself with the key components of this book. Think about how many hours you can consistently devote to GMAT study. We have found that most students have success with about three months of committed preparation before Test Day.

Consider the following statistic as you build your study plan: According to the GMAT testmaker, the average 600+ or 700+ scorer prepares for the GMAT for about 100 hours. We've designed this book to give you only the most essential content and strategies to help you focus your preparation. Working through this book thoroughly and taking and reviewing your online practice test should get you to about 35 hours of study. That 35 hours may be enough for some test takers but not for others. In any case, this study should give you an indication of where you stand relative to your GMAT goals. If you decide that you need more preparation, the most convenient way to bulk up your study plan is to acquire Kaplan's GMAT On Demand resources, which include approximately 160 hours of preparation. For more information on GMAT On Demand and the other preparation options (including instructor-led courses) available from Kaplan, see **KaplanGMAT.com.**

Schedule time for study, practice, and review. One of the most frequent mistakes in approaching study is to complete practice questions and tests but not review them thoroughly—review time is your best chance to gain points. It works best for many people to block out short, frequent periods of study time throughout the week. Check in with yourself frequently to make sure you're not falling behind your plan.

STEP 5: LEARN AND PRACTICE

Your book and Online Center come with many opportunities to develop and practice the skills you'll need on Test Day. Read each chapter of this book and complete the practice questions. Depending on how much time you have to study, you can do this work methodically, covering every chapter, or you can focus your study on those question types and content areas that are most challenging to you. You will inevitably need more work in some areas than in others, but know that the more thoroughly you prepare, the better your score will be.

Initially, your practice should focus on mastering the needed skills and not on timing. Add timing to your practice as you improve fundamental proficiency.

STEP 6: TAKE ANOTHER PRACTICE TEST

Once you've progressed in your GMAT studies, take another practice test to gauge your progress. Whether you started by taking the test in your Online Center or the pretest in this book, take your remaining practice test once you've had a chance to learn about and practice with each question type.

Review your practice test results thoroughly to make sure you continue to focus your study on the areas that are most important to your score. Allot time to review the detailed explanations so that you can learn from your mistakes before Test Day.

If you find that you would like access to more of Kaplan's CATs and quizzes, as well as in-depth instruction on the question types and strategies, look into the variety of course options available at **KaplanGMAT.com.**

Thanks for choosing Kaplan. We wish you the best of luck on your journey to business school.

KaplanGMAT.com

The material in this book is accurate and up-to-date at the time of printing. However, the Graduate Management Admission Council may have instituted changes in the test or test registration process after this book was published. Be sure to read carefully the materials you receive when you register for the test.

If there are any important late-breaking developments, we will post that information online at **KaplanGMAT.com.**

kaptest.com/publishing

If there are changes or corrections to the materials in this book, these can be found at **kaptest.com/ publishing.**

PART ONE

The GMAT

CHAPTER 1

Introduction to the GMAT

- GMAT Format
- GMAT Scoring
- GMAT Attitude
- GMAT Checklist

Let's start with the basics. The GMAT is, among other things, an endurance test. It is a computerized test, consisting of 150 minutes of multiple-choice math and verbal questions, a 30-minute analytical essay, and a 30-minute reasoning section. Add in the administrative details, plus two 8-minute breaks, and you can count on being in the testing center for about 4 hours.

It's a grueling experience, to say the least. And if you don't approach it with confidence and rigor, you'll quickly lose your composure. That's why it's so important that you take control of the test, just as you take control of the rest of your business school application process.

Here are the basics.

GMAT FORMAT

The GMAT begins with the Analytical Writing Assessment (the AWA). You are required to complete an essay, typing it into the computer using a simple word processing program. You are given 30 minutes for this essay, during which you have to analyze the reasoning behind a given argument, explain its weaknesses or flaws, and recommend how to correct them to improve the argument. Your own personal views on the topic are not relevant.

After the AWA, you have a 30-minute section called Integrated Reasoning. This section has 12 questions, each of which may require more than one response. The questions in this section ask you to draw conclusions based on information in tables, interpret graphs, understand information presented across different layouts, and sometimes find two answers leading to a single solution.

After these first two sections, there are two 75-minute multiple-choice sections—one Quantitative (Math) and one Verbal. The Quantitative section contains 37 questions in 2 formats, Problem Solving and Data Sufficiency, which are mixed together throughout the section. The Verbal section contains 41 questions in 3 formats, Reading Comprehension, Sentence Correction, and Critical Reasoning, which are also mixed throughout the section.

GMAT Exam Section	Questions	Time
Analytical Writing Assessment	1	30 min
Integrated Reasoning	12	30 min
Quantitative	37	75 min
Verbal	41	75 min
Total Testing Time		**3 hours, 30 minutes**

Order and Length of Sections on the GMAT

Some important things to note:

- After you complete the Integrated Reasoning section, you'll get an 8-minute break. Then, between the Quantitative and Verbal sections, you will get another 8-minute break.
- There are a few "experimental" questions scattered throughout the test. They look just like the other multiple-choice questions but won't contribute to your score.

We'll talk more about each of the question types in later chapters. For now, note the following: You'll be answering 90 multiple-choice questions in 3 hours. On average, that's 2 minutes per question, not counting the time it takes to answer multiple parts of Integrated Reasoning questions or to read the Reading Comprehension passages. Clearly, you'll have to move fast. But you can't let yourself get careless. Taking control of the GMAT means increasing the speed of your work without sacrificing accuracy.

GMAT SCORING

The most important score on the GMAT is the total score, which ranges from 200 to 800. This score is the GMAT result that schools look at primarily. The population of these scores follows a standard distribution: Most students score near the mean score, and more than half of all GMAT test takers score within 100 points of 550, the approximate mean. Pulling yourself out of that cluster is an important part of distinguishing your application: The top 10 business schools accept students with an average GMAT score of 720, the 94th percentile.

Percentile	Score
99%	760–800
94%	720
89%	700
77%	650
67%	620
48%	560

Some GMAT Percentiles vs. Total Scores

The total score is calculated from "scaled scores" from the Quantitative section (75 minutes, 37 questions) and Verbal section (75 minutes, 41 questions). Theoretically, these scores range from 1 to 60, but the extreme scores exist only to allow room for future expansion. Currently, possible scores range from about 11 to 51. These scores are meant to provide a timeless, absolute measure of skill. For example, a Quant score of 40 in 2004 represents the exact same level of ability as a Quant score of 40 does in 2014.

The scale might seem arbitrary to you. You may be wondering, "Why 11 to 51, of all possible scales?" One reason to have a scale such as this one is to avoid confusion with percentiles or percentages.

If scaled scores ranged from 0 to 100, for example, a score of 70 might be confused with answering 70 percent of the questions correctly.

While the scaled scores haven't changed over time, the population of test takers has. Quant performance has gone up over time, and Verbal performance has gone down. While Verbal section scores still follow a fairly even distribution, Quantitative scaled scores now skew high. In recent years, up to 12 percent of test takers received a 50 or 51 on the Quant section. Because of the shift over time and the nature of the population, percentiles don't match exactly to scaled scores. As that fact indicates, there is a third way of slicing and dicing GMAT performance: percentiles.

Schools view your percentile performance (which is the same thing as a "percent ranking") overall and on each section of the GMAT. The relationship between the section percentiles and the overall percentile is not simple. We're frequently asked, "One of my scaled scores is 83rd percentile and the other is 84th percentile. How can my overall score be 87th percentile?" This type of outcome is unproblematic. You can see why using a simple, albeit extreme, example. Imagine that of 100 students taking the test, 50 people got a 51 Quant and 11 Verbal, while the other 50 people got an 11 Quant and 51 Verbal. You take the same test and get 40 Quant and 40 Verbal. You'd be 50th percentile on each section, because 50 percent of test takers in this sample group scored worse than you. However, your total score would put you higher than anyone else on the test—99th percentile.

Quantitative			Verbal	
Percentile	Score		Percentile	Score
97%	51–60		99%	45–51
88%	50		98%	44
79%	49		96%	42
74%	48		94%	41
68%	47		91%	40
66%	46		89%	39
63%	45		85%	38
58%	44		83%	37
56%	43		81%	36

Some Percentiles vs. Scaled Scores for the
Quantitative and Verbal Sections

Now that we've cleared up that point of confusion, let's note two key takeaways about percentiles. The first is that your overall score is about balanced performance on the two sections. Generally, you will not win on the GMAT by nailing one section and hoping your performance will overcome a deficit on the other. The second key point is that, since Quant and Verbal percentiles aren't obvious from the overall score, admission officers often look at them specifically. Some admissions officers at top schools have remarked on panels, "We will look specifically at the Quantitative percentile on the GMAT. You should have at least an 80th percentile on that section as well as a strong overall score." Moreover, at specialized MBA and management programs, a Quantitative percentile of 90th or higher may be the norm.

So which of these measures is most important? The overall score of 200 to 800 is the most important score, since it's a balanced measure of absolute and relative performance. Next come percentiles, which admission officers often look at. In our experience, B-school admissions officers rarely mention paying attention to scaled scores.

The Analytical Writing Assessment (AWA) is scored separately from the rest of the GMAT. Unlike the total and scaled scores, AWA scores aren't available on Test Day. When you do get your score, it will take the form of a number from 1 to 6 in increments of 0.5 (you get a zero if you write off-topic or in a foreign language). The magic number here is 4. Although you should strive for the best score possible, an essay graded 4 is considered "satisfactory" according to the grading rubric, and an essay graded 3 is not.

AWA	
Percentile	Score
92%	6
81%	5.5
60%	5
44%	4.5
21%	4
13%	3.5
6%	3
5%	2.5
3%	0.5–2
0%	0

Percentiles vs. Scaled Scores for the AWA

Percentiles give a slightly different perspective on the AWA. An AWA score of 4 ranks at a shockingly low 21st percentile. To break the median, you have to score a 5 or higher. The good news is that few programs, in our experience, use the AWA score to differentiate candidate competitiveness. It's more of a reality check against the writing skills that you demonstrate in your application essays. In this vein, a little-noticed fact: Business schools receive the actual text of your AWA essay in the official score report. They're not going to spend too long examining your 30-minute analysis of an argument about whether additional taxation is in the greater interest of the citizens of Mauritania, but at least they have the option.

Lastly, you'll receive your score for the Integrated Reasoning section. As with the Quant and Verbal sections, Integrated Reasoning scores are available on Test Day. Like the AWA, the Integrated Reasoning section has its own scoring scale, independent from the 200 to 800 scale. You'll receive a score from 1 through 8, in whole-point increments. The magic number this time is 5, as this is the score at which you beat the median.

Integrated Reasoning	
Percentile	Score
92%	8
81%	7
67%	6
52%	5
37%	4
25%	3
12%	2
0%	1

Percentiles vs. Scaled Scores for the Integrated Reasoning Section

As of this writing, Integrated Reasoning is still a young section—it was introduced to the GMAT in summer of 2012. As a result, business schools don't weigh it nearly as heavily as they do the total 200 to 800 score. You want to show schools that you're in the better half of the Integrated Reasoning field, but at the same time, an exceptional 200 to 800 score will do more for your application than will an exceptional Integrated Reasoning score, and you should prioritize your study time accordingly.

The Integrated Reasoning section is very challenging for most test takers, in part because its scoring scale is so punishing. The 1 to 8 score is derived from just 12 questions, nearly all of which consist of multiple parts that must all be answered correctly in order to receive credit (i.e., there is no partial credit). Integrated Reasoning questions come in four types, which are described in more detail in the Integrated Reasoning chapter of this book: Graphics Interpretation, Multi-Source Reasoning, Table Analysis, and Two-Part Analysis.

Unlike the Quantitative and Verbal sections of the GMAT, the Integrated Reasoning section isn't adaptive: You'll see a predetermined sequence of 12 questions no matter how many you get right and wrong as you go along. However, despite not being adaptive, the Integrated Reasoning section does not let test takers skip questions or return to previously answered questions. As a result, it's often advantageous to guess and abandon a hard question early in the section to ensure that no easy questions are left unanswered at the end of the section.

SCORE REPORTS

Within 20 days after your test date, your official score report will be available online. You'll receive an email when yours is ready. Reports will only be mailed to candidates who request that service. The official score report includes your scores for the Analytical Writing Assessment (AWA), Integrated Reasoning, Verbal, and Quantitative sections, as well as your total score and percentile ranking.

Your report also includes the results of all the GMAT exams you've taken in the previous five years, including cancellations. Any additional reports are US$28 each. All score-report requests are final and cannot be canceled.

GMAT ATTITUDE

In the chapters that follow, we'll cover techniques for answering the GMAT questions. But you'll also need to go into the test with a certain attitude and approach. Here are some strategies.

USE THE NOTEBOARDS

Test takers are given noteboards, which are spiral-bound booklets of laminated paper, and a black wet-erase pen. Here are the specs so you know what to expect on Test Day.

Noteboard
- 5 sheets, 10 numbered pages
- Spiral-bound at top
- Legal-sized (8.5" × 14") in United States, Canada, and Mexico; A4 elsewhere
- First page has test instructions and is not suitable for scratchwork
- Pages 2–10 consist of a gridded work surface
- Pale yellow in United States, Canada, and Mexico; may be a different color elsewhere

Pen
- Black fine-print Staedtler wet-erase pen

You will not be given an eraser, and you are not allowed to reuse the noteboard. Each time you fill up your noteboard during the test, the administrator will replace your used noteboard with a clean one. You can also request a new pen, if necessary. The noteboard cannot be removed from the test room during or after the exam, and you must return it to the administrator when your exam is complete.

We know how important it is for test takers to be as prepared as possible for the actual testing experience. That's why we have always recommended that students use separate scratch material with our GMAT preparation program, including with the practice questions and tests in this book. Since the noteboards will be your only option on Test Day, we suggest that you use an eraser board (or anything with a similar surface) and a non-permanent marker while doing the practice tests. Although using them won't mimic the Test Day experience exactly, at least you'll get the feel of working in a comparable medium. Even if you practice with the noteboard and marker until you are comfortable, there are still some possible snags you may encounter on Test Day. Here are some tips on how to handle them:

1. **Erasable ink you're not supposed to erase:** Say you make a mistake during a calculation or you smudge your work with your hand. The noteboard's surface probably won't lend itself to quick-and-easy erasing (not surprisingly, since you are not meant to reuse it). You can't write on top of the smudge or error because you'll just be left with a blob of ink that you can't read. So what should you do? Just start over. Seriously. Think of it this way—you won't waste precious time in a futile attempt to save what is essentially a sinking ship. Left-handed test takers (and some right-handed ones, too) might find that their writing styles make them particularly susceptible to smudging. If this sounds like you, practicing with the eraser board will help you work out any such problems before Test Day.

2. **A problematic pen:** Difficulties with pens are not common. The test administrators are careful to provide good writing utensils so test takers don't have any extra anxieties. Keep in mind that you should recap your pen when you are not using it so that it doesn't dry out. However, you could get a pen that's simply dry from the get-go or dries out quickly no matter how careful you are. Don't sweat it. The best thing to do is just to get a new pen. Should you be saddled with a pen that leaves wayward blobs of ink, don't waste time with yours either. Ask the administrator for a new pen as soon as it starts to act up.

More Noteboard Strategies

Using one booklet for an entire section and requesting a replacement during breaks is the most efficient method for using the noteboards. Since you are given nine pages to write on, this technique can be used without difficulty, especially with planning and practice. However, should you need a new noteboard (or pen) during a section, hold the used one in the air to clarify immediately the nature of the request (rather than just raising your hand).

BE SYSTEMATIC

Use your noteboard to organize your thinking. If you eliminate choices, draw an answer choice grid, cross off choices as you rule them out, and guess intelligently. Make sure to leave enough time to answer every question in the section. You'll be penalized for questions you don't get to.

PACE YOURSELF

Of course, the last thing you want to happen is to run out of time before you've done all the questions. Pace yourself so that this doesn't happen. We're not saying you have to spend exactly 120 seconds, for instance, on every Critical Reasoning question. But you should have a sense of how much time to spend on each question. (We'll talk about general timing guidelines later.)

Before you go in to take the exam, get a sense of how long is too long to spend on a question. This is something you can do only with practice, so while working on the practice questions in this book, time yourself. (If you're using your watch, take it off and set it on the table in front of you.)

TURN OFF THE CLOCK

The timer in the corner of the GMAT screen can work to your advantage, but if you find yourself looking at it so often that it becomes a distraction, turn it off for 10 or 15 minutes and try to refocus. Even if you lose track a bit without the clock, there is no replacement for focus and accuracy. Some people work best with the clock off from the beginning. If that's you, be sure to check in with the clock every five questions. You don't want to fall too far behind. No matter what your preference is for the clock, when there are five minutes left, the clock turns on permanently, counts down the seconds, turns red, and flashes.

DON'T WASTE TIME ON QUESTIONS YOU CAN'T DO

Skipping a tough question is easier said than done. It's natural to want to plow through a test and answer every question as it appears. But that doesn't pay off here. We'll discuss in Chapter 2 why it's sometimes best to move on and avoid running out of time on a section. A strategic guess may be necessary to get a top score on the GMAT.

REMAIN CALM

It's imperative that you remain calm and composed during the test. You can't let yourself get rattled by one hard question to the degree that it throws off your performance on the rest of the section.

When you face a tough question, remember that you're surely not the only one finding it difficult. The test is designed to challenge everyone who takes it. Having trouble with a difficult question isn't going to ruin your score, but getting upset and letting it throw you off track will. When you understand that part of the testmaker's goal is to reward those who keep their composure, you'll recognize the importance of keeping your cool when you run into challenging material.

GMAT CHECKLIST

The GMAT is offered by appointment, at your convenience, almost every day of the year. You will be required to register online before making an appointment.

CHOOSE A TESTING CENTER

Before you register, find a testing center that's convenient for you and determine whether that site has available seats. Each testing center operates on its own schedule and can accommodate varying numbers of test takers. To locate a testing center near you, go to **mba.com**.

REGISTER AND SCHEDULE YOUR APPOINTMENT

Available time slots change continuously as people register for the test. You will find out what times are available at your chosen testing center when you register. You may be able to schedule an appointment within a few days of your desired test date, but popular dates (especially weekends) fill up quickly.

Admissions deadlines for business schools vary. Check with the schools and make your test appointment early enough to allow your scores to be reported before the schools' application deadlines.

You may register and schedule your appointment online, by phone, by mail, or by fax:

- Online: Go to **mba.com**.
- Phone (based on your location):
  - The Americas: Call toll-free (within the United States and Canada only) 800-717-GMAT (4628) or call the customer service line (952) 681-3680. The lines are operational from 7:00 a.m. to 7:00 p.m. Central Time.
  - Asia Pacific: +60 38318-9961, 9:00 a.m. to 6:00 p.m. AEST
  - China: 86-10-82345675, Monday to Friday, 8:30 a.m. to 5:30 p.m. China Standard Time
  - India: +91 120 439-7830, 9:00 a.m. to 6:00 p.m. Indian Standard Time
  - Europe/Middle East/Africa: +44 (0) 161 855 7219, 9:00 a.m. to 6:00 p.m. GMT
- Mail or fax (slowest options):
  - Download the Test Center List, Country Code List, and GMAT Appointment Scheduling form, available at **mba.com**.
  - Fill out the GMAT Appointment Scheduling form.
  - If you wish to fax your form, use one of the following fax numbers, based on your location:
    - The Americas: (952) 681-3681
    - Asia Pacific and India: +60 38319 1092
    - China: 86-10-61957800
    - Europe/Middle East/Africa: +44 (0) 161 855 7301
  - If you wish to mail your form, send your completed form to the following address. Keep in mind that mail from some countries can take as long as eight weeks to arrive in the United States:

    Pearson VUE
    Attention: GMAT Program
    Po Box 581907
    Minneapolis, MN 55458-1907, USA

The fee to take the GMAT is US$250 worldwide (at the time of printing). It is payable by credit card online or by mailing in a check. If you have questions about GMAT registration, visit **mba.com** or call 800-717-GMAT (4628).

Identify Yourself Correctly

When scheduling your test appointment, be sure that the spelling of your name and your stated date of birth match the ID you will present at the testing center. If those do not match, you will not be permitted to take the test, and your test fee will be forfeited.

RESCHEDULING OR CANCELING AN APPOINTMENT

If you need to reschedule the date, time, or location of your appointment, there is a US$50 fee (as this book goes to press) as long as you reschedule at least seven days before your original appointment. If you need to reschedule fewer than seven days before your original date, you have to pay the full registration amount again. Rescheduling can be done online at **mba.com** or by calling one of the numbers listed previously. If you reschedule over the phone, you may be subject to an additional fee. You cannot reschedule an appointment by mail or fax.

If you need to cancel your appointment, you will receive a US$80 refund (as this book goes to press) as long as you cancel at least seven days before your original appointment. If you cancel fewer than seven days before your original date, you forfeit the entire registration fee. For registration fees paid by credit card, the refund amount will be credited to the card. If the fee was paid by check or money order, you will receive a check in the mail. Cancellations can be made online at **mba. com** or by calling one of numbers listed previously, based on your location. If you cancel over the phone, you may be subject to an additional fee. You cannot cancel an appointment by mail or fax.

THE DAY OF THE TEST

You should arrive at your testing center 30 minutes before the time of your scheduled appointment. You must complete a number of security measures before you will be allowed to take the exam. A late arrival (15 minutes or more) may result in you being turned away from the testing center and forfeiting of your test fee.

Presentation of Proper Identification

You will be asked to present ID—no exceptions. The following are the only acceptable forms:

- Passport
- Government-issued driver's license
- Government-issued national/state/province identity card (including European ID card)
- Military ID card

If you aren't a citizen of the country in which you take your test, you'll probably need your passport. In some countries, a passport will always be required. Visit **mba.com** for the current requirements.

The ID must be current (not expired) and legible, and it should contain all four of the elements listed below. If you do not have one ID with all four of these elements, you will need to bring a second ID (also from the list above) that shows the missing elements.

1. Your name in the Roman alphabet. It must be exactly the same as what you provided when you made your appointment, including the order and placement of the names.
2. Your date of birth. The date of birth must also exactly match the date provided when you made your appointment.
3. A recent, recognizable photograph
4. Your signature

If these elements do not match what the test administrator has on file for you, you will not be allowed to take the GMAT, and your test fee will be forfeited.

Before you schedule your test appointment, make sure you understand all the requirements that are particular to your situation and have acquired or renewed the ID you will use. Also, note that if your ID is found to be fraudulent or invalid after you take the exam, your scores will be canceled and your test fee forfeited.

Palm Scan, Signature, and Photograph

Once your government-issued ID is approved, the administrator will take your palm scan, signature, and photograph using digital equipment. The testing rooms are also equipped with audio and video recorders, which are active during the exam. If you do not complete the entire check-in process or refuse to be recorded, you will not be allowed to take the GMAT, and your test fee will be forfeited.

Agreements

When you arrive at the center, you will be asked to agree to the GMAT Examination Testing Rules & Agreement. Once you are seated at a workstation, you will electronically confirm that you agree to the GMAT Non-Disclosure Agreement and General Terms of Use statement. If you do not agree, you will not be allowed to take the GMAT, and your test fee will be forfeited. If you are caught violating the agreement, the business schools that you're applying to will be informed of this fact.

Prohibited Items

The following items cannot be brought into the testing room:

- Electronics such as cell phones, media players, personal data assistants (PDAs), cameras, radios, and photographic devices
- Any timepieces, including wristwatches, stopwatches, and watch alarms
- Notes, scratch paper, books, pamphlets, dictionaries, translators, and thesauruses
- Pens and pencils
- Measuring tools such as rulers
- Calculators and watch calculators

Essentially, you can't bring anything that may cause distractions, provide aid during testing, or be used to remove exam content from the testing room. It is possible that your testing center has storage space available, such as lockers, where you can leave possessions that are prohibited from the testing room. However, this may not be the case at all centers. Call your testing center to inquire about storage and plan accordingly.

Disruptive Behavior

You will not be allowed to smoke, eat, drink, or use a cell phone in the testing room. In fact, you won't be allowed to use a phone or send a text message at all once the test has begun, even at breaks.

You also cannot leave the testing room without the administrator's permission. Some testing centers provide earplugs to keep noise to a minimum; if this interests you, call your testing center for details. Should you have any questions or problems during the exam, raise your hand and wait for the administrator to approach you.

Breaks

The length of your appointment is approximately four hours. Two breaks are scheduled into the exam—one after the Integrated Reasoning section and another after the Quantitative section. Each time you leave and return to the testing room, your palm will be scanned. If you exceed the allotted break time, the excess time will be deducted from the next section of your exam. For more information on administrative regulations and testing procedures, visit **mba.com**.

Bring the Names of Five Business Schools You Wish to Receive Your Scores

You may select up to five schools to receive your scores before you take the test. Your registration fee will cover that cost. Before Test Day, decide which schools you want to get your GMAT scores and bring that list with you. You will not be able to change the list once you have made your selection.

CHAPTER 2

Understanding the CAT

- The CAT Explained
- Are the First Questions More Important?
- The Importance of Pacing
- Other CAT Strategies

The GMAT is a computer-adaptive test, or CAT. The test is called "adaptive" because, in the course of a section, the test notices whether you answered the previous question correctly or incorrectly and "adapts" in its selection of the next question.

A few basic rules make the adaptive format possible.

- You're presented with one question at a time, and you must answer it to move on to the next question.
- You can't return to previously answered questions within a section.
- You can't skip questions—or rather, the only questions that can be skipped or omitted are any questions at the end of a section that you leave unanswered.
- Within a section (Quantitative or Verbal), the questions are not grouped by topic or type. You don't, for example, finish Reading Comprehension and then move on to Sentence Correction and then to Critical Reasoning; those three question types are interspersed with one another throughout the section.

THE CAT EXPLAINED

Here's how the adapting works. You start the section (Quantitative or Verbal) with a medium-difficulty question; about half of test takers get it right, and half get it wrong. Those who answer correctly get a harder question for the second item, and those who answer incorrectly get an easier item. This pattern repeats: Throughout the section, if you got the previous question right, generally you'll get a harder question next. Conversely, if you got the previous question wrong, generally you'll get an easier one next. This pattern reiterates so that you follow a generally upward, downward, or flat trajectory through the questions. The test homes in on the difficulty level that is best matched to your performance; at that difficulty level, generally, you'll get about half the questions correct and half incorrect. How high on the difficulty scale you end up is one of the criteria that determine your score, along with how many questions you answer and other factors.

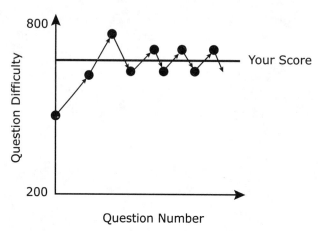

A Rough Schematic of How Adaptive Scoring Works on a CAT

The adaptive design of the test has two purposes:

1. **Accuracy:** A CAT is allegedly more accurate than a "linear" (i.e., nonadaptive) test because it zeroes in on a test taker's ability level. Lucky guesses cause the GMAT to give lucky testers harder questions that they cannot answer correctly, thus eliminating any gains resulting from chance. Conversely, unlucky arithmetic errors on tough problems give unlucky testers easier problems, and these unlucky testers should be able to get the easier questions right, thus correcting the nonrepresentative drop in score.

2. **Time:** CATs can be made shorter than comparable linear tests, and the shorter duration is a benefit both to you and the testmaker. The reason for this efficiency is that a CAT does not waste questions. If you get most of the questions right, you pretty much never see an easy one, and if you get most of the questions wrong, you pretty much never see a hard one. On a linear test such as the SAT, on the other hand, everyone gets the same mix of easy and hard questions. On such a test, students struggling on the easy questions will do little better than chance on the challenging problems, while high-scoring students will get close to 100 percent of the easy questions correct. Thus, giving low-scoring questions to high-scoring students (and vice versa) doesn't actually provide much useful statistical data. In this respect, many questions are "wasted," whereas the CAT can afford to be a much shorter test at equal accuracy.

Those points define the basic pattern of the CAT, but there are additional bells and whistles in the algorithm. One of the most important details to be aware of is that the test does not always adjust difficulty level question by question. Therefore, avoid the temptation to assess the difficulty level of a question you're on or to infer whether you got the previous question correct. Even if you could precisely assess a question's difficulty level (and you can't, in practice, for reasons we discuss partly later), you wouldn't be able to draw any conclusions, since the test doesn't always adapt immediately.

The experimental questions are another refinement to the CAT formula. Some of the questions in each section do not count toward your score. The testmaker must try future questions out on people who do not know that they are experimental in order to determine the validity and difficulty of the questions. We'll talk more about this topic later, but we'll give away one headline early: Do not try to guess which questions are experimental.

ARE THE FIRST QUESTIONS MORE IMPORTANT?

One of the most frequently asked questions about GMAT scoring is "Are the first 10 or so questions more important?"

As we've discussed, the GMAT adaptive algorithm starts with a medium-difficulty question. If you get it right, your next question is harder, and if you get it wrong, your next question is easier. The swings are relatively large at the beginning but then zero in on an estimate of your performance. For that reason, you may find it tempting to spend lots of extra time at the beginning of the test.

The short word on that idea: Don't.

The testmakers concede that the computer-adaptive testing algorithm uses the first 10 questions to obtain an initial estimate of your ability. The key word, though, is *initial*. As you continue to answer questions, the algorithm self-corrects by computing an updated estimate on the basis of all the questions you have answered, and then it administers items that are closely matched to this new estimate of your ability. Your final score is based on your responses, the difficulty of all the questions you answered, and the number of questions left unanswered. Taking additional time on the first 10 questions will not "game the system" and can hurt your ability to finish the test.

The testmakers insist that, despite persistent rumors to the contrary, you can't outsmart the GMAT by spending extra time at the beginning. The reason for this is timing: If you answer more questions correctly than you should in more time than you should, then you will face much harder questions, under more time pressure, in the remaining three quarters of the section. Your short-term gains will be erased.

However, you still want to adjust your test-prep strategy to account for those early swings. Specifically, remember that even when your test-taking skills have become so strong that most of your test will be made up of challenging, high-reward problems, you'll still have to go through some simpler problems to get there—don't rush or become overconfident just because those first few questions are easier.

A good comparison is to a sporting event. Are the first innings or the first quarter of a game more important than the following ones? Perhaps, since the early part of the game sets the tone for the game and gives the leading team options. But doing well during the first part of a game does not guarantee a win; you need to start strong *and* finish strong.

The cost of not finishing strong on the GMAT is substantial. If you don't answer all the questions, a penalty is assessed that will precipitously lower your score. In fact, this effect is more exaggerated in the case of high scorers. As an example, provided by GMAC, if you are at the 91st percentile but then fail to answer five questions, your score could drop to the 77th percentile. A score difference of that magnitude is substantial.

THE IMPORTANCE OF PACING

The GMAT is a test of both accuracy and speed. There is a substantial penalty for not finishing a section, as we've seen. But there is no need to think of the GMAT as a race. In fact, according to the testmakers, the GMAT is created to be optimally timed so that most test takers finish the first time they sit for the test. Those who don't finish the GMAT the first time often retake the test, and almost all finish the second time.

You want to be in the group that finishes the test on the first try. Also, while you don't want to rush or make sloppy guesses, you do need to finish the test on time in order to maximize your score.

The graph below is an illustration of the penalty incurred by test takers who leave a string of unanswered questions at the end of a CAT section. Even if you had previously been performing well on questions at a high level of difficulty, running out of time will lead to a severe drop in your score. Fortunately, pacing can be improved through practicing some key principles of time management.

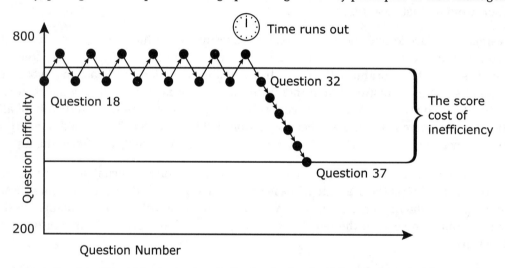

Spending Extra Time at the Beginning of a Section Can Lead to Failure at the End of the Section

You can pace yourself on both the Quantitative and Verbal sections, broadly speaking, by dividing each section into three parts:

- the first 10 questions,
- the last 10 questions, and
- everything in between.

Each part has its own strategy.

- **The first 10 questions:** Given what we've covered above, you now have an idea of how to pace yourself on the first 10 questions. To recap: The first questions are likely to produce some large swings in your score, but you may see larger swings later on, and it's important to finish just as strong as you start. The theme of these 10 questions: Proceed diligently, keep an eye out for pitfalls, and avoid preventable errors.

- **The middle segment:** Regardless of how the first 10 questions go, you're almost certain to find some challenges in this segment. Most test takers will "top out." Topping out means that you will be unable to solve any more difficult problems and you will begin to hover around your skill level, getting about half of the questions right and half of them wrong. The great danger at this point in the test is that you will feel you ought to be able to "get" every problem and you will spend too much time on some of them. Since time spent here takes away from the time you have for the later questions in the section, you may need to guess on a few questions to stay on pace. Fortunately, if you've budgeted your minutes well, you will have some time to give your guesses a little thought. The theme of the middle segment: Stay on pace, keep your morale high, and make shrewd guesses where necessary.

- **The final 10 questions** are the home stretch. You're trying to finish before the bell rings. Here you must pick your battles. Make an effort not to guess on more than one or two questions in a row. As the end draws nigh, alternate any guesses that you need to make, rather than saving them for a series at the end. Doing so will increase your options to solve without guessing, decrease the odds of accidentally running out of time, and most likely reduce the score drop from questions answered incorrectly. The theme of this segment: Choose your questions and finish on time.

Now you're done. You've maximized your payoff. It can be exciting to set a pace and stick to it, and guessing on the trickiest questions can reduce your anxiety and frustration.

OTHER CAT STRATEGIES

In addition to the strategies mentioned earlier about pacing, keep in mind other CAT-specific strategies that will have a direct, positive impact on your score:

- Because the level of difficulty of questions on the CAT is not predictable, always be on the lookout for answer-choice traps.
- Because each right or wrong answer affects the next question you get, the CAT does not allow you to return to questions you've already answered. In other words, you cannot go back to double-check your work. So be sure about your answers before moving on.
- If you're given a question you cannot answer, you'll have to guess. Guess intelligently and strategically by eliminating any answer choices that you know are wrong and guessing among those remaining.
- Don't get rattled if you keep seeing really tough questions. It can mean you're doing very well. Keep it up; you're on your way to a great GMAT score.

PART TWO

Pretest

CHAPTER 3

GMAT Pretest

HOW TO TAKE THIS TEST

Before taking this Pretest, find a quiet place where you can work uninterruptedly for a little over 2.5 hours. Make sure you have a comfortable desk, scratch paper, and something to write with. Have a watch or other timepiece that you can use to time yourself; to emulate test-like conditions, you should allow yourself 75 minutes for each of the two sections. You may take an 8-minute break between the sections.

This is not a full-length practice GMAT. Rather, this test comprises the two multiple-choice sections on the GMAT: the Quantitative and Verbal sections. These are the two sections that determine your 200–800 score, which is the most important score for business school admissions. (We have not included the Analytical Writing or Integrated Reasoning sections on this Pretest, as we believe it is a better use of your time to first learn about and practice these question types in the relevant chapters of this book. You will have the opportunity to practice these sections as part of a full-length practice test in your Online Center.)

This test is designed to accurately reflect the question types and content of the GMAT Quantitative and Verbal sections. The most important benefit you'll get from taking this test is the ability to assess your strengths and areas of opportunity. As you review this test, take note of the question types and topics that gave you the most trouble so that you can prioritize your studies in those areas for the maximum score improvement.

Since this test is not adaptive, the 200–800 score you will calculate at the end of the test is just a rough estimate of your ability level. Once you've spent some time learning the Kaplan Methods and strategies taught in this book, you should take a full-length computer-adaptive test in your Online Center to gauge your progress, to experience the test interface, and to get a more accurate sense of your score. Use this test primarily as a way to get familiar with the test content and assess your highest-yield areas for further study.

To make it easier to grade your test, use the answer sheet that follows to record your multiple-choice answers. You'll find the answer key and explanations following the test. As is the case throughout this book, answer choices are referred to in the answer key and explanations as **(A), (B), (C), (D),** and **(E)**, even though the test questions are formatted as you'll see them on Test Day: preceded by ovals, not letters.

Since the computer-adaptive GMAT does not allow test takers to skip questions or answer questions out of order, you can emulate that experience on this paper Pretest by answering each question in order, guessing where necessary, and not going back to check your work on previous questions.

Good luck!

GMAT PRETEST ANSWER SHEET

Remove (or photocopy) this answer sheet and use it to complete the practice test.

Quantitative

1. _____	20. _____
2. _____	21. _____
3. _____	22. _____
4. _____	23. _____
5. _____	24. _____
6. _____	25. _____
7. _____	26. _____
8. _____	27. _____
9. _____	28. _____
10. _____	29. _____
11. _____	30. _____
12. _____	31. _____
13. _____	32. _____
14. _____	33. _____
15. _____	34. _____
16. _____	35. _____
17. _____	36. _____
18. _____	37. _____
19. _____	

Verbal

1. _____	22. _____
2. _____	23. _____
3. _____	24. _____
4. _____	25. _____
5. _____	26. _____
6. _____	27. _____
7. _____	28. _____
8. _____	29. _____
9. _____	30. _____
10. _____	31. _____
11. _____	32. _____
12. _____	33. _____
13. _____	34. _____
14. _____	35. _____
15. _____	36. _____
16. _____	37. _____
17. _____	38. _____
18. _____	39. _____
19. _____	40. _____
20. _____	41. _____
21. _____	

Quantitative Section
37 Questions

Time—75 minutes

In the Quantitative section, there are two types of questions: Problem Solving and Data Sufficiency.

Directions: For each **Problem Solving** question, solve the problem and select the best of the answer choices given.

Each **Data Sufficiency** problem consists of a question and two statements, labeled (1) and (2), which contain certain data. Using these data and your knowledge of mathematics and everyday facts (such as the number of days in July or the meaning of the word *counterclockwise*), decide whether the data given are sufficient for answering the question and then select one of the following answering choices:

O Statement (1) ALONE is sufficient, but statement (2) alone is not sufficient to answer the question asked.

O Statement (2) ALONE is sufficient, but statement (1) alone is not sufficient to answer the question asked.

O BOTH statements (1) and (2) TOGETHER are sufficient to answer the question asked, but NEITHER statement ALONE is sufficient to answer the question asked.

O EACH statement ALONE is sufficient to answer the question asked.

O Statements (1) and (2) TOGETHER are NOT sufficient to answer the question asked, and additional data specific to the problem are needed.

<u>Note</u>: In Data Sufficiency problems that ask for the value of a quantity, the data given in the statements are sufficient only when it is possible to determine exactly one numerical value for the quantity.

Example:

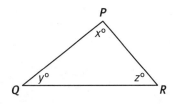

In $\triangle PQR$, what is the value of x?

(1) $PQ = PR$

(2) $y = 40$

Explanation: According to statement (1), $PQ = PR$; therefore, $\triangle PQR$ is isosceles and $y = z$. Since $x + y + z = 180$, it follows that $x + 2y = 180$. Since statement (1) does not give a value for y, you cannot answer the question using statement (1) alone. According to statement (2), $y = 40$; therefore $x + z = 140$. Since statement (2) does not give a value for z, you cannot answer the question using statement (2) alone. Using both statements together, since $x + 2y = 180$ and the value of y is given, you can find the value of x. Therefore, BOTH statements (1) and (2) TOGETHER are sufficient to answer the question, but NEITHER statement ALONE is sufficient.

For **all** questions in the Quantitative section you may assume the following:

Numbers: All numbers used are real numbers.

Figures:

- For Problem Solving questions, figures are drawn as accurately as possible. Exceptions will be clearly noted.
- For Data Sufficiency questions, figures conform to the information given in the question, but will not necessarily conform to the additional information given in statements (1) and (2).
- Lines shown as straight are straight, and lines that may appear jagged are also straight.
- The positions of points, angles, regions, etc., exist in the order shown, and angle measures are greater than zero.
- All figures lie in a plane unless otherwise indicated.

You may review these directions at any time during the Quantitative section.

1. If j and k are integers and $jk = 12$, what is the value of k?

    (1) $\dfrac{j}{6}$ is an integer.

    (2) $\dfrac{k}{2}$ is an integer.

    ○   Statement (1) ALONE is sufficient, but statement (2) is not sufficient.

    ○   Statement (2) ALONE is sufficient, but statement (1) is not sufficient.

    ○   BOTH statements TOGETHER are sufficient, but NEITHER statement ALONE is sufficient.

    ○   EACH statement ALONE is sufficient.

    ○   Statements (1) and (2) TOGETHER are NOT sufficient.

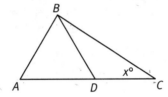

2. In the diagram above, if $AB = AD = BD = DC$, then $x =$

    ○   30

    ○   35

    ○   40

    ○   45

    ○   60

3. Tara has 12 coins in her pocket. How many of them are quarters?

    (1) The total value of the 12 coins is $1.80.

    (2) Tara has only quarters and dimes.

    ○   Statement (1) ALONE is sufficient, but statement (2) is not sufficient.

    ○   Statement (2) ALONE is sufficient, but statement (1) is not sufficient.

    ○   BOTH statements TOGETHER are sufficient, but NEITHER statement ALONE is sufficient.

    ○   EACH statement ALONE is sufficient.

    ○   Statements (1) and (2) TOGETHER are NOT sufficient.

GO ON TO THE NEXT PAGE ⇨

4. To meet a government requirement, a bottler must test 5 percent of its spring water and 10 percent of its sparkling water for purity. If a customer ordered 120 cases of spring water and 80 cases of sparkling water, what percent of all the cases must the bottler test before it can send the water out?

   O   6.5%
   O   7.0%
   O   7.5%
   O   8.0%
   O   8.5%

5. Company C sells a line of 25 products with an average retail price of $1,200. If none of these products sells for less than $420 and exactly 10 of the products sell for less than $1,000, what is the greatest possible selling price of the most expensive product?

   O $2,600
   O $3,900
   O $7,800
   O $11,800
   O $18,200

6. How many members of Group G are less than 25 years of age?

   (1) Exactly $\frac{3}{5}$ of the members of Group G are 25 years of age or older.
   (2) The 24 men in Group G constitute 30 percent of the group's membership.

   O   Statement (1) ALONE is sufficient, but statement (2) is not sufficient.
   O   Statement (2) ALONE is sufficient, but statement (1) is not sufficient.
   O   BOTH statements TOGETHER are sufficient, but NEITHER statement ALONE is sufficient.
   O   EACH statement ALONE is sufficient.
   O   Statements (1) and (2) TOGETHER are NOT sufficient.

GO ON TO THE NEXT PAGE ⟹

7. If $a - b = \dfrac{a^2 - b^2}{b^2 - a^2}$ and $b^2 - a^2 \neq 0$, then $b - a =$

   ○ −1

   ○ 0

   ○ 1

   ○ 2

   ○ It cannot be determined from the information given.

8. Andrea makes a certain trip in her car. On the first leg of her trip, she drives 40 miles per hour to her destination. On the second leg, she turns around and returns by the same route in 5 hours. How long does she spend driving on the first leg?

   (1) Andrea's average speed for the entire trip is 30 miles per hour.

   (2) The distance to her destination is 120 miles.

   ○ Statement (1) ALONE is sufficient, but statement (2) is not sufficient.

   ○ Statement (2) ALONE is sufficient, but statement (1) is not sufficient.

   ○ BOTH statements TOGETHER are sufficient, but NEITHER statement ALONE is sufficient.

   ○ EACH statement ALONE is sufficient.

   ○ Statements (1) and (2) TOGETHER are NOT sufficient.

9. If $p^3 \geq -125$ and p is an integer, what is the value of p?

   (1) $3p + 16 \leq 4$

   (2) $p^2 > 16$

   ○ Statement (1) ALONE is sufficient, but statement (2) is not sufficient.

   ○ Statement (2) ALONE is sufficient, but statement (1) is not sufficient.

   ○ BOTH statements TOGETHER are sufficient, but NEITHER statement ALONE is sufficient.

   ○ EACH statement ALONE is sufficient.

   ○ Statements (1) and (2) TOGETHER are NOT sufficient.

GO ON TO THE NEXT PAGE ⇒

10. A cube of white Styrofoam is painted red and then cut in half parallel to a pair of parallel sides to form two rectangular solids of equal volume. What percent of the surface area of each of the new solids is not painted red?

    ○   15%

    ○ $16\frac{2}{3}$%

    ○   20%

    ○   25%

    ○ $33\frac{1}{3}$%

11. How many multiples of 3 are there among the integers 15 through 105 inclusive?

    ○   30

    ○   31

    ○   32

    ○   33

    ○   34

12. In the equation $b = ka + 3$, k is a constant. If the possible solutions are in the form (a, b), is $(2, 3)$ a solution to the equation?

    (1) $(1, 4)$ is a solution of the equation $b = ka + 2$.

    (2) $(3, 5)$ is a solution of the equation $b = ka - 1$.

    ○   Statement (1) ALONE is sufficient, but statement (2) is not sufficient.

    ○   Statement (2) ALONE is sufficient, but statement (1) is not sufficient.

    ○   BOTH statements TOGETHER are sufficient, but NEITHER statement ALONE is sufficient.

    ○   EACH statement ALONE is sufficient.

    ○   Statements (1) and (2) TOGETHER are NOT sufficient.

GO ON TO THE NEXT PAGE

13. Ann and Bob drive separately to a meeting. Ann's average driving speed is greater than Bob's average driving speed by one-third of Bob's average driving speed, and Ann drives twice as many miles as Bob. What is the ratio of the number of hours Ann spends driving to the meeting to the number of hours Bob spends driving to the meeting?

   ○ $8:3$
   ○ $3:2$
   ○ $4:3$
   ○ $2:3$
   ○ $3:8$

14. If $0 < p < 1$, which of the following has the least value?

   ○ $\dfrac{1}{p^2}$

   ○ $\dfrac{1}{\sqrt{p}}$

   ○ $\dfrac{1}{p^2 + 1}$

   ○ $\dfrac{1}{\sqrt{p+1}}$

   ○ $\dfrac{1}{(p+1)^2}$

15. If $Z_1, Z_2, Z_3, \ldots, Z_n$ is a sequence of consecutive positive integers, is the sum of all the integers in this sequence odd?

   (1) $\dfrac{z_1 + z_2 + z_3 + \cdots + z_n}{n}$ is an odd integer.

   (2) n is odd.

   ○   Statement (1) ALONE is sufficient, but statement (2) is not sufficient.
   ○   Statement (2) ALONE is sufficient, but statement (1) is not sufficient.
   ○   BOTH statements TOGETHER are sufficient, but NEITHER statement ALONE is sufficient.
   ○   EACH statement ALONE is sufficient.
   ○   Statements (1) and (2) TOGETHER are NOT sufficient.

GO ON TO THE NEXT PAGE

16. Sets X and Y consist solely of positive integers. Each set contains at least two elements, and no element appears more than once within a set. Sets X and Y contain the same number of elements. Is the standard deviation of set X greater than the standard deviation of set Y?

    (1) The positive difference between the range of set X and the range of set Y is 12.

    (2) Each element of set Y is the square of an element of set X.

    O   Statement (1) ALONE is sufficient, but statement (2) is not sufficient.

    O   Statement (2) ALONE is sufficient, but statement (1) is not sufficient.

    O   BOTH statements TOGETHER are sufficient, but NEITHER statement ALONE is sufficient.

    O   EACH statement ALONE is sufficient.

    O   Statements (1) and (2) TOGETHER are NOT sufficient.

17. In a certain game, each player scores either 2 points or 5 points. If n players score 2 points and m players score 5 points, and the total number of points scored is 50, what is the least possible positive difference between n and m?

    O   1
    O   3
    O   5
    O   7
    O   9

18. Machine A can process 6,000 envelopes in 3 hours. Machines B and C working together but independently can process the same number of envelopes in $2\frac{2}{5}$ hours. If machines A and C working together but independently process 3,000 envelopes in 1 hour, then how many hours would it take machine B to process 12,000 envelopes?

    O   2
    O   3
    O   4
    O   6
    O   8

GO ON TO THE NEXT PAGE

19. If the probability of rain on any given day in City X is 50 percent, what is the probability that it rains on exactly 3 days in a 5-day period?

    ○ $\dfrac{8}{125}$

    ○ $\dfrac{2}{25}$

    ○ $\dfrac{5}{16}$

    ○ $\dfrac{8}{25}$

    ○ $\dfrac{3}{4}$

20. At a laboratory, white rats are fed 6 pellets of food per day, and black rats are fed 8 pellets of food per day. If the laboratory fed a total of 120 pellets of food to white and black rats on a certain day, were more black rats than white rats fed?

    (1) There are a total of 17 rats.
    (2) There are 8 white rats.

    ○ Statement (1) ALONE is sufficient, but statement (2) is not sufficient.
    ○ Statement (2) ALONE is sufficient, but statement (1) is not sufficient.
    ○ BOTH statements TOGETHER are sufficient, but NEITHER statement ALONE is sufficient.
    ○ EACH statement ALONE is sufficient.
    ○ Statements (1) and (2) TOGETHER are NOT sufficient.

21. Four different prime numbers, each less than 20, are multiplied together. What is the greatest possible result?

    ○ 21,879
    ○ 28,728
    ○ 40,755
    ○ 46,189
    ○ 49,742

GO ON TO THE NEXT PAGE ⇒

22. A baseball card collector has 1,100 cards that are in mint condition and 400 cards that are not. Of those cards in mint condition, 60 percent are rookie cards. If 740 of the cards in his collection are not rookie cards, then how many cards in the collection are rookie cards that are not in mint condition?

   ○   100
   ○   300
   ○   440
   ○   760
   ○   1,500

23. If m and n are both two-digit numbers, and $m - n = 11x$, is x an integer?

   (1) The tens digit and the units digit of m are the same.
   (2) $m + n$ is a multiple of 11.

   ○   Statement (1) ALONE is sufficient, but statement (2) is not sufficient.
   ○   Statement (2) ALONE is sufficient, but statement (1) is not sufficient.
   ○   BOTH statements TOGETHER are sufficient, but NEITHER statement ALONE is sufficient.
   ○   EACH statement ALONE is sufficient.
   ○   Statements (1) and (2) TOGETHER are NOT sufficient.

24. Which of the following must equal zero for all real numbers x?

   I. $x^3 - x^2$
   II. x^0
   III. x^1

   ○   None
   ○   I only
   ○   II only
   ○   I and II only
   ○   II and III only

GO ON TO THE NEXT PAGE

25. What is the value of x?

   (1) $x^2 - 4 = 20$

   (2) $-2x + \dfrac{\frac{8}{5}\sqrt{6}}{0.8} = -x$

   O   Statement (1) ALONE is sufficient, but statement (2) is not sufficient.
   O   Statement (2) ALONE is sufficient, but statement (1) is not sufficient.
   O   BOTH statements TOGETHER are sufficient, but NEITHER statement ALONE is sufficient.
   O   EACH statement ALONE is sufficient.
   O   Statements (1) and (2) TOGETHER are NOT sufficient.

26. The population of City A is three times the population of City B. Together, Cities A and B have twice the population of City C. What is the ratio of the population of City C to the population of City B?

   O   1:4
   O   1:2
   O   2:1
   O   3:1
   O   4:1

27. If the fraction $\dfrac{m}{n}$ is negative, which of the following CANNOT be true?

   O $\dfrac{n}{m} > \dfrac{m}{n}$
   O $mn < 0$
   O $n - m > 0$
   O $mn^3 > 0$
   O $m - n > 0$

GO ON TO THE NEXT PAGE

28. The speed of a train pulling out of a station is given by the equation $s = t^2 + t$, where s is the speed in kilometers per hour and t is the time in seconds from when the train starts moving. The equation holds for all situations where $0 \leq t \leq 4$. In kilometers per hour, what is the positive difference in the speed of the train 4 seconds after it starts moving compared to the speed 2 seconds after it starts moving?

   ○　0
   ○　6
   ○　14
   ○　20
   ○　38

29. If Rebecca made $60,000 last year after taxes and put all of this money toward living expenses, travel, and savings, how much did she spend on travel?

   (1) Rebecca's expenditure on travel was 20 percent of her expenditure on living expenses.

   (2) The total amount of money that Rebecca put towards living expenses and savings was 800 percent greater than the amount that she spent on travel.

   ○　Statement (1) ALONE is sufficient, but statement (2) is not sufficient.
   ○　Statement (2) ALONE is sufficient, but statement (1) is not sufficient.
   ○　BOTH statements TOGETHER are sufficient, but NEITHER statement ALONE is sufficient.
   ○　EACH statement ALONE is sufficient.
   ○　Statements (1) and (2) TOGETHER are NOT sufficient.

30. If Lisa walks t blocks in 3 minutes, how many minutes will it take her to walk s blocks at the same rate?

   ○　$\dfrac{s}{3t}$
   ○　$\dfrac{3s}{t}$
   ○　$\dfrac{3}{st}$
   ○　$\dfrac{3t}{s}$
   ○　$\dfrac{t}{3s}$

GO ON TO THE NEXT PAGE

31. A chemist has 10 liters of a solution that is 10 percent nitric acid by volume. He wants to dilute the solution to 4 percent strength by adding water. How many liters of water must he add?

    ○   15
    ○   18
    ○   20
    ○   25
    ○   26

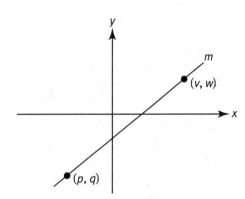

32. What is the slope of line *m* in the figure above?

    (1) $w - q = 14$
    (2) $p - v = -15$

    ○   Statement (1) ALONE is sufficient, but statement (2) is not sufficient.
    ○   Statement (2) ALONE is sufficient, but statement (1) is not sufficient.
    ○   BOTH statements TOGETHER are sufficient, but NEITHER statement ALONE is sufficient.
    ○   EACH statement ALONE is sufficient.
    ○   Statements (1) and (2) TOGETHER are NOT sufficient.

GO ON TO THE NEXT PAGE

33. If a^3, b^3, and c^3 are all positive, does $a^2 = \dfrac{b}{c^3}$?

    (1) $c = \dfrac{b}{(ac)^2}$

    (2) $c = \dfrac{b^{\frac{1}{3}}}{a^{\frac{2}{3}}}$

    O Statement (1) ALONE is sufficient, but statement (2) is not sufficient.
    O Statement (2) ALONE is sufficient, but statement (1) is not sufficient.
    O BOTH statements TOGETHER are sufficient, but NEITHER statement ALONE is sufficient.
    O EACH statement ALONE is sufficient.
    O Statements (1) and (2) TOGETHER are NOT sufficient.

34. Molly purchased Brand A binders at $8.00 apiece and Brand B binders at $5.60 apiece. If she bought a total of 12 binders for $84.00, how many Brand A binders did she buy?

    O 2
    O 5
    O 6
    O 7
    O 10

35. A local farmer grows wheat on land he rents for a fixed cost of $200,000 per year. The variable cost of growing one bushel of wheat is $10. In a certain year, the farmer grows and sells 50,000 bushels of wheat and makes a profit of $150,000, after paying the fixed cost to rent the land. If every bushel sold for the same price, what was the selling price, in dollars, of a bushel of wheat?

    O 3
    O 7
    O 11
    O 13
    O 17

GO ON TO THE NEXT PAGE

36. If a and b are integers and $a = |b + 2| + |3 - b|$, does $a = 5$?

   (1) $b < 3$
   (2) $b > -2$

   ○   Statement (1) ALONE is sufficient, but statement (2) is not sufficient.
   ○   Statement (2) ALONE is sufficient, but statement (1) is not sufficient.
   ○   BOTH statements TOGETHER are sufficient, but NEITHER statement ALONE is sufficient.
   ○   EACH statement ALONE is sufficient.
   ○   Statements (1) and (2) TOGETHER are NOT sufficient.

37. In a certain laboratory, chemicals are identified by a color-coding system. There are 20 different chemicals. Each is coded with either a single color or a unique two-color combination. If the order of colors in the pairs doesn't matter, what is the minimum number of different colors needed to code all 20 chemicals with either a single color or a unique pair of colors?

   ○   5
   ○   6
   ○   7
   ○   20
   ○   40

IF YOU FINISH BEFORE TIME IS CALLED, YOU MAY CHECK YOUR WORK ON
THIS SECTION ONLY. DO NOT TURN TO ANY OTHER SECTION IN THE TEST.

STOP

39

Verbal Section
41 Questions

Time—75 minutes

There are three types of questions in the Verbal section: Critical Reasoning, Reading Comprehension, and Sentence Correction.

Directions: For each question, select the best answer of the choices given.

Each of the **Critical Reasoning** questions is based on a short argument, a set of statements, or a plan of action.

Each of the **Reading Comprehension** questions is based on the content of a passage. After reading the passage, answer all questions pertaining to it on the basis of what is **stated** or **implied** in the passage.

Each of the **Sentence Correction** questions presents a sentence, part or all of which is underlined. Beneath the sentence you will find five ways of phrasing the underlined part. The first of these repeats the original; the other four are different. Follow the requirements of standard written English to choose your answer, paying attention to grammar, word choice, and sentence construction. Select the answer that produces the most effective sentence; your answer should make the sentence clear, exact, and free of grammatical error. It should also minimize awkwardness, ambiguity, and redundancy.

You may review these directions at any time during the Verbal section.

GO ON TO THE NEXT PAGE

1. Countries A and B are in competition to draw tourists to their countries. In Country A, about 2,500 violent crimes are reported per year. In Country B, about 1,000 violent crimes are reported per year. Trying to draw tourists away from Country A, officials in Country B use these violent crime statistics to claim it has a lower violent crime rate than Country A.

   Which of the following, if true, would most undermine Country B's argument that it has the lower violent crime rate?

   O   Most violent criminals in Country B are repeat offenders.

   O   White-collar crime is higher in Country B than in Country A.

   O   The population of Country A is 20 times greater than the population of Country B.

   O   Country B has fewer tourists than Country A.

   O   Country A has a better prison system than Country B.

2. It can be difficult for small investors to sell their shares of stock in companies whose policies they disagree with, because small investors' assets are less robust <u>than</u> large investors.

   O   than

   O   than those of

   O   than is true of

   O   compared with

   O   relatively to those of

3. The workers' union of GrainCorp, a grain-processing plant, is attempting to obtain a pay raise from GrainCorp management. To pressure GrainCorp management into accepting the union's proposal, the president of the union has proposed organizing a consumer boycott against SquareMart food stores, which are owned by MegaFood, the parent company of GrainCorp.

   The answer to which of the following questions is LEAST directly relevant to the union president's consideration of whether a boycott of SquareMart will lead to acceptance of the union's pay rate proposal?

   O   Would the loss of business at SquareMart stores materially affect MegaFood?

   O   Are the staple food products purchased by consumers at SquareMart stores readily available at other stores not owned by MegaFood?

   O   How many SquareMarts are within the region of the GrainCorp plant?

   O   Have other unions successfully employed the same strategy?

   O   Is MegaFood the only corporation that operates both grain-processing plants and food stores?

GO ON TO THE NEXT PAGE

Questions 4–7 are based on the following passage

An important feature of the labor market in recent years has been the increasing participation of women, particularly married women. Many analysts suggest, however, that women comprise a secondary labor market where rates of pay and promotion prospects are inferior to those available to men. The principal reason is that women

5   have, or are assumed to have, domestic responsibilities that compete with paid employment. Such domestic responsibilities are strongly influenced by social values, which require women to give priority to home and family over paid employment.

The difficulties that women face in the labor market and in their ability to reach senior positions in organizations are accentuated with the arrival of children. In order to

10   become full-time employees, women with children must overcome the problems of finding good, affordable child care and the psychological barriers of workplace marginality. Some women balance domestic and workplace commitments by working part-time. However, part-time work is a precarious form of employment. Women part-timers are often the first laid off in a difficult economy. These workers are often referred

15   to as the "reserve army" of female labor.

One researcher has found that approximately 80 percent of women in their twenties who have children remain at home. Such women who later return to work represent another sector of the workforce facing difficulties. When the typical houseworker returns to the labor market, she is unsure of herself in her new environment. This

20   doubt is accentuated by her recent immersion in housework, a very private form of work. Without recent employment experience, these women confront a restricted range of opportunities and will almost certainly be offered low-status jobs with poor prospects.

Even women professionals who interrupt their careers to have children experience

25   difficulties. Their technical skills may become rusty or obsolete, important networks of business contacts are broken, and their delayed return to work may mean that they are likely to come up for promotion well after the age that would be otherwise normal. Consequently, women, even those of high ability, may find themselves blocked in the lower echelons of an organization, overlooked, or even "invisible" to senior

30   management.

GO ON TO THE NEXT PAGE

4. The author of the passage is primarily concerned with

   O advocating changes in employers' practices towards women with children.

   O examining some of the reasons women rarely reach the higher echelons of paid labor.

   O describing the psychological consequences for women of working outside the home.

   O taking issue with those who believe women should not work outside the home.

   O analyzing the contribution of women to industry and business.

5. The passage provides information to support which of the following statements about women workers?

   O It is the responsibility of employers to provide child care accommodations for women workers with children.

   O Women in high-status positions are easily able to integrate career and children.

   O Conditions for working mothers are much better today than they were 20 years ago.

   O The decision to work outside the home is often the source of considerable anxiety for women with children.

   O With the expense of child care, it is often not profitable for women with children to work.

6. The author's discussion of women professionals in the last paragraph serves to

   O show that the difficulties of integrating careers and motherhood can be overcome.

   O indicate that even women of higher status are not exempt from the difficulties of integrating careers and children.

   O defend changes in the policies of employers towards working mothers.

   O modify a hypothesis regarding the increased labor force participation of women.

   O point out the lack of opportunities for women in business.

GO ON TO THE NEXT PAGE

7. According to the passage, men generally receive higher salaries and have a better chance of being promoted because women

   O   tend to work in industries that rely almost exclusively on part-time labor.

   O   lack the technical and managerial experience of their male counterparts.

   O   have responsibilities outside of the workplace that demand considerable attention.

   O   are the first to be laid off when the economy grows at a very slow pace.

   O   suffer discrimination in the male-dominated corporate environment.

8. Because the city's files covered only the years 1934 through <u>2002, so the potential buyers were unable to determine the year of originally</u> construction.

   O   2002, so the potential buyers were unable to determine the year of originally

   O   2002, and the potential buyers were unable to determine the year of originally

   O   2002, the potential buyers were unable to determine the year of original

   O   2002, therefore the potential buyers were unable to determine the year of originally

   O   2002; therefore, the potential buyers were unable to determine the year of original

9. Those who study ancient European history soon realize that <u>before Greece was Greece, it was a collection of small city-states</u> that were intensely jealous of one another and were only occasionally able to work together for common goals.

   O   before Greece was Greece, it was a collection of small city-states

   O   before there was Greece, it was a collection of small city-states

   O   before Greece, it was a collection of small city-states

   O   it was a collection of small city-states that was Greece

   O   Greece had become a collection of small city-states

GO ON TO THE NEXT PAGE

10. The local high school students have been clamoring for the freedom to design their own curricula. Allowing this would be as disastrous as allowing three-year-olds to choose their own diets. These students have neither the maturity nor the experience to equal that of the professional educators now doing the job.

Which of the following statements, if true, would most strengthen the above argument?

○ High school students have less formal education than those who currently design the curricula.

○ Three-year-olds do not, if left to their own devices, choose healthful diets.

○ The local high school students are less intelligent than the average teenager.

○ Individualized curricula are more beneficial to high school students than are the standard curricula, which are rigid and unresponsive to their particular strengths and weaknesses.

○ The ability to design good curricula develops only after years of familiarity with educational life.

11. <u>In order to document their contribution to the field of structural engineering, the curators at the university's art museum organized a comprehensive exhibition of the work of leading Swiss designers, including photographs, diagrams, and models of their most famous bridges and buildings.</u>

○ In order to document their contribution to the field of structural engineering, the curators at the university's art museum organized a comprehensive exhibition of the work of leading Swiss designers, including photographs, diagrams, and models of their most famous bridges and buildings.

○ In order to document the contribution of the Swiss to the field of structural engineering, the curators at the university's art museum organized a comprehensive exhibition of the work of leading Swiss designers, including photographs, diagrams, and models of their most famous bridges and buildings.

○ In order to document the contribution of the Swiss to the field of structural engineering, the curators at the university's art museum organized a comprehensive exhibition of the work of leading Swiss designers, including photographs, diagrams, and models of its most famous bridges and buildings.

○ In order to document their contribution to the structural engineering field, a comprehensive exhibition was organized by the curators at the university's art museum of their photographs, diagrams, and models of the most famous bridges and buildings of leading Swiss designers.

○ The curators at the university's art museum, in order to document their contribution to the field, organized a comprehensive exhibition of the work of leading Swiss designers, including photographs, diagrams, and models of their most famous bridges and buildings.

GO ON TO THE NEXT PAGE

Questions 12–14 are based on the following passage

A 1973 Supreme Court decision and related Senate hearings focused congressional criticism on the 1966 Freedom of Information Act. Its unconditional exemption of any material stamped "classified"—i.e., containing information considered relevant to national security—forced the Court to uphold nondisclosure in *EPA v. Mink*.
5   Justice Potter Stewart explained that the Act provided "no means to question a decision to stamp a document 'secret.'" Senate witnesses testified that the wording of certain articles in the Act permitted bureaucrats to discourage requests for newsworthy documents.

In response, a House committee drafted HR 12471, proposing several
10   amendments to the Act. A provision was reworded to ensure release of documents to any applicant providing a "reasonable description"—exact titles and numbers were no longer to be mandatory. The courts were empowered to review classified documents and rule on their status. The Senate companion bill, S 2543, included these provisions as well as others: standardization of
15   search and copy fees, sanctions against noncompliant federal employees, and a provision for nonexempt portions of a classified document to be released.

The Justice and Defense departments objected to the changes as "costly, burdensome, and inflexible." They argued that the time limits imposed on response "might actually hamper access to information." The Pentagon
20   asserted that judicial review of exemptions could pose a threat to national security. President Ford, upon taking office in August 1974, concurred.

HR 12471 passed in March 1974; S 2543 was approved in May after the adoption of further amendments to reduce the number of unconditional exemptions granted in 1966. The Hart Amendment, for instance, mandated
25   disclosure of law enforcement records, unless their release would interfere with a trial or investigation, invade personal privacy, or disclose an informer's identity. This amendment provoked another presidential objection: millions of pages of FBI records would be subject to public scrutiny, unless each individual section were proven exempt.

30   Before submitting the legislation to Ford, a joint conference of both houses amalgamated the two versions of the bill, while making further changes to incorporate Ford's criticisms. The administration of disciplinary sanctions was transferred from the courts to the executive branch; provisions were included to accord due weight to departmental expertise in the evaluation of "classified"
35   exemptions. The identity of confidential sources was in all cases to be protected. Ford nevertheless vetoed the bill, but the veto was overridden by a two-thirds vote in both houses.

GO ON TO THE NEXT PAGE

12. According to the passage, the Justice and Defense departments opposed the proposed revision of the Freedom of Information Act on the grounds that it

   O   was an attempt to block public access to information.

   O   would violate national security agreements.

   O   would pose administrative problems.

   O   was an attempt to curtail their own departmental power.

   O   would weaken the president's authority.

13. Which of the following statements, if true, supports the assertion that "judicial review of exemptions could pose a threat to national security" (lines 20–21)?

   O   Judges lack the expertise to evaluate the significance of military intelligence records.

   O   Many of the documents that are presently stamped "classified" contain information that is inaccurate or outdated.

   O   It would be time-consuming and expensive for judges to review millions of pages of classified records.

   O   Some judges are likely to rule on exemptions in accordance with vested interests of political action groups.

   O   The practice of judicial review of exemptions will succeed only if it meets with presidential approval.

14. Which of the following statements is in accordance with President Ford's position on disclosure of FBI records?

   O   FBI records should be exempt from the provisions of the Freedom of Information Act.

   O   FBI records should only be withheld from release if such release constitutes a threat to national security.

   O   It would be too expensive and time-consuming to identify exempt sections of FBI records.

   O   Protection of the identity of confidential sources is more important than the protection of personal privacy or investigative secrecy.

   O   FBI records should not be reviewed section by section before being released to the public.

GO ON TO THE NEXT PAGE

15. <u>Although some ornithologists contend that the precursors of birds are arboreal creatures that glide from tree to tree</u>, others believe that they were runners whose front limbs evolved into wings.

    ○   Although some ornithologists contend that the precursors of birds are arboreal creatures that glide from tree to tree

    ○   However it may be that some ornithologists contend that the precursors of birds were arboreal creatures that glide from tree to tree

    ○   Despite that the precursors of birds were, according to some ornithologists, arboreal creatures that glide from tree to tree

    ○   Although some ornithologists contend that the precursors of birds were arboreal creatures that glided from tree to tree

    ○   According to some ornithologists gliding from tree to tree, the precursors of birds are arboreal creatures, that

16. A recently published article on human physiology claims that Enzyme K contributes to improved performance in strenuous activities such as weight lifting and sprinting. The article cites evidence of above-average levels of Enzyme K in Olympic weight lifters and sprinters.

    Which of the following, if true, would most strengthen the article's conclusion?

    ○   Enzyme K levels tend to peak when people feel most alert.

    ○   Enzyme K has no other function in the human body.

    ○   Enzyme K levels are closely correlated with those of Enzyme L, a known stimulant.

    ○   Enzyme K helps weight lifters more than it helps sprinters.

    ○   Strenuous activities do not cause the human body to produce unusually high levels of Enzyme K.

17. The Dancing Doll line sold slightly more than $3.5 million worth of toys last year, 40 percent more than <u>the Teeny Tiny Trucks line did and nearly three times as much as the Basic Blocks line's sales</u>.

    ○   the Teeny Tiny Trucks line did and nearly three times as much as the Basic Blocks line's sales

    ○   the Teeny Tiny Trucks did and nearly three times what the Basic Blocks' sales were

    ○   the Teeny Tiny Trucks line sold and nearly three times as much as Basic Blocks' sales

    ○   the Teeny Tiny Trucks line and nearly three times as much as Basic Blocks' sales

    ○   the Teeny Tiny Trucks line sold and nearly three times as much as the Basic Blocks line sold

GO ON TO THE NEXT PAGE

18. Without hiding the fact that the destruction of Athens <u>was one of their most important objectives</u>, the multitudinous Persian army, led by Xerxes and nine of his generals, marched westward toward Greece in the spring and summer of 480 BCE.

    ○ was one of their most important objectives

    ○ was one of its most important objectives

    ○ was one of the objectives they considered to be most important

    ○ having been one of its most important objectives

    ○ is one of its most important objectives

19. The owner of a four-story commercial building discovered termites in the building's first and second floors and called an exterminator. The exterminator pumped gas into the walls on both the first and second floors. Due to the exterminator's work, the termites on those floors were killed quickly.

    Which of the following, if true, most seriously undermines the validity of the explanation for the speed with which the termites were killed?

    ○ The third floor had no termite infestation.

    ○ Even though the exterminator did not pump gas into the walls of the fourth story, the previously undiscovered termites there died as quickly as they did on the first and second stories.

    ○ The speed at which termites are killed increases as the concentration of an exterminator's gas increases.

    ○ The speed with which the exterminator's gas kills termites drops off sharply as the gas dissipates throughout the building's walls.

    ○ The exterminator's gas-pumping system works efficiently even when pumping gas into both the first and second stories of the building simultaneously.

GO ON TO THE NEXT PAGE ⇒

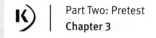

Questions 20–23 are based on the following passage

Modern methods of predicting earthquakes recognize that quakes, far from being geologic anomalies, are part of the periodic accumulation and discharge of seismic energy. As continents receive the horizontal thrust of seafloor plates, crustal strains develop. Accumulation of strain can take
5 anywhere from 100 years in certain coastal locations to over a millennium in some inland regions before a critical point is reached and a rupture occurs. In both areas, the buildup of strain is accompanied by long- and short-range precursory phenomena that are crucial to earthquake prediction.

Quakes along active faults—like those along the Pacific coasts—are usually
10 frequent; scientists designate such areas as quake-prone. However, when the time interval between quakes is great, as in inland regions, locating active faults is only a beginning. Geological scars of past subsidence, cracks, and offsets are useful in determining potential quake locations, as are seismicity gaps, areas where no small quakes have been recorded. Seismologists may
15 also consult the historical record. Primary sources range from eyewitness accounts of ancient quakes to recent official documentation of quake-related damage.

Once the perimeters of a quake-prone zone are established, a network of base stations can monitor precursory phenomena. Stations must extend over
20 a wide area yet be placed at measured intervals to obtain precise readings. Changes in geochemical readings (electric currents, radon concentrations) and in groundwater levels, as well as the occurrence of microearthquakes, are valuable precursors. Crustal movements—tilting, rising, and expansion or contraction of the ground's surface—can be read through triangulation and
25 leveling surveys taken over the course of decades. Theoretically, if an area's critical strain—the magnitude of strain necessary to produce a rupture—is known, subtracting the measured accumulated crustal strain from the critical strain will indicate a time frame for an impending quake.

Violent tilting and foreshocks are among phenomena classified as short-term
30 precursors. Many are still being identified as new quakes occur. Such precursors are valuable since their appearance can permit prediction of a quake to within hours of the primary rupture. Here, too, historical documents are useful. Seismologists recognized the liquefaction of sand as a precursor after a 1964 quake in Japan.

GO ON TO THE NEXT PAGE

20. According to the passage, a major difference between coastal regions and inland regions is that in coastal regions

    O   crustal strain does not occur.

    O   earthquakes are less numerous.

    O   critical points are reached more quickly.

    O   precursory phenomena are seldom observed.

    O   seafloor plate action is less powerful.

21. The primary purpose of the passage is to

    O   clarify the way in which earthquakes develop in inland locations.

    O   show that earthquakes are a result of the normal accumulation and discharge of seismic energy.

    O   discuss the accumulation of crustal strain in coastal regions.

    O   argue that precursory phenomena should be disregarded in attempts at quake prediction.

    O   describe methods of earthquake prediction and explain the importance of precursory phenomena.

22. The primary function of the third paragraph is to

    O   explain the relationship between accumulated and critical strain.

    O   describe the use of precise intervals in establishing networks of base stations.

    O   summarize the differences between earthquakes in coastal and inland regions.

    O   outline some of the methods used by seismologists to predict earthquakes.

    O   suggest that critical strain is not spread evenly along most major fault lines.

GO ON TO THE NEXT PAGE

23. According to the passage, knowledge of an area's critical strain can help seismologists

    O estimate the date of a future earthquake.
    O calculate the severity of an initial rupture.
    O measure the seismic force along a fault.
    O revise the distances between base stations.
    O predict the rate of future crustal movement.

24. Scoliosis, <u>a condition when the spine curves abnormally and throws the body out of line</u>, can cause heart and lung problems as well as physical deformity.

    O a condition when the spine curves abnormally and throws the body out of line
    O a condition in which an abnormal curvature of the spine throws the body out of line
    O a condition of the spine curving abnormally and in which the body is thrown out of line
    O where the body is thrown out of line by an abnormal curvature of the spine
    O a condition of an abnormal curvature of the spine throwing the body out of line

25. The state legislature has proposed a new law that would provide a tax credit to people who install alarm systems in their homes. Members of the legislature claim that the new law will reduce crime, citing studies showing that crime rates fall as the percentage of homes with alarm systems rises.

    Which of the following, if true, would cast the most doubt on the claim that the new law will reduce crime?

    O No law can prevent crime altogether.
    O The amount of the tax credit is so low relative to the cost of alarm systems that very few people will install alarm systems to obtain this credit.
    O Neighborhood crime prevention programs can reduce crime as effectively as alarm systems can.
    O The state would have to build more prisons to house all the people caught by the new alarm systems.
    O The state can afford to reduce taxes further.

GO ON TO THE NEXT PAGE ⇒

26. Corporation X spends a larger percentage of its revenue on insurance than Corporation Y does on employee salaries.

    O Corporation X spends a larger percentage of its revenue on insurance than Corporation Y does on employee salaries.

    O In Corporation X, a larger percentage of the revenues is spent on insurance than is spent on employee salaries in Corporation Y.

    O In Corporation X, they spend a larger percentage of revenues on insurance than Corporation Y does on employee salaries.

    O A larger percentage of Corporation X's revenue is spent on insurance than Corporation Y spends on employee salaries.

    O Of the Corporations X and Y, a higher percentage of revenues is spent on insurance by the former than the latter spends on employee salaries.

27. In a certain state, the rate at which inhabitants of City X contract a certain disease is significantly lower than the rate at which inhabitants of City Y contract the disease. So if a couple originally from City Y relocate to City X and raise a family there, their children will be significantly less likely to contract this disease than they would have, had they remained in City Y.

    Which of the following, if true, would most seriously weaken the conclusion drawn in the passage?

    O Many health experts do not believe that moving to City X will lead to a significant increase in the average person's immunity to the disease.

    O The mayor of City Y has falsely claimed that statistics relating to the incidence of the disease in his city are not accurate.

    O The lower incidence of the disease in City X can be ascribed mostly to genetically determined factors.

    O Some inhabitants of City Y possess a greater immunity to the disease than do the healthiest inhabitants of City X.

    O Smog levels in City X are significantly lower than those of any other city in the state.

28. Museum-goers who glanced up into the building's five-story atrium often notice birds nesting in the rafters, whose behavior was being studied by the museum's staff.

    O notice birds nesting in the rafters, whose behavior was being studied by the museum's staff

    O notice birds nesting in the rafters, which were being studied by the museum's staff

    O notice that birds, whose behavior was being studied by the museum's staff, are nesting in the rafters

    O noticed that birds, whose behavior was being studied by the museum's staff, were nesting in the rafters

    O noticed that birds, with the behavior that was being studied by the museum's staff, were nesting in the rafters

GO ON TO THE NEXT PAGE

29. Since 1993, when it passed a referendum <u>approving casino gambling, the town of Riverside, Missouri, was using</u> casino tax revenue to improve its streets, sewers, buildings, and other public works.

    ○ approving casino gambling, the town of Riverside, Missouri, was using

    ○ for the approving of casino gambling, the town of Riverside, Missouri, has used

    ○ approved casino gambling, the town of Riverside, Missouri, has used

    ○ approving casino gambling, the town of Riverside, Missouri, has used

    ○ approving casino gambling, the town of Riverside, Missouri, was to be using

30. Retail clothing stores should hold "one-day-only" sales to clear merchandise that has been returned because it is defective in some way. The stores should sell this merchandise for up to 70 percent less than the original retail price. Stores will find these sales to be an effective way of getting rid of defective merchandise as long as they inform customers that the discounted merchandise is nonreturnable.

    The author assumes which of the following about the "one-day-only" sale merchandise in predicting the effectiveness of these sales?

    ○ The defects in the merchandise are not so significant that customers will be unwilling to pay even the sale price.

    ○ The rate of returns when merchandise is new makes these "one-day-only" sales key to a store's profitability.

    ○ Too few shoppers purchase merchandise at full retail price.

    ○ If these sales become popular, stores will have to have them more often.

    ○ The majority of the "one-day-only" sale merchandise will be purchased by shoppers who would otherwise not shop at those stores.

31. Researchers have found that the human body can use protein derived from whey more efficiently than it can use <u>protein from other sources such as soy, eggs, or drinking milk</u>.

    ○ protein from other sources such as soy, eggs, or drinking milk

    ○ protein from other sources like soy, eggs, or drinking milk

    ○ protein from other sources such as soy, eggs, or milk

    ○ protein which it has derived from other sources such as soy, eggs, or drinking milk

    ○ its protein from other sources such as soy, eggs, or milk

GO ON TO THE NEXT PAGE

32. It was decided by the National Weather Service to purchase a forecasting system that combines 44 computers linked together with each other to form the world's sixth-largest supercomputer.

- ○ It was decided by the National Weather Service to purchase a forecasting system that combines 44 computers linked together with each other to form the world's sixth-largest supercomputer.

- ○ A forecasting system that combines 44 computers linked together with each other to form the world's sixth-largest supercomputer was selected to be purchased by the National Weather Service.

- ○ It was decided by the National Weather Service to purchase a forecasting system that links 44 computers together to form the world's sixth-largest supercomputer.

- ○ The National Weather Service decided to purchase a forecasting system that links 44 computers together to form the world's sixth-largest supercomputer.

- ○ The National Weather Service decided to purchase a forecasting system that combines 44 computers linked together with each other to form the world's sixth-largest supercomputer.

GO ON TO THE NEXT PAGE

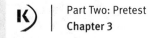
Questions 33–35 are based on the following passage

Contamination is the unintended presence of harmful substances or organisms in food. While it is true that recent scientific advances have resulted in safer foods, better methods of preservation, and improved storage practices, it is still necessary to guard against the practices that can
5   increase the likelihood of food contamination. Because food-borne illness poses a potentially serious threat to public health, preventing contamination of safe food needs to be a prime objective of every food service manager. Furthermore, a food service manager must possess accurate information on the different hazards associated with the contamination of food in the event
10 that a food-borne illness crisis does arise. A full understanding of the biological, chemical, and physical hazards allows the food service manager to implement the control measures necessary to minimize the health risks associated with food and, thus, to decrease the possibility of contamination.

The most serious risk associated with food is the biological hazard.
15 Biological hazards are dangers to food from pathogenic (disease-causing) microorganisms, such as bacteria, viruses, parasites, and fungi, and from toxins that occur in certain plants and fish. When biological hazards result in food-borne illnesses, these illnesses are generally classified as either infections or intoxications. A food-borne infection is a disease that results
20 from eating food containing living harmful microorganisms. One of the most frequently reported diseases of this type is salmonellosis, which results from the consumption of food contaminated with live pathogenic *Salmonella*.

The other major form of biologically induced food-borne illness is intoxication, which results when toxins, or poisons, from bacterial or mold
25 growth are present in ingested food and cause illness in the host (the human body). These toxins are generally odorless and tasteless and are capable of causing disease even after the microorganisms have been killed. *Staphylococcus* food intoxication is one of the most common types of food-borne illness reported in the United States.

GO ON TO THE NEXT PAGE

33. Which of the following best expresses the main idea of the passage?

    O   Despite recent scientific advances, food-borne illness continues to present a serious risk to public health.

    O   Although chemical and physical hazards can cause a food-borne illness, biological hazards pose the most serious risk of food contamination.

    O   Knowledge of contamination sources is essential for a food service manager to safely operate a food establishment.

    O   Biological, chemical, and physical hazards represent the main sources of food contamination.

    O   The illnesses caused by the contamination of food by biological hazards take the form of either a food-borne infection or a food-borne intoxication.

34. The author of the passage would most likely agree that a food service manager's comprehension of the nature of potential food hazards is

    O   crucial to the safety of a food service operation.

    O   necessarily limited due to the complexity of contamination sources.

    O   the primary factor in an employer's decision to hire that manager.

    O   utilized exclusively for the prevention of food-borne illness.

    O   vitally important but nearly impossible to attain.

35. According to the passage, pathogenic microorganisms

    O   are the most common form of biological hazard.

    O   can only trigger a food-borne illness when alive.

    O   are toxins that occur in certain plants and fish.

    O   include life forms such as bacteria and parasites.

    O   are difficult to detect because they are odorless and tasteless.

GO ON TO THE NEXT PAGE

36. The education offered by junior colleges just after World War II had a tremendous practical effect on family-run businesses throughout the country. After learning new methods of marketing, finance, and accounting, the sons and daughters of merchants returned home, often to increase significantly the size of the family's enterprise or to maximize profits in other ways.

Which of the following statements is best supported by the information above?

O The junior colleges principally emphasized methods of increasing the size of small businesses.

O The business methods taught in the junior colleges were already widespread before World War II.

O The business curricula at junior colleges did not include theoretical principles of management.

O Without the influence of junior colleges, many family-run businesses would have been abandoned as unprofitable.

O Business methods in many postwar family-run businesses changed significantly as a result of the junior colleges.

37. Since the new manufacturing process for plastic containers was introduced 10 years ago, the average size of plastic manufacturing plants <u>have dropped from 200,000 square feet to 50,000 square feet, an area that is about a football field's size</u>.

O have dropped from 200,000 square feet to 50,000 square feet, an area that is about a football field's size

O have dropped from 200,000 square feet to 50,000 square feet, about the size of a football field

O has dropped from 200,000 square feet to 50,000 square feet, about the size of a football field

O has dropped from 200,000 square feet down to 50,000 square feet, about the size of a football field's

O has dropped from 200,000 square feet down to 50,000 square feet, about a football field's size

GO ON TO THE NEXT PAGE →

38. A researcher has discovered that steel containing Element X is stronger and more flexible than ordinary steel because Element X reduces the occurrence of microscopic fractures. The level of Element X in much of the steel produced in Canada is naturally high because the ore deposits from which the steel is produced also contain Element X.

Which of the following can be correctly inferred from the statements above?

- O Steel from Canada is stronger and more flexible than steel from any other country.
- O Steel that is not from Canada is highly likely to develop microscopic fractures after years of use.
- O Producing steel from ore deposits containing Element X is the best way to make steel that is stronger and more flexible.
- O Some steel produced in Canada is less likely to develop microscopic fractures than other steel.
- O Steel produced from Canadian ore deposits contains the highest levels of Element X found in any steel.

39. The newly elected baseball commissioner has asked <u>that a federal arbitrator would mediate negotiations between representatives of the umpire's union, which has threatened</u> to go on strike, and lawyers representing major league franchise owners.

- O that a federal arbitrator would mediate negotiations between representatives of the umpire's union, which has threatened
- O that a federal arbitrator mediate negotiations between representatives of the umpire's union, which have threatened
- O of a federal arbitrator that he mediate negotiations between representatives of the umpire's union, which have threatened
- O a federal arbitrator that he mediate negotiations between representatives of the umpire's union, which has threatened
- O that a federal arbitrator mediate negotiations between representatives of the umpire's union, which has threatened

GO ON TO THE NEXT PAGE

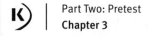

40. Sky Airlines recently announced aggressive cost-cutting measures <u>ranging from new airport check-in procedures that encourage passengers to use self-service kiosks and reductions</u> in the size of its fleet.

   ○ ranging from new airport check-in procedures that encourage passengers to use self-service kiosks and reductions

   ○ ranging from new airport check-in procedures that encourage passengers to use self-service kiosks and to reductions

   ○ such as improvement of airport check-in procedures, encouragement of passengers to use self-service kiosks and reducing

   ○ ranging from new airport check-in procedures that encourage passengers to use self-service kiosks to reducing

   ○ ranging from new airport check-in procedures that encourage passengers to use self-service kiosks to reductions

41. The latest census of the town in which Jacob's hardware store is located has revealed that the population of new residents has increased tenfold since 1980. Though Jacob has not encountered any new competition for business during this time period, his inventory records indicate that the average number of lawnmowers and snowblowers that he sells per year has risen only slightly over the average number of lawnmowers and snowblowers he sold yearly prior to 1980.

   Which of the following, if true, best explains the discrepancy outlined above?

   ○ Since 1980, many of the single-home properties have been subdivided into smaller single-home parcels.

   ○ Inflation has caused the prices of the machines to increase every year since 1980.

   ○ All of the housing built in Jacob's town since 1980 has been large apartment complexes.

   ○ The average snowfall since 1980 has decreased from 6 feet per year to 4 feet per year.

   ○ Jacob's store only carries two brands of lawnmowers and snowblowers.

IF YOU FINISH BEFORE TIME IS CALLED, YOU MAY CHECK YOUR WORK ON THIS SECTION ONLY. DO NOT TURN TO ANY OTHER SECTION IN THE TEST. **STOP**

60

CHAPTER 4

Pretest Answers and Explanations

HOW TO REVIEW THIS TEST

The primary purpose of this Pretest is to allow you to evaluate your strengths and weaknesses—or, as we call them, your areas of opportunity. If you have ample time before Test Day, you will benefit from working through each chapter in this book thoroughly, taking full advantage of the strategic explanations, and using your Online Center for further practice. If, however, you have more limited time to prepare, you may need to prioritize your studies to make sure you spend time addressing the areas in which you are struggling the most—thereby making the most of your opportunities for score improvement.

In either case, understanding your strengths and weaknesses is an essential starting point for your GMAT prep. Each of the explanations that follows is preceded by two labels: one label for the question type (e.g., Data Sufficiency, Sentence Correction) and one or more labels for the question topic (e.g., Arithmetic: Exponents, Verbs). These labels correspond to question types or content areas covered in this book. As you review the explanations, make note of what question types and topics you found most challenging. These are areas on which you will want to place special focus as you work through this book and your Online Center.

The explanations themselves are valuable learning tools. Review the questions you answered incorrectly *and* those you got right. Rework the questions you got wrong so you can be sure to know exactly what to do when you see a similar one in the future. For the questions you got correct, did you answer correctly for the right reasons, or did you follow a lucky hunch? Does the explanation offer an alternative, more efficient path to the right answer that you can add to your arsenal? Or maybe you aced the problem and should take note of your process so that you can repeat it on similar problems!

As you review these explanations, you may not initially understand everything that they describe. Don't worry about this at first—the GMAT tests many different concepts, and you haven't yet begun to learn all the valuable Kaplan Methods and strategies contained in this book. You may find it useful to return to these explanations later in your studies, once you've read and practiced with this book. It's likely that by that point, things that were once confusing to you will have become much clearer. It will also be a great confidence boost to see how far you've come in your mastery of the GMAT.

And finally, don't concern yourself too much with how you scored on this test. You've still got a lot to learn about the GMAT, but you have the best tools to help you on your journey—and taking and reviewing this Pretest is a first great step. Just remember to be patient with yourself as you make mistakes during your study. Everyone does; it's normal. But consider this: Every wrong answer you choose, *and then learn from*, reduces the chance that you'll get a similar question wrong on the one and only day when wrong answers matter. So make mistakes willingly and even happily now, while they don't count. Just resolve to learn from every one of them.

Happy studying!

ANSWER KEY

	Quantitative					Verbal			
1.	E		20.	D	1.	C		22.	D
2.	A		21.	D	2.	B		23.	A
3.	C		22.	A	3.	E		24.	B
4.	B		23.	C	4.	B		25.	B
5.	D		24.	A	5.	D		26.	A
6.	C		25.	B	6.	B		27.	C
7.	C		26.	C	7.	C		28.	D
8.	D		27.	D	8.	C		29.	D
9.	C		28.	C	9.	A		30.	A
10.	D		29.	B	10.	E		31.	C
11.	B		30.	B	11.	B		32.	D
12.	D		31.	A	12.	C		33.	C
13.	B		32.	C	13.	A		34.	A
14.	E		33.	D	14.	A		35.	D
15.	A		34.	D	15.	D		36.	E
16.	B		35.	E	16.	E		37.	C
17.	B		36.	C	17.	E		38.	D
18.	E		37.	B	18.	B		39.	E
19.	C				19.	B		40.	E
					20.	C		41.	C
					21.	E			

PRETEST SCORING TOOL

Using the answer key on the previous page, calculate the number of questions you answered correctly on the Quantitative and Verbal sections combined. The table below will give you an estimate of your score and the corresponding percentile ranking. Keep in mind also that this score is only a rough estimate, since by definition a paper-based test cannot adapt to your performance the way the computer-adaptive GMAT does. For practice taking full-length computer-adaptive tests, visit your Online Center.

Number Correct	Score Estimate	Percentile Estimate	Number Correct	Score Estimate	Percentile Estimate
78	740–800	99	38	380–430	13
77	730–780	98	37	370–420	11
76	720–770	97	36	360–410	10
75	710–760	96	35	350–400	9
74	700–750	94	34	340–390	8
73	690–740	92	33	330–380	7
72	680–730	90	32	330–380	7
71	680–730	90	31	320–370	6
70	670–720	88	30	310–360	5
69	660–710	85	29	300–350	4
68	660–710	85	28	300–350	4
67	650–700	84	27	290–340	3
66	640–690	81	26	280–330	3
65	630–680	79	25	270–320	3
64	620–670	74	24	260–310	2
63	610–660	73	23	250–300	2
62	600–650	70	22	240–290	2
61	590–640	67	21	230–280	2
60	580–630	63	20	220–270	1
59	570–620	60	19	210–260	1
58	560–610	57	18	200–250	1
57	550–600	54	17	200–240	1
56	540–590	51	16	200–230	1
55	530–580	48	15	200–220	1
54	530–580	48	14	200–210	0
53	520–570	45	13	200	0
52	510–560	40	12	200	0
51	500–550	39	11	200	0
50	490–540	36	10	200	0
49	480–530	34	9	200	0
48	470–520	31	8	200	0
47	470–520	31	7	200	0
46	460–510	29	6	200	0
45	450–500	26	5	200	0
44	440–490	23	4	200	0
43	430–480	21	3	200	0
42	420–470	19	2	200	0
41	410–460	17	1	200	0
40	400–450	16	0	200	0
39	390–440	14			

QUANTITATIVE SECTION EXPLANATIONS

1.   (E)

Question Type: Data Sufficiency
Question Topic: Number Properties: Factors and Multiples

This question stem states that j and k are integers and $jk = 12$. Think about sets of integers whose product is 12. The variables j and k could be any of the following sets of factors: 1 and 12; 2 and 6; 3 and 4. Remember, however, that j and k could also be negative.

Statement (1) tells you that j must equal ±6 or ±12. Since $jk = 12$, it follows that k must equal ±2 or ±1. But since you can't determine the unique value of k, the statement is insufficient to answer the question. Eliminate **(A)** and **(D)**.

Statement (2) tells you that k must be one of the integers ±2, ±4, ±6, or ±12. Again, you can't determine the unique value of k, so the statement is insufficient. Eliminate **(B)**.

Since the statements were both insufficient individually, you must now combine them. Comparing the possible values for k you determined by both statements, you have $k = ±2$. But you still can't determine whether k is positive or negative, so you can't answer the question. Choice **(E)** is correct.

2.   (A)

Question Type: Problem Solving
Question Topic: Geometry: Triangles

This question tests two common shapes: equilateral triangles and isosceles triangles. The key to this question, as in most geometry questions, is to put what the text of the question stem tells you into the figure so that you can visualize the relationships clearly. Four lines are of equal length:

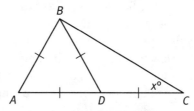

Because all the sides of triangle ABD are equal, its angles must all be 60°. And because $DC = BD$, the measure of angle DBC is the same as that of angle DCB:

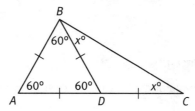

Now you could solve for x if you knew the measure of angle BDC; since the sum of the angles in a triangle is 180°, you can set up this equation: $180° = BDC + 2x°$. Can you figure angle BDC out? Absolutely. Supplementary angles add up to 180°. Since angle BDA is 60°, angle $BDC = 180° - 60° = 120°$.

$$180° = BDC + 2x°$$

Substitute BDC: $\qquad 180° = 120° + 2x°$

Subtract 120°: $\qquad 60° = 2x°$

Divide by 2: $\qquad 30° = x°$

Choice **(A)** is correct.

3.   (C)

Question Type: Data Sufficiency
Question Topic: Algebra: Systems of Linear Equations

This question stem leaves a lot of questions unanswered. All it tells you is that Tara has 12 coins. You can anticipate that the statements will give more information about the types of coins Tara has and enable you to set up one or more algebraic equations to solve for the number of quarters.

Statement (1) says that the total value of the coins is $1.80. It is possible that Tara has 6 quarters and 6 nickels. Tara could also have 7 quarters and 5 pennies. Statement (1) is insufficient. You can eliminate **(A)** and **(D)**.

Now, take a look at Statement (2), forgetting anything you read in Statement (1). Statement (2) says Tara has only quarters and dimes. So of the 12 coins she has, there could be 5 quarters and 7 dimes. She could also have 8 quarters and 4 dimes. Statement (2) is insufficient. You can eliminate **(B)**.

Now take the statements together. Because Statement (2) says that she only has quarters and dimes, you could say that q is the number of quarters Tara has and d is the number of dimes Tara has. From the question stem you know that $q + d = 12$. From Statement (1), if you say that the total value is 180 cents, then $25q + 10d = 180$. Now you have two different linear equations that contain two variables. By applying the rules that govern systems of linear equations, you know that these two equations will have a solution with a single value for q and a single value for d. You could solve them using combination or substitution, but since this is Data Sufficiency, you don't need to waste time solving for the exact values. Since there is only one possible value for q, the statements taken together are sufficient to answer the question. Choice **(C)** is correct.

4.   (B)

Question Type: Problem Solving
Question Topic: Proportions: Percents

You are asked to find the percentage of all cases that must be tested. The total number of cases is $120 + 80 = 200$. For the spring water, the bottler must test $0.05(120) = 6$ cases, and for the sparkling water, it must test $0.1(80) = 8$ cases. The total number of cases to be tested for the spring and sparkling water combined is $6 + 8 = 14$, which is $\frac{14}{200} = \frac{7}{100} = 7\%$ of all cases. Choice **(B)** is correct.

5. (D)

Question Type: Problem Solving
Question Topic: Math Formulas: Averages

Since the 25 products sell at an average price of $1,200, to buy one of each, you'd have to spend 25 × $1,200 = $30,000. You want to find the greatest possible selling price of the most expensive product. The way to maximize this price is to minimize the prices of the other 24 products. Ten of these products sell for less than $1,000, but all sell for at least $420. This means that (in trying to minimize the price of 24 items) you sell 10 at $420. That leaves 14 more that sell for $1,000 or more. So in order to keep minimizing the price of these other items, you'll price these at $1,000. That means that out of the $30,000 you know it will take at least 10($420) + 14($1,000) = $18,200 to purchase the 24 other items. The final, most expensive item can thus cost as much as $30,000 − $18,200 = $11,800. Choice **(D)** is correct.

6. (C)

Question Type: Data Sufficiency
Question Topic: Proportions: Ratios, Percents

The question stem gives no information, so look at the statements.

Statement (1) says that $\frac{3}{5}$ of the members are 25 years of age or older, so the remaining $\frac{2}{5}$ of the members must be under 25 years of age. However, this statement does not give the actual number of members. It is therefore impossible to determine how many people $\frac{2}{5}$ constitutes. Statement (1) is insufficient, so you should eliminate **(A)** and **(D)**.

Statement (2) allows you to determine the total membership of the group (24 = 0.3G, so G = 80), but it tells you nothing about the members' ages. Statement (2) taken by itself is also insufficient, so eliminate **(B)**.

Combining Statements (1) and (2), you know the total number of members (80) from Statement (2), and you know what fraction of those members are under 25 years of age $\left(\frac{2}{5}\right)$ from Statement (1). You could thus easily calculate the total number of members under age 25 to be $\frac{2}{5}(80) = 32$. The statements combined are sufficient, so choice **(C)** is correct.

7. (C)

Question Type: Problem Solving
Question Topic: Algebra: Isolating a Variable, Quadratic Equations

$x − y = −(y − x)$ is an important idea for the GMAT. You will most frequently use this property to re-express algebraic expressions to match the given answer choices, but here it shows up in the question stem: $a^2 − b^2 = −(b^2 − a^2)$. Notice also that the given equation involves $a − b$, but you're solving for $b − a$, which you can also express as $−(a − b)$.

$$a - b = \frac{a^2 - b^2}{b^2 - a^2}$$

Use the property $a^2 - b^2 = -(b^2 - a^2)$:

$$a - b = \frac{-(b^2 - a^2)}{(b^2 - a^2)}$$

Cancel common factors:

$$a - b = \frac{-1}{1}$$

$$a - b = -1$$

Multiply by -1:

$$-(a - b) = -(-1)$$

$$b - a = 1$$

Choice **(C)** is correct.

8. (D)

Question Type: Data Sufficiency
Question Topic: Math Formulas: Rates and Speed

This is a Value question: How long is the first leg of the trip? This question involves rates, which is one of the common math formulas you should memorize for Test Day: Distance = Rate × Time.

Make a table to organize the information you know:

	distance	rate	time
First Leg	d	40 mph	t
Second Leg	d	r	5 hours

The question asks for the time (t) of the first leg of the trip. Since you already have the rate, if you knew the distance (d), you would be able to solve for t. Thus, any piece of information that allows you to determine d will give you sufficiency.

Statement (1) gives a value for the average speed for the entire trip; this allows you to determine the rate of the second leg of the trip, which in turn allows you to find d. Thus, the statement is sufficient. Although you wouldn't do the math on Test Day, let's look at how this works. You know that Average speed = $\frac{\text{Total distance}}{\text{Total time}}$, and you have the average speed (30 mph), the total distance ($2d$), and the total time ($t + 5$). This is one equation with two variables, but remember that you have another equation relating d and t: Using the formula Distance = Rate × Time, you can say $d = 40t$. Thus, with two variables and two equations, you could solve for each of the variables. Statement (1) is sufficient, so you should eliminate **(B)**, **(C)**, and **(E)**.

Statement (2) is also sufficient. This gives a value for d, which is exactly what you need to solve directly for t. Since both statements are sufficient individually, choice **(D)** is correct.

9.   (C)

Question Type: Data Sufficiency
Question Topic: Arithmetic: Exponents, Inequalities

From the question stem, you know that p must be an integer greater than or equal to −5. To have sufficiency, you need information that will allow you to narrow this range down to one possible value for p.

Statement (1) gives you an inequality that you could solve for p, resulting in the inequality $p \leq -4$. The information in the question, $p^3 \geq -125$, tells you that $p \geq -5$. Since p is an integer, it could be either −4 or −5. You cannot find a single value for p, and Statement (1) is insufficient. You can eliminate **(A)** and **(D)**.

Statement (2) tells you that $p^2 > 16$, so you know that $p > 4$ or that $p < -4$. The information in the question stem, $p^3 \geq -125$, tells you that $p \geq -5$. So p could be either any integer greater than 4, or it could be −5. This does not allow you to find a single value for p, so Statement (2) is insufficient. You can eliminate choice **(B)**.

Combining Statements (1) and (2), you have $p < -4$. Taken in conjunction with the question itself, which tells you that $p \geq -5$, you know that p must equal −5. Choice **(C)** is correct.

10.   (D)

Question Type: Problem Solving
Question Topic: Geometry: Solids

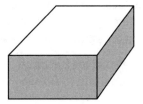

In the figure above, meant to represent one of the two half cubes, the three unseen sides (the back, bottom, and left side) are also shaded. Only the top—the surface that used to be "inside" the cube—is still white. Count up the surfaces, calling a full cube face (a face on the original cube) 1 unit. Then find the areas of the faces of the half cube.

You have the bottom and top here, which makes 2 square units. Each of the other four faces has an area of half a square unit, so that's $4 \times \frac{1}{2}$, or another 2 square units. The total surface area of the cube, then, is 2 + 2 = 4 square units. One whole cube face (the top), which has an area of 1 square unit, is still white, so $\frac{1}{4}$, or 25 percent, of the surface area is not red. The answer is **(D)**.

11.   (B)

Question Type: Problem Solving
Question Topic: Statistics: Sequences of Integers; Number Properties: Multiples

It wouldn't be too ridiculously time-consuming just to list out all the multiples of 3 in question (15, 18, 21, 24, 27, … 102, 105) and then count them. You have on average two minutes per question on the Quantitative section, and it would take about that long—perhaps less—to solve the problem that way. The key here would be to begin that solution quickly and not waste 90 seconds looking for a faster way.

If you happen to see the faster way, then of course that's a great solution. As with many hard GMAT questions, the solution involves factoring. Since these numbers are all multiples of 3, they can all be re-expressed as 3 × something:

$$15 = 3 \times 5;\ 18 = 3 \times 6;\ 21 = 3 \times 7;\ 24 = 3 \times 8;\ \ldots\ 102 = 3 \times 34;\ 105 = 3 \times 35.$$

So, counting the multiples of 3 in the list of 15 through 105 is exactly the same as counting the numbers 5 through 35. Now 35 − 5 = 30, but don't forget to add 1 to that result to account for the fact that both endpoints are included in the set. (Counting 1 through 10, for instance, there are not 10 − 1 = 9 numbers but 9 + 1 = 10 numbers.) The correct answer is 31, choice **(B)**.

12. (D)

Question Type: Data Sufficiency
Question Topic: Algebra: Isolating a Variable

This problem illustrates a Data Sufficiency pitfall that can trap even the most math-savvy GMAT student. If you don't remember that your goal is to determine whether the question can be answered, rather than whether it can be answered affirmatively, you can get all the math right and still pick the wrong answer.

Here's the math part of the solution: To determine whether any particular ordered pair (a, b) is a solution to the equation $b = ka + 3$, you need to find the value of k. Specifically, to find out if $(2, 3)$ is a solution, you need to know whether $3 = 2k + 3$. That's the same as asking whether $0 = 2k$, or, more simply, whether $k = 0$.

Statements (1) and (2) say that $(1, 4)$ and $(3, 5)$, respectively, are solutions of other equations that also involve k. Plugging the appropriate ordered pair into the equation in Statement (1) gives you $k = 2$. So you can give a definite answer to the question—the answer is definitely "no."

Doing the same thing for Statement (2) also gives $k = 2$ and also gives a definite negative response. Since each statement is sufficient to give a definitive answer to the question, the correct answer is **(D)**.

13. (B)

Question Type: Problem Solving
Question Topic: Math Formulas: Rates and Speed; Proportions: Ratios

With multiple unknowns (the two speeds, two distances, and two times), this is a great question to use the strategy of Picking Numbers. Since Ann drives $\frac{1}{3}$ faster than Bob, pick a number for Bob's speed that's a multiple of 3, such as 3. You can say that Bob drives 3 miles per hour. Then Ann drives $\frac{1}{3}$ faster, or 4 miles per hour. Now, the other information you have to consider is how far each travels. Ann drives twice as far as Bob. You can pick 12 as the number of miles she drives (it's a multiple of both 3 and 4, the numbers you've already chosen). If Ann drives 12 miles, then Bob drives 6 miles. So now how much time will each spend driving? Ann will drive 12 miles at 4 miles per hour:

4 miles per hour × A hours = 12 miles

$$4A = 12$$

$$A = 3$$

Bob will drive for 6 miles at 3 miles per hour:

3 miles per hour × B hours = 6 miles

$$3B = 6$$

$$B = 2$$

So the ratio of the amount of time that Ann will drive to the amount of time that Bob will drive is 3:2. Choice **(B)** is correct.

Notice that **(D)** is the correct ratio reversed. Be careful to note exactly what you are looking for. You would solve for **(A)** if you multiplied the distance by the speed instead of dividing. Choice **(E)** is simply the reverse of **(A)**.

14. (E)

Question Type: Problem Solving
Question Topic: Arithmetic: Exponents and Radicals

Since there are variables in the answer choices, Picking Numbers is a workable approach.

Before you start solving, remember to consider the question. You're looking for the answer choice with the least value. And look at those answers ... all fractions with the same numerator, 1. Positive fractions with the same numerator get smaller as the denominator increases. Likewise, they get larger as the denominator shrinks. For instance, $\frac{1}{2}$ is twice as large as $\frac{1}{4}$ and ten times larger than $\frac{1}{20}$. So you can re-express the question as follows: Which has the *largest denominator*?

Your answer choices will have you both squaring and taking the square root of your fraction p. So you want to build this fraction out of a numerator and denominator that are small (so the numbers don't get unwieldy when squared) and perfect squares (so you can easily take a square root). The two numbers that fit the best are 1 and 4. So say that p equals $\frac{1}{4}$.

(A)'s denominator is now $\left(\frac{1}{4}\right)^2$, which is $\frac{1}{16}$. **(B)**'s denominator is $\sqrt{\frac{1}{4}}$, or $\frac{1}{2}$. **(B)**'s denominator is considerably larger. **(C)**'s denominator is $1\frac{1}{16}$, which is much larger still. So far **(C)** is the winner.

(D) is hard to compare to **(C)** directly, so move on to something easier—a comparison of **(C)** to **(E)**. **(E)**'s denominator is $\left(\frac{5}{4}\right)^2$, or $\frac{25}{16}$, or $1\frac{9}{16}$. That's bigger than **(C)**.

Now you have to compare **(D)** to **(E)**. Notice that the expressions are very similar. **(D)** takes the square root of $p + 1$, whereas **(E)** squares it. $p + 1$ is $\frac{5}{4}$, which is bigger than 1. Squaring a number greater than 1 produces a larger result; taking the square root of a number greater than 1 produces a smaller result. So **(E)** has the largest denominator and, therefore, is the least of the answer choices.

15. (A)

Question Type: Data Sufficiency
Question Topic: Number Properties: Sequences, Odds and Evens

A sequence of consecutive positive integers is just a string of regular counting numbers (such as 3, 4, 5, 6 or 101, 102, 103). Whether you do so while analyzing the question stem or while evaluating the statements, you'll have to experiment to see what happens to the sum of the terms when the sequence starts with an odd or an even number and when the sequence has an odd or an even number of terms. The best way to do this is to pick simple numbers, knowing that the results you come up with will always hold true due to the predictability of the rules that govern odd and even numbers. (Just remember to pick more than one set of numbers and to pick different kinds of numbers.)

Here Statement (2) looks much simpler, so turn to it first. n is the number of terms (that's what Z_n in the question stem tells you), so the sequence has an odd number of terms, but not necessarily an odd sum. For instance, the sum of {2, 3, 4} is odd, but the sum of {1, 2, 3} is even. So Statement (2) is insufficient, and you can eliminate **(B)** and **(D)**.

Statement (1) says that dividing the sum of the terms by the number of terms yields an odd integer. You may have recognized that this statement paraphrases the average formula: $\frac{\text{Sum of terms}}{\text{# of terms}} = \text{Average}$. Statement (1) thus means that the average of the numbers in the sequence is an odd integer. It also implies that the sequence has an odd number of terms, because the average of an even number of consecutive integers cannot be an integer. Pick simple numbers to see the pattern, and you'll notice that sequences in which the middle term is odd have an odd average. The statement tells you that $\frac{Z_1 + Z_2 + Z_3 + \ldots + Z_n}{n} = \text{odd}$. You can get rid of the denominator by multiplying both sides by n: $Z_1 + Z_2 + Z_3 + \ldots + Z_n = n \times \text{odd}$. Since n is odd, $Z_1 + Z_2 + Z_3 + \ldots + Z_n$, = odd × odd. When you multiply an odd number by another odd number, the result is always an odd number. Therefore, $Z_1 + Z_2 + Z_3 + \ldots + Z_n$, the sum of all of the integers in the sequence, is odd. Statement (1) alone is sufficient, and choice **(A)** is correct.

16. (B)

Question Type: Data Sufficiency
Question Topic: Statistics: Standard Deviation

Standard deviation is a measure of dispersion—in other words, how spread out the elements of a set are.

Statement (1) tells you that one of the sets has a larger range than the other, which is insufficient for two reasons. The first is that you don't know whether X or Y is the larger-range set. The second, and more important, is that even if you did know which one had the larger range, you still wouldn't know how spread out the set was. For example, the range of one set could be much larger due to one distant number, but its standard deviation could be smaller because most of the set elements are much closer to the mean, thus making the overall dispersion of the data smaller. Eliminate choices **(A)** and **(D)**.

Statement (2) is sufficient because squares of positive integers are always larger than the integers; thus, the set must contain larger numbers that are further apart. (The integer 1 is an exception to this rule, but this set must contain at least two distinct positive integers, so at least one of those integers is greater than 1.) If you're unsure, you can test this statement yourself by Picking Numbers for each set. Statement (2) alone is sufficient, so choice **(B)** is correct.

17. (B)

Question Type: Problem Solving
Question Topic: Algebra: Translating Words into Expressions and Equations

Here's a great example of a question that rewards you if you are in the habit of analyzing before you do math.

Studying the question stem, you see that players are restricted to scoring either 2 or 5 points and that the sum of all the points is 50. You're asked to find the least possible difference between n and m, which is to say that you need to get the number of 2-point scorers as close as possible to the number of 5-point scorers. How could you approach this if no straightforward math occurs to you? What strategy could you use? With multiple variables in the question stem, you can use Picking Numbers.

As long as the number of possibilities is reasonably small and you've analyzed the problem so that you aren't working randomly, trial and error is a fine approach. You could start off with a nice clear set and give all 50 points to the 5-point players. So $m = 10$ and $n = 0$. Clearly, a difference of 10 is possible. But is it the *least* possible difference? No. For one thing, 10 is not an answer choice. So you'll need to change these numbers. You might try one lower and have $m = 9$. That would be 45 points, leaving 5. But players who score only 2 points can't combine for 5. So $m = 9$ is not permissible. How about $m = 8$? That's 40 points, leaving 10. The 10 points can be scored by the other players, if $n = 5$. That's a difference of $8 - 5 = 3$, which is an answer choice.

But **(B)** isn't the smallest answer choice given, so you have to keep going. Try $m = 6$, as you discovered that odd values of m won't be permissible. That's 30 points, leaving 20. In that case, $n = 10$. The difference is now $10 - 6 = 4$. You're not getting smaller numbers at this point but bigger ones. So **(B)** is as small as you can get.

18. (E)

Question Type: Problem Solving
Question Topic: Math Formulas: Combined Rates and Combined Work

You're asked for the time it takes machine B to process 12,000 envelopes. You'll need to be careful about the size of the job, as the data are given for different-sized jobs.

Machines B and C together can process 6,000 envelopes in $2\frac{2}{5}$ (or $\frac{12}{5}$) hours. Using the combined work equation, you can say that $\frac{BC}{B+C} = \frac{12}{5}$ for 6,000 envelopes. So you could solve for B if you knew how long C took by itself. To know that, you'll use the fact that machines A and C together take 1 hour for 3,000 envelopes, or 2 hours for 6,000. So $\frac{AC}{A+C} = 2$. Since machine A alone takes 3 hours for 6,000, that's $\frac{3C}{3+C} = 2$. So $3C = 6 + 2C$. That means $C = 6$. Plugging that back into $\frac{BC}{B+C} = \frac{12}{5}$, you get $\frac{6B}{B+6} = \frac{12}{5}$. Cross multiplying gives $30B = 12B + 72$. Subtract $12B$ from each side to get $18B = 72$, or $B = 4$. But since that amount of time was only for 6,000 envelopes, you need to double that to 8 hours for 12,000 envelopes. Choice **(E)** is correct.

19. (C)

Question Type: Problem Solving
Question Topic: Statistics: Probability

For this question, use the probability formula:

$$\text{Probability} = \frac{\text{Number of desired outcomes}}{\text{Number of possible outcomes}}$$

First, determine the number of possible outcomes of rain for City X over a 5-day period. There are two possibilities for each day—rain or no rain—so the total number of possible outcomes would be $2 \times 2 \times 2 \times 2 \times 2 = 32$.

Next, determine the desired outcomes. One approach is to list the ways in which you could get rain on exactly 3 days. They are as follows:

RRRNN, RRNRN, RRNNR, RNRRN, RNRNR, RNNRR, NRRRN, NRRNR, NRNRR, NNRRR

There are 10 desired outcomes in all, and a systematic run-through of the possibilities should account for them all. There are other ways to count the ways in which you could have gotten rain on 3 days out of 5. Perhaps you recognized this as a combinations question: You are choosing 3 days out of 5 to have rain. That's $_5C_3$, or

$$\frac{5!}{3!(5-3)!} = \frac{5!}{3!2!} = \frac{5 \times 4 \times 3 \times 2 \times 1}{3 \times 2 \times 1 \times 2 \times 1} = 10$$

So the probability is $\frac{10}{32} = \frac{5}{16}$, and choice **(C)** is the correct answer.

20. (D)

Question Type: Data Sufficiency
Question Topic: Algebra: Systems of Linear Equations, Translating Words into Expressions and Equations

This Yes/No Data Sufficiency question asks simply whether more black rats than white were fed. Note that for sufficiency you don't need to calculate the actual numbers of rats, as long as you know you can answer the question in one definitive way.

According to the stem, white rats are fed 6 pellets of food per day and black rats are fed 8 pellets of food per day. Since a total of 120 pellets were used on a particular day, you can set up this equation, where w and b represent the number of white rats and black rats, respectively: $6w + 8b = 120$. This is one linear equation. If you had another distinct linear equation involving w and/or b, you would be able to calculate how many rats were white and how many were black.

Statement (1) lets you set up the equation $b + w = 17$. Now you have two equations and two unknowns; you can solve for each variable and see which is larger. Remember, if you had to solve, you would solve for one variable in terms of another and then substitute, like this: $w = 17 - b$, so $120 = 6(17 - b) + 8b$. Then solve this equation to get b. But try to learn the math concepts tested on the GMAT well enough that you never have to waste time solving on Data Sufficiency. Statement (1) is sufficient, so you can eliminate **(B)**, **(C)**, and **(E)**.

The information in Statement (2) allows you to answer the question more directly. Multiplying the number of white rats by 6 pellets per white rat would give you the total number of pellets fed to white rats on that day. Subtracting that product from 120 would give you the number of pellets fed to black rats on that day. Dividing that difference by 8 pellets per black rat would give you the number of black rats, which you could compare to the number of white rats and thus answer the question. Of course, the numbers themselves are immaterial—all you care about is the sufficiency of the information. Statement (2) is also sufficient. Choice **(D)** is correct.

21. (D)

Question Type: Problem Solving
Question Topic: Number Properties: Factors and Primes

To find the greatest product, you could multiply the greatest four primes less than 20. If you suspect that such a solution would be far too much calculation, that's a great GMAT instinct—look for a pattern that will help you get to the solution more efficiently. Since a prime number, by definition, has no factors other than 1 and itself, $19 \times 17 \times 13 \times 11$ cannot have any other prime factors. So you can eliminate any answer that's a multiple of a smaller prime. This is a chance to use what you know about factoring and divisibility rules. **(B)** and **(E)** are clearly multiples of 2, and **(C)** is clearly a multiple of 5. Testing for multiples of 3 is fairly straightforward—the digits must sum to a multiple of 3. The digits of **(A)** sum to 27, so **(A)** is a multiple of 3. Since **(D)** is the only answer choice you haven't eliminated, it must be correct.

22. (A)

Question Type: Problem Solving
Question Topic: Math Formulas: Overlapping Sets

These overlapping set problems are often best solved by organizing the data into a chart:

	Rookie	Not Rookie	Total
Mint	0.6(1,100) = 660		1,100
Not Mint			400
Total		740	

Then you can just add or subtract to fill in the other spots until you arrive at your answer:

	Rookie	Not Rookie	Total
Mint	660	440	1,100
Not Mint	100	300	400
Total	760	740	1,500

He has 100 rookie cards that are not in mint condition. Choice **(A)** is correct.

23. (C)

Question Type: Data Sufficiency
Question Topic: Number Properties: Multiples

If you have trouble finding an approach to a difficult Data Sufficiency problem, you may want to rephrase the given information. Here, m and n are both greater than or equal to 10 and less than or equal to 99. You're supposed to determine if their difference is a multiple of 11.

Statement (1) implies that m is a two-digit multiple of 11. At this point, you can use Picking Numbers to show that this statement is insufficient. If $m = 22$ and $n = 11$, then $m - n$ is a multiple of 11, but if $m = 22$ and $n = 18$, then $m - n$ is not a multiple of 11. Statement (1) is insufficient, so you can eliminate **(A)** and **(D)**.

If $m + n$ is a multiple of 11, as Statement (2) says, then m could be 10 and n could be 12, and $m - n$ will not be a multiple of 11. But m could also be 22 and n could be 11, in which case $m - n$ is a multiple of 11. Statement (2) is also insufficient, so you can eliminate **(B)**.

Putting the statements together, m must be a multiple of 11 from Statement (1), and that means that n must be a multiple of 11 in order to make Statement (2) true (if you're unsure, you can use Picking Numbers to try out a few examples to confirm this rule). And any multiple of 11 minus a multiple of 11 is a multiple of 11 (remember, it's fine if $x = 0$).

If you find the unknowns too abstract to deal with, use Picking Numbers. Pick any two- or three-digit multiple of 11 to represent $m + n$, per Statement (2). Then pick any two-digit multiple of 11 to represent m, per Statement (1). The difference between those two numbers will be n. If you then subtract n from m, the difference will still be a multiple of 11. And remember, there's nothing special about the number 11 here; the same properties would be true with multiples of another number (if you want, you can use Picking Numbers to try out a few examples to confirm this rule). The statements together are sufficient, so choice **(C)** is correct.

24. (A)

Question Type: Problem Solving
Question Topic: Arithmetic: Exponents

For a Roman numeral problem, you want to find the statement that appears in the most answer choices and work with it first. If you can eliminate it, you can quickly reduce the number of possible choices.

Here, statement II shows up three times, so you can start there. By definition, any number raised to the exponent zero is equal to 1, so x^0 cannot equal zero. Thus, you can eliminate **(C)**, **(D)**, and **(E)**. Based on the remaining choices, you can see that either statement I must equal zero or none of the statements must equal zero.

The next step is to evaluate statement I. You can use Picking Numbers: If x is 1, then $x^3 - x^2$ is $1 - 1 = 0$. But if you try $x = 2$, you find that $x^3 - x^2 = 2^3 - 2^2 = 8 - 4 = 4$. So this statement might be equal to zero, but it doesn't have to be. You can eliminate **(B)**. In fact, none of the statements has to equal zero, so **(A)** is correct.

25. (B)

Question Type: Data Sufficiency
Question Topic: Algebra: Isolating a Variable, Quadratic Equations

The question stem gives you no information about x, so move on to the statements.

Statement (1) gives you a quadratic, not a linear, equation. Adding 4 to both sides of the equation $x^2 - 4 = 20$, you have $x^2 = 24$, so x could be either $\sqrt{24}$ or $-\sqrt{24}$. Statement (1) is insufficient, so you can eliminate **(A)** and **(D)**.

Statement (2) gives you a complicated-looking equation containing the variable x. A closer look, however, reveals that this is just a single-variable linear equation with x. You can solve for the one value of x, although you don't need to solve now—just knowing that you could is enough. Keep in mind that when a GMAT question gives you a square root sign, as this one does with $\sqrt{6}$, the square root symbol refers to the principal, or positive, square root of 6. So unlike Statement (1), which leaves us unable to determine whether x is positive or negative, Statement (2) gives us enough information to solve for a single, definitive value for x. Statement (2) is sufficient, so choice **(B)** is correct.

26. (C)

Question Type: Problem Solving
Question Topic: Proportions: Ratios

Let a be the population of City A, let b be the population of City B, and let c be the population of City C. Since a is three times larger than b, $a = 3b$, and the population of A and B together is $3b + b$, or $4b$.

Furthermore, since the population of A and B together (which you've calculated to be $4b$) is twice the population of C, you can write the equation $4b = 2c$, or $c = 2b$. Dividing both sides by b gives $\frac{c}{b} = 2$, so the ratio of c to b is 2:1.

Alternatively, you could solve this problem by Picking Numbers. For City A, pick any small number easily divisible by 3; in fact, picking 3 works well. If the population of A is 3, then the population of B must be 1, and their combined population must be 4. (Don't worry if the populations seem unrealistic. Remember, it's permissibility and manageability that matter, not realism.) Since C's population is half that of A and B together, it must be 2. Thus the ratio of C to B is 2:1, and the answer is **(C)**.

27. (D)

Question Type: Problem Solving
Question Topic: Number Properties: Positives and Negatives

This is a number properties question, so Picking Numbers will work. Since m divided by n must be negative, one of the two numbers m or n must be negative, and the other must be positive. So you'll test two pairs of numbers: You can try $m = 3$, $n = -1$ and $m = -3$, $n = 1$. Because the question asks, "Which of the following . . . ," start with choice **(E)** and work your way up through the answer choices.

(E): Using the first pair of values, $m - n = 3 - (-1) = 4$. That's greater than zero, so **(E)** could be true; there is no need to test the second pair of values. You can eliminate **(E)**.

Testing **(D)**, you find

$$(3)(-1)^3 = (3)(-1) < 0, \text{ and } (-3)(1)^3 = (-3)(1) < 0$$

Both pairs give values less than zero, so **(D)** is not true in either case. **(D)** looks good, but on a "cannot be"/"must be" problem, you need to make sure you didn't get a false positive. This can be confirmed either by testing the other choices or by recognizing an important pattern: Here, since one and only one of the two numbers must be negative, and any negative number cubed will still be negative, mn^3 will either involve multiplying a positive m times a negative n^3 or a negative m times a positive n^3 and, therefore, the product mn^3 could never be positive. Choice **(D)** is correct.

28. (C)

Question Type: Problem Solving
Question Topic: Algebra: Isolating a Variable

As in many GMAT word problems, the initial presentation is a little confusing. Don't try to comprehend everything all at once. When you read the question stem the first time, focus on understanding the basic situation. Here, you're given a formula for figuring out the speed of a train at any given time. You're asked for the difference between the speed at 4 seconds and the speed at 2 seconds.

To answer this question, all you need to do is use the formula you're given to calculate the speeds, then subtract.

Speed formula:	$s = t^2 + t$
Solve for $t = 4$ seconds:	$s = 4^2 + 4 = 16 + 4 = 20$
Solve for $t = 2$ seconds:	$s = 2^2 + 2 = 4 + 2 = 6$
Difference:	$20 - 6 = 14$

Choice **(C)** is correct.

29. (B)

Question Type: Data Sufficiency
Question Topic: Proportions: Percents; Algebra: Systems of Linear Equations

Call Rebecca's expenditure on travel t, her expenditure on living expenses l, and the amount of her savings s. Then you know that $60,000 = t + l + s$, and you need the value of t to have sufficiency.

Statement (1) tells you that $t = 0.2l$, or $5t = l$, and you can substitute in the original equation. Now you have $60{,}000 = t + 5t + s$, but without the value of s, you can't solve for t. In other words, there are three unknowns but only two linear equations. So Statement (1) is insufficient and you can eliminate **(A)** and **(D)**.

Statement (2) tells you that $t + 8t = l + s$, so you can substitute in the original equation. This becomes $60{,}000 = t + (t + 8t)$, which is a single-variable equation you could easily solve for t. Statement (2) is sufficient, so choice **(B)** is correct.

30. (B)

Question Type: Problem Solving
Question Topic: Algebra: Translating Words into Expressions and Equations

Use the formula Distance = Speed × Time. In this case, you want to find the time required to walk s blocks, so divide both sides of the formula by speed to get $\frac{\text{Distance}}{\text{Speed}} = \text{Time}$. You are told that the distance is s blocks, so you just need to find Lisa's speed.

If you go back to the distance formula and divide both sides by time, you see that Speed $= \frac{\text{Distance}}{\text{Time}}$. Lisa walked t blocks in 3 minutes, so her speed is $\frac{t\,\text{blocks}}{3\,\text{minutes}} = \frac{t}{3}$ blocks per minute. So $\frac{\text{Distance}}{\text{Speed}} = \frac{s\,\text{blocks}}{\frac{t}{3}\,\text{blocks per minute}} = (s)\left(\frac{3}{t}\right) = \frac{3s}{t}$ minutes. Choice **(B)** is correct.

Sound complicated? Picking Numbers makes fast work of this problem. Pick a manageable number of blocks to walk in 3 minutes: 3 blocks in 3 minutes sounds pretty straightforward, so say $t = 3$. Now, let s equal 2. The question then is "If Lisa can walk 3 blocks in 3 minutes, how many minutes does it take her to walk 2 blocks?" 3 blocks in 3 minutes is 1 block per minute; 2 blocks will take 2 minutes.

Plug $t = 3$ and $s = 2$ into the answer choices. Only **(B)** yields the number you want, 2. So **(B)** is correct.

31. (A)

Question Type: Problem Solving
Question Topic: Proportions: Mixtures

In "changing mixture" problems, the first thing to identify is which components change and which stay the same. In this case, water is being added, so its volume, as well as that of the total mixture, is changing; however, nitric acid is neither added nor removed, so that volume is constant.

You can calculate the volume of that original nitric acid content with a simple equation—multiply the volume by the percent concentration.

$$(\text{Volume}_1)(\text{Concentration}_1) = \text{Acid}_1$$

The same formula applies to the new solution that you'll have after more water is added.

$$(\text{Volume}_2)(\text{Concentration}_2) = \text{Acid}_2$$

But the amount of acid is unchanged between mixtures. Thus, you can set the two expressions equal to each other:

$$(\text{Volume}_1)(\text{Concentration}_1) = \text{Acid}_1 = \text{Acid}_2 = (\text{Volume}_2)(\text{Concentration}_2)$$

$$(\text{Volume}_1)(\text{Concentration}_1) = (\text{Volume}_2)(\text{Concentration}_2)$$

Plugging in the values from the question stem, you get this:

$$(10\%)(10) = (4\%)(V_2)$$

$$\frac{10}{100} \times 10 = \frac{4}{100} \times V_2$$

$$\frac{\cancel{100}}{4} \times \frac{10}{\cancel{100}} \times 10 = V_2$$

$$V_2 = 25$$

Note that **(D)** is a trap answer for those who stop too soon; this question is asking how much water was *added*, not what the final volume was. Since you started with 10 liters of liquid and ended with 25, you added 15 liters of water, so **(A)** is correct.

32. (C)

Question Type: Data Sufficiency
Question Topic: Geometry: Coordinate Geometry

This is a Value question dealing with coordinate geometry. You are given the two points (p, q) and (v, w) on a line, and asked for the slope. According to the slope formula, the slope of the line going through the points (p, q) and (v, w) is $\frac{w - q}{v - p}$. If you knew the values of each of p, q, v, and w, you would have sufficient information to find the slope. You would also have sufficiency if you knew the value of $w - q$ and $v - p$.

Statement (1) gives you the value of $w - q$. If you knew $v - p$ also, this would be sufficient, but this statement alone doesn't give you any information about v or p. Statement (1) is insufficient. You can eliminate **(A)** and **(D)**.

Statement (2) gives you the value of $p - v$. So you can find the value of $v - p$ because $v - p = -(p - v)$. If you knew $w - q$ also, this would be sufficient, but this statement alone doesn't give you any information about w or q. Statement (2) is insufficient. You can eliminate **(B)**.

Together, however, the two statements tell a different story. You know the value of $w - q$, and you can find the value of $v - p$, since $v - p = -(p - v)$. You can divide the value of $w - q$ by the value of $v - p$ to get the slope of the line. The statements together are sufficient, so the correct answer is **(C)**.

33. (D)

Question Type: Data Sufficiency
Question Topic: Algebra: Isolating a Variable; Arithmetic: Exponents

The fact that a^3, b^3, and c^3 are all positive means that a, b, and c are all positive. Knowing this, consider the statements.

Statement (1) gives you an equation with a, b, and c. Simplifying the denominator of the right side of the equation $c = \frac{b}{(ac)^2}$, you have $c = \frac{b}{a^2c^2}$. Multiplying both sides of the equation by a^2, you have $a^2c = \frac{b}{c^2}$. Dividing both sides of the equation by c, you have $a^2 = \frac{b}{c^3}$. This is the exact equation that the question stem asks about. Statement (1) leads to the answer "yes" to the question. Statement (1) is sufficient. You can eliminate **(B)**, **(C)**, and **(E)**.

Statement (2) gives you another equation with a, b, and c. This equation is also equivalent to the equation in the question stem. Notice that in the fraction on the right side of the equation, the numerator and denominator are both raised to fractional exponents with denominators of 3. A denominator of 3 in an exponent tells you that cube roots are involved. Therefore, to get rid of the fractional exponents, you'll need to cube both sides of the equation. Start on the left, where c becomes c^3. Now cube the right side. Remember that to cube a fraction, all you have to do is cube the numerator and the denominator separately. Start with the numerator. When you raise a number that already has an exponent to another exponent, you multiply the exponents together. So the numerator becomes $b^{\left(\frac{1}{3}\times 3\right)}= b^1 = b$. The denominator becomes $a^{\left(\frac{2}{3}\times 3\right)}= a^2$. Thus, $c^3 = \dfrac{b}{a^2}$. Multiplying both sides of the equation $c^3 = \dfrac{b}{a^2}$ by a^2, you have $a^2c^3 = b$. Dividing both sides of the equation $a^2c^3 = b$ by c^3, you have $a^2 = \dfrac{b}{c^3}$. This is the exact equation that the question stem asks about. Statement (2) leads to the answer "yes" to the question, so Statement (2) is also sufficient. Since each statement is sufficient by itself, the correct answer is **(D)**.

34. (D)

Question Type: Problem Solving
Question Topic: Algebra: Systems of Linear Equations

This classic word problem illustrates the importance of studying the question stem and answer choices, as well as determining what's asked, before starting to work on the problem. It's tempting to write down $a = 8.00$ and $b = 5.60$, because you're given price first. But you aren't asked for price; you're asked for the number of Brand A binders. So those two equations will make your life quite complicated, as you'd now need two new variables for the number of binders.

By determining what you're asked before you start solving, though, you know to let a equal the number of Brand A binders and to let b equal the number of Brand B binders. For the number of binders purchased, you have $a + b = 12$, and for the amount spent, you have $\$8a + \$5.60b = \$84$.

To use combination to solve the equations, you need one of the variables to have the same coefficient in both equations so that it will cancel out. If you multiply the first equation by 8, you get $8a + 8b = 96$.

So you can write the two equations as follows:

$$8a + 8b = 96$$

$$8a + 5.60b = 84$$

If you subtract the bottom equation from the top one, you get $(8a - 8a) + (8b - 5.60b) = 96 - 84$, or $2.4b = 12$. If you divide both sides by 2.4, you are left with $b = 5$. Thus, Molly must have purchased $12 - b = 12 - 5 = 7$ Brand A binders. Choice **(D)** is the correct answer.

This is also a great Backsolving opportunity. Let's say you started with **(B)**. That means Molly would have bought 5 Brand A binders at $8 apiece and $12 - 5 = 7$ Brand B binders at $5.60 apiece. That's $5 \times \$8 = \$40.00$ for the Brand A binders and $7 \times \$5.60 = \$39.20$ for the Brand B binders. You get $\$40.00 + \$39.20 = \$79.20$, which is less than she actually spent. She needs more of the expensive Brand A binders, so **(A)** and **(B)** are eliminated.

You would next test choice **(D)**: She buys 7 Brand A binders at $8 apiece and 12 − 7 = 5 Brand B binders at $5.60 apiece. That's 7 × $8 = $56.00 for the Brand A binders and 5 × $5.60 = $28.00 for the Brand B binders. You add $56.00 + $28.00 = $84.00, which is exactly what you're looking for. Choice **(D)** is correct.

35. (E)

Question Type: Problem Solving
Question Topic: Algebra: Translating Words into Expressions and Equations

Studying the question stem and the answer choices would allow you to make some quick eliminations with no calculation at all. You're told that the farmer makes a profit selling his wheat and that his costs include $10 per bushel. To make a profit, he would have to sell each bushel for more than $10 apiece. Otherwise, he'd lose money on every bushel sold. So **(A)** and **(B)** can be thrown away immediately.

Backsolving is a straightforward approach to this problem. You would start with **(D)**, since **(B)** has already been eliminated. The 50,000 bushels sold for $13 each give $650,000 of revenue. The farmer's costs are $10 per bushel, or $500,000, plus $200,000 rent. That's a total of $700,000 of costs but only $650,000 of revenue. So selling wheat at $13/bushel still loses the farmer money. **(E)**, as the only number larger than 13, must be correct.

Algebraically, if p = selling price per bushel in dollars and Profit = Revenue − Fixed cost − Variable cost, the following equation can be written: $150,000 = 50,000p − 200,000 − (50,000 × 10)$. Solving this for p will result in $850,000 = 50,000p$, or $p = 17$. This is choice **(E)**.

36. (C)

Question Type: Data Sufficiency
Question Topic: Arithmetic: Absolute Value, Inequalities; Number Properties: Integers

This question stem contains variables, so you can try Picking Numbers. Substitute 5 for a into the equation with absolute value signs and test out values for b that make the equation true. You will find that $a = 5$ when $−2 \leq b \leq 3$. You will therefore have sufficiency if you know that b must or must not lie within this range. If you didn't think to do this analysis up front, you could use Picking Numbers to test out each statement.

You can evaluate Statement (1) by Picking Numbers that meet the constraint of the statement. If $b = 0$, then $a = 5$. But if $b = −3$, then $a = 7$. Since a may or may not equal 5, this statement is insufficient. Eliminate **(A)** and **(D)**.

Statement (2) says that $b > −2$. If $b = 1$, then $a = 5$. But if $b = 9$, then $a = 17$. Since a may or may not equal 5, the statement is insufficient. Eliminate **(B)**.

When you consider Statements (1) and (2) together, you know that $−2 < b < 3$, so all possible values for b will result in 5 as the value for a. The answer to the question is "yes," and choice **(C)** is correct.

37. (B)

Question Type: Problem Solving
Question Topic: Statistics: Combinations and Permutations

Because the order of colors in the pairs doesn't matter, the number of two-color codes that can be made will be the number of ways one can select two colors from the total number of colors; that is, you would use the combinations formula to determine how many two-color codes can be created.

Since you're asked for the minimum possible number of colors, you'll have to Backsolve a little differently. If you test **(B)** and discover that 6 colors are enough to code all 20 chemicals, that wouldn't prove that 5 isn't also enough. So you'll have to start with **(A)**. If 5 is enough, **(A)** is the right answer because there's nothing smaller. If 5 isn't enough, you'll test **(B)** and work your way up if necessary.

If you have 5 colors, there are 5 possible single-color codes. As for the two-color codes, you can use the combinations formula to calculate $_5C_2$. That's $\frac{5!}{2!(5-2)!} = \frac{5!}{2!3!} = \frac{5\times4\times3\times2\times1}{2\times1\times3\times2\times1} = 10$. So the total of one- and two-color codes is 5 + 10 = 15. That's not enough for all 20 chemicals, so you'll try **(B)**.

If you have 6 colors, there are 6 possible single-color codes. For the number of two-color codes, you can calculate $_6C_2$. That's $\frac{6!}{2!(6-2)!} = \frac{6!}{2!4!} = \frac{6\times5\times4\times3\times2\times1}{2\times1\times4\times3\times2\times1} = 15$. So the total of one- and two-color codes is 6 + 15 = 21. That's enough for your 20 chemicals, so **(B)** is correct.

If guessing on this problem, you could have eliminated **(D)** and **(E)**. Because some chemicals will use pairs of colors, there is no need to have as many colors as chemicals, as in **(D)**, or more colors than chemicals, as in **(E)**.

VERBAL SECTION EXPLANATIONS

1.   (C)

Question Type: Critical Reasoning
Question Topic: Weaken

Country B has fewer violent crimes, but that doesn't necessarily mean that it has a lower crime rate, or fewer violent crimes per person. If the populations of the two countries are similar, or if B has more residents, then B does in fact have a lower crime rate. However, if A's population is substantially larger than B's, A may in fact have the lower crime rate. The question stem asks you to identify the fact that will most undermine, or weaken, the argument. Thus, a good prediction would be "Country A has many more people in it than Country B." Choice **(C)** fits the bill: Country A has 2.5 times more crimes but a population 20 times larger. That means Country A actually has a crime rate that's one-eighth that of Country B.

(A), **(B)**, and **(E)** aren't relevant to the relative rates of violent crime in the two countries. **(D)** is out of scope because it doesn't tell us which country has more people in it.

2.   (B)

Question Type: Sentence Correction
Question Topic: Comparison

The fact that the word *than* is underlined is a clue that there may be a comparison problem here. As written, the sentence actually compares the assets of small investors to the large investors themselves, which doesn't make sense. You need to compare either investors to investors or assets to assets. Only **(B)** and **(E)** make the comparison clear: *small investors' assets* are being compared to *those of large investors*. Those two differ at the beginning: *than/relatively to*. The correct construction is only *less . . . than*. **(E)**, as well as **(D)**, can be eliminated on those grounds. Choice **(B)** is correct.

3.   (E)

Question Type: Critical Reasoning
Question Topic: Evaluation

You need to find the one question that does not help you decide whether the boycott of SquareMart would lead to the acceptance of the pay rate proposal. The question stem itself gives you a lot of information. There's one important piece of evidence in the stimulus—namely that SquareMart and the company that employs the union workers in question are owned by the same parent company. As with any question that asks you to evaluate a plan, you need to consider other factors that might influence the situation and whether the proposed solution would be effective.

With **(A)**, if a loss of business would hurt the parent company's bottom line, the boycott would put a great deal of pressure on management and would be more likely to work. Similarly, if SquareMart were an insignificant piece of the MegaFood empire, the boycott wouldn't work. So this is an important question. **(B)** raises the possibility that SquareMart might be the only place some people can buy staple items. That would make the boycott less likely to succeed, as people couldn't refuse to patronize the store. If, per **(C)**, there are many SquareMarts in the area, then a boycott could be easily organized and highly effective. But if no SquareMart stores are nearby, the union members may not be able to execute a successful boycott. For one thing, they wouldn't be customers themselves and couldn't take their business away from a store that they already didn't use! As for **(D)**, if boycotts have been successful before, they may well be so again. And if they've failed in the past, they'd be more likely to fail now. **(E)** is the correct answer, as whether other companies have a similar corporate structure has no bearing on the likelihood of the boycott's success.

On the left, we've shown how keywords help you to identify the major elements of the passage and its structure and what you could skim over. On the right, we've shown what you might be thinking as you read the passage strategically.

Passage for Questions 4–7

An **important** feature of the labor market in recent years has been the increasing participation of women ... Many analysts **suggest, however,** that women comprise a **secondary** labor market where rates of pay and promotion prospects are **inferior** to those available to men. The **principal reason** is that women have, or are **assumed** to have, domestic responsibilities ...

The **difficulties** that women face in the labor market ... are **accentuated** with the arrival of children ... Some women balance domestic and workplace commitments by working part-time. **However,** part-time work is a **precarious** form of employment ...

... Such women who later return to work represent **another** sector of the workforce facing **difficulties** ... these women confront a **restricted** range of opportunities and **will almost certainly** be offered **low-status** jobs with **poor** prospects.

Even women professionals who interrupt their careers to have children experience **difficulties** ... **Consequently,** women, even those of **high ability,** may find themselves **blocked** in the **lower** echelons of an organization, **overlooked,** or even **"invisible"** to senior management.

Analysis

The topic is clear right at the start—women in the labor market.

Women don't seem to be paid or promoted as much, and domestic responsibilities seem to take the blame. (Note the "assumed," though ... that opens the door for the author to put the blame somewhere else later.)

Children don't help much. And part-time work is not a good solution. Note how the "distancing" word choices of ¶1 ("analysts suggest" and "assumed") are gone.

We are now looking at the author's own viewpoint.

Lots of detail here, but the keywords at the end of the paragraph make it clear:

Women who return to work don't get good offers.

Women professionals have it no better.

(Note all the negative emphasis words at the end of the paragraph.)

Passage Map

Here is a sample Passage Map you might have created as you took notes on each paragraph:

¶1: Women face inferior job prospects—domestic responsibilities blamed

¶2: Children make things tough; part-time work precarious

¶3: No good prospects on return to work

¶4: High-ability professionals struggle too

Topic: Women in the labor market

Scope: Difficulties faced by __↑ ⟵⎤

Purpose: Explain the causes behind _____⎦

4. (B)

Question Type: Reading Comprehension
Question Topic: Global

The right answer to Global questions must reflect the passage's topic, scope, purpose, and overall point of view. Your prediction for the answer would be something like "Explain the difficulties faced by women in the labor market." **(B)** is the only choice that fits.

(A) incorrectly broadens the scope to employers' practices in general, whereas the author is concerned only with pay and promotion. Besides, the author restricts himself to discussing the current state of affairs; he doesn't advocate anything.

(C) takes a detail in paragraphs 2 and 3 and wrongly blows it up into the author's primary concern.

(D) and **(E)** are completely off the topic, and contrary to what **(D)** says, the author doesn't take issue with others' views.

5. (D)

Question Type: Reading Comprehension
Question Topic: Inference

Lines 9–11 suggest that it is up to working women themselves, not employers **(A)**, to make child care arrangements. You might anticipate that the author of this passage would agree with **(A)**, but no support for this position is actually given. That's an important aspect of GMAT Inference questions—the right answer isn't just *probably* true but *definitely* true.

(B) is a 180 trap, meaning that it is the exact opposite of what the passage states. Paragraph 4 says that women in high-status positions, such as professionals, face problems advancing their careers while caring for their children.

The passage doesn't compare conditions for today's working mothers with those that existed 20 years ago, so eliminate **(C)**.

Choice **(D)** is based on lines 18–19, which say, "When the typical houseworker returns to the labor market, she is unsure of herself in her new environment." **(D)** is correct.

Although lines 10–11 imply that reasonably priced child care can be difficult to find, **(E)**, the passage doesn't go so far as to suggest that the expense of child care often makes it unprofitable for mothers to work.

6. (B)

Question Type: Reading Comprehension
Question Topic: Logic

The gist of paragraph 4 is that even women of high ability and status—professionals—face career problems if they decide to have children.

(A) is a 180 trap. The point of paragraph 4 is to explain that even the most able women may *not* be able to "overcome" the difficulties "of integrating career and motherhood."

Paragraph 4 does not address labor policies **(C)** or increasing female participation in the labor force **(D)**. Moreover, the author doesn't ever "defend changes" or "modify a hypothesis."

(E) is too vague. Paragraph 4 draws a definite link between career opportunities and children: It's not about a general lack of career opportunities for women. Choice **(B)** is correct.

7. (C)

Question Type: Reading Comprehension
Question Topic: Detail

The question sends you to the second sentence of paragraph 1, which discusses "pay and promotion prospects ... inferior to those available to men." Context is key for detail-oriented questions. The very next sentence blames the disparity on "domestic responsibilities." That fits only with **(C)**.

The passage states that some women work part-time (line 12), not that women in general tend to get work in industries that rely on part-time labor **(A)**.

Paragraph 4 indicates that *some* women—those who took time off to raise children—can lack technical skills. But **(B)** suggests that *all* women lack those skills. Furthermore, paragraph 4 is not the part of the passage addressed by the question stem.

According to lines 13–14, women who work part-time, not women in general (as choice **(D)** says), are likely to be laid off in an economic slowdown. Besides, this fact has nothing to do with inferior pay and promotion rates.

(E) is outside the scope of the passage: The author doesn't discuss general workplace discrimination against women.

8. (C)

Question Type: Sentence Correction
Question Topic: Other (Clauses and Connectors)

There are two splits among these choices, one at the beginning and one at the end. The former is *so/and/the/therefore*. Since the sentence already contains a connecting word that links the two clauses (that word is *because*), no other such word is needed. Only **(C)** can be correct. Had you started with the difference at the end, you'd be comparing *originally* to *original*. Since the word modified is a noun (*construction*), you need an adjective; **(A)**, **(B)**, and **(D)** must be eliminated.

9. (A)

Question Type: Sentence Correction
Question Topic: Pronouns; Usage/Style

The underlined portion includes the pronoun *it*. At first glance, it seems like *it* could refer either to *Greece* or to the phrase *ancient European history*. However, the logical structure of the sentence clearly identifies the pronoun: "Before *A* was *X*, it was *Y*," makes the meaning of *it* unambiguously *Greece*. Things look good, but you might still be hesitant; you should check the rest of the answers.

(E) removes the *it*, playing it safe. However, **(E)** incorrectly uses the past perfect tense; *had become* would imply that becoming city-states happened before some other event, but there isn't a second past event anywhere else in the sentence. **(B)**, **(C)**, and **(D)**, meanwhile, keep the *it* but eliminate the sentence structure in **(A)** that identifies the pronoun; in all three, *it* seems to refer to *European history*, which logically cannot be a *collection of small city-states*.

10. (E)

Question Type: Critical Reasoning
Question Topic: Strengthen

First, you have to understand the argument. The author claims that high school students should not design their own curricula, because they don't have the maturity or experience of professional educators. What if experience and maturity weren't necessary for the design of good curricula? The author's argument would completely fall apart. So to strengthen it, you need the answer to explain why curriculum design requires both experience and maturity. **(E)** does exactly that and is the correct answer.

(A) just restates the last piece of evidence, and right answers on the GMAT always deal with the assumption, not the evidence. **(B)** reinforces the author's rhetorical flourish about three-year-olds, but that is just window dressing, not the heart of the author's point; you didn't need to bring three-year-olds into your paraphrase at all. So **(B)** does not strengthen the main argument. The comparison made in **(C)** is irrelevant; teenagers who don't go to the local high school are outside the scope of the argument, which is about what one needs to design curricula. Besides which, "intelligence" is not exactly the same thing as "experience and maturity." **(D)** is also out of scope, as it discusses what kind of curriculum is best, not who designs it (and if anything, **(D)** weakens the argument, as it suggests that there needs to be a change in curriculum design).

11. (B)

Question Type: Sentence Correction
Question Topic: Pronouns; Modification

When faced with choices that are this long, it may be easier to scan two answers at a time rather than all five at once. Scanning **(A)** and **(B)**, notice *their contribution* versus *the contribution of the Swiss*. So pronoun ambiguity may be the issue. Is *their* ambiguous? It sure is, as it may refer either to *leading Swiss designers* or to *the curators*. Eliminate answers that repeat that error; a quick scan shows those to be **(A)**, **(D)**, and **(E)**. Comparing the two that remain shows you only one difference: *their most famous bridges* versus *its most famous bridges*. *Its* could only possibly refer to the museum, which makes no logical sense—these are the designers' buildings. So **(B)** is correct. Also note the passive construction of **(D)**: "organized by the curators." **(D)** also has a modification error: The modifying phrase that begins the sentence is intended to describe the curators, but "exhibition" is the first noun following the comma.

EXPLANATIONS

On the left, we've shown how keywords help you to identify the major elements of the passage and its structure and what you could skim over. On the right, we've shown what you might be thinking as you read the passage strategically.

Passage for Questions 12–14

A 1973 Supreme Court decision and related Senate hearings focused congressional **criticism** on the 1966 Freedom of Information Act. ...

In **response**, a House committee drafted HR 12471, **proposing** several amendments to the Act. ... The Senate companion bill, S 2543, included these provisions as well as others ...

The Justice and Defense departments **objected** ... They **argued** that ... The Pentagon **asserted** that judicial review of exemptions could pose a **threat** to national security. President Ford, upon taking office in August 1974, **concurred**.

HR 12471 **passed** in March 1974; S 2543 was **approved** in May after the adoption of further amendments ... The Hart Amendment, **for instance** ... This amendment **provoked** another presidential **objection** ...

Before submitting the legislation to Ford, a joint conference of both houses amalgamated the two versions of the bill, while making further changes to **incorporate Ford's criticisms**. ... Ford **nevertheless vetoed** the bill, **but** the veto was **overridden** by a two-thirds vote in both houses.

Analysis

A whole lot of detail about the Freedom of Information Act. We learn that Congress didn't like it.

Congress responds by proposing some laws. Don't worry about what those laws are until you get a question about them.

Now the executive branch gets in the game. Seems that it didn't like the changes.

The laws were passed anyway, and the president was not thrilled.

Congress tried to compromise with the president, but he still vetoed the bill. It passed anyway, however.

Passage Map

Here is a sample Passage Map you might have created as you took notes on each paragraph:

¶1: F.I.A. criticized by Congress

¶2: Congress proposes new laws

¶3: President doesn't like proposed changes

¶4: Laws pass anyway

¶5: Compromise rejected; law passes

Topic: Freedom of Information Act

Scope: Changes to _____

Purpose: Describe the history of _____

88

12. (C)

Question Type: Reading Comprehension
Question Topic: Detail

Lines 17–18 say that the Justice and Defense departments objected to revision as "costly, burdensome, and inflexible." They opposed revision, in other words, for administrative reasons.

According to lines 18–19, the Justice and Defense departments argued that changes "might actually hamper access to information." But they did not go so far as to suggest that the revision was an attempt to limit public access to information **(A)**.

Although the Pentagon thought that revision might pose national security problems, it didn't argue that changes violated specific national security agreements **(B)**.

(D) and **(E)** are beyond the scope: Neither the Justice nor the Defense department protested revision on the grounds that it would weaken either its power or presidential authority. Choice **(C)** is correct.

13. (A)

Question Type: Reading Comprehension
Question Topic: Strengthen

The Pentagon doesn't offer much justification for its assertion that judicial review would cause national security problems. You know that the president agreed, but you don't learn why. You need an answer that explains the connection between judges and national security dangers. **(A)** does this; if judges don't have the necessary expertise, they might release information that would endanger national security.

(B) and **(C)** don't explain the danger posed by judicial review. **(D)** may seem tempting, but no explicit link is drawn between political interests and security concerns. (Compare that to the use of "military intelligence" in **(A)**.) Same problem with **(E)**—there's no reason given to think that presidential approval necessarily has anything to do with national security. Perhaps the president would disapprove for other reasons.

14. (A)

Question Type: Reading Comprehension
Question Topic: Application

Lines 27–29 indicate that Ford was opposed to the release of FBI records. He didn't want them to be open to public scrutiny.

(B) and **(E)**—180 answer choices—wrongly suggest that Ford was open to the idea of a release of FBI records.

(C) is incorrect. Based on lines 27–29, you can infer that Ford perceived barriers to exemption of individual FBI records, but you can't assume that expense was one of these barriers.

There is no hint in the passage that Ford believed it was more important to protect confidential sources than personal privacy or investigative secrecy **(D)**. Paragraph 4 tells you that all three are protected by the Hart amendment, but no distinction like **(D)**'s is drawn. Choice **(A)** is correct.

15. (D)

Question Type: Sentence Correction
Question Topic: Verbs

Since the sentence is about *precursors,* or forerunners, and since the non-underlined part of the sentence uses the past tense verb *were,* the answer has to use *were,* not *are* as in **(A)** and **(E)**. Also, *however it may be that* in **(B)** and *despite that* in **(C)** are unidiomatic. **(E)** drops the contrast altogether. Note that **(E)** also makes it seem that the ornithologists are the ones gliding from tree to tree. **(D)** is correct.

16. (E)

Question Type: Critical Reasoning
Question Topic: Strengthen

Because the article claims that Enzyme K causes better performance, this is an example of a causality argument—an "*X* causes *Y*" situation. The evidence is that Olympic weight lifters and sprinters have above-average levels of Enzyme K. This is evidence only of correlation. It could be that the strenuous activities of weight lifting and sprinting produce Enzyme K (as part of the body's recovery process, perhaps). In other words, it could be that "*Y* causes *X*." The author assumes that high levels of the enzyme cause better athletic performance (*X* does cause *Y*), not that athletic performance produces the enzyme (*Y* does not cause *X*). Your prediction, then, would be something like "The enzyme does, in fact, aid athletic performance," or "Athletic performance does not, in fact, produce the enzyme." **(E)** matches the second prediction. It removes "*Y* causes *X*" as a possibility, making it more likely that "*X* caused *Y*."

(A) simply adds another correlation, this time between Enzyme K and alertness. It does nothing to strengthen the causal relationship in the argument. **(B)**, which states that Enzyme K doesn't do anything *other* than help the body perform strenuous activities, is tempting. But consider the possibility that Enzyme K simply has no function in the body at all. Enzyme K could be a useless byproduct of other biological processes. Choice **(B)** requires the assumption that every bodily enzyme has at least one function. Without that additional fact, **(B)** doesn't work as a strengthener. If anything, **(C)** weakens the argument by raising the possibility that the improved performance is actually caused by another enzyme whose levels are correlated with those of Enzyme K. **(D)** is an irrelevant comparison; both weight lifters and sprinters are presented as equal evidence.

17. (E)

Question Type: Sentence Correction
Question Topic: Comparison; Parallelism

The word *than* preceding the underlined portion of the sentence tells you that the underlined portion is a comparison. Items compared must be parallel. Here, the money the Dancing Doll (DD) line received from sales is compared to that received by the Teeny Tiny Trucks (TT) and Basic Blocks (BB) lines, so all of these quantities should be stated the same way. Only the name of the toy line and the amount should change from item to item, and the verb form used should be consistent throughout. Since **(A)** includes *did* with the TT sales but no verb with the BB sales, these forms are not parallel; eliminate **(A)**.

(B) is not parallel because it uses *did* with TT sales and *were* with BB sales. **(C)** includes *sold* with TT sales but no additional verb with BB, so it's out. **(D)** uses *Basic Blocks' sales*—something not parallel to *Dancing Dolls line* and *Teeny Tiny Trucks line*. Only **(E)** uses exactly the same form for all three items, so it is correct.

18. **(B)**

Question Type: Sentence Correction
Question Topic: Pronouns; Verbs

If you saw the pronoun error as you read, you quickly eliminated **(A)** and **(C)**, as the pronoun refers to the singular *army*, not to the plural *Xerxes and nine of his generals*. You could also have seen that pronoun agreement was being tested by scanning the answer choices, as *their/its* is the only difference between **(A)** and **(B)**. The other major split among the answer choices is a 3-1-1—*was/having been/is*. The sentence is clearly set in the past (it's describing 480 BCE). So the present *is* and the present perfect *having been* are wrong; **(D)** and **(E)** can be eliminated. Only **(B)** remains, and it is correct. To continue training your ear to spot awkward sentences, compare **(C)** to **(B)**.

19. **(B)**

Question Type: Critical Reasoning
Question Topic: Weaken

The question stem tells you very clearly what you are to weaken—the explanation for the speed with which the termites were killed. Reading the stimulus tells you the reason: Gas was pumped directly into the walls in the first and second floors. This is another classic example of the GMAT's cause-and-effect arguments. Your prediction should be along the lines of "Something other than the direct pumping of gas was responsible for the speedy deaths." **(B)** does this. It doesn't outright tell you what the other factor was. But if termites died with equal speed on floors into which no gas was being pumped, then it's pretty likely that the direct pumping wasn't the cause of the rapid deaths.

Taken by itself, **(A)** is irrelevant. **(C)** and **(D)** appear to support, rather than weaken, the argument, because they suggest that a higher density of gas kills termites more rapidly. **(E)** doesn't weaken the argument because it offers no information to help you compare the speed of termite deaths in gassed and nongassed areas of the building.

On the left, we've shown how keywords help you to identify the major elements of the passage and its structure and what you could skim over. On the right, we've shown what you might be thinking as you read the passage strategically.

Passage for Questions 20–23

Modern methods of predicting earthquakes **recognize** that quakes, **far from** being geologic anomalies, are part of the periodic ... long- and short-range precursory phenomena that are **crucial** to earthquake prediction.

Quakes along active faults ... are usually frequent ... **However** ... locating active faults is **only a beginning** [detail] are **useful** in determining potential quake locations, as are [more detail]. **Seismologists may also** [again, detail].

Once the perimeters of a quake-prone zone are established, a network of base stations can monitor precursory phenomena. ... [science detail] are **valuable precursors**. ... **Theoretically**, if an area's critical strain [complicated detail] is known ... will indicate a time frame for an impending quake.

Violent tilting and foreshocks are among phenomena classified as short-term precursors. ... Such precursors are **valuable since** ...

Analysis

Stay focused on the big picture: Quakes aren't anomalies but part of a cycle. There are long- and short-range phenomena that allow quakes to be predicted.

Lots of ways to predict quake locations.

Steering clear of the complicated detail, you see *why* it's here: predicting a quake's time frame.

Short-term precursors.

Passage Map

Here is a sample Passage Map you might have created as you took notes on each paragraph:

¶1: *Quakes are predictable*

¶2: *Predicting where*

¶3: *Predicting when*

¶4: *Short-term precursors*

Topic: *Predicting earthquakes*

Scope: *Precursors useful in*

Purpose: *Describe*

EXPLANATIONS

20. (C)

Question Type: Reading Comprehension
Question Topic: Detail

Paragraph 1 contrasts coastal regions, where crustal strains build rapidly, with inland regions, where strains build more slowly. **(C)** paraphrases that distinction.

(A) flatly contradicts the passage—the first paragraph states that crustal strain is great in coastal regions. **(B)** contradicts the passage—quakes are less numerous in *inland* areas. **(D)** also contradicts the passage—you can infer that in coastal areas, which experience frequent quakes, precursory phenomena must be common. **(E)** contradicts the passage—paragraph 1 indicates that coastal regions confront thrusting sea floor plates.

21. (E)

Question Type: Reading Comprehension
Question Topic: Global

Choice **(E)** encompasses the passage's topic and scope plus the content of all four paragraphs—the importance of precursors.

(A) is too narrow—the passage says little about earthquakes in inland areas. **(B)** mentions introductory information in paragraph 1, but it neglects the passage's topic—methods of earthquake prediction. **(C)** has the same problem as **(A)**—it's too narrow. Coastal regions are only part of the picture in this passage. **(D)** is also too narrow, and it's inconsistent with the passage. Precursory phenomena are key to earthquake prediction.

22. (D)

Question Type: Reading Comprehension
Question Topic: Logic

Paragraph 3 lists a lot of details that are useful for predicting when an earthquake will strike. That fits very nicely with **(D)**.

(A) and **(B)** are the sorts of answers you can fall for if your reading becomes too detail oriented. They both represent details in paragraph 3 but not the main function of the paragraph. **(C)** addresses details in paragraphs 1 and 2. The paragraph never suggests "that critical strain is not spread evenly along most major fault lines," **(E)**.

23. (A)

Question Type: Reading Comprehension
Question Topic: Detail

"Strain" is mentioned in paragraph 1, but the question asks about "critical strain," which is discussed only at the end of paragraph 3. There, you read "critical strain will indicate a time frame for an impending quake." That fits perfectly with **(A)**.

There is nothing anywhere about calculating "the severity of an initial rupture," **(B)**. It's unclear what the term *seismic force* means, so **(C)** is no good. **(D)** refers to an unrelated detail from the beginning of the paragraph. **(E)** is tempting because "crustal movement" is discussed in the context, but it is ultimately wrong because it leaves out the idea of predicting a time frame for the next earthquake.

EXPLANATIONS

24. (B)

Question Type: Sentence Correction
Question Topic: Other (Which, Where, and When)

When should be used only for references to a time, and *where* should be used only for references to a place, so **(A)** and **(D)** are incorrect. **(C)** and **(E)** are both awkward, and they use the unidiomatic phrase *a condition of.* Choice **(B)** is correct.

25. (B)

Question Type: Critical Reasoning
Question Topic: Weaken

This argument has elements of both causality ("*X* causes *Y*") and plans/proposals/predictions. So there are many good ways to approach this question. As with all Weaken questions, begin by understanding the argument. You are to believe that a new law that will give people a tax credit if they install an alarm system will reduce crime. The evidence is a correlation between lower crime and more alarm systems. There are several assumptions. Perhaps you noticed that the link between alarm systems and low crime is only a correlation. The argument assumes that the alarm systems are causing the reduction in crime. There's also the assumption that the tax credit will cause more alarm systems to be installed. Or you could look at this argument through the plan/proposal/prediction lens and say that it assumes that there's nothing self-defeating about the plan.

To weaken the first assumption, you'd look for an answer that says, "The drop in crime noted by the studies was caused by something other than installation of alarm systems." To weaken the second, you'd say, "The tax credit won't lead to more alarm installations." To weaken the third, you'd say, "Explain why the tax credit won't lead to lower crime, even though alarm sales correlate with low crime." Choice **(B)** fits nicely with the second two, as it explains how the tax credit would fail to result in more alarm system installations. It turned out that the right answer wasn't built on the first assumption. But kudos to you for noticing it, as differentiating between correlation and causation will serve you well on many GMAT questions.

(A) uses extreme language and is also out of scope; the issue is whether this particular law can reduce crime, not whether crime can ever be eradicated. **(C)** presents an irrelevant comparison. Even if it is true, it does not provide any reason why the new tax law would not reduce crime. **(D)** is out of scope. The possible need for more prisons is irrelevant to the author's conclusion that alarm systems will lower crime rates. **(E)** actually makes the proposal more likely to work and thus strengthens the assumption.

26. (A)

Question Type: Sentence Correction
Question Topic: Comparison

The sentence compares the percentage of revenue that Corporation X spends on insurance with the percentage that Corporation Y spends on salaries. Since these two things have the same form, the comparison is clear and grammatically correct. **(A)** is the right answer. In **(B)**, the phrase *In Corporation X* modifies the rest of the sentence, illogically making it seem as if X spends a percentage of its revenue on employee salaries in Corporation Y. It also needlessly uses the passive voice. In **(C)**, *they* has no clear antecedent; because *corporation* is singular, *they* seems to refer to some other, unspecified subject. **(D)** compares Corporation X's percentage with Corporation Y's actual amount. **(E)** is awkwardly worded and seems to compare a percentage to an amount.

27. (C)

Question Type: Critical Reasoning
Question Topic: Weaken

To weaken the argument, you need to find the choice that contradicts its key assumption. The conclusion is that moving from City Y to City X will lower the likelihood of contracting the disease, since the disease occurs at a much lower rate in City X. The assumption is that living in City X reduces the risk of contracting the disease; in other words, environmental factors (such as lifestyle, air quality, or health care costs) in City X are responsible for the low incidence of the disease. Whenever you have to weaken a cause-and-effect assumption, you want to look for an answer that suggests another cause. In this case, then, your prediction would be "a reason other than the environment in City X that explains the lower incidence of the disease." That's what **(C)** gives you; if genetic factors are the reason for the lower incidence of the disease, moving won't help. Moving might change your environment but will not change your genes.

(A) is out of scope; the rates of incidence in the two cities, not the opinion of professionals, are at issue here. Also, this type of "appeal to authority" is rarely correct on the GMAT. **(B)** would strengthen the argument; the statistics state that the incidence is higher in City Y, and if the mayor were proven to have falsely suggested otherwise, it would still make sense to move to City X, where the incidence is lower. **(D)** is irrelevant. Even if true, it would not imply that the risk for the average person is lower in City Y. **(E)** is out of scope; you have no information on whether smog has anything to do with the disease in question. Furthermore, this would, if anything, strengthen the conclusion by providing at least one sense in which City X is a more healthful place to live.

28. (D)

Question Type: Sentence Correction
Question Topic: Verbs; Modification

There are two problems with this sentence. First, the unchangeable verb *glanced* is in the past tense, but the underlined *notice* is in the present tense. Since museum-goers would have *noticed* the birds at the same time that they *glanced up,* both verbs must be in the past tense. So *notice* must become the past tense *noticed.* On this basis, you can eliminate **(A)**, **(B)**, and **(C)**.

The other problem involves modification, as evidenced by the changing position and wording of the modifying phrase among the answer choices. The clause that begins *whose behavior* is intended to describe *birds,* as *rafters* do not have behavior. This also gets rid of **(A)**. **(B)** solves the problem but by changing the meaning, so it should be eliminated. **(C)** and **(D)** get the modification right. **(E)** attempts to do so but rewrites the modifier awkwardly. **(D)** is correct.

EXPLANATIONS

EXPLANATIONS

29. (D)

Question Type: Sentence Correction
Question Topic: Verbs; Usage/Style

The word *since* in a sentence is a big clue that verb tenses are being tested. Sure enough, there's a 1-3-1 split at the end of the choices involving verbs: *was using/has used/was to be using*. When was the casino tax revenue used? *Since 1993* lets you know that the use of the revenue began in the past but is still continuing, so eliminate **(A)** and **(E)**. The other split is at the beginning: *approving/for the approving of/approved*. **(B)** is awkward, and it should be tossed for that. **(C)** incorrectly changes the active participle *approving* to the passive *approved*. **(D)** is the correct answer.

Look out for words like *since, during, before,* and *after*. They indicate sequence of events, so noticing them will make verb tense questions much easier.

30. (A)

Question Type: Critical Reasoning
Question Topic: Assumption

This question stem gives you a lot of information. You know not only that it's an Assumption question but also that the conclusion is a prediction about the effectiveness of a "one-day-only" sale. Treat predictions just like plans and proposals—the central assumption is that there's nothing inherently self-defeating about the prediction. As you read, you'll hunt for anything that catches your eye as a possible problem.

The prediction is that "one-day-only" sales will be a good way of getting rid of merchandise that has previously been returned as defective. The stores will offer steep discounts and be clear that the merchandise is nonreturnable. If you don't see the potential problem that the assumption has to clear up (namely, that people might not want to buy defective merchandise in the first place), the Denial Test can lead you to the right answer.

If **(A)** were negated, then no one would be willing to pay even the sale price for the defective merchandise. If that were the case, then the sale wouldn't be effective. So this is the right answer. If **(B)** were negated, then the stores would be profitable without the sales. That doesn't damage the argument, as the author is only speculating about the store's ability to get rid of defective merchandise. **(C)** isn't necessary for similar reasons; the store could be selling plenty of merchandise and still need to clear out the returns. If **(D)** is negated, then the store could get away with having very few sales. That hardly implies that the sales are failing to meet their goal of clearing out defective merchandise. In fact, it would seem to indicate the sales' success. **(E)** is out of scope, as the issue of who would buy the merchandise doesn't matter—it only matters whether it would be bought.

31. (C)

Question Type: Sentence Correction
Question Topic: Parallelism; Comparison

The underlined portion contains a list of three sources of protein. Whenever you see a list, check for parallel structure. The three sources must have parallel forms, but *soy, eggs,* and *drinking milk* do not. A parallel construction would be *soy, eggs, or milk*. So **(A)**, **(B)**, and **(D)** are out. **(E)** adds *its*, which seems to refer to *the human body*. The sentence is not about protein in the human body but rather protein that the human body can use, so **(E)** can be eliminated. Note the *like* in **(B)** is incorrectly used—on the GMAT, *like* cannot mean "for example." Choice **(C)** is correct.

32. (D)

Question Type: Sentence Correction
Question Topic: Verbs; Usage/Style

While this sentence is long and wordy, you needn't be intimidated as long as you scan for differences. There's a pretty clear 2-1-2 split right at the start: *It was decided by the National Weather Service/A forecasting system/The National Weather service decided.* The first of these, *It was decided by . . .*, is passive construction and not preferred by the GMAT. That eliminates **(A)** and **(C)**. What about **(B)**? It's structured slightly differently, but does it share the passive voice error? It does! The whole thing reads "A forecasting system . . . *was selected* to be purchased by the National Weather Service." Eliminate **(B)** as well. Comparing **(D)** to **(E)**, you see this difference: *links 44 computers together* versus *combines 44 computers linked together with each other.* **(E)** is redundant. Just saying *linked together* is enough—if things are "linked together," they are already "combined" and "with each other." (This redundancy error is shared by **(A)**, **(B)**, and **(E)**.) Choice **(D)** remains, and it is correct.

EXPLANATIONS

On the left, we've shown how keywords help you to identify the major elements of the passage and its structure and what you could skim over. On the right, we've shown what you might be thinking as you read the passage strategically.

Passage for Questions 33–35

Contamination is the unintended presence of harmful substances or organisms in food. **While ... it is still necessary to guard against** the practices that can increase the likelihood of food contamination. **Because** food-borne illness poses a potentially **serious threat** to public health, **preventing** contamination of safe food needs to be a **prime objective** ... **Furthermore** ...

The **most serious** risk associated with food is the biological hazard. Biological hazards are ... One of the **most frequently** reported diseases of this type is salmonellosis ...

The **other major** form of biologically induced food-borne illness is intoxication ... *Staphylococcus* food intoxication is one of the **most common** types ...

Analysis

Food contamination seems to be the topic. It's a serious threat, so managers need to guard against it.

Biological hazards and the most common disease

Another kind—food-borne intoxication

Passage Map

Here is a sample Passage Map you might have created as you took notes on each paragraph:

¶1: Food contamination a potentially serious threat

¶2: Biological hazards

¶3: Food-borne intoxication

Topic: Food contamination

Scope: Sources of

Purpose: Describe

33. (C)

Question Type: Reading Comprehension
Question Topic: Global

You need the answer that reflects the passage's topic, scope, purpose, and overall structure. **(A)** and **(E)** may be tempting but only tell parts of the story. **(A)** is the point of paragraph 1, and **(E)** is the point of paragraphs 2 and 3. **(C)** correctly expresses the gist of all three paragraphs working together. The last two paragraphs summarize the knowledge of contamination sources, and the first paragraph discusses why this knowledge is essential.

(B) and **(D)** both distort paragraphs 2 and 3, as well as leaving out paragraph 1.

34. (A)

Question Type: Reading Comprehension
Question Topic: Inference

The author discusses food service managers in paragraph 1. The author uses a lot of strong, prescriptive language: "preventing contamination of safe food needs to be a prime objective of every food service manager" and "a food service manager must possess accurate information on the different hazards associated with the contamination of food." The author clearly thinks that a food service manager's comprehension of food hazards is very important. This fits perfectly with **(A)**.

(B) is a distortion. Although the sources of contamination seem varied and complex, there is nothing here to suggest that a diligent food service manager can gain only a limited understanding of contamination.

(C) misses the scope of the passage by focusing on the decision to *hire* a manager. Even if you infer that a manager's understanding of these issues must be a consideration in hiring, since it's so important, you still can't say it's the *primary* consideration.

(D) uses the extreme word *exclusively* and consequently is too extreme. In fact, the author states that prevention is only part of the battle—knowledge is also necessary so that a manager knows what to do "in the event that a . . . crisis does arise."

(E)'s pessimism is reminiscent of **(B)**. A clear understanding of the author's purpose and tone allows you to eliminate choices like these that don't match either. The first few words of **(E)** are on the right track; in fact, "vitally important" is synonymous with **(A)**'s "crucial." But the whole choice needs to fit, and the rest of **(E)** misses the point.

35. (D)

Question Type: Reading Comprehension
Question Topic: Detail

The striking term *pathogenic organisms* that appears in the question stem is relatively easy to locate in paragraph 2. Correct choice **(D)** comes right out of lines 15–17, with the keywords *such as* acting as the link between pathogenic microorganisms and bacteria and parasites. Even in a passage with lots of unfamiliar terms, it all boils down to good strategic reading. Take a look at the wrong choices. In **(A)**, the passage doesn't tell you what the most common form is. Nothing in paragraph 2 suggests **(B)**, but paragraph 3 actually suggests the opposite—some microorganisms can cause disease even after being killed. A careful reading of the sentence in which "pathogenic organisms" appears shows that **(C)** distorts the meaning of the sentence. Toxins are not the same

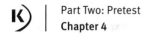
as pathogenic microorganisms. **(E)**—how hard it is to detect pathogenic organisms—is outside the scope, as only the detection of toxins is mentioned.

36. (E)

Question Type: Critical Reasoning
Question Topic: Inference

This question asks, "Which of the following statements is best supported by the information above?" In other words, what can be inferred from the stated material? The author in this question asserts that junior college education had a big impact on family-run businesses after WWII, as the new methods of accounting, marketing, and finance allowed business size to grow and profits to be maximized.

It's difficult to make a specific prediction on most Inference questions. It's often best to say, "The answer *must* be true based on the stimulus; it won't go beyond the scope or read a detail in an extreme way."

In **(A)**, the disqualifying word is *principally*. The information presented does not specify what the junior colleges emphasized. This choice reads too much into the fact that often family businesses increased in size because of the newly acquired knowledge. **(B)** is wrong because you really can't infer how popular or widespread these methods were before the war. For all you know, these could have been revolutionary techniques or well-kept secrets. In **(C)**, you know junior colleges taught new methods of marketing and finance and stuff like that; you do not know how much management theory was or was not presented. This choice relies on data you aren't given—a sure sign of an incorrect or unwarranted inference. **(D)** takes the facts in the stimulus too far. You're told that profits increased thanks to the influence of junior colleges, so you could infer that family-run businesses would have been less profitable without them. But there's a world of difference between *less profitable* and *unprofitable*. **(E)** is certainly true. Business methods did change because of the education—the stimulus calls them "new methods," after all. It's a common mistake to throw out an answer because it seems somehow "too obvious." Some Inference answers are tough to prove, but many are very straightforward.

37. (C)

Question Type: Sentence Correction
Question Topic: Verbs; Modification

Notice the descriptive phrase *of plastic manufacturing plants* between the subject *size* and the verb phrase *have dropped*. That's your clue to check for subject-verb agreement. In fact, *size* is singular, but *have dropped* is plural. **(A)** and **(B)** contain *have* and should be eliminated. There's also another split: The *down* in **(D)** and **(E)** is redundant with *dropped*. If something has dropped, it's gone down! This quickly leaves you with only **(C)**. To improve your ear's ability to spot awkward phrasing, check out the end of **(A)**, **(D)**, and **(E)**. **(D)**'s ending is not only awkward but also redundant, as the implied word at the end is *size*: "about the size of a football field's [size]."

38. (D)

Question Type: Critical Reasoning
Question Topic: Inference

You need to find the choice that must logically follow if the stimulus is true. If making steel with Element X reduces the level of microscopic fractures, and if some Canadian steel contains Element X, it follows that some Canadian steel will be less likely to develop such fractures. So **(D)** can be inferred.

(A) is too extreme to be inferred. It *might* be true, but nothing says that at least one other country can't produce steel as strong and flexible as Canada's. **(B)** wrongly introduces the idea of "years of use"; you know nothing about when these fractures would start to appear. Furthermore, the stimulus only tells you about some Canadian steel. You know nothing about steel from other countries. Perhaps many countries make steel with Element X; perhaps none do. You just don't know. **(C)** and **(E)** are both too extreme. The stimulus never says that there isn't a better steel out there somewhere, nor does it say that Canadian ore has more Element X than any other kind, only that it has a lot.

39. (E)

Question Type: Sentence Correction
Question Topic: Other (Subjunctive Mood; Which, Where, and When)

There are clear differences at the beginning of the choices: *that a federal arbitrator/of a federal arbitrator/a federal arbitrator*. In **(C)**, *asked of* is unidiomatic. For verbs like *ask*, there are two correct forms: *ask + object + to* or *ask + that + (subject of clause) + (infinitive without to)*. The former construction is attempted by **(D)**, but this choice uses *that* inappropriately. **(A)**, **(B)**, and **(E)** try the latter, but **(A)** uses *would* inappropriately. **(B)** and **(E)** both open correctly, but they differ at the end; **(B)** uses *have*, while **(E)** uses *has*. The verb in question is part of a modifying clause that describes *union*, so the singular *has* is correct. Eliminate **(B)** (and **(C)**, if you haven't already eliminated it). **(E)** is the correct answer.

Note that all verbs that are synonyms of *request* or *order*, such as *ask*, *mandate*, or *require*, can be used in either of the two ways described in this explanation: "The GMAT requires test takers to be on time," or "The GMAT requires that test takers be on time."

40. (E)

Question Type: Sentence Correction
Question Topic: Parallelism

The sentence contains two parallel elements—procedures and reductions—that are incorrectly joined by the construction *from ... and*. The construction should be *from ... to*. Eliminate **(A)** and **(B)**. **(C)** changes the parallel structure format with *such as*, but *reducing* is not parallel with *improvement* and *encouragement*. Moreover, *reducing* can't be followed by the preposition *in* from the original sentence. Eliminate **(C)**. **(D)** correctly uses *from ... to* but includes the nonparallel *procedures* and *reducing*. That leaves **(E)**, which is correct.

41. (C)

Question Type: Critical Reasoning
Question Topic: Explain

As with any Explain question, you should make sure that you understand what the discrepant pieces of information are. The stimulus tells you that despite no increase in competition and a large increase in local population, a hardware store has seen little increase in snowblower or lawnmower sales. Your prediction should be "the answer that explains why snowblower and lawnmower sales have not gone up, even though there are more people and the same number of competitors."

(A) doesn't explain the slow sales, because although the area to be mown or blown may not be increasing, the number of people responsible for doing the job is going up; there's no reason to think that they're all sharing equipment. **(B)** doesn't explain things because wages may have risen right along with inflation. Inflation tells you nothing about relative buying power or the demand for equipment. **(C)** is the correct answer, because apartment-dwellers don't require snowblowers or lawnmowers. The maintenance crews of the buildings do, but sales have increased a little—so those sales are accounted for in the stimulus. **(D)** may explain the slow sales of snowblowers (they may be used less and therefore need replacement less often) but not of lawnmowers. **(E)** is ruled out by the stimulus, which explicitly says that Jacob's store has no competition; there's no better selection anywhere else in town.

PART THREE

Verbal Section and Strategies

CHAPTER 5

Verbal Section Overview

- Composition of the Verbal Section
- Pacing on the Verbal Section
- How the Verbal Section Is Scored
- Core Competencies on the Verbal Section
- Introduction to Strategic Reading

COMPOSITION OF THE VERBAL SECTION

A little more than half of the multiple-choice questions that count toward your overall score appear in the Verbal section. You have 75 minutes to answer 41 Verbal questions in three formats: Reading Comprehension, Sentence Correction, and Critical Reasoning. These three types of questions are mingled throughout the Verbal section, so you never know what's coming next. Here's what you can expect to see:

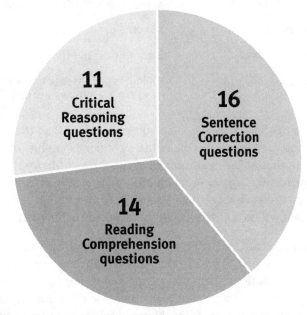

The Approximate Mix of Questions on the GMAT Verbal Section: 11 Critical Reasoning Questions, 14 Reading Comprehension Questions, and 16 Sentence Correction Questions

You may see more of one question type and fewer of another. Don't worry. It's likely just a slight difference in the types of "experimental" questions you get.

In the next three chapters, you'll learn strategies for each of these question types. But first, let's look at some techniques for managing the Verbal section as a whole.

PACING ON THE VERBAL SECTION

The GMAT will give you four Reading Comprehension passages. Two will likely be longer and have four questions each, and two will likely be shorter and have three questions each. With less than two minutes per question on the Verbal section, where will you find the time to read those passages?

Part of the answer is that the Reading Comprehension chapter of this book will give you great tips about how to read the passages efficiently. Another big part, though, is how you will handle Sentence Correction. Follow the Kaplan Method for Sentence Correction, which you will see in the chapter devoted to that question type, and through practice you will bring your average time down to 60 seconds per Sentence Correction question. Moving through Sentence Correction questions quickly and efficiently will allow you the time you'll need to read long Reading Comprehension passages and take apart complex arguments in Critical Reasoning.

Here are Kaplan's timing recommendations for the Verbal section of the GMAT. While it's far more important at first that you practice to build accuracy and mastery of the strategies, it's also a good idea to keep these timing recommendations in mind. By incorporating more and more timed practice as you progress in your GMAT prep, you will grow comfortable with these timing guidelines, and following them will contribute greatly to your success on Test Day.

Verbal Section Timing	
Question Type	**Average Time You Should Spend**
Sentence Correction	1 minute per question
Critical Reasoning	2 minutes per question
Reading Comprehension	4 minutes per passage and a little less than 1.5 minutes per question

Following these timing guidelines will also help you pace yourself so that you have time to work on the questions at the end of the section. One of the most persistent bits of bad advice out there is that you should take more time at the beginning of the test. Don't fall for this myth! Running short of time at the end of the test will cost you much more than you may gain from a few extra right answers up front. The testmakers impose heavy score penalties for not reaching all questions in a section, and long strings of wrong answers due to guessing or rushing will hurt your score as well.

What this all means is that you are under some conflicting pressures. It might seem like a good idea to take extra time at the beginning to ensure that you get all the early questions right, since then the test would give you those difficult, high-value questions. But if you use up a lot of time early on, you won't have time to finish, and your score will suffer a severe penalty. Just a handful of unanswered final questions can lower a score from the mid-90th percentile to the mid-70th percentile. Plus, if you spend all that time early on, you won't have time to solve the hard questions you may receive as a result of your careful work, so you won't be able to take advantage of their extra value.

So if taking more time at the beginning isn't a good idea, does that mean you should rush through the beginning? This is also not the case. Rushing almost guarantees that you will miss some crucial aspect of a question. If you get a lot of midlevel questions wrong, the test will never give you those difficult, high-value questions that you want to reach.

If you are stuck on a question, make a guess. Even the best test takers occasionally guess, and it's still possible to achieve an elite score if you are strategic about when and how you guess. If you start to fall behind pace, look for good guessing questions. That way you'll reach the end of the section and have the time to earn the points for all the questions that you are capable of answering correctly and efficiently. What kinds of questions are good candidates for guessing? Ones that you know play to your weaknesses, ones that require lots of reading, or ones that look like they will involve separate evaluation of each answer choice.

STRATEGIC GUESSING

Whether you've run short of time or encountered a question that totally flummoxes you, you will have to guess occasionally. But don't simply guess at random. First, try to narrow down the answer choices. This will greatly improve your chances of guessing the right answer. When you guess, you should follow this plan:

1. **Eliminate answer choices you know are wrong.** Even if you don't know the right answer, you can often tell that some of the answer choices are wrong. For instance, on Sentence Correction questions, you can eliminate answer choice **(A)** as soon as you find an error in the original sentence, thus reducing the number of choices to consider.

2. **Avoid answer choices that make you suspicious.** These are the answer choices that just "look wrong" or conform to a common wrong-answer type. For example, if an answer choice in a Reading Comprehension question mentions a term you don't remember reading, chances are it is wrong. (The next three chapters contain more information about common wrong-answer types on the Verbal section.)

3. **Choose one of the remaining answer choices.** The fewer options you have to choose from, the higher your chances of selecting the right answer.

EXPERIMENTAL QUESTIONS

Some questions on the GMAT are experimental. These questions are not factored into your score. They are questions that the testmaker is evaluating for possible use on future tests. To get good data, the testmakers have to test each question against the whole range of test takers—that is, high and low scorers. Therefore, you could be on your way to an 800 and suddenly come across a question that feels out of line with how you think you are doing.

Don't panic; just do your best and keep on going. The difficulty level of the experimental questions you see has little to do with how you're currently scoring. Remember, there is no way for you to know for sure whether a question is experimental or not, so approach every question as if it were scored.

Keep in mind that it's hard to judge the true difficulty level of a question. A question that seems easy to you may simply be playing to your personal strengths and be very difficult for other test takers. So treat every question as if it counts. Don't waste time trying to speculate about the difficulty of the questions you're seeing and what that implies about your performance. Rather, focus your energy on answering the question in front of you as efficiently as possible.

HOW THE VERBAL SECTION IS SCORED

The Verbal section of the GMAT is quite different from the Verbal sections of paper-and-pencil tests you may have taken. The major difference between the test formats is that the GMAT computer-adaptive test (CAT) adapts to your performance. Each test taker is given a different mix of questions, depending on how well he or she is doing on the test. In other words, the questions get harder or easier depending on whether you answer them correctly or incorrectly. Your GMAT score is not determined by the number of questions you get right but rather by the difficulty level of the questions you get right.

When you begin a section, the computer

- assumes you have an average score (about 550), and
- gives you a medium-difficulty question. About half the people who take the test will get this question right, and half will get it wrong. What happens next depends on whether you answer the question correctly.

If you answer the question correctly,

- your score goes up, and
- you are given a slightly harder question.

If you answer the question incorrectly,

- your score goes down, and
- you are given a slightly easier question.

This pattern continues for the rest of the section. As you get questions right, the computer raises your score and gives you harder questions. As you get questions wrong, the computer lowers your score and gives you easier questions. In this way, the computer homes in on your score.

If you feel like you're struggling at the end of the section, don't worry! Because the CAT adapts to find the outer edge of your abilities, the test will feel hard; it's designed to be difficult for everyone, even the highest scorers.

CORE COMPETENCIES ON THE VERBAL SECTION

Unlike most subject-specific tests you have taken throughout your academic career, the scope of knowledge that the GMAT requires of you is fairly limited. In fact, you don't need any background knowledge or expertise beyond fundamental math and verbal skills. While mastering those fundamentals is essential to your success on the GMAT—and this book is concerned in part with helping you develop or refresh those skills—the GMAT does *not* primarily seek to reward test takers for content-specific knowledge. Rather, the GMAT is a test of high-level thinking and reasoning abilities; it uses math and verbal subject matter as a platform to build questions that test your critical thinking and problem solving capabilities. As you prepare for the GMAT, you will notice that similar analytical skills come into play across the various question types and sections of the test.

Kaplan has adopted the term "Core Competencies" to refer to the four bedrock thinking skills rewarded by the GMAT: Critical Thinking, Pattern Recognition, Paraphrasing, and Attention to the Right Detail. The Kaplan Methods and strategies presented throughout this book will help you demonstrate these all-important skills. Let's dig into each of the Core Competencies in turn and discuss how each applies to the Verbal section.

CRITICAL THINKING

Most potential MBA students are adept at creative problem solving, and the GMAT offers many opportunities to demonstrate this skill. You probably already have experience assessing situations to see when data are inadequate; synthesizing information into valid deductions; finding creative solutions to complex problems; and avoiding unnecessary, redundant labor.

In GMAT terms, a critical thinker is a creative problem solver who engages in critical inquiry. One of the hallmarks of successful test takers is their skill at asking the right questions. GMAT critical thinkers first consider what they're being asked to do, then study the given information and ask the right questions, especially, "How can I get the answer in the most direct way?" and "How can I use the question format to my advantage?"

For instance, as you examine a Reading Comprehension passage, you'll interrogate the author: "Why are you writing about Walt Whitman?" or "Why have you included this detail in paragraph 2?" For Sentence Correction questions, you'll ask: "Why do three of the five answer choices share the same grammatical construction?" or "Is there a better way to express the idea?" For Critical Reasoning, you'll ask the author of the argument: "What's your main point?" or "What evidence have you presented to convince me to agree with you?"

Those test takers who learn to ask the right questions become creative problem solvers—and GMAT champs. Let's see how to apply the GMAT Core Competency of Critical Thinking to a sample Critical Reasoning question:

1. One problem with labor unions today is that their top staffs consist of college-trained lawyers, economists, and labor relations experts who cannot understand the concerns of real workers. One goal of union reform movements should be to build staffs out of workers who have come up from the ranks of the industry involved.

    The argument above depends primarily upon which one of the following assumptions?

    O   Higher education lessens people's identification with their class background.

    O   Union staffs should include more people with first-hand industrial supervisory experience.

    O   Some people who have worked in a given industry can understand the concerns of workers in that industry.

    O   Most labor unions today do not fairly represent workers' interests.

    O   A goal of union reform movements should be to make unions more democratic.

This question asks you to identify what the author is assuming. You'll learn more about assumptions in the Critical Reasoning chapter of this book, but for now, know that an "assumption" is something the author *must* believe but doesn't state directly. A skilled critical thinker will approach this task by asking questions to uncover the author's unstated assumption.

First of all, what does the author want to see happen? The author argues that unions should get more "workers who have come up through the ranks" into leadership. What's her reason for this claim? She asserts that the lawyers and experts don't understand what real workers worry about.

So if her solution is to get more rank-and-file workers into top union staffs, then what must she think these rank-and-file are capable of? The author is assuming that, unlike the college-trained experts, "workers who have come up through the ranks" can understand the concerns of the "real workers" whom the unions are supposed to represent. Scanning the answer choices, the one that matches this prediction is choice **(C)**.

Notice how efficiently you can move through a question like this one when you engage in critical inquiry—no rereading, no falling for answer choice traps, no time wasted. As you move through this book, you'll learn how to identify the most helpful questions to ask depending on how the test question is constructed.

PATTERN RECOGNITION

Most people fail to appreciate the level of constraint standardization places on testmakers. Because the testmakers must give reliable, valid, and comparable scores to many thousands of students each year, they're forced to reward the same skills on every test. They do so by repeating the same kinds of questions with the same traps and pitfalls, which are susceptible to the same strategic solutions.

Inexperienced test takers treat every problem as if it were a brand-new task, whereas the GMAT rewards those who spot the patterns and use them to their advantage. Of course Pattern Recognition is a key business skill in its own right: Executives who recognize familiar situations and apply proven solutions to them will outperform those who reinvent the wheel every time.

Even the smartest test taker will struggle if he approaches each GMAT question as a novel exercise. But the GMAT features nothing novel—just repeated patterns. Kaplan knows this test inside and out, and we'll show you which patterns you will encounter on Test Day. You will know the test better than your competition does. Let's see how to apply the GMAT Core Competency of Pattern Recognition to a sample Sentence Correction question:

2. A major pharmaceutical company, in cooperation with an international public health organization and the medical research departments of two large universities, is expected to announce tomorrow that it will transfer the rights to manufacture a number of tuberculosis drugs to several smaller companies.

   O   is expected to announce tomorrow that it will transfer the
   O   are expected to announce tomorrow that they will transfer their
   O   are expected to announce tomorrow that they will transfer the
   O   is expected to announce tomorrow that they will transfer the
   O   is expected to announce tomorrow that there would be a transfer of the

Many people will look at this problem and start thinking about grammar classes they haven't had for years. Then they'll plug every answer choice back into the sentence to see which one works best. Did you find yourself doing that during the Pretest in this book?

There are two important patterns at work in this question that you should recognize from now on: First, choice **(A)** on Sentence Correction questions will always repeat the underlined portion of the original sentence. You should only ever choose **(A)** if there's no error in the original sentence. If you've already read the original sentence, there's never any reason to spend time reading through choice **(A)**.

Second, notice the pronoun *it* in the underlined portion. Pronouns are one of seven grammar and usage topics that together make up 93 percent of the Sentence Correction issues on the GMAT.

Whenever a pronoun appears in the underlined portion of the sentence, you should check whether it's correct. Here, ask yourself what *it* refers to. In this case, *it* is the pharmaceutical company. Notice in scanning the answer choices that they, too, fall into patterns: Some use *it*, and others use *they*. Recognizing this pattern lets you know what question to ask next: "To refer to a company, is the correct pronoun *it* or *they*?" For a singular noun, the correct pronoun is *it*. Eliminate choices **(B)**, **(C)**, and **(D)**, which all use *they*.

Having narrowed down the choices to just two, **(A)** and **(E)**, you can eliminate choice **(E)** because it uses an awkward, lengthy phrase that makes it less clear *who* will "transfer the rights." The answer is **(A)**; the sentence is correct as written.

Notice how efficiently you can find the correct answer when you recognize the patterns. Meanwhile, your competition, not recognizing how the GMAT works, would waste time floundering through each answer choice in turn.

PARAPHRASING

The third Core Competency is Paraphrasing: The GMAT rewards those who can reduce difficult, abstract, or polysyllabic prose to simple terms. Paraphrasing is, of course, an essential business skill: Executives must be able to define clear tasks based on complicated requirements and accurately summarize mountains of detail.

The test isn't going to make it easy for you to understand questions and passages. But you won't be overwhelmed by the complicated prose of Critical Reasoning or Reading Comprehension questions if you endeavor to make your own straightforward mental translations. Habitually putting complex ideas and convoluted wording into your own simple, accurate terms will ensure that you "get it"— that you understand the information well enough to drive to the correct answer.

Let's see how to apply the GMAT Core Competency of Paraphrasing to the first paragraph of a sample Reading Comprehension passage. You will return to this passage in full in the Reading Comprehension chapter of this book. For now, use the first paragraph to see how Paraphrasing helps you synthesize ideas by putting them in your own words:

> The informal sector of the economy involves activities that, in both developed and underdeveloped countries, are outside the arena of the normal, regulated economy and thus escape official recordkeeping. These activities, which include such practices as off-the-books hiring and cash payments, occur mainly in service industries like construction, hotels, and restaurants. Many economists think that the informal sector is an insignificant supplement to the larger formal economy. They base this belief on three assumptions that have been derived from theories of industrial development. But empirical evidence suggests that these assumptions are not valid.

One of the most crucial ways to paraphrase on the GMAT is to summarize the main idea of a paragraph. When you learn about Passage Mapping in the Reading Comprehension chapter of this book, you will see how helpful it is to write a short summary of each paragraph. Clearly, however, you do not want to waste time copying down whole sentences or phrases from the passage verbatim. Paraphrasing helps you simultaneously identify quick, short ways to record main ideas and reinforce your understanding of those ideas.

You don't need to be an expert on economic policy to identify the main ideas in this paragraph and put them into your own words. The paragraph defines the informal sector, gives examples, then sets the stage for a debate between "many economists" and the author over how big or important the informal sector is.

On Test Day, you might write the following shorthand notes in your Passage Map for this paragraph:

¶1: Informal sector jobs; examps; econs think insig (based on 3 assumps); author disagrees

As you work through the Verbal chapters of this book, you will learn more about Paraphrasing for Reading Comprehension passages. You will also develop techniques for Paraphrasing the content of Critical Reasoning questions and interpreting the gist of what a Sentence Correction sentence is trying to say so that you can choose the answer choice that most accurately and concisely expresses that meaning.

ATTENTION TO THE RIGHT DETAIL

Details present a dilemma: Missing them can cost you points. But if you try to absorb every fact in a Reading Comprehension passage or Critical Reasoning stimulus, you may find yourself swamped, delayed, and still unready for the questions that follow, because the relevant and irrelevant details are all mixed together in your mind. Throughout this book, you will learn how to discern the essential details from those that can slow you down or confuse you. The GMAT testmakers reward examinees for paying attention to "the right details"—the ones that make the difference between right and wrong answers.

Attention to the Right Detail distinguishes great administrators from poor ones in the business world as well. Just ask anyone who's had a boss who had the wrong priorities or who was so bogged down in minutiae that the department stopped functioning.

Not all details are created equal, and there are mountains of them on the test. Learn to target only what will turn into correct answers. Let's see how to apply the GMAT Core Competency of Attention to the Right Detail to a sample Critical Reasoning question:

3. Police officers in Smith County who receive Special Weapons and Tactics (SWAT) training spend considerable time in weapons instruction and practice. This time spent developing expertise in the use of guns affects the instincts of Smith County officers, making them too reliant on firearms. In the past year in Smith County, in 12 of the 14 cases in which police officers shot a suspect while attempting to make an arrest, the officer involved had received SWAT training, although only five percent of the police force as a whole in the county had received such training.

   Which of the following, if true, most strengthens the argument above?

   O   In an adjacent county, all of the cases in which police shot suspects involved officers with SWAT training.

   O   SWAT training stresses the need for surprise, speed, and aggression when approaching suspects.

   O   Only 15 percent of Smith County's SWAT training course is devoted to firearms lessons.

   O   Among officers involved in the arrest of suspects in Smith County in the past year, the proportion who had received SWAT training was similar to the proportion who had received SWAT training in the police force as a whole.

   O   Some Smith County officers without SWAT training have not been on a firing range in years.

You will learn more about strengthening arguments in the Critical Reasoning chapter of this book; for now, focus on finding the detail that makes a difference.

SWAT training, the author concludes in the second sentence, is making Smith County officers too reliant on firearms. The evidence in the third sentence presents you with many different numbers and figures. However, the important thing to note here is the shift in scope between the conclusion, which is about Smith County police officers in general, and the evidence, which is about the 14 cases that involved shootings during an arrest.

That "scope shift" signals that you've found the right detail to focus on. If the author is using data from arrests to make a point about the effects of SWAT training on the police force as a whole, it will make a difference if, for example, disproportionately many officers involved in making arrests have received SWAT training. Since you're looking for the answer choice that strengthens the argument, you need one that equates officers making arrests to officers at large.

Answer choice **(D)** is the correct answer. If **(D)** is true, then the officers in the 14 cases are representative of officers as a whole, and the argument is strengthened.

Notice that paying Attention to the Right Detail—the one that the question hinges upon—enables you to form a prediction of what the correct answer will contain. Selecting an answer then becomes a straightforward matter of finding the choice that matches your prediction, rather than a time-consuming process of debating the pros and cons of each answer choice in turn. Throughout this book you will learn to distinguish the important from the inconsequential on the GMAT.

INTRODUCTION TO STRATEGIC READING

Since you're reading this book and aspire to go to business school, it goes without saying that you can read. What needs saying is that the way of reading for which you've been rewarded throughout your academic and professional careers is likely not the best way to read on Test Day.

Normally, when you read for school, pleasure, or even work, the main things you try to get from the text are the facts—the story, who did what, what's true or false. That way of reading may have served you well throughout your life, but on the GMAT you must read strategically.

Because Kaplan knows the test so well, we've identified the key structures that will get you points on the test. More importantly, we've identified the keywords that signal those structures and tell you what to do with them. Strategic Reading means using structural keywords to zero in on what the test will ask you about. Usually, it's great to read in order to broaden your horizons. On Test Day, you haven't got time for anything that doesn't pay off in right answers.

KEYWORDS

- Keywords determine the structure of a passage.
- Keywords highlight lines in the text that are crucial to the author's message.

As you see from the bullet points, keywords help you see the structure of the passage. That, in turn, tells you what part of the text is crucial to the author's point of view, which is what the test consistently rewards you for noticing.

On the GMAT, questions could give the same facts, but the correct answers could vary depending on the author's point of view. To see how this works, take a look at the following two facts about Bob:

> Bob got a great GMAT score.
>
> He is going to East Main State Business School.

The meaning depends on the keyword that links these facts. Fill in the supported inference for each case:

> Bob got a great GMAT score. Therefore, he is going to East Main State Business School.
>
> Supported inference about East Main State: _____
>
> Bob got a great GMAT score. Nevertheless, he is going to East Main State Business School.
>
> Supported inference about East Main State: _____

For the first example, you can infer that East Main State must be a good school, or at least Bob must think it is; because he got a good score, that's where he's going. Based on the second example, however, you can infer that East Main State must not be the kind of school where people with good scores usually go; it must not be very competitive to get in there. Notice that the facts didn't change. The keywords "therefore" and "nevertheless" made all the difference to the correct GMAT inference.

This distinction is important because almost all GMAT questions hinge on keywords. Because it cannot reward test takers for outside knowledge, the GMAT cannot ask what you already know about East Main State—but it *will* ask questions to assess how well you understand what the author says about East Main State.

In Reading Comprehension and Critical Reasoning, keywords highlight the author's opinion and logic, and they may indicate contrast, illustration, continuation, and sequence. As you continue your GMAT prep, pay close attention to keywords you encounter and what they tell you about the relationship between the information that comes before and after the keywords. Here are the most important categories of keywords and some examples of words that fall into each category.

KEYWORD CATEGORIES

Contrast: Nevertheless, despite, although, but, yet, on the other hand

Continuation: Furthermore, moreover, additionally, also, and

Logic: Therefore, thus, consequently, it follows that, because, since

Illustration: For example, we can see this by, this shows, to illustrate

Sequence/Timing: First, second, finally, in the 1920s, several steps, later

Emphasis/Opinion: Unfortunately, happily, crucial, very important, a near disaster, unsuccessful, she even _____

To see how keywords separate the useful from the useless on the GMAT, take a look at the following Critical Reasoning question—without the answer choices for the moment. You will learn more about analyzing arguments in the Critical Reasoning chapter of this book, but for now, the following questions will guide you through the process of breaking down an argument using keywords:

What does this word tell us about the relationship between "artistic quality" and "marketing tool"? _____

What does this word tell us about the purpose of this sentence? _____

4. In recent years, many advertisements have won awards for their artistic quality. But since advertising must serve as a marketing tool, advertising executives must exercise their craft with an eye to the effectiveness of their advertisement. For this reason, advertising is not art.

What reason is this phrase referring to?

_____

_____

Paraphrase this argument: _____

_____

_____

_____

The argument above depends on which of the following assumptions?

What is the author assuming? _____

_____

Let's walk through the above questions in boxes, starting with the question that refers to the word "but." You may have noted that "but" is a contrast keyword. This tells you that the author believes the terms "artistic quality" and "marketing tool" to be opposed or incompatible.

The next question refers to the word "since," which falls under the logic category of keywords. Like the word "because," "since" signals a reason; in terms of an argument, "since" introduces the author's evidence.

The phrase "for this reason" refers to the evidence that came immediately beforehand—that ad executives must be concerned with effectiveness. "For this reason" also signals that the final sentence contains the argument's conclusion.

The next box asks you to paraphrase the argument. This means that you should put the evidence and conclusion into your own succinct words: Ads aren't art [conclusion] because they must take effectiveness into account [evidence].

Before looking at the answer choices, you need to predict exactly what you're looking for: "What is the author assuming?" Look for the gap in your paraphrase above. The author must believe that something you have to judge based on its effectiveness cannot be art.

Now take a look at the answer choices and identify which one matches your prediction.

4. In recent years, many advertisements have won awards for their artistic quality. But since advertising must serve as a marketing tool, advertising executives must exercise their craft with an eye to the effectiveness of their advertisement. For this reason, advertising is not art.

    The argument above depends on which of the following assumptions?

    O   Some advertisements are made to be displayed solely as art.
    O   Some advertising executives are more concerned than others with the effectiveness of their product.
    O   Advertising executives ought to be more concerned than they currently are with the artistic dimension of advertising.
    O   Something is not "art" if its creator must be concerned with its practical effect.
    O   Artists are not concerned with the monetary value of their work.

Choice **(D)** matches the prediction and is the correct answer.

By attending to the keywords, you zeroed in on just what's important to the testmakers—with no wasted effort or rereading. Strategic Reading embodies all four GMAT Core Competencies: Critical Thinking, Pattern Recognition, Paraphrasing, and Attention to the Right Detail.

CHAPTER 6

Critical Reasoning

A study of 20 overweight men revealed that each man experienced significant weight loss after adding SlimDown, an artificial food supplement, to his daily diet. For three months, each man consumed one SlimDown portion every morning after exercising and then followed his normal diet for the rest of the day. Clearly, anyone who consumes one portion of SlimDown every day for at least three months will lose weight and will look and feel his best.

Which one of the following is an assumption on which the argument depends?

○ The men in the study will gain back the weight if they discontinue the SlimDown program.

○ No other dietary supplement will have the same effect on overweight men.

○ The daily exercise regimen was not responsible for the effects noted in the study.

○ Women won't experience similar weight reductions if they adhere to the SlimDown program for three months.

○ Overweight men will achieve only partial weight loss if they don't remain on the SlimDown program for a full three months.

Above is a typical Critical Reasoning question. In this chapter, we'll look at how to apply the Kaplan Method to this question, discuss the logical structures being tested, and go over the basic principles and strategies that you want to keep in mind on every Critical Reasoning question. But before you move on, take a minute to think about what you see in this question and answer some questions about how you think it works:

• The question refers to the paragraph as an "argument." What does this term mean?

• What does it mean for an argument to depend on an assumption?

• Notice that the question comes after the argument. Is it a better idea to read the argument or the question first?

• What GMAT Core Competencies are most essential to success on this question?

PREVIEWING CRITICAL REASONING

THE QUESTION REFERS TO THE PARAGRAPH AS AN "ARGUMENT." WHAT DOES THIS TERM MEAN?

Over 70 percent of Critical Reasoning questions are based on arguments, so understanding what they are and how they work will be of great help on Test Day.

When the GMAT refers to an *argument*, it doesn't mean a conversation that involves two people shouting at each other. An argument in Critical Reasoning means any piece of text in which an author puts forth a set of ideas or a point of view and attempts to support it. A statement such as "Small dogs make better pets than large dogs," is not an argument—it's just an opinion. An argument must make some attempt to persuade. For instance, if the opinion statement above included a reason or two to support its point of view, then it would become a simple argument: "Small dogs make better pets than large dogs because they are easier to clean up after and generally have longer life spans than large dogs." Later in this chapter, you will learn to refer to these main parts of the argument as the *conclusion* (the author's main point) and the *evidence* (the support for that point).

WHAT DOES IT MEAN FOR AN ARGUMENT TO DEPEND ON AN ASSUMPTION?

In everyday life, the verb *to assume* is used to mean "to take for granted" or "to presume" that something is the case. Likewise, to *depend on* something is to "need" or "rely on" that thing. Fortunately, the meaning of the word *assumption* in the context of a GMAT argument is much the same. Critical Reasoning questions that ask for an argument's assumption could be paraphrased as follows: "What important fact does the author of the argument take for granted but not directly state?" or "What else would need to be true in order for this argument to hold?" Throughout this chapter, you will see how identifying the central assumption is key to answering Critical Reasoning questions that involve arguments.

NOTICE THAT THE QUESTION COMES AFTER THE ARGUMENT. IS IT A BETTER IDEA TO READ THE ARGUMENT OR THE QUESTION FIRST?

It might be your natural instinct to start reading from the beginning of the paragraph, but the most efficient approach is to read the question (which we call the "question stem") before the paragraph that precedes it (which we call the "stimulus"). By starting with the question stem and identifying the task it poses, you will be able to read the stimulus strategically—targeting the information you need to answer the question without wasting time rereading.

WHAT GMAT CORE COMPETENCIES ARE MOST ESSENTIAL TO SUCCESS ON THIS QUESTION?

As you may have surmised from the previous paragraphs, Critical Reasoning questions are full of rewards for test takers with a firm handle on all four Core Competencies—the bedrock analytical skills that the GMAT measures. Critical Thinking will enable you to analyze the structure of arguments such as the one at the beginning of this chapter and identify any gaps or errors in the author's logic. Your Pattern Recognition skills will help you take advantage of patterns of argumentation that come up again and again, as well as enable you to spot common wrong answer types quickly. Paraphrasing is essential to untangling tough text, such as the description of study results in this stimulus, by putting it in your own words. Finally, Attention to the Right Detail will let you zero in on the most important parts of Critical Reasoning stimuli, often signaled by keywords, and determine which facts are crucial to the correct answer. In this chapter, you will learn how to apply these skills to every type of Critical Reasoning question you may see on Test Day.

Here are the main topics we'll cover in this chapter:

- Question Format and Structure
- The Basic Principles of Critical Reasoning
- The Kaplan Method for Critical Reasoning
- Critical Reasoning Question Types
- Advanced Strategies: Three Special Cases

QUESTION FORMAT AND STRUCTURE

About 11 Critical Reasoning questions appear on the Verbal section of the GMAT. Critical Reasoning (CR) tests reasoning skills involved in making arguments, evaluating arguments, and formulating or evaluating a plan of action. These questions are based on materials from a variety of sources, though you will not need to be familiar with any subject matter beforehand.

Specifically, you are measured on your ability to reason in the following areas:

- **Understanding the argument's construction:** Recognizing the basic structure of an argument, properly drawn conclusions, underlying assumptions, explanatory hypotheses, or parallels between structurally similar arguments
- **Evaluating the argument:** Analyzing an argument, recognizing elements that would strengthen or weaken it, identifying reasoning errors or aspects of the argument's development
- **Formulating and evaluating a plan of action:** Recognizing the relative appropriateness, effectiveness, and efficiency of different plans of action, as well as factors that would strengthen or weaken a proposed plan of action

The directions for Critical Reasoning questions are short and to the point. They look like this:

Directions: Select the best of the answer choices given.

On the GMAT, in business school, and in your career, you'll need the ability to recognize and understand complex reasoning. It's not enough to sense whether an argument is strong or weak; you'll need to analyze precisely why it is so. This presumes a fundamental skill that's called on by nearly every Critical Reasoning question—the ability to isolate and identify the various components of any given argument. And that brings us to the basic principles of Critical Reasoning.

THE BASIC PRINCIPLES OF CRITICAL REASONING

Here are the basic skills that you need to succeed on CR questions.

UNDERSTAND THE STRUCTURE OF AN ARGUMENT

As you learned earlier in this chapter, an argument is an author's attempt to convince you of a point. You must know how arguments are structured so that you can break them down into their core components. Every GMAT argument is made up of two basic parts:

1. The conclusion (the point that the author is trying to make)
2. The evidence (the support that the author offers for the conclusion)

Success on these questions hinges on your ability to identify the parts of the argument. There is no general rule about where the conclusion and evidence appear in the argument—the conclusion could be first, followed by the evidence, or it could be the other way around. Consider the following CR stimulus:

> The Brookdale Public Library will require extensive physical rehabilitation to meet the new building codes passed by the town council. For one thing, the electrical system is inadequate, causing the lights to flicker sporadically. Furthermore, there are too few emergency exits, and those few that exist are poorly marked and sometimes locked.

Suppose that the author of this argument was allowed only one sentence to convey her meaning. Do you think she would waste her time with the following statement? Would she walk away satisfied that her main point was communicated?

> The electrical system [at the Brookdale Public Library] is inadequate, causing the lights to flicker sporadically.

No. Given a single opportunity, she would have to state the first sentence to convey her real purpose:

> The Brookdale Public Library will require extensive physical rehabilitation...

That is the conclusion. If you pressed the author to state her reasons for making that statement, she would then cite the electrical and structural problems with the building. That is the evidence for her conclusion.

But does that mean that an evidence statement like "The electrical system is inadequate," can't be a conclusion? Not necessarily—it's just not the conclusion for this particular argument. Every idea, every new statement, must be evaluated in the context of the stimulus in which it appears.

For the statement above to serve as the conclusion, the stimulus could be the following:

> The electrical wiring at the Brookdale Public Library was installed more than 40 years ago and appears to be corroded in some places [evidence]. An electrician, upon inspection of the system, found a few frayed wires as well as some blown fuses [evidence]. Clearly, the electrical system at the Brookdale Public Library is inadequate [conclusion].

To succeed in Critical Reasoning, you'll have to be able to determine the precise function of every sentence in the stimulus. The easiest way to do this is to use structural signals, or "keywords" as we call them at Kaplan, to identify conclusion and evidence. You read about keywords in the Verbal Section Overview chapter of this book. Keywords such as *because, for, since, as a result of,* and *due to* are clear indications of evidence; keywords such as *therefore, hence, thus, so, clearly,* and *consequently* usually signal the conclusion. Notice how the word *clearly* in the argument above provides a strong signal that the last sentence is the conclusion.

Not every Critical Reasoning stimulus will have these keywords, but most do; look for them every time, because using them to identify the conclusion and evidence will greatly increase not only your ability to get the right answer but also your ability to do so quickly.

STUDY THE QUESTION FIRST

As you learned earlier in this chapter, you should always look over the question stem before you read the stimulus. Doing so will give you some idea of what you need to look for as you read. Suppose the question with the first library argument above asked:

> The author supports her point about the need for rehabilitation at the Brookdale Library by citing which of the following?

If you had read the question before the stimulus, you'd know what to look for in advance—only the evidence, the "support," provided. You wouldn't have to pay much attention to the conclusion at all! But suppose the question were this:

> The author's main point is best expressed by which of the following?

In this case you'd do the opposite—you'd focus only on the conclusion and wouldn't care much about the evidence.

Reading the question first allows you to save valuable time because you will know how to attack the stimulus. As you'll soon see, this technique will be especially handy when you have a great working knowledge of the strategies for the different types of Critical Reasoning questions.

READ STRATEGICALLY

As you learned in the Verbal Section Overview chapter of this book, Strategic Reading means reading for structure and for the author's point of view, since these are the things the GMAT most rewards test takers for noticing. On Critical Reasoning questions in particular, this means using keywords to identify the most important parts of the stimulus (often an argument) and paraphrasing the main ideas. Let's examine how to read strategically on Critical Reasoning questions.

Paraphrase the Argument

In Critical Reasoning, you should paraphrase the author's main argument to yourself after reading the stimulus. As you learned in the Verbal Section Overview chapter, Paraphrasing serves as a valuable test. If you can't accurately paraphrase the stimulus, you probably don't understand it yet. Frequently, the authors in Critical Reasoning say pretty simple things in complex ways. So if you mentally translate the verbiage into a simpler form, the whole thing will become more manageable.

In the first library argument, for instance, there's no advantage to grappling with the full complexity of the author's stated conclusion:

> The Brookdale Public Library will require extensive physical rehabilitation to meet the new building codes passed by the town council.

Instead, you want to paraphrase a much simpler point: The library will need fixing up to meet new codes.

Similarly, the evidence is pretty bulky:

> For one thing, the electrical system is inadequate, causing the lights to flicker sporadically. Furthermore, there are too few emergency exits, and those few that exist are poorly marked and sometimes locked.

You could paraphrase it like this: The library's electrical system is bad, and the emergency exits are too few, hard to find, and locked.

So the whole argument might be said simply as follows: The library's electrical system is bad, and the emergency exits are too few, hard to find, and locked. Therefore, the library will need fixing up to meet new codes.

Often, by the time you begin reading through the answer choices, you run the risk of losing sight of the gist of the stimulus. So restating the argument in your own words will not only help you get the author's point in the first place but also help you hold onto it until you've found the correct answer. Keep in mind that it's the *meaning* of the answer choices that matters. Since Critical Reasoning questions hinge on logic, you will be better able to choose the correct answer if you have paraphrased the ideas in the stimulus; doing so will keep you from becoming derailed if the correct choice doesn't use the exact wording you might expect.

Hunt for Potential Problems with the Argument

You must read actively, not passively, on the GMAT. Active readers are always thinking critically, analyzing what they're reading, and forming reactions as they go along. Instead of accepting an argument at face value, they look for potential problems. This pays huge dividends on most Critical Reasoning questions.

Here are some common potential problems in Critical Reasoning questions:

- **Shifts of scope:** The argument suddenly introduces a new term or idea that wasn't mentioned before and isn't connected to the rest of the argument.
- **Mistaking correlation for causation:** Just because two things happen at the same time doesn't mean that one caused the other.
- **Plans and predictions:** Could there be something inherently self-defeating about a proposed course of action? Any unintended consequences? Any important factors unaccounted for? The GMAT asks many questions about plans and predictions because they are like miniature business plans.

Consider the argument about the library again. Seems pretty reasonable at first glance—good lighting and working emergency exits are pretty important for a public building. But the critical reader might ask, "Wait a second—I've got a lot of information about the problems but no information about the codes. Do the codes apply to flickering lights, for example?"

Since part of what you're called on to do here is to evaluate arguments, don't let yourself fall into the bad habits of the passive reader—reading solely for the purpose of getting through the stimulus. Those who read this way invariably find themselves having to read stimuli two or even three times. Then they're caught short on time. Read the stimulus right the first time—with a critical eye and an active mind.

Answer the Question Being Asked

One of the most disheartening experiences in Critical Reasoning is to understand the author's argument fully but then supply an answer to a question that wasn't asked.

The classic example of this error occurs on "Strengthen/Weaken" questions, one of the common CR question types we will cover in this chapter. When you're asked to strengthen or weaken an argument, you can be sure that there will be at least one answer choice that does the opposite of what's asked. Choosing such a wrong choice is less a matter of failing to understand the argument than of failing to remember the task at hand.

The question stem will always ask for something very specific. It's your job to follow the testmakers' line of reasoning to the credited response.

Also, as you read the question stem, be on the lookout for words such as *not* and *except*. These little words are easy to miss, but they entirely change the kind of statement you're looking for among the choices.

Try to Predict an Answer

This principle, which is really an extension of the last one, is crucial. You must approach the answer choices with at least a faint idea of what the answer should look like. That is, predict the answer in your own mind before looking at the choices. This isn't to say you should ponder the question for minutes—it's still a multiple-choice test, so the right answer is on the screen. Just get in the habit of framing an answer in your head.

Once you have made a prediction, scan the choices. Sure, the correct choice on the exam will be worded differently and may be more fleshed out than your prediction. But if it matches your thought, you'll know it in a second. And you'll find that there's no more satisfying feeling in Critical Reasoning than predicting correctly and then finding the correct answer quickly and confidently.

Continuing with the library situation, suppose you were asked this question:

> The author's argument depends on which of the following assumptions about the new building codes?

Having hunted for potential problems and realized that the argument gave no information about whether the codes applied to the problems in the library, you could quickly predict that the answer must say something like "The new building codes apply in this situation." Then an answer like this one would jump off the screen as clearly correct:

O   The new codes apply to existing buildings, as well as to buildings under construction.

Alternatively, the correct answer could be worded like this:

O   The new codes require that all buildings have stable electrical systems as well as clearly marked, easily accessible emergency exits.

The most effective predictions are vague enough to fit with unexpected ideas (such as "existing buildings" in the example above) but specific enough about the scope of the argument to allow you to eliminate most wrong answers.

Keep the Scope of the Stimulus in Mind

When you're at the point of selecting one of the answer choices, focus on the scope of the stimulus. Most of the wrong choices for CR questions are wrong because they are "outside the scope." In other words, the wrong answer choices contain elements that don't match the author's ideas or that go beyond the context of the stimulus.

Some answer choices are too narrow, too broad, or have nothing to do with the author's points. Others are too extreme to match the scope—they're usually signaled by such words as *all, always, never, none,* and so on. For arguments that are moderate in tone, correct answers are more qualified and contain such words as *usually, sometimes,* and *probably.*

To illustrate the concept of scope, let's look again at the question mentioned above:

> The author's argument depends on which of the following assumptions about the new building codes?

Let's say one of the answer choices read as follows:

O   The new building codes are far too stringent.

Knowing the scope of the argument would help you to eliminate this choice very quickly. You know that this argument is just a claim about what the new codes will require: that the library be rehabilitated. It's not an argument about whether the requirements of the new codes are good, or justifiable, or ridiculously strict. That kind of value judgment is outside the scope of this argument.

Recognizing scope problems is a great way to eliminate wrong answers quickly. However, don't jump to eliminate an answer choice simply because it introduces a new term into discussion. A common error is to think that scope is purely about terminology. It's much more about the impact of the ideas in the answer choice on the ideas in the stimulus. If it has the right impact, the answer is within the scope, regardless of its terminology. This fact reinforces the importance of paraphrasing the contents of stimuli to see how the ideas relate to one another.

THE KAPLAN METHOD FOR CRITICAL REASONING

Now it's time to learn how to orchestrate all of these basic principles into a consistent protocol for approaching Critical Reasoning questions. Kaplan has developed a Method for Critical Reasoning that you can use to attack each and every CR question.

The Kaplan Method for Critical Reasoning

1. **Identify the question type.**

2. **Untangle the stimulus.**

3. **Predict the answer.**

4. **Evaluate the choices.**

STEP 1: IDENTIFY THE QUESTION TYPE

As you read in the introduction of basic Critical Reasoning principles, reading the question stem first is the best way to focus your reading of the stimulus. Determine the question type, and you'll know exactly what you're looking for. The majority of the rest of this chapter is devoted to a thorough analysis of each type of CR question, including practice questions for each type. There may also be other important information in the question stem—possibly the conclusion of the argument or a particular aspect of the stimulus that you will need to focus on.

STEP 2: UNTANGLE THE STIMULUS

With the question stem in mind, read the stimulus. Read actively, paraphrasing to make sure you understand the construction of the stimulus and hunting for any potential problems. Even though over 70 percent of CR stimuli contain arguments, other types of stimuli will not contain arguments. Depending on the type of question that you identified in Step 1 of the Method, you will look to gather different information from the stimulus.

STEP 3: PREDICT THE ANSWER

Form an idea of what the right answer choice should say or do. How you form your prediction will vary depending on the specific question type. For some question types, it can be difficult to form a specific prediction of what the correct answer choice will say, but based on your analysis in Steps 1 and 2, you will always know at least what function the correct answer will accomplish. On the next page is a chart that summarizes how to predict answers for different question types; you will learn about and practice all of these in depth later in this chapter.

STEP 4: EVALUATE THE CHOICES

Attack each answer choice critically. Keep your prediction in mind and see whether the answer choices match it. If you don't find a "clear winner," read through the answers that you haven't eliminated yet. You know what you *like* about each; now focus on what might be *wrong*.

STEPS 3 AND 4, BY QUESTION TYPE

You will look for different things in Steps 3 and 4 of the Method, depending on the question type.

- **Assumption:** Identify the argument's central assumption and hunt for the answer choice that matches your prediction. If that fails, use the Denial Test on each answer choice.
- **Strengthen/Weaken:** Identify the argument's central assumption and predict an answer explaining why that assumption is more (for a Strengthen question) or less (for a Weaken question) likely to be true.
- **Evaluation:** Identify the argument's central assumption and hunt for the answer choice that identifies missing information that would help assess the validity of that assumption.
- **Flaw:** Identify the argument's central assumption and predict the error in the argument's reasoning.
- **Explain:** Predict the answer that explains how two seemingly discrepant facts can both be true. If it's difficult to form a specific prediction, work through the answers one by one, eliminating choices that are clearly wrong, until you find the one that reconciles both parts of the supposed paradox.
- **Inference:** It's often difficult to form a prediction beyond "the right answer *must be true* based on what the stimulus states." Work through the answers one by one, eliminating choices that are clearly wrong.
- **Bolded Statement:** Predict an answer based on the logic and structure of the stimulus.

Now let's apply the Kaplan Method to the Critical Reasoning question you saw at the beginning of the chapter:

A study of 20 overweight men revealed that each man experienced significant weight loss after adding SlimDown, an artificial food supplement, to his daily diet. For three months, each man consumed one SlimDown portion every morning after exercising, then followed his normal diet for the rest of the day. Clearly, anyone who consumes one portion of SlimDown every day for at least three months will lose weight and will look and feel his best.

Which one of the following is an assumption on which the argument depends?

O The men in the study will gain back the weight if they discontinue the SlimDown program.

O No other dietary supplement will have the same effect on overweight men.

O The daily exercise regimen was not responsible for the effects noted in the study.

O Women won't experience similar weight reductions if they adhere to the SlimDown program for three months.

O Overweight men will achieve only partial weight loss if they don't remain on the SlimDown program for a full three months.

Step 1: Identify the Question Type

The question stem indicates directly that this is an Assumption question. Don't worry if you don't yet know much about Assumption questions; we will cover them in depth later in this chapter. For now, just focus on applying each step of the Method. You know from the mention of an "assumption" in this question stem that the argument in the stimulus will be missing a link in the chain of reasoning—some piece of support that the author takes for granted without which the conclusion wouldn't be valid. You will now turn to the stimulus, ready to find that link.

Step 2: Untangle the Stimulus

Sentence 1 introduces a study of 20 men who used a certain food supplement product. All 20 lost weight. Sentence 2 describes how they used it: once a day, for three months, after morning exercise. So far so good; it feels as if the argument is building up to something. The keyword *clearly* usually indicates that some sort of conclusion follows, and that's the case here: In sentence 3, the author predicts that anyone who has one portion of the product daily for three months will lose weight, too.

You might paraphrase the argument like this:

> Each of 20 overweight men lost weight after taking SlimDown every morning after exercise (but otherwise eating normally). So anyone who consumes SlimDown will lose weight.

Reading strategically, do you see any scope shifts or other potential problems? Sure—what happened to the exercise? It's in the evidence as part of the study regimen but is totally dropped from the conclusion. That's a pretty significant change in scope, and you can use that scope shift as the basis for your prediction in Step 3.

You could also look at the argument even more abstractly:

> A bunch of guys did *A* and *B* and had *X* result. So if someone does *A*, they'll get *X* result too.

This argument structure seems pretty weak: Who says *A* (SlimDown) caused *X* (weight loss)? Why couldn't *B* (exercise) have been the cause? The argument asserts that there could only be one cause for a certain effect even though other causes might, in reality, be possible. This kind of sloppy thinking about causality is a common GMAT pattern that you can use to help form your paraphrase.

You can use this insight to make a prediction in Step 3, too. No matter how abstract or concrete your prediction is, you arrive at the same basic issue—that the author isn't accounting for the exercise. There's rarely one "perfect way" to figure out the right answer; as long as you read critically, you'll be moving in the right direction.

Step 3: Predict the Answer

You've realized that the argument forgot to consider the exercise. So you might predict something like "The author assumes exercise doesn't matter." That's it. There's no need to paraphrase with something fancy or complicated. A simple paraphrase, as long as it reflects the scope of the stimulus, is enough to help you find the right answer.

Step 4: Evaluate the Choices

Judge the answer choices based on how well they fulfill the requirements of your prediction. Sure enough, only **(C)** even mentions the exercise regimen. Reading it closely, you see it fits the prediction perfectly, clearing up the question of whether the exercise caused the weight loss.

Since the difficulty of Critical Reasoning is often in the answer choices (rather than the stimulus), you can't let them make you indecisive. Predicting the answer lets you know exactly what you're looking for, so you'll know it when you see it. You can choose **(C)** with confidence and move on.

CRITICAL REASONING QUESTION TYPES

Now that you're familiar with the basic principles of Critical Reasoning and the Kaplan Method, let's look at the most common types of questions. Certain question types appear again and again on the GMAT, so it pays to understand them beforehand.

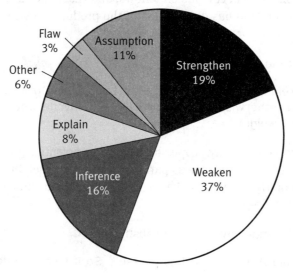

The Approximate Distribution of GMAT Critical Reasoning Questions

You have seen many references to arguments so far in this chapter, and indeed analyzing arguments is the most important—though not the *only*—skill you need possess for Critical Reasoning on the GMAT. Of the question types listed in the pie chart above, Assumption, Strengthen, Weaken, and Flaw questions are based on arguments. Another question type, Evaluation, is also based on arguments, but these questions are rare and are included in the "Other" category in the pie chart. For these five question types based on arguments, the way you will analyze the argument is quite similar. In all cases, the correct answer will depend on identifying and understanding the argument's conclusion, evidence, and central assumption.

GMAT ARGUMENTS

- GMAT arguments (given in the stimuli) are usually two to four sentences long.
- GMAT arguments vary in soundness: Some are (intentionally) flawed.
- To untangle the stimulus, find the conclusion, evidence, and the author's central assumption.

Let's examine in depth Kaplan's strategies for the different types of CR questions based on arguments, starting with Assumption questions.

ASSUMPTION QUESTIONS

Assumption questions ask you for a piece of support that isn't explicitly stated but is necessary for the argument to remain valid. When a question asks you for what's missing from the argument or what the argument depends on, then it's asking you to find the author's necessary assumption.

Untangling the Stimulus for Assumption Questions

By first analyzing the question stem, you'll know what to look for in the stimulus. For Assumption questions—and all questions based on arguments—untangling the stimulus consists of identifying the three parts of a GMAT argument: conclusion, evidence, and assumption.

CONCLUSION

The conclusion is the main point of the author's argument. It's the thing that the author is seeking to convince you of. There are three ways to identify the conclusions of arguments:

- **Conclusion keywords or phrases:** As you learned in the Verbal Section Overview chapter of this book, keywords are clues to the structure of a passage or argument. They tell you how the author's ideas relate to one another. Keywords and phrases that signal an argument's conclusion include the following: *thus, therefore, so, hence, consequently, in conclusion, clearly, for this reason.*

- **The one-sentence test:** You can also identify the author's conclusion by asking, "If the author had to boil this entire argument down to one sentence that retains his main point, which sentence would it be?"

- **Fact vs. opinion:** The conclusion of the argument is always a reflection of the author's opinion. This opinion can take several forms; it could be the author's plan, proposal, prediction, or value judgment, or simply her interpretation or analysis of the evidence. Whereas the conclusion is always an opinion, the evidence is usually (but not always) factual in nature.

EVIDENCE

Evidence is provided to support the conclusion. GMAT arguments usually have little filler, so what isn't the conclusion is typically evidence. Evidence can take the form of data, such as statistics, surveys, polls, or historical facts. Sometimes, however, the evidence is merely a conjecture or an opinion. The best way to identify an argument's evidence is by examining its function within the argument: Any material in the stimulus that provides support for the author's conclusion is evidence.

ASSUMPTION

All GMAT arguments contain one or more assumptions; identifying the assumptions is the most essential step when answering any Critical Reasoning question based on an argument. An assumption is the unstated evidence necessary to make the argument work. It bridges the gap between two pieces of the argument, usually between conclusion and evidence but occasionally between two unconnected pieces of evidence. Without the assumption, the argument falls apart. You can think of it as something the author *must* believe but doesn't directly state.

You can visualize the relationship between the various parts of an argument as follows:

Evidence + Assumption(s) → Conclusion

Predicting the Answer for Assumption Questions

As you saw in the question about SlimDown diet supplement earlier in this chapter, you can usually predict an answer to an Assumption question. Your prediction is simply the argument's assumption, which you've already identified when you untangled the stimulus during Step 2 of the Kaplan Method.

Let's practice the whole process of untangling the stimulus and predicting the answer using this simple stimulus:

> Allyson plays volleyball for Central High School. Therefore, Allyson must be over 6 feet tall.

The conclusion is the second sentence (signaled by the keyword *therefore*), and the evidence is the first. Is there a gap, or assumption, in this argument? Well, who's to say that all high school volleyball players have to be over 6 feet tall? So you can confidently predict that the answer to an Assumption question would say something like this:

> All volleyball players at Central High School are over 6 feet tall.

But what if the assumption doesn't just jump out at you? How can you track it down? One of the most common ways the GMAT uses assumptions is to cover over a scope shift in the argument. Notice how the argument above starts by talking about playing volleyball and then all of a sudden is talking about being over 6 feet tall. Look closely at the terms in each part of the argument. Could the scope of the evidence be slightly different than that of the conclusion?

Consider this seemingly solid argument:

> Candidate A won the presidential election, carrying 40 out of 50 states.
> Clearly, Candidate A has a strong mandate to push for her legislative agenda.

At first glance, this sounds pretty good. But take a close look at the terms of the argument. The evidence is a win representing a sizeable majority of states. The conclusion is about a strong mandate for an agenda. Even if you don't notice the subtle difference between these two things, you could still make a prediction like this: "Candidate A's big victory means she has a mandate for her agenda." You'd be much more likely to recognize the right answer between these two possibilities:

- ○ No other candidate in the last 24 years has won as many states as did Candidate A.
- ○ Most of the people who voted for Candidate A support her legislative agenda.

The first answer choice doesn't deal with Candidate A's agenda at all. The second one shows a connection between her victory and her agenda, so it must be the right answer.

But what if you still aren't sure that your answer choice is correct? Or what if the assumption is so subtle that you can't predict the answer at all? In those cases, you can use the Denial Test.

The Denial Test

An assumption must be true in order for the conclusion to follow logically from the evidence. Therefore, in an Assumption question, you can test each answer choice by negating it—in other words, imagining that the information given in the answer choice is false. If this negation makes the author's argument fall apart, then the answer choice is a necessary assumption.

If the argument is unaffected, then the choice is wrong. Let's look at what you predicted earlier as the assumption in the volleyball argument:

> All volleyball players at Central High School are over 6 feet tall.

Now let's negate it:

> Some volleyball players at Central High School are not over 6 feet tall.

Would Allyson still have to be over 6 feet tall? Not anymore. That's why that prediction would be a necessary assumption. Keep in mind not to be too extreme when negating answer choices. The denial of *hot* isn't *cold* but rather *not hot*. Similarly, the denial of *all are* isn't *none are* but rather *some aren't*.

Now let's take another look at the answer choices for the question about Candidate A:

- ○ No other candidate in the last 24 years has won as many states as did Candidate A.
- ○ Most of the people who voted for Candidate A support her legislative agenda.

And now we'll negate them:

- ○ Some candidates in the last 24 years have won as many states as did Candidate A.

Could Candidate A still enjoy a strong mandate? Definitely. Just because others in the past were as popular doesn't mean that she doesn't enjoy support for her agenda as well.

- ○ A majority of those who voted for Candidate A do not actually support her legislative agenda.

Now can Candidate A claim a mandate for her agenda? No, she can't. That's why the second choice is the correct answer for this Assumption question.

Give the Denial Test a try on your own using the following argument. Negate each answer choice and then ask yourself, "Can the evidence still lead to the conclusion?"

> I live in the city of Corpus Christi, so I also live in Texas.
>
> The argument assumes which of the following:
>
> - ○ Corpus Christi is the only city in Texas.
> - ○ The only city named Corpus Christi is located in Texas.
> - ○ If you have not been to Corpus Christi, you have not been to Texas.

The argument here is short and sweet, but it has all the essential elements of any GMAT argument. The conclusion is signaled by the keyword *so*: The author lives in Texas. The author's evidence is the claim in the first part of the sentence: He lives in Corpus Christi.

Rather than predict the correct answer right away, let's test the answer choice statements using the Denial Test.

Negation of statement (A): Corpus Christi is not the only city in Texas.

Does that threaten the argument? No. There could be other cities in Texas, and it could still be valid to say that living in Corpus Christi proves that the author lives in Texas. The evidence could still lead to the conclusion, so choice **(A)** is not the assumption.

Negation of statement (B): There is at least one other city named Corpus Christi that is not located in Texas.

If this is true, does the conclusion still follow logically from the evidence? No. In this case, if there is another town named Corpus Christi located in, say, California or Florida, it would no longer be logically valid to say that the author must live in Texas because he lives in Corpus Christi. Choice **(B)** is a necessary assumption for the argument.

Negation of statement (C): If you have not been to Corpus Christi, you still could have been to Texas.

Note that when you are denying an if/then statement, you should deny the "then," or result, portion of the statement. What impact does this negation have on the argument? None. Someone else could visit other cities in Texas, and still it may or may not be valid for the author to say, "I live in Texas because I live in Corpus Christi." Choice **(C)** is not the necessary assumption.

Argument Analysis Exercise

Answers on the following page

Now it's time to put all these skills together and practice breaking down some arguments. First find the conclusion, then identify the evidence that supports that conclusion, and finally determine the central assumption. Once you've identified the assumption, try the Denial Test to confirm that the assumption you've identified is necessary for the argument to hold:

1. Over the past 10 years, some businesses located in country X have moved manufacturing or assembly operations to country Y. But a proposed change to the laws of country Y would raise the minimum per-hour wage in country Y to approximately the same level as the equivalent rate in country X. Hence, if the change were to come into effect, very few businesses in country X would move manufacturing or assembly operations to country Y.

Conclusion:

Evidence:

Assumption(s):

2. In percentage terms, the total population of the United States grew faster from 1790 until 1890 than it did from 1890 to 1990. In 1890, the Census Bureau declared that the continental United States was settled to an extent that a frontier line could not be marked on a map. So, it seems safe to say that the existence of extensive space for an expansion of agricultural settlement is necessary for increases in national population.

Conclusion:

Evidence:

Assumption(s):

Argument Analysis Exercise: Answers

1. **Conclusion:** Country X businesses aren't likely to move to country Y.

   Evidence: Country Y is proposing to raise its minimum wage.

   Assumption: The only, or primary, reason for businesses to relocate to country Y is cheaper labor.

2. **Conclusion:** Countries need space for more agriculture in order to have national population growth.

   Evidence: The U.S. population grew more slowly after the frontier was closed.

   Assumptions: (In this case, the author is taking several things for granted.) Frontier space was primarily used for agriculture; agriculture is the reason for the population growth from 1790 to 1890; the example of the U.S. is representative of other countries, and there are no examples elsewhere that contradict this argument; statements about rates of growth translate to statements about absolute growth.

Sample Question Stems

There are many ways to write a Critical Reasoning question. Any wording that suggests that you need to find a missing but vital piece of information indicates an Assumption question. Assumption questions are worded in some of the following ways:

- Which one of the following is assumed by the author?
- Upon which one of the following assumptions does the author rely?
- The argument depends on the assumption that...
- Which one of the following, if added to the passage, would make the conclusion logical?
- The validity of the argument depends on which one of the following?
- The argument presupposes which one of the following?

APPLYING THE KAPLAN METHOD: ASSUMPTION QUESTIONS

Now let's use the Kaplan Method for Critical Reasoning to solve an Assumption question:

> When unemployment rates are high, people with full-time jobs tend to take fewer and shorter vacations. When unemployment rates are low, people tend to vacation more often and go away for longer periods of time. Thus, it can be concluded that full-time workers' perceptions of their own job security influence the frequency and duration of their vacations.
>
> The argument above assumes that
>
> O the people who take the longest vacations when unemployment rates are low have no fear of losing their jobs
>
> O travel costs are lower during times of low unemployment
>
> O most people prefer to work full-time jobs
>
> O workers' perceptions of their own job security are in some way related to the unemployment rate
>
> O workers' fears of losing their jobs have increased recently

Step 1: Identify the Question Type

The word "assumes" in the question stem is a clear indication of an Assumption question.

Step 2: Untangle the Stimulus

"Thus" signals the argument's conclusion. You could paraphrase it as follows: How much vacation time full-time workers take depends on how secure they feel in their jobs. The author's evidence for this conclusion is the relationship between vacations and unemployment. When unemployment is high, workers take fewer and shorter vacations; when unemployment is low, the opposite happens.

Step 3: Predict the Answer

To find the central assumption, use Critical Thinking to link the terms in the evidence with the terms in the conclusion. If the evidence centers on employment levels and vacations, and if the conclusion centers on job security and vacations, then the central assumption must center on the connection between employment levels and job security.

Step 4: Evaluate the Choices

Choice **(D)** matches this prediction perfectly by bridging the terms of the evidence with the terms of the conclusion. The Denial Test can help confirm **(D)** as the correct answer; if there were no relationship between workers' perceptions of job security and the unemployment rate, then it would no longer make sense for the author to use evidence about the unemployment rate to support a conclusion about workers' perceptions of job security. **(D)** is an assumption necessary for the argument to hold.

The other choices are all incorrect in some definable way. It's great practice to identify exactly why each wrong choice is wrong. Doing so will help you develop your Pattern Recognition skills so you can identify common wrong answer types on Test Day. **(A)** is too extreme ("*no* fear of losing their jobs") to be the necessary assumption. **(B)** introduces the idea of travel costs, which are far outside the scope of the stimulus and have no necessary connection to job security in the conclusion. **(C)** similarly steps outside the scope; whether those people who work full-time jobs prefer to work them is irrelevant. **(E)** tells us that workers' perceptions of their job security have deteriorated lately, but that has no necessary connection to the unemployment rate. Remember that the assumption must successfully link the evidence to the conclusion. The correct answer is **(D)**.

TAKEAWAYS: ASSUMPTION QUESTIONS

- On Assumption questions, identify the argument's conclusion and evidence, determine the central assumption, and predict the answer. Evaluate the answer choices and select the one that matches your prediction.
- If you read the answer choices and can't find your prediction, try eliminating choices by asking whether they are necessary for the argument to hold.
- The Denial Test discriminates between right and wrong answers; when you deny the correct answer to an Assumption question, the argument falls apart.

PRACTICE SET: ASSUMPTION QUESTIONS

Answers and explanations at end of chapter

1. Burger Land, a nationwide fast-food chain, recently announced a special promotion dramatically reducing the price of its most popular burger, the Big and Beefy. This development has provoked a strong response by the nation's nutritionists. Citing the extremely high levels of cholesterol in the Big and Beefy, they predict that the price reduction will have a negative impact on the health of our citizens.

    The nutritionists' argument assumes which of the following?

    O   Some consumers induced by the price reduction to purchase the Big and Beefy would otherwise have consumed food lower in cholesterol than the Big and Beefy.

    O   Reducing fat consumption is the most important factor in improving one's diet.

    O   Burger Land could not have increased sales of the Big and Beefy by reducing its cholesterol content and appealing to health-conscious consumers.

    O   Other fast-food companies will not respond to Burger Land's announcement by reducing the price of their own high-cholesterol burgers.

    O   Lost revenue due to the price reduction in the Big and Beefy will be offset by an increase in the number of burgers sold.

2. In Country X, all citizens eligible to vote must do so or face stiff fines. Because voting in Country X is mandatory, over 99 percent of the eligible voters voted in the last election. Thus, the winner of the last election is truly the people's choice.

    Which of the following identifies an assumption in the author's argument?

    O   In Country X, voters are allowed to vote for a candidate of their choice.

    O   If Country X did not make voting mandatory, few people would vote.

    O   Only in countries where voting is mandatory do people vote the way they wish to vote.

    O   Country X is a true democracy, despite the fact that all people are forced to vote.

    O   Only in countries where voting is not mandatory do the winners of elections truly reflect the people's choice.

3. In the next four years, the number of doctors, nurses, and other health care workers will increase significantly worldwide. Even so, the average compensation received by such professionals will not decline but rather is likely to increase. This is due, at least partly, to the fact that the median age of the world's population will increase steadily in this same period of time.

    The argument above depends logically upon which of the following assumptions?

    O   The increase in the number of health care workers will be responsible for the increase in the average life span.

    O   The compensation of doctors and physical therapists who treat the elderly will increase more than that of other health care workers.

    O   As a group, older people receive more attention from health care workers than do younger people.

    O   Geriatrics, a branch of medicine focusing on the health problems of older people, is the most expensive element of American health care.

    O   Increase in the median age of the population will occur in all regions of the world.

STRENGTHEN AND WEAKEN QUESTIONS

Determining an argument's necessary assumption, as you've just seen, is required to answer an Assumption question. But it also is required to answer two other common types of question: Strengthen and Weaken.

In the real world, we can weaken someone's argument by attacking her evidence. But the GMAT is testing not your ability simply to find evidence but rather your ability to analyze how that evidence is used. The right answer to a Weaken question on the GMAT will always weaken the connection between the evidence and the conclusion—in other words, the assumption.

The answer to many Weaken questions is the one that reveals an author's assumption to be unreasonable or untrue; conversely, the answer to many Strengthen questions provides additional support for the argument by affirming the truth of an assumption.

Let's return to a stimulus we've seen before and consider it in the context of Strengthen and Weaken questions:

> Allyson plays volleyball for Central High School. Therefore, Allyson must be over 6 feet tall.

Remember which assumption holds this argument together? It is that all volleyball players for Central High are over 6 feet tall. That assumption makes or breaks the argument. So if you're asked to weaken the argument, you'll want to attack that assumption:

> Which one of the following, if true, would most weaken the argument?

Prediction: Not all volleyball players at Central High School are over 6 feet tall.

Correct Answer:

> O   Some volleyball players at Central High School are under 6 feet tall.

Notice that we don't have to prove the conclusion wrong, just make it less likely. We've called into doubt the author's basic assumption, thus damaging the argument. Allyson still *could* be over 6 feet tall, but now she doesn't have to be.

What if the question asked you to strengthen the argument? Again, the key would be the necessary assumption:

> Which one of the following, if true, would most strengthen the argument?

Prediction: All volleyball players at Central High School are over 6 feet tall.

Correct Answer:

> O   No member of the Central High School volleyball team is under 6'2".

Here, by confirming the author's assumption, you've in effect bolstered the argument.

TAKEAWAYS: STRENGTHEN AND WEAKEN QUESTIONS

- The first steps to answering Strengthen and Weaken questions are the same as those for Assumption questions.
- Strengtheners make the conclusion more likely to follow from the evidence, while weakeners make it less so.

Strengthening and Weakening Arguments Exercise

Answers on the following page

Now it's time to put all these skills together and practice analyzing arguments and identifying possible strengtheners and weakeners. Find the conclusion, evidence, and assumption for each of the following arguments. Then predict what a correct answer choice might contain for a Strengthen question and for a Weaken question.

1. Mountain biking on trails is soaring in popularity in the United States. The number of mountain bikes sold in the United States has increased 133 percent over the past four years. In addition, bike stores in the United States last year reported that mountain bikes accounted for more than 65 percent of their total sales, far more than in previous years, even though sales of other bikes have been strong.

Conclusion:

Evidence:

Assumption(s):

Predict strengtheners:

Predict weakeners:

2. A shoe manufacturer developed a man-made material that looked and felt just like natural leather. Over the course of a year, the manufacturer made its entire shoe line in both natural leather and man-made leather. During the year when both lines were sold, the man-made leather shoes outsold the natural leather shoes. The shoe manufacturer concluded that its customers prefer man-made leather to natural leather.

Conclusion:

Evidence:

Assumption(s):

Predict strengtheners:

Predict weakeners:

3. According to a recent study, the majority of people in a large city believe that most homeless people are drug addicts who could get jobs if they wanted to work. However, the public is misinformed. The city's Coalition for the Homeless estimates that over 85 percent of the homeless population is moderately to severely mentally ill.

Conclusion:

Evidence:

Assumption(s):

Predict strengtheners:

Predict weakeners:

Strengthening and Weakening Arguments Exercise: Answers

1. **Conclusion:** Mountain biking on trails is getting a lot more popular.

   Evidence: Stores are selling more mountain bikes and mountain bikes are a greater proportion of their overall bike sales.

   Assumption: The people who are buying mountain bikes must be using them on trails.

   Possible strengthener: Most of the people who are driving the increase in mountain bike sales are involved in trail cycling.

   Possible weakener: People who buy mountain bikes tend to use them in urban or suburban settings, rather than on trails.

2. **Conclusion:** Customers prefer man-made leather to natural leather.

   Evidence: A shoe company made their full line of shoes in both natural and man-made, and the man-made outsold the real.

   Assumption: People are buying man-made leather because they prefer it, not for some other reason.

   Possible strengthener: There were not other reasons (i.e., price, availability, lack of adequate labeling in the store) for the customers to purchase the man-made instead of the natural leather.

   Possible weakener: There were other reasons (i.e., price, availability, lack of adequate labeling in the store) for the customers to purchase the man-made instead of the natural leather.

3. **Conclusion:** The public is misinformed in its belief that the homeless are drug addicts who don't want to work.

   Evidence: An estimate from Coalition for the Homeless that says the vast majority of homeless people are mentally ill.

   Assumption: If a homeless person is severely mentally ill, he is not a drug addict who is able to work.

   Possible strengthener: Moderate to severe mental illness makes it impossible to obtain or maintain employment.

   Possible weakener: Even the mentally ill are capable of maintaining employment if they want to.

Sample Stems

The stems associated with these two question types are usually self-explanatory. Here's a list of some you can expect to see on Test Day:

Weaken:

- Which one of the following, if true, would most weaken the argument above?
- Which one of the following, if true, would most seriously damage the argument above?
- Which one of the following, if true, casts the most doubt on the argument above?
- Which of the following, if true, would most seriously call into question the plan outlined above?

Strengthen:

- Which one of the following, if true, would most strengthen the argument?
- Which one of the following, if true, would provide the most support for the conclusion in the argument above?
- The argument above would be more persuasive if which one of the following were found to be true?

It's also common for the question stem to refer explicitly to part of the argument. You might, for example, see something like this:

> Which of the following, if true, casts the most doubt on the author's conclusion that the Brookdale Public Library does not meet the requirements of the new building codes?

Reading the question stem first, here we would be told outright what the author's conclusion is, making the untangling of the stimulus much easier to manage.

When you identify the question type during Step 1 of the Method, make sure you fully understand what effect the correct answer will have on the argument. Wrong answers that have the opposite of the desired effect are called 180s, and they're extremely common on Strengthen and Weaken questions. If you're asked to weaken an argument, watch out for wrong answers that would strengthen it. Asked to strengthen? Be wary of weakeners. Pay close attention to what the question asks and jot it down in your scratchwork so you can avoid this trap.

APPLYING THE KAPLAN METHOD: STRENGTHEN AND WEAKEN QUESTIONS

Now let's use the Kaplan Method for Critical Reasoning to solve a Strengthen or Weaken question:

> Due to recent success, Lawton, a contractor, can be more selective than in the past regarding the types of clients he chooses to service. If he restricts his business to commercial clients and only those residential clients requiring $10,000 of work or more, he would cease doing most of the kind of residential work he currently does, which would allow him to earn a higher average profit margin per job.
>
> Which of the following, if true, would most strengthen the conclusion that limiting his service in the manner cited would increase Lawton's average profit margin per job?
>
> O Lawton's recent success is due primarily to an upsurge in the number of residential clients he services.
>
> O Lawton's commercial clients would prefer that he focus more of his time and energy on their projects and less on the concerns of his residential clients.
>
> O Residential work for which Lawton cannot bill more than $10,000 comprises a significant proportion of his low-profit-margin work.
>
> O Due to the use of a more efficient cost-accounting system, Lawton's average profit margin per job has increased in each of the last three years.
>
> O Commercial jobs typically take longer to complete than residential jobs.

Step 1: Identify the Question Type

In addition to containing the telltale word "strengthen," the question stem helps you by identifying the conclusion. When the GMAT gives you a gift like this, accept it!

Step 2: Untangle the Stimulus

The conclusion has been handed to you by the question stem: By restricting his work to commercial projects and expensive ($10,000+) residential projects, Lawton will increase his average profit margin. The only evidence is the first sentence, which informs you that due to recent success, Lawton can restrict his work to certain clients if he chooses.

Step 3: Predict the Answer

The evidence proves that Lawton can be selective. However, it does not establish that restricting his business will actually improve his profit margin. The author's claim depends on an assumption: Inexpensive residential jobs have lower profit margins than do commercial jobs and pricey residential jobs.

Step 4: Evaluate the Choices

Answer choice **(C)** supports the assumption, thereby strengthening the argument, and is the correct answer.

Wrong answer choices on Strengthen and Weaken questions commonly provide facts that are outside the scope of the argument; since such choices have no direct bearing on the argument presented, there's no way they could strengthen or weaken it. **(A)** is out of scope because the source of Lawton's recent success is irrelevant and has no connection to higher profit margins. **(B)** discusses the preferences of Lawton's commercial clients, which are also outside the scope. **(D)** credits a new accounting system with an increase in Lawton's profit margin per job. This statement doesn't tell us whether expensive jobs have a higher profit margin than do small residential jobs, so it doesn't help the argument. Furthermore, **(D)** focuses on past improvements, which have no bearing on whether his future plans will be successful. **(E)** tells us that commercial jobs will take longer to complete, but the profit margin of the jobs, not their duration, is what matters in this argument. Choice **(C)** is correct.

TAKEAWAYS: STRENGTHEN AND WEAKEN QUESTIONS

- On Strengthen and Weaken questions, determine the argument's conclusion, evidence and assumption. Predict the strengthening or weakening answer based on the assumption.
- Weakening an argument is not the same as disproving a conclusion—and strengthening is not the same as proving it. A weakener tips the scale toward doubting the conclusion, while a strengthener tips the scale toward believing in the validity of the conclusion.
- The words "if true" in the question stem remind you that the correct answers should be treated as facts that can make the argument more or less likely to be true.
- Some Critical Reasoning questions provide the conclusion in the stem; use such cases to your advantage.
- Common wrong answers in Critical Reasoning include out-of-scope, 180s, and irrelevant comparisons.

PRACTICE SET: STRENGTHEN AND WEAKEN QUESTIONS

Answers and explanations at end of chapter

4. The threatened prosecution of businesses flying 20-by-38-foot garrison flags, which are traditionally to be flown on national holidays, instead of the smaller post flags, which can be flown at any time, is unconscionable. Legal technicalities of this sort should never restrict patriotic expression.

    Which of the following, if true, would most seriously weaken the argument above?

    O   Many people find the garrison flags' size to be distracting and ill suited to neighborhood aesthetics.

    O   The businesses that are flying garrison flags do so primarily to attract customers.

    O   The raising and lowering of different-sized flags on the correct days of the year is a laborious and time-consuming procedure.

    O   The regulations that govern the correct display of the nation's flags are part of an old and time-honored tradition.

    O   The symbolic significance of a flag's size is not generally understood by most of the customers patronizing these businesses.

5. Any college football player who uses steroids should be banned from competition. The national agency with the responsibility to preserve the natural competitive balance between players enforces rules specifically mandating that no player be allowed to use drugs to gain a competitive advantage. Studies show that steroid users tend to have much greater strength and weight than non-users.

    Which of the following statements, if true, would most strengthen the argument?

    O   Users of steroids often suffer from acne, extreme nervousness, and reduced sexual potency.

    O   Increased strength is more useful than increased weight to college football players.

    O   Superior strength and weight give college football players a significant competitive advantage.

    O   Steroid use is much more prevalent in college football than in college baseball.

    O   Random drug testing of athletes has been shown to be effective in the detection of drug use by athletes.

6. The state legislature has proposed a law that requires all new cars sold in the state to be equipped with airbags for both front-seat passengers. The auto industry has lobbied against the proposed law, pointing out that the airbags would prevent only a small percentage of serious injuries because in most accidents, serious injuries can be avoided by the use of seat belts.

Which of the following, if true, would most weaken the argument put forth by the auto industry?

- O The government has a duty to protect the welfare of its citizens.
- O The number of accidents per mile driven in the state is substantially higher than that for the rest of the nation.
- O The cost of equipping automobiles with airbags will be passed on to the consumer in the form of higher prices.
- O Most serious injuries occur when front-seat passengers are not wearing their seat belts.
- O Because the law would apply only to new cars, it would take nearly a decade for the majority of the state's cars to become equipped with airbags.

7. Artistic success as an actor is directly dependent on how well an actor has developed his craft. This has been demonstrated by the discovery of a positive relationship between the number of classes taken by an actor and the number of professional productions in which that actor has appeared in the past two years.

Each of the following, if true, casts doubt on the author's argument about artistic success for actors EXCEPT:

- O The figures for the number of classes taken were based solely on information provided by actors.
- O Success as an actor cannot necessarily be judged exclusively by recent credits.
- O For most successful actors, it is not the quantity but the quality of their classes that has helped to develop their craft.
- O There is no relationship between the number of professional productions in which an actor has appeared and true artistic success.
- O Most successful actors have taken only a small number of intensive classes.

EVALUATION QUESTIONS

Evaluation is a rare Critical Reasoning question type. An Evaluation question asks you to identify information that would help you assess an argument's strength. The correct answer won't strengthen or weaken the author's reasoning or supply a missing assumption. Instead, the right answer will specify the kind of evidence that would help you judge the validity of the author's argument.

Since the needed information will usually fill a gap in the argument, the correct answer to an Evaluation question typically relates in some way to the assumption. For example, whereas a Weaken answer choice might state: "Businesses relocate their operations to country Y primarily to reduce labor costs," an Evaluation answer choice would instead claim that it would be most useful to know "whether factors besides labor costs affect the decisions of certain businesses to relocate their operations to country Y." Incorrect Evaluation answer choices are often out of scope; the information they ask for would have little or no effect on the argument.

Sample Stems

Here are some example question stems that indicate an Evaluation question:

- Which of the following would it be most useful to know in order to evaluate the argument?
- The answer to which of the following questions would be most important in evaluating the proposal?
- Which of the following would it be most useful to determine in order to evaluate the argument?
- To evaluate the author's reasoning, it would be most useful to compare ...
- Which of the following must be studied in order to evaluate the argument presented above?

APPLYING THE KAPLAN METHOD: EVALUATION QUESTIONS

Now let's use the Kaplan Method for Critical Reasoning to solve an Evaluation question:

> Mullein has been employed as an expectorant for centuries and is still greatly praised for this purpose by herbalists. However, mullein roots and seeds are believed to contain rotenone, a compound that is used as an insecticide and fish toxin and that has been shown to be a causative factor in Parkinson's disease. Therefore, the use of mullein leaf tea for the treatment of dry coughs is not as safe as has previously been believed.
>
> Which of the following would be most useful to know in order to evaluate the truth of the argument's conclusion?
>
> O   Whether mullein roots and seeds are effective as pesticides
> O   Whether mullein roots and seeds contain other toxic chemicals besides rotenone
> O   Whether there are other agents besides rotenone involved in the etiology of Parkinson's disease
> O   Whether there are safer herbs that are effective expectorants
> O   Whether mullein leaves contain rotenone in sufficient quantities to contribute to Parkinson's disease

Step 1: Identify the Question Type

The word "evaluate" signals that this is an Evaluation question. Evaluation questions are similar to Strengthen/Weaken questions: You must find the answer choice that impacts the validity of the argument's conclusion.

Step 2: Untangle the Stimulus

Like Strengthen/Weaken questions, Evaluation questions are built around an argument's central assumption, so you should, as usual, begin by identifying the conclusion and evidence. The conclusion is the last sentence: Using mullein leaf tea for coughs is not as safe as was once thought. The evidence is that mullein roots and seeds are believed to contain rotenone, a substance that causes Parkinson's disease. This argument contains a scope shift: The evidence is about "mullein roots and seeds," while the conclusion is about "mullein leaf tea." The scope shift signals the central assumption: A compound contained in the roots and seeds of the mullein plant must also be contained in its leaves.

Step 3: Predict the Answer

In order to evaluate whether the conclusion is strong or weak, you would need to know whether the assumption that mullein leaves contain rotenone is true. Specifically, you would need to know whether mullein leaves contain enough rotenone to cause Parkinson's disease.

Step 4: Evaluate the Choices

(E) matches this prediction and is the correct answer. **(A)** and **(B)** are incorrect because the toxicity of mullein roots and seeds is beside the point. The argument's conclusion concerns the leaves of the mullein plant, not the roots and seeds. **(C)** is incorrect because other chemicals that cause Parkinson's disease are outside the scope of the argument, which concludes that mullein leaves are unsafe due to their assumed rotenone content. Finally, the "safer herbs" mentioned in **(D)** are again outside the scope. The argument is about mullein; other herbs are irrelevant. Choice **(E)** is correct.

TAKEAWAYS: EVALUATION QUESTIONS

- Evaluation questions ask you to determine what information would most help to evaluate the argument.
- Untangle the stimulus the same way you do for other argument-based questions: Identify the conclusion, evidence, and assumption(s).
- Choose the answer choice that would best fill in the gap in logic created by the central assumption.

Practice Set: Evaluation Questions
Answers and explanations at end of chapter

8. Herbed Wellness, a manufacturer of herbal products, wants its new headache remedy to be as effective as possible while using only natural ingredients. A controlled study has found that 58 percent of headache sufferers obtain complete headache relief from a dose of caffeine equivalent to that typically found in a cup of coffee. Therefore, even though the vast majority of its customers are health-conscious avoiders of coffee, Herbed Wellness should add caffeine to its new herbal headache treatment; doing so will prove both efficacious and cost-effective.

The answer to which of the following questions would be most useful in evaluating the claim that caffeine will be efficacious in relieving headaches among Herbed Wellness customers?

  O Is the headache relief provided by caffeine as long-lasting as that provided by over-the-counter drugs such as aspirin?

  O What percentage of the study participants were regular coffee drinkers who suffer from caffeine-withdrawal headaches?

  O Is caffeine less expensive per dose than the individual herbs used in the headache formulation?

  O Does synthetic caffeine qualify as a natural substance?

  O What percentage of Herbed Wellness customers will shun the new headache remedy if it contains caffeine?

9. A study of more than 5,000 people showed that those who lived at high latitudes, where UV exposure is minimal, had higher cancer rates than did those who lived near the equator, where UV exposure is, on average, far greater. One of the effects of UV radiation on humans is that it stimulates vitamin D manufacture in exposed skin. These results are consistent with other studies demonstrating that cancer patients often have lower than average vitamin D levels. Therefore, high blood levels of vitamin D reduce the risk of cancer in humans.

The answer to which of the following questions would be most useful to know in order to evaluate the validity of the argument's conclusion?

  O Does seasonal affective disorder, experienced more frequently by those living at high latitudes than by those living at the equator, predispose its sufferers to cancer?

  O Do high blood levels of vitamin D reduce the incidence of the common cold?

  O Can blood levels of vitamin D be raised through supplementation, thus reducing the risk of sunburn due to UV exposure?

  O Does exposure to UV radiation prevent cancer in other mammals, such as laboratory rats?

  O Are wintertime low vitamin D levels responsible for the flu season phenomenon?

FLAW QUESTIONS

Flaw questions are the final question type that is based on stimuli that consist of arguments. These questions are similar to Weaken questions, but instead of asking you for some new fact that, if true, would make the argument questionable, Flaw questions ask what's already wrong with the argument. So your prediction should focus on reasoning errors the author makes.

The good news is that the GMAT uses a handful of common flaws over and over:

- Confusing correlation and causation
- Confusing percent and actual value
- Unsupportable scope shifts between evidence and conclusion
- Inappropriate analogies (comparing things that aren't comparable)
- Overlooked alternatives
- Inappropriate conflation/distinction of terms

More important than memorizing all the items on this list, however, is understanding what unites them. All of these flaws center on the author's assumption, so you should handle them similarly to how you've handled all the other argument-based questions so far: by identifying the conclusion, evidence, and assumption. The correct answer to a Flaw question will describe the logical flaw inherent in the argument's assumption.

Sample Stems

Here are some example question stems that indicate a Flaw question:

- Which of the following is a flaw in the reasoning above?
- The argument above is vulnerable to which of the following criticisms?

APPLYING THE KAPLAN METHOD: FLAW QUESTIONS

Now let's use the Kaplan Method for Critical Reasoning to solve a Flaw question:

> The public service advertising campaign promoting the use of helmets has improved bicycle safety dramatically. Over the past 12 months, the number of serious bicycling injuries has been reduced by nearly 70 percent. Unfortunately, helmet usage has not reduced the number of all types of bike injuries. While serious head trauma has decreased by nearly 85 percent, broken bones now represent 20 percent of all reported bicycling injuries. This is a significant increase from last year's 14 percent.

> The reasoning in the argument is flawed because the argument does which of the following?

- ○ It fails to include information about any types of bicycle injuries other than head trauma and broken bones.
- ○ It implies that the same conclusion can result from two different sets of causes.
- ○ It fails to take into account any possible increase in the number of people riding bicycles over the past 12 months.
- ○ It presumes that an increase in the percentage of injuries involving broken bones precludes a decrease in the actual number of such injuries.
- ○ It ignores the fact that a 70 percent overall decrease in injuries would not allow for an 85 percent decrease in one specific type of injury.

Step 1: Identify the Question Type

The question stem alerts you to the idea that this argument is flawed, so Flaw is definitely the question type here.

Step 2: Untangle the Stimulus

The author concludes that the number of broken-bone bicycle injuries has gone up from last year to this year. The evidence for this is that broken bones made up 20 percent of this year's total bicycle-related injuries but were only 14 percent of last year's total.

Step 3: Predict the Answer

As soon as you see both percentages and numbers mentioned in the stimulus for a Flaw question, beware. In the Quantitative section, you will learn, if you have not already, that you must be careful when working with percents. Twenty percent is guaranteed to equal a higher number than 14 percent only if those percentages are of the same total. And since the total number of injuries is much lower this year than last year, 20 percent of a much lower total could actually equal a lower number than 14 percent of last year's higher total.

If you're having trouble seeing this, you can use the Quant strategy of Picking Numbers. Suppose there were 100 bicycle injuries last year. That means that 14 percent, or 14 total, of those injuries involved broken bones. You know that this year, injuries have been reduced by 70 percent. In this example, that means there were a total of 30 bicycle injuries this year. Twenty percent of the new, lower total is 6 broken-bone injuries, a significantly lower number than last year's 14. The flaw here is the author's assumption that an increase in percentage cannot be consistent with a decrease in actual number.

Step 4: Evaluate the Choices

Only **(D)** accurately captures the logical flaw in this argument—confusing percent and actual value. **(D)** is the correct answer.

The fact that the author mentions only two types of injuries, as **(A)** says, is not a flaw in the argument, which concerns only whether or not the number of broken bones has been reduced. Other types of injuries are out of scope. Since two sets of causes aren't discussed, you can rule out **(B)**. Causation does figure in many GMAT flaws, but not this one. **(C)** might seem tempting, since it does relate to the "percentage versus actual number" issue, but if the total number of bicyclists increased over the past year, the reduction in the number of total injuries would actually be greater. And since a 70 percent overall decrease in injuries could, in fact, allow for an 85 percent decrease in one specific type of injury, **(E)** can be ruled out as well. **(D)** is the correct answer.

TAKEAWAYS: FLAW QUESTIONS

- Flaw questions ask you to describe how the author's reasoning has gone awry. Identifying the author's assumption will reveal the flawed thinking.
- Some classic flaws include mistaking correlation for causation and confusing actual value with percent.
- On Flaw questions, determine the conclusion, evidence, and central assumption(s). Then predict an answer describing the reasoning error in the author's assumption.

PRACTICE SET: FLAW QUESTIONS

Answers and explanations at end of chapter

10. Our legislature is considering passing legislation to ban skateboarding on city streets, citing safety concerns. However, a review of public health records reveals that the legislature's concern is misplaced. Each year, many more people are injured while jogging than are injured while skateboarding. So in fact, skateboarding is safer than jogging.

    Which of the following indicates a flaw in the reasoning above?

    O   It fails to distinguish professional skateboarders who attempt very dangerous maneuvers from amateurs who are comparatively cautious.

    O   It assumes without warrant that no one who skateboards also jogs.

    O   It fails to consider the number of people who skateboard as compared with the number of people who jog.

    O   It ignores the possibility that other activities cause even more injuries than either skateboarding or jogging.

    O   It fails to address the issue and instead attacks the character of the legislature.

11. We favor the registration of all firearms, regardless of type. The National Rifle Association has done a good job of persuading its members that registration is the first step toward confiscation of all weapons. Nonsense. Americans register, among other things, their cars, their dogs, and the births of their children. Yet, confiscation of cars, cocker spaniels, and infants has never been a great problem.

    Which one of the following best describes the major flaw in the author's reasoning?

    O   He ignores the danger to the general public posed by unregulated weapons sales.

    O   He ignores the potential for bureaucratic mismanagement of any such registration effort.

    O   He ignores the existence of dog catchers, tow trucks, and child-welfare officers.

    O   He ignores the differences between firearms and other items that make the former a more likely target for confiscation.

    O   He ignores the expertise of the members of the National Rifle Association.

EXPLAIN QUESTIONS

Questions based on arguments (Assumption, Strengthen, Weaken, Evaluation, and Flaw) make up over 70 percent of all Critical Reasoning questions, but you will likely run into other question types on Test Day that are not necessarily based on arguments.

Explain question stimuli are not argumentative. Rather, they present a seeming discrepancy and ask you to find an explanation for the paradox. Your Paraphrasing skills and Attention to the Right Detail are the key to this question type—in your own simple but accurate words, restate not only the details in the stimulus but also the nature of the apparent contradiction. Once you've summed up the nature of the discrepancy, look for an answer choice that explains how the apparently contradictory facts in the stimulus could both be true.

It's sometimes difficult to predict exactly what the correct answer will contain, since an apparent contradiction can often be resolved in a number of different ways. On questions for which there could be multiple ways for the testmakers to phrase the correct answer, predictions must be in the form of characterizing what the right answer will mean or do, not the words it will use. Again, Paraphrasing is crucial.

Sample Stems

Here are some example question stems that indicate an Explain question:

- Which of the following would best explain the discrepancy above?
- Which of the following would best resolve the paradox described above?

APPLYING THE KAPLAN METHOD: EXPLAIN QUESTIONS

Now let's use the Kaplan Method for Critical Reasoning to solve an Explain question:

> A series of experiments was conducted in which rats of various ages were placed in a series of mazes and timed to see how long it took them to find their way out. In the first set of runs, the younger rats made their way out of the mazes an average of 30 percent faster than the older rats. Three days later, however, when the same rats were placed in the same mazes, the older rats were faster than the younger rats by nearly 40 percent.
>
> Which of the following hypotheses best accounts for the findings of the experiment?
>
> O   A rat's sense of smell becomes less acute as it gets older.
> O   The older rats had been used in earlier experiments.
> O   Older rats have a better-developed sensory memory, which allows them to "remember" the mazes three days later.
> O   Younger rats become frustrated when faced with repeated dead ends in a maze, while older rats do not.
> O   Older rats tire more easily than younger rats.

Step 1: Identify the Question Type

The wording of this stem is less direct than most question stems, but any question that asks you to account for a certain set of potentially contradictory findings is an Explain question.

Step 2: Untangle the Stimulus

When untangling the stimulus, paraphrase the given information and make sure you understand the paradox. Indeed, the findings of the experiments described in this stimulus seem to be contradictory: At first it seems that younger rats are capable of completing mazes more quickly, and then it appears that older ones are.

Step 3: Predict the Answer

There could be a couple of reasons why this happened, so it's difficult to predict the exact answer here. But no matter how the right answer is phrased, you know that it will probably be something about older rats that allows them to perform better the second time around.

Step 4: Evaluate the Choices

If rats develop sensory memories as they get older, this would explain how the older rats, which were initially slower, were later able to complete the mazes more quickly: They "remembered" the route. This is what **(C)** indicates, so it's the correct answer.

Remember that for an answer choice to be correct, it must relate logically to *both* parts of the seeming contradiction in the stimulus. All the incorrect choices here explain only one side of the story or the other; in other words, they fail to resolve the paradox. If rats use their sense of smell to negotiate mazes, then **(A)** might explain why the older rats were slower initially, but it would not explain why they completed the mazes faster three days later. **(B)** might explain why the older rats finished the mazes faster in the later runs (assuming that the earlier experiments also involved mazes), but it wouldn't explain why they initially took longer than the younger ones. If **(D)** were true, you would expect older, more patient rats to finish more quickly every time. **(E)** might explain why the older rats took longer the first time, but it wouldn't explain why they finished more quickly the second time. Choice **(C)** is correct.

TAKEAWAYS: EXPLAIN QUESTIONS

- Explain questions require test takers to choose an answer choice that best explains why all the information in the stimulus is true.

- In many instances, the Explain question stimulus contains a paradox or discrepancy. The correct answer reconciles the information in the stimulus without contradicting it.

- On Explain questions, identify the seeming paradox and predict an answer that addresses the paradox but does not contradict the evidence at hand.

PRACTICE SET: EXPLAIN QUESTIONS

Answers and explanations at end of chapter

12. At a large manufacturing corporation, the ratio of the annual job-related injury insurance premium per employee to average employee annual net pay increased between 1978 and 2003. Yet, the annual number of job-related injuries per employee during that time decreased by more than 30 percent.

    Which of the following, if true, best explains the discrepancy outlined above?

    ○ From 1978 to 2003, the severity of job-related injuries at the corporation decreased significantly due to compliance with new workplace safety rules.

    ○ The number of employees at the corporation decreased between 1978 and 2003.

    ○ During the 1978–2003 period, inflation significantly eroded the purchasing power of the dollar.

    ○ The corporation did not change its insurance provider during the 1978–2003 period.

    ○ Between 1978 and 2003, health care costs per job-related injury rose sharply, pressuring insurance providers to raise premiums.

13. Music industry executives have claimed that online file-sharing networks are significantly hurting their business because potential consumers are getting music for free that they would otherwise purchase. However, after file-sharing networks started to become popular, CD sales actually increased.

    Which of the following, if true, best explains the apparent contradiction described above?

    ○ File-sharing networks carry a more complete variety of music than most traditional music stores.

    ○ The few people using file-sharing networks already purchased more music than most people.

    ○ Many people prefer to store their music as computer files rather than maintain large CD collections.

    ○ Many consumers have purchased music by artists they discovered through file-sharing networks.

    ○ Music available on file-sharing networks is of the same audio quality as music on commercially produced CDs.

INFERENCE QUESTIONS

A common question type in both Critical Reasoning and Reading Comprehension is the Inference question. The process of inferring is a matter of considering one or more statements as evidence and then drawing a conclusion from them. A valid inference is something that must be true if the statements in the stimulus are true. Not *might* be true, not *probably* is true, but *must* be true.

Think of an inference as a conclusion that you draw based on the information, or evidence, given. It is your job on these questions to choose the inference that requires no assumption whatsoever; the correct answer will follow directly from the stimulus. But the answer to an Inference question is just as likely to be drawn from only one or two details as it is to take into account the stimulus as a whole. For this reason, it can be very difficult to predict an exact answer. Nevertheless, you can make a general prediction: The answer is the one that *must* be true based on the facts in the stimulus. You can use this prediction to help eliminate choices answer by answer, ruling out options that clearly don't match the facts as you paraphrased them. This is the beauty of a multiple-choice test—find four wrong answers, and you've also found the right one!

Let's examine a somewhat expanded version of the volleyball team argument:

> Allyson plays volleyball for Central High School, despite the team's rule against participation by nonstudents. Therefore, Allyson must be over 6 feet tall.

Wrong answer:

O   Allyson is the best player on the Central High School volleyball team.

Certainly Allyson *might* be the best player on the team. It's tempting to think that this would *probably* be true—otherwise the team would not risk whatever penalties violating the rule might entail. But *must* it be true? No. Allyson could be the second best. Or the third best. Or perhaps the coach owed Allyson's dad a favor. We have no support for the idea that she's the best on the team, so we can't infer this answer choice from the stimulus.

Valid inference:

O   Allyson is not a student at Central High School.

Clearly, if Allyson plays volleyball *despite* the team's rule against participation by nonstudents, she must not be a student. Otherwise, she wouldn't be playing despite the rule; she'd be playing in accordance with the rule. But note that this inference is not a necessary assumption of the argument because the conclusion about Allyson's height doesn't depend on it.

So be careful: Unlike an assumption, an inference need not have anything to do with the author's conclusion. In fact, many Inference stimuli don't have conclusions at all—they consist not of arguments but of a series of facts. Make sure you are prepared for Inference questions, as they require a different approach than do other Critical Reasoning questions. Remember, everything that you need will be contained in the stimulus, so focus on the information as it's presented and avoid answers that twist the facts (or make up new ones).

Sample Stems

Inference questions probably have the most varied wording of all the Critical Reasoning question stems. Some question stems denote inference fairly obviously. Others are more subtle, and still others may look like other question types entirely. The bottom line is that if a question asks you to take the stimulus as fact and find something based on it, then you're looking at an Inference question. Here's a quick rundown of various Inference question stems that you may see on your test:

- Which one of the following can be inferred from the argument above?
- Which one of the following is implied by the argument above?
- The author suggests that _____.
- If all the statements above are true, which one of the following must also be true?
- The statements above, if true, support which of the following?
- Which of the following is best supported by the statements above?
- Which of the following is the conclusion toward which the author is probably moving?
- The statements above best support which of the following conclusions?

APPLYING THE KAPLAN METHOD: INFERENCE QUESTIONS

Now let's use the Kaplan Method for Critical Reasoning to solve an Inference question:

> A new electronic security system will only allow a single person at a time to pass through a secure door. A computer decides whether or not to unlock a secure door on the basis of visual clues, which it uses to identify people with proper clearance. The shape of the head, the shape and color of the eyes, the shape and color of the lips, and other characteristics of a person's head and face are analyzed to determine his or her identity. Only if the person trying to open a secure door has the required clearance will the door unlock. Because this new system never fails, an unauthorized person can never enter a secure door equipped with the system.

> If the statements above are true, which of the following conclusions can be most properly drawn?

> O The new system is sure to be enormously successful and revolutionize the entire security industry.

> O The new system can differentiate between people who are seeking to open a secure door and people passing by a secure door.

> O No two people have any facial features that are identical, for example, identical lips.

> O High costs will not make the new security system economically unviable.

> O The new computer system is able to identify some slight facial differences between people who look very similar, such as identical twins.

Step 1: Identify the Question Type

Since the stem asks you to accept the statements as true and draw a conclusion on the basis of them, this is an Inference question.

Step 2: Untangle the Stimulus

When untangling the stimulus of an Inference question, briefly paraphrase the important facts to ensure you understand them. The stimulus tells you that a new electronic security system is completely fail-safe and will never allow an unauthorized person through a door equipped with the system. The system allows an authorized person to enter solely on the basis of the person's appearance and facial features.

Step 3: Predict the Answer

Attempting to predict the correct inference is difficult here, but on the GMAT, remember that an inference is something that must be true, not just something that could or might be true. It's crucial to approach the answer choices with this definition in mind.

Step 4: Evaluate the Choices

(A) is out of scope. There is no evidence of how the security industry is going to respond to the new system, so you can't say that this statement must be true based on what the stimulus states. **(B)** also doesn't need to be true. The new system doesn't need to differentiate between people passing by the door and people trying to enter, so long as it lets authorized people in and keeps unauthorized people out. **(C)** is too extreme. According to the stimulus, the security system examines multiple facial features to determine identity. You don't know that any *one* feature cannot be the same. All you know is that *all* of the features can't be the same. As for **(D)**, costs are outside the scope of this stimulus, since the stimulus only discusses the likelihood that unauthorized people will be able to get past the security system and through a secure door.

That means the correct inference must be **(E)**: If one twin is authorized and the other isn't, you know the system must be able to tell them apart, because the stimulus states that the security system never fails. Thus, **(E)** must be true.

TAKEAWAYS: INFERENCE QUESTIONS

- Inference stimuli seldom contain complete arguments. Rather, they contain statements from which you must make a deduction.
- On an Inference question, you want the choice that *must* follow from the stimulus—not a choice that *might* or *could* follow.
- On Inference questions, determine which answer choice must be true, based on the stimulus.
- An inference need not be based on the entire stimulus. An inference may follow from a single sentence or fact.
- Some Inference question stems require you to complete a train of thought.

PRACTICE SET: INFERENCE QUESTIONS

Answers and explanations at end of chapter

14. The number of wild tigers living in India dropped from an estimated 40,000 at the turn of the century to 2,000 in 1970. Although determined conservation efforts have halted the precipitous decline, the survival of the wild tiger in India is uncertain even now. Still, it is beyond doubt that if the tiger is to survive in the wild at all, its best chance is in India.

The statements above, if true, support which of the following?

O   There are now more than 2,000 wild tigers surviving in India.

O   There are fewer than 2,000 wild tigers living in the wild outside of India.

O   If tigers fail to survive in the wild in India, the species will become extinct.

O   It is impossible for a tiger raised in captivity to ever successfully adapt to life in the wild.

O   The survival of the wild tiger in countries other than India is also endangered.

15. A local department store hires college students for one month every spring to audit its unsold inventory. It costs the department store 20 percent less to pay wages to students than it would cost to hire outside auditors from a temporary service. Even after factoring in the costs of training and insuring the students against work-related injury, the department store spends less money by hiring its own auditors than it would by hiring auditors from the temporary service.

The statements above, if true, best support which of the following assertions?

O   The amount spent on insurance for college-student auditors is more than 20 percent of the cost of paying the college students' basic wages.

O   It takes 20 percent less time for the college students to audit the unsold inventory than it does for the outside auditors.

O   The department store pays its college-student auditors 20 percent less than the temporary service pays its auditors.

O   By hiring college students, the department store will cause 20 percent of the auditors at the temporary service to lose their jobs.

O   The cost of training its own college-student auditors is less than 20 percent of the cost of hiring auditors from the temporary service.

16. For many years, polls have shown that most American taxpayers fear the fines and late fees that can follow an Internal Revenue Service (IRS) audit. The move to fashion a friendlier public image for the IRS in order to increase the operating efficiency of the agency may be counterproductive because _____.

   O   many taxpayers are only concerned with receiving their refund checks

   O   a friendlier public image for the IRS will increase voluntary compliance with tax laws

   O   the timely collection of taxes could not be maintained if most taxpayers did not have a respectful fear of the IRS

   O   fewer taxpayers fear the IRS today than feared it 10 years ago

   O   collecting delinquent taxes does not necessarily cost the government more than collecting taxes on time

BOLDED STATEMENT QUESTIONS

Bolded Statement questions are usually based on stimuli that contain arguments, but the way you will analyze these arguments is different from what you have learned for other argument-based questions. Bolded Statement questions focus more on the structure than the substance of the stimulus.

A Bolded Statement question asks for the role that specific sentences play in an argument. The relevant sentences are, as the name implies, written in bold font. The answers to these questions will be abstract, using language such as "The first provides a counterexample to an opinion, while the second reaffirms that opinion by dismissing the counterexample." This technical language can make these questions seem intimidating.

Fortunately, these questions are rare, appearing only occasionally on the tests of high-scoring test takers. Moreover, if you do see any of these questions on Test Day, they shouldn't be nearly as difficult as they look. Remind yourself that Bolded Statement questions test the same core skill as much of the rest of the Critical Reasoning section: the ability to identify the evidence and the conclusion of an argument.

One caution: Unlike most GMAT stimuli, Bolded Statement questions often contain multiple arguments. Make sure that you note not only which parts of the argument are evidence and which are conclusions but also which evidence is connected to which conclusion. In addition, use keywords in the stimulus to identify which conclusion (if any) the author agrees with. Once you've done so, you should be able to make a prediction about the role of the bolded statements. Then you can turn these difficult questions into points.

Sample Stem

Bolded Statement question stems can't really avoid referring directly to the part(s) of the argument in bold type, so these stems are among the easiest to identify. A Bolded Statement question stem will look something like this example:

- The portions of the argument in **boldface** play which of the following roles?

APPLYING THE KAPLAN METHOD: BOLDED STATEMENT QUESTIONS

Now let's use the Kaplan Method for Critical Reasoning to solve a Bolded Statement question:

> Auto Manufacturer: For the past three years, the Micro has been our best-selling car. This year, however, sales of the Micro have been down for two consecutive quarters. Therefore, we are going to make certain features, like leather seats and CD players, standard on the Micro, rather than require buyers to pay extra for them. **This will make the Micro more attractive to buyers, thus stimulating sales.**
>
> Auto Dealer: Most people who buy the Micro do so because of its low cost. **Adding new standard features will raise the base price of the Micro,** costing us sales.
>
> In the argument above, the two statements in **bold** play which of the following roles?
>
> O   The first is a conclusion; the second suggests that this conclusion is based on evidence that is irrelevant to the issue at hand.
>
> O   The first presents a hypothesis; the second casts doubt on the evidence on which that hypothesis is based.
>
> O   The first provides a conclusion; the second weakens the assumption on which that conclusion relies.
>
> O   The first offers evidence that is disproved by the second.
>
> O   The first presents a conclusion; the second supports the conclusion but offers a different interpretation of how it will impact the speakers' business.

Step 1: Identify the Question Type

This stem offers standard language for a Bolded Statement question—it asks you to determine the roles played in the arguments by each of the boldface statements.

Step 2: Untangle the Stimulus

The stimulus is organized as a dialogue. This is a rare stimulus format, but it does occasionally turn up on the GMAT. Here, the manufacturer has devised a solution to revive flagging sales of the Micro: to make certain features standard that used to cost buyers extra. The auto dealer, on the other hand, posits that adding new standard features will increase the price of the Micro, thereby hurting sales.

Step 3: Predict the Answer

Predict the answer by identifying the function of each of the bolded statements within the context of the argument-counterargument structure. The first bolded statement is a prediction that serves as the auto manufacturer's conclusion: Adding more standard features to the Micro will stimulate sales. The manufacturer's conclusion relies on one of two assumptions: either that the added features will not result in an increase to the Micro's base price, or that car buyers interested in the Micro are willing and able to pay more for a version of the car with added features. However, as the auto dealer states, people who buy the Micro do so primarily because of its low price. Because the addition of more standard features will result in an increase in price, the manufacturer's proposal will actually lower sales. The second bolded statement, therefore, weakens the manufacturer's prediction by challenging his assumption.

Step 4: Evaluate the Choices

Only **(C)** matches this analysis of the arguments. **(A)** begins correctly, but the second bolded statement does not challenge any of the manufacturer's evidence (that the Micro was the best-selling model for three years, that sales of the Micro have been down for two quarters, and that the company is planning to add new standard features to the Micro). **(B)** can also be eliminated for this reason. **(D)** is incorrect because the first bolded statement is not the manufacturer's evidence but his conclusion. **(E)** might also have appealed to you, since the auto dealer does offer a different point of view on how these new standard features will affect sales of the Micro. However, the dealer's point of view is actually the opposite of the manufacturer's conclusion, so saying that the second statement "supports the conclusion" of the first is incorrect. Answer choice **(C)** is correct.

TAKEAWAYS: BOLDED STATEMENT QUESTIONS

- Bolded Statement questions commonly ask test takers to choose the answer that finds a connection between the two parts of the stimulus that are in boldface.
- Predicting will help you deal with the wordy and difficult answer choices.
- On Bolded Statement questions, identify the purpose of every sentence in the stimulus and select the answer that matches your description of the bolded statements.
- The most challenging questions may present multiple points of view, often the author's argument and a counterargument.

PRACTICE SET: BOLDED STATEMENT QUESTIONS

Answers and explanations at end of chapter

17. An increased number of candidates running for a political position, one opinion says, is likely to raise the percentage of voters. **The larger the number of candidates who run for a given position, the better the chances that a voter will find a candidate that adequately represents his or her political opinions.** In the reality of the political world, however, the opposite is likely to be the case. **As more candidates enter the election process, the differences between their declared positions on political matters tend to become less obvious.**

    In the argument given, the two portions in **boldface** play which of the following roles?

    O   The first explains an opinion that was raised, and the second further supports that opinion by elaborating on the explanation.

    O   The first raises an opinion, and the second raises another opinion contrary to the first opinion.

    O   The first explains an opinion that was raised, and the second raises another opinion contrary to the first opinion.

    O   The first raises an opinion, and the second supplies evidence that supports that opinion.

    O   The first explains an opinion that was raised, and the second undermines that opinion by contradicting the explanation.

18. Social worker: Typically, physicians in the United States who promote specialized services do not charge as much as do physicians who do not promote their services at all. **Every time physicians are allowed to promote without restriction, the number of physicians promoting their specialty service has gone up, and patients have paid less for these consultations.** Recent changes in regulations of such promotions have lifted the requirement that the amount charged for a consultation appear on the promotion. An effect of this change will be that physicians will no longer be inclined to reduce their fees when they start to promote, and **many physicians who promote their services will increase their charges to patients.**

    In the above argument, the two parts in **boldface** play which of the following roles?

    O   The first makes a general claim that the social worker takes to be the truth; the second is proposed as an outcome resulting from the general claim's truth.

    O   The first supplies an action and a consequence that the social worker argues will be replicated; the second recognizes a situation that would cause the action and consequence to fall apart.

    O   The first supplies an action and a consequence that the social worker perceives will no longer hold true; the second gives an explanation to support that perception.

    O   The first provides clarification that the social worker presents in advocacy of a prediction; the second is that prediction.

    O   The first recognizes a perspective that opposes the point that the social worker advocates; the second is that point.

ADVANCED STRATEGIES: THREE SPECIAL CASES

Throughout this chapter, you have learned about the standard Critical Reasoning question types on the GMAT. Recognizing these formulaic question types enables you to read strategically—that is, to read for the details that make the difference between right and wrong answers. But the arguments in CR stimuli follow patterns as well. Recognizing common argument structures will allow you to analyze stimuli and predict correct answers more efficiently.

These advanced techniques are no substitute for knowing how to identify the conclusion, evidence, and assumptions in arguments—the ability to break down arguments into their component parts remains essential—but the three special cases we are about to discuss can help you zero in on the author's central assumption with speed and accuracy. When you understand the kind of argument an author is making, you can anticipate what kind of assumptions he or she is likely to make.

The three special cases are Causality; Representativeness; and Plans, Proposals, and Predictions. Causality and Representativeness are classic argument structures, and Plans, Proposals, and Predictions are classic argument conclusions that function in predictable ways.

Let's begin by discussing how to identify a causal argument and use that knowledge to your advantage on Critical Reasoning questions.

CAUSALITY

A causal argument is an assertion that a certain cause produced a certain effect. In other words, X caused Y, X made Y happen, or Y is the result of X. The author's assertion of causality may be explicit (e.g., "The drought led to large-scale crop failures," or "The new city plan is responsible for these underdeveloped downtown blocks.") or implicit (e.g., "Since the introduction of the new radiator design, brand X cars have seen an 8 percent increase in incidents of overheating. Customer dissatisfaction will remain high until we announce a redesign."). Examine the following example of a conclusion that contains a claim of causality:

> Married people have been shown in several important studies to have higher
> levels of happiness than single people. Therefore, marriage causes happiness.

This argument draws its validity from a stated cause-effect relationship (namely, that marriage causes happiness). A conclusion that X caused Y relies on certain assumptions: (1) that nothing else—A, B, C, etc.—could have caused Y; (2) that Y was not the cause of X; and (3) that the apparent relationship between X and Y wasn't just a coincidence. An author who makes any of these assumptions may be confusing correlation and causation.

Causal conclusions often appear in Weaken stimuli. There are three ways to weaken causal arguments based on the assumptions listed above. Let's try them out with the following cause-effect statement:

"Marriage causes happiness."

X = cause (marriage); Y = effect (happiness)

Patterns for weakening a causal argument:

> **Alternative explanation:** It wasn't *X* that caused *Y*; it was actually *Z* that caused *Y*.
>
> "Marriage doesn't cause happiness; in fact, financial security (which correlates strongly with marriage) was the real cause of the happiness reported in the surveys."
>
> **Causality reversed:** It wasn't *X* that caused *Y*; it was actually *Y* that caused *X*.
>
> "Marriage doesn't cause happiness; in fact, people who are already happy are significantly more likely to marry."
>
> **Coincidence:** It wasn't *X* that caused *Y*; any correlation between *X* and *Y* is a coincidence, since they have no direct relationship.
>
> "Marriage doesn't cause happiness; other studies that looked at the same group of people over time found that people reported similar levels of happiness before and after getting married. Any seeming correlation between marriage and happiness is coincidental or based on other factors."

In Weaken questions involving causality, the first of these three weakeners (alternative explanation) is the most common. It can be difficult to predict the specific alternative cause that will appear in the correct answer. You do know, however, that the right answer will provide a plausible explanation other than the one the author assumes to be true. The introduction of a plausible alternative cause undermines the author's conclusion.

APPLYING THE KAPLAN METHOD: CAUSALITY

Now let's use the Kaplan Method for Critical Reasoning to solve a question involving causality:

> For the past year, a network television talk-show host has been making fun of the name of a particular brand of chainsaw, the Tree Toppler. The ridicule is obviously taking its toll: In the past 12 months, sales of the Tree Toppler have declined by 15 percent, while the sales of other chainsaws have increased.
>
> Which of the following, if true, casts the most serious doubt on the conclusion drawn above?
>
> O   The talk-show host who is ridiculing the Tree Toppler name actually owns a Tree Toppler.
>
> O   The number of product complaints from owners of the Tree Toppler has not increased in the past year.
>
> O   The average price of all chainsaws has increased by 10 percent in the past year.
>
> O   The number of stores that sell the Tree Toppler has remained steady for the past year.
>
> O   A year ago, a leading consumer magazine rated the Tree Toppler as "intolerably unsafe."

Step 1: Identify the Question Type

Because this stem asks you to "cast doubt" on the conclusion, this is a Weaken question.

Step 2: Untangle the Stimulus

For the last year, a talk-show host has been ridiculing Tree Toppler chainsaws. Over that time, Tree Toppler sales have fallen while other chainsaws' sales have risen. The author concludes that the talk-show host's jokes must have caused the declining Tree Toppler sales.

Step 3: Predict the Answer

To weaken an argument in which *X* is claimed to have caused *Y*, consider whether *Y* might actually have caused *X* (i.e., reversal) or whether something else might have caused *Y* (i.e., alternative cause). In this case, it seems unlikely that the decline in sales caused the on-air ridicule; the host is making fun of the chainsaw's name, not its declining sales. Therefore, the correct answer to this Weaken question will probably offer some alternative explanation for the decline in Tree Toppler sales.

Step 4: Evaluate the Choices

(E) provides that alternative explanation. If a prominent magazine rates a chainsaw as unsafe, that could certainly deter people from purchasing it, and a subsequent decline in sales would be reasonable to expect. **(E)** matches the prediction and is the correct answer.

If you hadn't immediately recognized **(E)** as a match for your prediction, you could still find the right answer by eliminating answer choices that miss the mark. Even if the talk-show host actually owns a Tree Toppler, as **(A)** says, the decline in sales could still be caused by the host's on-air ridicule; **(A)** is out of scope. **(B)** is a 180 because it actually strengthens the argument by eliminating a potential alternative explanation for the decline in sales. **(C)** might be tempting, but the argument actually mentions that sales of other chainsaws have increased, so an increase in the purchase price of *all* chainsaws is not a reasonable alternative explanation. **(D)** also strengthens the argument by eliminating another alternative explanation for the decline in sales (that fewer stores are carrying the Tree Toppler). Choice **(E)** is the correct answer.

Note that relevant alternative explanations for a causal relationship may, at first glance, appear to be outside the scope of the argument. But this is precisely because the author failed to recognize that there was an alternative possibility. Before you move to the answer choices, come up with two or three specific alternative explanations. Focus on the *effect* each answer choice has on the alleged causal relationship. By weakening the causal relationship, the correct answer choice will undermine the logic of the argument.

TAKEAWAYS: CAUSALITY

When a GMAT argument uses evidence of a correlation to support a conclusion of causation ($X \rightarrow Y$), consider whether:

1. Something else is the cause of one or both of the correlated items ($Z \rightarrow Y$; or $Z \rightarrow X$ and Y).
2. Causality is reversed; the purported effect is actually the cause ($Y \rightarrow X$).
3. The correlation is mere coincidence (*X* and *Y* are unrelated).

PRACTICE SET: CAUSALITY

Answers and explanations at end of chapter

19. Our architecture schools must be doing something wrong. Almost monthly we hear of domes and walkways collapsing in public places, causing serious injuries. In their pursuit of some dubious aesthetic, architects design buildings that sway, crumble, and even shed windows into our cities' streets. This kind of incompetence will disappear only when the curricula of our architecture schools devote less time to so-called artistic considerations and more time to the basics of good design.

Which of the following, if true, would most seriously weaken the argument above?

○ All architecture students are given training in basic physics and mechanics.

○ Most of the problems with modern buildings stem from poor construction rather than poor design.

○ Less than 50 percent of the curriculum at most architecture schools is devoted to aesthetics.

○ Most buildings manage to stay in place well past their projected life expectancies.

○ Architects study as long and as intensively as most other professionals.

20. Parents of high school students argue that poor attendance is the result of poor motivation. If students' attitudes improve, regular attendance will result. The administration, they believe, should concentrate less on making stricter attendance policies and more on increasing students' learning.

Which of the following, if true, would most effectively weaken the parents' argument?

○ Motivation to learn can be improved at home, during time spent with parents.

○ The degree of interest in learning that a student develops is a direct result of the amount of time he or she spends in the classroom.

○ Making attendance policies stricter will merely increase students' motivation to attend classes, not their interest in learning.

○ Showing a student how to be motivated is insufficient; the student must also accept responsibility for his or her decisions.

○ Unmotivated students do not perform as well in school as other students.

21. Attempts to blame the mayor's policies for the growing inequality of wages are misguided. The sharp growth in the gap in earnings between college and high school graduates in this city during the past decade resulted from overall technological trends that favored the skills of more educated workers. The mayor's response to this problem cannot be criticized, as it would hardly be reasonable to expect him to attempt to slow the forces of technology.

Which of the following, if true, casts the most serious doubt on the conclusion drawn in the last sentence above?

O   The mayor could have initiated policies that would have made it easier for less-educated workers to receive the education necessary for better-paying jobs.

O   Rather than cutting the education budget, the mayor could have increased the amount of staff and funding devoted to locating employment for graduating high school seniors.

O   The mayor could have attempted to generate more demand for products from industries that paid high blue-collar wages.

O   Instead of reducing the tax rate on the wealthiest earners, the mayor could have ensured that they shouldered a greater share of the total tax burden.

O   The mayor could have attempted to protect the earnings of city workers by instituting policies designed to reduce competition from foreign industries.

REPRESENTATIVENESS

When GMAT arguments include evidence in the form of surveys, studies, polls, anecdotes, or experiments, a key issue is often the representativeness of the group used as evidence. You may be familiar with the idea of representativeness from a statistics or research methods class. This concept is no different on the GMAT. In order to be representative, a sample must be large enough, the survey length must have covered an adequate amount of time, and the population surveyed cannot be biased in some flawed way.

In GMAT arguments, the author always believes that her evidence leads to her conclusion. Therefore, the author who uses this kind of statistical evidence always assumes the evidence is relevant to the scope of the conclusion. But in order for this to be the case, the sample used in the evidence must be representative of the group to which the conclusion is applied. Oftentimes on GMAT questions, the sample will prove to be too small for, or outside the scope of, the conclusion.

APPLYING THE KAPLAN METHOD: REPRESENTATIVENESS

Now let's use the Kaplan Method for Critical Reasoning to solve a question involving representativeness:

> Candidate A was widely believed to be the favorite in her state's gubernatorial race. Candidate B, the incumbent governor, had figured prominently in a corruption scandal during the previous year. Although he was ultimately never charged with a crime, Candidate B received very negative coverage in local and national media. A poll of registered voters in the state showed that a majority supported Candidate A and would vote for her. In fact, election day "exit polls" of those who voted showed that most had voted for Candidate A, and so she was expected to win. However, once the votes were counted, Candidate B was shown to have won a narrow victory. Clearly, respondents to the polls were not being honest when they claimed to have supported Candidate A.

The argument above depends on which of the following assumptions?

O   It is difficult to predict the degree to which an incumbent candidate's support will be affected by negative media coverage.

O   The negative media coverage made supporters of Candidate B reluctant to express their views in public, and so they claimed to support Candidate A when they actually had voted for Candidate B.

O   No voter ever changes his or her mind about whom to vote for.

O   Candidate B successfully used the fact that he had not been charged with a crime to restore his good image with the voting public.

O   The sample of voters surveyed in the exit poll was representative of those who voted in the election.

Step 1: Identify the Question Type

This question directs you to find an assumption on which the argument depends, so this is definitely an Assumption question.

Step 2: Untangle the Stimulus

The argument concludes that respondents to recent election exit polls and pre-election polls were not being honest when they claimed to have supported Candidate A for governor. The evidence for this is that despite a strong showing in these polls, Candidate A still lost the election.

Step 3: Predict the Answer

This conclusion is based in part on the results of two polls, so those polls need to have been conducted with representative samples in order for the conclusion to be valid. After all, what if the polls had both been conducted outside campaign rallies for Candidate A or in Candidate A's hometown? The sample group for the polls needs to be an adequate cross section of the voting population, and since this argument stakes its conclusion on the polls, the author of the argument must be assuming that the sample is indeed representative.

This question shows you that Kaplan's strategy for representativeness is not restricted to Strengthen and Weaken questions. On Test Day, if you're asked an Assumption question and you notice that the stimulus focuses on a study, survey, poll, or experiment, know that a choice that essentially says, "The sample was representative," is likely to be correct.

Step 4: Evaluate the Choices

(E) matches this prediction perfectly and is the correct answer. If you used the Denial Test to negate **(E)**, by stating that the poll's sample group was *not* representative, then the author's conclusion that voters must have lied can no longer be valid. If the people who participated in the polls were not representative of the larger voting population, then there would be no particular reason to expect the poll and voting results to be similar. **(E)** is therefore a necessary assumption of the argument.

(A) is not necessary to the argument because the author doesn't base her conclusion on a prediction drawn from the press coverage. Rather, the author bases her conclusion on a prediction drawn from the polling data. **(B)**, if true, would strengthen the argument, but this isn't a Strengthen question; the right answer to an Assumption question must be something upon which the argument relies. While the argument asserts that people polled lied about whom they voted for, it does not depend on any particular reason why they did so. **(C)** is far too extreme; the argument's point that the polls' respondents lied is not undone if one or two people simply changed their minds. As for **(D)**, the author doesn't necessarily assume anything about *how* Candidate B was able to eke out a victory. Choice **(E)** is correct.

TAKEAWAY: REPRESENTATIVENESS

When you see an argument based on the findings of a study, survey, experiment, or analogy, compare the population of the evidence with that of the conclusion.

PRACTICE SET: REPRESENTATIVENESS

Answers and explanations at end of chapter

22. In recent years, Doberman attacks on small children have risen dramatically. Last year saw 35 such attacks in the continental United States alone, an increase of almost 21 percent over the previous year's total. Clearly, then, it is unsafe to keep dogs as pets if one has small children.

    Which of the following, if true, would most strengthen the argument above?

    ○ No reasonable justification for these attacks by Dobermans has been discovered.

    ○ Other household pets, such as cats, don't display the same violent tendencies.

    ○ The number of Doberman attacks on small children will continue to rise in the coming years.

    ○ A large percentage of Doberman attacks could have been avoided if the Dobermans had been leashed or muzzled.

    ○ The behavior that Dobermans exhibit toward small children is representative of the behavior of dogs in general.

23. A social worker surveyed 200 women, each of whom had recently given birth to her first child. Half of the women surveyed had chosen to give birth in a hospital or obstetrics clinic; the other half had chosen to give birth at home under the care of certified midwives. Of the 100 births that occurred at home, only 5 presented substantial complications, whereas 17 of the hospital births presented substantial complications. The social worker concluded from the survey that the home is actually a safer environment in which to give birth than a hospital or clinic.

    Which of the following, if true, most seriously calls the social worker's conclusion into question?

    ○ Women who give birth in hospitals and clinics often have shorter periods of labor than do women who give birth at home.

    ○ Many obstetricians discourage patients from giving birth at home.

    ○ All of the women in the study who had been diagnosed as having a high possibility of delivery complications elected to give birth in a hospital.

    ○ Women who give birth at home tend to experience less stress during labor than women who deliver in hospitals.

    ○ Pregnant doctors prefer giving birth in a hospital.

24. A team of pediatricians recently announced that pet birds are more likely to bite children under age 13 than people of any other age group. The team's finding was based on a study showing that the majority of all bird bites requiring medical attention involved children under 13. The study also found that the birds most likely to bite are cockatiels and parakeets.

Which of the following, if true, would most weaken the pediatricians' conclusion that birds are more likely to bite children under age 13 than people of any other age group?

O   More than half of bird bites not requiring medical attention, which exceed the number requiring such attention, involve people aged 13 and older.

O   The majority of bird bites resulting in the death of the bitten person involve people aged 65 and older.

O   Many serious bird bites affecting children under age 13 are inflicted by birds other than cockatiels and parakeets.

O   Most bird bites in children under age 13 that require medical attention are far less serious than they initially appear.

O   Most parents can learn to treat bird bites effectively if they avail themselves of a small amount of medical information.

PLANS, PROPOSALS, AND PREDICTIONS

Once you start identifying plans, proposals, and predictions in Critical Reasoning stimuli, you'll realize that many arguments contain conclusions in these forms. All three have a future orientation and indicate the author's opinion.

Plans and proposals are found in conclusions that begin, "Thus, we should . . ." or "It's in the company's best interest to . . . ." When a conclusion takes the form of a plan or proposal, the author is likely assuming that the plan or proposal is helpful and practical under the current circumstances. GMAT questions often test whether we realize that it may not be helpful or currently practical.

Critical Reasoning stimuli involving plans or proposals almost invariably offer only one reason for the plan or proposal. In other words, because of *X*, we should do *Y*.

So, what must the author be assuming about that evidence? That it's the only, or at least the most important, factor to consider. Thus, any answer that introduces an alternative and competing consideration weakens the argument. Any answer that rules out a possible alternative consideration strengthens it.

Think about how you might weaken the following proposal:

> Sam often oversleeps because he reaches over and turns off the alarm before he's fully awake. To fix this problem, Sam proposes buying a second alarm clock.

Sam's proposal is inherently flawed because it fails to consider some important factors: Sam might put the second clock right next to the first one and just shut it off, too. Alternatively, Sam might have to plug the second clock in too far from his bed. Then, he couldn't hear it, so it wouldn't be of any help. Either way, there's an intervening consideration that suggests the plan will fail or will be self-defeating.

This happens in the business world all the time. For example, a sales manager might say, "Let's do *X* and increase sales. That will make us profitable." The operations manager might then respond, "Doing *X* would cost too much; this plan will lose money." The problem is not that the sales manager is unreasonable in claiming that proposal *X* would increase sales—it might, in fact, do so; however, the operations manager raises other concerns that the sales manager failed to see that could undermine proposal *X*'s chance of success.

Predictions are no different on CR questions than they are in real life; they use the future tense: "So-and-so will win the Oscar," "The economy will show modest growth," or "We will not be able to meet the production deadline." GMAT authors base their predictions on past and current trends or situations. In order to weaken such an argument, you want to find an answer choice that says that the trend will change. To strengthen it, look for an answer choice that says, "Future events will unfold as expected."

APPLYING THE KAPLAN METHOD: PLANS, PROPOSALS, AND PREDICTIONS

Now let's use the Kaplan Method for Critical Reasoning to solve a question involving a plan, proposal, or prediction:

> Several people have died while canoeing during high water on a nearby river in recent years. The local police have proposed a ban on canoeing when the river reaches flood stage. Opponents of the ban argue that the government should ban an activity only if it harms people other than those who willingly participate in the activity, and they therefore conclude that the proposed ban on high-water canoeing is unwarranted.
>
> Which of the following, if true, most seriously weakens the opponents' conclusion?
>
> O Sailboats are not allowed on a nearby lake when winds exceed 50 miles per hour.
>
> O Several other local governments have imposed similar bans on other rivers.
>
> O Several police officers have been seriously injured while trying to rescue canoeists who were stranded on the river while attempting to canoe during high water.
>
> O More canoeists drown while canoeing rivers at normal water levels than while canoeing rivers at high water levels.
>
> O Statistics provided by the U.S. National Park Service show that fewer people drown on rivers with high-water canoeing bans than on rivers without such bans.

Step 1: Identify the Question Type

The stem contains the obvious keyword "weakens," but it also asks you to weaken the opponents' conclusion in particular. Keep this information in mind—there may be more than one argument in the stimulus.

Step 2: Untangle the Stimulus

The government shouldn't ban an activity that poses no risk to people who don't voluntarily participate. Therefore, the opponents argue, the government should not ban high-water canoeing.

Step 3: Predict the Answer

To weaken the argument, you need an answer choice that explains why the opponents' proposal should, on its own terms, be rejected. Here, the opponents assume that high-water canoeing does not harm anyone who does not willingly participate in the canoeing. To weaken the conclusion, look for an answer choice suggesting that canoeing during flood stage does in fact threaten people other than those who have chosen to canoe.

Step 4: Evaluate the Choices

(C) offers such a suggestion by stating that police officers, none of whom consented to expose themselves to the dangers of canoeing in high water, were in fact harmed as a result of such canoeing.

Choice **(A)** is out of scope; it isn't clear how sailing on a lake during high wind is relevant to canoeing on a river during high water. This statement tells us nothing about whether high-water canoeing poses risks to non-canoers. And just because, as **(B)** says, other governments have also enacted the bans, that doesn't mean that the bans are necessarily reasonable. The opponents might still have a valid argument. Therefore, **(B)** is also out of scope. **(D)** offers an irrelevant comparison: That more canoeists drown while the river is at normal levels may simply be due to the fact that there are more canoeists at that time to begin with. That has no bearing on whether canoeing should be banned at high water levels. And **(E)** might be tempting, but it doesn't show that the opponents' proposal to abolish the ban won't work *on its own terms*. **(E)** doesn't give an example of non-canoeists harmed by the canoeing. Choice **(C)** is the correct answer.

TAKEAWAYS: PLANS, PROPOSALS, AND PREDICTIONS

When you see a question regarding a statement about the future, identify assumptions about the feasibility, usefulness, and relevance of the future conditions.

- To weaken an argument whose conclusion is a plan or proposal, show that the plan or proposal, on its own terms, will not work.
- To weaken an argument whose conclusion is a prediction, show why the prediction is unlikely to come to pass.
- To weaken an objection to a plan, proposal, or prediction, seek evidence that it *will* work or come true.

PRACTICE SET: PLANS, PROPOSALS, AND PREDICTIONS

Answers and explanations at end of chapter

25. A team of researchers at a university hospital has developed a chemical test that detects breast tumors in the early stages of development. In order to save lives, the researchers want to make the test a routine part of examinations at the hospital. However, a spokesperson for the hospital argued that because virtually all breast tumors are detectable by self-examination, the chemical test would have little impact on the breast cancer death rate.

    Which of the following, if true, would most seriously weaken the hospital spokesperson's argument?

    O   Fatal breast tumors are often not revealed by self-examination until it is too late for effective treatment.

    O   Breast tumors are usually discovered at an earlier stage of development than are lung tumors.

    O   Mammograms are currently in wide use as a breast cancer test and cost much less than the chemical test.

    O   Because men are not typically victims of breast cancer, the new test would benefit only half of the population.

    O   Most women learn how to check for signs of breast cancer from magazines and not from doctors.

26. Thousands who suffer heart attacks each year die before reaching a hospital or clinic where they can benefit from the drugs that dissolve clots found in coronary arteries. The Food and Drug Administration recently approved a new blood clot–dissolving agent, which a spokesperson claimed could save the lives of many people who would otherwise join this group of heart attack victims.

    Which of the following statements, if true, would most weaken the argument above?

    O   The new agent must be administered by a team of doctors in a hospital or clinic setting.

    O   Many heart attack victims die unnecessarily even though they reach a hospital or clinic in time.

    O   The new agent can be effectively administered prior to the victim's arrival at a hospital or clinic.

    O   The Food and Drug Administration has already approved agents that are at least as effective as the new drug in dissolving blood clots.

    O   The new blood clot–dissolving agent causes kidney damage and irregular heart rates in some patients.

27. According to a recent study, advertisements in medical journals often contain misleading information about the effectiveness and safety of new prescription drugs. The medical researchers who wrote the study concluded that the advertisements could result in doctors' prescribing inappropriate drugs to their patients.

    The researchers' conclusion would be most strengthened if which of the following were true?

    O   Advertisements for new prescription drugs are an important source of revenue for medical journals.

    O   Editors of medical journals are often unable to evaluate the claims made in advertisements for new prescription drugs.

    O   Doctors rely on the advertisements as a source of information about new prescription drugs.

    O   Advertisements for new prescription drugs are typically less accurate than medical journal articles evaluating those same drugs.

    O   The Food and Drug Administration, the government agency responsible for drug regulation, reviews advertisements for new drugs only after the ads have already been printed.

CRITICAL REASONING QUIZ

Answers and explanations at end of chapter

28. To avoid the appearance of conflicts of interest, the board of a major U.S. stock exchange is considering a new policy that would ban former top executives of the exchange from taking positions at publicly traded companies for a period of two years after leaving the stock exchange. Critics of the plan say the policy is unfair because it would likely prevent former top executives of the exchange from earning a decent living.

Which of the following statements, if true, would most strengthen the prediction made by the critics of the proposed company policy?

O The labor union that represents most of the stock exchange's employees has made public statements that threaten a strike if the policy is adopted.

O Former employees of the exchange most often work for publicly traded companies after leaving the exchange.

O Low-level managers at the exchange have an average tenure of 13 years, one of the longest in the industry.

O Low-level managers at the exchange most often leave their jobs for positions with the state or federal government.

O Former top executives of the exchange have a particular set of skills such that they are usually only able to find work with publicly traded companies.

29. The increase in taxes on cigarettes next month will not limit the use of addictive tobacco products to the extent that health advocates hope. Many cigarette smokers will shift their spending to cigars and chewing tobacco when the law takes effect.

Which of the following, if true, would most strongly weaken the argument above?

O Cigars and chewing tobacco can satisfy the nicotine cravings of most cigarette smokers.

O The taste, smell, and texture of cigars and chewing tobacco are sufficiently different from those of cigarettes to deter cigarette smokers from using them.

O Many health advocates themselves use tobacco products.

O The government might also impose significant taxes on cigars and chewing tobacco over the course of two years.

O Cigars and chewing tobacco are often more expensive than cigarettes.

30. The percentage of local businesses with more than 10 employees is higher in Grandview City than in any other city in the state. However, the percentage of local businesses with 15 employees or more is higher in Lakeshore City, which is in the same state, than in any other city in the state.

    If the statements above are true, then which of the following must also be true?

    O   The percentage of local businesses with more than 18 employees is higher in Lakeshore City than in any other city in the state.

    O   The state has more local businesses with more than 10 employees than any other state in the country.

    O   The number of local businesses with 15 or more employees is greater in Lakeshore City than in Grandview City.

    O   Some local businesses in Grandview City have 11 to 14 employees.

    O   The average number of employees per business is higher in Lakeshore City than in Grandview City.

31. It appears that the number of people employed by a typical American software firm decreased in the 1980s and 1990s. This trend is borne out by two studies, conducted 20 years apart. In a large 1980 sample of randomly chosen American software firms, the median size of the firms' workforce populations was 65. When those same firms were studied again in 2000, the median size was 57.

    Which of the following points to the most serious logical flaw in the reasoning above?

    O   The median number of employees in American firms in many industries decreased during the 1980s and 1990s.

    O   During the 1980s and 1990s, many software firms increased the extent to which they relied on subcontractors to write code.

    O   The data in the studies refer only to companies that existed in 1980.

    O   The studies focused on the number of employees, but there are many ways of judging a firm's size, such as revenues and profits.

    O   The median number of employees is not as sound a measure of the number of employees employed in an industry as is the mean number of employees, which accounts for the vast size of the few large firms that dominate most industries.

32. The Ministry of Tourism in country X began an expensive television advertising campaign in country Y two years ago. Since that time, the number of visitors to country X from country Y has increased by more than 8 percent. Clearly, the Ministry of Tourism's campaign is responsible for the increase.

Which of the following, if true, would most weaken the argument above?

O   The advertisements sponsored by the Ministry of Tourism in country X were panned by the country Y media for lack of imagination.

O   A devaluation of the currency in country X two years ago made travel there more affordable for residents of country Y.

O   Increasing political turmoil in country X will lead to a decrease in visitors from country Y next year.

O   The number of visitors from country Y to country Z increased by more than 8 percent over the past two years.

O   Over the past two years, the advertisement campaign launched by the Ministry of Tourism in country X cost more money than residents of country Y spent traveling in country X.

33. A study of children's television-watching habits by the federal Department of Education found that children aged 7–10 who watched more than 25 hours of television per week performed worse in school than children of the same age who watched fewer than 25 hours of television per week. Therefore, parents of children aged 7–10 should prohibit their children from watching more than 25 hours of television per week.

Which of the following, if true, would best strengthen the argument above?

O   A separate study, by a renowned graduate school of education, found that when parents prohibited their children from watching any television, the children's reading scores increased rapidly and significantly and stayed high indefinitely.

O   Children who watched more than 25 hours of television per week also performed worse on measures of physical fitness than children who watched fewer than 25 hours per week.

O   The television shows that children aged 7–10 are most likely to watch are saturated with advertisements for products, such as toys and candy, of little educational value.

O   The Department of Education study gave appropriate weight to children of backgrounds representative of children nationwide.

O   Children who develop a habit of extensive television watching are more likely than others to maintain that habit as an adult.

34. Cable Television Executive: **Our service and reliability have increased dramatically over the past year.** Our customer service line is receiving 30 percent fewer reports of interrupted service, and the number of subscribers canceling their accounts is barely half of what it was last year.

    Cable Television Customer: That doesn't mean your service and reliability have improved. **It's possible that customers don't bother to call your customer service line to report problems because they never get any assistance when they do.** And the drop-off in the number of canceled accounts could reflect the fact that nearly all of your dissatisfied customers have already canceled their accounts.

    In the argument above, the two portions in boldface play which of the following roles?

    O   The first is evidence designed to lead to a conclusion; the second offers further evidence in support of that conclusion.

    O   The first is evidence designed to lead to a conclusion; the second offers evidence designed to cast doubt on that conclusion.

    O   The first is a conclusion; the second offers evidence in support of that conclusion.

    O   The first is a conclusion; the second offers evidence designed to cast doubt on that conclusion.

    O   The first is a conclusion; the second is an alternative conclusion based on the same evidence.

35. Opponents of the laws prohibiting nonprescription narcotic drugs argue that in a free society, people have the right to take risks as long as the risks do not constitute a harm to others who have not elected to take such risks. These opponents conclude that it should be each person's decision whether or not to use narcotic drugs.

    Which of the following, if true, most seriously weakens the conclusion drawn above?

    O   Some narcotic drugs have been shown to have medicinal qualities.

    O   There are laws that govern the use of prescription drugs.

    O   Studies have shown that people who use nonprescription drugs are much more likely to perpetrate a violent crime when intoxicated than when sober.

    O   People who use narcotic drugs are twice as likely to die of an overdose as of natural causes.

    O   The rate of drug overdoses is higher in countries that do not have laws governing the use of narcotic drugs than in countries that do have such laws.

36. In a survey of undergraduates, two-fifths admitted to having cheated on an exam at least once during their education. However, the survey may underestimate the proportion of undergraduates who have cheated, because _____.

Which of the following best completes the passage above?

O   some undergraduates who have cheated at least once might have claimed on the survey never to have cheated

O   some undergraduates who have never cheated might have claimed on the survey to have cheated

O   some undergraduates who claimed on the survey to have cheated at least once may have cheated on multiple occasions throughout their education

O   some undergraduates who claimed on the survey to have cheated at least once may have been answering honestly

O   some students who are not undergraduates have probably cheated at least once during their education

37. During the last 18 years, the number of people who live or work in the Dry River Valley, which is prone to flash flooding, has continually increased, as has traffic on local roads and bridges. However, the number of people caught in flash floods has decreased, even though the annual number of floods has increased slightly.

Which of the following, if true, best explains the decrease described above?

O   Flash floods are more likely to happen in the first hour of a rainstorm than afterward.

O   Flash floods killed some people in the Dry River Valley in every one of the last 18 years.

O   Better meteorological technology, combined with a better understanding of the conditions conducive to flash flooding, has increasingly improved local authorities' ability to predict when and where flash floods will occur.

O   Many people work in the Dry River Valley but live elsewhere.

O   A law that went into effect 18 years ago mandated that all new homes built in the valley be built on raised foundations, making those homes much less susceptible to flood damage.

38. Colleges in Tycho City have failed to prepare their students for the business world. A recent study revealed that the majority of college graduates in Tycho City could not write a simple business letter.

    Which of the following, if true, would provide additional evidence in support of the claim above?

    ○   A majority of students attending colleges in Tycho City are business majors.

    ○   The State College in neighboring Twyla Township has recently improved its business program by adding courses in business writing.

    ○   Most Tycho City college graduates move outside the Tycho City area after they graduate.

    ○   Most Tycho City college students live in on-campus dormitories.

    ○   The majority of college graduates living in Tycho City received their college degrees from institutions located in Tycho City.

ANSWERS AND EXPLANATIONS

1. A	14. E	27. C
2. A	15. E	28. E
3. C	16. C	29. B
4. B	17. E	30. D
5. C	18. C	31. C
6. D	19. B	32. B
7. A	20. B	33. D
8. B	21. A	34. D
9. A	22. E	35. C
10. C	23. C	36. A
11. D	24. A	37. C
12. E	25. A	38. E
13. D	26. A	

1. **(A)**

Burger Land, a nationwide fast-food chain, recently announced a special promotion dramatically reducing the price of its most popular burger, the Big and Beefy. This development has provoked a strong response by the nation's nutritionists. Citing the extremely high levels of cholesterol in the Big and Beefy, they predict that the price reduction will have a negative impact on the health of our citizens.

The nutritionists' argument assumes which of the following?

○ Some consumers induced by the price reduction to purchase the Big and Beefy would otherwise have consumed food lower in cholesterol than the Big and Beefy.

○ Reducing fat consumption is the most important factor in improving one's diet.

○ Burger Land could not have increased sales of the Big and Beefy by reducing its cholesterol content and appealing to health-conscious consumers.

○ Other fast-food companies will not respond to Burger Land's announcement by reducing the price of their own high-cholesterol burgers.

○ Lost revenue due to the price reduction in the Big and Beefy will be offset by an increase in the number of burgers sold.

Step 1: Identify the Question Type

The word "assumes" in the question stem signals that this is an Assumption question. We're looking for an unstated piece of information that links the evidence to the conclusion. The stem also tells us that we should focus on the nutritionists' argument.

Step 2: Untangle the Stimulus

In Assumption questions, we first need to find the argument's conclusion and evidence. The conclusion is the nutritionists' prediction: Cheaper Big and Beefy burgers will negatively impact citizens' health. The evidence is that the Big and Beefy is extremely high in cholesterol and that Burger Land plans to significantly lower the price of the Big and Beefy.

Step 3: Predict the Answer

This stimulus contains a scope shift, or change in topic between evidence and conclusion. To spot scope shifts, look for a brand-new term or idea that appears for the first time in the conclusion without having been mentioned in the evidence. Here, the conclusion introduces the idea of citizens' health being harmed, so we need to figure out why, given the evidence, the author thinks a negative impact on the population's health is likely. The author makes two assumptions: (1) that eating a lot of cholesterol is bad for one's health, and (2) that the drop in price will entice people to purchase Big and Beefy burgers instead of lower-cholesterol food they would otherwise have eaten. (For this author's argument to work, it's not enough that Big and Beefy burgers are unhealthy; they've got to be less healthy than the foods they replace.) An answer choice that states either of these assumptions will be correct.

Step 4: Evaluate the Choices

(A) matches the second of our predicted assumptions: The reduced price will cause at least some people to purchase the Big and Beefy rather than other lower-cholesterol foods. This is the correct answer. **(B)** falls outside the scope of the argument, which is concerned not with "fat consumption" but with the very high levels of cholesterol the burgers contain. **(C)** is incorrect because other approaches the burger chain could have taken are outside the scope. The argument is concerned only with the potential consequences of the move they actually made, which was to reduce the price of one particular burger. **(D)** is incorrect because other fast-food companies are outside the scope. We're interested specifically in Burger Land. Finally, **(E)** is incorrect because lost revenues at Burger Land are irrelevant. What is important is the health impact of one specific burger that the company produces, not the company's finances. Choice **(A)** is correct.

2. **(A)**

In Country X, all citizens eligible to vote must do so or face stiff fines. Because voting in Country X is mandatory, over 99 percent of the eligible voters voted in the last election. Thus, the winner of the last election is truly the people's choice.

Which of the following identifies an assumption in the author's argument?

O   In Country X, voters are allowed to vote for a candidate of their choice.

O   If Country X did not make voting mandatory, few people would vote.

O   Only in countries where voting is mandatory do people vote the way they wish to vote.

O   Country X is a true democracy, despite the fact that all people are forced to vote.

O   Only in countries where voting is not mandatory do the winners of elections truly reflect the people's choice.

Step 1: Identify the Question Type

The question stem contains the classic telltale word "assumption," so we can be confident that this is an Assumption question.

Step 2: Untangle the Stimulus

The argument concludes that the winner of the election is the people's choice. This is based on the evidence that nearly every eligible voter voted in the election and that voting is mandatory in Country X.

Step 3: Predict the Answer

But just because everyone voted doesn't mean that the winner is truly the people's choice. In fact, if voting is compulsory, people might be forced to vote in an election in which they don't prefer *any* of the candidates. The author's claim about the election depends on the assumptions that citizens of Country X are able to vote for whomever they like, that their votes express their preference, and that their votes will be tallied honestly and accurately.

Step 4: Evaluate the Choices

(A) reflects our prediction nearly verbatim. **(B)** tells us that Country X may be justified in requiring its citizens to vote, but that does nothing to prove that the winner of the election is the people's choice. As for **(C)**, even if people vote for candidates of their choice in countries where voting is *not* mandatory, this argument could still be made. **(C)** also doesn't demonstrate anything about Country X specifically, so it's not the assumption we're looking for. **(D)** is tempting—but it requires the assumption that a "true democracy" is one in which the winner of any election is "the people's choice." Because the term "true democracy" is not defined in the answer choice or in the stimulus, **(D)** is out of scope. **(E)** is the exact opposite of what we're seeking, because it would suggest that the winner of the election in Country X would *not* be the people's choice. Choice **(A)** is the correct answer.

3. **(C)**

In the next four years, the number of doctors, nurses, and other health care workers will increase significantly worldwide. Even so, the average compensation received by such professionals will not decline but rather is likely to increase. This is due, at least partly, to the fact that the median age of the world's population will increase steadily in this same period of time.

The argument above depends logically upon which of the following assumptions?

- ○ The increase in the number of health care workers will be responsible for the increase in the average life span.
- ○ The compensation of doctors and physical therapists who treat the elderly will increase more than that of other health care workers.
- ○ As a group, older people receive more attention from health care workers than do younger people.
- ○ Geriatrics, a branch of medicine focusing on the health problems of older people, is the most expensive element of American health care.
- ○ Increase in the median age of the population will occur in all regions of the world.

Step 1: Identify the Question Type

The question stem instructs us to seek an assumption on which the argument depends.

Step 2: Untangle the Stimulus

First identify the conclusion: The number of health care workers is about to rise, as is the average compensation of those workers. Next, find the evidence: The median age of the world and, by extension, the number of elderly people are increasing.

Step 3: Predict the Answer

To find the central assumption, link the terms of the evidence with the terms of the conclusion. The conclusion centers on more workers who'll get more money. The evidence centers on more elderly. The assumption, which links the evidence and the conclusion, must center on the idea that the elderly are especially likely to require the services of health care workers.

Step 4: Evaluate the Choices

(C) is the best match for our prediction and, thus, the correct answer. **(A)** gets the cause-and-effect relationship from the argument in the wrong order, since the author argues that the increase in life span will be responsible for an increase in the number of health care workers. **(B)** draws an irrelevant comparison. The author argues that the average compensation received by all health care workers will increase. **(D)** certainly doesn't have to be true—the conclusion can still follow from the evidence even if there are elements of American health care that are more expensive than geriatrics. **(E)** is similarly extreme. It need not be true that the median age of the population will increase in every corner of the globe. Choice **(C)** is the correct answer.

EXPLANATIONS

4.   **(B)**

The threatened prosecution of businesses flying 20-by-38-foot garrison flags, which are traditionally to be flown on national holidays, instead of the smaller post flags, which can be flown at any time, is unconscionable. Legal technicalities of this sort should never restrict patriotic expression.

Which of the following, if true, would most seriously weaken the argument above?

○   Many people find the garrison flags' size to be distracting and ill suited to neighborhood aesthetics.

○   The businesses that are flying garrison flags do so primarily to attract customers.

○   The raising and lowering of different-sized flags on the correct days of the year is a laborious and time-consuming procedure.

○   The regulations that govern the correct display of the nation's flags are part of an old and time-honored tradition.

○   The symbolic significance of a flag's size is not generally understood by most of the customers patronizing these businesses.

Step 1: Identify the Question Type

The word "weaken" in the question stem signals that this is a Weaken question. We need the answer choice that makes the argument's conclusion less likely to be true.

Step 2: Untangle the Stimulus

We start by finding the conclusion, evidence, and assumption. The conclusion is the first sentence, which states that businesses should not be prosecuted for flying large garrison flags rather than smaller post flags. The evidence is the second sentence: Legal technicalities should not restrict patriotic expression. The author of this argument assumes that businesses are flying the garrison flags out of a sense of patriotism, rather than for some other reason.

Step 3: Predict the Answer

Because this is a Weaken question, the correct answer will make the central assumption less likely to be true. We'll look for a choice stating that businesses fly the larger flags for some reason other than patriotism.

Step 4: Evaluate the Choices

(B) matches our prediction: If businesses are flying large garrison flags to attract customers, they are not doing so out of a sense of patriotism. Because the argument's evidence hinges on "patriotic expression," the conclusion that these businesses should not be prosecuted is thus greatly weakened. This is the correct answer. **(A)** is incorrect because it falls outside the scope of the argument, which is concerned not with "neighborhood aesthetics" but with the permissibility of flying the larger flags. **(C)** is incorrect because it is a slight strengthener, not a weakener. The fact that abiding by the proper flag calendar and switching back and forth between the larger and smaller flags is "laborious and time-consuming" could be cited as an additional reason businesses should not be prosecuted for sticking to the larger flags. **(D)** is out of scope. It, like **(A)**, provides a reason that businesses should perhaps not be allowed to fly whichever flag they like with impunity, but this reason—longstanding tradition—has nothing to do with the scope of the argument, which focuses on patriotic expression. **(E)** is out of scope. Whether or not business patrons understand the "symbolic significance" of a flag's size has no effect on the conclusion that business owners ought not to be prosecuted for flying the larger flags. Choice **(B)** is correct.

5.   **(C)**

Any college football player who uses steroids should be banned from competition. The national agency with the responsibility to preserve the natural competitive balance between players enforces rules specifically mandating that no player be allowed to use drugs to gain a competitive advantage. Studies show that steroid users tend to have much greater strength and weight than non-users.

Which of the following statements, if true, would most strengthen the argument?

○   Users of steroids often suffer from acne, extreme nervousness, and reduced sexual potency.

○   Increased strength is more useful than increased weight to college football players.

○   Superior strength and weight give college football players a significant competitive advantage.

○   Steroid use is much more prevalent in college football than in college baseball.

○   Random drug testing of athletes has been shown to be effective in the detection of drug use by athletes.

Step 1: Identify the Question Type

The word "strengthen" gives this one away as a Strengthen question.

Step 2: Untangle the Stimulus

A Strengthen question is built around the argument's assumption. "Strengthen the argument" means "strengthen the conclusion," but we'll be strengthening the argument's conclusion specifically by affirming its central assumption.

The author concludes that steroid users should be banned from college football. The evidence comes in two parts. First, the rules forbid football players to use drugs to obtain a "competitive advantage." The second piece of evidence is that steroids cause big increases in strength and weight.

Step 3: Predict the Answer

The author's conclusion depends on the assumption that having "greater strength and weight" provides athletes with a "competitive advantage." (It's possible that added bulk could be a drawback for a college player; perhaps speed and flexibility are more important.) To strengthen the argument, look for an answer choice that suggests that players derive a benefit from the extra size and strength that steroids provide.

Step 4: Evaluate the Choices

(C) matches our prediction perfectly and is the correct answer. **(A)** introduces several negative side effects of steroids, all of which fall outside the scope of the argument. **(B)** offers an irrelevant comparison between increased strength and increased weight. It doesn't matter which of these two qualities is more important to a college football player; it only matters whether these qualities provide a competitive advantage. **(D)** is another irrelevant comparison, this time between college football and college baseball. The argument is about steroid use among football players, so baseball is beside the point. The "prevalence" of steroid use is also out of scope. **(E)** is incorrect because methods of drug detection fall outside the scope of the argument. It doesn't matter how players are caught. Choice **(C)** is correct.

6. **(D)**

The state legislature has proposed a law that requires all new cars sold in the state to be equipped with airbags for both front-seat passengers. The auto industry has lobbied against the proposed law, pointing out that the airbags would prevent only a small percentage of serious injuries because in most accidents, serious injuries can be avoided by the use of seat belts.

Which of the following, if true, would most weaken the argument put forth by the auto industry?

○ The government has a duty to protect the welfare of its citizens.

○ The number of accidents per mile driven in the state is substantially higher than that for the rest of the nation.

○ The cost of equipping automobiles with airbags will be passed on to the consumer in the form of higher prices.

○ Most serious injuries occur when front-seat passengers are not wearing their seat belts.

○ Because the law would apply only to new cars, it would take nearly a decade for the majority of the state's cars to become equipped with airbags.

Step 1: Identify the Question Type

From the question stem, we know not only that we are to weaken the argument but also that the argument will be "put forth by the auto industry."

Step 2: Untangle the Stimulus

The auto industry's conclusion is a prediction that airbags would prevent only a small percentage of serious injuries. The evidence for this is signaled by the word "because": In most accidents, serious injuries can be avoided by the use of seat belts. Note: Neither the legislature nor the laws are anywhere in our conclusion or evidence, so they will only be associated with wrong choices. This is why it helps to read the question stem as closely and carefully as possible.

Step 3: Predict the Answer

Both the evidence and the conclusion use the phrase "serious injuries," so there's no scope shift there. Thus, the question that needs answering is whether cars need airbags to prevent these serious injuries. The auto industry says no, because seat belts can protect most people. But in order to be protected by a seat belt, a person must wear a seat belt. (Compare that with an airbag, which works even when the driver of a car irresponsibly fails to protect himself.) The industry never gives us any statistics about the percentage of people who buckle up; that most people wear seat belts is a necessary assumption. To weaken the argument, find a statement that suggests that people don't really wear them.

Step 4: Evaluate the Choices

Only **(D)** suggests that people are not consistently wearing their seat belts, so it's an ideal weakener. **(A)** and **(E)** talk about government or laws, which would put those choices outside the scope of the argument. **(B)** tells us that this state has a disproportionately high number of accidents, but without a connection to seat belts or airbags, **(B)** is outside the scope. **(C)** is also outside the scope: The auto industry doesn't predict anything about profits or costs; the only prediction is about the airbags' ability to prevent serious injuries. Choice **(D)** is the correct answer.

7. **(A)**

Artistic success as an actor is directly dependent on how well an actor has developed his craft. This has been demonstrated by the discovery of a positive relationship between the number of classes taken by an actor and the number of professional productions in which that actor has appeared in the past two years.

Each of the following, if true, casts doubt on the author's argument about artistic success for actors EXCEPT:

O The figures for the number of classes taken were based solely on information provided by actors.

O Success as an actor cannot necessarily be judged exclusively by recent credits.

O For most successful actors, it is not the quantity but the quality of their classes that has helped to develop their craft.

O There is no relationship between the number of professional productions in which an actor has appeared and true artistic success.

O Most successful actors have taken only a small number of intensive classes.

Step 1: Identify the Question Type

In the question stem, the phrase "casts doubt on" indicates that this is a Weaken question. The word "EXCEPT" tells us that the correct answer, in this case, is the one that does *not* weaken the argument. Look for an answer that strengthens the argument or that has no effect on it at all.

Step 2: Untangle the Stimulus

The conclusion is the first sentence, which states that an actor's "artistic success" depends on the "development of his craft." (Note: It is easy to identify the second sentence as evidence supporting the first sentence because it begins with "this has been demonstrated by.") The evidence is that there is a positive correlation between the number of classes taken and the number of professional appearances by an actor.

Step 3: Predict the Answer

In this argument, two central assumptions bridge the terms of the evidence to those of the conclusion: first, that the number of classes taken is equivalent to how well developed an actor's craft is and, second, that artistic success correlates to the number of productions an actor has appeared in. If an answer choice attacks either of these assumptions, it can be eliminated as a weakener.

Step 4: Evaluate the Choices

First, examine the choices looking for answers that sever the link between taking a large number of classes and having a well-developed craft. **(C)** effectively attacks this assumption by suggesting that the sheer number of classes is not enough to guarantee developed craft. **(E)** points out that an actor can achieve success even if he takes only a few classes. Both of these choices can be eliminated. Next, examine the choices seeking answers that sever the link between professional productions and artistic success. **(B)** suggests that success is determined by more than an actor's résumé, and **(D)** destroys the relationship explicitly. This leaves **(A)**, which has no effect on the author's argument because it doesn't matter who provides the figures on the number of classes taken. Choice **(A)** is the correct answer.

8. **(B)**

Herbed Wellness, a manufacturer of herbal products, wants its new headache remedy to be as effective as possible while using only natural ingredients. A controlled study has found that 58 percent of headache sufferers obtain complete headache relief from a dose of caffeine equivalent to that typically found in a cup of coffee. Therefore, even though the vast majority of its customers are health-conscious avoiders of coffee, Herbed Wellness should add caffeine to its new herbal headache treatment; doing so will prove both efficacious and cost-effective.

The answer to which of the following questions would be most useful in evaluating the claim that caffeine will be efficacious in relieving headaches among Herbed Wellness customers?

- ○   Is the headache relief provided by caffeine as long-lasting as that provided by over-the-counter drugs such as aspirin?
- ○   What percentage of the study participants were regular coffee drinkers who suffer from caffeine-withdrawal headaches?
- ○   Is caffeine less expensive per dose than the individual herbs used in the headache formulation?
- ○   Does synthetic caffeine qualify as a natural substance?
- ○   What percentage of Herbed Wellness customers will shun the new headache remedy if it contains caffeine?

Step 1: Identify the Question Type

The phrase "most useful in evaluating the claim" tells us that this is a rare Evaluation question. Evaluation questions are very similar to Strengthen/Weaken questions: We must find the answer choice that impacts the validity of the argument's conclusion. This question specifically asks us to evaluate the claim that caffeine will be effective in relieving headaches among Herbed Wellness customers.

Step 2: Untangle the Stimulus

Evaluation questions are argument-based questions, so we begin by identifying the conclusion and evidence. The conclusion of this argument is the rather lengthy last sentence, but the question stem directs us to a specific piece of that sentence. We are supposed to examine the claim that caffeine will provide effective headache relief to Herbed Wellness customers. For our purposes, then, that claim is the conclusion. The evidence for caffeine's effectiveness as a headache remedy is the study demonstrating that 58 percent of participants obtained headache relief from an amount of caffeine typically found in a cup of coffee.

Step 3: Predict the Answer

Whenever an argument contains a study or a sample, we should check to be certain that the sample is representative of the group it is supposed to shed light on. In this argument, the question becomes whether the study participants are representative of Herbed Wellness customers. The only bit of information we have about those customers is that they tend to avoid coffee. Did the study participants also habitually avoid coffee, then? If they did not, their behavior differs from that of Herbed Wellness customers, and the study does not provide us with a proper sample from which to draw a conclusion. It follows that in order to determine whether caffeine will indeed be an effective remedy for Herbed Wellness customers, we need to know whether or not the study participants also habitually avoided coffee.

Step 4: Evaluate the Choices

(B) matches our prediction and is the correct answer. Whether the study participants are representative of Herbed Wellness customers depends on whether they are habitual coffee drinkers. **(A)** is incorrect because how long the headache relief provided by caffeine lasts is outside the scope of the argument, as are other headache remedies besides caffeine. **(C)** is incorrect because the question stem directs us to evaluate the claim of caffeine's efficacy, not its cost-effectiveness. **(D)** is incorrect because whether the caffeine the company uses is considered "natural" has no bearing on whether it is effective in relieving headaches. Finally, **(E)** is incorrect because whether customers actually buy the new headache remedy has no impact on its potential effectiveness in relieving their headaches. Choice **(B)** is the correct answer.

9. **(A)**

A study of more than 5,000 people showed that those who lived at high latitudes, where UV exposure is minimal, had higher cancer rates than did those who lived near the equator, where UV exposure is, on average, far greater. One of the effects of UV radiation on humans is that it stimulates vitamin D manufacture in exposed skin. These results are consistent with other studies demonstrating that cancer patients often have lower than average vitamin D levels. Therefore, high blood levels of vitamin D reduce the risk of cancer in humans.

The answer to which of the following questions would be most useful to know in order to evaluate the validity of the argument's conclusion?

O   Does seasonal affective disorder, experienced more frequently by those living at high latitudes than by those living at the equator, predispose its sufferers to cancer?

O   Do high blood levels of vitamin D reduce the incidence of the common cold?

O   Can blood levels of vitamin D be raised through supplementation, thus reducing the risk of sunburn due to UV exposure?

O   Does exposure to UV radiation prevent cancer in other mammals, such as laboratory rats?

O   Are wintertime low vitamin D levels responsible for the flu season phenomenon?

Step 1: Identify the Question Type

The word "evaluate" indicates that this is an Evaluation question. The correct answer will contain a question relevant to the strength of the conclusion. Like Assumption, Strengthen, Weaken, and Flaw questions, Evaluation questions are built around assumptions in the stimuli.

Step 2: Untangle the Stimulus

Begin by identifying the conclusion, evidence, and assumption(s). The conclusion is signaled by the word "Therefore": High vitamin D levels reduce human cancer risk. The evidence comes in two main parts. First, the sun stimulates vitamin D production. People who live near the equator, where it's sunny, have lower cancer rates than do people who live in high latitudes and get less sun. Second, people suffering from cancer have unusually low vitamin D levels.

The author makes several assumptions here. One is that people living at higher latitudes have lower blood vitamin D levels. We know that people at high latitudes get less sun—but it's possible that their UV-related vitamin D deficit is offset by some other factor. The next assumption is that differing vitamin D levels, if in fact they do differ between people at high and low latitudes, contribute to the differing cancer rates in these populations. Third, the author assumes that the low vitamin D levels observed in cancer patients are not an effect of the cancer or of treatment for the cancer. Finally, the author assumes that there are no other differences between people in high latitudes and people in low latitudes that could affect their cancer risk.

Step 3: Predict the Answer

Whenever an argument includes a causal conclusion (*X* caused *Y*), consider two possibilities: an alternative cause (*Z* caused *Y*) or a reversal of causality (*Y* caused *X*). In this case, both possibilities could be relevant. To assess the strength of the argument, we would want to know, first, whether some factor unrelated to vitamin D could account for the difference in cancer rates between people at high and low latitudes (that's an alternative cause). Second, we would want to know whether the low levels of vitamin D observed in cancer sufferers were a cause of the cancer, as opposed to an effect of the cancer (that's a reversal of causality). An answer choice that addresses either of these two issues is correct.

Step 4: Evaluate the Choices

(A) matches our prediction and is the correct answer. If seasonal affective disorder does predispose humans to cancer, the conclusion that a low vitamin D level is responsible is greatly weakened. On the other hand, if seasonal affective disorder has no impact on cancer rates, then an alternative cause is ruled out, and the conclusion that vitamin D controls cancer risk is strengthened. **(B)** is outside the scope of the argument, which concerns cancer risk, not the risk of contracting a common cold. The method of raising vitamin D levels mentioned in **(C)** is likewise outside the scope, as are the "other mammals" mentioned in **(D)** and the "flu season phenomenon" mentioned in **(E)**. Choice **(A)** is the correct answer.

10. **(C)**

Our legislature is considering passing legislation to ban skateboarding on city streets, citing safety concerns. However, a review of public health records reveals that the legislature's concern is misplaced. Each year, many more people are injured while jogging than are injured while skateboarding. So in fact, skateboarding is safer than jogging.

Which of the following indicates a flaw in the reasoning above?

○   It fails to distinguish professional skateboarders who attempt very dangerous maneuvers from amateurs who are comparatively cautious.

○   It assumes without warrant that no one who skateboards also jogs.

○   It fails to consider the number of people who skateboard as compared with the number of people who jog.

○   It ignores the possibility that other activities cause even more injuries than either skateboarding or jogging.

○   It fails to address the issue and instead attacks the character of the legislature.

Step 1: Identify the Question Type

The word "flaw" in the question stem indicates that this is a Flaw question. We'll be looking for the argument's faulty assumption.

Step 2: Untangle the Stimulus

In Flaw questions, just as in Assumption questions, we need to identify the argument's conclusion and evidence. In this argument, the conclusion is the final sentence: Skateboarding is safer than jogging. The evidence is that more people are injured while jogging than while skateboarding.

Step 3: Predict the Answer

In Flaw questions, we expect that the conclusion will not follow logically from the evidence because the author makes an inappropriate assumption. Here, the author incorrectly assumes that a higher number of people injured means a higher percentage of people injured, which is not necessarily the case. Picking Numbers clarifies the issue. Let's say that 100 people skateboard in a given city, while 10,000 people jog. In that case, if 200 people are injured by jogging while only 10 are injured by skateboarding, jogging would actually be the far safer sport because 2 percent of joggers but 10 percent of skateboarders have sustained injuries. The flaw in the argument, then, is that it fails to provide us with the relative numbers of joggers versus skateboarders.

Step 4: Evaluate the Choices

(C) matches our prediction and is correct. **(A)** is an irrelevant comparison between professional and amateur skateboarders. **(B)** is incorrect because the evidence explicitly states that more people are hurt while jogging than while skateboarding. Even if some people do engage in both activities, the conclusion is based on evidence about which activity they were doing when they were injured, so it makes no difference whether there is any overlap between joggers and skateboarders. **(D)** is incorrect because activities other than jogging and skateboarding are outside the scope of the stimulus. **(E)** is incorrect because there is no attack on anybody's character in the argument. Choice **(C)** is correct.

11. (D)

We favor the registration of all firearms, regardless of type. The National Rifle Association has done a good job of persuading its members that registration is the first step toward confiscation of all weapons. Nonsense. Americans register, among other things, their cars, their dogs, and the births of their children. Yet, confiscation of cars, cocker spaniels, and infants has never been a great problem.

Which one of the following best describes the major flaw in the author's reasoning?

- ○ He ignores the danger to the general public posed by unregulated weapons sales.
- ○ He ignores the potential for bureaucratic mismanagement of any such registration effort.
- ○ He ignores the existence of dog catchers, tow trucks, and child-welfare officers.
- ○ He ignores the differences between firearms and other items that make the former a more likely target for confiscation.
- ○ He ignores the expertise of the members of the National Rifle Association.

Step 1: Identify the Question Type

"Major flaw" in the question stem indicates that we're looking at a Flaw question.

Step 2: Untangle the Stimulus

This author concludes that contrary to what the NRA argues, confiscation of registered firearms is not likely to be a problem. The author supports this conclusion by drawing an analogy: Other items that are registered (e.g., cars, dogs, children) are not likely to be confiscated, so the same can be said for firearms.

Step 3: Predict the Answer

Flaws in arguments almost always result from the author making faulty assumptions. So what's the assumption? In an argument that proceeds by analogy, as this one does, the assumption is always that the two things being compared are sufficiently alike. That is what the author is assuming. That assumption is probably not valid, since guns are very different from cars, dogs, and babies when it comes to the likelihood of confiscation.

Step 4: Evaluate the Choices

And that's exactly what **(D)** says. As for **(A)**, unregulated weapons sales aren't an issue in this argument, which simply attempts to prove that registration of weapons won't lead to their confiscation. Similarly, how the registration effort proceeds, an issue introduced by **(B)**, is not integral to the argument in any way. **(C)** focuses on dogs, cars, and children. Any observation about dogs, cars, and children is secondary to the major flaw, which is that the argument ignores whether they are relevant points of comparison to begin with. **(E)** introduces the irrelevant issue of expertise. There's nothing here to demonstrate that the members of the NRA are experts on the issue of registration and confiscation of weapons. Choice **(D)** is the correct answer.

12. (E)

At a large manufacturing corporation, the ratio of the annual job-related injury insurance premium per employee to average employee annual net pay increased between 1978 and 2003. Yet, the annual number of job-related injuries per employee during that time decreased by more than 30 percent.

Which of the following, if true, best explains the discrepancy outlined above?

- ○ From 1978 to 2003, the severity of job-related injuries at the corporation decreased significantly due to compliance with new workplace safety rules.
- ○ The number of employees at the corporation decreased between 1978 and 2003.
- ○ During the 1978–2003 period, inflation significantly eroded the purchasing power of the dollar.
- ○ The corporation did not change its insurance provider during the 1978–2003 period.
- ○ Between 1978 and 2003, health care costs per job-related injury rose sharply, pressuring insurance providers to raise premiums.

Step 1: Identify the Question Type

The phrase "explain the discrepancy" indicates that this is an Explain question. Our task will be to resolve an apparent contradiction in the stimulus.

Step 2: Untangle the Stimulus

Explain questions typically do not involve arguments. Rather, the stimulus will present us with two seemingly contradictory statements. Our job is to reconcile them without changing any of the information we are given. Here, the apparent contradiction is that, between 1978 and 2003, the cost of insurance premiums came to represent a greater proportion of workers' net pay. Over that same period, the number of job-related injuries per employee decreased. We would expect premiums to drop as the risk of injury drops; we need to explain the fact that they instead went up. It may also be the case that wages went down, while insurance premiums stayed the same, causing the ratio of insurance premiums to net pay to be higher.

Step 3: Predict the Answer

There must be some reason, unrelated to the number of workplace injuries, for the increase in the ratio of insurance premiums to net pay. Insurance premiums are typically tied to health care costs. So it may be that those job-related injuries that occurred in 2003 were more expensive to treat than those that occurred in 1978, either because those that occurred in 2003 were more severe or because diagnostic or other medical costs per injury increased during the stated time period.

Step 4: Evaluate the Choices

(E) matches our prediction exactly: The cost of treating an average workplace injury went way up. This would cause premiums to rise even if fewer workers were getting hurt on the job. **(E)** is the correct answer. **(A)** is incorrect because it is the opposite of what we want, or a 180. If the severity as well as the number of injuries decreased, then we would expect treatment costs, and thus insurance premiums, to decrease as well. **(B)** is incorrect because we're given the insurance premium per employee as well as the injury rate per employee. We don't have to calculate either of those numbers, so the actual number of workers employed by the manufacturing corporation is not relevant. **(C)** may sound tempting because inflation could certainly cause insurance premiums to increase, but it should also cause wages to increase at a similar rate. Therefore, since what is increasing is the ratio of the insurance premium to net pay, inflation is irrelevant. **(D)** is incorrect because, like choice **(A)**, it is the opposite of what we need. If the company had changed its insurance provider, that might account for the increased premiums. But if the company retained the same provider, we would expect the premiums to remain the same. Choice **(E)** is correct.

13. (D)

Music industry executives have claimed that online file-sharing networks are significantly hurting their business because potential consumers are getting music for free that they would otherwise purchase. However, after file-sharing networks started to become popular, CD sales actually increased.

Which of the following, if true, best explains the apparent contradiction described above?

○ File-sharing networks carry a more complete variety of music than most traditional music stores.

○ The few people using file-sharing networks already purchased more music than most people.

○ Many people prefer to store their music as computer files rather than maintain large CD collections.

○ Many consumers have purchased music by artists they discovered through file-sharing networks.

○ Music available on file-sharing networks is of the same audio quality as music on commercially produced CDs.

Step 1: Identify the Question Type

Since the question stem asks us to "explain the apparent contradiction," we can be sure this is an Explain question.

Step 2: Untangle the Stimulus

Rather than dissecting the stimulus looking for conclusion, evidence, and assumption, let's examine the stimulus not as an argument but as a set of statements presenting a contradiction. The discrepancy here is that CD sales have actually increased despite the fact that more people are gaining access to music for free.

Step 3: Predict the Answer

It is usually difficult to predict precisely how a discrepancy will be explained, but we can predict precisely what effect the right answer will have: It must explain how CD sales could increase, even while people have more access to free music.

Step 4: Evaluate the Choices

(A) doesn't help because it doesn't explain why more CDs are being sold in traditional music stores. **(B)** mentions music that has already been purchased, so it doesn't explain why CD sales have increased *after* file-sharing networks grew in popularity. **(C)** deepens the mystery because it suggests that people would be unwilling to purchase more CDs. **(D)** suggests that many people discovered new artists through file sharing, but rather than just listen to these artists on file-sharing networks, they then purchased more music by these artists. This could certainly explain why CD sales increased after the file-sharing networks became popular, so this is our correct answer. **(E)** equalizes electronic music and music on CDs when it comes to audio quality, so why would people purchase more CDs after beginning to share music electronically for free? Choice **(D)** is correct.

14. (E)

The number of wild tigers living in India dropped from an estimated 40,000 at the turn of the century to 2,000 in 1970. Although determined conservation efforts have halted the precipitous decline, the survival of the wild tiger in India is uncertain even now. Still, it is beyond doubt that if the tiger is to survive in the wild at all, its best chance is in India.

The statements above, if true, support which of the following?

- ○ There are now more than 2,000 wild tigers surviving in India.
- ○ There are fewer than 2,000 wild tigers living in the wild outside of India.
- ○ If tigers fail to survive in the wild in India, the species will become extinct.
- ○ It is impossible for a tiger raised in captivity to ever successfully adapt to life in the wild.
- ○ The survival of the wild tiger in countries other than India is also endangered.

Step 1: Identify the Question Type

Whenever we are asked to make a deduction based on the stimulus, we have an Inference question.

Step 2: Untangle the Stimulus

The stimulus for an Inference question will typically not be an argument. Instead of looking for evidence and conclusion, we simply take the statements in the stimulus at face value and paraphrase them to make sure we understand the situation they describe. Here we're told that conservation efforts have stopped the decline of wild tigers in India, the number of which decreased from 40,000 in 1900 to 2,000 in 1970. Moreover, while tigers are still endangered in India, that country is nonetheless the wild tiger's best chance for survival.

Step 3: Predict the Answer

The answer to an Inference question is often difficult to predict because there are any number of deductions we might make from the stimulus. Instead, we must go through the answer choices, carefully checking each against the information in the stimulus, until we find the one that must be true based only on the information we are given.

Step 4: Evaluate the Choices

(A) cannot be the correct answer because the stimulus mentions nothing about the number of wild tigers existing in India at the present time; we only have numbers for 1900 and 1970. **(B)** is also incorrect because it mentions the number of tigers living outside India, about which we have no information. We cannot glean an inference this precise from this stimulus. For example, it's possible that Malaysia and Thailand each have 900 wild tigers, but it's also possible that Thailand has 3,000 but is losing 500 a year. We can't infer the statement in **(B)** without bringing in imagined outside information. **(C)** is too extreme. The stimulus does say that India is the best chance of the wild tiger's survival, but it does not go so far as to say that India is the tiger's only hope. Perhaps there is another location where tigers could survive in the wild, and failing that, perhaps they could be bred at zoos. **(D)** is incorrect because the stimulus gives us no information about tigers raised in captivity. By process of elimination, **(E)** must be the right answer. Indeed, the stimulus tells us that the wild tiger's best chance of survival is in India, even though it is endangered there. It follows that it must be endangered elsewhere as well. Because choice **(E)** states a deduction we can draw from the stimulus, it is correct.

15. **(E)**

A local department store hires college students for one month every spring to audit its unsold inventory. It costs the department store 20 percent less to pay wages to students than it would cost to hire outside auditors from a temporary service. Even after factoring in the costs of training and insuring the students against work-related injury, the department store spends less money by hiring its own auditors than it would by hiring auditors from the temporary service.

The statements above, if true, best support which of the following assertions?

O   The amount spent on insurance for college-student auditors is more than 20 percent of the cost of paying the college students' basic wages.

O   It takes 20 percent less time for the college students to audit the unsold inventory than it does for the outside auditors.

O   The department store pays its college-student auditors 20 percent less than the temporary service pays its auditors.

O   By hiring college students, the department store will cause 20 percent of the auditors at the temporary service to lose their jobs.

O   The cost of training its own college-student auditors is less than 20 percent of the cost of hiring auditors from the temporary service.

Step 1: Identify the Question Type

Since the question stem is asking us to make an assertion supported by the statements in the stimulus, this is an Inference question.

Step 2: Untangle the Stimulus

Sometimes Critical Reasoning questions look more like math word problems. Any time we see numbers and statistics, we need to pay close attention, especially to the distinction between actual numbers and percentages. For this question, the stimulus confirms that what the department store pays student auditors in wages is 20 percent less than the cost of hiring outside auditors. And we also know that even after we add the costs of training and insuring the students (costs not involved with hiring outside auditors), the cost to the store is still less than hiring the outside auditors.

Step 3: Predict the Answer

Based on the statements here, it must be true that the costs of training and insuring the students are not more than 20 percent of the cost of hiring the outside auditors. If they were, then the 20 percent savings in wages would be outweighed by those extra costs, and hiring outside auditors would be cheaper.

Step 4: Evaluate the Choices

Therefore, **(E)** is correct. **(A)** mentions the relationship between the students' wages and the cost of their insurance, but this relationship is not mentioned in the stimulus, so we can't infer anything about it. By the same token, **(B)** can be eliminated because it discusses the amount of time the employees take to audit the inventory, when the stimulus only concerns the cost to the department store. **(C)** distorts the 20 percent statistic from the stimulus. That statistic compares what the department store spends on student employees to what the store spends on outside auditors. What the temp service pays the auditors is totally irrelevant. **(D)** is yet another distortion of the 20 percent statistic. We can't say for sure that *any* of the outside auditors will lose their jobs if they are not hired by the department store. Choice **(E)** is the correct answer.

16. **(C)**

For many years, polls have shown that most American taxpayers fear the fines and late fees that can follow an Internal Revenue Service (IRS) audit. The move to fashion a friendlier public image for the IRS in order to increase the operating efficiency of the agency may be counterproductive because _____.

○ many taxpayers are only concerned with receiving their refund checks

○ a friendlier public image for the IRS will increase voluntary compliance with tax laws

○ the timely collection of taxes could not be maintained if most taxpayers did not have a respectful fear of the IRS

○ fewer taxpayers fear the IRS today than feared it 10 years ago

○ collecting delinquent taxes does not necessarily cost the government more than collecting taxes on time

Step 1: Identify the Question Type

Questions that ask us to fill in a blank in a stimulus are Inference questions, since we must complete the author's line of reasoning, based on the information given.

Step 2: Untangle the Stimulus

In this stimulus, the author states that the IRS's attempt to be friendlier in order to increase its operating efficiency may be counterproductive. The author also cites polls indicating that a majority of taxpayers fear the fines and fees accompanying an IRS audit.

Step 3: Predict the Answer

It's up to us to determine why the IRS being friendlier could compromise its operating efficiency rather than enhance it. Even if we can't predict the correct inference exactly, seeing the word "counterproductive" should make us look for an answer that shows why the new program will not work.

Step 4: Evaluate the Choices

(C) tells us that in order to ensure the timely collection of taxes, taxpayers need to have some fear of the IRS. If the IRS becomes too friendly and taxpayers no longer fear the IRS, then the timely collection of taxes will suffer. And that of course would defeat the IRS's stated goal of increasing its operating efficiency. Therefore, **(C)** is correct. **(A)** introduces the idea of refund checks, which is far outside the scope and has no bearing on an argument about the IRS being able to collect taxes efficiently. **(B)** suggests that the IRS wouldn't have to audit quite as much, since more people will cooperate. This would make the IRS's plan quite successful, not counterproductive. As for **(D)**, it's irrelevant whether or not more people feared the IRS 10 years ago. If people still fear the IRS, then becoming friendlier may still be productive. **(E)** suggests that becoming friendlier wouldn't necessarily help the IRS save money and efficiency, but it certainly doesn't suggest that becoming friendlier might cost them anything, either. Choice **(C)** is correct.

17. (E)

An increased number of candidates running for a political position, one opinion says, is likely to raise the percentage of voters. **The larger the number of candidates who run for a given position, the better the chances that a voter will find a candidate that adequately represents his or her political opinions.** In the reality of the political world, however, the opposite is likely to be the case. **As more candidates enter the election process, the differences between their declared positions on political matters tend to become less obvious.**

In the argument given, the two portions in boldface play which of the following roles?

○   The first explains an opinion that was raised, and the second further supports that opinion by elaborating on the explanation.

○   The first raises an opinion, and the second raises another opinion contrary to the first opinion.

○   The first explains an opinion that was raised, and the second raises another opinion contrary to the first opinion.

○   The first raises an opinion, and the second supplies evidence that supports that opinion.

○   The first explains an opinion that was raised, and the second undermines that opinion by contradicting the explanation.

Step 1: Identify the Question Type

Any question that asks us to identify the roles played by statements in boldface is a Bolded Statement question. Our task is to find the structure of the stimulus and to determine the structural functions of the statements in bold type.

Step 2: Untangle the Stimulus

This stimulus includes two contradictory opinions: the author's opinion, stated in the third sentence, and the "one opinion" the author is arguing against (we'll call this the opponent's opinion), stated in the first sentence. The opponent believes that the more candidates there are running for office, the more voters will turn out at the polls. The first bolded statement serves as the opponent's evidence: More voters will turn out because the more candidates there are, the more likely voters are to find one they like and consequently want to vote for. The author counters the opponent, implying that in actual practice, the more candidates there are, the fewer voters will turn out. The second bolded statement serves as the author's evidence: The more candidates there are, the more alike they all look to voters.

Step 3: Predict the Answer

Both bolded statements, then, are evidence—the first for the opponent's position and the second for the author's.

Step 4: Evaluate the Choices

(E) matches our prediction, though the wording of this choice makes it a bit tricky. The first bolded statement definitely explains why the opponent holds the position he does. So far, so good. We know that the second bolded statement is the author's evidence. Because the author is contradicting the opponent, the author's evidence does in fact serve to "undermine" the opponent's view. Finally, the second bolded statement directly contradicts the first bolded statement. The first says that the more candidates there are, the more likely a voter will be to find one she likes. The second says that the more candidates there are, the more similar they start to seem, which implies that it will be more difficult for voters to find candidates they like. It follows that the final piece of choice **(E)**, "by contradicting [the first bolded statement]," is also correct and **(E)** is the correct answer. **(A)** is incorrect because the second bolded statement supports the author's view, not the opponent's. **(B)** is incorrect because both bolded statements are evidence for an opinion, not the opinion itself. **(C)** is incorrect because the second statement is, again, evidence for an opinion, not the opinion itself. **(D)** is incorrect because the first bolded statement is evidence, and the second is evidence for the author, not the opponent. Choice **(E)** is correct.

18. (C)

Social worker: Typically, physicians in the United States who promote specialized services do not charge as much as do physicians who do not promote their services at all. **Every time physicians are allowed to promote without restriction, the number of physicians promoting their specialty service has gone up, and patients have paid less for these consultations.** Recent changes in regulations of such promotions have lifted the requirement that the amount charged for a consultation appear on the promotion. An effect of this change will be that physicians will no longer be inclined to reduce their fees when they start to promote, and **many physicians who promote their services will increase their charges to patients.**

In the above argument, the two parts in **boldface** play which of the following roles?

O   The first makes a general claim that the social worker takes to be the truth; the second is proposed as an outcome resulting from the general claim's truth.

O   The first supplies an action and a consequence that the social worker argues will be replicated; the second recognizes a situation that would cause the action and consequence to fall apart.

O   The first supplies an action and a consequence that the social worker perceives will no longer hold true; the second gives an explanation to support that perception.

O   The first provides clarification that the social worker presents in advocacy of a prediction; the second is that prediction.

O   The first recognizes a perspective that opposes the point that the social worker advocates; the second is that point.

Step 1: Identify the Question Type

This is definitely a Bolded Statement question since it asks us to identify the roles played in the argument by the statements in boldface.

Step 2: Untangle the Stimulus

The social worker begins by stating that patients pay less for consultations with doctors who promote their specialties. Whenever doctors have been allowed to promote without restriction, more doctors have promoted, and patients have paid less. But under the new laws, the ads no longer have to say how much consultations cost. The social worker thinks this change means patients will pay more for care. The social worker asserts that doctors who promote their specialties will raise their fees and overall costs for patients will rise.

Step 3: Predict the Answer

The first boldface statement describes a cause-and-effect relationship that has existed in the past, but will no longer exist. The second statement shows why this relationship is unlikely to exist in the future.

Step 4: Evaluate the Choices

According to **(C)**, the first of the two bolded statements "supplies an action and a consequence"—i.e., a cause and an effect—that the author believes "will no longer hold true" in the future. **(C)** says that the second bolded statement provides evidence that this cause-effect relationship will not continue. This matches our prediction straight down the line. **(A)** is incorrect because the second bolded statement does not describe "an outcome resulting from" the truth of the first bolded statement. **(B)** mischaracterizes the first bolded statement; the social worker does not believe that the cause-effect relationship "will be replicated." Answer choice **(D)** inaccurately states that the first statement is evidence in support of the second statement. And **(E)** doesn't work, since nobody is arguing against the social worker's position. **(C)** is correct.

19. (B)

> Our architecture schools must be doing something wrong. Almost monthly we hear of domes and walkways collapsing in public places, causing serious injuries. In their pursuit of some dubious aesthetic, architects design buildings that sway, crumble, and even shed windows into our cities' streets. This kind of incompetence will disappear only when the curricula of our architecture schools devote less time to so-called artistic considerations and more time to the basics of good design.

> Which of the following, if true, would most seriously weaken the argument above?

> ○ All architecture students are given training in basic physics and mechanics.

> ○ Most of the problems with modern buildings stem from poor construction rather than poor design.

> ○ Less than 50 percent of the curriculum at most architecture schools is devoted to aesthetics.

> ○ Most buildings manage to stay in place well past their projected life expectancies.

> ○ Architects study as long and as intensively as most other professionals.

Step 1: Identify the Question Type

The phrase "most seriously weaken" in the question stem tells us that we have a Weaken question.

Step 2: Untangle the Stimulus

The stimulus will contain an argument; we need to pick out the conclusion, evidence, and assumption. The conclusion is the last sentence, which states that a shift away from aesthetics in architecture schools' curricula is necessary for buildings to be more soundly constructed. The evidence is the frequency with which parts of buildings collapse. Note that this is a causal argument: The author assumes that architecture schools' artistic considerations, rather than something else, are directly responsible for the crumbling buildings because the time devoted to them prevents architects from learning good design principles.

Step 3: Predict the Answer

The correct answer for this Weaken question will contradict the assumption that aesthetic considerations are causing buildings to be poorly designed and thus to crumble. We'll simply scan the choices for one that provides an alternate cause for the decay of the city's buildings.

Step 4: Evaluate the Choices

(B) provides an alternate cause, poor building construction, and is thus the correct answer. **(A)** is outside the scope and therefore incorrect. Even if students are currently instructed in basic physics and mechanics, they may not be spending enough time learning good design principles. **(C)** is incorrect because we have no information to indicate how great a percentage of time spent studying aesthetics the author of this argument would consider too much. Perhaps "less than 50 percent" is still too much. **(D)** is incorrect because it fails to provide us with any new and relevant information. The author merely complains that some buildings are collapsing. The fact that "most" are not collapsing does not take away the fact that some are falling down. Finally, **(E)** is an irrelevant comparison between architects and other professionals. Choice **(B)** is correct.

20. (B)

Parents of high school students argue that poor attendance is the result of poor motivation. If students' attitudes improve, regular attendance will result. The administration, they believe, should concentrate less on making stricter attendance policies and more on increasing students' learning.

Which of the following, if true, would most effectively weaken the parents' argument?

○ Motivation to learn can be improved at home, during time spent with parents.

○ The degree of interest in learning that a student develops is a direct result of the amount of time he or she spends in the classroom.

○ Making attendance policies stricter will merely increase students' motivation to attend classes, not their interest in learning.

○ Showing a student how to be motivated is insufficient; the student must also accept responsibility for his or her decisions.

○ Unmotivated students do not perform as well in school as other students.

Step 1: Identify the Question Type

The word "weaken" in the stem clearly indicates a Weaken question.

Step 2: Untangle the Stimulus

The parents conclude that poor motivation by schools causes poor attendance by students and that increasing students' learning will boost their attitudes, thus making them more likely to regularly attend school.

Step 3: Predict the Answer

Notice that the parents' argument is essentially causal in nature. According to the parents, the cause is poor motivation, and the effect is poor attendance. Whenever you're asked to weaken a causal argument, always consider the three classic alternative explanations: (1) reverse the cause and effect ("poor attendance causes poor motivation"), (2) find an alternative cause for the effect ("anything other than poor motivation would cause poor attendance"), or (3) chalk it up to coincidence ("whatever the cause of the poor attendance, it isn't poor motivation"). You may not know exactly what the right answer will say, but you can expect it to do one of these three things.

Step 4: Evaluate the Choices

(B) posits that the author has confused a cause with an effect—that bad attendance causes bad motivation. That's reversal of causality, one of the classic weakeners. **(B)** is the correct answer. **(A)** suggests that parents can be vital to the development of motivation, but this has no direct link to attendance, so it doesn't weaken the argument. **(C)** is a 180. It agrees with the parents' position that a stricter policy will not lead to increased learning, the very position you are asked to weaken, so it doesn't have any effect; the parents aren't looking for the school to tighten attendance policies, so finding out that such tightening won't increase their motivation does nothing to the parents' argument. **(D)** introduces the idea of accepting responsibility, which sounds like a good thing overall but has no direct bearing on improving attendance. Finally, **(E)** mentions that unmotivated students have poorer performance, but the parents are only interested in ways to get students to improve their attendance, not their performance in school. Choice **(B)** is correct.

21. (A)

Attempts to blame the mayor's policies for the growing inequality of wages are misguided. The sharp growth in the gap in earnings between college and high school graduates in this city during the past decade resulted from overall technological trends that favored the skills of more educated workers. The mayor's response to this problem cannot be criticized, as it would hardly be reasonable to expect him to attempt to slow the forces of technology.

Which of the following, if true, casts the most serious doubt on the conclusion drawn in the last sentence above?

○   The mayor could have initiated policies that would have made it easier for less-educated workers to receive the education necessary for better-paying jobs.

○   Rather than cutting the education budget, the mayor could have increased the amount of staff and funding devoted to locating employment for graduating high school seniors.

○   The mayor could have attempted to generate more demand for products from industries that paid high blue-collar wages.

○   Instead of reducing the tax rate on the wealthiest earners, the mayor could have ensured that they shouldered a greater share of the total tax burden.

○   The mayor could have attempted to protect the earnings of city workers by instituting policies designed to reduce competition from foreign industries.

Step 1: Identify the Question Type

If you're ever asked to "cast doubt" on an argument, you're being asked to weaken it.

Step 2: Untangle the Stimulus

Here the argument concludes that the mayor's policies are not responsible for the growing inequality of wages in the city. The argument instead attempts to blame overall technological trends that favored the skills of more educated workers and thus enabled college graduates to earn more money than high school grads.

Step 3: Predict the Answer

To weaken an argument in which an author says that *X* did *not* cause *Y*, think about strengthening the idea that *X did* cause *Y*. Since the author is attempting to blame technological trends and not the mayor's policies, try to find an answer indicating that the mayor's policies did play a role.

Step 4: Evaluate the Choices

This is exactly what **(A)** does, making **(A)** the correct answer. If the mayor's policies neglected to even the playing field between better-educated workers and their less-educated counterparts, then the mayor does share some of the responsibility for the wage gap, and the author's argument is severely impaired. **(B)** misses the point. The point is not that the less-educated workers are unemployed; it's that the jobs they do have don't pay as much as those of better-educated workers. **(C)** takes too many leaps to be correct. In order to choose **(C)**, we'd have to assume that less-educated workers were all concentrated in blue-collar jobs, and we'd also have to assume that creating more demand for products from those blue-collar industries would result in higher wages for blue-collar employees. **(D)** introduces the tax rate, which is completely outside the scope of the argument, and **(E)** deals with city workers, which doesn't help or hurt the argument because city workers aren't necessarily better or less educated than other workers, so we don't know whether city workers are even a part of the wage gap problem. Choice **(A)** is correct.

22. (E)

In recent years, Doberman attacks on small children have risen dramatically. Last year saw 35 such attacks in the continental United States alone, an increase of almost 21 percent over the previous year's total. Clearly, then, it is unsafe to keep dogs as pets if one has small children.

Which of the following, if true, would most strengthen the argument above?

○   No reasonable justification for these attacks by Dobermans has been discovered.

○   Other household pets, such as cats, don't display the same violent tendencies.

○   The number of Doberman attacks on small children will continue to rise in the coming years.

○   A large percentage of Doberman attacks could have been avoided if the Dobermans had been leashed or muzzled.

○   The behavior that Dobermans exhibit toward small children is representative of the behavior of dogs in general.

Step 1: Identify the Question Type

The word "strengthen" indicates that we'll need to support the argument's conclusion by making its central assumption more likely to be true.

Step 2: Untangle the Stimulus

The conclusion is signaled by the keyword "clearly" in the last sentence: If one has small children, it is unsafe to keep dogs as pets. The evidence is data indicating an increase in attacks on small children by Dobermans.

Step 3: Predict the Answer

Whenever an argument contains a sample or a study, suspect a representativeness issue. In this argument, we have evidence about Dobermans, but the conclusion is about dogs in general. The author must be assuming that Dobermans are representative of dogs in general. To strengthen the argument, we'll look for the answer choice that supports (or simply restates as fact) this assumption. Note that we could have simply treated this question as a scope shift from "Dobermans" in the evidence to "dogs" in the conclusion. Indeed, the problem of representativeness often simply amounts to a scope shift: One group mentioned in the evidence is assumed to be representative of a different group mentioned in the conclusion.

Step 4: Evaluate the Choices

(E) matches our prediction and is correct. **(A)** is incorrect because it is outside the scope. The reason for the Doberman attacks is irrelevant. **(B)** again falls outside the scope. We're interested in dogs, not "other household pets." **(C)** is again irrelevant to the argument. If Doberman attacks continue to increase, then we can certainly conclude that Dobermans are unsafe to have around young children, but we cannot necessarily conclude that all dogs are unsafe in this regard. Finally, **(D)** is a 180, since it weakens rather than strengthens the argument. If the Doberman attacks cited as evidence could have been prevented with muzzles or leashes, then perhaps it would be safe to keep Dobermans (and other dogs) around small children as long as such safety measures are in place. Choice **(E)** is the correct answer.

23. (C)

A social worker surveyed 200 women, each of whom had recently given birth to her first child. Half of the women surveyed had chosen to give birth in a hospital or obstetrics clinic; the other half had chosen to give birth at home under the care of certified midwives. Of the 100 births that occurred at home, only 5 presented substantial complications, whereas 17 of the hospital births presented substantial complications. The social worker concluded from the survey that the home is actually a safer environment in which to give birth than a hospital or clinic.

Which of the following, if true, most seriously calls the social worker's conclusion into question?

O   Women who give birth in hospitals and clinics often have shorter periods of labor than do women who give birth at home.

O   Many obstetricians discourage patients from giving birth at home.

O   All of the women in the study who had been diagnosed as having a high possibility of delivery complications elected to give birth in a hospital.

O   Women who give birth at home tend to experience less stress during labor than women who deliver in hospitals.

O   Pregnant doctors prefer giving birth in a hospital.

Step 1: Identify the Question Type

Since we need to call the social worker's conclusion into question, we need to weaken it.

Step 2: Untangle the Stimulus

The social worker's conclusion is that it is safer to give birth at home than at a hospital or clinic. The evidence for this is a survey in which some women chose to give birth at a hospital and others chose home birth. Overall, the hospital births presented more substantial medical complications than did the home births.

Step 3: Predict the Answer

We can successfully undermine the social worker's conclusion if we undermine the evidence on which it's based, namely, the study. If we find an answer choice that tells us that the survey is invalid or that the sample studied in the survey is unrepresentative, then any conclusion based on the survey would be in doubt.

Step 4: Evaluate the Choices

(C) tells us that the hospital births presented more complications simply because the women who chose to give birth at the hospital were predisposed to complications. This suggests that these women would have had complications no matter where they gave birth, which undermines the conclusion that a hospital is less safe than a home as a place to give birth. Thus, choice **(C)** is the correct answer. **(A)** is out of scope. A shorter labor can still be more dangerous, so this isn't a valid weakener. Just because obstetricians discourage home birth, as **(B)** says, doesn't mean that the home is more or less safe than a hospital; there could be plenty of reasons why the obstetricians would discourage home birth. **(D)** strengthens the argument by telling us that women who give birth at home experience less stress, which could potentially make their births go more smoothly. **(E)** also goes outside the scope of the argument. Pregnant doctors might *prefer* to give birth in a hospital simply because they are more familiar with the hospital environment, not because a hospital is necessarily safer. Choice **(C)** is correct.

24. (A)

A team of pediatricians recently announced that pet birds are more likely to bite children under age 13 than people of any other age group. The team's finding was based on a study showing that the majority of all bird bites requiring medical attention involved children under 13. The study also found that the birds most likely to bite are cockatiels and parakeets.

Which of the following, if true, would most weaken the pediatricians' conclusion that birds are more likely to bite children under age 13 than people of any other age group?

- More than half of bird bites not requiring medical attention, which exceed the number requiring such attention, involve people aged 13 and older.
- The majority of bird bites resulting in the death of the bitten person involve people aged 65 and older.
- Many serious bird bites affecting children under age 13 are inflicted by birds other than cockatiels and parakeets.
- Most bird bites in children under age 13 that require medical attention are far less serious than they initially appear.
- Most parents can learn to treat bird bites effectively if they avail themselves of a small amount of medical information.

Step 1: Identify the Question Type

This stem contains a wealth of helpful information. Not only do we see the telltale keyword "weaken" indicating the question type, but we also have the conclusion of the argument stated directly in the stem. Part of our job is already done.

Step 2: Untangle the Stimulus

The basic conclusion of the pediatricians is that pet birds are more likely to bite young children than older people. The evidence for this is a study, which should ring alarm bells for representativeness issues. The study indicates that when we look at injuries that required medical attention, we see that most of the injuries were to young children.

Step 3: Predict the Answer

But not all bird bites necessarily require medical attention, so in order for this study's results to prove that birds are more likely to bite young children *overall*, we need proof that the bird bites requiring medical attention are representative of all bird bites. So to weaken this argument, let's find a choice that essentially says, "Bites that require medical attention are *not* representative of bites in general."

Step 4: Evaluate the Choices

You'll then be drawn to choice **(A)**: Looking at *all* bird bite injuries reveals that most of them don't require medical attention, and of those that don't, more than half of them are suffered by people over the age of 13. **(A)** would actually indicate that birds are just as likely, if not *more likely*, to bite people over the age of 13 as to bite younger children. Thus, choice **(A)** is the correct answer. Just because senior citizens are more likely to *die from* bird bites, as **(B)** says, doesn't mean that they're more likely to be bitten in the first place. **(C)** improperly seizes on the last sentence of the argument, which is a tangential statement that has no bearing on the overall conclusion. **(D)** is off base because the argument deals with the likelihood that a bird will bite someone, not with the likelihood that the bite is serious. **(E)** commits a similar error by dealing with treatment; this argument is only concerned with the relative frequency of bird bites occurring in the first place and not with the treatment plans for bites that have already occurred. Choice **(A)** is correct.

25. (A)

A team of researchers at a university hospital has developed a chemical test that detects breast tumors in the early stages of development. In order to save lives, the researchers want to make the test a routine part of examinations at the hospital. However, a spokesperson for the hospital argued that because virtually all breast tumors are detectable by self-examination, the chemical test would have little impact on the breast cancer death rate.

Which of the following, if true, would most seriously weaken the hospital spokesperson's argument?

○ Fatal breast tumors are often not revealed by self-examination until it is too late for effective treatment.

○ Breast tumors are usually discovered at an earlier stage of development than are lung tumors.

○ Mammograms are currently in wide use as a breast cancer test and cost much less than the chemical test.

○ Because men are not typically victims of breast cancer, the new test would benefit only half of the population.

○ Most women learn how to check for signs of breast cancer from magazines and not from doctors.

Step 1: Identify the Question Type

In addition to using the word "weaken" to signal the question type, this question stem points us to the "spokesperson's argument."

Step 2: Untangle the Stimulus

The spokesperson's conclusion is a prediction that the chemical test will have little impact on the breast cancer death rate. The spokesperson's evidence is that virtually all breast tumors are detectable by self-examination.

Step 3: Predict the Answer

The spokesperson assumes that the chemical test has no advantage over self-examination. Because this is a Weaken question, we need the answer choice that contradicts this assumption—so we'll scan for a choice that cites an advantage of the chemical test.

Step 4: Evaluate the Choices

(A) suggests a possible advantage of the chemical test. The stimulus states that the chemical test "detects breast tumors in the early stages of development." If it is true that self-examination reveals those same tumors too late for effective treatment, then the chemical test might in fact have an impact on the breast cancer death rate, and the conclusion is weakened. This is the correct answer. **(B)** is an irrelevant comparison between breast tumors and lung tumors. **(C)** introduces a different diagnostic tool, mammograms, which are outside the scope of the question of whether the chemical test would have any positive impact relative to self-examination. **(D)** is outside the scope. The fact that men typically do not contract breast cancer is irrelevant to the question of whether the chemical test would positively impact the breast cancer death rate. **(E)** is again outside the scope. Where women learn to do breast exams has no bearing on the assumption that the chemical test has no advantage over those exams. Choice **(A)** is the correct answer.

26. (A)

Thousands who suffer heart attacks each year die before reaching a hospital or clinic where they can benefit from the drugs that dissolve clots found in coronary arteries. The Food and Drug Administration recently approved a new blood clot–dissolving agent, which a spokesperson claimed could save the lives of many people who would otherwise join this group of heart attack victims.

Which of the following statements, if true, would most weaken the argument above?

O The new agent must be administered by a team of doctors in a hospital or clinic setting.

O Many heart attack victims die unnecessarily even though they reach a hospital or clinic in time.

O The new agent can be effectively administered prior to the victim's arrival at a hospital or clinic.

O The Food and Drug Administration has already approved agents that are at least as effective as the new drug in dissolving blood clots.

O The new blood clot–dissolving agent causes kidney damage and irregular heart rates in some patients.

Step 1: Identify the Question Type

The word "weaken" in the question stem is the clearest indication of a Weaken question.

Step 2: Untangle the Stimulus

The argument we're seeking to weaken is that of the FDA spokesperson, who claims that the new blood clot–dissolving agent approved by the FDA could save the lives of people who would otherwise die of their heart attacks before reaching a hospital or clinic.

Step 3: Predict the Answer

The spokesperson's conclusion can be characterized as a prediction. Before evaluating the choices, let's determine what would have to happen in order for that prediction to come true. In order for the blood clot–dissolving agent to save these lives that the spokesperson mentions, it would have to be administered before people get to the hospital, since that's the critical life-saving window. So to weaken the argument, we need an answer that demonstrates that this won't happen.

Step 4: Evaluate the Choices

It doesn't get much more straightforward than **(A)**, which is the correct answer. If the agent must be administered in the hospital, then it doesn't do this group of people any good, since they ordinarily die before they can get to the hospital. **(B)** doesn't weaken the argument because it doesn't tell us that the new dissolving agent won't help these heart-attack victims. **(C)** strengthens the argument by suggesting that paramedics will have a chance to save victims without having to bring them to the hospital first. **(D)** has no effect; even if there are other agents out there, that doesn't mean that this new agent won't be helpful. And **(E)** does introduce some potentially nasty side effects, but the spokesperson doesn't argue that the new agent won't cause side effects; he merely argues that the drug will save lives. Choice **(A)** is correct.

27. (C)

According to a recent study, advertisements in medical journals often contain misleading information about the effectiveness and safety of new prescription drugs. The medical researchers who wrote the study concluded that the advertisements could result in doctors' prescribing inappropriate drugs to their patients.

The researchers' conclusion would be most strengthened if which of the following were true?

○   Advertisements for new prescription drugs are an important source of revenue for medical journals.

○   Editors of medical journals are often unable to evaluate the claims made in advertisements for new prescription drugs.

○   Doctors rely on the advertisements as a source of information about new prescription drugs.

○   Advertisements for new prescription drugs are typically less accurate than medical journal articles evaluating those same drugs.

○   The Food and Drug Administration, the government agency responsible for drug regulation, reviews advertisements for new drugs only after the ads have already been printed.

Step 1: Identify the Question Type

The phrase "most strengthened" tells us that this is a Strengthen question.

Step 2: Untangle the Stimulus

The researchers' argument concludes with a prediction: Doctors will prescribe inappropriate drugs to their patients. This is apparently because advertisements in medical journals often contain misleading information about certain drugs.

Step 3: Predict the Answer

To strengthen this argument, you want a choice that gives a reason or reasons why the prediction will come to pass. What circumstances would lead to inappropriate prescriptions? Since the inaccurate information comes from medical journals, doctors will probably be more likely to prescribe inappropriate drugs if they base their decisions on what they read in the journals.

Step 4: Evaluate the Choices

If doctors rely on the ads in medical journals to learn about new drugs, as **(C)** suggests, then inaccurate information could very well lead to faulty prescriptions. So, **(C)** is correct. **(A)** tells us why the journals carry the ads, but it doesn't strengthen the idea that doctors will use them to make inappropriate prescriptions. **(B)** could explain why the ads are published despite the inaccurate and misleading information contained in them, but like **(A)**, **(B)** does not provide a bridge to doctors' inappropriate prescriptions. **(D)** makes an irrelevant comparison between the accuracy of ads and that of articles. **(E)**, like **(B)**, explains how an ad can make it to print with inaccurate information, but **(E)** doesn't tell us how an inaccurate ad necessarily translates to a faulty prescription by a doctor, so **(E)** can't strengthen the researchers' prediction. Choice **(C)** is the correct answer.

28. (E)

To avoid the appearance of conflicts of interest, the board of a major U.S. stock exchange is considering a new policy that would ban former top executives of the exchange from taking positions at publicly traded companies for a period of two years after leaving the stock exchange. Critics of the plan say the policy is unfair because it would likely prevent former top executives of the exchange from earning a decent living.

Which of the following statements, if true, would most strengthen the prediction made by the critics of the proposed company policy?

O   The labor union that represents most of the stock exchange's employees has made public statements that threaten a strike if the policy is adopted.

O   Former employees of the exchange most often work for publicly traded companies after leaving the exchange.

O   Low-level managers at the exchange have an average tenure of 13 years, one of the longest in the industry.

O   Low-level managers at the exchange most often leave their jobs for positions with the state or federal government.

O   Former top executives of the exchange have a particular set of skills such that they are usually only able to find work with publicly traded companies.

Step 1: Identify the Question Type

We're looking to strengthen the argument here—specifically the prediction made by the critics of a policy. So as we examine the stimulus, the critics' argument will be most helpful.

Step 2: Untangle the Stimulus

A new policy would ban former top executives of a major stock exchange from working for publicly traded companies for two years after leaving the exchange. Critics of the policy contend that the policy will prevent the top executives from earning a decent living.

Step 3: Predict the Answer

Since we're strengthening the prediction, let's look for an answer choice that makes it more likely that the former top execs can't earn a decent living. A good prediction is "something that explains why top executives must work at publicly traded companies in order to make a decent living."

Step 4: Evaluate the Choices

So we should definitely select **(E)**, which states that former top executives of the firm can usually only find work at publicly traded companies because of their particular skill set. If this were true, then a two-year ban on working for publicly traded companies would mean no work for most former top executives (and by extension, no decent living), thus strengthening the prediction stated by critics of the plan. Whether or not the union strikes has no bearing on the effect the new policy would have on the former executives if enacted; thus **(A)** is incorrect. **(B)** simply states that most former employees of the exchange work for publicly traded companies; it does not tell us that they could not make a decent living elsewhere if need be. **(C)** and **(D)** refer to low-level managers, and the prediction only discusses top executives; thus both are outside the scope and incorrect. Choice **(E)** is correct.

29. (B)

The increase in taxes on cigarettes next month will not limit the use of addictive tobacco products to the extent that health advocates hope. Many cigarette smokers will shift their spending to cigars and chewing tobacco when the law takes effect.

Which of the following, if true, would most strongly weaken the argument above?

○ Cigars and chewing tobacco can satisfy the nicotine cravings of most cigarette smokers.

○ The taste, smell, and texture of cigars and chewing tobacco are sufficiently different from those of cigarettes to deter cigarette smokers from using them.

○ Many health advocates themselves use tobacco products.

○ The government might also impose significant taxes on cigars and chewing tobacco over the course of two years.

○ Cigars and chewing tobacco are often more expensive than cigarettes.

Step 1: Identify the Question Type

The wording is a little strange ("most strongly weaken"), but this is ultimately a Weaken question.

Step 2: Untangle the Stimulus

The conclusion in this argument is a prediction. According to the conclusion, many current cigarette smokers will shift their spending to cigars and chewing tobacco because of an impending increase in taxes on cigarettes. We could also look at this as a causality argument, as it asserts that the price of cigarettes affects smoking behavior.

Step 3: Predict the Answer

If you are using the plan/proposal/prediction approach, your prediction would be "something that explains why cigarette smokers won't use cigars or chewing tobacco, even though taxes on cigarettes will increase." And if you are approaching this argument focusing on causality, your prediction would likely be "another factor that affects smoking behavior." (The other two ways of weakening causality aren't very reasonable here—smoking behavior doesn't affect the price one pays for cigarettes, and we know from the stimulus that the price of cigarettes isn't set by coincidence.)

Step 4: Evaluate the Choices

(B) effectively weakens the author's prediction: If the differences in taste, smell, and texture will deter smokers from using cigars and chewing tobacco, then it is unlikely that cigarette smokers will shift their spending to them even if taxes are raised. They may find cigarette smoking prohibitively expensive, but they won't be likely to switch to other tobacco products, no matter how much cheaper those products are. And if you were looking for a new factor that affects smoking behavior, here there are three: taste, smell, and texture. **(A)** is a 180. It strengthens the author's prediction in the last sentence: If cigars and chewing tobacco satisfy the same nicotine cravings as cigarettes, then it is likely that cigarette smokers will buy them instead if taxes on cigarettes are raised. **(C)** is outside the scope, because the personal habits of health advocates have no bearing on the author's prediction. **(D)** is similarly outside the scope: The author's prediction is concerned only with the spending of consumers next month, not in two years. **(E)** is tempting at first glance, but it doesn't provide enough information to weaken the argument. Will cigars and chewing tobacco still be more expensive than cigarettes after the tax increase? Without more specific information, **(E)** doesn't weaken the argument. Choice **(B)** is correct.

30. (D)

The percentage of local businesses with more than 10 employees is higher in Grandview City than in any other city in the state. However, the percentage of local businesses with 15 employees or more is higher in Lakeshore City, which is in the same state, than in any other city in the state.

If the statements above are true, then which of the following must also be true?

○ The percentage of local business with more than 18 employees is higher in Lakeshore City than in any other city in the state.

○ The state has more local businesses with more than 10 employees than any other state in the country.

○ The number of local businesses with 15 or more employees is greater in Lakeshore City than in Grandview City.

○ Some local businesses in Grandview City have 11 to 14 employees.

○ The average number of employees per business is higher in Lakeshore City than in Grandview City.

Step 1: Identify the Question Type

This question asks us to choose the answer that makes a valid deduction from the stimulus, so it is an Inference question.

Step 2: Untangle the Stimulus

Usually, the stimulus of an Inference question will not include an argument. We just need to read and understand the statements in the stimulus and take note of any connections between them. This stimulus really just provides two related pieces of information: Grandview has the highest percentage of businesses with 11+ employees, while Lakeshore has the highest percentage with 15+.

Step 3: Predict the Answer

Grandview has the highest percentage of businesses with 11+ employees, but not the highest percentage with 15+. The only way that's possible is if Grandview has at least a few businesses with 11–14 employees. We might use Picking Numbers to make this deduction more obvious. For instance, let's say that both Grandview and Lakeshore have 100 businesses. If Grandview has 25 businesses with 11+ employees, and Lakeshore has 20 businesses with 15+ employees, Lakeshore could still have the higher percentage of 15+ employee businesses if Grandview has more than 5 businesses with 11–14 employees. What "must be true" is that Grandview has at least a few businesses with 11–14 employees. We'll be looking for an answer choice that says so.

Step 4: Evaluate the Choices

(D) matches our prediction perfectly and is the correct answer. **(A)** is incorrect because businesses with more than 18 employees are outside the scope of the stimulus. **(B)** introduces an irrelevant comparison between states. We're only interested in two specific cities within one state, not in any other states. **(C)** is a bit tricky, but the actual number of businesses is outside the scope; we're concerned only with percentages, not raw numbers. Finally, **(E)** introduces another irrelevant point. We care only about businesses with very specific numbers of employees, not about the average number of employees per business. Choice **(D)** is the correct answer.

31. (C)

It appears that the number of people employed by a typical American software firm decreased in the 1980s and 1990s. This trend is borne out by two studies, conducted 20 years apart. In a large 1980 sample of randomly chosen American software firms, the median size of the firms' workforce populations was 65. When those same firms were studied again in 2000, the median size was 57.

Which of the following points to the most serious logical flaw in the reasoning above?

O   The median number of employees in American firms in many industries decreased during the 1980s and 1990s.

O   During the 1980s and 1990s, many software firms increased the extent to which they relied on subcontractors to write code.

O   The data in the studies refer only to companies that existed in 1980.

O   The studies focused on the number of employees, but there are many ways of judging a firm's size, such as revenues and profits.

O   The median number of employees is not as sound a measure of the number of employees employed in an industry as is the mean number of employees, which accounts for the vast size of the few large firms that dominate most industries.

Step 1: Identify the Question Type

Since the question stem asks for a "logical flaw," we're dealing with a Flaw question here.

Step 2: Untangle the Stimulus

The argument concludes that the typical American software firm employs fewer people in the 2000s than it did in the 1980s and 1990s. This conclusion is supported by two studies; in order for the conclusion to be valid, both studies need to be representative.

Step 3: Predict the Answer

The sample in the 1980 study seems legitimate: It was large and randomly chosen. However, notice the problem with the 2000 study: It uses the same firms as in the 1980 study. The firms are no longer randomly chosen, nor does the sample size account for the many software firms that presumably sprang up between 1980 and 2000. In other words, the sample in the second survey was not representative of all American software firms.

Step 4: Evaluate the Choices

This prediction matches **(C)**, which pinpoints a problem with the representativeness of the 2000 survey. If the firms surveyed included only those that also existed 20 years ago, then no information is included about firms that have come into existence since then. If the survey is not based on information about all American software firms, including those that have come into existence over the last 20 years, then the survey is not representative, and any conclusions drawn from those results are called into question. **(A)**'s focus on many industries is outside the scope of the argument, which is concerned only with the number of people employed by a typical American software firm. **(B)** gives a plausible explanation of why the median size of firms is decreasing, but it fails to describe a flaw in the argument. **(D)** is irrelevant: The survey is concerned with the firm's size in terms of workforce population. All other measures of a firm's size are outside the scope. Finally, **(E)** is not a flaw in this argument. While it may be true that the mean is a better measure for total workforce population in an industry, this argument concerns the number of employees in *a typical firm* in one industry, not across the industry as a whole. Choice **(C)** is correct.

32. (B)

The Ministry of Tourism in country X began an expensive television advertising campaign in country Y two years ago. Since that time, the number of visitors to country X from country Y has increased by more than 8 percent. Clearly, the Ministry of Tourism's campaign is responsible for the increase.

Which of the following, if true, would most weaken the argument above?

- ○ The advertisements sponsored by the Ministry of Tourism in country X were panned by the country Y media for lack of imagination.
- ○ A devaluation of the currency in country X two years ago made travel there more affordable for residents of country Y.
- ○ Increasing political turmoil in country X will lead to a decrease in visitors from country Y next year.
- ○ The number of visitors from country Y to country Z increased by more than 8 percent over the past two years.
- ○ Over the past two years, the advertisement campaign launched by the Ministry of Tourism in country X cost more money than residents of country Y spent traveling in country X.

Step 1: Identify the Question Type

The question stem clearly indicates that this is a Weaken question.

Step 2: Untangle the Stimulus

The conclusion is that the Ministry of Tourism's ad campaign is responsible for the increase in the number of visitors from country Y to country X. The evidence is that since the ad campaign began running, the number of visitors from country Y to country X has gone up by more than 8 percent.

Step 3: Predict the Answer

This is a very straightforward causal argument. While there are three classic alternatives to a causal argument (reverse cause and effect, find an alternative cause, or suggest coincidence), the most common way of weakening a causal argument is to exploit the second alternative—citing another possible cause for the phenomenon. So let's look for an answer choice that offers another explanation for the increase of tourism from country Y.

Step 4: Evaluate the Choices

And **(B)** offers that alternative explanation. If travel to country X became more affordable at the same time that tourism to country X increased, it is possible that the devaluation in currency is responsible for this increase rather than the Ministry of Tourism's ad campaign. While it does not *disprove* that the ad campaign was the cause of the increase, it certainly weakens the author's argument by presenting another potential cause of the increase. **(A)** does not effectively weaken the argument. Just because the media panned the ads does not mean they could not have spurred the increase in tourism. The prediction in **(C)** is irrelevant to the author's argument about the past efficacy of the Ministry of Tourism's ad campaign. **(D)** ventures outside the scope by bringing up tourism in country Z. And **(E)** is irrelevant: The author is only concerned with establishing a causal relationship between the ad campaign and increased tourism, not with whether the campaign was cost-effective. Choice **(B)** is the correct answer.

33. (D)

A study of children's television-watching habits by the federal Department of Education found that children aged 7–10 who watched more than 25 hours of television per week performed worse in school than children of the same age who watched fewer than 25 hours of television per week. Therefore, parents of children aged 7–10 should prohibit their children from watching more than 25 hours of television per week.

Which of the following, if true, would best strengthen the argument above?

○ A separate study, by a renowned graduate school of education, found that when parents prohibited their children from watching any television, the children's reading scores increased rapidly and significantly and stayed high indefinitely.

○ Children who watched more than 25 hours of television per week also performed worse on measures of physical fitness than children who watched fewer than 25 hours per week.

○ The television shows that children aged 7–10 are most likely to watch are saturated with advertisements for products, such as toys and candy, of little educational value.

○ The Department of Education study gave appropriate weight to children of backgrounds representative of children nationwide.

○ Children who develop a habit of extensive television watching are more likely than others to maintain that habit as an adult.

Step 1: Identify the Question Type

Here, we're clearly asked to strengthen the argument; question stems don't get much more straightforward than this.

Step 2: Untangle the Stimulus

As soon as you read the words "a study," know that you're probably dealing with a classic representativeness argument. The argument concludes that parents of children aged 7–10 should limit their kids' TV watching to 25 hours per week. The evidence is a study indicating that kids aged 7–10 who watched more than 25 hours a week did worse in school.

Step 3: Predict the Answer

In order to strengthen an argument that relies on a survey as evidence, look for an answer choice that states that the sample used in the survey is representative of the population mentioned in the conclusion.

Step 4: Evaluate the Choices

(D) validates the representativeness of the sample directly. The author's conclusion is about all parents of children aged 7–10. A study that "gives appropriate weight" to kids with diverse backgrounds is therefore more representative. (D) is the correct answer. (A) is out of scope because it deals with parents who prohibit their children from watching *any* television, rather than parents who hold their kids to a 25-hour-per-week limit. (B) is not relevant because it concerns physical fitness tests, not school performance. (C) does nothing to suggest that parents should limit their children's television watching to 25 hours per week. It merely offers one reason that the shows kids watch are of little educational value. And (E) is outside the scope. The argument is not concerned with the habits of these children as they age; it deals only with the school performance of children from age 7 to 10. Choice (D) is correct.

34. (D)

Cable Television Executive: **Our service and reliability have increased dramatically over the past year.** Our customer service line is receiving 30 percent fewer reports of interrupted service, and the number of subscribers canceling their accounts is barely half of what it was last year.

Cable Television Customer: That doesn't mean your service and reliability have improved. **It's possible that customers don't bother to call your customer service line to report problems because they never get any assistance when they do.** And the drop-off in the number of canceled accounts could reflect the fact that nearly all of your dissatisfied customers have already canceled their accounts.

In the argument above, the two portions in boldface play which of the following roles?

O   The first is evidence designed to lead to a conclusion; the second offers further evidence in support of that conclusion.

O   The first is evidence designed to lead to a conclusion; the second offers evidence designed to cast doubt on that conclusion.

O   The first is a conclusion; the second offers evidence in support of that conclusion.

O   The first is a conclusion; the second offers evidence designed to cast doubt on that conclusion.

O   The first is a conclusion; the second is an alternative conclusion based on the same evidence.

Step 1: Identify the Question Type

This stem offers standard language for a Bolded Statement question—it asks us to determine the roles played in the arguments by each of the boldface statements.

Step 2: Untangle the Stimulus

The cable television executive uses evidence of fewer customer complaints and cancellations to conclude that the cable company's service has improved over the past year. The customer disagrees, providing an alternative explanation for the executive's evidence. According to the customer, there are fewer cancellations because all the dissatisfied customers have already canceled their accounts, and the decreased number of complaints indicates that frustrated customers have just given up.

Step 3: Predict the Answer

The first bolded statement is the cable executive's conclusion, and the second bolded statement is evidence from the customer that would support a contradictory conclusion.

Step 4: Evaluate the Choices

(D) is correct; the second statement is designed to cast doubt on the validity of the conclusion in the first. Since the first bolded statement represents the executive's conclusion, we can eliminate **(A)** and **(B)**, which characterize this statement as evidence. The customer clearly disagrees with the executive, so we can eliminate **(C)**. **(E)** is tricky; the second statement does provide an alternate explanation of some of the evidence, but the second statement is not a conclusion, merely a possible interpretation. Always read diligently so that you can avoid half-right, half-wrong answer choices. Choice **(D)** is correct.

35. **(C)**

Opponents of the laws prohibiting nonprescription narcotic drugs argue that in a free society, people have the right to take risks as long as the risks do not constitute a harm to others who have not elected to take such risks. These opponents conclude that it should be each person's decision whether or not to use narcotic drugs.

Which of the following, if true, most seriously weakens the conclusion drawn above?

- ○ Some narcotic drugs have been shown to have medicinal qualities.
- ○ There are laws that govern the use of prescription drugs.
- ○ Studies have shown that people who use nonprescription drugs are much more likely to perpetrate a violent crime when intoxicated than when sober.
- ○ People who use narcotic drugs are twice as likely to die of an overdose as of natural causes.
- ○ The rate of drug overdoses is higher in countries that do not have laws governing the use of narcotic drugs than in countries that do have such laws.

Step 1: Identify the Question Type

The phrase "weakens the conclusion" in the question stem announces that this is a Weaken question.

Step 2: Untangle the Stimulus

As in all argument-based questions, we need to find the conclusion and evidence. The conclusion is the last sentence: Use of nonprescription narcotic drugs should be everyone's personal decision. The evidence is that people have the right to take risks as long as taking those risks doesn't hurt anyone besides themselves.

Step 3: Predict the Answer

In a Weaken question, the correct answer will challenge the argument's central assumption. The opponents assume that nonprescription narcotics pose risks only to the people who use them. If narcotics could harm non-users, however, then narcotic use would not be a permissible risk; individuals would no longer have the right to use those drugs. Because this is a Weaken question, we'll look for an answer choice that says that taking narcotics *can* in fact harm others besides the drug users themselves.

Step 4: Evaluate the Choices

(C) does the job perfectly. If people are more likely to commit violent crimes while under the influence of drugs, then others are at risk from the drug use, and the conclusion that it is everyone's personal right to choose whether to use drugs is greatly weakened. **(C)** is thus the correct answer. **(A)** is incorrect because it introduces the idea of medicinal qualities, which is outside the scope of the argument. The prescription drugs in **(B)** are likewise outside the scope of the argument, which is concerned only with nonprescription drugs. **(D)** has no bearing on the argument since it describes only a risk to the user of the drug, rather than a risk to others. Finally, **(E)** is an irrelevant comparison between two different sets of countries. The laws of those countries have no bearing on the argument because rates of overdose only indicate personal risk, not risk to others. Choice **(C)** is the correct answer.

EXPLANATIONS

36. (A)

In a survey of undergraduates, two-fifths admitted to having cheated on an exam at least once during their education. However, the survey may underestimate the proportion of undergraduates who have cheated, because _____.

Which of the following best completes the passage above?

○ some undergraduates who have cheated at least once might have claimed on the survey never to have cheated

○ some undergraduates who have never cheated might have claimed on the survey to have cheated

○ some undergraduates who claimed on the survey to have cheated at least once may have cheated on multiple occasions throughout their education

○ some undergraduates who claimed on the survey to have cheated at least once may have been answering honestly

○ some students who are not undergraduates have probably cheated at least once during their education

Step 1: Identify the Question Type

Here, we have an Inference question that asks us to complete the final sentence of a brief argument.

Step 2: Untangle the Stimulus

The portion of the sentence we need to complete begins with the keyword "because." That tells us that whatever is to fill in the blank must provide evidence for what came before it in the sentence. The author's conclusion is that the survey may have underestimated the proportion of undergraduates who cheated. We know from the first sentence that two-fifths of the students *reported* having cheated at least once. The author implies that there are additional unreported cheaters out there.

Step 3: Predict the Answer

Our prediction cannot be too specific, but its criteria are crystal clear. The one correct answer will provide a reason to think that there are additional, unreported cheaters among the undergraduate population.

Step 4: Evaluate the Choices

(A) is a perfect match for our prediction: Some undergrads may have cheated but lied about it on the survey. If we were looking for a reason why the survey might *overestimate* the proportion of undergrads cheating, **(B)** would be correct. **(C)** refers to multiple cases of cheating per student; the survey is only dealing with the proportion of students who have cheated at least once. **(D)** gives a reason why we might believe the survey is accurate, which is the opposite of what we want, and **(E)** introduces students who are not undergrads, which is out of the scope of the survey. Choice **(A)** is correct.

EXPLANATIONS

37. (C)

During the last 18 years, the number of people who live or work in the Dry River Valley, which is prone to flash flooding, has continually increased, as has traffic on local roads and bridges. However, the number of people caught in flash floods has decreased, even though the annual number of floods has increased slightly.

Which of the following, if true, best explains the decrease described above?

○ Flash floods are more likely to happen in the first hour of a rainstorm than afterward.

○ Flash floods killed some people in the Dry River Valley in every one of the last 18 years.

○ Better meteorological technology, combined with a better understanding of the conditions conducive to flash flooding, has increasingly improved local authorities' ability to predict when and where flash floods will occur.

○ Many people work in the Dry River Valley but live elsewhere.

○ A law that went into effect 18 years ago mandated that all new homes built in the valley be built on raised foundations, making those homes much less susceptible to flood damage.

Step 1: Identify the Question Type

This is an Explain question. We can anticipate seeing a paradox or unusual coincidence described in the stimulus. Our task is to resolve the seemingly disparate pieces of information in order to explain the anomalous result.

Step 2: Untangle the Stimulus

The stimulus tells us about two increases—the number of people and the number of flash floods—in the Dry River Valley. The keyword "However" signals the seeming discrepancy: Despite those increases, the number of people caught in flash floods has gone down. Let's think critically about how we can reconcile these facts.

Step 3: Predict the Answer

Sometimes we can know exactly what the right answer choice is going to say, but that's rare for Explain questions. Here, the stimulus involves numbers (of residents, floods, and flood victims), but it doesn't state any actual values. Picking Numbers can help us visualize the situation in the stimulus.

Pick numbers that are permissible and manageable. Let's say that 18 years ago, there were 1,000 people, 10 floods, and 100 flood victims in the valley. Following the information in the stimulus, let's say there are now 2,000 people, 20 floods, and 50 victims.

	18 years ago	now
people	1,000	2,000
floods	10	20
people caught in floods	100	50

This shows that the floods are now less dangerous.

	18 years ago	now
proportion of people caught in floods	1 in 10	1 in 40
people caught per flood	10	2.5

The correct answer will explain this change. It will provide a reason why the floods have been less dangerous.

Step 4: Evaluate the Choices

(C) gives us the explanation we need: More accurate advance notice of floods allows local authorities to better prevent people from getting caught. **(A)** may be true of flash flooding in general, but it doesn't give us any difference between the floods now and those 18 years ago. **(B)** is outside the scope of the question, which deals with people *caught* in the floods, not people killed by them. **(D)** doesn't explain the difference either, as there's no reason to think that flash floods somehow selectively avoid commuters. **(E)** is also out of scope, since the argument does not focus on property damage. Choice **(C)** is correct.

38. (E)

Colleges in Tycho City have failed to prepare their students for the business world. A recent study revealed that the majority of college graduates in Tycho City could not write a simple business letter.

Which of the following, if true, would provide additional evidence in support of the claim above?

O   A majority of students attending colleges in Tycho City are business majors.

O   The State College in neighboring Twyla Township has recently improved its business program by adding courses in business writing.

O   Most Tycho City college graduates move outside the Tycho City area after they graduate.

O   Most Tycho City college students live in on-campus dormitories.

O   The majority of college graduates living in Tycho City received their college degrees from institutions located in Tycho City.

Step 1: Identify the Question Type

To "provide additional evidence in support" of an argument is to strengthen it, so this is a Strengthen question.

Step 2: Untangle the Stimulus

The argument concludes that colleges in Tycho City don't do a good job of preparing their grads for the business world, because the majority of college grads living in Tycho City couldn't write a simple business letter. Since this argument is based on a study, there is likely a representativeness problem.

Step 3: Predict the Answer

In this argument, the author makes a Scope shift between the evidence and the conclusion: The evidence is based on "college graduates in Tycho City," while the conclusion refers to the supposed failings of "colleges in Tycho City." In order for the conclusion to hold, it must be true that the college grads in the study are representative of colleges in Tycho City—that is, that those people actually attended school in Tycho City. Look for an answer that bolsters that assumption.

Step 4: Evaluate the Choices

(E) properly strengthens the argument by reinforcing the assumption. In other words, **(E)** demonstrates that the sample studied is actually representative of colleges in Tycho City. **(A)** has no effect on the argument. While the argument concerns whether students are prepared for the business world, it is not relevant what the students are majoring in. **(B)** is outside the scope. What some other college is doing does not affect an argument about the effectiveness of Tycho City college programs. **(C)** actually weakens the argument. If most Tycho City college graduates leave the Tycho City area after graduation, then it is unlikely that a study of graduates in Tycho City is representative of graduates of Tycho City colleges. Be careful of 180 answers in Strengthen/Weaken questions. Finally, **(D)** is irrelevant, since where the students live has no effect on whether or not they're adequately prepared for the business world. Choice **(E)** is the correct answer.

GMAT BY THE NUMBERS: CRITICAL REASONING

Now that you've learned how to approach Critical Reasoning questions on the GMAT, let's add one more dimension to your understanding of how they work.

Take a moment to try the following question. The next page features performance data from thousands of people who have studied with Kaplan over the decades. Through analyzing this data, we will show you how to approach questions like this one most effectively and how to avoid similarly tempting wrong answer choice types on Test Day.

> Wunderlich Park has a strict regulation that requires mountain bicyclists to wear helmets. Recently, a group of bicyclists acknowledged that helmets may prevent injuries to the wearer, but protested claiming the park should only regulate activities that may hurt a third party. Hence, the bicyclists argued that they should have the right to refrain from wearing helmets.
>
> Which of the following, if true, most seriously weakens the conclusion in the passage?
>
> O   Ninety percent of bicyclists who use Wunderlich Park prefer to wear a helmet to protect themselves in case of an accident.
>
> O   Lawyers for Wunderlich Park have warned that the repeal of the helmet regulation would lead to an increase in general admission park entrance fees to cover the legal expenses associated with personal injury lawsuits.
>
> O   Motorcyclists in a neighboring county are required to wear a helmet while on the road.
>
> O   Parks that require the use of helmets have a lower percentage of accidents resulting in deaths than parks that don't require the use of helmets.
>
> O   More bicyclists who do not wear helmets are seriously injured in accidents than bicyclists who do wear helmets.

EXPLANATION

The argument's conclusion is presented in the final sentence, introduced by the keyword "hence": The bicyclists claim that they shouldn't have to wear helmets in the park. But despite the wording of the question, it isn't really the *conclusion* itself that the testmakers want you to weaken—rather, you must weaken the *logic supporting that conclusion*. According to this argument, the reason why cyclists shouldn't be made to wear helmets is that the park should not restrict an activity that doesn't harm others. The right answer, therefore, will show how not wearing a helmet actually does harm someone else.

The correct answer—choice **(B)**—does just that; it shows how cyclists' not wearing helmets would in fact harm non-cyclists: The harm would be financial.

QUESTION STATISTICS

10% of test takers choose **(A)**

46% of test takers choose **(B)**

2% of test takers choose **(C)**

23% of test takers choose **(D)**

19% of test takers choose **(E)**

Sample size = 3,132

The three most commonly selected wrong answers are wrong because they do not address the entire argument, only the general sense of the conclusion. Answer choices **(D)** and **(E)** both give good reasons to wear a helmet, but they suggest that only the cyclist is at risk, not someone else. Choice **(A)** discusses cyclists' preferences, but the argument about when to permit regulation has to do only with whether others would be harmed, not with personal preference. You can see that answers that ignore an argument's reasoning are popular, and as such are very common. Learn to avoid them, and you'll go a long way to improving your GMAT score.

MORE GMAT BY THE NUMBERS ...

To see more questions with answer choice statistics, be sure to review the full-length CATs in your Online Center.

CHAPTER 7

Reading Comprehension

It can be inferred from the passage that supporters of the Alvarez and Courtillot theories would hold which of the following views in common?

O   The KT boundary was formed over many thousands of years.

O   Large animals such as the dinosaurs died out gradually over millions of years.

O   Mass extinction occurred as an indirect result of debris saturating the atmosphere.

O   It is unlikely that the specific cause of the Cretaceous extinctions will ever be determined.

O   Volcanic activity may have been triggered by shock waves from the impact of an asteroid.

Above is a typical Reading Comprehension question. For now, don't worry that we haven't given you the passage this question refers to. In this chapter, we'll look at how to apply the Kaplan Method to this question, discuss the types of questions the GMAT asks about reading passages, and go over the basic principles and strategies that you want to keep in mind on every Reading Comprehension question. But before you move on, take a minute to think about what you see in the structure of this question and answer some questions about how you think it works:

- What does it mean to draw an inference from a GMAT passage?

- How much are you expected to know about the subject matter of the passages before you take the test?

- What can you expect to see in a GMAT passage that discusses two related theories?

- What GMAT Core Competencies are most essential to success on this question?

PREVIEWING READING COMPREHENSION

WHAT DOES IT MEAN TO DRAW AN INFERENCE FROM A GMAT PASSAGE?

You may remember from the Critical Reasoning chapter the definition of an "inference" on the GMAT: An inference is something that *must* be true, based on the information provided. There are two important parts to this definition:

(1) A valid GMAT inference *must* be true. This sets a high standard for what you consider a valid inference. It is sometimes difficult to determine whether a statement in an answer choice must always be true, but you can also approach these questions by eliminating the four answer choices that *could* be false. Keep both of these tactics in mind for questions that ask for an inference.

(2) A valid GMAT inference is based on the passage. By definition, an inference won't be explicitly stated in the passage; you will have to understand the passage well enough to read between the lines. But just because it isn't directly stated doesn't mean an inference could be anything under the sun. On the GMAT, any inference you draw will be unambiguously supported by something that is stated in the passage. It may take some Critical Thinking to figure out, but you will always be able to pinpoint exactly why a valid inference must be true.

HOW MUCH ARE YOU EXPECTED TO KNOW ABOUT THE SUBJECT MATTER OF THE PASSAGES BEFORE YOU TAKE THE TEST?

Familiarity with the subject matter is not required. GMAT passages contain everything you need to answer GMAT questions. In fact, many Reading Comp questions contain wrong answer choices based on information that is actually true but not mentioned in the passage. So if you know the subject, be careful not to let your prior knowledge influence your answer. And if you don't know the subject, be happy—some wrong answer traps won't be tempting to you!

Reading Comprehension is designed to test not your prior knowledge but your critical reading skills. Among other things, it tests whether you can do the following:

- Summarize the main idea of a passage.
- Understand logical relationships between facts and concepts.
- Make inferences based on information in a text.
- Analyze the logical structure of a passage.
- Deduce the author's tone and attitude about a topic from the text.

Note that none of these objectives relies on anything other than your ability to understand and apply ideas found in the passage. This should be a comforting thought: Everything you need is right there in front of you. In this chapter, you will learn strategic approaches to help you make the best use of the information the testmakers provide.

WHAT CAN YOU EXPECT TO SEE IN A GMAT PASSAGE THAT DISCUSSES TWO RELATED THEORIES?

Because the GMAT cannot ask you purely factual questions that might reward or punish you for your outside knowledge, it tends to focus its questions on the opinions or analyses contained in the passages. Since this question asks you what Alvarez's and Courtillot's theories have in common, this means that they must agree on at least one thing. You can anticipate, however, that the two theories are largely *not* in agreement with each other.

This is a common structure for a GMAT passage: The author discusses more than one explanation of the same phenomenon, describing each in turn or perhaps comparing them directly, usually summarizing the relevant evidence and explaining why disagreement exists among the explanations' proponents. When a passage contains multiple opinions, keep track of who is making each assertion and how the assertion relates to the other opinions in the passage: Does it contradict, agree with, or expand upon what came before? Another important thing to note is whether the author takes a side—does the author prefer one viewpoint to another? Does he offer his own competing argument?

WHAT GMAT CORE COMPETENCIES ARE MOST ESSENTIAL TO SUCCESS ON THIS QUESTION?

Since the GMAT constructs Reading Comprehension passages in similar ways and asks questions that conform to predictable "types," you can learn to anticipate how an author will express her ideas and what the GMAT testmakers will ask you about a passage. The more you practice and the more you focus on structure as you read, the stronger your Pattern Recognition skills will become.

Critical Thinking is also essential. As you read, you should ask yourself why the author is including certain details and what the author's choice of transitional keywords implies about how the ideas in the passage are related.

The best test takers learn how to pay Attention to the Right Detail. Reading Comp passages are typically filled with more details than you could reasonably memorize—and more, in fact, than you will ever need to answer the questions. Since time is limited, you must prioritize the information you assimilate from the passage, focusing on the big picture but allowing yourself to return to the passage to research details as needed.

Practice Paraphrasing constantly as you read, both to keep yourself engaged and to make sure you understand what's being discussed. Developing this habit will make taking notes much easier, since you've already distilled and summarized the most important information in your head. You'll learn later in this chapter how to take concise and well-organized notes in the form of a Passage Map.

Here are the main topics we'll cover in this chapter:

- Question Format and Structure
- The Basic Principles of Reading Comprehension
- The Kaplan Method for Reading Comprehension
- Reading Comprehension Question Types

QUESTION FORMAT AND STRUCTURE

The directions for Reading Comprehension questions look like this:

Directions: The questions in this group are based on the content of a passage. After reading the passage, choose the best answer to each question. Base your answers only according to what is stated or implied in the text.

In Reading Comp, you are presented with a reading passage (in an area of business, social science, biological science, or physical science) and then asked three or four questions about that text. You are not expected to be familiar with any topic beforehand—all the information you need is contained in the text in front of you. In fact, if you happen to have some previous knowledge about a given topic, it is important that you not let that knowledge affect your answers. Naturally, some passages will be easier to understand than others, though each will present a challenge. The passages will have the tone and content that one might expect from a scholarly journal.

You will see four Reading Comp passages—most likely two shorter passages with 3 questions each and two longer passages with 4 questions each, for a total of approximately 14 questions. However, as is usual for the computer-adaptive GMAT, you will see only one question at a time on the screen, and you will have to answer each question before you can see the next question. The passage will appear on the left side of the screen. It will remain there until you've answered all of the questions that relate to it. If the text is longer than the available space, you'll be given a scroll bar to move through it. Plan to take no longer than 4 minutes to read and make notes on the passage and a little less than 1.5 minutes to answer each question associated with the passage.

TAKEAWAYS: QUESTION FORMAT AND STRUCTURE

- GMAT passages are between one and five paragraphs in length.
- You will usually see two shorter and two longer passages in the Verbal section.
- Usually, you will get three questions for a shorter passage and four questions for a longer passage. You can answer only one at a time and can't go back to previous questions.
- The passages usually have the tone and content that one might expect from a scholarly journal.
- You are not expected to have prior knowledge of the subject matter in the passage.
- The passage stays on the screen for all questions that pertain to it.
- You should spend 4 minutes per passage and a little less than 1.5 minutes per question.

THE BASIC PRINCIPLES OF READING COMPREHENSION

In daily life, most people read to learn something or to pass the time pleasantly. Neither of these goals has much to do with the GMAT. On Test Day, you have a very specific goal—to get as many right answers as you can. So your reading needs to be tailored to that goal. There are really only two things a Reading Comp question can ask you about: the "big picture" of the passage or its "little details."

Since the passage is right there on the screen, you don't need to worry much about the "little details" as you read. (In fact, doing so may hinder your ability to answer questions, as you'll soon see.) So your main goal as you read is to prepare yourself to get the "big-picture" questions right, while leaving yourself as much time as possible to find the answers to the "little-detail" questions.

Here are the four basic principles you need to follow to accomplish this goal.

LOOK FOR THE TOPIC AND SCOPE OF THE PASSAGE

Think of the topic as the first big idea that comes along. Almost always, it will be right there in the first sentence. It will be something broad, far too big to discuss in the 150–350 words that most GMAT passages contain. Here's an example of how a passage might begin:

> The great migration of European intellectuals to the United States in the second quarter of the 20th century prompted a transmutation in the character of Western social thought.

What's the topic? The migration of European intellectuals to the United States in the second quarter of the 20th century. It would also be okay to say that the topic is the effects of that migration on Western social thought. Topic is a very broad concept, so you really don't need to worry about how exactly you word it. You just need to get a good idea of what the passage is talking about so you feel more comfortable reading.

Now, as to scope. Think of scope as a narrowing of the topic. You're looking for an idea that the author might reasonably focus on for the length of a GMAT passage. If the topic is "the migration of European intellectuals to the United States in the second quarter of the 20th century," then perhaps the scope will be "some of the effects of that migration upon Western social thought." It will likely be even more specific: "one aspect of Western social thought affected by the migration." But perhaps something unexpected will come along. Might the passage compare two different migrations? Or contrast two different effects? Think critically about what's coming and look for clues in the text that let you know on what specific subject(s) the author intends to focus.

Finding the scope is critically important to doing well on Reading Comp. As in Critical Reasoning, many Reading Comp wrong answers are wrong because they are outside the scope of the passage. It's highly unlikely that there will be a "topic sentence" that lays out plainly what the author intends to write about—but the first paragraph probably will give some indication of the focus of the rest of the passage.

Note that some passages are only one paragraph long. In these cases, the topic can still appear in the first sentence. The passage will probably (but not necessarily) narrow in scope somewhere in the first third of the paragraph, as the author doesn't have much text to work with and needs to get down to business quickly.

GET THE GIST OF EACH PARAGRAPH AND ITS STRUCTURAL ROLE IN THE PASSAGE

The paragraph is the main structural unit of any passage. At first, you don't yet know the topic or scope, so you have to read the first paragraph pretty closely. But once you get a sense of where the passage is going, all you need to do is understand what role each new paragraph plays. Ask yourself the following:

- Why did the author include this paragraph?
- What's discussed here that's different from the content of the paragraph before?
- What bearing does this paragraph have on the author's main idea?
- What role do the details play?

Notice that last question—don't ask yourself, "What does this mean?" but rather, "Why is it here?" Many GMAT passages try to swamp you with tedious, dense, and sometimes confusing details. Consider this paragraph, which might appear as part of a difficult science-based passage:

> The Burgess Shale yielded a surprisingly varied array of fossils. Early chordates were very rare, but there were prodigious numbers of complex forms not seen since. *Hallucigenia*, so named for a structure so bizarre that scientists did not know which was the dorsal and which the ventral side, had fourteen legs. *Opabinia* had five eyes and a long proboscis. This amazing diversity led Gould to believe that it was highly unlikely that the eventual success of chordates was a predictable outcome.

This is pretty dense stuff. But if you don't worry about understanding all of the science jargon and instead focus on the gist of the paragraph and *why* the details are there, things get easier. The first sentence isn't that bad:

> The Burgess Shale yielded a surprisingly varied array of fossils.

A quick paraphrase is that the "Burgess Shale," whatever that is, had a lot of different kinds of fossils. The passage continues:

> Early chordates were very rare, but there were prodigious numbers of complex forms not seen since. *Hallucigenia*, so named for a structure so bizarre that scientists did not know which was the dorsal and which the ventral side, had fourteen legs. *Opabinia* had five eyes and a long proboscis.

When you read this part of the passage strategically, asking what its purpose is in context, you see that this is just a list of the different kinds of fossils and some facts about them. There were not a lot of "chordates," whatever they are, but there was lots of other stuff.

> This amazing diversity led Gould to believe that it was highly unlikely that the eventual success of chordates was a predictable outcome.

Notice that the beginning of this sentence tells us *why* those intimidatingly dense details are there; they are the facts that led Gould to a belief—namely that the rise of "chordates" couldn't have been predicted. So, on your noteboard, you'd jot down something like this:

Evidence for Gould's belief—chordate success not predictable.

Notice that you don't have to know what any of these scientific terms mean in order to know why the author brings them up. Taking apart every paragraph like this allows you to create a map of the passage's overall structure. We'll call this a "Passage Map" from here on—we'll discuss Passage Mapping in detail later in this chapter. Making a Passage Map will help you acquire a clear understanding of the "big picture." It will give you a sense of mastery over the passage, even when it deals with a subject you don't know anything about.

To break down paragraphs and understand the structural function of each part, look for keywords, or structural words or phrases that link ideas to one another. You got an overview of the categories of keywords in the Verbal Section Overview chapter of this book. Let's now dig a little deeper into how keywords can help you distinguish the important things (such as opinions) from the unimportant (such as supporting examples) and to understand why the author wrote each sentence.

Types of keywords:

- **Contrast** keywords such as *but, however, nevertheless,* and *on the other hand* tell you that a change or disagreement is coming.

- **Continuation** keywords such as *moreover, also,* and *furthermore* tell you that the author is continuing on the same track or general idea.

- **Logic** keywords, which you've seen to be very important in Critical Reasoning stimuli, alert you to an author's reasoning. **Evidence** keywords let you know that something is being offered in support of a particular idea. The specifics of the support are usually unimportant for the first big-picture read, but you do want to know what the idea is. Examples of evidence keywords are *since, because,* and *as.* **Conclusion** keywords such as *therefore* and *hence* are usually *not* associated with the author's main point in Reading Comp. Rather, they indicate that the next phrase is a logical consequence of the sentence(s) that came before.

- **Illustration** keywords let you know that what follows is an example of a broader point. One example, of course, is *example*. *For instance* is another favorite in GMAT passages.

- **Sequence/Timing** is a broader category of keywords. These are any words that delineate lists or groupings. *First, second,* and *third* are obvious examples. But you could also get a chronological sequence (*17th century, 18th century,* and *today*). Science passages may also group complicated phenomena using simpler sequence keywords (*at a high temperature* and *at a low temperature*, for example).

- **Emphasis** and **Opinion** keywords can be subtler than those in the other categories, but these are perhaps the most important keywords of all. Emphasis keywords are used when the author wants to call attention to a specific point. These come in two varieties: generic emphasis keywords, such as *very* and *critical,* and charged emphasis keywords, such as *beneficial* or *dead end.* Opinion keywords point to the ideas in a passage; these opinions are frequently the focus of GMAT questions. Be sure to distinguish between the author's opinions and those of others. Others' opinions are easier to spot and will be triggered by words such as *believe, theory,* or *hypothesis.* The author's opinion is more likely to reveal itself in words that imply a value judgment, such as *valid* or *unsupported.* (If the passage expresses something in the first person, such as *I disagree,* that's also a clear sign.)

As you might have guessed, reading the passage strategically doesn't mean simply going on a scavenger hunt for keywords. Rather, it means using those keywords to identify the important parts of the passage—its opinions and structure—so you can focus on them and not on little details. Keywords also help you predict the function of the text that follows. Let's see how this works by taking a look at a simple example. Say you saw a passage with the following structure on Test Day. What kinds of details can you anticipate would fill each of the blanks?

Bob is very excited to go to East Main State Business School because _____

_____. Furthermore, _____

_____. Moreover, _____

_____. However, _____.

You learn about Bob's attitude toward East Main State Business School through the word *excited,* which is an emphasis keyword. After *because* (a logic keyword) will be a reason that East Main State is a great place to go to school or some reason it's special to Bob. After *furthermore* and *moreover* (continuation keywords) will be additional reasons or elaborations of the reason in the first sentence. After *however* will come some drawback or counterexample that undermines the previous string of good things about East Main State. You may not be able to predict the exact content of the details that fill the blanks, but you can predict the tone and purpose of the details. Reading this way is valuable because the GMAT testmakers are more likely to ask you why the author put the details in, not what's true about them.

Reading for keywords seems straightforward when the passage deals with subject matter that's familiar or easy to understand. But what if you were to see the following passage about a less familiar topic? How can you decode the structure of the following paragraph?

> Recent studies suggest that mirror neurons play an important role in the learning
> process because _____. Furthermore, _____
> _____. Moreover, _____
> _____. However, _____.

Here the emphasis keyword *important* lets you know why the author cares about mirror neurons: They're important for learning. The details that would fill these blanks are probably dense and intimidating for the non-neurologist, but the strategic reader will still be able to understand the passage well enough to answer the questions correctly. Notice that the structure is identical to the paragraph about Bob, so the details that fill the blanks will serve the same purpose as those you predicted previously. You can anticipate what they will be and why the author is including them. Reading strategically allows you to take control of the passage; you will know where the author is going and what the GMAT will consider important, even if you know nothing about the subject matter of the passage.

LOOK FOR OPINIONS, THEORIES, AND POINTS OF VIEW—ESPECIALLY THE AUTHOR'S

An important part of strategic reading is distinguishing between factual assertions and opinions or interpretations. It's the opinions and interpretations that Reading Comp questions are most often based on, so you should pay the most attention to them. Let's say you come upon a paragraph that reads:

> The coral polyps secrete calcareous exoskeletons, which cement themselves into an underlayer of rock, while the algae deposit still more calcium carbonate, which reacts with sea salt to create an even tougher limestone layer. All of this accounts for the amazing renewability of the coral reefs despite the endless erosion caused by wave activity.

In a sense, this is just like the Burgess Shale paragraph; it begins with a lot of scientific jargon and later tells us why that jargon is there. In this case, it shows us how coral reefs renew themselves. But notice a big difference—the author doesn't tell us how someone else interprets these facts. He could have written "scientists believe that these polyps account for ... ," but he didn't. This is the author's own interpretation.

It's important to differentiate between the author's own voice and other people's opinions. GMAT authors may disagree with other people but won't contradict themselves. So the author of the Burgess Shale passage might well disagree with Gould in the next paragraph. But the author of the Coral Reef passage has laid his cards on the table—he definitely thinks that coral polyps and algae are responsible for the renewability of coral reefs.

Spotting the opinions and theories also helps you to accomplish the goal of reading for structure. Once you spot an idea, you can step back from the barrage of words and use Critical Thinking to dissect the passage, asking, "Why is the author citing this opinion? Where's the support for this idea? Does the author agree or disagree?"

Consider how you would read the following paragraph strategically:

> Abraham Lincoln is traditionally viewed as an advocate of freedom because he issued the Emancipation Proclamation and championed the Thirteenth Amendment, which ended legal slavery in the United States. And indeed this achievement cannot be denied. But he also set uncomfortable precedents for the curtailing of civil liberties.

A strategic reader will zero in on the passage's keywords and analyze what each one reveals about the structure of the passage and the author's point of view. Here the keyword *traditionally* lets you know how people usually think about Lincoln. You might already anticipate that the author is setting up a contrast between the traditional view and her own. Sure enough, the keyword *but* makes the contrast clear: The author asserts that despite his other accomplishments, Lincoln in fact restricted civil liberties. And the word *uncomfortable* is an opinion keyword indicating that the author is not at all pleased with Lincoln because of it. However, the author already tempered her criticism with the phrase *this achievement cannot be denied*, meaning that she won't go so far as to say that Lincoln was an enemy of freedom.

At this point, the strategic reader can anticipate where the passage's structure will lead, just as you did on the earlier passages dealing with Bob at East Main State and mirror neurons. Given how this opening paragraph ends, you can predict that the author will spend at least one paragraph describing these "uncomfortable precedents" and how they restricted civil liberties. It might even be possible, since she uses the word *precedents*, that she goes on to describe how later governments or leaders used Lincoln's actions as justification for their own restrictions.

This is the power of predictive, strategic reading: By using keywords to anticipate where the author is heading, you will not only stay more engaged as you read, but you'll also develop a better understanding of the structure of the passage and the author's point of view—the very things that pay off in a higher GMAT score.

Put together, the passage's structure and the opinions and theories it contains will lead you to understand the author's primary purpose in writing the passage. This is critical, as most GMAT passages have a question that directly asks for that purpose. For the Lincoln passage, you might get a question like this:

Which of the following best represents the main idea of the passage?

O The Emancipation Proclamation had both positive and negative effects.
O Lincoln's presidency laid the groundwork for future restrictions of personal freedoms.
O The traditional image of Lincoln as a national hero must be overturned.
O Lincoln used military pressure to influence state legislatures.
O Abraham Lincoln was an advocate of freedom.

Just from a strategic reading of the first few sentences, you could eliminate **(A)** as being a distortion of the first and third sentences, **(C)** as being too extreme because of the *cannot be denied* phrase, **(D)** as out of scope—either too narrow or just not present in the passage at all, and **(E)** as missing the author's big point—that Lincoln helped restrict civil liberties. And just like that, you can choose **(B)** as the right answer and increase your score.

DON'T OBSESS OVER DETAILS

On the GMAT, you'll need to read only for short-term—as opposed to long-term—retention. When you finish the questions about a certain passage, that passage is over and done with. You're promptly free to forget everything about it.

What's more, there's certainly no need to memorize—or even fully comprehend—details. You *do* need to know why they are there so that you can answer big-picture questions, but you can always go back and reread them in greater depth if you're asked a question that hinges on a detail. And you'll find that if you have a good sense of the passage's scope and structure, the ideas and opinions in the passage, and the author's purpose, then you'll have little problem navigating through the text as the need arises.

Furthermore, you can even hurt your score by reading the details too closely. Here's how:

- **Wasted time.** Remember, there will only be three or four questions per passage. The testmakers can't possibly ask you about all the little details. So don't waste your valuable time by focusing on minutiae you will likely not need to know. If you do, you won't have nearly enough time to deal with the questions.

- **Tempting wrong answers.** Attempting to read and understand fully every last detail can cause your mind to jumble all the details—relevant and irrelevant alike—together in a confusing mess. Since most of the wrong answers in GMAT Reading Comp are simply distortions of details from the passage, they will sound familiar and therefore be tempting to uncritical readers. The strategic reader doesn't give those details undue importance and thus isn't tempted by answer choices that focus on them. Instead, he takes advantage of the open-book nature of the test to research specific details only when asked.

- **Losing the big picture.** It's very easy to miss the forest for the trees. If you get too drawn into the small stuff, you can pass right by the emphasis and opinion keywords that you'll need to understand the author's main purpose.

Here's a great trick for cutting through confusing, detail-laden sentences: Focus on the subjects and verbs first, throwing away modifying phrases, and don't worry about fancy terminology. Let's revisit some dense text from before:

> The coral polyps secrete calcareous exoskeletons, which cement themselves into an underlayer of rock, while the algae deposit still more calcium carbonate, which reacts with sea salt to create an even tougher limestone layer. All of this accounts for the amazing renewability of the coral reefs despite the endless erosion caused by wave activity.

Now look at what happens if you paraphrase these sentences, distilling them to main subjects and verbs, ignoring modifiers, and not worrying about words you don't understand:

> Coral polyps (whatever they are) secrete something . . . and algae deposit something. This accounts for the amazing renewability of the coral reefs.

The structure of this paragraph has suddenly become a lot more transparent. Now the bulkiness of that first sentence won't slow you down, so you can understand its role in the big picture.

TAKEAWAYS: THE BASIC PRINCIPLES OF READING COMPREHENSION

The basic principles of Reading Comprehension are the following:

- Look for the topic and scope of the passage.
- Get the gist of each paragraph and its structural role in the passage.
- Look for opinions, theories, and points of view—especially the author's.
- Don't obsess over details.

Let's now put all these basic principles together to analyze a passage similar to one you may see on Test Day. However, unlike passages you'll see on Test Day, the following text has been formatted to approximate the way a strategic reader might see it—important keywords and phrases are in bold, the main ideas are in normal type, and the supporting details are grayed out. Take a moment to read only the bold and regular text: Identify what the keywords tell you about the structure, paraphrase the crucial text, and practice predicting what the grayed-out portions contain.

> The United States National Park Service (NPS) is in the **unenviable** position of being charged with two missions that are **frequently at odds with one another**. Created by an act of Congress in 1916, the NPS is mandated to maintain the country's national parks in "absolutely unimpaired" condition, while somehow
> 5 ensuring that these lands are available for "the use ... and pleasure of the people." As the system of properties (known as units) managed by the NPS has grown over the years—a system now encompassing seashores, battlefields, and parkways—so has its popularity with the vacationing public. **Unfortunately**, the maintenance of the system has not kept pace with the record number of visits, and many of the
> 10 properties are in **serious** disrepair.
>
> **Several** paths can be taken, perhaps simultaneously, to **alleviate the deterioration** of the properties within the system. Adopting tougher requirements for admission could reduce the number of additional units that the NPS manages. Congress has on occasion added properties without any input from the NPS itself.
> 15 It is debatable whether all of these properties, which may be of importance to the constituents of individual representatives of Congress, pass the test of "national significance." **Furthermore**, some of the units now in the NPS (there are close to 400) receive few visitors, and there is no reason to think that this trend will reverse itself. These units can be removed from the system, and their fates can
> 20 be decided by local public and private concerns. The liberated federal funds could then be rerouted to areas of greater need within the system.
>
> **Another approach** would be to attack the root causes of the deterioration. Sadly, a great deal of the dilapidated condition of our national parks and park lands can be attributed not to overuse, but to misuse. Visitors should be educated about
> 25 responsible use of a site. Violators of these rules must be held accountable and fined harshly. There are, of course, already guidelines and penalties set in place, but studies strongly indicate that enforcement is lax.

From the first sentence, you can already tell a lot about this passage. The Park Service has an "unenviable" (opinion keyword) dilemma. You can predict that the author will state (in the grayed-out text of the first paragraph) what that dilemma is.

You get more opinion from the author in the final sentence of paragraph 1. "Unfortunately," (opinion keyword), the Park Service can't maintain the parks with so many visitors. The problem is apparently "serious" (emphasis keyword). On Test Day you would jot some brief notes on your noteboard about the main idea of the first paragraph:

¶1: NPS problem: lots of visitors = hard to maintain lands

From the first sentence of the second paragraph, where do you anticipate that this passage will go? The phrase "alleviate the deterioration" indicates that the author will discuss some possible solutions to the Park Service's problem. Now is a good time to ask yourself whether this author is likely to express a preference for one of those solutions in particular. It seems that this author will probably describe the solutions without supporting one over the others, since she says there are "several" and that they might work at the same time. In the middle of the second paragraph, the word "Furthermore" is a continuation keyword, signaling that the paragraph continues to describe a proposed solution and why it might be effective. This is all you need to know about this paragraph from your initial read-through. Take down some notes for later reference:

¶2: Possible solutions; details about the first

Right off the bat, the third paragraph indicates that the author will describe "another approach." If you need to know details about this other approach, you can always return to the passage to research the answer to a question.

¶3: 2nd solution details

Just from this quick analysis, notice how much you already understand about the structure of the passage and the author's point of view. You effectively know what the grayed-out parts of the passage accomplish, even though you can't recite the details they contain. You are now in a strong position to approach the questions that accompany this passage, knowing that you can always return to the passage to clarify your understanding of any relevant details. Let's look at this first question:

Which of the following best describes the organization of the passage as a whole?

O   The author mentions a problem, and opposing solutions are then described.

O   The various factors that led to a problem are considered, and one factor is named the root cause.

O   A historical survey is made of an institution, followed by a discussion of the problem of management of the institution.

O   A problem is described, and two possibly compatible methods for reducing the problem are then outlined.

O   A description of a plan and the flaws of the plan are delineated.

This question asks for the organization of the entire passage. Fortunately, you already have the passage structure in your notes, so there's no need to go back to the passage itself to answer this question. The author begins by introducing a problem, then advances two potential solutions to that problem. The solutions are complementary, as the author states in line 11 that they can be undertaken "simultaneously." Choice **(D)** matches this prediction and is the correct answer.

If you weren't sure about the answer, you could always eliminate incorrect answer choices by finding the specific faults they contain. **(A)** cannot be correct because it calls the two solutions "opposing."

(B) is incorrect because the focus of the passage is not on the "factors" leading to the problem but rather on solutions to the problem. **(C)** is incorrect because the passage gives no "historical survey" of the National Park Service; the only bit of historical data given is the date of its founding (1916). Finally, **(E)** is incorrect because the passage does not focus on the strengths and drawbacks of a single proposed plan of action; instead, it considers several different suggestions. Moreover, the passage never discusses the flaws of any of these possible solutions. Choice **(D)** is correct.

Let's now look at one more question about this passage:

> The author is primarily concerned with
>
> O   analyzing the various problems that beset the NPS
> O   summarizing the causes of deterioration of NPS properties
> O   criticizing the NPS's maintenance of its properties
> O   encouraging support for increased funding for the NPS
> O   discussing possible solutions for NPS properties' deterioration

This question asks for the author's purpose in writing the passage. As was the case in the previous question, you've already thought through the author's purpose as you read the passage strategically. Again, this question does not require specific research beyond the notes you've already taken.

The author is concerned with advancing two possible solutions to the dilemma faced by the National Park Service. Choice **(E)** matches your prediction perfectly and is correct.

(A) is incorrect because only one problem is discussed, not "various" problems. **(B)** is incorrect because it is the solutions, not the causes, of the National Park Service's problem that are the focus of the passage. **(C)** is incorrect because the author is not critical of the NPS. Indeed, the word "unenviable" in the first sentence actually signals sympathy with the NPS's plight. **(D)** is incorrect because there is no discussion of funding in the passage. **(E)** is the correct answer.

THE KAPLAN METHOD FOR READING COMPREHENSION

Many test takers read the entire passage closely from beginning to end, taking detailed notes and making sure that they understand everything, and then try to answer the questions from memory. But this is *not* what the best test takers do.

The best test takers attack the passages and questions critically in the sort of aggressive, energetic, and goal-oriented way you've learned earlier. Working this way pays off because it's the kind of pragmatic and efficient approach that the GMAT rewards—the same type of approach that business schools like their students to take when faced with an intellectual challenge.

To help this strategic approach become second nature to you, Kaplan has developed a Method that you can use to attack each and every Reading Comp passage and question.

The Kaplan Method for Reading Comprehension

1. **Read the passage strategically.**

2. **Analyze the question stem.**

3. **Research the relevant text.**

4. **Make a prediction.**

5. **Evaluate the answer choices.**

STEP 1: READ THE PASSAGE STRATEGICALLY

Like most sophisticated writing, the prose you will see on the GMAT doesn't explicitly reveal its secrets. Baldly laying out the *why* and *how* of a passage up front isn't a hallmark of GMAT Reading Comprehension passages. And even more important (as far as the testmakers are concerned), if the ideas were blatantly laid out, the testmakers couldn't ask probing questions about them. So to set up the questions—to test how you think about the prose you read—the GMAT uses passages in which authors hide or disguise their reasons for writing and challenge you to extract them.

This is why it's essential to start by reading the passage strategically, staying on the lookout for structural keywords and phrases. With this strategic analysis as a guide, you should construct a Passage Map—a brief summary of each paragraph and its function in the passage's structure. You should also note the author's topic, scope, and purpose. Start by identifying the topic and then hunt for scope, trying to get a sense of where the passage is going, what the author is going to focus on, and what role the first paragraph is playing. As you finish reading each paragraph, jot down a short note about its structure and the role it plays in the passage. This process is similar to how you took notes on each paragraph of the National Park Service passage above. When you finish reading the passage, double-check that you got the topic and scope right (sometimes passages can take unexpected turns) and note the author's overall purpose.

The topic will be the first big, broad idea that comes along. Almost always, it will be right there in the first sentence. There's no need to obsess over exactly how you word the topic; you just want a general idea of what the author is writing about so the passage gets easier to understand.

The scope is the narrow part of the topic that the author focuses on. If the author expresses his own opinion, then the thing he has an opinion about is the scope. Your statement of the scope should be as narrow as possible while still reflecting the passage as a whole. Your scope statement should also answer the question "What about this topic interests the author?" Identifying the scope is crucial because many wrong answers are outside the scope of the passage. Remember that even though the first paragraph usually narrows the topic down to the scope, there probably won't be a "topic sentence" in the traditional sense.

The purpose is what the author is seeking to accomplish by writing the passage. You'll serve yourself well by picking an active verb for the purpose. Doing so helps not only by setting you up to find the right answer—many answer choices contain active verbs—but also by forcing you to consider the author's opinion. Here are some verbs that describe the purpose of a "neutral" author: *describe*, *explain*, *compare*. Here are some verbs for an "opinionated" author: *advocate*, *argue*, *rebut*, *analyze*.

After you finish reading, your Passage Map should look something like this example:

¶1: NPS problem: lots of visitors = hard to maintain lands

¶2: Possible solutions; details about the first

¶3: 2nd solution details

Topic: National Park Service Dilemma

Scope: Reasons and possible solutions

Purpose: Describe two

You don't want to take any more than four minutes to read and write your Passage Map. After all, you get points for answering questions, not for creating nicely detailed Passage Maps. The more time you can spend working on the questions, the better your score will be. But creating a Passage Map and identifying the topic, scope, and purpose will prepare you to handle those questions efficiently and accurately.

It generally works best to create your Passage Map paragraph by paragraph. Don't write while you're reading, since you'll be tempted to write too much. But it's also not a good idea to wait until you've read the whole passage before writing anything, since it will be more difficult for you to recall what you've read. Analyze the structure as you read and take a few moments after you finish each paragraph to summarize the main points. Include details that are provided as evidence only when keywords indicate their importance. A line or two of paraphrase is generally enough to summarize a paragraph.

Your Passage Map can be as elaborate or as brief as you need it to be. Don't waste time trying to write out entire sentences if fragments and abbreviations will do. And notice in the above example how effective arrows can be. For example, there's no sense writing out the purpose as "Describe two solutions to the National Park Service's dilemma resulting from the dual imperative to keep lands unimpaired and also to allow for their recreational use," when some simple notes with arrows are just as helpful to you.

STEP 2: ANALYZE THE QUESTION STEM

Only once you have read the passage strategically and jotted down your Passage Map should you read the first question stem. The second step of the Kaplan Method is to identify the question type; the most common question types are Global, Detail, Inference, and Logic. We will cover each of these question types in detail later in this chapter. For now, know that you will use this step to ask yourself, "What should I do on this question? What is being asked?" Here are some guidelines for identifying each of the main question types:

- **Global.** These question stems contain language that refers to the passage as a whole, such as "primary purpose," "main idea," or "appropriate title for the passage."
- **Detail.** These question stems contain direct language such as "according to the author," "the passage states explicitly," or "is mentioned in the passage."
- **Inference.** These question stems contain indirect language such as "most likely agree," "suggests," or "implies."
- **Logic.** These question stems ask for the purpose of a detail or paragraph and contain language such as "in order to," "purpose of the second paragraph," or "for which of the following reasons."

In addition to identifying the question type, be sure to focus on *exactly* what the question is asking. Let's say you see this question:

> The passage states which of the following about the uses of fixed nitrogen?

Don't look for what the passage says about "nitrogen" in general. Don't even look for "fixed nitrogen" alone. Look for the *uses* of fixed nitrogen. (And be aware that the GMAT may ask you to recognize that *application* is a synonym of *use*.)

Finally, the GMAT occasionally asks questions that do not fall into one of the four major categories. These outliers make up only about 8 percent of GMAT Reading Comp questions, so you will probably see only one such question or maybe none at all. If you do see one, don't worry. These rare question types usually involve paraphrasing or analyzing specific points of reasoning in the passage. Often they are extremely similar to question types you know from GMAT Critical Reasoning. Because you can use your Passage Map to understand the passage's structure and Kaplan's strategies for Critical Reasoning to deconstruct the author's reasoning, you will be prepared to handle even these rare question types.

STEP 3: RESEARCH THE RELEVANT TEXT

Since there just isn't enough time to memorize the whole passage, you shouldn't rely on your memory to answer questions. Treat the GMAT like an open-book test, knowing you can return to the passage as needed. However, don't let that fact make you over-reliant on research in the passage. Doing so could lead to lots of rereading and wasted time. For some question types, you are just as likely to find all the information you need to answer the question correctly using only your Passage Map. Here is how you should focus your research for each question type:

- **Global.** The answer will deal with the passage as a whole, so you should review your Passage Map and the topic, scope, and purpose you noted.
- **Detail.** Use the specific reference in the question stem to research the text. Look for the detail to be associated with a keyword.
- **Inference.** For questions that include specific references, research the passage based on the clues in the question stem. For open-ended questions, refer to your topic, scope, and purpose; you may need to research in the passage as you evaluate each answer choice.
- **Logic.** Use the specific reference in the question stem to research the text. Use keywords to understand the passage's structure. Refer to your Passage Map for the purpose of a specific paragraph.

STEP 4: MAKE A PREDICTION

As you have seen in the Critical Reasoning chapter of this book, predicting the answer before you look at the answer choices is a powerful strategy to increase your efficiency and accuracy. The same is true for GMAT Reading Comp. Making a prediction allows you to know what you're looking for before you consider the answer choices. Doing so will help the right answer jump off the screen at you. It will also help you avoid wrong answer choices that might otherwise be tempting. Here is how you should form your prediction for each question type:

- **Global.** Use your Passage Map and topic, scope, and purpose as the basis of your prediction.
- **Detail.** Predict an answer based on what the context tells you about the detail.
- **Inference.** Remember that the right answer *must* be true based on the passage. (Since many valid inferences could be drawn from even one detail, it's often best not to make your prediction more specific than that.)
- **Logic.** Predict an answer that focuses on *why* the paragraph or detail was used, not on *what* it says.

STEP 5: EVALUATE THE ANSWER CHOICES

Hunt for the answer choice that matches your prediction. If only one choice matches, it's the right answer.

If you can't find a match for your prediction, if more than one choice seems to fit your prediction, or if you weren't able to form a prediction at all (this happens for some open-ended Inference questions), then you'll need to evaluate each answer choice, looking for errors. If you can prove four answers wrong, then you can confidently select the one that remains, even if you aren't completely sure what you think about it. This is the beauty of a multiple-choice test—knowing how to eliminate the four wrong answers is as good as knowing how to identify the correct one.

Here are some common wrong answer traps to look out for:

- **Global.** Answers that misrepresent the scope or purpose of the passage and answers that focus too heavily on details from one part of the passage
- **Detail.** Answers that distort the context or focus on the wrong details entirely
- **Inference.** Answers that include extreme language or exaggerations of the author's statements, distortions of the passage's meaning, or the exact opposite of what might be inferred
- **Logic.** Answers that get the specifics right but the purpose wrong

Look out for out-of-scope answer choices and for "half-right/half-wrong" choices, which are mostly okay except for one or two words. Some answer choices are very tempting because they have the correct details and the right scope, but they have a *not, doesn't,* or other twist that flips their meanings to the opposite of what the question asks for. Watch out for these "180s."

Now let's apply the Kaplan Method to an actual GMAT-length passage and some of its questions. One of the questions that follow is the same one you saw at the beginning of the chapter. Read the passage strategically and practice making a Passage Map. You can try your hand at the questions and then compare your analysis to ours, or you can let our analysis below guide you through the steps of the Kaplan Method. For now, don't worry if you're not quite sure how to identify the question types; we will cover those thoroughly later in this chapter. For now, concentrate on analyzing what the question asks of you and using the Method to take the most efficient path from question to correct answer.

Questions 1–2 are based on the following passage

Since 1980, the notion that mass extinctions at the end of the Cretaceous period 65 million years ago resulted from a sudden event has slowly gathered support, although even today there is no scientific consensus. In the Alvarez scenario, an asteroid struck the earth, creating a gigantic crater. Beyond the immediate effects
5 of fire, flood, and storm, dust darkened the atmosphere, cutting off plant life. Many animal species disappeared as the food chain was snapped at its base.

Alvarez's main evidence is an abundance of iridium in the KT boundary, a thin stratum dividing Cretaceous rocks from rocks of the Tertiary period. Iridium normally accompanies the slow fall of interplanetary debris, but in KT boundary
10 strata, iridium is 10–100 times more abundant, suggesting a rapid, massive deposition. Coincident with the boundary, whole species of small organisms vanish from the fossil record. Boundary samples also yield osmium isotopes, basaltic sphericles, and deformed quartz grains, all of which could have resulted from high-velocity impact.

15 Paleontologists initially dismissed the theory, arguing that existing dinosaur records showed a decline lasting millions of years. But recent studies in North America, aimed at a comprehensive collection of fossil remnants rather than rare or well-preserved specimens, indicate large dinosaur populations existing immediately prior to the KT boundary. Since these discoveries, doubts about
20 theories of mass extinction have lessened significantly.

Given the lack of a known impact crater of the necessary age and size to fit the Alvarez scenario, some scientists have proposed alternatives. Courtillot, citing huge volcanic flows in India coincident with the KT boundary, speculates that eruptions lasting many thousands of years produced enough atmospheric debris to cause
25 global devastation. His analyses also conclude that iridium in the KT boundary was deposited over a period of 10,000–100,000 years. Alvarez and Asaro reply that the shock of an asteroidal impact could conceivably have triggered extensive volcanic activity. Meanwhile, exploration at a large geologic formation in Yucatan, found in 1978 but unstudied until 1990, has shown a composition consistent with
30 extraterrestrial impact. But evidence that the formation is indeed the hypothesized impact site remains inconclusive.

1. It can be inferred from the passage that supporters of the Alvarez and Courtillot theories would hold which of the following views in common?

    O   The KT boundary was formed over many thousands of years.

    O   Large animals such as the dinosaurs died out gradually over millions of years.

    O   Mass extinction occurred as an indirect result of debris saturating the atmosphere.

    O   It is unlikely that the specific cause of the Cretaceous extinctions will ever be determined.

    O   Volcanic activity may have been triggered by shock waves from the impact of an asteroid.

2. The author mentions "recent studies in North America" (lines 16–17) primarily in order to

   ○ point out the benefits of using field research to validate scientific theories.

   ○ suggest that the asteroid impact theory is not consistent with fossil evidence.

   ○ describe alternative methods of collecting and interpreting fossils.

   ○ summarize the evidence that led to wider acceptance of catastrophic scenarios of mass extinction.

   ○ show that dinosaurs survived until the end of the Cretaceous period.

Step 1: Read the Passage Strategically

Here's an example of how the passage should be analyzed. We've reprinted the passage as seen through the lens of strategic reading. On the left is the passage as you might read it, with keywords and important points in bold. On the right is what you might be thinking as you read.

PASSAGE

... **the notion** that mass extinctions at the end of the Cretaceous period 65 million years ago resulted from a sudden event **has slowly gathered support, although** even today there is **no** scientific **consensus**. In the **Alvarez scenario**, [bunch of details about an asteroid]

Alvarez's main evidence is [lots of detail]

Paleontologists initially dismissed the theory, arguing that [something] last[ed] **millions of years. But** recent studies ... **doubts** about theories of mass extinction **have lessened significantly**.

ANALYSIS

The first sentence is rich with information for the strategic reader. Not only do you get the topic (*mass extinctions at the end of the Cretaceous period*—whatever that is), but you also get an idea (*the notion that [the mass extinction] resulted from a sudden event*), the fact that some people agree with it (*slowly gathered support*), and the fact that not everyone does (*no scientific consensus*). You can predict that the passage will go on to talk not only about the support but also about why not everyone agrees. You also get one specific theory (*the Alvarez scenario*) and an elaborate description of what that is—it seems to involve an asteroid.

The keywords are pretty clear—here's some evidence in support of one "sudden event" theory.

You don't need to focus too much on what the evidence is until there's a question about it.

With *dismissed the theory*, it's clear that this paragraph shows why some would oppose the "sudden event" idea (just as you predicted). Note that *millions of years*, not normally a keyword, creates contrast with "sudden event." Then the keyword *But* announces a change in direction: The recent studies lend support for the "sudden event" theory, so *doubts have lessened significantly*.

Given the **lack** of [evidence] to **fit the Alvarez scenario, some scientists have proposed alternatives. Courtillot, citing** [evidence], **speculates** that eruptions ... cause[d] global devastation. **His analyses also conclude** [something about iridium]. **Alvarez and Asaro reply ... But evidence ... remains inconclusive**.

Alvarez lacks some evidence still, so there are some other theories. Courtillot says something about volcanoes and iridium. It looks like Alvarez makes a counterargument to Courtillot, too. But there isn't enough evidence either way, so the author doesn't pick a "winner."

Your Passage Map would look something like this:

¶1: Mass ext. & sudden event—Alvarez/asteroid

¶2: Alvarez evidence

¶3: Initial disagreement, recent studies, now less doubt

¶4: Courtillot/volcanoes; Alvarez reply; not enough evidence to choose

Topic: Mass extinctions at end of Cret. period

Scope: Theories about ⬑

Purpose: Describe two "sudden event" theories

This isn't the only way to word the Passage Map, of course. Anything along these lines would work—so long as you note that there are two theories and that the author doesn't ultimately prefer one to the other.

Step 2: Analyze the Question Stem

Now it's time to move to the questions and identify the question type. **Question 1** is what you will learn to call an Inference question: It uses the phrase *can be inferred*. Luckily, this Inference question contains clues that point you to a specific part of the passage. This will save you a lot of time. **Question 2** is a Logic question. The phrase *in order to* indicates that you're asked to identify *why* the author includes this detail.

Step 3: Research the Relevant Text

Question 1 asks you to find something that must be true according to both the Alvarez and the Courtillot theories. Our Passage Map shows that the Alvarez theory takes all of paragraph 2 and some of paragraph 4. That's too much to reread closely. But the Courtillot theory is mentioned only once, in paragraph 4 lines 22–26. Probably the most efficient way to research this question is to read through those two sentences and then deal with paragraph 2, doing focused research on each answer choice as needed.

Question 2 refers to lines 16–17, which are in paragraph 3. Since this is a Logic question, it's best to begin your research with the Passage Map. Here's what the Map has to say about paragraph 3:

¶3: Initial disagreement, recent studies, now less doubt

So the "recent studies in North America" are either part of the initial disagreement or a reason that theories of mass extinction are less doubted now. Already, the word *recent* suggests the latter. But if you weren't confident about that, you could read the context of lines 16–17. The keywords *initially dismissed the theory* [*of mass extinction*] from the sentence before and from the sentence after (*Since these discoveries, doubts about theories of mass extinctions have lessened significantly.*) seal the deal.

Step 4: Make a Prediction

The answer to **Question 1**, as you know, must be consistent with both theories. Since you researched Courtillot's theory, you can quickly eliminate any answer choice that disagrees with it.

Question 2 asks *why* the "recent studies in North America" were mentioned. Your research shows you that they provide the evidence that reduces doubt about theories of mass extinction. So an easy prediction would be something like "reasons why theories of mass extinction are doubted less than they used to be."

Step 5: Evaluate the Answer Choices

Question 1—**(A)** says that the KT boundary was formed over thousands of years, and that's consistent with Courtillot (line 26). What about Alvarez? Scanning through paragraph 2 for anything about "KT boundary" and time, you read in lines 9–11: "KT boundary ... rapid, massive deposition." The word *rapid* is the only time signal at all, and it hardly fits with *many thousands of years*. Eliminate **(A)**. Perhaps you could eliminate **(B)** right away if you remembered that both theories are in the "sudden event" camp. But if not, your Passage Map saves the day—*dinosaurs died out gradually over millions of years* fits with *dinosaur records showed a decline lasting millions of years* in paragraph 3. But your Map shows that to be evidence *against* Alvarez, not in support. So **(B)** is gone.

Debris saturating the atmosphere is consistent with Courtillot (line 24). What about Alvarez? Line 9 says *slow fall of interplanetary debris*. So both theories involve *debris*. Does it saturate the atmosphere? Not explicitly. But this is an Inference question, and you shouldn't expect to see things repeated explicitly from the passage. You do see that there was a *massive deposition* ... and *massive* would suggest that there's a lot of this debris, so it's plausible that it saturated the atmosphere. There's not enough evidence to rule out **(C)**, so you can leave it alone for now.

(D) is the opposite of what Courtillot (as well as Alvarez) is trying to do, so this is a quick big-picture elimination. **(E)** is consistent with Alvarez's reply (lines 26–28). But this is a reply to Courtillot's theory—not his theory itself. The passage gives no indication of whether Courtillot would agree with this claim, so **(E)** is eliminated. Only **(C)** is left standing, so it must be right.

Note that you can prove **(C)** to be the right answer without proving *why* it's right. To prove why **(C)** is correct, you'd not only have to connect all the dots in paragraph 2, you'd have to tie it all to *mass extinctions* by going back to details from paragraph 1. It's much more efficient to eliminate **(A)**, **(B)**, **(D)**, and **(E)**.

Question 2—Your predicted answer from Step 4 ("reasons why theories of mass extinction are doubted less than they used to be") leads directly to **(D)**, the correct answer.

(A) sounds nice on its own, but the context has nothing to do with the benefits of field research in a specific way. **(B)** is the opposite of why those studies are introduced—it is in fact the old belief that these studies dispel. **(C)** and **(E)** focus on the details in lines 16–17 themselves—**(C)** in a distorted way—but not on *why* those details are there.

READING COMPREHENSION QUESTION TYPES

Though you might be inclined to classify Reading Comp according to the kinds of passages that appear—business, social science, biological science, or physical science—it's more effective to do so by question type. While passages differ in their content, you can read them in essentially the same way, employing the same strategic reading techniques for each.

Now that you're familiar with the basic principles of Critical Reasoning and the Kaplan Method, let's look at the most common types of questions. Certain question types appear again and again on the GMAT, so it pays to understand them beforehand.

The four main question types on GMAT Reading Comp are **Global, Detail, Inference**, and **Logic**. Let's walk through each of these question types in turn, focusing on what they ask and how you can approach them most effectively.

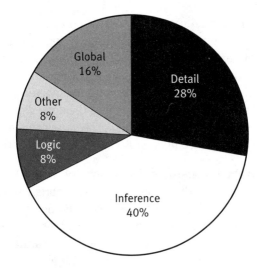

The Approximate Distribution of GMAT Reading Comprehension Questions

GLOBAL QUESTIONS

Any question that explicitly asks you to consider the passage as a whole is a Global question. Here are some examples:

- Which of the following best expresses the main idea of the passage?
- The author's primary purpose is to ...
- Which of the following best describes the organization of the passage?
- Which of the following would be an appropriate title for this passage?

The correct answer will be consistent with the passage's topic, scope, purpose, and structure. If you've jotted these down on your noteboard (and you should!), then it will only take a few seconds to select the right answer.

The GMAT will probably word the answer choices rather formally, so by "few seconds," we mean closer to 45 than to 10. But that's still significantly under your average time per question, meaning that you can spend more time dealing with the trickier Inference questions.

Most wrong answers will either get the scope wrong (too narrow or too broad) or misrepresent the author's point of view. Be wary of Global answer choices that are based on details from the first or last paragraph. These are usually traps laid for those who wrongly assume that GMAT passages are traditional essays with "topic sentences" and "concluding sentences."

Often answer choices to Global questions asking about the author's purpose will begin with verbs; in this case, the most efficient approach is to scan vertically to eliminate choices with verbs that are inconsistent with the author's purpose. Common wrong answers misrepresent a neutral author by using verbs that indicate an opinionated stance.

TAKEAWAYS: GLOBAL QUESTIONS

- Step 1 of the Kaplan Method provides you with the information you need to predict the answer to Global questions.
- Use your Passage Map, topic, scope, and purpose to predict an answer. Then search the answer choices.
- If you can't find your prediction among the answer choices, eliminate wrong answer choices that misrepresent the scope.
- When all of the answer choices start with a verb, try a vertical scan, looking for choices that match your prediction or looking to eliminate choices that misrepresent the author's purpose.

DETAIL QUESTIONS

Detail questions ask you to identify what the passage explicitly says. Here are some sample Detail question stems:

- According to the passage, which of the following is true of X?
- The author states that ...
- The author mentions which of the following in support of X?

It would be impossible to keep track of all of the details in a passage as you read through it the first time. Fortunately, Detail stems will always give you clues about where to look to find the information you need. Many Detail stems include specific words or phrases that you can easily locate in the passage. A Detail stem might even highlight a sentence or phrase in the passage itself. Using these clues, you can selectively reread parts of the passage to quickly zero in on the answer—a more efficient approach than memorization.

So between highlighting, references to specific words or phrases, and your Passage Map, locating the detail that the GMAT is asking about is usually not much of a challenge. What, then, could these questions possibly be testing? They are testing whether you understand that detail *in the context of the passage.* The best strategic approach, then, is to read not only the sentence that the question stem sends you to but also the sentences before and after it. Consider the following question stem:

> According to the passage, which of the following is true of the guinea pigs discussed in the highlighted portion of the passage?

Let's say that the highlighted portion of the passage goes like this:

> ... a greater percentage of the guinea pigs that lived in the crowded, indoor, heated area survived than did the guinea pigs in the outdoor cages.

If you don't read for context, you might think that something like this could be the right answer choice:

> O   Guinea pigs survive better indoors.

But what if you read the full context, starting one sentence before?

> Until recently, scientists had no evidence to support the hypothesis that low temperature alone, and not other factors such as people crowding indoors, is responsible for the greater incidence and severity of influenza in the late fall and early winter. Last year, however, researchers uncovered several experiment logs from a research facility whose population of guinea pigs suffered an influenza outbreak in the winter of 1945; these logs documented that a greater percentage of the guinea pigs that lived in the indoor, heated area survived than did the guinea pigs in the outdoor cages.

Now you could identify this as the right answer:

> O   Researchers discovered that some guinea pigs survived better indoors than outdoors during a flu outbreak.

By reading not just the highlighted portion of the passage but the information before it, you realize that it's not necessarily true that guinea pigs always survive better indoors; only a specific subset did. If you had picked an answer that matched the first prediction, you would be distorting the facts—you need to understand the information *in context.*

Make sure that you read entire sentences when answering Detail questions. Notice here that the question stem sends you to the end of the last sentence, but it's the "no evidence" and "however" at the *beginning* of the sentences that form the support for the right answer.

TAKEAWAYS: DETAIL QUESTIONS

- On Detail questions, use your Passage Map to locate the relevant text in the passage. If necessary, read that portion of the passage again. Then predict an answer.
- On Detail questions, never pick an answer choice just because it sounds familiar. Wrong answer choices on Detail questions are often distortions of actual details in the passage.
- All of the information needed to answer Detail questions is in the passage.

INFERENCE QUESTIONS

Reading Comp Inference questions, like Critical Reasoning Inference questions, ask you to find something that must be true based on the passage but is not mentioned *explicitly* in the passage. In other words, you need to read "between the lines." Here are some sample Inference question stems:

- Which of the following is suggested about X?
- Which of the following can be most reasonably inferred from the passage?
- The author would most likely agree that ...

Inference questions come in two types. The first uses key phrases or highlighting to refer to a specific part of the passage. To solve this kind of question, find the relevant detail in the passage and consider it in the context of the material surrounding it. Then make a flexible prediction about what the correct answer will state.

Consider the following Inference question, once again asking about the guinea pigs we discussed earlier:

> Which of the following is implied about the guinea pigs mentioned in the highlighted portion of the passage?

Just like last time, you want to review the context around the highlighted portion. Doing so, you'll find that "until recently," there was "no evidence" that temperature affected the flu; "however," last year these guinea pig records appeared. The logical inference is not explicitly stated, but you can easily put the information from the two sentences together. The answer will be something like this:

O Their deaths provided new evidence that influenza may be more dangerous in lower temperatures.

Other Inference questions make no specific references, instead asking what can be inferred from the passage as a whole or what opinion the author might hold. Valid inferences can be drawn from anything in the passage, from big-picture issues like the author's opinion to any of the little details. But you will probably be able to eliminate a few answers quickly because they contradict the big picture.

Then you'll investigate the remaining answers choice by choice, looking to put each answer in one of three categories—(1) proved right, (2) proved wrong, or (3) not proved right but not proved wrong either. It's distinguishing between the second and third categories that will lead to success on Inference questions. Don't throw away an answer because you aren't sure about it or "don't like it."

If you can't find material in the passage that proves an answer choice wrong, don't eliminate it. Since the correct answer to an Inference question is something that *must* be true based on the passage, you can often find your way to the correct answer by eliminating the four choices that *could* be false.

TAKEAWAYS: INFERENCE QUESTIONS

- On Inference questions, search for the answer choice that follows from the passage.
- When it's difficult to predict a specific answer to an Inference question, you still know that "the right answer *must* be true based on the passage."
- Wrong answer choices on Inference questions often use extreme language, or they exaggerate views expressed in the passage.

LOGIC QUESTIONS

Logic questions ask why the author does something—why he cites a source, why he includes a certain detail, why he puts one paragraph before another, and so forth. Another way of thinking of Logic questions is that they ask not for the purpose of the passage as a whole but for the purpose of a part of the passage. As a result, any answer choice that focuses on the actual content of a detail will be wrong.

Here are some sample Logic question stems:

- The author mentions X most probably in order to ...
- Which of the following best describes the relationship of the second paragraph to the rest of the passage?
- What is the primary purpose of the third paragraph?

Most Logic questions can be answered correctly from your Passage Map—your written summary of each paragraph and the passage's overall topic, scope, and purpose. If the question references a detail, as does the first sample question stem above, then you should read the context in which that detail appears as well—just as you should for any Detail or Inference question that references a specific detail.

TAKEAWAYS: LOGIC QUESTIONS

- On Logic questions, predict the correct answer using the author's purpose and your Passage Map.
- Answer choices that focus too heavily on specifics are usually wrong—it's not content that's key in Logic questions but the author's motivation for including the content.

"OTHER" QUESTIONS

As you saw from the pie chart earlier, approximately 8 percent of Reading Comp questions will not fall neatly into the four main categories described above. On such questions, strategic reading of the question stem becomes even more important, since you'll need to define precisely what the question is asking you to do, and you may not be able to identify any specific "pattern" that the question falls into. But even within these rare "Other" question types, you can prepare yourself to see questions of the following varieties:

"Critical Reasoning" Questions

Occasionally in Reading Comp, you might find a question that seems more like one of the common Critical Reasoning question types, such as an **Assumption, Strengthen, Weaken,** or **Flaw** question. These questions refer to arguments, just as they do in Critical Reasoning—although unlike in Critical Reasoning, a particular argument will usually be confined to just one paragraph or portion of the Reading Comp passage, rather than the entire passage focusing on a single argument.

When you see questions like this, you should research the portion of the passage that includes the argument referenced by the question stem. Just as you would in Critical Reasoning, identify the conclusion and relevant evidence; then use the central assumption to form a prediction for the right answer.

Parallelism Questions

These questions ask you to take the ideas in a passage and apply them through analogy to a new situation. For example, a passage might describe a chain of economic events that are related causally, such as reduced customer spending leading to a slowdown of industrial production, which in turn leads to the elimination of industrial jobs. A Parallelism question might then ask you the following:

> Which of the following situations is most comparable to the economic scenario described the passage?

In this case, the correct answer will describe a scenario that is logically similar to the one in the passage. Don't look for a choice that deals with the same subject matter as the passage, as such choices are often traps. Parallelism questions are more concerned with structure than substance, so the correct answer will provide a chain of causally connected events, such as water pollution from a factory causing the death of a certain type of algae, which in turn causes a decline in the fish population that relied on that type of algae as its primary food source.

Application Questions

Application questions ask you to identify an example or application of something described in the passage. For instance, if the passage describes a process for realigning a company's management structure, an Application question could give you five answer choices, each of which describes the structure of a given company. Only the correct answer choice will accurately reflect the process described in the passage.

Application questions function similarly to Parallelism questions, except that whereas Parallelism questions ask you to identify an analogous logical situation (irrespective of subject matter), Application questions ask you to apply information or ideas directly, within the same subject area (rather than by analogy or metaphor).

Question Type Identification Exercise

Answers found on the page following this exercise

Identifying the question type during Step 2 of the Kaplan Method for Reading Comprehension is a chance for you to put yourself in control of the entire process that follows: how to research, what to predict, and, thus, how to evaluate answer choices. Use the Core Competency of Pattern Recognition to analyze keywords in the question stem and determine what the question is asking you to do. Based on this analysis, choose the correct question type from the list of choices.

1. The passage implies which of the following about XXXXXXX?

    O   Global
    O   Detail
    O   Inference
    O   Logic
    O   Other

2. According to the passage, each of the following is true of XXXXXXX EXCEPT

    O   Global
    O   Detail
    O   Inference
    O   Logic
    O   Other

3. The author mentions XXXXXXX in order to

    O   Global
    O   Detail
    O   Inference
    O   Logic
    O   Other

4. The author's primary objective in the passage is to

   ○ Global
   ○ Detail
   ○ Inference
   ○ Logic
   ○ Other

5. The author makes which of the following statements concerning XXXXXXX?

   ○ Global
   ○ Detail
   ○ Inference
   ○ Logic
   ○ Other

6. An appropriate title for the passage would be

   ○ Global
   ○ Detail
   ○ Inference
   ○ Logic
   ○ Other

7. Which of the following statements about XXXXXXX can be inferred from the passage?

    O   Global
    O   Detail
    O   Inference
    O   Logic
    O   Other

8. Which of the following, if true, would most weaken the theory proposed by XXXXXXX?

    O   Global
    O   Detail
    O   Inference
    O   Logic
    O   Other

9. Which of the following best states the central idea of the passage?

    O   Global
    O   Detail
    O   Inference
    O   Logic
    O   Other

10. Which of the following situations is most comparable to XXXXXXX as it is presented in the passage?

   O   Global

   O   Detail

   O   Inference

   O   Logic

   O   Other

11. The passage provides support for which of the following assertions about XXXXXXX?

   O   Global

   O   Detail

   O   Inference

   O   Logic

   O   Other

12. The author indicates explicitly that which of the following has been XXXXXXX?

   O   Global

   O   Detail

   O   Inference

   O   Logic

   O   Other

13. The author would most likely agree with which of the following?

   ○ Global
   ○ Detail
   ○ Inference
   ○ Logic
   ○ Other

14. The author refers to XXXXXXX most probably in order to

   ○ Global
   ○ Detail
   ○ Inference
   ○ Logic
   ○ Other

15. Which of the following represents the clearest application of XXXXXXX's theory as described in the passage?

   ○ Global
   ○ Detail
   ○ Inference
   ○ Logic
   ○ Other

16. The passage is primarily concerned with

   O   Global
   O   Detail
   O   Inference
   O   Logic
   O   Other

Question Type Identification Exercise: Answers

1. C

When you see "implies" or "suggests," know that you're facing an Inference question.

2. B

When you see direct, categorical language like "according to the passage," know that you're facing a Detail question.

3. D

The phrase "in order to" means that this is a Logic question. Logic questions deal with the author's motivations. If a question asks you why the author includes a paragraph, brings up a detail, or cites a source, know that you are facing a Logic question.

4. A

The phrase "primary objective" means that this is a Global question.

5. B

The phrase "makes which of the following statements" signals that this is a Detail question.

6. A

The phrase "title for the passage" means that we must base our answer on the whole passage, so this is a Global question.

7. C

The word "inferred" means that this is an Inference question.

8. E (Weaken)

The word "weaken" means that this is a Weaken question, one of the rarer question types in Reading Comp.

9. A

The phrase "central idea of the passage" means that this is a Global question.

10. E (Parallelism)

The phrase "most comparable to" means that this is a Parallelism question.

11. C

The phrase "passage provides support for" means that this is an Inference question.

12. B

The phrase "indicates explicitly" means that this is a Detail question.

13. C

The phrase "most likely agree" signals an Inference question.

14. D

The phrase "in order to" means that this is a Logic question.

15. E (Application)

The phrase "represents the clearest application of" means that this is an Application question. Application questions ask you to find the answer choice that is most consistent with a description, theory, or process described in the passage.

16. A

The phrase "passage is primarily concerned" means that this is a Global question.

READING COMPREHENSION QUIZ

Answers and explanations at end of chapter

Now it's time to apply the skills you've learned in this chapter to the following Reading Comprehension Quiz. Follow the Kaplan Method consistently so this strategic approach can become second nature by Test Day.

Note that the GMAT will give you three or four questions per passage, drawing those questions adaptively from a larger pool of up to six to eight problems. (The computer considers both your current score level and the distribution of question types you've seen so far.) For several passages on this quiz, we've given you more than four questions so that you can see the full range of questions the GMAT might ask about a given passage. But remember that on Test Day, you'll see only three or four.

Furthermore, remember that on Test Day, you can't take notes on the computer screen or skip forward and back between questions. So challenge yourself now not to take notes in this book (use separate scratch paper or a wet-erase noteboard like the one you'll use at the testing center) and to do the questions in order.

Questions 1–3 are based on the following passage

Due to the laws and mechanics of the American presidential election system, the plurality winner of a state's popular vote generally gains that state's entire electoral vote. Thus, the winner of the national election is not necessarily the most popular candidate. In the 30 presidential elections from 1880 to 2000, there were two

5 occasions in which the winner of the presidential election did not win a plurality of the popular votes and ten occasions in which the president chosen by this system did not receive the majority of votes cast. Some critics believe that the electoral process should be replaced by a system that might better choose a president who is the most popular candidate among voters. Proposed alternatives include multiple

10 rounds of elections, "approval voting," and "rank voting."

In the approval voting system, each voter can cast votes for as many candidates as he or she wishes. A voter can select one candidate whom he or she favors, or a voter who disapproves of certain candidates can vote for every candidate except the ones whom he or she opposes. The Secretary General of the United Nations is elected using approval

15 voting, and, in a 1990 statewide referendum using the approval voting system, Oregon voters chose from five options for school financing. The approval voting system, however, can be confusing, and it can, theoretically, work against candidates who take strong stands on the issues and therefore attract disapproval.

Rank voting is known more formally as "Borda voting" after its first known

20 proponent, Jean Charles Borda. In this scheme, each voter can rank candidates from first to last. Depending on the number of candidates, each position would represent a number of points. For instance, if there were five candidates, the candidate ranked first would get five points, the candidate ranked second would get four points, and so on. The candidate with the most points in the end would be the winner. Rank voting

25 is used in the United States by the Associated Press to choose the best college sports teams, and a variant is used in most Australian elections. The rank system is advocated by a number of noted scholars, but it is criticized by some because the candidate ranked first by a majority of voters can still lose. For example, a

candidate who is ranked second by 80 percent of the voters could end up with more
30 points than one who is ranked first by 52 percent of the voters.

Although alternative voting systems offer noteworthy alternatives to the current process, there is not enough support for an alternative system in the United States to make its adoption likely in the near future on a national scale.

1. Which of the following best describes the main function of the first paragraph?

   O To lament the nondemocratic nature of the U.S. presidential election system, and to provide alternatives to elections as a means of selecting presidents

   O To show that the winner of a U.S. presidential election isn't necessarily the most popular candidate, and to explain that some critics suggest modifying the system

   O To describe alternatives for the current U.S. presidential election system, and to advocate the acceptance of one alternative

   O To attack the results of U.S. presidential elections, and to warn of the dangers of not adopting an alternative election system

   O To advocate a sweeping reform of the U.S. presidential election system, and to provide evidentiary support for such a reform

2. It can be inferred from the passage that in a U.S. presidential election, the selection of the candidate most popular among the voters

   O is more important than the other results that might be generated from the use of a particular election system.

   O would be attained through the use of the approval system for presidential elections.

   O has occurred in only a minority of U.S. presidential elections since 1880.

   O is critical to the maintenance of democratic institutions in the United States.

   O might be achieved through multiple rounds of elections.

3. The primary purpose of the passage as a whole is to

   O advocate a new system for electing presidents in the United States.

   O explain how the winner of the popular vote can lose the electoral vote.

   O argue that the current electoral system should be replaced with a rank voting system.

   O describe alternatives to the current U.S. presidential election system.

   O demonstrate that the current system of electing U.S. presidents is out-of-date.

Questions 4–6 are based on the following passage

The informal sector of the economy involves activities that, in both developed and underdeveloped countries, are outside the arena of the normal, regulated economy and thus escape official recordkeeping. These activities, which include such practices as off-the-books hiring and cash payments, occur mainly in service
5   industries like construction, hotels, and restaurants. Many economists think that the informal sector is an insignificant supplement to the larger formal economy. They base this belief on three assumptions that have been derived from theories of industrial development. But empirical evidence suggests that these assumptions are not valid.

10   All three assumptions are, essentially, hypotheses about the character of the labor process at different levels of development. The first is that informal activities are transitory, being a consequence of the imperfect penetration of modern capitalism into less developed regions, and are thus destined to disappear with the advance of industrialization. The second is that the principal reason for the
15   continuing existence of an informal sector is to keep a redundant segment of the labor force alive through jobs invented to fit in the interstices of the modern economy. The third is that the informal sector is primarily a feature of peripheral economies such as those of Latin America, Africa, and most of Asia.

Data collected from both developed and underdeveloped countries, however,
20   reveal that the informal sector is neither disappearing with industrialization, limited in function to being an employment alternative of last resort, nor exclusively or particularly a Third World phenomenon. Informal sector employment rates in many countries have remained constant in the postwar era. Moreover, if the informal economy were exclusively a refuge from destitution, two facts would logically follow:
25   First, average income levels among the informally employed would be significantly lower than among workers in formal activities; second, those who found employment in formal activities would never leave voluntarily in order to move into the informal economy. But neither of these predictions is supported by data.

4.   The primary purpose of this passage is to

O   compare the economies of developed and underdeveloped countries.

O   suggest that economists should develop a new framework for studying the global economy.

O   criticize the notion that the informal economy is primarily a Third World phenomenon.

O   dispute a widely held view of the relationship between the formal and informal sectors of the world economy.

O   argue that workers in the informal economy are almost as well paid as those in the formal economy.

5. From the passage, which of the following can be inferred about employment opportunities in the informal economy?

○ Workers employed in the informal economy generally receive much lower wages than do workers in the formal economy.

○ Some workers have purposely chosen to work in the informal economy rather than in the formal economy.

○ The number of workers employed in the informal economy has remained stable over the last few centuries.

○ Employment opportunities in the informal economy will decline as agriculture is displaced by industry.

○ The informal economy has created no employment for workers who would otherwise be unemployable.

6. The author states which of the following about activities in the informal economy?

○ They are an insignificant aspect of the global economy.

○ They provide income for workers who are unemployable in the formal economy.

○ They are a consequence of capitalist penetration of less developed economies.

○ They thrive mainly in underdeveloped countries in Asia, Africa, and Latin America.

○ They consist of such unregulated practices as off-the-books hiring and cash payments.

Questions 7–12 are based on the following passage

The Big Bang model posits that the universe was created in a primordial fireball between 10 and 20 billion years ago. The model attempts to reconstruct the behavior of the early universe using only the rules of general relativity, elementary particle physics, and basic thermodynamics. Matching these claims with
5 observations of the universe today shows its validity.

The Big Bang produced a universe made almost entirely of hydrogen and helium. For the first few seconds of the universe's existence, its temperature was so high—over 10 billion degrees—and energetic electrons, neutrinos, and positrons so abundant that subatomic particles such as neutrons and protons were constantly
10 transmuted into one another. As the universe cooled, these transmutations ceased. Most of the matter took the form of the most stable particle, the proton, leaving a universe where the ratio of protons to neutrons was about seven to one.

After a few minutes, the temperature of the universe fell to about 1 billion degrees, cool enough for these protons and neutrons to bond and form nuclei.
15 Deuterons were formed as each neutron found a proton partner. Most deuterons then joined another deuteron to form a helium nucleus. As the universe continued to expand and cool, its density became too low to allow further fusion into heavier elements, and so almost all the neutrons were incorporated into helium. Only 0.01 percent of the deuterons formed remained unpaired, and an even smaller
20 percentage had fused into elements heavier than helium, such as lithium.

Because only one neutron was formed for every seven protons, six-sevenths of all protons remained isolated. These remaining protons formed hydrogen nuclei containing one proton each. The Big Bang model predicts that about three-quarters of the total mass of the universe will be hydrogen and the remaining quarter
25 helium. This simple prediction matches observations very well.

7. The author is primarily concerned with

○ explaining how the evolution of the universe is incompatible with the implications of the Big Bang model.

○ chronicling the events that followed the creation of matter by the Big Bang.

○ explaining how helium was formed in the early life of the universe.

○ illustrating specific propositions of a model and showing how they have been supported by observation.

○ showing how the ratios of protons to neutrons created in the Big Bang dictated the final ratio of hydrogen to helium in the universe.

8. In the fourth paragraph, the author introduces information about the Big Bang model's prediction for the molecular composition of the universe in order to

○ obviate the claim that six-sevenths of all protons remained isolated.

○ show that the remaining quarter of the total mass of the universe must be helium.

○ provide evidence for the veracity of the Big Bang model.

○ describe the means by which remaining protons formed hydrogen nuclei.

○ predict the results of a Big Bang.

9. According to the passage, which of the following was true during the first few seconds of the universe's existence?

I. The great majority of neutrons were incorporated into helium molecules.

II. The temperature was not high enough to allow for the formation of deuterons.

III. Vast numbers of subatomic particles rapidly metamorphosed into other types of particles.

○ None

○ I only

○ III only

○ II and III only

○ I, II, and III

10. The author uses the first paragraph to introduce

    O a scientific model that the passage will show to be supported by modern evidence.

    O a theory of the origin of the universe that the passage will describe and attempt to refute.

    O a description of the theoretical basis for a scientific model and the modern evidence undermining it.

    O an attempt to use recent evidence to revive a discarded scientific model.

    O a detailed description of an appealing but unsupported theoretical model.

11. The author would most likely agree with the position that

    O models of the creation of the universe that were made before the Big Bang model was created failed because they did not take into account the behavior of subatomic particles.

    O no credence can be given to a scientific model unless it is possible to produce supporting data through a series of controlled experiments.

    O the Big Bang was part of a cycle of expansion and contraction in the universe.

    O it is beneficial to use the statistical evidence at hand when judging the veracity of scientific models for which the process cannot be repeated in a laboratory.

    O the simplicity of the Big Bang theory accounts for its accuracy.

12. According to the passage, a helium nucleus

    O could only be created early in the universe's history.

    O has a low density due to the cooling and expansion of the universe.

    O is more stable than a lithium nucleus.

    O has four times the mass of a hydrogen nucleus.

    O consists of exactly two neutrons and two protons.

Questions 13–17 are based on the following passage

Parfleche is the French name for the Plains peoples' *hoemskot 'eo*—an envelope-shaped rawhide container for storing clothes, food, and personal items. The *parfleche* served not only as a practical and durable storage solution, but also as a decorative object of spiritual significance. Among certain tribes, most notably

5 the Cheyenne and Arapaho, *parfleches* were decorated by the women's painting society, whose members among the Cheyenne were known as *moneneheo*, the Selected Ones. Although similar in their economic and social importance to craftsmen's guilds in medieval and Renaissance Western Europe, the painting society also had a spiritual or religious nature. The shamanistic society required application for

10 admission and held its members to high artistic and moral standards. The society further displayed its importance by defining aspects of Cheyenne wealth and status.

Painting on rawhide was fraught with challenges. If painting was attempted while the prepared hide was too moist, the applied paint bled, but if the hide was too dry, the skin did not absorb the pigments. This restricted the time frame in which

15 painting could best be completed, which meant that designs had to be visualized

fully before the work started. Moreover, every aspect of creating a *parfleche* was
a sacred act. Each design element, for instance, was a syntagma—a linguistic or
visual unit intended to convey meaning—freighted with symbolic referents. For
example, diamond shapes represented the *ha 'kot*, the grasshopper, an abundant

20 grass eater itself symbolic of the bison, the sacred source of food, shelter, tools,
and clothing. The tools used were also symbolic: The shape of the "flesher" used to
prepare the hide represented lightning bolts—emblematic of the masculine essence
of spirit. The flesher removed the flesh from the hide, transforming it into a spiritual
container that would hold earthly matter (the people's material goods).

25 Even the position of the *parfleche* in the lodge held symbolic significance. It
was stored beneath the bed of older women, not only because they were careful
guardians, but also because they were closer to Grandmother Earth, from whose
union with the lightning spirit the animals and plants of the middle world came to
provide food and shelter. The symbolism of every aspect of the *parfleche,* therefore,

30 from the interpretable design work on its outside to its storage place within the
lodge, reflects the Cheyenne belief in a complementary worldview: the blending of
the masculine spirit and the feminine physical matter.

13. According to the passage, one reason why there was a limited time frame in which to
paint a prepared rawhide was that

- ○ the pigments dried quickly and thus had to be applied with speed to avoid
  cracking.
- ○ if the hide was too dry, it absorbed too much paint.
- ○ if the hide was too moist, it rejected the pigments.
- ○ the designs had to be fully visualized before painting was started.
- ○ if the hide was too moist, the paint bled.

14. The main purpose of the passage is to

- ○ describe a tool used among Native Americans when working with rawhide.
- ○ rebut a commonly held view about the symbolism of the *parfleche* for the
  Plains peoples.
- ○ analyze the societies of the Cheyenne and Arapaho people.
- ○ propose a new method for analyzing the use of symbolism in Native American
  art.
- ○ discuss the spiritual and symbolic importance of a rawhide container and its
  decorations to several Plains tribes.

15. According to the author, the Cheyenne women's painting society was unlike Western
European guilds of the Middle Ages and the Renaissance in that

- ○ application for membership was required.
- ○ the group had significant economic standing in the community.
- ○ the group had significant social standing in the community.
- ○ the women's painting society was religious in nature.
- ○ the society had an influence on social standing and material valuation.

16. You can most reasonably conclude that the Cheyenne definition of the term *moneneheo* (line 6) reflects

    O the high status some women enjoyed as artists in Cheyenne culture.

    O the shamanistic spiritual origins of the women's painting society.

    O the notion that artists were chosen by the gods to perform their tasks.

    O the self-restrictive nature of the women's painting society.

    O a woman's skill in using rawhide tools such as the "flesher."

17. The author describes the symbolic meanings of the diamond shape most likely in order to

    O indicate how precious the completed *parfleche* was to its owner.

    O prove that the grasshopper was superior to the bison in Cheyenne religion.

    O illustrate the visual complexity of the abstract forms used in creating a *parfleche.*

    O provide an example of the many layers of symbolism involved in creating a *parfleche.*

    O demonstrate the relationship between the symbolic shapes of the tools and the abstract designs used in creating a *parfleche.*

Questions 18–23 are based on the following passage

Prior to the nineteenth century, both human and animal populations were limited by the finite resources (such as food) to which they had access. When the enormous increases in prosperity ushered in by the Industrial Revolution essentially freed many Western nations from these constraints, scientists of the time expected
5 a Malthusian explosion in population. However, an inverse relationship between prosperity and reproduction was soon noted; the average size of families fell. The trend continues to this day and has spread to recently industrialized portions of the world.

Early biologists tried to explain the transition to smaller families by drawing
10 comparisons to the animal world. Animals that have many young tend to live in hostile, unpredictable environments. Since the odds against any given offspring's survival are high, having many offspring increases the chance that at least one or two of them will survive. In contrast, animals that have fewer children but invest more resources in childrearing tend to live in stable, less hostile environments.
15 While the young of these "high-investment" species enjoy the benefits of a relatively safe environment, they need to compete with animals whose young are equally unlikely to perish early in life. Therefore, the biologists observed, progeny that have acquired the skills they need to compete while sheltered by a family have an advantage over their less prepared competitors. By analogy, if people living in
20 a prosperous environment produced only a few, pampered children, those children would out-compete the progeny of parents who had stretched their resources too widely.

Critics of this theory argue that there are limitations in conflating animal and human behavior. They argue instead that changes in social attitudes are adequate
25 to explain this phenomenon. To a family in a society that is tied to the land, a large

number of children is a great boon. They increase family income by being put to work early, and usually some can be persuaded to care for their parents into old age. As a society becomes richer, and as physical labor becomes less important, education may extend into the early twenties, making children economically
30   unattractive as they now consume family assets rather than produce them. Meanwhile, plans such as pensions and Social Security mitigate the need for children to care for their parents into their dotage.

18. The primary purpose of the passage is to

    O   criticize explanations of human behavior that are based solely on observations taken from the animal world.

    O   show why the expected population explosion following the Industrial Revolution did not occur before the Industrial Revolution.

    O   demonstrate how family size was influenced by both environmental restraints and social attitudes before and after the Industrial Revolution.

    O   present two alternative theories that explain why family size tends to shrink with increased prosperity.

    O   argue that studies based on social attitudes are more effective than models based on evolutionary advantages in accounting for demographic patterns.

19. According to the passage, which of the following is true of a Malthusian explosion in population?

    O   Its occurrence has been limited to those areas of the globe that have remained preindustrial.

    O   It is inevitable in societies making the transition from an economy based on agriculture to one based on industry.

    O   It was predicted by at least some who lived through the Industrial Revolution in the West.

    O   Social scientists have only recently reached consensus on the question of why it fails to occur in recently industrialized countries.

    O   It was avoided in Western society because the wealth created by industrialization allowed families to support children through extended periods of education.

20. The last paragraph performs which of the following functions in the passage?

    O   It presents an alternate explanation for the phenomenon described in the first paragraph.

    O   It criticizes the explanation presented in the second paragraph.

    O   It describes how social attitudes change as societies become richer.

    O   It explains a phenomenon presented in the second paragraph.

    O   It argues that changing social attitudes are sufficient to explain the phenomenon described in the first paragraph.

21. The passage mentions each of the following as a possible reason average family size might fall in recently industrialized nations EXCEPT:

    O   extended periods of education that make children a drain on family resources

    O   well-fed, advantaged children who out-compete those in less advantaged families

    O   improved social care of the elderly

    O   changed social attitudes

    O   increased demand for physical laborers in recently industrialized economies

22. The information in the passage suggests that which of the following animals would be most likely to have many young?

    O   A plant eater that lives in drought-susceptible grassland and is fiercely protective of its offspring.

    O   An omnivore whose population is restricted to several small islands that are threatened by human encroachment.

    O   A meat eater that has no natural predators but must migrate long distances to maintain its supply of food.

    O   A scavenger that competes with few other species for territory and food.

    O   A filter feeder that is prey for many creatures in the seasonal streams and lakes where it lives.

23. The author mentions a decrease in the importance of physical labor (line 28) in order to

    O   give an example of the factors that may lead to changes in social attitudes toward family size.

    O   demonstrate why those who anticipated a Malthusian explosion in population in industrialized Europe were incorrect.

    O   show how family structures adjust to meet the demands of a changing economy.

    O   rebut the claims of those who argue that there are limitations in conflating human and animal behavior.

    O   illustrate how larger families can increase family income.

Questions 24–29 are based on the following passage

Generally, interspecific matings represent an evolutionary dead end, producing sterile offspring, if any at all. For some species of birds, however, such pairings may indeed bring evolutionary advantages to the participants. In the case of the female collared flycatchers of Gotland, three distinct factors may work to make interspecific
5   pairings with pied flycatcher males reproductively beneficial.

In many instances, female collared flycatchers nest with male pied flycatchers while continuing to mate with other collared flycatchers, in effect parasitizing the pied flycatchers, who invest in rearing and fledging any offspring. Often, more than half of the offspring raised by interspecific flycatcher pairs are, in fact, not hybrids.
10   Furthermore, an estimated 65 percent of the hybrid offspring of the resident pied flycatcher male are male. Because hybrid females are sterile and males are not, this male bias minimizes the primary disadvantage of interspecific matings: sterile offspring. Habitat specialization may be a third mechanism: These pairings tend to occur in the late spring when the coniferous woods favored by the pied flycatcher
15   provide a greater availability of food than the deciduous woods where the collared flycatchers tend to live. Together, these factors form a mechanism to improve substantially the reproductive success of female collared flycatchers beyond what would be expected of interspecific mating with pied flycatcher males.

Although all three of these mechanisms appear to act in concert to form a single
20   elaborate mechanism specifically evolved to circumvent the usual disadvantages of interspecific mating, studies have shown similar motivations for the behavior of female collared flycatchers mating within the species. According to Professor Siever Rohwer, collared flycatcher females will choose to nest with subordinate collared flycatcher males that inhabit good territory because collared flycatcher females
25   must pair-bond in order to be successful in raising offspring. To engender the best offspring, however, the females will continue to copulate with higher-quality collared males with whom they are not paired. Thus, females seem to be nesting with males of any species with the best territories available at the time, but they will continue to mate with more attractive males outside of their pair bonds.

30   A highly unusual behavior, interspecific mating seems to provide certain reproductive advantages to the collared flycatcher female. However, it remains unclear whether the mating behavior of female collared flycatchers evolved to circumvent the usual problems with interspecific mating or whether the behavior is simply an extension of how female collared flycatchers behave when mating within
35   their own species.

24. The author's primary purpose is to

  O criticize the basis of a scientific theory.

  O defend a hypothesis concerning bird-mating behaviors.

  O point out the need for further study of female collared flycatchers.

  O describe two possible explanations for the interspecific mating behavior of female collared flycatchers.

  O defend an unpopular view of a natural phenomenon.

25. According to the passage, female collared flycatchers' mating with male pied flycatchers could be explained by any of the following reasons EXCEPT:

    O Food is more available in pied flycatcher territories during the mating season.

    O Male pied flycatchers can help raise offspring successfully, even if the offspring are not theirs.

    O Male pied flycatchers sire more female offspring than do collared flycatcher males, increasing the reproductive success of the female collared flycatcher.

    O Females are known to nest with subordinate males while pursuing extra-pair copulation with higher-quality males.

    O Females enjoy greater reproductive success by pair-bonding with an inferior male than by not pair-bonding at all.

26. The bias toward male offspring resulting from the mating of collared flycatcher females and pied flycatcher males is presented as evidence that

    O collared flycatcher females that mate with pied flycatcher males have more dominant male offspring.

    O the offspring from extra-pair matings with collared flycatcher males are more frequently male.

    O female flycatchers are not deterred from interspecific pairing by the likelihood of sterile hybrid offspring.

    O males are produced to reduce interspecific inbreeding in future generations.

    O interspecific breeding is normal in all varieties of flycatchers.

27. It can be inferred from the passage that

    O food resources are an important determinant of success in raising offspring.

    O having 50 percent male offspring is not optimal for collared flycatcher pairs.

    O flycatchers generally mate for life.

    O males do not vary in the benefits they provide to their offspring.

    O over half of all females engage in extra-pair matings.

28. Professor Rohwer would most likely agree with which of the following statements?

   O   All traits related to particular functions have evolved only for those particular
       functions.

   O   Flycatchers represent the best population for studies of bird-mating behavior.

   O   Behaviors may appear functional even under conditions other than those
       under which the behaviors evolved.

   O   Evolution has played no role in shaping the behavior of interspecifically paired
       flycatchers.

   O   Hybridization is generally beneficial.

29. The mating behavior of female collared flycatchers paired with subordinate male
    flycatchers is offered as

   O   an unwarranted assumption behind the adaptive explanation of interspecific
       matings.

   O   an alternative explanation for pair matings of collared females with pied
       males.

   O   evidence supporting the hypothesis of adaption for interspecific breeding.

   O   a discredited mainstream explanation for why hybridization is a dead end.

   O   proof in support of the theory that collared and pied flycatchers are separate
       species.

Questions 30–35 are based on the following passage

A regimen of intrauterine AZT (zidovudine) as a means of reducing the chances
of HIV transmission from mother to child was first described in a study known as
Protocol 076, the results of which were published in the *New England Journal of
Medicine* in November 1994. The trial found that administration of AZT to HIV-
5   positive women during pregnancy and delivery, and to their babies after birth,
reduced the transmission of HIV to the infants by two-thirds, compared with a
placebo. The study was acclaimed as one of the first successful instances of a
prophylaxis preventing HIV transmission—particularly "vertical" transmission, or
transmission from mothers to infants. The study, prematurely ended so that all the
10   subjects on placebos could be switched to AZT, led to the recommendation that all
pregnant women with HIV take AZT.

The validity of the study's results, however, is debatable. Since Protocol 076
examined only women who had fairly high numbers of T-cells—the white blood
cells that coordinate immune response—and who had previously taken AZT for less
15   than six months, the same regimen might not succeed for other pregnant women
with HIV. Moreover, the study administered large doses of AZT without examining
whether lower doses, more economically feasible for uninsured or underinsured
women, might be effective. Further, the trial design did not account for important
variables: in particular, whether the subjects' viral load—the amount of HIV in their
20   bodies—might have contributed to the difference in transmission rates. Since the
exact mechanism and timing of vertical transmission of the HIV virus are unknown,
it cannot be ruled out that viral load influences rates of vertical transmission.

Also, the study did not consider the long-term impact of AZT, which is toxic, on
the babies themselves. There have been few studies of AZT's effect on HIV-positive
25 infants and none on its effects on uninfected babies. Since the majority of the
babies born to HIV-positive women are HIV-negative, and since HIV may mutate
into drug-resistant strains following a break in medication, the value of a short-term
"zap" with AZT becomes suspect.

30. The author questions the results of Protocol 076 for which of the following reasons?

   O   The number of T-cells was not considered in choosing subjects for the study.

   O   The trial was discontinued, and the control group of women on placebo was
       shifted to AZT.

   O   Seventy-five percent of babies born to women in the placebo group were free
       of infection with HIV.

   O   Different transmission rates could have been influenced by different amounts
       of HIV in the women's bodies.

   O   The exact mechanism and timing of HIV transmission are unknown.

31. The author of this passage would be LEAST likely to challenge the benefits of
    intrauterine AZT for which of the following HIV-positive women and/or their future
    children?

   O   A woman who has used the regimen successfully in a previous pregnancy

   O   A woman whose T-cell count is dangerously low and who plans to continue
       taking AZT after her baby is born

   O   A woman who is matched with the study's subjects in terms of ethnicity and
       socioeconomic status

   O   A woman who has lost a previous infant to HIV and who wants to be sure
       that her next child is healthy

   O   A woman whose T-cell count is not low and who has not taken AZT before

32. The passage implies that the "viral loads" of the subjects in the study are significant
    because

   O   all the subjects had relatively high viral loads, so the study's results may not
       apply to other groups of women.

   O   the viral loads of babies whose mothers had received the placebo were just
       as high as those of babies whose mothers had received AZT.

   O   viral load must be measured if researchers are to understand the exact
       mechanism and timing of transmission of HIV.

   O   the viral loads of women in the placebo group may have been different from
       those of women in the AZT group.

   O   viral load may be a critical factor in determining transmission, but the
       researchers wrongly assumed that it was the only factor.

33. The primary purpose of the passage is to

    ○ document recent problems with HIV and AIDS treatment.

    ○ expose medical errors caused by careless methodology in an important clinical trial.

    ○ raise doubts about a course of treatment based on a groundbreaking study.

    ○ describe the process of vertical transmission of HIV and suggest preventive therapy.

    ○ evaluate treatment possibilities for pregnant women with HIV.

34. The author of the passage would be most likely to agree with which of the following statements?

    ○ Medications harmful to one group of patients are probably not harmful to another.

    ○ Recommendations based on a conditional experiment must be qualified.

    ○ The study should not have been prematurely ended.

    ○ Clinical trials that may harm patients are unethical.

    ○ No HIV-positive woman should take AZT during pregnancy.

35. The primary function of the second paragraph is to

    ○ refute issues.

    ○ evaluate solutions.

    ○ describe results.

    ○ support action.

    ○ identify problems.

ANSWERS AND EXPLANATIONS BEGIN ON NEXT PAGE

ANSWERS AND EXPLANATIONS

1.	B	10.	A	19.	C	28.	C
2.	E	11.	D	20.	A	29.	B
3.	D	12.	E	21.	E	30.	D
4.	D	13.	E	22.	E	31.	E
5.	B	14.	E	23.	A	32.	D
6.	E	15.	D	24.	D	33.	C
7.	D	16.	A	25.	C	34.	B
8.	C	17.	D	26.	C	35.	E
9.	C	18.	D	27.	A		

On the left, we've shown how keywords help you to identify the major elements of the passage and its structure and what you could skim over. On the right, we've shown what you might be thinking as you read the passage strategically.

Passage for Questions 1–3

Due to the laws and mechanics of the **American presidential election system**, the plurality winner of a state's popular vote generally gains that state's entire electoral vote. **Thus**, the winner of the national election is not necessarily the most popular candidate. In the 30 presidential elections from 1880 to 2000, there were two occasions in which the winner of the presidential election did not win a plurality of the popular votes and ten occasions in which the president chosen by this system did not receive the majority of votes cast. **Some critics believe** that the electoral process should be replaced by a system that might better choose a president who is the most popular candidate among voters. **Proposed alternatives** include multiple rounds of elections, "approval voting," and "rank voting."

In the **approval voting system**, each voter can cast votes for as many candidates as he or she wishes. A voter can select one candidate whom he or she favors, or a voter who disapproves of certain candidates can vote for every candidate except the ones whom he or she opposes. The Secretary General of the United Nations is elected using approval voting, and, in a 1990 statewide referendum using the approval voting system, Oregon voters chose from five options for school financing. The approval voting system, **however**, can be confusing, and it can, theoretically, work against candidates who take strong stands on the issues and therefore attract disapproval.

Analysis

The topic, the American presidential election system, is announced in the first sentence.

A quirky effect of the current system: The winner isn't necessarily the most popular candidate. This leads the critics to suggest that a different system might be better.

Because the author enumerates the possible alternative systems at the end of the opening paragraph, we expect to see at least some of them discussed in later paragraphs.

Indeed, here's the first alternative we'll hear about: approval voting, which simply seems to be a system allowing voters to cast votes for multiple candidates they approve of.

Here we get a couple of examples of elections run according to approval voting.

The word "however" indicates contrast. We've been hearing that approval voting is a system that is in fact in use, but the author believes that it nevertheless has a couple of drawbacks.

Rank voting is known more formally as "Borda voting" after its first known proponent, Jean Charles Borda. **In this scheme**, each voter can rank candidates from first to last. Depending on the number of candidates, each position would represent a number of points. **For instance**, if there were five candidates, the candidate ranked first would get five points, the candidate ranked second would get four points, and so on. The candidate with the most points in the end would be the winner. Rank voting is used in the United States by the Associated Press to choose the best college sports teams, and a variant is used in most Australian elections. The rank system is **advocated** by a number of noted scholars, **but it is criticized** by some because the candidate ranked first by a majority of voters can still lose. **For example**, a candidate who is ranked second by 80 percent of the voters could end up with more points than one who is ranked first by 52 percent of the voters.

Although alternative voting systems offer **noteworthy alternatives** to the current process, there is **not enough support** for an alternative system in the United States to make its adoption likely in the near future on a national scale.

Now the author proceeds to discuss a second alternative: rank voting. The words "in this scheme" indicate that we're about to be given a description of the rank voting method.

Here we get specific examples of elections using rank voting.

Like approval voting, rank voting apparently has its pros and cons.

The keyword "Although" signals a contrast: The author thinks there are "noteworthy" methods that could replace the current one, but they aren't likely to be put into use anytime soon.

Passage Map

¶1: *American presidential election system = electoral system*

   Problem: candidate with most popular vote can lose

   Critics favor alternatives

¶2: *Approval voting: can vote for several candidates*

   Drawback: can be confusing

¶3: *Rank voting: voters rank choices*

   Drawback: candidate ranked 1st by majority could still lose

¶4: *Author likes alternatives, but they probably won't be adopted soon*

Topic: American presidential election system

Scope: Problem with, and alternatives to, the current system

Purpose: Describe problem with current electoral system and two potential alternatives

1. **(B)**

    Which of the following best describes the main function of the first paragraph?

    - ○ To lament the nondemocratic nature of the U.S. presidential election system, and to provide alternatives to elections as a means of selecting presidents
    - ○ To show that the winner of a U.S. presidential election isn't necessarily the most popular candidate, and to explain that some critics suggest modifying The system
    - ○ To describe alternatives for the current U.S. presidential election system, and to advocate the acceptance of one alternative
    - ○ To attack the results of U.S. presidential elections, and to warn of the dangers of not adopting an alternative election system
    - ○ To advocate a sweeping reform of the U.S. presidential election system, and to provide evidentiary support for such a reform

Step 2: Analyze the Question Stem

Because we are asked for the function of a chunk of the passage, this is a Logic question. Specifically, we are asked to deduce the role played by the first paragraph.

Step 3: Research the Relevant Text

A glance at our Passage Map will suffice in this case. We shouldn't have to go back to the passage text itself.

Step 4: Make a Prediction

The first paragraph, we noted in our Passage Map, describes the American presidential election system, states that there is a problem with the current system that has caused it to receive some criticism, and lists several proposed alternatives.

Step 5: Evaluate the Answer Choices

(B) matches our prediction and is the correct answer. The fact that the winner of a U.S. presidential election isn't necessarily the most popular candidate is the "problem" we recorded in our Passage Map. **(A)** is incorrect because the author takes a very neutral tone. The initial verb, "to lament," is sufficient to throw this one out. Moreover, the author never describes the U.S. presidential election system as "nondemocratic." **(C)** is incorrect because the author does not "advocate" for either of the proposed alternatives. **(D)** is incorrect because the author does not "attack" election results. **(E)** is similar to **(C)**; again, the author does not "advocate" making a change to the current system. Choice **(B)** is correct.

2. **(E)**

It can be inferred from the passage that in a U.S. presidential election, the selection of the candidate most popular among the voters

- ○ is more important than the other results that might be generated from the use of a particular election system.
- ○ would be attained through the use of the approval system for presidential elections.
- ○ has occurred in only a minority of U.S. presidential elections since 1880.
- ○ is critical to the maintenance of democratic institutions in the United States.
- ○ might be achieved through multiple rounds of elections.

Step 2: Analyze the Question Stem

The word "inferred" signals that this is an Inference questions. The correct answer must be true based only on information in the passage. Note that the question asks us specifically about the selection of the most popular candidate in U.S. presidential elections.

Step 3: Research the Relevant Text

We can use our Passage Map to confirm that the question stem points to the first paragraph, where the author discusses the current practice used in American presidential elections. We read that under the current system, the winner of the popular vote is not necessarily the winner of an election and that critics have proposed alternative systems that would make the winner more likely to be the popular favorite, including multiple rounds of elections, approval voting, and rank voting.

Step 4: Make a Prediction

While it is difficult to make a specific prediction because the sentence in the question stem could be completed in multiple ways, the correct answer will be in accord with the information we have gleaned from the first paragraph about the U.S. presidential election system.

Step 5: Evaluate the Answer Choices

(A) cannot be correct because there is nothing in the first paragraph to indicate that electing the most popular candidate is "more important" than any other result of a particular election system. **(B)** might be tempting, because we read about the possibility of using approval voting in the last sentence of the first paragraph. However, we can throw out this choice as extreme. The author merely states that approval voting is one of the systems that the critics believe "might" better choose the most popular candidate; there is no indication that the approval voting system would definitely have this effect. **(C)** cannot be correct according to the numbers given in the first paragraph. In 20 of 30 presidential elections, the winner has received the majority of votes cast, and in 28 of 30, he has received the plurality of votes cast. Either way, that's the majority of elections since 1880. **(D)** is outside the scope. There is no mention of anything being "critical to the maintenance of democratic institutions." That leaves **(E)**, which corrects the extreme language of **(B)**. It is true, according to the last few lines of the first paragraph, that selecting the most popular candidate "might" be achieved through multiple rounds of elections. Choice **(E)** is correct.

3. **(D)**

    The primary purpose of the passage as a whole is to

    ○   advocate a new system for electing presidents in the United States.
    ○   explain how the winner of the popular vote can lose the electoral vote.
    ○   argue that the current electoral system should be replaced with a rank voting system.
    ○   describe alternatives to the current U.S. presidential election system.
    ○   demonstrate that the current system of electing U.S. presidents is out-of-date.

Step 2: Analyze the Question Stem

The phrase "primary purpose" indicates that this is a Global question. We need to ascertain the author's purpose in writing the passage.

Step 3: Research the Relevant Text

The only research we'll need to do will be to consult our statements of topic, scope, and purpose.

Step 4: Make a Prediction

We said that the author's purpose is to describe a problem with the current U.S. electoral system, as well as two alternatives that have been proposed.

Step 5: Evaluate the Answer Choices

(D) matches our prediction and is the correct answer. **(A)** is incorrect because the author isn't "advocating" for anything. The tone of the passage is fairly neutral. **(B)** is a classic wrong answer type called "faulty use of detail." The passage definitely discusses how the winner of the popular vote can lose the electoral vote, but it goes on to discuss the two proposed alternative election systems. Watch out for answer choices that, like this one, provide you with only part of the passage when you're looking for a choice that encompasses the entire thing. **(C)** is incorrect because the author does not make any recommendations. **(E)** is incorrect because the passage makes no mention of the idea that the current electoral system is "out-of-date." Choice **(D)** is correct.

· On the left, we've shown how keywords help you to identify the major elements of the passage and its structure and what you could skim over. On the right, we've shown what you might be thinking as you read the passage strategically.

Passage for Questions 4–6

The **informal sector of the economy** involves activities that, in both developed and underdeveloped countries, are outside the arena of the normal, regulated economy and thus escape official recordkeeping. These activities, which include such practices as off-the-books hiring and cash payments, **occur mainly** in service industries like construction, hotels, and restaurants. **Many economists** think that the informal sector is an insignificant supplement to the larger formal economy. They base this belief on **three assumptions** that have been derived from theories of industrial development. **But** empirical evidence suggests that these assumptions are **not valid.**

All three assumptions are, essentially, hypotheses about the character of the labor process at different levels of development. The **first** is that informal activities are transitory, being a consequence of the imperfect penetration of modern capitalism into less developed regions, and are thus destined to disappear with the advance of industrialization. The **second** is that the principal reason for the continuing existence of an informal sector is to keep a redundant segment of the labor force alive through jobs invented to fit in the interstices of the modern economy. The **third** is that the informal sector is primarily a feature of peripheral economies such as those of Latin America, Africa, and most of Asia.

Analysis

The author begins by describing the informal sector of the economy, which will be the topic of the passage.

Economists think the informal sector is not important, based on three assumptions.

The author of the passage disagrees with the economists' assumptions, citing evidence to the contrary.

The second paragraph outlines the three assumptions made by the economists mentioned above.

The author's opinion doesn't figure into this paragraph—it only identifies the three assumptions.

EXPLANATIONS

Data collected from both developed and underdeveloped countries, **however**, reveal that the informal sector is neither disappearing with industrialization, limited in function to being an employment alternative of last resort, nor exclusively or particularly a Third World phenomenon. Informal sector employment rates in many countries have remained constant in the postwar era. **Moreover**, if the informal economy were exclusively a refuge from destitution, two facts would logically follow: First, average income levels among the informally employed would be significantly lower than among workers in formal activities; second, those who found employment in formal activities would never leave voluntarily in order to move into the informal economy. **But** neither of these predictions is supported by data.

Here the author discusses how the "data" refute the first of the economists' assumptions (transitory)...

and the second (redundant)...

and the third (peripheral).

The author further develops the rebuttal.

Passage Map

¶1: Description of informal sector

Economists think it's unimportant, due to three assumptions

¶2: Economists' assumptions about the informal sector:

(1) transitory

(2) created for those who cannot find jobs within the formal economy (redundant)

(3) a feature of developing economies (peripheral)

¶3: Economists' assumptions are all incorrect

Reasons given to refute the first two

Topic: Informal sector of the economy

Scope: Economists' belief and assumptions about the informal sector

Purpose: To show the economists are incorrect in their assumptions and thus in their belief that the informal sector is insignificant

4. **(D)**

The primary purpose of this passage is to

O compare the economies of developed and underdeveloped countries.

O suggest that economists should develop a new framework for studying the global economy.

O criticize the notion that the informal economy is primarily a Third World phenomenon.

O dispute a widely held view of the relationship between the formal and informal sectors of the world economy.

O argue that workers in the informal economy are almost as well paid as those in the formal economy.

Step 2: Analyze the Question Stem

The phrase "primary purpose" signals that this is a Global question. We need the author's reason for writing the passage.

Step 3: Research the Relevant Text

For this question, we'll simply consult our notes on topic, scope, and purpose. We shouldn't have to go back to the passage itself.

Step 4: Make a Prediction

We noted that the author's purpose in writing the passage is to demonstrate that the economists are wrong in thinking the informal sector of the economy to be "insignificant" compared to the formal sector.

Step 5: Evaluate the Answer Choices

(D) matches our prediction. The "widely held view" is that of the economists. **(A)** is outside the scope of the passage, which focuses on the economists' assumptions about the informal sector of the economy. **(B)** is again outside the scope. The author makes no recommendation as to what the economists "should" do. **(C)** is a classic faulty use of detail. The idea that the informal sector is a Third World phenomenon is certainly mentioned and criticized in the passage (specifically, in paragraph 3), but this isn't the purpose of the entire passage. **(E)** is another faulty use of detail. The pay rates of informal- and formal-sector workers are mentioned in the third paragraph, but again, this doesn't constitute the purpose of the entire passage. Choice **(D)** is correct.

5.   **(B)**

From the passage, which of the following can be inferred about employment opportunities in the informal economy?

O   Workers employed in the informal economy generally receive much lower wages than do workers in the formal economy.

O   Some workers have purposely chosen to work in the informal economy rather than in the formal economy.

O   The number of workers employed in the informal economy has remained stable over the last few centuries.

O   Employment opportunities in the informal economy will decline as agriculture is displaced by industry.

O   The informal economy has created no employment for workers who would otherwise be unemployable.

Step 2: Analyze the Question Stem

The word "inferred" signals an Inference question. This question stem provides us with a context clue: "employment opportunities in the informal economy."

Step 3: Research the Relevant Text

Unless a question specifically mentions a different point of view, it is asking for the author's perspective. We can safely confine our research to the first and third paragraphs and leave out the second, which describes the economists' assumptions. In the first paragraph, we learn that informal sector occupations are typically service jobs such as construction, hotel, or restaurant jobs. In the third paragraph, we learn that informal sector jobs are not jobs "of last resort," because they don't necessarily pay a great deal less than formal sector jobs and because some workers actually move "voluntarily" from the formal to the informal sector.

Step 4: Make a Prediction

While it is difficult to make a precise prediction for this question, the correct answer will follow from our research. We'll check the answer choices against it one at a time.

Step 5: Evaluate the Answer Choices

(A) states the opposite of the wage information we found in the third paragraph. **(B)** paraphrases the last couple of lines of the passage: Data support the idea that some workers do voluntarily move from formal sector employment to informal sector employment. This is the correct answer. **(C)** is too extreme. We learn in the third paragraph that "informal sector employment rates in many countries have remained constant in the postwar era," but we have no support for the idea that such employment has remained stable for "centuries." **(C)** also confuses employment rates (which are percentages) with the number employed. **(D)** restates one of the economists' assumptions. It is the economists, not the author, who believe that the informal sector will disappear with increasing industrialization. **(E)** is extreme. While the author debunks the economists' assumption that the informal sector is "limited in function to being an employment alternative of last resort," she never goes so far as to say that not a single job for an otherwise unemployable person has been created in the informal sector. Choice **(B)** is correct.

6. **(E)**

    The author states which of the following about activities in the informal economy?

    ○ They are an insignificant aspect of the global economy.
    ○ They provide income for workers who are unemployable in the formal economy.
    ○ They are a consequence of capitalist penetration of less developed economies.
    ○ They thrive mainly in underdeveloped countries in Asia, Africa, and Latin America.
    ○ They consist of such unregulated practices as off-the-books hiring and cash payments.

Step 2: Analyze the Question Stem

This Detail question asks us for something the author "states" explicitly. All we need to do is go back to the passage and look up the "activities in the informal economy."

Step 3: Research the Relevant Text

The "activities" that take place in the informal economy are mentioned at the beginning of the first paragraph. We learn that they are typically "off-the-books" and that they include hiring and cash payments in the construction, hotel, and restaurant industries.

Step 4: Make a Prediction

We'll look for an answer choice that mentions any of the details we gleaned from our research. Remember that for a Detail question, the correct answer has to come from the passage nearly verbatim.

Step 5: Evaluate the Answer Choices

(E) restates what we read in the first paragraph and is the correct answer. **(A)** is incorrect because it is the economists, not the author, who believe that informal sector activities are "insignificant." **(B)** is incorrect because, again, it states one of the economists' assumptions, not the author's opinion. Similarly, **(C)** and **(D)** are incorrect because they present the economists' beliefs, not the author's. Choice **(E)** is correct.

On the left, we've shown how keywords help you to identify the major elements of the passage and its structure and what you could skim over. On the right, we've shown what you might be thinking as you read the passage strategically.

Passage for Questions 7–12

The Big Bang model **posits** that the universe was created in a primordial fireball between 10 and 20 billion years ago. The model **attempts** to reconstruct the behavior of the early universe using only the rules of general relativity, elementary particle physics, and basic thermodynamics. Matching these claims with observations of the universe today **shows its validity**.

The Big Bang produced a universe made almost entirely of hydrogen and helium. For the **first few seconds** of the universe's existence, its temperature was **so high**—over 10 billion degrees—and energetic electrons, neutrinos, and positrons **so abundant** that subatomic particles such as neutrons and protons were constantly transmuted into one another. As the universe **cooled**, these transmutations ceased. Most of the matter took the form of the most stable particle, the proton, leaving a universe where the ratio of protons to neutrons was about seven to one.

After a few minutes, the **temperature** of the universe **fell** to about 1 billion degrees, **cool enough** for these protons and neutrons to bond and form nuclei. Deuterons were formed as each neutron found a proton partner. Most deuterons then joined another deuteron to form a helium nucleus. As the universe **continued to** expand and **cool**, its density became too low to allow further fusion into heavier elements, and so almost all the neutrons were incorporated into helium. Only 0.01 percent of the deuterons formed remained unpaired, and an even smaller percentage had fused into elements heavier than helium, such as lithium.

Analysis

The topic appears right away: the Big Bang model.

The word "attempts" begs the question of whether the model succeeds.

Aha! Indeed, the Big Bang model succeeded. And current observations demonstrate this.

Lots of details about the Big Bang. Since we don't want to read details too closely, we could try to get away just with saying "details about the Big Bang" in our map, but then paragraph 3 would be the same thing. So, we have to find some way of grouping these details. The passage gives us two sequences that let us do so easily: time (*first few seconds*) or temperature (*so high* and *cooled*).

Once again, a ton of details about the Big Bang. If we're using the time sequence, then this is the next *few minutes*. If we're using the temperature sequence, then the universe continues to *cool*. Happily, we don't need to understand a thing about particle physics to understand the basic structure of the passage!

EXPLANATIONS

Because only one neutron was formed for every seven protons, six-sevenths of all protons remained isolated. These remaining protons formed hydrogen nuclei containing one proton each. The Big Bang model **predicts** that about three-quarters of the total mass of the universe will be hydrogen and the remaining quarter helium. This simple **prediction matches** observations **very well**.

Still more details! These focus on the fact that the model's predictions match observations, which (as we remember from paragraph 1) is why the model can be said to be valid.

Passage Map

¶1: Introduce Big Bang model of the universe's creation; it is valid

¶2: First seconds: temperature and energy high

¶3: After a few minutes: cooler, more stable

¶4: Observation confirms BB model

Topic: Big Bang Model

Scope: Validity of (B.B.M.)

Purpose: Demonstrate (the validity of the B.B.M.)

7.   **(D)**

The author is primarily concerned with

O   explaining how the evolution of the universe is incompatible with the implications of the Big Bang model.

O   chronicling the events that followed the creation of matter by the Big Bang.

O   explaining how helium was formed in the early life of the universe.

O   illustrating specific propositions of a model and showing how they have been supported by observation.

O   showing how the ratios of protons to neutrons created in the Big Bang dictated the final ratio of hydrogen to helium in the universe.

Step 2: Analyze the Question Stem

The phrase "primarily concerned" in the question stem lets us know that this is a Global question.

Step 3: Research the Relevant Text

Using our Passage Map—particularly the topic, scope, and purpose—we should be able to predict the correct answer without having to reread any of the passage.

Step 4: Make a Prediction

From our scope and purpose notes, we can predict that the correct answer will say that the author is "demonstrating the Big Bang model's validity."

Step 5: Evaluate the Answer Choices

(D) is the only choice to mention that the passage addresses how observation supports the model's propositions. **(D)** is the correct answer. **(A)** is a 180 trap; it claims that the Big Bang model isn't valid. Change *incompatible* to *compatible*, and it would be correct. **(B)** focuses on the details from paragraphs 2 and 3 but does not address how those details fit within the passage as a whole. **(C)** claims that the passage is focused mainly on helium; the word *helium* certainly shows up a bit in paragraphs 3 and 4, but it isn't the scope of the passage as a whole. **(E)** distorts details given in the passage. The author of the passage uses the ratios of hydrogen and helium to show us how well the Big Bang model matches observations. Choice **(D)** is correct.

8. **(C)**

In the fourth paragraph, the author introduces information about the Big Bang model's prediction for the molecular composition of the universe in order to

- ○ obviate the claim that six-sevenths of all protons remained isolated.
- ○ show that the remaining quarter of the total mass of the universe must be helium.
- ○ provide evidence for the veracity of the Big Bang model.
- ○ describe the means by which remaining protons formed hydrogen nuclei.
- ○ predict the results of a Big Bang.

Step 2: Analyze the Question Stem

This is a Logic question, because we are asked why the author used a specific piece of information. The question stem gives us a perfect reference—"the Big Bang model's prediction for the molecular composition of the universe"—to guide our research.

Step 3: Research the Relevant Text

The reference from the question stem leads us to paragraph 4. Our Passage Map paraphrased paragraph 4 as showing that observation confirms the Big Bang model. Note that by doing our research in the Passage Map first, we save ourselves from spending time rereading unnecessarily.

Step 4: Make a Prediction

From our research we can predict that the correct answer will say that the author included the details of the paragraph in order to "show us why the Big Bang model is valid."

Step 5: Evaluate the Answer Choices

Our prediction matches very nicely with **(C)**; this is the correct answer. The word *obviate* in **(A)** means "to avoid or eliminate." The author believes it's true that six-sevenths of all protons remained isolated, so **(A)** doesn't make sense. **(B)** mixes things up; the author isn't using the Big Bang model to prove that the universe is made up of certain kinds of molecules; instead, the author is using the molecular makeup of the universe to argue that the Big Bang model is valid. **(D)** incorrectly states that the author's objective in this paragraph is to explain the *how* of hydrogen nucleus formation. The details of nucleus formation are discussed only to help the author make the case that the Big Bang theory is sound. **(E)** is wrong because the author, in the fourth paragraph, is not out to predict the results of a Big Bang, but rather to validate the Big Bang model's predictions. Choice **(C)** is correct.

9. **(C)**

According to the passage, which of the following was true during the first few seconds of the universe's existence?

    I. The great majority of neutrons were incorporated into helium molecules.

   II. The temperature was not high enough to allow for the formation of deuterons.

  III. Vast numbers of subatomic particles rapidly metamorphosed into other types of particles.

  O None
  O I only
  O III only
  O II and III only
  O I, II, and III

Step 2: Analyze the Question Stem

The phrase "according to" in the stem signals a Detail question. So the right answer must be something that the author explicitly states. We also see that we're looking for something that "was true during the first few seconds" of the universe.

Step 3: Research the Relevant Text

The Passage Map focuses our research on paragraph 2, specifically lines 7–10. We should notice that this sentence emphasizes temperatures that are "so high" and particles "so abundant" that constant change was the order of the day (or, at least, its first few seconds).

Step 4: Make a Prediction

The correct answer will agree with the ideas expressed in lines 7–10. Anything else must be incorrect because that's the only place we learn about the "first few seconds."

Step 5: Evaluate the Answer Choices

For Roman numeral questions, we should start with the statement that appears most frequently in the answer choices, which in this case is III. Lines 8–10 provide support for Statement III. Each phrase and idea in Statement III matches directly with a phrase or idea from the passage: "vast numbers" matches with "so abundant," "rapidly metamorphosed" matches with "constantly transmuted," and "subatomic particles" matches with, well, "subatomic particles." Since Statement III is correct, eliminate **(A)** and **(B)**. Next evaluate Statement II, as it appears in two of the remaining three choices. Researching line 7 shows that the temperature was "high" during the first few seconds of the universe's existence. So, the phrase "not high enough" kills Statement II. That eliminates **(D)** and **(E)**, leaving only **(C)**. Choice **(C)** is the correct answer.

Note that both Statements I and II refer to details from paragraph 3, which the time/sequence keywords show to describe not the first few seconds of the universe's existence but rather the few minutes thereafter.

EXPLANATIONS

10. (A)

The author uses the first paragraph to introduce

O   a scientific model that the passage will show to be supported by modern evidence.

O   a theory of the origin of the universe that the passage will describe and attempt to refute.

O   a description of the theoretical basis for a scientific model and the modern evidence undermining it.

O   an attempt to use recent evidence to revive a discarded scientific model.

O   a detailed description of an appealing but unsupported theoretical model.

Step 2: Analyze the Question Stem

This question stem asks for the purpose not of the whole passage, but of one of its parts. That makes this a Logic question. The stem makes clear reference to the first paragraph.

Step 3: Research the Relevant Text

As the question focuses on the whole of the first paragraph, our research can be focused on our Passage Map. We wrote that paragraph 1 tells us what the Big Bang model is and that it's valid, supported by observation of the universe.

Step 4: Make a Prediction

A reasonable prediction would be something like this: The author uses the first paragraph to introduce the Big Bang model and claim that it's valid.

Step 5: Evaluate the Answer Choices

(A) matches our prediction perfectly. Every other answer choice gets the detail right ("theory" or "model") but the purpose wrong: "refute," "undermining," "discarded," and "unsupported" are all negative terms, while the author's only purpose is to be positive. Choice **(A)** is correct.

11. (D)

The author would most likely agree with the position that

O   models of the creation of the universe that were made before the Big Bang model was created failed because they did not take into account the behavior of subatomic particles.

O   no credence can be given to a scientific model unless it is possible to produce supporting data through a series of controlled experiments.

O   the Big Bang was part of a cycle of expansion and contraction in the universe.

O   it is beneficial to use the statistical evidence at hand when judging the veracity of scientific models for which the process cannot be repeated in a laboratory.

O   the simplicity of the Big Bang theory accounts for its accuracy.

Step 2: Analyze the Question Stem

The word "agree" makes this an Inference question, so the right answer *must* be true based on the passage but is likely not mentioned explicitly. This stem contains no reference to a particular detail or paragraph.

Step 3: Research the Relevant Text

When the test asks you an Inference question without providing a particular reference to guide your research, prepare yourself to evaluate the answers by refreshing your memory on the topic, scope, and purpose.

Step 4: Make a Prediction

We cannot anticipate the exact wording of the correct answer, but since we are asked what the author would agree with, we know the right answer will be in line with "The Big Bang model corresponds well with the observed universe; the model seems valid."

Step 5: Evaluate the Answer Choices

(A) can be eliminated for two reasons. First, the passage only mentions the Big Bang model, not any others. So there's no way we can state with confidence why any of those other models failed. Second, the author only ever uses *positive* opinion keywords, such as "validity." So an answer about why something "failed" can't be correct. **(B)** is a 180 wrong answer trap. The author gives credence to the Big Bang model, not by "a series of controlled experiments," but by "matching … claims with observations." **(C)** is incorrect because although the passage does mention "expansion" in line 17, there is no support for "contraction" or for "a cycle." (Here is a case of something that is generally believed to be true in the world outside the GMAT but that is not actually supported by the passage.) The wording of **(D)** is convoluted and dense, but the passage supports everything here: "statistical evidence at hand" could well refer to "0.01 percent," "six-sevenths," or "three-quarters." The author is indeed "judging the veracity of a scientific model." The passage discusses the creation of the universe and its behavior, a "process which cannot be repeated in a laboratory." But, more important than any of that is the fact that if the author *didn't* believe **(D)**, there's no way he could say that the Big Bang model is valid. **(D)** is correct. **(E)** is a distortion of the last sentence. The author may agree that the Big Bang model is simple but not that this is what "accounts for its accuracy." According to paragraphs 1 and 4, it is the model's match with observation that demonstrates its validity. The correct answer is **(D)**.

EXPLANATIONS

12. (E)

According to the passage, a helium nucleus

O   could only be created early in the universe's history.

O   has a low density due to the cooling and expansion of the universe.

O   is more stable than a lithium nucleus.

O   has four times the mass of a hydrogen nucleus.

O   consists of exactly two neutrons and two protons.

Step 2: Analyze the Question Stem

The phrase "according to" announces this as a Detail question, and the question gives us a clear reference for our research: "helium nucleus."

Step 3: Research the Relevant Text

We know that the passage grows increasingly detail oriented in the third and fourth paragraphs. A quick scan reveals mention of the helium nucleus in line 16. The key to researching a detail is its context. Here, the sentence on the helium nucleus (lines 15–16) tells us that it is formed of two deuterons. And the sentence right before that tells us that deuterons are made up of one neutron and one proton.

Step 4: Make a Prediction

Our research shows that a good prediction for the correct answer choice is one that says the helium nucleus is made up of two deuterons or two protons and two neutrons.

Step 5: Evaluate the Answer Choices

The correct answer, **(E)**, uses almost exactly the language of our prediction. **(A)** is too extreme. The passage does say that fusion stopped after the first few minutes. But it doesn't say that fusion could *never* happen under *any* other circumstance. Moreover, **(A)** distorts the passage, which claims that "fusion *into heavier elements*" stopped—not that fusion into helium itself stopped. **(B)** is a tricky distortion. The sentence following the reference to the helium nucleus says, "As the universe continued to expand and cool, its density became too low ...." But "its" refers to the universe, not the helium nucleus. Both **(C)** and **(D)** are out of scope, mentioned nowhere in the passage. **(D)**, interestingly, happens to be a fact—you may recall from high school chemistry that a helium nucleus has four times the mass of a hydrogen nucleus. However, that fact is not mentioned in this passage, and it is not the correct response to a question asking for what's true "according to the passage." This answer is a good example of our caution against bringing in outside knowledge. Choice **(E)** is correct.

On the left, we've shown how keywords help you to identify the major elements of the passage and its structure and what you could skim over. On the right, we've shown what you might be thinking as you read the passage strategically.

Passage for Questions 13–17	**Analysis**
Parfleche is the French name for **the Plains peoples'** *hoemskot 'eo*—an envelope-shaped rawhide container for storing clothes, food, and personal items. The *parfleche* served **not only** as a **practical** and durable storage solution, **but also** as a decorative object of **spiritual significance**. Among certain tribes, **most notably** the Cheyenne and Arapaho, *parfleches* were decorated by the women's painting society, whose members among the Cheyenne were known as *moneneheo*, the Selected Ones. **Although similar** in their **economic and social** importance to craftsmen's guilds in medieval and Renaissance Western Europe, the painting society **also** had a **spiritual or religious** nature. The shamanistic society required application for admission and held its members to **high artistic and moral standards**. The society **further** displayed its importance by defining aspects of Cheyenne wealth and status.	The topic, the *parfleche*, is addressed and defined in the first sentence.

The "not only ... but also" structure indicates that the author will focus on the spiritual significance of the *parfleche*.

Another contrast: The group that made *parfleche* was economic/social "but also" spiritual/religious. |
| Painting on rawhide was **fraught with challenges**. If painting was attempted while the prepared hide was too moist, the applied paint bled, but if the hide was too dry, the skin did not absorb the pigments. This restricted the time frame in which painting could best be completed, which meant that designs had to be visualized fully before the work started. **Moreover, every aspect** of creating a *parfleche* was a **sacred** act. Each design element, **for instance**, was a syntagma—a linguistic or visual unit intended to convey meaning—freighted with symbolic referents. **For example**, diamond shapes represented the *ha 'kot*, the grasshopper, an abundant grass eater itself symbolic of the bison, the sacred source of food, shelter, tools, and clothing. The tools used were **also symbolic**: The shape of the "flesher" used to prepare the hide represented lightning bolts—emblematic of the masculine essence of spirit. The flesher removed the flesh from the hide, transforming it into a spiritual container that would hold earthly matter (the people's material goods). | Making of *parfleche*: difficult; highly symbolic; even tools symbolic. |

EXPLANATIONS

Even the **position** of the *parfleche* in the lodge held **symbolic** significance. It was stored beneath the bed of older women, **not only because** they were careful guardians, **but also because** they were closer to Grandmother Earth, from whose union with the lightning spirit the animals and plants of the middle world came to provide food and shelter. The symbolism of every aspect of the *parfleche*, **therefore**, from the interpretable design work on its outside to its storage place within the lodge, reflects the Cheyenne belief in a complementary worldview: the blending of the masculine spirit and the feminine physical matter.

Parfleche kept by mature women (considered spiritual people). Conclusion: *parfleche* reflects masculine/feminine blend.

Passage Map

¶1: *Intro to the* **parfleche** *and the people who created it*

¶2: *The process and symbolism involved in making the* **parfleche**

¶3: *The* **parfleche** *as a symbol of the Cheyenne worldview*

Topic: The **parfleche**

Scope: The spiritual significance of the production, decoration, and use of the **parfleche**

Purpose: To explain the cultural and spiritual significance of the **parfleche** *to the Plains peoples*

13. (E)

According to the passage, one reason why there was a limited time frame in which to paint a prepared rawhide was that

- ○ the pigments dried quickly and thus had to be applied with speed to avoid cracking.
- ○ if the hide was too dry, it absorbed too much paint.
- ○ if the hide was too moist, it rejected the pigments.
- ○ the designs had to be fully visualized before painting was started.
- ○ if the hide was too moist, the paint bled.

Step 2: Analyze the Question Stem

The phrase "According to the passage … " indicates that this is a Detail question. The stem gives us a clear reference for our research: "limited time frame in which to paint a prepared rawhide."

Step 3: Research the Relevant Text

Using our Passage Map, we can refer to the second sentence of the second paragraph, where the author was discussing the difficulties in creating the *parfleche.*

Step 4: Make a Prediction

The second sentence of paragraph 2 provides everything we need for a prediction of the correct answer: "If painting was attempted while the prepared hide was too moist, the applied paint bled, but if the hide was too dry, the skin did not absorb the pigments."

Step 5: Evaluate the Answer Choices

(E) agrees perfectly with the first half of this statement. **(A)** is unsupported by the passage. **(B)** and **(C)** are both 180 wrong answer traps, since the sentence actually said that when the hides are too dry, they would not absorb paint. **(D)** is a distortion; it reverses the cause-and-effect relationship described in the passage. The reason that the designs had to be visualized in advance was the limited time during which the hides could be painted, not the other way around. Choice **(E)** is the correct answer.

14. (E)

The main purpose of the passage is to

○ describe a tool used among Native Americans when working with rawhide.

○ rebut a commonly held view about the symbolism of the *parfleche* for the Plains peoples.

○ analyze the societies of the Cheyenne and Arapaho people.

○ propose a new method for analyzing the use of symbolism in Native American art.

○ discuss the spiritual and symbolic importance of a rawhide container and its decorations to several Plains tribes.

Step 2: Analyze the Question Stem

The wording here—"main purpose of the passage"—makes this one of the most common Global question stems that appear on the GMAT.

Step 3: Research the Relevant Text

Since we paraphrased the author's purpose while creating our Passage Map, we can simply refer to that; there is no need to go back to the passage itself.

Step 4: Make a Prediction

The Passage Map tells us that the author wrote this passage to explain the *parfleche* and its "spiritual significance" to certain Indian tribes.

Step 5: Evaluate the Answer Choices

(E) best summarizes this and properly reflects the author's tone. Notice that **(E)** doesn't use the word "*parfleche*" but rather its definition. Looking for the right words in Reading Comp answer choices is misguided; always look for the answer choice that matches the meaning or idea that you've predicted. **(A)** is too narrow in scope; it reflects only one detail from the text instead of the passage as a whole. **(C)** is too broad in scope; our author is focused on one aspect of Cheyenne culture. **(B)** and **(D)** are not correct because the author of this passage does not take a stand on or disagree with anyone about the symbolism of the *parfleche* or the methods used for studying it. Choice **(E)** is the correct answer.

15. **(D)**

According to the author, the Cheyenne women's painting society was unlike Western European guilds of the Middle Ages and the Renaissance in that

- ○ application for membership was required.
- ○ the group had significant economic standing in the community.
- ○ the group had significant social standing in the community.
- ○ the women's painting society was religious in nature.
- ○ the society had an influence on social standing and material valuation.

Step 2: Analyze the Question Stem

This is another Detail question, again with a clear reference point for research during the upcoming Step 3. Here, we are asked what, in the author's words, distinguished the Cheyenne women's society that made the *parfleche* from medieval guilds.

Step 3: Research the Relevant Text

As expected, the contrast is highlighted for us by a keyword—in this case "Although"—in the passage. The Cheyenne group was similar to guilds in economic and social importance, but different because the Cheyenne painters' group was "spiritual or religious."

Step 4: Make a Prediction

The correct answer will highlight the Cheyenne groups' spiritual side.

Step 5: Evaluate the Answer Choices

Thus, **(D)** is the correct answer choice. **(A)** is outside the scope of this passage, since while we know that the women's painting society required application for membership, we do not know that the guilds were any different in their requirements. **(B)**, **(C)**, and **(E)** all describe ways in which the women's painting society was similar to the Western European guilds. Choice **(D)** is correct.

EXPLANATIONS

16. **(A)**

You can most reasonably conclude that the Cheyenne definition of the term *moneneheo* (line 6) reflects

- O   the high status some women enjoyed as artists in Cheyenne culture.
- O   the shamanistic spiritual origins of the women's painting society.
- O   the notion that artists were chosen by the gods to perform their tasks.
- O   the self-restrictive nature of the women's painting society.
- O   a woman's skill in using rawhide tools such as the "flesher."

Step 2: Analyze the Question Stem

The wording of this question stem is a bit unusual, but a moment's reflection tells us that this is an Inference question. Inference questions ask what must be true based on the passage. In this case, the passage gives us information indicating why the Cheyenne would refer to the women's painting society members as *moneneheo*. The question simply wants us to paraphrase that information accurately.

Step 3: Research the Relevant Text

The question stem refers to the word *moneneheo* in the line 6, where the author tells us that it refers to the members of the women's painting society and translates as "the Selected Ones." The author goes on to explain the society's high importance and the "high artistic and moral standards" required for admission and membership.

Step 4: Make a Prediction

Predicting an answer to the question, we would say that the Cheyenne term reflects respect for the society member's status, talent, importance, etc. Remember, we aren't trying to predict the *words* of the answer but, rather, its meaning.

Step 5: Evaluate the Answer Choices

Choice **(A)**, with its emphasis on status, matches our prediction nicely. Although we are told that the *moneneheo* is a shamanistic organization, we learn nothing about its origins, so **(B)** is out of scope. Choice **(C)** requires a leap from the use of "selected" to the notion that the gods do the selecting. Nothing the author writes supports this leap. The author mentions no sense in which the term *moneneheo* refers to anything "self-restrictive" on the part of the women's painting society; **(D)** is out of scope. The author draws no association between the term and the skinning tool or "flesher" (which is, in any case, not mentioned until the end of paragraph 2); thus, **(E)** is also out of scope. Choice **(A)** is correct.

17. (D)

The author describes the symbolic meanings of the diamond shape most likely in order to

○ indicate how precious the completed *parfleche* was to its owner.

○ prove that the grasshopper was superior to the bison in Cheyenne religion.

○ illustrate the visual complexity of the abstract forms used in creating a *parfleche*.

○ provide an example of the many layers of symbolism involved in creating a *parfleche*.

○ demonstrate the relationship between the symbolic shapes of the tools and the abstract designs used in creating a *parfleche*.

Step 2: Analyze the Question Stem

This is an archetypal GMAT Logic question. We are referred to a detail—here, the "diamond shape"—and asked why the author includes it in the passage. Notice that the wording of the question, ending with "in order to …" means that the answer choices must begin with verbs.

Step 3: Research the Relevant Text

The diamond shape was among the symbols mentioned in the second paragraph. It is located in a sentence that begins with the illustration keywords "For example." The sentence goes on to tell us that the diamond represents the grasshopper, which in turn represents the bison, which in turn is sacred, and so on.

Step 4: Make a Prediction

Our research tells us that this answer must begin with a verb meaning "illustrate" or "give an example of" and continue by saying something about the symbolic meanings of the *parfleche*.

Step 5: Evaluate the Answer Choices

Choice **(D)** matches the prediction and is correct. Given the verbs that begin each answer choice, only **(C)** and **(D)** are really in the running. **(C)** distorts the purpose of the diamond-shape example beyond what we read in the passage. Closer reading shows answers **(A)**, **(B)**, and **(E)**, already suspect for having the wrong purpose verbs, to be even worse. **(A)** addresses the value of the *parfleche* to its owner, a topic touched on nowhere in the passage. **(B)** suggests an unsupported, and rather ridiculous, comparison between the grasshopper and bison as characterized in Cheyenne culture. **(E)** tries to apply the diamond-shape example to the tool-use example that comes later in the paragraph. **(D)** is the correct answer.

On the left, we've shown how keywords help you to identify the major elements of the passage and its structure and what you could skim over. On the right, we've shown what you might be thinking as you read the passage strategically.

Passage for Questions 18–23

Prior to the nineteenth century, both human and animal **populations** were **limited by the finite resources** (such as food) to which they had access. When the **enormous increases in prosperity** ushered in by the Industrial Revolution essentially freed many Western nations from these constraints, **scientists** of the time **expected** a Malthusian **explosion in population. However,** an inverse relationship between prosperity and reproduction was soon noted; the average size of families fell. **The trend continues** to this day and has spread to recently industrialized portions of the world.

Early biologists tried to explain the transition to smaller families by drawing **comparisons to the animal world.** Animals that have many young tend to live in hostile, unpredictable environments. Since the odds against any given offspring's survival are high, having many offspring increases the chance that at least one or two of them will survive. In contrast, animals that have fewer children but invest more resources in childrearing tend to live in stable, less hostile environments. While the young of these "high-investment" species enjoy the benefits of a relatively safe environment, they need to compete with animals whose young are equally unlikely to perish early in life. Therefore, the biologists observed, progeny that have acquired the skills they need to compete while sheltered by a family have an advantage over their less prepared competitors. **By analogy,** if people living in a prosperous environment produced only a few, pampered children, those children would out-compete the progeny of parents who had stretched their resources too widely.

Analysis

The first sentence announces the topic: population size.

"However" signals a discrepancy between what scientists expected (a population explosion) and what really happened (a decrease in family size). We can expect the rest of the passage to present one or more explanations for this discrepancy.

Here comes the first explanation, put forth by early biologists, who compare patterns of human reproduction to different animal species' reproduction strategies.

The biologists argue that animals living in environments with few resources have many offspring, while animals living in richer environments have fewer, pampered offspring.

The biologists claim that the number of offspring humans have also depends on how resource-rich their environment happens to be.

Critics of this theory argue that there are limitations in conflating animal and human behavior. **They argue instead** that **changes in social attitudes** are adequate to explain this phenomenon. To a family in a society that is tied to the land, a large number of children is a great boon. They increase family income by being put to work early, and usually some can be persuaded to care for their parents into old age. As a society becomes richer, and as physical labor becomes less important, education may extend into the early twenties, making children economically unattractive as they now consume family assets rather than produce them. **Meanwhile**, plans such as pensions and Social Security mitigate the need for children to care for their parents into their dotage.

The third paragraph introduces an opposing point of view. Critics of the early biologists argue that shrinking family size in the context of new-found prosperity has more to do with changes in social attitudes than with natural selection.

The passage ends without introducing the author's own perspective. We're simply left with two competing explanations for the unexpected decline in family size after the Industrial Revolution, the biologists' and the critics'.

Passage Map

¶1: *Population growth paradox: scientists' expectations vs. reality*

¶2: *Early biologists' explanation: family size depends on how resource-rich the environment is*

¶3: *Critics' explanation: changes in social attitudes cause family size to decline*

Topic: *Family size/population growth*

Scope: *Why industrialized, prosperous nations have shrinking families*

Purpose: *Describe two different explanations for why families tend to decrease in size with increasing prosperity*

EXPLANATIONS

18. (D)

The primary purpose of the passage is to

○ criticize explanations of human behavior that are based solely on observations taken from the animal world.

○ show why the expected population explosion following the Industrial Revolution did not occur before the Industrial Revolution.

○ demonstrate how family size was influenced by both environmental restraints and social attitudes before and after the Industrial Revolution.

○ present two alternative theories that explain why family size tends to shrink with increased prosperity.

○ argue that studies based on social attitudes are more effective than models based on evolutionary advantages in accounting for demographic patterns.

Step 2: Analyze the Question Stem

This Global question asks us for the passage's "primary purpose."

Step 3: Research the Relevant Text

A quick look at our notes on topic, scope, and purpose will suffice. There's no need to go back to the passage itself to answer a Global question.

Step 4: Make a Prediction

Our notes say that the author's purpose is to describe two different explanations for why families tend to decrease in size with increasing prosperity. In evaluating the choices, it will also help to recall that the author's point of view in this passage is entirely neutral.

Step 5: Evaluate the Answer Choices

In evaluating the choices for a "primary purpose" question, it is often useful to start with a scan of the initial verb. **(D)** starts with the verb "present," which is perfectly neutral and very close to our description of the author's purpose, which we said is to "describe" two alternate explanations. This should be the choice we read first. When we do, we find that is a perfect match for our prediction. **(D)** is in fact the correct answer. **(A)** is incorrect because the author doesn't "criticize" anything. **(B)** is incorrect because events that occurred "before the Industrial Revolution" are outside the scope of the passage. **(C)** is incorrect because the author fails to "demonstrate" that either or both of the explanations described have any merit. **(E)** is incorrect because the author doesn't "argue" for or against anything. Choice **(D)** is correct.

19. (C)

According to the passage, which of the following is true of a Malthusian explosion in population?

○   Its occurrence has been limited to those areas of the globe that have remained preindustrial.

○   It is inevitable in societies making the transition from an economy based on agriculture to one based on industry.

○   It was predicted by at least some who lived through the Industrial Revolution in the West.

○   Social scientists have only recently reached consensus on the question of why it fails to occur in recently industrialized countries.

○   It was avoided in Western society because the wealth created by industrialization allowed families to support children through extended periods of education.

Step 2: Analyze the Question Stem

"According to" signals that this is a Detail question. The correct answer will simply paraphrase a detail mentioned in the passage.

Step 3: Research the Relevant Text

The "Malthusian explosion in population" is mentioned in the first paragraph, where we really only learn two things about it: (1) It was "expected" by scientists at the time of the Industrial Revolution, and (2) it didn't actually happen.

Step 4: Make a Prediction

For Detail questions, what we've found through our research amounts to our prediction. We need an answer choice that says either that a Malthusian population explosion was expected, or that it did not actually occur, or both.

Step 5: Evaluate the Answer Choices

(C) matches our prediction and is the correct answer. **(A)** is incorrect because "preindustrial areas of the globe" are outside the scope of the passage. All we know is that there has not been a population explosion in industrialized nations; what has happened elsewhere is not discussed in the passage. **(B)** is the opposite of what we need. The first paragraph of the passage states that a Malthusian population explosion, though believed to be inevitable during or after the Industrial Revolution, did not actually occur. As for **(D)**, the closest thing to "social scientists" mentioned in the passage would be the "critics" of the early biologists. However, the passage does not state whether there is a "consensus" among these critics' views or when such a "consensus" was arrived at. **(D)** is thus outside the scope of the passage. Finally, **(E)** is a distortion. The population explosion was avoided, according to the passage, for one of the two possible reasons put forth by the "early biologists" and their "critics," respectively. While the critics' explanation does include extended education as an economic liability that helps convince people in industrialized nations to have fewer children, the author of the passage does not endorse the critics' explanation as correct. Choice **(C)** is the correct answer.

EXPLANATIONS

20. **(A)**

The last paragraph performs which of the following functions in the passage?

O It presents an alternate explanation for the phenomenon described in the first paragraph.

O It criticizes the explanation presented in the second paragraph.

O It describes how social attitudes change as societies become richer.

O It explains a phenomenon presented in the second paragraph.

O It argues that changing social attitudes are sufficient to explain the phenomenon described in the first paragraph.

Step 2: Analyze the Question Stem

This question asks us for the function of the final paragraph and is thus a Logic question. Logic questions are essentially code for "Why did the author bother to include this part of the passage?"

Step 3: Research the Relevant Text

Because we are being asked for the function of the third paragraph in the passage as a whole, we should cast a quick glance at our Passage Map. The first paragraph introduces the curious fact that family size has declined in industrialized nations, the second paragraph gives the early biologists' explanation for this phenomenon, and the third paragraph presents the critics' explanation.

Step 4: Make a Prediction

The author's point of view in this passage is completely neutral; there is no endorsement of one or the other explanation for decreasing family size. The third paragraph, then, simply describes one of two possible explanations.

Step 5: Evaluate the Answer Choices

(A) matches our prediction and is the correct answer. The "phenomenon described in the first paragraph" is the decline in family size in industrialized nations. **(B)** is incorrect because the function of the third paragraph is simply to present another explanation. The author of the passage doesn't "criticize" either explanation (though the critics do). **(C)** is incorrect because while the critics' argument is precisely that social attitudes change as societies become wealthier, this is again not necessarily the author's opinion. We must always keep the author's perspective in mind when answering Logic questions. **(D)** is incorrect because the "phenomenon" explained in the third paragraph was originally presented in the first paragraph, not the second. Finally, **(E)** is incorrect for the same reason that **(B)** and **(C)** are incorrect: The idea that changing social attitudes are sufficient to explain decreasing family size in industrialized nations is not endorsed by the author. The third paragraph simply presents the critics' argument; the author doesn't evaluate that argument at all. Choice **(A)** is the correct answer.

21. (E)

The passage mentions each of the following as a possible reason average family size might fall in recently industrialized nations EXCEPT:

O extended periods of education that make children a drain on family resources

O well-fed, advantaged children who out-compete those in less advantaged families

O improved social care of the elderly

O changed social attitudes

O increased demand for physical laborers in recently industrialized economies

Step 2: Analyze the Question Stem

This question asks for the one answer choice not specifically mentioned in the passage, so we have a Detail EXCEPT question.

Step 3: Research the Relevant Text

We'll need to look up each answer choice to rule out those that are mentioned in the passage. The question stem directs us to the second and third paragraphs, as those paragraphs contain the explanations for why family size tends to fall in industrialized nations.

Step 4: Make a Prediction

For Detail EXCEPT questions, we'll have to look up the answer choices individually. We're looking for that answer choice that is *not* mentioned in the passage.

Step 5: Evaluate the Answer Choices

(A) is incorrect because lengthy education that makes children a drain on family resources is mentioned in the third paragraph as part of the critics' explanation. **(B)** is incorrect because advantaged children out-competing disadvantaged ones comes up at the end of the second paragraph as part of the early biologists' explanation. **(C)** is incorrect because improved social care of the elderly is mentioned during the critics' explanation in the third paragraph. The "changed social attitudes" in **(D)** form the crux of the critics' explanation, so **(D)** is incorrect. **(E)** must, by default, be the correct answer. Indeed, the second-to-last sentence in the third paragraph states that in industrialized societies, physical labor becomes less important, not more so. **(E)** states the opposite of what the passage says and is therefore correct.

EXPLANATIONS

22. (E)

The information in the passage suggests that which of the following animals would be most likely to have many young?

○ A plant eater that lives in drought-susceptible grassland and is fiercely protective of its offspring.

○ An omnivore whose population is restricted to several small islands that are threatened by human encroachment.

○ A meat eater that has no natural predators but must migrate long distances to maintain its supply of food.

○ A scavenger that competes with few other species for territory and food.

○ A filter feeder that is prey for many creatures in the seasonal streams and lakes where it lives.

Step 2: Analyze the Question Stem

The word "suggests" in the question stem signals an Inference question.

Step 3: Research the Relevant Text

The question stem directs us to the early biologists' comparison, in the second paragraph, of human family sizes to the reproductive patterns of animals living in different environments. We learn that animals that have many young "tend to live in hostile, unpredictable environments," while animals that have fewer young "tend to live in stable, less hostile environments" and "invest more resources in childrearing."

Step 4: Make a Prediction

The question asks for an animal that has many young. We can expect the correct answer to describe an animal that lives in a harsh environment. Moreover, while the passage does not explicitly say so, we can infer that the animal with many young will provide minimal care for its offspring.

Step 5: Evaluate the Answer Choices

(E) matches our prediction and is the correct answer. An animal that lives in "seasonal streams and lakes" certainly lives in an unpredictable environment, since those bodies of water are prone to drying up. Moreover, the presence of many predators certainly contributes to a very harsh environment. **(A)** might look tempting because a drought-susceptible grassland definitely qualifies as a hostile and unpredictable environment, but we would not expect an animal that has many offspring to be "fiercely protective" of those offspring. **(A)** is thus a perfect example of a half-right/half-wrong answer choice. **(B)** is incorrect because while the islands are threatened by human encroachment, they may nevertheless constitute a stable, friendly natural environment. **(C)** is incorrect because even though the meat eater has to migrate in search of food, there is no suggestion that food is ever unavailable, and the lack of predators implies a non-hostile environment. **(D)** is incorrect because little competition again suggests a non-hostile environment. Choice **(E)** is correct.

23. (A)

The author mentions a decrease in the importance of physical labor (line 28) in order to

- O give an example of the factors that may lead to changes in social attitudes toward family size.
- O demonstrate why those who anticipated a Malthusian explosion in population in industrialized Europe were incorrect.
- O show how family structures adjust to meet the demands of a changing economy.
- O rebut the claims of those who argue that there are limitations in conflating human and animal behavior.
- O illustrate how larger families can increase family income.

Step 2: Analyze the Question Stem

The phrase "in order to" indicates that this is a Logic question. Specifically, we are asked why the author mentions a decrease in the importance of physical labor.

Step 3: Research the Relevant Text

The question stem sends us to line 28, which is in the middle of the third paragraph. That paragraph begins with the critics' argument, which is that "changes in social attitudes are adequate to explain" shrinking family size in industrialized nations. The rest of the paragraph contains the critics' evidence for their position.

Step 4: Make a Prediction

Physical labor's diminishing importance is a social phenomenon that helps to bring about a change in social attitudes, so it is essentially a piece of evidence for the critics' argument.

Step 5: Evaluate the Answer Choices

(A) matches our prediction and is the correct answer. **(B)** is a distortion. The critics' argument counters that of the early biologists, not the argument of those scientists alive at the time of the Industrial Revolution who predicted a Malthusian population explosion. **(C)** is another distortion. It's family size that the critics contest must change to meet the demands of a changing economy, not family "structures." **(D)** falls outside the scope of the passage. The author doesn't rebut any argument; the tone of the passage is perfectly neutral. Finally, **(E)** is another distortion. The critics argue that large families can increase family income in preindustrial societies "tied to the land." But a decrease in the importance of physical labor happens in industrial societies, not in preindustrial ones. Choice **(A)** is correct.

On the left, we've shown how keywords help you to identify the major elements of the passage and its structure and what you could skim over. On the right, we've shown what you might be thinking as you read the passage strategically.

Passage for Questions 24–29

Generally, interspecific matings represent an evolutionary **dead end**, producing sterile offspring, if any at all. For some species of birds, **however**, such pairings may indeed bring evolutionary advantages to the participants. **In the case of** the female collared flycatchers of Gotland, **three distinct factors** may work to make interspecific pairings with pied flycatcher males reproductively **beneficial**.

In many instances, female collared flycatchers nest with male pied flycatchers while continuing to mate with other collared flycatchers, in effect parasitizing the pied flycatchers, who invest in rearing and fledging any offspring. **Often**, more than half of the offspring raised by interspecific flycatcher pairs are, **in fact**, not hybrids. **Furthermore**, an estimated 65 percent of the hybrid offspring of the resident pied flycatcher male are male. **Because** hybrid females are sterile and males are not, this male bias minimizes the primary disadvantage of interspecific matings: sterile offspring. Habitat specialization may be **a third mechanism**: These pairings tend to occur in the late spring when the coniferous woods favored by the pied flycatcher provide a greater availability of food than the deciduous woods where the collared flycatchers tend to live. **Together**, these factors form a mechanism to **improve substantially** the reproductive success of female collared flycatchers beyond what would be expected of interspecific mating with pied flycatcher males.

Analysis

"Generally" implies that there will be an exception. Usually, interspecific mating doesn't work.

The female collared flycatcher is the exception. We're going to see three reasons why.

Why interspecific mating works for female collared flycatchers:

1. They get pied flycatchers to raise their collared flycatcher offspring.

2. The offspring aren't all sterile.

3. Pied flycatchers live where the food is.

These factors seem to work together.

Although all three of these mechanisms appear to act in concert to form a single elaborate mechanism specifically evolved to circumvent the usual disadvantages of interspecific mating, **studies have shown similar motivations** for the behavior of female collared flycatchers mating within the species. **According to** Professor Siever Rohwer, collared flycatcher females will choose to nest with subordinate collared flycatcher males that inhabit good territory **because** collared flycatcher females must pair-bond in order to be successful in raising offspring. To engender the best offspring, **however**, the females will continue to copulate with higher-quality collared males with whom they are not paired. **Thus**, females **seem to** be nesting with males of any species with the best territories available at the time, **but they will** continue to mate with more attractive males outside of their pair bonds.

> "Although … similar motivations": Female collared flycatchers act the same way when mating with male collared flycatchers.

> Pair with males that have good nests; mate with others, too.

A **highly unusual** behavior, interspecific mating **seems to provide** certain reproductive **advantages** to the collared flycatcher female. **However**, it **remains unclear** whether the mating behavior of female collared flycatchers evolved to circumvent the usual problems with interspecific mating or whether the behavior is simply an extension of how female collared flycatchers behave when mating within their own species.

> The author is wrapping up.

> "However" shows the central unanswered question: Did female collared flycatchers evolve this way because of interspecific mating or just because they act this way generally?

EXPLANATIONS

Passage Map

¶1: *Interspecific mating—usually evolutionary dead end/sterile offspring; FCF is exception*

¶2: *3 advantages of interspecific mating for FCF*

¶3: *FCF nests/mates same way intraspecifically, too. Same advantages*

¶4: *Question—did FCF evolve this way for interspecific mating or just in general?*

Topic: *Interspecific mating—female collared flycatcher exception*

Scope: *FCF's interspecific and intraspecific mating behaviors and their evolutionary advantages*

Purpose: *Describe FCF's mating/nesting behavior and pose an unanswered question about its origins*

24. (D)

The author's primary purpose is to

O   criticize the basis of a scientific theory.

O   defend a hypothesis concerning bird-mating behaviors.

O   point out the need for further study of female collared flycatchers.

O   describe two possible explanations for the interspecific mating behavior of female collared flycatchers.

O   defend an unpopular view of a natural phenomenon.

Step 2: Analyze the Question Stem

"Primary purpose" signals that this is a Global question.

Step 3: Research the Relevant Text

No research within the passage is required. We just need to consult our Passage Map, specifically our statement of the author's purpose.

Step 4: Make a Prediction

Our statement of the author's purpose said that the author was describing the mating behavior of the female collared flycatcher and posing a question about it. Two possible explanations are presented: (1) Interspecies mating brings distinct benefits, and (2) interspecies mating is just an extension of normal behavior. With that background, we're more than ready to assess the choices.

Step 5: Evaluate the Answer Choices

(D) best summarizes the author's purpose. **(A)** is incorrect because the author never takes a stand on either explanation and so does not "criticize" anything. Similarly, **(B)** and **(E)** are wrong because the author does not "defend" anything. The author never calls for further research, so **(C)** is not correct either.

25. (C)

According to the passage, female collared flycatchers' mating with male pied flycatchers could be explained by any of the following reasons EXCEPT:

○ Food is more available in pied flycatcher territories during the mating season.

○ Male pied flycatchers can help raise offspring successfully, even if the offspring are not theirs.

○ Male pied flycatchers sire more female offspring than do collared flycatcher males, increasing the reproductive success of the female collared flycatcher.

○ Females are known to nest with subordinate males while pursuing extra-pair copulation with higher-quality males.

○ Females enjoy greater reproductive success by pair-bonding with an inferior male than by not pair-bonding at all.

Step 2: Analyze the Question Stem

"According to the passage" is a clear indication that this is a Detail question. Just make sure you didn't miss the "EXCEPT" at the end of the stem. Here, the four wrong answers will all have been cited in the text. The correct answer will not. Remember, the correct answer to a Detail EXCEPT question may contradict the text or fall outside the scope of the passage. The right answer might also repeat a piece of information that appears in the text but that has no relevance to the question posed in the stem (i.e., make a faulty use of detail). Here, the wrong answers will give possible explanations for the female collared flycatcher's unusual mating behavior.

Step 3: Research the Relevant Text

The female collared flycatcher's nesting and mating behaviors are explained in the second and third paragraphs. While the question asks specifically about explanations for the interspecific mating behaviors, remember that the third paragraph told us that the motivations for intraspecific mating behaviors were similar.

Step 4: Make a Prediction

We cannot predict what the correct answer will say, but we know that the four wrong answers will be supported by text from paragraphs 2 or 3.

Step 5: Evaluate the Answer Choices

The coniferous forests where the pied flycatchers live are indeed richer in food late in the season, as **(A)** suggests. Females may use the pied males for their help in rearing young—including those sired by other males—as **(B)** says. But as for **(C)**, the passage says that pied males mating with collared females father more males than females. So, **(C)** directly contradicts paragraph 2, making **(C)** the correct answer. **(D)** and **(E)** are both supported by paragraph 3. Choice **(C)** is correct.

26. (C)

The bias toward male offspring resulting from the mating of collared flycatcher females and pied flycatcher males is presented as evidence that

- ○ collared flycatcher females that mate with pied flycatcher males have more dominant male offspring.
- ○ the offspring from extra-pair matings with collared flycatcher males are more frequently male.
- ○ female flycatchers are not deterred from interspecific pairing by the likelihood of sterile hybrid offspring.
- ○ males are produced to reduce interspecific inbreeding in future generations.
- ○ interspecific breeding is normal in all varieties of flycatchers.

Step 2: Analyze the Question Stem

The language of the question stem indicates that this is a Logic question. This stem goes out of its way to be helpful, though, by telling us that the detail at issue—the predominance of male offspring from male pied and female collared flycatcher mates—is presented as evidence. Our job will simply be to research what it is used as evidence for.

Step 3: Research the Relevant Text

The reference to the offspring of male pied and female collared flycatcher mates leads us to paragraph 2. We're told that the male offspring are not sterile, thus minimizing a typical downside to interspecies mating.

Step 4: Make a Prediction

The correct answer will tell us that the male offspring bias is evidence that a typical disadvantage—sterile offspring—of interspecies mating is not present when female collared flycatchers and male pied flycatchers mate.

Step 5: Evaluate the Answer Choices

(C) matches the prediction nicely. It is correct. (A) is out of scope; the dominance of offspring is not discussed. (B) is a distortion; it is the interspecific hybrids, not pure collared flycatchers, that show a male bias in their offspring. (D) is incorrect because no argument is ever made about future generations of interspecific breeding. And (E) is incorrect because the passage does not comment on the regularity of interspecific breeding by any bird other than the female collared flycatcher. The answer is (C).

27. **(A)**

It can be inferred from the passage that

   ○   food resources are an important determinant of success in raising offspring.

   ○   having 50 percent male offspring is not optimal for collared flycatcher pairs.

   ○   flycatchers generally mate for life.

   ○   males do not vary in the benefits they provide to their offspring.

   ○   over half of all females engage in extra-pair matings.

Step 2: Analyze the Question Stem

Here's an open-ended Inference question. The stem references no specific detail or part of the passage. We will begin our evaluation of the answers with reference to what we know about the topic, scope, and purpose overall.

Step 3: Research the Relevant Text

Given that there is no reference to guide our research within the passage, we should simply review our topic, scope, and purpose summaries. We may have to do further research choice by choice.

Step 4: Make a Prediction

Lacking a point of reference in the passage, we cannot make a prediction beyond saying that the correct answer will follow from the passage and agree with the author. That should be enough to help us find the correct answer or, at least, eliminate one or more of the wrong ones.

Step 5: Evaluate the Answer Choices

The second paragraph points out that the greater abundance of food in pied flycatcher habitats late in the mating season is a mechanism that makes interspecies pairings reproductively beneficial. If food were not relevant to the success of raising offspring, it could not be a mechanism to make interspecific mating reproductively beneficial. So **(A)** is true based on the passage; this is the exact criterion for the correct answer in an Inference question.

All four wrong answers either fall outside the scope of anything addressed by the passage or out-and-out contradict the passage. **(B)** is not mentioned—the percentage of male offspring is discussed only in relation to interspecific pairs. Mating for life is never mentioned either, putting **(C)** outside the scope. The fact that females *do* choose males on the basis of reproductive benefits makes **(D)** incorrect; it contradicts what the passage implies. Lastly, we have no basis for knowing the proportion of females that engage in extra-pair matings, so **(E)** is also outside the scope. Choice **(A)** is correct.

28. (C)

Professor Rohwer would most likely agree with which of the following statements?

○   All traits related to particular functions have evolved only for those particular functions.

○   Flycatchers represent the best population for studies of bird-mating behavior.

○   Behaviors may appear functional even under conditions other than those under which the behaviors evolved.

○   Evolution has played no role in shaping the behavior of interspecifically paired flycatchers.

○   Hybridization is generally beneficial.

Step 2: Analyze the Question Stem

This is also an Inference question, as signaled by the phrase "most likely agree with ... ." The key is to spot that it is Professor Rowher's opinion that we are drawing our inference from.

Step 3: Research the Relevant Text

Rohwer's opinion is discussed in the third paragraph, where the passage demonstrates the similarities between the female collared flycatcher's interspecies and intraspecies mating behavior. Rowher's point is that pair-bonding is essential to the female collared flycatcher's success in rearing young. The implication is that the female collared flycatcher will nest with one male and mate with others regardless of whether she is engaged in intra- or interspecies mating.

Step 4: Make a Prediction

The correct answer will have to address the context in which the author cites Rowher. The point is that it may be the necessity of pair-bonding, rather than an adaptation that favors interspecific mating, that drives the birds' behavior.

Step 5: Evaluate the Answer Choices

Our prediction supports **(C)** as the correct answer. **(B)** and **(E)** are out of scope: The relative benefits of studying flycatchers rather than other birds is not discussed, nor is Rohwer's opinion on the benefits of hybridization. **(A)** and **(D)** contradict, at least by implication, the message of the passage; they also include the phrases "*all* traits" and "played *no* role," which flag extreme statements. Choice **(C)** is correct.

29. (B)

The mating behavior of female collared flycatchers paired with subordinate male flycatchers is offered as

- ○ an unwarranted assumption behind the adaptive explanation of interspecific matings.
- ○ an alternative explanation for pair matings of collared females with pied males.
- ○ evidence supporting the hypothesis of adaption for interspecific breeding.
- ○ a discredited mainstream explanation for why hybridization is a dead end.
- ○ proof in support of the theory that collared and pied flycatchers are separate species.

Step 2: Analyze the Question Stem

Here, we have another Logic question. Like all Logic stems, this one gives us a clear reference to guide our research. The female collared flycatchers that pair with subordinates are mentioned in the third paragraph. Remember that Logic questions ask *why* the author included the detail, not *what* she said about it.

Step 3: Research the Relevant Text

The third paragraph is about the female collared flycatcher's intraspecies nesting and mating behaviors. The specific fact highlighted by the author was that the female collared flycatcher behaves similarly when mating with male collared flycatchers as it does when mating with pied males. The author's point is that the female collared flycatcher's behavior may not have evolved exclusively in support of interspecies mating.

Step 4: Make a Prediction

While we don't know the wording that the correct answer will use, we can anticipate that it will address the position that the female collared flycatcher's behavior is possibly explained by more than just adaptation to interspecific mating.

Step 5: Evaluate the Answer Choices

The prediction leads us to **(B)**. Paragraph 2 had explained how the female collared flycatcher's behavior is well adapted to the special problems of interspecies mating, so paragraph 3 qualifies as an "alternative explanation." Stated evidence can never be an assumption (which is unstated), so **(A)** is incorrect. The evidence in question does not support the adaptive explanation for interspecies breeding—in fact, it does just the opposite—so **(C)** is a wrong answer choice. This evidence is also not an explanation for why hybridization is a dead end; thus, **(D)** is wrong. Lastly, that the collared and pied flycatchers are separate species is a given in the passage; otherwise, the pairing of pied males and collared females could not be called interspecific. Moreover, this evidence has nothing to do with this issue, making **(E)** incorrect. The correct answer is **(B)**.

EXPLANATIONS

On the left, we've shown how keywords help you to identify the major elements of the passage and its structure and what you could skim over. On the right, we've shown what you might be thinking as you read the passage strategically.

Passage for Questions 30–35

A regimen of intrauterine AZT (zidovudine) as a means of reducing the chances of HIV transmission from mother to child was **first** described in a study known as Protocol 076, the results of which were published in the *New England Journal of Medicine* in November 1994. **The trial found** that administration of AZT to HIV-positive women during pregnancy and delivery, and to their babies after birth, reduced the transmission of HIV to the infants by two-thirds, compared with a placebo. The study was **acclaimed** as one of the **first successful instances** of a prophylaxis preventing HIV transmission— **particularly** "vertical" transmission, or transmission from mothers to infants. The study, prematurely ended so that all the subjects on placebos could be switched to AZT, **led to the recommendation** that all pregnant women with HIV take AZT.

The **validity** of the study's results, **however**, is **debatable**. **Since** Protocol 076 examined only women who had fairly high numbers of T-cells—the white blood cells that coordinate immune response— and who had previously taken AZT for less than six months, the same regimen might not succeed for other pregnant women with HIV. **Moreover**, the study administered large doses of AZT without examining whether lower doses, more economically feasible for uninsured or underinsured women, might be effective. **Further**, the trial design did not account for important variables: **in particular**, whether the subjects' viral load—the amount of HIV in their bodies—might have contributed to the difference in transmission rates. **Since** the exact mechanism and timing of vertical transmission of the HIV virus are unknown, it **cannot be ruled out** that viral load influences rates of vertical transmission.

Analysis

An early HIV-prevention study.

AZT reduced transmission from HIV-positive mother to her child.

Study led to recommendation for all HIV-positive pregnant women to take AZT.

Author's not so sure about this study.

Several reasons to doubt study: "Since," "Moreover," "Further."

Author emphasizes viral load—"in particular"—as a factor that could reduce effectiveness of AZT.

Also, the study **did not consider** the long-term impact of AZT, which is toxic, on the babies themselves. There have been few studies of AZT's effect on HIV-positive infants and none on its effects on uninfected babies. **Since** the majority of the babies born to HIV-positive women are HIV-negative, **and since** HIV may mutate into drug-resistant strains following a break in medication, the **value** of a short-term "zap" with AZT **becomes suspect**.

"Also"—this means we'll see more criticism of the study.

The study failed to look at the effects of AZT on the babies.

Author concludes that value of AZT is "suspect."

Passage Map

¶1: *AZT—early study said HIV-positive pregnant women should take it; prevent transmission to child*

¶2: *Study flawed—only used on those with high T-cell counts, ignored(?) lower dosage, and, especially, ignored viral load*

¶3: *Study flawed II—ignored effect on babies; Conclusion—AZT maybe not so great*

Topic: *AZT and HIV transmission prevention*

Scope: *A study that recommended AZT use*

Purpose: *Critique the study in order to question AZT's value*

30. (D)

The author questions the results of Protocol 076 for which of the following reasons?

○ The number of T-cells was not considered in choosing subjects for the study.

○ The trial was discontinued, and the control group of women on placebo was shifted to AZT.

○ Seventy-five percent of babies born to women in the placebo group were free of infection with HIV.

○ Different transmission rates could have been influenced by different amounts of HIV in the women's bodies.

○ The exact mechanism and timing of HIV transmission are unknown.

Step 2: Analyze the Question Stem

This is a Detail question, but with slightly unusual wording. We don't see "According to the passage," but we can see from the way that the question is asked that we will find the correct answer stated somewhere in the text. The research clue is "The author questions the results ..."

Step 3: Research the Relevant Text

We know that the author gave reasons to doubt the validity of the study in paragraphs 2 and 3. If we've made a Passage Map, we should have these reasons summarized on our noteboard.

Step 4: Make a Prediction

It's hard to say exactly which of the reasons for questioning the study the correct answer will cite, but we can be certain it will be one of the following: The study used only high T-cell patients, it ignored lower dosage possibilities, it ignored the patients' viral loads, or it failed to study the effect of AZT on the babies.

Step 5: Evaluate the Answer Choices

The passage states that the potential effects of viral load, or the amount of HIV in patients' bodies, were not considered in this study (lines 18–20). So **(D)** is correct. Don't be misled by the fact that the answer didn't use the term "viral load." It instead uses the term's definition, which the passage provides in the same sentence that mentions "different transmission rates."

(A) is a distortion. The passage implies that the women in the study were, in fact, selected on the basis of T-cell counts. The author was unhappy that it was limited to those with high counts. **(B)** is a faulty use of detail. It is true that the trial was discontinued and all subjects were shifted to AZT, but the author doesn't present this fact as a problem with the study. **(C)** is simply outside the scope. We're told that the majority of babies born to HIV-positive women are born HIV-negative, but the 75 percent figure comes out of nowhere. **(E)** is another faulty use of detail. The author does state that the mechanism and timing of vertical transmission (from mother to child) are unknown, but he does so in order to emphasize why viral load is such an important issue, not as grounds for criticizing the study. The answer is **(D)**.

31. **(E)**

The author of this passage would be LEAST likely to challenge the benefits of intrauterine AZT for which of the following HIV-positive women and/or their future children?

- ○ A woman who has used the regimen successfully in a previous pregnancy
- ○ A woman whose T-cell count is dangerously low and who plans to continue taking AZT after her baby is born
- ○ A woman who is matched with the study's subjects in terms of ethnicity and socioeconomic status
- ○ A woman who has lost a previous infant to HIV and who wants to be sure that her next child is healthy
- ○ A woman whose T-cell count is not low and who has not taken AZT before

Step 2: Analyze the Question Stem

This is an Inference question with an important twist. We are used to seeing questions that ask what the author would "most likely agree with," but this question asks us to apply what we've learned about the author's opinion. We'll research with an eye to language that tells us the type of patient for whom AZT is most likely to work.

Step 3: Research the Relevant Text

The passage states (in lines 12–15) that the only women included in Protocol 076 had fairly high T-cell counts and had taken AZT for less than six months. So, the author would be unlikely to dispute that a woman with a similar T-cell level and a similar history of AZT use would experience a positive outcome similar to those of the women in the study.

Step 4: Make a Prediction

We'll look for an answer describing a woman who fits the criteria from our research step.

Step 5: Evaluate the Answer Choices

(E) matches the criteria from the second paragraph nicely. It's the correct answer. **(A)** is wrong because the author says that AZT might become less effective if taken after a hiatus in use (paragraph 3). **(B)** is wrong because the study only looked at women with high T-cell counts (paragraph 2); AZT might not help women with low counts. **(C)** is outside the scope: The author never discusses ethnic and socioeconomic factors. As for **(D)**, whether or not a mother has lost a previous child to HIV, or wants a healthy child this time, is not relevant to the potential success of the treatment. The correct answer is **(E)**.

32. (D)

The passage implies that the "viral loads" of the subjects in the study are significant because

   ○   all the subjects had relatively high viral loads, so the study's results may not apply to other groups of women.

   ○   the viral loads of babies whose mothers had received the placebo were just as high as those of babies whose mothers had received AZT.

   ○   viral load must be measured if researchers are to understand the exact mechanism and timing of transmission of HIV.

   ○   the viral loads of women in the placebo group may have been different from those of women in the AZT group.

   ○   viral load may be a critical factor in determining transmission, but the researchers wrongly assumed that it was the only factor.

Step 2: Analyze the Question Stem

This Inference question ("the passage implies") gives us a clear reference for our research. Not surprisingly, it takes us back to the author's consideration of viral load, something he emphasized as a "particular" problem with the study's design.

Step 3: Research the Relevant Text

The author states in paragraph 2 that "the trial design did not account for important variables: in particular, whether subjects' viral loads—the amounts of HIV in their bodies—might have contributed to the difference in transmission rates." In other words, the author is saying that it is possible that the women in the AZT group may have had different viral loads than the women in the placebo group.

Step 4: Make a Prediction

The correct answer will follow directly from the passage. It must address the fact that the study's failure to account for viral load may have created an unrepresentative sample in the test group.

Step 5: Evaluate the Answer Choices

(D) expresses this idea and is the correct answer. (A) and (B) are both outside the scope—the passage does not supply any information about what the relative viral loads of the women or the babies actually were. Be careful with an answer like (A); we were told that all of the subjects had high T-cell counts and the results might not be broadly applicable. Don't confuse details; do research. (C) may be true, but it doesn't answer the question at hand: Why was the viral load of the test subjects significant? (E) is a half-right/half-wrong answer. Viral load may indeed be a critical factor, but the researchers did not consider it in selecting test and control group subjects. Choice (D) is correct.

33. (C)

The primary purpose of the passage is to

O   document recent problems with HIV and AIDS treatment.

O   expose medical errors caused by careless methodology in an important clinical trial.

O   raise doubts about a course of treatment based on a groundbreaking study.

O   describe the process of vertical transmission of HIV and suggest preventive therapy.

O   evaluate treatment possibilities for pregnant women with HIV.

Step 2: Analyze the Question Stem

This is a typical Global question. Even though some questions may contain tougher answer choices than others, the question types themselves function the same way throughout the test.

Step 3: Research the Relevant Text

No textual research is required. We'll just need to consult our Passage Map, particularly our summaries of the author's scope and purpose.

Step 4: Make a Prediction

The most important word in our summary of the purpose is the verb. Here, we used "critique." We may not find that exact word in our correct answer, but the verb used will have to indicate that the author is trying to caution us against accepting the completely rosy view of AZT given by the study.

Step 5: Evaluate the Answer Choices

(C) is correct. The verb phrase "raise doubts" matches our interpretation of the author's purpose. Notice that no other answer begins with as appropriate a verb. **(A)** is outside the scope: The passage deals with only one HIV/AIDS treatment method, not all such treatments in general. **(B)** is wrong because, while the passage does cite problems with the design of a clinical trial, **(B)** is too extreme in characterizing the design as "careless" or as having "medical errors." **(D)** is outside the scope: The process of vertical transmission is mentioned, but it is neither described in detail nor is it the purpose of the passage. **(E)** is outside the scope: The author is only looking at one treatment possibility—intrauterine AZT. The correct answer is **(C)**.

EXPLANATIONS

34. (B)

The author of the passage would be most likely to agree with which of the following statements?

○ Medications harmful to one group of patients are probably not harmful to another.

○ Recommendations based on a conditional experiment must be qualified.

○ The study should not have been prematurely ended.

○ Clinical trials that may harm patients are unethical.

○ No HIV-positive woman should take AZT during pregnancy.

Step 2: Analyze the Question Stem

Here's a broadly worded Inference question. It doesn't give us any specific clues for research, but importantly, it tells us that the correct answer is something that must follow from the author's opinion.

Step 3: Research the Relevant Text

Lacking any exact research reference, we should go back to the Passage Map and refresh our memory of the author's scope and purpose.

Step 4: Make a Prediction

We'll use the author's scope and purpose to pick out the correct answer or, at least, to eliminate choices that the author would either disagree with or have no opinion about.

Step 5: Evaluate the Answer Choices

(B) is correct: It follows from the author's criticisms of Protocol 076, which studied only women with high T-cell counts who had been taking AZT for less than six months. The author believes this study was insufficient to recommend giving AZT to all pregnant women with HIV. **(A)** is wrong because the author never suggests that AZT, which is known to be toxic (paragraph 3), is probably harmless to some people. **(C)** is incorrect. There is no evidence that the author thinks the study should have been continued. Any complaints he makes about it involve its setup, not its termination. **(D)** is outside the scope: The ethics of this trial are not in question. **(E)** is extreme. The author suggests a cautious attitude toward treating HIV-positive pregnant women with AZT, but he never rules it out entirely. Choice **(B)** is correct.

35. (E)

The primary function of the second paragraph is to

- ○ refute issues.
- ○ evaluate solutions.
- ○ describe results.
- ○ support action.
- ○ identify problems.

Step 2: Analyze the Question Stem

This Logic question asks us for the author's purpose in writing paragraph 2.

Step 3: Research the Relevant Text

For Logic questions that ask about complete paragraphs, the best approach is to consult your notes for that paragraph in your Passage Map.

Step 4: Make a Prediction

For paragraph 2, our Passage Map read: "Study flawed—only used on those with high T-cell counts, ignored(?) lower dosage, and, especially, ignored viral load." The correct answer will say something along the lines of "describe flaws" or "outline shortcomings."

Step 5: Evaluate the Answer Choices

(E), "identify problems," accurately reflects the content of paragraph 2 and is the correct answer. All of the wrong answers miss the point of the paragraph.

GMAT BY THE NUMBERS: READING COMPREHENSION

Now that you've learned how to approach Reading Comprehension questions on the GMAT, let's add one more dimension to your understanding of how they work.

Take a few minutes to read the following passage and try the questions associated with it. The next pages feature performance data from thousands of people who have studied with Kaplan over the decades. Through analyzing this data, we will show you how to approach questions like these most effectively and how to avoid similarly tempting wrong answer choice types on Test Day.

Introduced in 1978, video laserdiscs were technologically more advanced than video cassettes—they offered better picture quality without degradation over time—yet video cassettes and recorders were far more successful commercially, at least in part because relatively few movies were ever released on laserdisc. As this example illustrates, superior technology is no guarantee of success in the home audio and video market.

In home audio, vinyl records were the dominant format until the 1970s, when audio cassette tapes were introduced. Cassette tapes offered no better sound quality than vinyl records (in fact, some believed they offered lower quality), yet this format became widely successful for reasons having little to do with technical advancements in sound quality. Cassettes were more portable than records, and the ability to record from records onto cassettes made the two formats complementary. In addition to buying pre-recorded records and tapes, consumers could now make copies of vinyl records and listen to them outside the home. Thus, cassette tape sales grew even as vinyl remained a popular format.

The rise of audio compact discs (CDs) was quite different. Introduced in 1983, CDs clearly offered higher sound quality than records or cassettes, yet they were not an immediate success. However, CDs were persistently and aggressively marketed by the industry, and by the 1990s they had become the most popular audio format. The dominant position of CDs was further cemented later in the 1990s by the advent of new technology that allowed consumers to create their own CDs at home—thus combining one of the best features of audio cassettes with the higher sound quality of CDs.

In home video, after the failure of laserdiscs, video cassettes remained the dominant format until the advent of digital video discs (DVDs). Introduced in 1997, DVDs quickly gained widespread popularity. These discs were based on a technology similar to that of laserdiscs and offered several clear advantages over video cassettes, including better picture quality and better search features. Yet perhaps the real key to their rapid rise was the fact that manufacturers quickly made many titles available on DVD. This combination of better technology and smart marketing helped the DVD avoid the fate of the laserdisc.

1. The passage is primarily concerned with which of the following?

    ○ Contrasting the success of DVDs with the failure of laserdiscs

    ○ Describing the crucial role played by technology in the home audio and video market

    ○ Questioning the wisdom of introducing new audio or video formats

    ○ Illustrating that there is more than one path to success in the home audio and video market

    ○ Proving that good marketing is the only way to guarantee success in the home audio and video market

2. The author of this passage would most likely agree that

    ○ better technology alone will never cause the success of a new audio or video format.

    ○ a combination of better technology and good marketing is the best way to ensure success when introducing a new format.

    ○ there is no perfectly reliable way to predict the success or failure of new audio and video formats.

    ○ companies in the home audio or video industry should invest less in product research and development than in marketing.

    ○ consumer behavior is inherently irrational.

3. According to the passage, which strategy is LEAST likely to produce a successful media format?

   O   Aggressively marketing a brand new format
   O   Cautiously testing the market by releasing titles sparingly
   O   Relying on word-of-mouth advertising
   O   Creating a new format based on earlier technology
   O   Introducing a product that works with existing products

EXPLANATION: QUESTION 1

It is crucial not to get lost in the details of a Reading Comprehension passage but to keep your eyes focused on the author's main idea. The last sentence of the first paragraph makes it clear that the passage will focus on how superior technology does not guarantee commercial success. Each body paragraph contains an example to support this point of view. The paragraphs describe many technical details but also provide other reasons for commercial success: flexibility of use (cassettes), aggressive marketing (CDs), wide availability (DVDs). The correct answer—choice **(D)**—reflects the idea that success is determined by several factors.

QUESTION STATISTICS

8% of test takers choose **(A)**

19% of test takers choose **(B)**

2% of test takers choose **(C)**

64% of test takers choose **(D)**

7% of test takers choose **(E)**

Sample size = 2,163

Many test takers focus too much on what the details say, rather than what idea the details support. The testmakers understand this tendency, and they craft answer choices that reflect only the details. You can see how the most tempting wrong answer—choice **(B)**—accurately describes the details but misses the overall point that factors other than technology have an important influence. Also note how the second- and third-most popular wrong answers also miss the overall point by focusing on individual paragraphs instead of the entire passage: **(A)** focuses only on the fourth paragraph and **(E)** on the third. Although not a commonly selected wrong answer on this question, **(C)** is also wrong because it misconstrues the main idea, claiming that improved formats are not a good idea rather than simply insufficient for success.

EXPLANATION: QUESTION 2

Despite the vague wording of this question stem, the GMAT has a very specific standard for what defines the correct answer to Inference questions such as this one—and knowing that standard allows you to successfully avoid the common traps. From the testmaker's point of view, an inference is valid only if it unambiguously *must* be true. So the right answer will be something that the author *must* agree with. If there's any room for doubt, or if it's possible that the author might not agree, the choice is wrong.

QUESTION STATISTICS

29% of test takers choose **(A)**

46% of test takers choose **(B)**

23% of test takers choose **(C)**

1% of test takers choose **(D)**

1% of test takers choose **(E)**

Sample size = 2,150

It's easy to see why unpopular choices **(D)** and **(E)** are wrong. The author neither makes directives to companies nor casts aspersions on consumers. But why are the two most commonly selected answers wrong? The reason is that they are too extreme.

It's very easy for an all-or-nothing statement to be possibly false. **(A)** claims that better technology will never cause the success of a new format. But the author only says that better technology "is no guarantee of success." A lack of a guarantee doesn't mean that something will *never* happen, so **(A)** is incorrect. **(B)** also goes too far by claiming that superior technology and good marketing is the *best* way to ensure success. The author clearly thinks that combining good technology with good marketing is better than having good technology alone. But this doesn't rule out the possibility that some other approach might be better still. In fact, marketing is not mentioned as part of the reason for the success of audio cassettes.

Notice how **(C)** uses more cautious wording, saying that no formula for success is "perfectly reliable." Given that the author mentions three different ways that new formats succeeded (flexibility of use, aggressive marketing, wide availability of titles), it makes sense for the author to agree that there's no one perfect way. That's why **(C)** is correct. Learn to avoid extreme language like "never" and "best" and to embrace hedged language like "no perfectly reliable," and you'll be well ahead of your competition and well on the way to a higher GMAT score.

EXPLANATION: QUESTION 3

Notice that the question explicitly tells you to base your answer on the content of the passage. Many test takers let their own opinions cloud their analysis and thus wander into traps. This question asks you to find the strategy most likely to fail. The first and fourth paragraphs both mention that the laserdisc probably failed because not enough titles were available. That makes a cautious, slow release of titles a recipe for failure, which is why **(B)** is correct.

QUESTION STATISTICS

3% of test takers choose **(A)**

70% of test takers choose **(B)**

18% of test takers choose **(C)**

6% of test takers choose **(D)**

3% of test takers choose **(E)**

Sample size = 2,122

(A) and **(E)** are mentioned in the passage as reasons that new formats succeeded—CDs were aggressively marketed, and cassettes complemented vinyl—so it's no wonder that few test takers choose those answers. Neither **(C)** nor **(D)** is mentioned in the passage, which is why these choices are wrong—there's no support for either. But you can see from the question statistics that **(C)** is a popular choice. That is because you might look at "word-of-mouth advertising" and think that it isn't a sufficiently "aggressive" marketing strategy. This may be true in the real world (although if you're a savvy buzz marketer, you might disagree), but there is nothing *in the passage* to suggest that a word-of-mouth marketing campaign couldn't be aggressive. Stick with what's supported by the passage, and you'll be successful on Test Day.

MORE GMAT BY THE NUMBERS ...

To see more questions with answer choice statistics, be sure to review the full-length CATs in your Online Center.

CHAPTER 8

Sentence Correction

> Several consumer protection agencies have filed suit, seeking to bar distributors from advertising treatments for baldness <u>that brings no discernible improvement and may even result in potential harm</u>.
>
> ○ that brings no discernible improvement and may even result in potential harm
>
> ○ that bring no discernible improvement and may even prove harmful
>
> ○ bringing no discernible improvement and even being harmful
>
> ○ that brings no discernible improvement and may even potentially result in harm being done
>
> ○ that bring no discernible improvement, maybe even resulting in harm

Above is a typical Sentence Correction question. In this chapter, we'll look at how to apply the Kaplan Method to this question, discuss the grammar rules being tested, and go over the basic principles and strategies that you want to keep in mind on every Sentence Correction question. But before you move on, take a minute to think about what you see in this question and answer some questions about how you think it works:

- What skills and concepts does this question test?

- How does answer choice **(A)** relate to the given sentence?

- What other patterns do you notice in the answer choices?

- What GMAT Core Competencies are most essential to success on this question?

PREVIEWING SENTENCE CORRECTION

WHAT SKILLS AND CONCEPTS DOES THIS QUESTION TEST?

Many students, upon seeing Sentence Correction questions for the first time, think of them as "grammar" questions. It's true that correct answers often fix grammar mistakes, but you don't need to know the names of grammar rules or of different verb conjugations. What is it that you're being asked to do on Sentence Correction questions? These questions ask you to pick the answer that most clearly, correctly, or effectively gets across the idea of the sentence.

Sentence Correction questions cover a range of grammatical errors, some of which are so obscure that even good writers commit them. However, you don't have to be a grammar expert to do well on this section. All you need is a mode of attack and some knowledge about what does—and does not—constitute good GMAT grammar. Most of this chapter focuses on these common errors and how you can identify the answer choice that the GMAT considers correct.

Another key element in GMAT Sentence Correction is style, or what the directions for this question type call "effectiveness of expression." That means English that is clear and exact and without awkwardness, ambiguity, or redundancy. (Note that it doesn't have to be interesting. In fact, the test is set up to see whether you get worn down by difficult, often boring prose or whether you rise above that to stay involved—and awake.)

HOW DOES ANSWER CHOICE (A) RELATE TO THE GIVEN SENTENCE?

Each Sentence Correction sentence will contain an underlined portion and ask you which of the choices best fits in place of that underlined portion. Answer choice **(A)** will always repeat exactly that underlined part of the sentence. So, choice **(A)** is correct when there's no error. Recognizing this pattern means that you never need to spend any time reading choice **(A)** once you've read the original sentence. Given the statistically random distribution of correct answers across the five choices, you can anticipate that choice **(A)**—the sentence is correct as written—will be correct approximately 20 percent of the time.

WHAT OTHER PATTERNS DO YOU NOTICE IN THE ANSWER CHOICES?

Spotting patterns in how the answer choices are presented is the bedrock of the Kaplan Method for Sentence Correction. As you scan through these answer choices, you'll see that they tend to split easily into groups based on the varying ways they handle the grammatical issues in the sentence. Two of the choices start with *that bring*, two with *that brings*, and one with *bringing*.

We will return to analyze this particular question fully once we've learned the Kaplan Method, but for now just know that we call this phenomenon a "split"—certain patterns in how the answer choices are constructed allow us to place them into groups, sometimes even eliminating two or three answer choices solely on the basis of this categorization. Most Sentence Correction questions have a 3-2 or 2-2-1 split. This strategic, pattern-oriented approach will allow you to narrow the choices down to the one correct answer with the confidence and speed of an expert.

WHAT GMAT CORE COMPETENCIES ARE MOST ESSENTIAL TO SUCCESS ON THIS QUESTION?

Pattern Recognition and Attention to the Right Detail are the Core Competencies central to Sentence Correction questions. The typical Sentence Correction question contains two or more errors. The testmakers reward you for being able to quickly spot and correct these problems that impair effective communication. Time is of the essence with these questions; the sentences vary in length and complexity, so you'll have to move considerably faster on the short ones to leave time for the long ones. Knowing the main types of grammatical errors that show up repeatedly on Sentence Correction questions and being able to analyze the patterns in how the answer choices are presented will help you move through these questions efficiently and accurately.

Here are the main topics we'll cover in this chapter:

- Question Format and Structure
- The Kaplan Method for Sentence Correction
- Commonly Tested Grammar on the GMAT

QUESTION FORMAT AND STRUCTURE

The GMAT Verbal Reasoning section includes about 16 Sentence Correction questions, which are mixed in with Critical Reasoning and Reading Comprehension.

The directions for Sentence Correction questions look like this:

> **Directions:** Each Sentence Correction question presents a sentence, part or all of which is underlined. Below each sentence you will find five ways to phrase the underlined portion. The first answer choice repeats the original version, while the other four choices are different. If the original seems best, choose the first answer choice. If not, choose one of the revisions.
>
> In choosing an answer, follow the norms of standard written English: grammar, word choice, and sentence construction. Choose the answer that produces the most effective sentence, aiming to eliminate awkwardness, ambiguity, redundancy, and grammatical error.

Sentence Correction tests your command of standard written English—the rather formal language that is used in textbooks and scholarly periodicals. It's the language that's used to convey complex information precisely, as opposed to the casual language that we use for everyday communication. The good news is that you do *not* need to know every grammar rule for these questions. Errors reflecting certain rules show up repeatedly on the GMAT. Focus on mastering these commonly tested rules—that's how to get the biggest bang for your study-time buck.

THE KAPLAN METHOD FOR SENTENCE CORRECTION

Now it's time to learn how to bring together all of the strategies you read about above into a consistent protocol for approaching Sentence Correction questions. Kaplan has developed a Method for Sentence Correction that you can use to attack each and every Sentence Correction question. Through regular practice, this method will become second nature by Test Day.

The Kaplan Method for Sentence Correction

1. **Read the original sentence carefully, looking for errors.**

2. **Scan and group the answer choices.**

3. **Eliminate choices until only one remains.**

STEP 1: READ THE ORIGINAL SENTENCE CAREFULLY, LOOKING FOR ERRORS

Read the sentence. Look for things that sound wrong but also keep your eyes peeled for signs of the classic errors that the GMAT loves to repeat. If you spot an error, eliminate **(A)** immediately. If you don't spot an error the first time through, don't bother rereading. You're no more likely to spot a problem the second time around—especially because there may not be an error at all! Instead, move straight to Step 2.

STEP 2: SCAN AND GROUP THE ANSWER CHOICES

Instead of wasting time reading each answer choice individually, quickly scan and compare the answers with one other. If you spotted an error in Step 1, sort the answer choices into two groups: those that do not fix the error (which you can eliminate) and those that appear to fix it.

If you *didn't* spot an error, try to zero in on a grammatical or stylistic difference that splits the answer choices into distinct groups. This will let you identify one of the issues that the question is testing. Once you know what is being tested, you can apply your knowledge of English grammar to determine which group is correct—thereby eliminating multiple answers at once.

STEP 3: ELIMINATE CHOICES UNTIL ONLY ONE REMAINS

If more than one choice remains, go back to Step 2 and scan again to find another difference. Then eliminate accordingly. Repeat this process until only one answer remains.

Important Pacing Tip: If more than one choice remains after you have eliminated all of the answers that you are sure are wrong, just go with your best guess. If you don't know the rule by Test Day, you probably won't successfully teach it to yourself while taking the exam. You'll get a much higher score by investing that time in other questions. If you are working on a quiz or a practice test, of course, reading the answer explanation closely will help you to learn the important rules so you can use them successfully on Test Day.

Now let's apply the Kaplan Method to the Sentence Correction question you saw earlier:

> Several consumer protection agencies have filed suit, seeking to bar distributors from advertising treatments for baldness <u>that brings no discernible improvement and may even result in potential harm</u>.
>
> O   that brings no discernible improvement and may even result in potential harm
> O   that bring no discernible improvement and may even prove harmful
> O   bringing no discernible improvement and even being harmful
> O   that brings no discernible improvement and may even potentially result in harm being done
> O   that bring no discernible improvement, maybe even resulting in harm

Step 1: Read the Original Sentence Carefully, Looking for Errors

The underlined phrase is a clause that is describing something in the first part of the sentence. (The use of the word *that* is a good clue that you are working with a clause.) What in the first part of the sentence "brings no discernible improvement" and may cause harm? *Treatments.* But you can't say *treatments brings*.

You've found a problem with this sentence (subject-verb agreement), so **(A)**, the original structure, can't be correct. The correct answer will fix the subject-verb agreement problem without introducing other errors.

Step 2: Scan and Group the Answer Choices

Now you'd quickly scan the choices, looking for any that repeat the error. That's **(D)**.

If you didn't spot the error at first, you'd look for the main differences among the choices. Here, you have a 2-2-1 split: Two say *brings*, two say *bring*, and one says *bringing*. Which is correct?

Step 3: Eliminate Choices Until Only One Remains

If you spotted the error, you eliminated **(A)** and **(D)** as wrong, which leaves *bring* and *bringing*.

If you didn't spot the error, you'd now look at your groups of answer choices. Two answer choices say *brings*, two say *bring*—one is plural, the other singular. This is very likely about subject-verb agreement, one of the testmakers' favorite types of errors. So what *brings* no improvement? Is it *baldness*? There's an *of* before *baldness*, so *baldness* can't be the subject. Plus "Baldness brings no discernible improvement" just doesn't make sense. It has to be *treatments*. You'd eliminate **(A)** and **(D)** and turn your attention to *bring/bringing*.

You'd eliminate *bringing*, either because you recognize that the continuous tense is awkward and unnecessary here or because you know that on the GMAT, *-ing* forms are almost always wrong in verb questions. Plus, only one answer choice uses *bringing*, so eliminate it and move on.

Scanning between **(B)** and **(E)**, you spot a difference at the end: *and may even prove harmful* versus *maybe even resulting in harm*. *Prove* is parallel with *bring*, and *resulting* is not. Eliminate **(E)**. That leaves only one answer, **(B)**.

TAKEAWAYS: THE KAPLAN METHOD FOR SENTENCE CORRECTION

- If you don't spot an error in the sentence, immediately scan the answer choices for differences. Focus on one error at a time. Usually you will find a 3-2 or 2-2-1 split somewhere in the wording.

- Some differences will provide an easier basis by which to eliminate than others. If you see a difference but can't determine which alternative is better, see if there are other differences that you can use.

- Knowing how to spot the differences in the answer choices is only half the battle. Learning the testmakers' favorite errors, so that you can figure out which version is correct, is the other half.

PRACTICE SET: THE KAPLAN METHOD FOR SENTENCE CORRECTION

Answers and explanations at end of chapter

1. The rise in the number of new housing starts in the final two quarters of last
    year <u>suggest that the sluggish economy should continue its recovery into the first
    quarter of this year, but</u> weak job growth in the private sector continues to worry
    some economists.

    O   suggest that the sluggish economy should continue its recovery into the first
        quarter of this year, but

    O   suggest that the sluggish economy will continue to recover in the first quarter
        of this year, but that

    O   suggest that the sluggish economy is continuing to recover in the first quarter
        of this year, but

    O   suggests that the sluggish economy should continue its recovery into the first
        quarter of this year, but that

    O   suggests that the sluggish economy will continue to recover in the first
        quarter of this year, but

2. The green flash, an atmospheric refractive phenomenon whereby the top edge
    of a setting sun will momentarily turn green, rarely is seen by the naked eye,
    primarily <u>on account of requiring</u> specific favorable conditions to occur.

    O   on account of requiring
    O   on account of their requiring
    O   because they require
    O   because it requires
    O   because of requiring

3. A new study has found that college students <u>had been more involved in
    on-campus political activities during the last few years than at any time</u> in the
    past two decades.

    O   had been more involved in on-campus political activities during the last few
        years than at any time

    O   had been more involved in on-campus political activities during the last few
        years than at any other time

    O   have been more involved in on-campus political activities during the last few
        years than at any other time

    O   have been more involved in on-campus political activities during the last few
        years than at any time

    O   are more involved in on-campus political activities during the last few years
        as compared to any other time

4. Depending on which scholar you consult, Christopher Columbus, Leif Ericson, or the Chinese eunuch Zheng Ho <u>is credited with being the first explorer from the Eurasian continent to have traveled to the New World by ship</u>.

    O   is credited with being the first explorer from the Eurasian continent to have traveled to the New World by ship

    O   is credited to be the first explorer from the Eurasian continent to have traveled to the New World by ship

    O   is credited to have been the first explorer from the Eurasian continent to have traveled to the New World by ship

    O   are credited with being the first explorers from the Eurasian continent to have traveled to the New World by ship

    O   are credited to be the first explorers from the Eurasian continent to have traveled to the New World by ship

5. Noting that <u>its revenues had fallen due to a recent</u> prolonged slump in CD sales, the music-store chain announced that it would be forced to raise prices at all of its outlets.

    O   its revenues had fallen due to a recent

    O   its revenues have fallen due to a recently

    O   its revenues are falling due to a recently

    O   their revenues are falling due to a recent

    O   their revenues had fallen due to a recent

COMMONLY TESTED GRAMMAR ON THE GMAT

Doing well on Sentence Correction questions begins with knowing how to approach them and then learning the errors that appear most frequently. Test takers who learn the most commonly tested patterns on GMAT Sentence Correction will be able to answer these questions confidently and efficiently. In this section, we'll look at the seven most commonly tested areas of grammar and usage:

- Verbs
- Pronouns
- Modification
- Parallel Structure
- Comparisons
- Usage/Idioms
- Miscellaneous Errors

It's important to master these areas of grammar and usage, but keep in mind that many questions, particularly those of higher difficulty, will test multiple concepts. Many questions contain more than one error. Using the Kaplan Method for Sentence Correction will give you an efficient way to focus on one error at a time. With both knowledge of these commonly tested areas and mastery of the Kaplan Method, you'll be able to handle all, even the toughest, Sentence Correction questions.

VERBS

Subject-Verb Agreement

A sentence is defined as an independent sequence of words that contains a subject and a verb. Verbs must agree with their subjects. Singular subjects have singular verbs, and plural subjects have plural verbs. If you're a native English speaker, this is probably so automatic that you may wonder why the GMAT tests it at all. But the testmakers craftily separate subject and verb with lots of text to make it harder to recognize whether the subject and verb agree. Also, it is sometimes hard to tell whether the subject is singular or plural. You should look out for the following common subject-verb agreement issues:

- Long modifying phrases or clauses following the subject
- Phrases and clauses in commas between the subject and the verb
- Subjects joined by *either/or* and *neither/nor*
- Sentences in which the verb precedes the subject
- Collective nouns, such as *majority, committee, audience, team, group, flock, family,* especially when followed by a prepositional phrase containing a plural noun ("the group of legislators"):
  - Collective nouns take a singular verb when the members of the collective act as a unit ("the flock of geese is flying south") or are non-countable ("a lot of water was spilled").
  - When the members of the collective act as individuals, the collective noun takes a plural verb ("the majority of voters favor the proposal"; "a number of solutions are possible").

Subject-Verb Agreement Exercise

Answers on the following page

Correct each of the following subject-verb errors.

1. The depletion of natural resources, in addition to the rapid increase in utilization of these resources, have encouraged many nations to conserve energy.

2. There is, without a doubt, many good reasons to exercise.

3. Among the many problems plaguing suburbanites is the ubiquity of shopping malls, the increasing cost of gasoline, and the unavailability of mortgages.

4. The neighbors told police investigators that neither Annette nor her brother are capable of telling the truth.

5. The assembly of delegates intend to scrutinize the governor's policy decisions.

Subject-Verb Agreement Exercise: Answers

1. *Depletion* is the subject. Correct by changing *have* to *has* or by changing *in addition to* to *and*.

2. There *are* many good reasons. A good strategy for checking subject-verb agreement is to ignore, temporarily, any parts of the sentence that are set off by commas.

3. If the sentence ended at *malls, is* would be correct. But because there is more than one problem listed, *are* is the correct verb here.

4. "Neither Annette nor her brother *is* capable." In *or/nor* constructions, the verb agrees with the subject to which it is closest. So if it were "Neither Annette nor her friends," *are* would be called for.

5. Even though *delegates* is plural, the subject of the sentence, *assembly*, is a singular noun referring collectively to the group. *Assembly* therefore takes a singular verb: "The assembly *intends* to scrutinize."

Verb Tense

A verb tense indicates the order in which separate actions or events occur. Deciding which verb tense is appropriate in a given situation isn't just a matter of grammar; it's also a question of logic. Many GMAT sentences are long and complicated, involving or implying several different actions. The correct tenses make the sequence of events clear.

To determine whether the verbs in a sentence are in the proper tenses, pick one event as a standard and measure every other event against it. Ask yourself whether the other events are supposed to have happened before the standard event took place, after it took place, or while it took place. Those aren't mutually exclusive options, by the way: It is possible in English to have one action start before a second action and continue during that second action.

A frequent GMAT verb error is the inappropriate use of *-ing* forms: "I am going, I was going, I had been going," and so on. As far as the GMAT is concerned, the only reason to use an *-ing* form is to emphasize that an action is continuing or that two actions are occurring simultaneously. To remember this rule, think of the word *during* and its *-ing* ending. Other than that, pick a simpler tense—one that doesn't use the *-ing* form. In other words, avoid *-ing* forms as much as possible.

Most Commonly Tested Verb Tenses

- **Simple Present**—*I am*—Used for an action happening now, with no contextual information about when it started.
- **Simple Past**—*I was*—Used for an action that happened at a specified time in the past.
- **Simple Future**—*I will*—Used for an action that will happen in the future.
- **Past Perfect**—*I had been*—Used for an action that happened *before* another past action (e.g., "I had been on the subway for 30 minutes before I realized that I was going the wrong direction.").
- **Present Perfect**—*I have been*—Used for an action that started in the past but is still continuing now (e.g., "I have been on the subway for two hours now, and I still don't know where I'm going!") or for past events that happened at an unspecified time (e.g. "He has read *Don Quixote* seven times.").

There are other verb tenses in the English language, but these are the ones that are tested most often on the GMAT.

Verb Tense Exercise

Answers on the following page

Correct the verb tenses in each sentence.

1. The criminal escaped from custody and is believed to flee the country.

2. Some archaeologists believe that the Minoans of 3,700 years ago had practiced a religion that involved human sacrifice.

3. If the experiment works, it will be representing a quantum leap forward for pharmaceutical chemistry.

4. He had seen that movie recently, so he doesn't want to see it tonight.

5. By the time she retires, she will save enough money to allow her to live comfortably.

6. She already closed the door behind her when it occurred to her that she wasn't able to get back in later.

Verb Tense Exercise: Answers

1. The *criminal escaped* correctly uses simple past tense to refer to an event that happened at a specific time. The believing happens now, so simple present *is believed* is correct. However, the fleeing happened at an unknown and unspecified time in the past, so the present perfect should be used: "... is believed to have fled the country."

2. Here, there's no indication the Minoans practiced human sacrifice for a while and then did something else. So use the simple past *practiced* instead of the past perfect *had practiced*.

3. The experiment won't *be representing* a quantum leap; it will *represent* a quantum leap.

4. *Had* plus a past tense verb is used to indicate which of two things that went on in the past occurred earlier. That's not necessary in this sentence. "He saw that movie recently, so he doesn't want to see it tonight." ("He had seen the movie recently, so he didn't want to see it tonight," also works, although it changes the meaning of the sentence to indicate that the desire happened earlier tonight instead of happening now.)

5. Here, we're indicating an action that began in the past but will end in the future. Think of it this way: At some future time, what will have happened? "... she will have saved enough money."

6. *Closed, occurred,* and *wasn't able to get back in* are all in the simple past tense. But you need to indicate that she first closed the door and then something occurred to her—namely, that she wouldn't be able to do something in the future. "She had already closed the door behind her when it occurred to her that she wouldn't be able to get back in later."

APPLYING THE KAPLAN METHOD: VERBS

Now let's use the Kaplan Method on a Sentence Correction question dealing with verbs:

> The governor's approval ratings <u>has been extremely high until</u> a series of corruption scandals rocked his administration last year.

- ○ has been extremely high until
- ○ have been extremely high until
- ○ had been extremely high until
- ○ were extremely high as
- ○ had been extremely high as

Step 1: Read the Original Sentence Carefully, Looking for Errors

Whenever a sentence contains an underlined verb, you need to make sure that it agrees with its subject and is in the correct tense. Here, the underlined portion contains a singular verb, "has been," that disagrees with the plural subject, "ratings." The verb is also is in the wrong tense—"has been" indicates that the ratings are still high, but the sentence contradicts that. You can eliminate answer choice **(A)** immediately.

Step 2: Scan and Group the Answer Choices

Now it's time to look for a split in the answer choices. You see that the choices begin with many different verb forms: two "had been," one "were," one "have been," and one "has been." That's not a very helpful split. If you don't find a split at the beginnings of the answer choices, look for a split at the ends. Answer choices **(A)**, **(B)**, and **(C)** end with "until," whereas **(D)** and **(E)** end with "as"; a 3-2 split.

Step 3: Eliminate Choices Until Only One Remains

You eliminated answer choice **(A)** because the subject, "ratings," is plural, so the singular verb, "has been," cannot be correct. But verb tense is also at issue here. The correct verb tense is "had been extremely high," because the past perfect tense is used to indicate that something had already happened in the past before something else happened in the past. Here, the governor's ratings *had been* high, until scandals *rocked* his administration. This eliminates **(B)** and **(D)**. And **(E)** can be eliminated, since changing the preposition from "until" to "as" loses the sense that the scandals occurred before, and led to, the reversal in the governor's approval ratings. For the record, note that **(D)** also contains this error. The GMAT will often give you multiple opportunities to eliminate answer choices. This leaves **(C)** as the only flawless answer.

TAKEAWAYS: VERBS

- A complete sentence consists, at minimum, of a subject and a verb.
- The verb must agree with the subject of the sentence; plural subjects take plural verbs and singular subjects take singular verbs.
- The verb tense must match the meaning of the sentence as a whole.
- Don't fall for needlessly complicated verb tenses. Go for the simplest verb tense that makes sense given the time frame of the sentence.
- Use the past perfect tense (*had done, had seen*) to indicate something that happened prior to another past event.
- Use the present perfect tense for an action that happened at an unspecified time in the past (*have read, has said*) or an action that started in the past and has continued until the present time (*have lived, has been, have had*).
- Use the present perfect continuous tense (*have been studying, has been waiting*) for an action that started in the past and is still continuing now.

PRACTICE SET: VERBS

Answers and explanations at end of chapter

6. After all the research that has been conducted in the last 30 years, it is readily apparent that <u>there are, without question, a wealth of good reasons to do aerobic exercise regularly</u>.

   ○ there are, without question, a wealth of good reasons to do aerobic exercise regularly

   ○ there are, without question, a wealth of good reasons to exercise aerobically regularly

   ○ there are, without question, a wealth of good reasons to engage regularly in aerobic exercise

   ○ there is, without question, a wealth of good reasons to engage regularly in aerobic exercise

   ○ there is, without question, a wealth of good reasons to do regular aerobic exercises

7. As state governments <u>become less and less able to support higher education in the coming years, universities have been becoming</u> more and more dependent on alumni networks, corporate sponsorships, and philanthropists.

   ○ become less and less able to support higher education in the coming years, universities have been becoming

   ○ are becoming less and less able to support higher education in the coming years, universities have become

   ○ become less and less able to support higher education in the coming years, universities will become

   ○ become less and less able to support higher education in the coming years, universities have become

   ○ are becoming less and less able to support higher education in the coming years, universities will become

8. The most common breed of rabbit, *Oryctolagus cuniculus*, <u>is native to Europe but was accidentally introduced into the Australian continent in the 1850s, causing</u> decades of habitat destruction and crop devastation before its numbers were finally brought under control by bounty hunters.

   O is native to Europe but was accidentally introduced into the Australian continent in the 1850s, causing

   O is a native of Europe but was accidentally introduced into the Australian continent in the 1850s, which caused

   O was a native of Europe but was accidentally introduced into the Australian continent in the 1850s, causing

   O had been native to Europe but was accidentally introduced into the Australian continent in the 1850s, which caused

   O had been a native of Europe but was accidentally introduced into the Australian continent in the 1850s, causing

9. A recent spate of news reports questioning the long-term health benefits of high-fat diets <u>have done little to convince its practitioners that they should follow more traditional weight-loss plans</u>.

   O have done little to convince its practitioners that they should follow more traditional weight-loss plans

   O have done little to convince their practitioners to follow more traditional weight-loss plans

   O has done little to convince its practitioners to follow more traditional weight-loss plans

   O has done little to convince practitioners of these diets to follow more traditional weight-loss plans

   O has done little to convince practitioners of these diets they should follow more traditional weight-loss plans

ADVANCED PRACTICE SET: VERBS

Answers and explanations at end of chapter

10. Some economists contend that the way markets react to financial news <u>are based as much on irrational fears and expectations than on</u> sound fiscal analyses.

   - ○ are based as much on irrational fears and expectations than on
   - ○ are based as much on their irrational fears and expectations as they are on
   - ○ is based as much on irrational fears and expectations than on
   - ○ is based as much on irrational fears and expectations as on
   - ○ has been based on irrational fears and expectations as much as

11. The newspaper reported that <u>some homes that were destroyed and severely damaged in the hurricane last year were</u> built too close to the coastline.

   - ○ some homes that were destroyed and severely damaged in the hurricane last year were
   - ○ some homes that were destroyed or severely damaged in the hurricane last year had been
   - ○ some homes the hurricane destroyed and severely damaged last year have been
   - ○ last year the hurricane destroyed or severely damaged some homes that have been
   - ○ last year some of the homes that were destroyed or severely damaged in the hurricane have been

12. The activism of state citizens, who have demanded safer road conditions as well as stiffer penalties for intoxicated drivers, <u>have led to a significant decrease in the number</u> of traffic accidents.

   - ○ have led to a significant decrease in the number
   - ○ have led to significant decreases in the amount
   - ○ has led to a significant decrease in the number
   - ○ has been significant in the decrease in the number
   - ○ has significantly decreased the amount

PRONOUNS

Pronoun errors are one of the most common Sentence Correction issues on the GMAT. Luckily, the GMAT doesn't test every kind of pronoun error. Common errors fall into two categories: reference and agreement. Pronoun reference errors mean that a given pronoun does not refer to—or stand for—a specific noun or pronoun in the sentence (its antecedent). The pronouns that cause the most trouble on the GMAT are *it, its, they, their, them, which*, and *that*.

For pronoun agreement errors, it's a question of numbers: Perhaps a pronoun that refers to a singular noun is not in singular form, or a pronoun that refers to a plural noun is not in plural form.

As usual, the GMAT presents camouflaged examples of these two mistakes. Whenever you see a pronoun in the underlined portion of a sentence, look out for the following:

- Pronouns, such as *it* and *they*, that are often misused on the GMAT (and in everyday life)
- Pronouns that don't clearly refer to a specific noun
- Pronouns that don't agree in number or gender with their antecedents

Pronoun Agreement Exercise

Answers on the following page

Correct the following common pronoun reference errors.

1. Beatrix Potter's stories depict animals in an unsentimental and humorous manner, and she illustrated them with delicate watercolor paintings.

2. There is no known cure for certain forms of hepatitis; they hope, though, that a cure will be found soon.

3. If the partners cannot resolve their differences, the courts may have to do it.

4. In order to boost their name recognition, the Green Party sent canvassers to a busy shopping mall.

5. It is now recognized that the dangers of nuclear war are much graver than that of conventional warfare.

6. One of the men complained about the noise in the hallway, and they don't want to identify themselves.

Pronoun Agreement Exercise: Answers

1. *She* is clearly intended to refer to Beatrix Potter, but notice that the proper noun *Beatrix Potter* doesn't appear anywhere in this sentence; a pronoun cannot refer to a modifier, even a possessive modifier such as *Beatrix Potter's*. There's a second problem as well: It's not clear whether the *them* that are illustrated are the stories or the animals. Here's a rewrite that solves all the problems: "Beatrix Potter not only wrote stories that depicted animals in an unsentimental and humorous manner, but also illustrated each story with delicate watercolor paintings."

2. It's unclear what *they* refers to. The only plural noun is *forms*, but it can't be the *forms of hepatitis* that are hoping for a cure. It must be *scientists* or some other group of people: "scientists hope to find a cure soon."

3. *It* is the unclear pronoun here. There's no singular noun in the sentence for *it* to refer to. The main clause should read: "... the courts may have to do so."

4. A pronoun or possessive should match the form of the noun it refers to. Use *its* and not *their* in place of the Green Party, because *party*, like *audience*, is a singular noun that stands for a collective group: "In order to boost its name recognition, the Green Party ..."

5. *Dangers* is plural, so the pronoun "that" should be plural as well: "... than those of conventional warfare."

6. The antecedent of "they" and "themselves" is "one," so the pronouns do not agree in number or gender with their antecedent. Because the gender of "one" is male ("one of the men"), the pronouns should be changed to "he" and "himself," and the verb "don't" should be changed to the singular "doesn't."

APPLYING THE KAPLAN METHOD: PRONOUNS

Now let's use the Kaplan Method on a Sentence Correction question dealing with pronouns:

Despite <u>the platform of the opposition party supporting the measure, they keep</u> voting against campaign finance reform in Congress.

- O   the platform of the opposition party supporting the measure, they keep
- O   the opposition party's platform supporting the measure, they keep
- O   the opposition party's platform which supports the measure, it keeps
- O   support of the measure being in the opposition party's platform, it keeps
- O   the opposition party's platform supporting the measure, party members keep

Step 1: Read the Original Sentence Carefully, Looking for Errors

Pattern Recognition and Attention to the Right Detail are essential to spotting pronoun issues in Sentence Correction. Here, you should be paying attention to the word "they" in the underlined portion of the sentence. Colloquially, it's common to use "they" as a nebulous pronoun with no clear antecedent. On the GMAT, though, such usage is always wrong. In this sentence, it isn't clear who "they" refers to, so you know that's an issue that needs to be fixed by the correct answer.

Step 2: Scan and Group the Answer Choices

The beginnings of the answer choices don't yield much in the way of splits, but the ends definitely do: **(A)** and **(B)** end with "they," **(C)** and **(D)** end with "it," and **(E)** dispenses with pronouns entirely. You have a 2-2-1 split.

Step 3: Eliminate Choices Until Only One Remains

The pronoun use here is wrong, because the sentence does not contain an antecedent plural noun to which "they" could refer. So, **(A)** and **(B)** are incorrect. **(C)** and **(D)** contain the singular pronoun "it"—but once again, the pronoun reference is confusing and wrong. It's not the *party platform* that keeps voting against the measure, as these choices imply. Both **(C)** and **(D)** can be eliminated. Only choice **(E)**, which avoids faulty pronoun reference and makes it clear that *party members* keep voting against the measure, makes sense and is the correct answer.

TAKEAWAYS: PRONOUNS

- A pronoun is a word that stands for a noun.
- A pronoun must refer unambiguously to a specific noun, known as its *antecedent*.
- A pronoun must agree in number and gender with the noun it replaces.
- When you see a pronoun underlined in the original sentence, focus on that pronoun and determine whether it is being used correctly.
- The pronouns that cause the most trouble on the GMAT are *it*, *they*, *its*, *their*, *them*, *which*, and *that*.
- Never use *they* to refer to a third-person singular noun on the GMAT, even if you don't know or don't want to specify gender.

PRACTICE SET: PRONOUNS

Answers and explanations at end of chapter

13. The government <u>has imposed sanctions and restricted foreign aid to a renegade nation last month after it violated</u> the terms of a worldwide arms control treaty.

    ○ has imposed sanctions and restricted foreign aid to a renegade nation last month after it violated

    ○ has imposed sanctions on and restricted foreign aid to a renegade nation last month after it violated

    ○ imposed sanctions on and restricted foreign aid to a renegade nation last month after that nation violated

    ○ imposed sanctions and restricted foreign aid to a renegade nation last month after violating

    ○ had imposed sanctions and restricted foreign aid to a renegade nation last month after it had violated

14. Every one of the police reports <u>have been filed so that they can be located by their case number, the date they were created, or the victim's last name</u>.

    ○ have been filed so that they can be located by their case number, the date they were created, or the victim's last name

    ○ have been filed so that they can be located by their case numbers, the dates they were created, or by the victims' last names

    ○ has been filed so that they can be located by their case number, the date they were created, or the victim's last name

    ○ has been filed so that it can be located by its case number, the date it was created, or the victim's last name

    ○ has been filed so that it can be located by its case number, the date it was created, or by the victim's last name

15. <u>Although swimming can cause cramps in a swimmer's legs or feet, they</u> can usually be avoided if the swimmer avoids overexertion and performs stretching exercises before entering the pool.

   ○   Although swimming can cause cramps in a swimmer's legs or feet, they

   ○   Cramps in a swimmer's legs or feet caused by swimming

   ○   Swimming can cause cramps in a swimmer's legs or feet, which

   ○   The fact that swimming can cause cramps in a swimmer's legs or feet

   ○   Swimming can cause cramps in a swimmer's legs or feet, although they

16. Some mathematicians argue that <u>to permit a candidate to win an election because they have won a plurality vote is like ranking a student</u> who earned three As and two Fs higher than one who got two As and three Bs.

   ○   to permit a candidate to win an election because they have won a plurality vote is like ranking a student

   ○   permitting a candidate to win an election because they have won a plurality of votes is like ranking a student

   ○   permitting candidates to win elections because they have won a plurality of votes is like to rank a student

   ○   permitting candidates to win elections because they have won a plurality of votes is like ranking a student

   ○   to permit candidates to win elections because they have won a plurality of votes is like ranking students

ADVANCED PRACTICE SET: PRONOUNS

Answers and explanations at end of chapter

17. According to a recently enacted law, any organization that engages in lobbying activities is required either to notify <u>their members about the percentage of dues that are used for lobbying activities or</u> pay a proxy tax.

   - O   their members about the percentage of dues that are used for lobbying activities or
   - O   their members about the percentage of dues they use for lobbying activities or to
   - O   their members about the percentage of dues that are used for lobbying activities or they should
   - O   its members about the percentage of dues that are used for lobbying activities or it should
   - O   its members about the percentage of dues that is used for lobbying activities or to

18. The chief executive officer met with the board of directors to consider the possibility of a hostile takeover attempt by a competitor and <u>how they would have to respond to deal with them</u>.

   - O   how they would have to respond to deal with them
   - O   how to deal with them if action would become necessary
   - O   what action would be required for dealing with such an event
   - O   what action would be necessary to deal with such an event
   - O   the necessity of taking action in order to deal with it

19. Arguing that the dominance of an economic theory has more to do with the persuasive skills of <u>its expositors than with its</u> accuracy in predicting economic events, Professor McCloskey examines the rhetorical practices of economists.

   - O   its expositors than with its
   - O   these expositors than its
   - O   its expositors compared to its
   - O   the theory's expositors than their
   - O   its expositors than with their

MODIFICATION

A modifier is a word, phrase, or clause that describes another part of the sentence. It should be placed as close as possible to whatever it is modifying. Adjectives modify nouns; adverbs modify verbs, adjectives, or other adverbs. Modifiers describe the word that they are right next to. (The only exception is the case of two modifiers; one has to be first.) The GMAT often creates modification errors by making a modifier appear to describe a word that it actually doesn't. Use Pattern Recognition to help you spot modification errors on the GMAT.

The most common GMAT modification error is a long modifier at the beginning of the sentence. It should modify the subject of the sentence but will likely not do so properly. Another common modification error is a long modifier that appears in the middle or at the end of a sentence. Often such a modifier on the GMAT will logically describe something elsewhere in the sentence, but grammatically a modifying phrase must modify the word that comes immediately before or after it. The result of a misplaced modifier is a nonsensical sentence. Also look out for the following:

- Sentences beginning or ending with descriptive phrases
- *That/which* clauses, especially ones that come at the end of sentences

Modification Exercise

Answers on the following page

In each of the following sentences, first identify what each clause or phrase is modifying. Then, fix each error you find.

1. Upon landing at the airport, the hotel sent a limousine to pick us up.

2. Based on the most current data available, the company made plans to diversify its holdings.

3. Small and taciturn, Joan Didion's presence often goes unnoticed by those she will later write about.

4. I took several lessons to learn how to play tennis without getting the ball over the net even once.

5. The house overlooked the lake, which was set back from the shore.

Modification Exercise: Answers

1. The sentence seems to be saying that the *hotel* landed at the airport. Your common sense will tell you that *upon landing at the airport* really intends to modify the unnamed *we*, instead. So you could say, "Upon landing at the airport, we were met by a limousine the hotel had sent."

2. As written, it sounds as though the company was based on current data. *Based on the most current data available* modifies the subject *company*. Obviously, though, what was based on the data were the *plans*, not the company. "Based on the most current data available, plans were made to diversify the company's holdings."

3. It's Joan Didion—not her presence—who is small and taciturn. "Small and taciturn, Joan Didion often goes unnoticed ...."

4. As written, *without getting the ball over the net* is describing *how to play tennis*. The intended meaning is much more likely to be "I took many tennis lessons before I could get the ball over the net even once."

5. The misplaced modifying clause produces an absurd image: a lake that's set back from its own shore. Of course, the *which* clause should follow *the house*: "The house, which was set back from the shore, overlooked the lake."

APPLYING THE KAPLAN METHOD: MODIFICATION

Now let's use the Kaplan Method on a Sentence Correction question dealing with modification:

Subjects tend to be vividly but disturbingly portrayed in Egon Schiele's portraits, often his closest friends and relatives.

- O Subjects tend to be vividly but disturbingly portrayed in Egon Schiele's portraits, often his closest friends and relatives
- O Subjects tend to be vividly but disturbingly portrayed in Egon Schiele's portraits, who were often his closest friends and relatives
- O Subjects of Egon Schiele's portraits, often his closest friends and relatives, tend to be vividly but disturbingly portrayed
- O In Egon Schiele's portraits, the subjects, often his closest friends and relatives, tend to be vividly but disturbingly portrayed
- O Vividly but disturbingly, the subjects portrayed in Egon Schiele's portraits tended to be his closest friends and relatives

Step 1: Read the Original Sentence Carefully, Looking for Errors

The entire sentence is underlined, but don't let that intimidate you. Use the Kaplan Method as you normally would and look for common errors. In this case, the error is a misplaced modifier at the end of the sentence. (Keep in mind that misplaced modifiers can occur anywhere in a sentence, not just at the beginning.) Here, the modifier is the final phrase set off by a comma, "often his closest friends and relatives." This phrase should refer to "subjects," but it's placed right next to "portraits." Always ask yourself when you see a modifier, "What should this word or phrase refer to? Is it as close to that word or phrase as possible?"

Step 2: Scan and Group the Answer Choices

As you scan, be on the lookout for where the modifier is placed. In these answer choices, the modifying phrase appears in several different positions. Any choice placing it far from the word it modifies—"subjects"—should be eliminated. In **(B)**, the modifying clause, "who were often his closest friends and relatives," seems to refer to *portraits* rather than *subjects*. Choice **(B)** retains the same problem as **(A)**, so you can eliminate it. Choice **(D)** places the modifier immediately after "subjects," so this is likely to be your answer.

Step 3: Eliminate Choices Until Only One Remains

In choice **(C)**, "subjects of Egon Schiele's portraits" seems to be one syntactical unit, so the phrase "often his closest friends and relatives" appears correctly to modify *subjects*, even though it is not directly adjacent to *subjects*. However, **(C)** is wrong because it is unclear whether "tend to be vividly but disturbingly portrayed" refers to how these subjects are displayed in the portraits, or elsewhere; perhaps biographers of Schiele depict them in this manner.

Finally, choice **(E)** is incorrect because the adverbial phrase "Vividly but disturbingly" appears to refer to the verb "tended" rather than to the adjective "portrayed," making it seem as if the subjects' tendency to be Egon's friends is what's vivid and disturbing. Only choice **(D)** properly addresses this misplaced modifier problem; it is therefore your correct answer. Moreover, choice **(D)**, unlike **(C)**, makes it clear that the vivid but disturbing portrayal is in the portaits themselves.

TAKEAWAYS: MODIFICATION

- Adjectives modify nouns; adverbs modify verbs, adjectives, or other adverbs.
- A modifying phrase must clearly refer to what it modifies. It should be placed as close as possible to what it modifies.
- Many GMAT modification errors involve misplaced modifiers at the beginning of the sentence. When there is a modifying phrase at the beginning of the sentence, make sure that the subject of that phrase is what follows the comma.
- Misplaced modifiers can also occur at the middle and end of a sentence, and they may or may not be set off by commas.
- When a particular modifying word or phrase appears in many different positions in the answer choices, determine exactly what it is meant to modify and pick the choice that places it where it belongs.

Practice Set: Modification

Answers and explanations at end of chapter

20. In an effort to determine whether changes in diet and exercise can reverse coronary heart disease, <u>1,800 elderly heart patients will participate in a Medicare program costing $12,960,000 over the next three years to reduce lifestyle-related risk factors</u>.

    O 1,800 elderly heart patients will participate in a Medicare program costing $12,960,000 over the next three years to reduce lifestyle-related risk factors

    O $12,960,000 will be spent by Medicare over the next three years in a program to reduce lifestyle-related risk factors in 1,800 elderly patients

    O over the next three years $12,960,000 will be spent on 1,800 patients by Medicare on a program to reduce lifestyle-related risk factors

    O Medicare is to spend $12,960,000 over the next three years on a program for reducing lifestyle-related risk factors in 1,800 elderly heart patients

    O Medicare will spend $12,960,000 over the next three years on a program to reduce lifestyle-related risk factors in 1,800 elderly heart patients

21. Children often pick up on gender norms very early in life, as many parents discover when <u>their toddlers recoil at toys that have only been designed to appeal to toddlers of the opposite sex</u>.

    O their toddlers recoil at toys that have only been designed to appeal to toddlers of the opposite sex

    O only their toddlers recoil at toys that have been designed to appeal to toddlers of the opposite sex

    O their toddlers recoil at toys that have been designed to appeal to toddlers of the opposite sex only

    O toys that have only been designed to appeal to toddlers of the opposite sex cause their toddlers to recoil

    O only toys that have been designed to appeal to toddlers of the opposite sex cause their toddlers to recoil

22. <u>Based on the candidates' performances in the televised debates</u>, many pundits predicted that the rival was likely to score an upset defeat over the incumbent senator.

- O   Based on the candidates' performances in the televised debates
- O   Basing it on the candidates' performances in the televised debates
- O   Basing their assessments on the candidates' performances in the televised debates
- O   With the candidates' performances in the televised debates used as a basis
- O   By the assessments of the candidates' performances in the televised debates that they made

23. Hoping to avert another situation in which the candidate who won the popular vote could lose the electoral vote, <u>it was proposed by Congress</u> that the Electoral College be abolished.

- O   it was proposed by Congress
- O   there was a proposal by Congress
- O   a proposal was made by Congress
- O   Congress proposed
- O   Congress will have proposed

ADVANCED PRACTICE SET: MODIFICATION

Answers and explanations at end of chapter

24. Cheered by better-than-expected opening week box office returns, <u>it was decided by the movie's producer to give bonuses to the entire cast</u>.

   ○ it was decided by the movie's producer to give bonuses to the entire cast

   ○ the entire cast was given bonuses by the movie's producer

   ○ the movie's producer decided to give the entire cast bonuses

   ○ the decision of the movie's producer was to give the entire cast bonuses

   ○ bonuses to the entire cast were given by the movie's producer

25. States now have an incentive to lower the blood alcohol level <u>that constitutes drunk driving by a federal law that withholds</u> highway funds from those states that don't enforce the applicable standard.

   ○ that constitutes drunk driving by a federal law that withholds

   ○ that constitutes drunk driving, because a federal law withholds

   ○ that constitutes drunk driving, because a federal law withheld

   ○ which constitutes drunk driving by a federal law that withholds

   ○ which constitutes drunk driving, because a federal law withholds

26. <u>Using a seismic survey, hydrocarbons can be located even though they are buried far beneath Earth's surface</u>.

   ○ Using a seismic survey, hydrocarbons can be located even though they are buried far beneath Earth's surface

   ○ Hydrocarbons can be located even though they are buried far beneath Earth's surface, using a seismic survey

   ○ Locating hydrocarbons that are buried far beneath Earth's surface, a geophysicist can use a seismic survey

   ○ Buried far beneath Earth's surface, hydrocarbons can be detected using a seismic survey

   ○ Using a seismic survey, a geophysicist can locate hydrocarbons even though they are buried far beneath Earth's surface

PARALLELISM

The basic concept behind parallelism is pretty simple: Ideas with the same importance and function—nouns, verbs, phrases, or whatever—should be expressed in the same grammatical form. There are two types of constructions that test parallel structure on the GMAT:

- Lists of items or a series of events
- Two-part constructions such as *from* X *to* Y, *both* X *and* Y, *either* X *or* Y, *prefer* X *to* Y, *not only* X *but also* Y, and *as much* X *as* Y

Prepositions, articles, and auxiliaries can begin a list without needing to be repeated throughout. But if they are repeated, they must be in every element of the list.

- Correct: "Will you travel by plane, car, or boat?"
- Also correct: "Will you travel by plane, by car, or by boat?"
- Incorrect: "Will you travel by plane, car, or by boat?"

Analogies, similes, and other comparisons all require parallel structure.

- He was as brazen as his brother was diffident.
- Seeing her smile was like feeling the warmth of the sun.

Parallelism Exercise

Answers on the following page

For each of the following sentences, put parallel items into the same form.

1. The city's decay stems from governmental mismanagement, increasing unemployment, and many businesses are relocating.

2. Tourists' images of France range from cosmopolitan to the pastoral.

3. Excited about visiting New York, Jasmine minded neither riding the subways nor to cope with the crowded sidewalks.

4. To visualize success is not the same as achieving it.

5. I remember my aunt making her own dandelion wine and that she played the fiddle.

6. In my favorite Armenian restaurant, the menu is fascinating and the entrées exquisite.

Parallelism Exercise: Answers

1. *Many businesses are relocating* should be written as *business relocation* to parallel *governmental mismanagement* and *increasing unemployment*.

2. If you say *the* pastoral, you have to say *the* cosmopolitan. Or you could say "… from cosmopolitan to pastoral."

3. To parallel *riding*, you need *coping*—not *to cope*.

4. *To visualize* should be *visualizing* to parallel *achieving*. Alternately, *achieving* could be written as *to achieve* to parallel *to visualize*.

5. Change *my aunt making* to *that my aunt made* to be parallel with *that she played*. Another possibility is to change *that she played* to *playing* to match *making*.

6. *The menu* is singular, but *entrées* is plural, so you must say *are exquisite* to parallel the phrase *is fascinating*.

APPLYING THE KAPLAN METHOD: PARALLELISM

Now let's use the Kaplan Method on a Sentence Correction question dealing with parallelism:

> Pablo Picasso's genius is only fully revealed when one considers the various facets of his work as they developed through many artistic phases, beginning with his Red <u>period, continuing through his Blue period, and finishing with his period of Cubism</u>.

- O period, continuing through his Blue period, and finishing with his period of Cubism
- O period, continuing through his Blue period, and finishing with his Cubist period
- O period, and continuing through his Blue period and his Cubist period
- O period phase, his Blue period phase, and his phase of Cubism
- O period, his Blue period, and his period of Cubism

Step 1: Read the Original Sentence Carefully, Looking for Errors

The original sentence contains a list, so your Pattern Recognition skills should tell you to check for parallel structure. Because the first two items in the list contain "Red period" and "Blue period," you should expect the third item in the list to follow the adjective-noun pattern and contain "Cubist period." Instead, this sentence ends with "period of Cubism," breaking the pattern and making choice **(A)** incorrect.

Step 2: Scan and Group the Answer Choices

Choices **(B)** and **(C)** end with "his Cubist period," while **(A)** and **(E)** reference "his period of Cubism" and **(D)** ends with the similar construction "his phase of Cubism." You have a 3-2 split.

Step 3: Eliminate Choices Until Only One Remains

You've established that **(A)** is incorrect, so eliminate **(D)** and **(E)** as well. This leaves only **(B)** and **(C)** with the correct parallel construction "cubist period." The list should also contain the parallel phrases, "beginning … continuing … and finishing." **(C)** is wrong because it drops "finishing," which alters the meaning and also destroys the parallel structure. Only **(B)** exhibits parallel structure throughout the list and is the correct answer.

TAKEAWAYS: PARALLELISM

- Items in a list must have parallel form.
- Many two-part constructions set up parallel elements. Examples: "not only A but also B," "from A to B," and "either A or B."
- The key to handling parallel structure questions is consistency.
- Analogies, metaphors, similes, and other comparisons all require parallel structure.

PRACTICE SET: PARALLELISM

Answers and explanations at end of chapter

27. <u>The creation of an independent treasury, establishing lower tariffs, and purchasing</u> the Oregon Territory, all credited to the presidency of James Knox Polk, are among the significant accomplishments that persuade historians to rank this former governor of Tennessee as an above-average president.

- ◯ The creation of an independent treasury, establishing lower tariffs, and purchasing
- ◯ The creation of an independent treasury, establishing lower tariffs, as well as purchasing
- ◯ The creation of an independent treasury, the establishment of lower tariffs, and the purchase of
- ◯ Creating an independent treasury, the establishment of lower tariffs, and purchasing
- ◯ Creating an independent treasury, the establishing of lower tariffs, and the purchasing of

28. The rapid-rail lines that were recently introduced in southern California have had positive effects: <u>not only have they lowered pollution levels, they have helped in decongesting</u> the region's freeway system, which had been operating far above its capacity.

- ◯ not only have they lowered pollution levels, they have helped in decongesting
- ◯ the lines have not only lowered pollution levels, but also helped to decongest
- ◯ not only have pollution levels been lowered, but they have helped to decongest
- ◯ lines have lowered pollution levels, as well as helped in decongesting
- ◯ not only have they lowered pollution levels, but also have they helped decongest

29. A national study evaluating the need for gun control is currently attempting to document where criminals purchase guns, how gun owners are trained in the use of firearms, and <u>what character traits are common to persons who are liable to turn</u> to violence to resolve problems.

    ○   what character traits are common to persons who are liable to turn

    ○   what are the character traits common to persons who are liable to turning

    ○   the common character traits of persons who are liable to turn

    ○   the traits of character common to persons who are liable to turn

    ○   the traits of character that are common to persons who are liable to turn

30. <u>Hearing Kenneth Branagh deliver the "St. Crispin's Day" speech in *Henry V* is to be mesmerized by a great performer, with seemingly</u> boundless emotional energy.

    ○   Hearing Kenneth Branagh deliver the "St. Crispin's Day" speech in *Henry V* is to be mesmerized by a great performer, with seemingly

    ○   Hearing Kenneth Branagh deliver the "St. Crispin's Day" speech in *Henry V* is to be mesmerized by a great performer, one with seeming

    ○   Hearing Kenneth Branagh deliver the "St. Crispin's Day" speech in *Henry V* is being mesmerized by a great performer, one with seeming

    ○   To hear Kenneth Branagh deliver the "St. Crispin's Day" speech in *Henry V* is being mesmerized by a great performer, with seemingly

    ○   To hear Kenneth Branagh deliver the "St. Crispin's Day" speech in *Henry V* is to be mesmerized by a great performer, one with seemingly

ADVANCED PRACTICE SET: PARALLELISM

Answers and explanations at end of chapter

31. By the time they completed their journey, the young explorers had overcome their fears, sharpened their survival <u>skills, and had developed a healthy respect</u> for nature's potential destructiveness.

    O   skills, and had developed a healthy respect

    O   skills, and developed a healthy respect

    O   skills and a healthy respect developed

    O   skills, developing a healthy respect

    O   skills, all the while developing a healthy respect

32. <u>However much Americans may agree that</u> the financing of elections with special interest money undermines democracy and that campaign finance reform would produce better government, it has been very difficult to push such measures through a Congress that has been elected using the old financing system.

    O   However much Americans may agree that

    O   Despite agreement among Americans to the fact

    O   Although Americans agree

    O   Even though Americans may agree

    O   There is agreement among Americans that

33. South Pacific Vacations has a package tour to Sydney, Australia, for $999 per person, including airfare from Los Angeles, <u>spending five nights at the Mega Hotel, and to take a harbor cruise, and round-trip airfare from New York is</u> an additional $400.

    O   spending five nights at the Mega Hotel, and to take a harbor cruise, and round-trip airfare from New York is

    O   spending five nights at the Mega Hotel, and taking a harbor cruise; and in addition round-trip airfare from New York is

    O   five nights at the Mega Hotel, and a harbor cruise; round-trip airfare from New York is

    O   with five nights at the Mega Hotel, and a harbor cruise, with round-trip airfare from New York being

    O   to spend five nights at the Mega Hotel, and to take a harbor cruise; round-trip airfare from New York is

COMPARISONS

Faulty comparisons account for a significant number of errors in GMAT Sentence Correction questions. Most relate to the very simple idea that you can't compare apples to oranges. Of course, you want to compare things that are grammatically similar, but you also want to compare things that are logically similar. You can't logically compare, say, a person to a quality or an item to a group. You have to compare one individual to another, one quality to another, one group to another.

Use Attention to the Right Detail and Pattern Recognition to keep an eye out for the following:

- Key comparison words such as *like, as, compared to, less than, more than, other, that of,* and *those of*
- Long modifying phrases between compared elements. Don't be distracted! Ignore the modifying phrase at first so you can see the compared elements clearly.

Compared items must be parallel in terms of construction. If a preposition, article, or auxiliary is in one compared item, it needs to be in the other:

- Incorrect: I would do anything for my mother but not my boss.

- Correct: I would do anything for my mother but not for my boss.

Comparisons Exercise

Answers on the following page

Fix the comparisons in the sentences below.

1. Like a black bear that I once saw in the Buenos Aires Zoo, the Central Park Zoo polar bear's personality strikes me as being sadly neurotic.

2. The article questioned the popularity of jazz compared to classical music.

3. The challenger weighed 20 pounds less than that of the defender.

4. The Boston office contributes less to total national sales than any other U.S. branch.

5. The host paid more attention to his celebrity guest than the others.

Comparisons Exercise: Answers

1. *Like* creates a comparison, and you can compare only similar things. Here, you have to compare bears to bears or personalities to personalities. "Like a black bear I once saw in the Buenos Aires Zoo, the Central Park Zoo polar bear strikes me as being sadly neurotic."

2. "The article questioned the popularity of jazz compared to *that of* classical music."

3. "The challenger weighed 20 pounds less than the defender did," or "The challenger's weight was 20 pounds less than that of the defender."

4. There are two ways to read this sentence as it's written. We could be comparing the Boston office's contribution to national sales and other branches' contributions, but we also could be comparing the Boston office's contribution to national sales and the Boston office's contribution to those other branches. The former comparison is more logical, so we clarify: "... than any other U.S. branch *does*."

5. A similar problem—you need to repeat the verb after *than* ("than *he paid to* the others") or refer to the verb by placing *to* after *than* ("than *to* the others").

APPLYING THE KAPLAN METHOD: COMPARISONS

Now let's use the Kaplan Method on a Sentence Correction question dealing with comparisons:

<u>Like most other marsupial species and all other kangaroo species, the diet of the swamp wallaby consists</u> of leaves and other sorts of vegetation.

- ○ Like most other marsupial species and all other kangaroo species, the diet of the swamp wallaby consists

- ○ Like those of most other marsupial species and all other kangaroo species, the diets of the swamp wallaby consists

- ○ Just like the diet of most other marsupial species and all other kangaroo species, the diet of the swamp wallaby consists

- ○ Similar to the diets of most other marsupial species and all other kangaroo species, the swamp wallabies have a diet which consists

- ○ Like most other marsupial species and all other kangaroo species, the swamp wallaby has a diet consisting

Step 1: Read the Original Sentence Carefully, Looking for Errors

This sentence begins with the word "Like," which signals that you have a comparison to check. Look at the items being compared and make sure they are comparable. In the original sentence, *species* are compared to a *diet*. That's an incorrect comparison.

Step 2: Scan and Group the Answer Choices

All the answer choices contain "like" or "similar to," so they all contain comparisons. As you examine each choice, look to ensure that it makes a proper comparison. Notice how Attention to the Right Detail—to the words that signal a comparison—has helped you to quickly form a strategy for this question.

Step 3: Eliminate Choices Until Only One Remains

The incorrect comparison in the original sentence means that you would automatically eliminate **(A)**. Aside from sounding awkward, **(B)** contains a subject/verb agreement problem—the plural noun "diets" takes the singular verb "consists," which is incorrect. **(C)** should be eliminated because in the introductory phrase "diet" should be plural; also, there's no reason to use "Just like" rather than "Like." In addition, "Like" is preferable to "Similar to" in **(D)**, which also incorrectly compares *diets* to *wallabies*. Only **(E)** correctly compares the swamp wallaby to other species.

TAKEAWAYS: COMPARISONS

- Items being compared must be both grammatically and logically comparable.
- Compared items must have parallel form.
- The key to handling comparison questions is to make sure that the comparisons are correct and avoid any possibility of ambiguity.
- Don't let intervening phrases or clauses distract you from what is being compared.

PRACTICE SET: COMPARISONS

Answers and explanations at end of chapter

34. Recent surveys indicate that, contrary to popular belief, total abstinence from alcohol does not correlate <u>as strongly with good health as with moderate drinking</u>.

   ○   as strongly with good health as with moderate drinking

   ○   strongly with good health, like moderate drinking does

   ○   as strongly with good health as does moderately drinking

   ○   as strongly with good health as does moderate drinking

   ○   as strongly with good health as moderate drinking

35. Unlike <u>its fellow Baltic nations, Latvia and Lithuania, the economy of Estonia grew at an astonishing rate in the late 1990s, and at the end of the decade it was placed</u> on the fast track to join the European Union.

   ○   its fellow Baltic nations, Latvia and Lithuania, the economy of Estonia grew at an astonishing rate in the late 1990s, and at the end of the decade it was placed

   ○   its fellow Baltic nations, Latvia and Lithuania, Estonia grew at an astonishing rate economically in the late 1990s, and at the end of the decade earned itself a place

   ○   its fellow Baltic nations, Latvia and Lithuania, Estonia's economy grew at an astonishing rate in the late 1990s, and at the end of the decade they were placed

   ○   Latvia and Lithuania, its fellow Baltic nations, the economy of Estonia grew at an astonishing rate in the late 1990s, and at the end of the decade it was placed

   ○   its fellow Baltic nations, Latvia and Lithuania, Estonia experienced economic growth at an astonishing rate in the late 1990s, and at the end of the decade it earned a place

36. <u>No less significant than</u> international pressures are the constraints that domestic culture and ideology impose on decision making by national political figures.

   O   No less significant than

   O   The things that are just as significant as

   O   Just like the significant

   O   Not lesser than the significance of

   O   What are as significant as

37. Golden and Labrador Retrievers have enjoyed wide popularity as guide dogs because their dispositions are more suited to companion work <u>than</u> most other breeds.

   O   than

   O   than is true of

   O   than are those of

   O   in comparison to

   O   as compared to

ADVANCED PRACTICE SET: COMPARISONS

Answers and explanations at end of chapter

38. Unlike other primates, which are born with <u>fully formed craniums, a newborn human baby's cranium</u> consists of eight bones that take years to fuse together fully, allowing the brain to grow much larger during those early years.

- O   fully formed craniums, a newborn human baby's cranium
- O   fully formed craniums, newborn human babies have craniums that
- O   a fully formed cranium, a human baby's cranium
- O   fully formed craniums, a human is born with a cranium that
- O   a fully formed cranium, the cranium of a newborn human baby

39. The legal considerations that have forced some universities to revise their affirmative action admissions programs are similar to <u>the revisions that certain large businesses have recently made to their affirmative action hiring practices</u>.

- O   the revisions that certain large businesses have recently made to their affirmative action hiring practices
- O   the affirmative action hiring practices that certain large business recently have revised
- O   those that have recently forced certain large businesses to revise their affirmative action hiring practices
- O   those recent revisions that have been made by certain large businesses to their affirmative action hiring practices
- O   what certain large businesses have done to their affirmative action hiring practices in the recent past.

40. During the Civil War, nearly three times as many Americans lost their lives from infections that could have been prevented with antiseptic techniques <u>than</u> were killed on the battlefield.

- O   than
- O   than those who
- O   than the number who
- O   as the number who
- O   as

IDIOMS AND USAGE

The frequently tested principle of idioms concerns forms of expression that have established themselves in standard English as the "right" way to say things. There's no grammar rule that applies here; it's just that these particular expressions are generally agreed upon as correct by English speakers.

If you're a native English speaker, you probably know most idioms already. You'll hear them and be able to instinctively tell what's "right" and what's not. For example, if someone were to say to you, "I am aware about these problems, because I saw the newscast yesterday," you'd pick up on the error right away. The correct idiom is "aware *of*," not "aware *about*." But some idioms are commonly, through incorrectly, used in informal English. For example, your brother says to you, "Here's a tip—Mom prefers platinum over gold." Did you spot the error? The correct idiom is "prefers X *to* Y." So it's a good idea to review idioms and to keep a list of those you encounter but don't know.

If you're a nonnative English speaker, you'll likely know fewer idioms. Jot down all the idioms that you come across and make sure you know all the correct forms. Also, look out for the following:

- Prepositions (*to*, *from*, *at*, *over*, etc.) in the underlined portion of the sentence. Their usage is often dictated by idiomatic rules.
- Verbs whose idiomatic usage you've seen frequently tested. Common examples are *prefer*, *require*, and *regard*.

You will also need to know how to correct problems with usage and style. As tested on the GMAT, usage and style questions reward students for correcting both the syntax and diction of sentences. The GMAT will always prefer active voice and clear, direct style. Look out for the following:

- Unneccessary passive voice: "John wrote the letter" is better than "The letter was written by John."
- Unnecessary wording and redundancy. For example, the word "because" is better than the phrase "in view of the fact that."
- Awkward, choppy, or clunky phrasing: Use your "ear" to help you identify sentences and phrases that simply don't read well.

Idioms and Usage Exercise, Part I

Answers on the page following the exercises

Fill in the blank with the correct word or phrase that completes the idiom correctly in the sentence. In some cases, the correct idiom may not require any additional words.

1. He modestly *attributed* his business's success _____ good luck.

2. My dictionary *defines* "idiom" _____ the usual way in which the words of a particular language are joined together.

3. Alexander Graham Bell is *credited* _____ inventing the telephone.

4. Some color-blind people cannot *distinguish* red _____ green.

5. Other color-blind people cannot *distinguish* _____ yellow _____ blue.

6. Although his story seems incredible, I *believe* it _____ the truth.

7. She is *regarded* _____ an expert on public health policy.

8. He is *considered* _____ a close friend of the president.

9. I like to *contrast* my plaid pants _____ a lovely paisley jacket.

10. According to Aristotle, contentment is *different* _____ happiness.

11. The oldest rocks on Earth are *estimated* _____ 4.6 billion years old.

12. Louisiana's legal system is *modeled* _____ the Napoleonic code.

13. I don't mean for my comments to be *perceived* _____ criticism.

14. Cigarette ads *aimed* _____ children have been banned by the FDA.

15. The mass extinction of dinosaurs has been *linked* _____ a large meteor impact.

16. Don't *worry* _____ all GMAT idioms; just memorize the ones that your ear doesn't recognize.

Idioms and Usage Exercise, Part II

Answers on the page following the exercises

Fill in the blank with the correct word or phrase that completes the idiom correctly in the sentence. In some cases, the correct idiom may not require any additional words.

1. I sold more glasses of lemonade _____ my neighbor sold.

2. She sold as many glasses of lemonade _____ she could.

3. The bigger they come, _____ they fall, or so it is said.

4. According to my diet, I can have either cake or/and ice cream, but not both.

5. Given my choice, I would have both cake _____ ice cream.

6. I must decide between one _____ the other.

Part Three: Verbal Section and Strategies
Sentence Correction

7. Neither the coach _____ the players <u>was/were</u> happy with the team's performance.

8. I couldn't decide <u>if/whether</u> he was kidding or not.

9. <u>Between/Among</u> the three candidates, he has the <u>more/most</u> impressive record.

10. There are <u>less/fewer</u> students in class today than there were yesterday.

11. However, the <u>amount/number</u> of students enrolled in this class has increased.

12. People are forbidden <u>from entering/to enter</u> the park at night.

13. The ruling prohibits the defendant <u>from discussing/to discuss</u> the case.

14. Most politicians do not want to be seen associating <u>with/among</u> convicted felons.

15. We should treat others <u>as/like</u> we would want them to treat us.

16. I would prefer a salty treat <u>like/such as</u> potato chips <u>over/to</u> a candy bar.

17. Scores on the GMAT range from 200 _____ 800.

18. Most local residents view the monument _____ an eyesore.

19. In the United States, there is less opposition _____ the use of genetically modified foods than in Europe.

20. Stress can lower one's resistance _____ cold and flu viruses.

21. The rise in inflation has become so significant _____ constitute a threat to the economic recovery.

22. The actress's performance was so poignant _____ the entire audience was moved to tears.

23. Just try _____ do as well as you can on the test.

Idioms and Usage Exercise, Part I: Answers

1. He modestly *attributed* his business's success *to* good luck.
2. My dictionary *defines* "idiom" *as* the usual way in which the words of a particular language are joined together.
3. Alexander Graham Bell is *credited* *with* inventing the telephone.
4. Some color-blind people cannot *distinguish* red *from* green.
5. Other color-blind people cannot *distinguish* *between* yellow *and* blue.
6. Although his story seems incredible, I *believe* it *to be* the truth.
7. She is *regarded* *as* an expert on public health policy.
8. He is *considered* a close friend of the president. *[This blank takes nothing.]*
9. I like to *contrast* my plaid pants *with* a lovely paisley jacket.
10. According to Aristotle, contentment is *different* *from* happiness.
11. The oldest rocks on Earth are *estimated* *to be* 4.6 billion years old.
12. Louisiana's legal system is *modeled* *after* the Napoleonic code.
13. I don't mean for my comments to be *perceived* *as* criticism.
14. Cigarette ads *aimed* *at* children have been banned by the FDA.
15. The mass extinction of dinosaurs has been *linked* *to* a large meteor impact.
16. Don't *worry* *about* all GMAT idioms; just memorize the ones that your ear doesn't recognize.

Idioms and Usage Exercise, Part II: Answers

1. I sold more glasses of lemonade *than* my neighbor sold.
2. She sold as many glasses of lemonade *as* she could.
3. The bigger they come, *the harder* they fall, or so it is said.
4. According to my diet, I can have either cake *or* ice cream, but not both.
5. Given my choice, I would have both cake *and* ice cream.
6. I must decide between one *and* the other.
7. Neither the coach *nor* the players *were* happy with the team's performance.
8. I couldn't decide *whether* he was kidding or not.
9. *Among* the three candidates, he has the *most* impressive record.
10. There are *fewer* students in class today than there were yesterday.
11. However, the *number* of students enrolled in this class has increased.
12. People are forbidden *to enter* the park at night.
13. The ruling prohibits the defendant *from discussing* the case.
14. Most politicians do not want to be seen associating *with* convicted felons.
15. We should treat others *as* we would want them to treat us.
16. I would prefer a salty treat *such as* potato chips *to* a candy bar.
17. Scores on the GMAT range from 200 *to* 800.
18. Most local residents view the monument *as* an eyesore.
19. In the United States, there is less opposition *to* the use of genetically modified foods than in Europe.

20. Stress can lower one's resistance **to** cold and flu viruses.

21. The rise in inflation has become so significant **as to** constitute a threat to the economic recovery.

22. The actress's performance was so poignant **that** the entire audience was moved to tears.

23. Just try **to** do as well as you can on the test.

APPLYING THE KAPLAN METHOD: IDIOMS AND USAGE

Now let's use the Kaplan Method on a Sentence Correction question dealing with idioms and usage:

> Growth in the industry is at an all-time low, with total employment <u>at less than 68,000 people and fewer</u> companies in the field than there have been during any of the past ten years.
>
> O   at less than 68,000 people and fewer
> O   at fewer than 68,000 people and fewer
> O   lesser than 68,000 people and fewer
> O   fewer than 68,000 people and less
> O   at less than 68,000 people and there are less

Step 1: Read the Original Sentence Carefully, Looking for Errors

Notice that underlined portion of the sentence contains the words "less" and "fewer." These words are often tested on the GMAT because they are often used incorrectly, so be sure to pay attention to them. Doing so will save you valuable time. "Less" can only refer to non-countable items, such as soup or confidence. "Fewer" must refer to countable items, such as chairs or peanuts. In this sentence, since "people" and "companies" can both be counted, "fewer" is appropriate.

Step 2: Scan and Group the Answer Choices

Even if that didn't occur to you as the issue in the sentence, you should note that some of the choices use "less" (or "lesser") and others use "fewer" and group accordingly into a 3-2 split.

Step 3: Eliminate Choices Until Only One Remains

You would eliminate choice **(A)** because the original sentence uses the non-countable adjective "less" to describe the countable noun "people." Choices **(C)** and **(E)** make the similar errors (and choice **(C)**'s "lesser than" is thoroughly unidiomatic), so eliminate them as well. Choice **(D)** uses "less" to describe the countable noun "companies," so it is incorrect. Only in choice **(B)** are both countable nouns modified by the countable adjective "fewer," making it the correct answer.

TAKEAWAYS: IDIOMS AND USAGE

- Avoid verbosity and redundancy.
- Avoid passive verbs wherever possible.
- Avoid clunky, choppy, or awkward-sounding sentences.
- Use the correct idioms.
- There really are no rules when it comes to idioms, which are simply word combinations that, based on common usage, have established themselves as correct in standard written English. Many GMAT idiom questions require you to use the right prepositions.

PRACTICE SET: IDIOMS AND USAGE

Answers and explanations at end of chapter

41. <u>When a product costs more, be it</u> a bottle of wine or a handbag, the more likely it is to be esteemed by consumers.

   ○ When a product costs more, be it

   ○ When a product costs more, whether it is

   ○ As a product becomes more and more costly, like

   ○ The more a product costs, like

   ○ The more a product costs, whether it is

42. Mary Shelley is widely credited <u>for the invention of a new literary genre; many scholars consider her first and only novel, *Frankenstein*, to be</u> the first science fiction story.

   ○ for the invention of a new literary genre; many scholars consider her first and only novel, *Frankenstein*, to be

   ○ for inventing a new literary genre; many scholars consider her first and only novel, *Frankenstein*, as being

   ○ to have invented a new literary genre; many scholars regard her first and only novel, *Frankenstein*, to be

   ○ with the invention of a new literary genre; many scholars regard her first and only novel, *Frankenstein*, to be

   ○ with the invention of a new literary genre; many scholars consider her first and only novel, *Frankenstein*,

43. <u>The percentage of people aged 25–44 living alone increased abruptly between 1990 and 1995 and</u> continued to rise more slowly over the next five years.

   ○ The percentage of people aged 25–44 living alone increased abruptly between 1990 and 1995 and

   ○ There was an abruptly increased percentage of people aged 25–44 who lived alone between 1990 and 1995 and they

   ○ The percentage of people aged 25–44 who lived alone increased abruptly between 1990 and 1995 and has

   ○ There has been an abrupt increase in the percentage of people aged 25–44 living alone between 1990 and 1995 and it

   ○ Between 1990 and 1995, there was an abrupt increase in the percentage of people aged 25–44 who lived alone which

ADVANCED PRACTICE SET: IDIOMS AND USAGE

Answers and explanations at end of chapter

44. The macabre nature of *Macbeth*, together with the widespread belief that real-life tragedies have accompanied many productions, <u>has made the name of the play so dreaded that not even the least superstitious members of most casts dare</u> utter it.

   ○ has made the name of the play so dreaded that not even the least superstitious members of most casts dare

   ○ have made the name of the play so dreaded, even the least superstitious members of most casts will not dare to

   ○ have made the play's name sufficiently dreaded, so that even the less superstitious members of most casts will not dare to

   ○ have made the name of the play sufficiently dreaded, so that not even the least superstitious members of most casts dare

   ○ has made the name of the play is dreaded, so that even the least superstitious members of most casts dare not

45. The university's board of trustees, <u>being worried over declining student enrollments and their failing</u> to secure additional funding from the state, has formed a committee to determine what cuts need to be made to staff and programs.

   ○ being worried over declining student enrollments and their failing

   ○ worrying over declining student enrollments and also the failure

   ○ worried about declining student enrollments and the failure

   ○ in that they are worried about the decline in student enrollments and the failure

   ○ because of its worry concerning the decline of student enrollments and, as well as concerning the failure

MISCELLANEOUS ERRORS

Most Sentence Correction errors fall into the categories we've just reviewed. Through our research, we've seen three other types of errors that show up with enough frequency on the GMAT to merit a word here.

Which, Where, When

The GMAT likes to test your understanding of the use of the relative pronouns *which*, *where*, and *when*. While the usage of these words may be flexible in informal speech, there are specific rules for how they are used on the GMAT:

- On the GMAT, "which" needs to be preceded by a comma and refer to the noun just before the comma, or else its use is wrong (except when it follows a preposition, as in the phrase "in which").
- On the GMAT, "where" must refer to an actual location, or else its use is wrong.
- On the GMAT, "when" must refer to an actual time or else its use is wrong.

Subjunctive Mood

The subjunctive mood is the form of a verb used to describe a situation that is contrary to fact. You will see the subjunctive mood used in sentences that describe an order or recommendation. The subjunctive mood is also used in sentences that present hypothetical situations. Here are the rules to keep in mind when you see one of these types of sentences:

- **Orders and recommendations:** With verbs such as *order, recommend, demand, insist,* etc., what follows the verb should be *that,* a new subject, and the infinitive form of a verb but without the "to." Example: He *demanded* that the door *be* opened.
- **Hypothetical situations:** When contemplating hypothetical or contrary-to-fact situations, use *were* and *would.* Example: If I *were* rich, I *would* quit my job.

Clauses and Connectors

The GMAT uses compound and complex sentences to test your knowledge of clauses and connectors. Recall that a clause is a group of words that contains a subject and a verb. When two clauses appear in a sentence, the clauses should be connected by one, and only one, connector (*because, although, as, but,* etc.). The connector used should make sense with the rest of the sentence.

Miscellaneous Errors Exercise

Answers on the following page

For each of the following sentences, correct the error related to one of the three listed categories of miscellaneous errors.

1. After the mediation session, the victim said he was now in a state where he could forgive the offender.

2. The order from the vice president was that all employees will work through the weekend to finish the project.

3. If she was more competent, she would be promoted more quickly.

4. Many citizens agree that austerity measures are necessary, few are happy about the ones that were enacted.

5. She invited me to join her at the sushi restaurant which just opened next to Carlotta's Bistro on Main Street.

Miscellaneous Errors Exercise: Answers

1. "Where" can only refer to a place, and "a state (of mind)" is not a place. Use "in which" instead.

2. The verb in an order should be in the infinitive form, without the "to": *The order from the vice president was that all employees work through the weekend to finish the project.*

3. Use "were" and "would" with hypothetical situations: *If she were more competent, she would be promoted more quickly.*

4. The two clauses in this sentence need to be related by a connector: *Many citizens agree that austerity measures are necessary, although few are happy about the ones that were enacted.*

5. "Which" is only correct when it appears immediately after a comma or as part of a phrase like "in which." "That" is the correct word in this case: *She invited me to join her at the sushi restaurant that just opened next to Carlotta's Bistro on Main Street.*

APPLYING THE KAPLAN METHOD: MISCELLANEOUS ERRORS

Now let's use the Kaplan Method on a Sentence Correction question dealing with miscellaneous errors:

> <u>More and more couples wait before trying to start</u> a family, the average age of first-time parents is increasing.

- ○ More and more couples wait before trying to start
- ○ As more and more couples wait before trying to start
- ○ As more and more couples wait before trying and starting
- ○ Although more and more couples wait before trying to start
- ○ Being that more and more couples are waiting before trying to start

Step 1: Read the Original Sentence Carefully, Looking for Errors

This sentence contains two complete clauses, each with its own subject and verb. The subject of "wait" is "couples," and the subject of "is increasing" is "age." Two complete clauses should be joined with a conjunction, but this sentence has no conjunction and is thus a run-on. The correct answer will provide the sentence with a conjunction. Choice **(A)** is incorrect.

Step 2: Scan and Group the Answer Choices

Choices **(B)** and **(C)** introduce "As" at the beginning of the sentence. Choice **(D)** substitutes "Although," and choice **(E)** uses "Being that."

Step 3: Eliminate Choices Until Only One Remains

The GMAT testmakers consider "Being that" to be awkward and wordy, and an answer choice containing it will invariably be wrong. Recognizing this pattern makes choice **(E)** easy to eliminate. Choice **(D)** adds the conjunction "Although," which certainly sounds better than "Being that" but which indicates a contrast and therefore doesn't make logical sense. "Because" would be a more appropriate connector than "Although." Choices **(B)** and **(C)** both start with "As," which does make logical sense as a conjunction for this sentence. Choice **(C)** changes "trying to start" to "trying and starting," which is an idiomatically incorrect construction. The correct answer is choice **(B)**, which adds an appropriate conjunction and does not create any new errors.

TAKEAWAYS: MISCELLANEOUS ERRORS

- Memorize the rules for "which," "where," and "when" and apply them with rigor on Test Day.
- Memorize the situations in which the subjunctive is used and the rules for how to handle them.
- Clauses and connectors must be used correctly on the GMAT. Avoid missing or redundant connectors.

PRACTICE SET: MISCELLANEOUS ERRORS

Answers and explanations at end of chapter

46. The United States' trade deficit with China rose in 2003 to $123 billion, <u>which is 17 percent more than the previous year</u> and more than 10 times the U.S.-China trade deficit in 1998.

   O   which is 17 percent more than the previous year

   O   which is 17 percent higher than it was the previous year

   O   17 percent higher than the previous year's figure was

   O   an amount that is 17 percent more than the previous year was

   O   an amount that is 17 percent higher than the previous year's figure

47. The two-party political system is one <u>where the electorate gives its votes largely to only two major parties and where</u> one or the other party can usually win a majority in the legislature.

   O   where the electorate gives its votes largely to only two major parties and where

   O   in which the electorate largely gives only its votes to two major parties and where

   O   where the electorate gives largely its votes to only two major parties and in which

   O   in which the electorate gives its votes largely to only two major parties and in which

   O   in which the electorate largely gives only its votes to two major parties and in which

48. Most financial advisers <u>recommend that stock portfolios should be reviewed</u> at least once a year, if only to make sure that changes do not need to be made.

   O   recommend that stock portfolios should be reviewed

   O   recommend you to review your stock portfolio

   O   recommend that stock portfolios be reviewed

   O   are recommending that stock portfolios are reviewed

   O   have a recommendation to review stock portfolios

49. The United States <u>would achieve a 10 percent reduction in gasoline consumption, if Congress will raise</u> fuel economy standards to 31.3 miles per gallon for passenger cars and to 24.5 mpg for light trucks.

    ○ would achieve a 10 percent reduction in gasoline consumption, if Congress will raise

    ○ will achieve a 10 percent reduction in gasoline consumption, if Congress were to raise

    ○ will have achieved a 10 percent reduction in gasoline consumption, if Congress will raise

    ○ would achieve a 10 percent reduction in gasoline consumption, if Congress were to raise

    ○ would achieve a 10 percent reduction in gasoline consumption, if Congress were raising

50. Because the moon's distance from Earth varies, <u>so the gravitational pull between the two bodies differ</u>, as do the size and times of oceanic tides.

    ○ so the gravitational pull between the two bodies differ

    ○ so the gravitational pull between the two bodies differs

    ○ the gravitational pull between the two bodies differs

    ○ therefore the gravitational pull between the two bodies differ

    ○ therefore the gravitational pull between the two bodies differs

SENTENCE CORRECTION QUIZ

Answers and explanations at end of chapter

51. With a boiling temperature of –195.8 degrees Celsius, <u>nitrogen composes approximately 78 percent of the volume of the atmosphere</u>.

    ○   nitrogen composes approximately 78 percent of the volume of the atmosphere

    ○   nitrogen is composing the volume of 78 percent of the atmosphere

    ○   the atmosphere is approximately 78 percent nitrogen, as measured by volume

    ○   nitrogen is composed of 78 percent of the atmosphere's volume

    ○   the atmosphere is composed, in terms of volume, of 78 percent nitrogen

52. At more than 800 pages in length, the <u>novelist's life stands revealed in the new biography, which sets the standard for research</u>.

    ○   novelist's life stands revealed in the new biography, which sets the standard for research

    ○   new biography is setting standards of research on the novelist's life

    ○   standard for research has been set by a new biography on the novelist

    ○   new biography about the novelist sets the standard for research

    ○   novelist's life is revealed in a standard-setting new biography

53. Because women buy approximately 80 percent of ties sold in the United States, <u>they are often displayed</u> near perfume or women's clothing departments.

    ○   they are often displayed

    ○   ties are often being displayed

    ○   the displaying of ties is often

    ○   ties are often displayed

    ○   they often can be found

54. Although the British were responsible for the early European settlement <u>of both Australia and the United States, Australia is having much closer political and cultural links with Britain than the United States is having</u>.

- ○ of both Australia and the United States, Australia is having much closer political and cultural links with Britain than the United States is having

- ○ in both Australia and the United States, they are closer in their political and cultural links in Australia than in the United States

- ○ of both nations, Australia has much closer political and cultural links to Britain than the United States has

- ○ in both nations, Australia is politically and culturally linked to Britain in a much closer fashion than the United States

- ○ of both Australia and the United States, they have much closer political and cultural links to it than the United States has

55. <u>Each of the major setbacks the Germans suffered in June 1944—the fall of Rome, the collapse of Army Group Center on the Eastern Front, and the breaching of the Atlantic Wall at Normandy—were powerful shocks</u> signaling the inability of the German war machine to compete on multiple fronts.

- ○ Each of the major setbacks the Germans suffered in June 1944—the fall of Rome, the collapse of Army Group Center on the Eastern Front, and the breaching of the Atlantic Wall at Normandy—were powerful shocks

- ○ The fall of Rome, the collapse of Army Group Center on the Eastern Front, and the breaching of the Atlantic Wall at Normandy—each of them major setbacks the Germans suffered in June 1944—were powerful shocks

- ○ Powerful shocks—the fall of Rome, the collapse of Army Group Center on the Eastern Front, and the breaching of the Atlantic Wall at Normandy—each a major setback for the Germans in June 1944, was such

- ○ The major setbacks suffered by the Germans in June 1944—the fall of Rome, the collapse of Army Group Center on the Eastern Front, and the breaching of the Atlantic Wall at Normandy—each were powerful shocks

- ○ Each of the major setbacks the Germans suffered in June 1944—the fall of Rome, the collapse of Army Group Center on the Eastern Front, and the breach of the Atlantic Wall at Normandy—was a powerful shock

56. Adult pelicans store fish in a deep, expandable pouch below the lower mandible, <u>of which the young feed</u>.

    O   of which the young feed
    O   being for the feeding of the young
    O   from which the young feed
    O   that it feeds the young from
    O   young feed from

57. Anthony Trollope, one of the most famous English novelists of the nineteenth century, also <u>wrote travel books, some based on his undertaking of journeys</u> while an employee of the postal service.

    O   wrote travel books, some based on his undertaking of journeys
    O   wrote travel books, some based on journeys he undertook
    O   undertook journeys, having based travel books on them
    O   based travel books on journeys undertaken
    O   wrote travel books, some based on journeys which he was to undertake

58. A federal government survey taken in 1997 showed that during the 12 months preceding the survey, 36 percent of the U.S. population had tried marijuana, cocaine, or other illicit drugs, 71 percent of the population <u>were smoking cigarettes, and 82 percent</u> tried alcoholic beverages.

    O   were smoking cigarettes, and 82 percent
    O   had smoked cigarettes, and 82 percent had
    O   smoked cigarettes, and that 82 percent
    O   smoked cigarettes, and 82 percent had
    O   will be smoking cigarettes, and 82 percent

59. Like Art Nouveau jewelry designers, the <u>Art Deco movement used art materials suitable for expressing</u> the new stylistic language of the 1920s, one dominated by an interplay of geometric forms.

- O   Art Deco movement used art materials suitable for expressing
- O   Art Deco movement was expressed through the use of materials suitable for the
- O   artists of the Art Deco movement used materials suitable for expressing
- O   Art Deco movement's materials were used by artists to suitably express
- O   artists of the Art Deco movement also used suitable materials for the expression of

60. Amtrak, a government-owned corporation, schedules passenger rail service, <u>payments to privately owned firms to run trains, and bears all administrative costs, such as</u> those incurred by the purchase of new equipment and by the sale of tickets.

- O   payments to privately owned firms to run trains, and bears all administrative costs, such as
- O   pays privately owned firms to run trains, and is bearing all administrative costs, such as
- O   pays privately owned firms to run trains, and bears all administrative costs, such as
- O   pays privately owned firms to run trains, and bears all administrative costs, being inclusive of
- O   pays privately owned firms to run trains, and the bearer of all costs of administration, for example

61. In feudal Korea, <u>cattle were traditionally used as beasts of burden, rather than as a food source, and fish were</u> the primary source of protein in the typical diet.

- O   cattle were traditionally used as beasts of burden, rather than as a food source, and fish were
- O   cattle were being used as beasts of burden, rather than as a food source, and fish were providing
- O   cattle were traditionally used as beasts of burden, rather than a food source, with fish being
- O   the traditional use of cattle was as beasts of burden, rather than for the provision of food, and fish were
- O   cattle were traditionally used for beasts of burden, rather than for a food source, and fish were

62. The term "support staff" is often used to describe employees <u>that perform lower-level tasks but also are providing</u> essential administrative duties for executive-level managers.

   O   that perform lower-level tasks but also are providing
   O   performing lower-level tasks but also providing
   O   who perform lower-level tasks, but are also providing
   O   that performs lower-level tasks but also provide
   O   who perform lower-level tasks but also provide

63. National Women's History Month <u>began as a single week and as a local event when, in 1978, Sonoma County, California, sponsored</u> a women's history week to promote the teaching of women's history—a neglected subject in elementary and high school curricula at that time.

   O   began as a single week and as a local event when, in 1978, Sonoma County, California, sponsored
   O   began as a single week local event sponsoring, in Sonoma County, California,
   O   begins with a single week in 1978 sponsoring the local Sonoma County, California of
   O   will have began in 1978 as a single week local event when Sonoma County, California was in sponsorship of
   O   was begun in 1978 when, in Sonoma County, California, there was to be a sponsorship of

64. <u>People with schizophrenia experience miscarriages at a higher rate of frequency than people without schizophrenia, whose overactive immune systems tend to be indiscriminately rejecting</u> the foreign DNA of the fetus.

   O People with schizophrenia experience miscarriages at a higher rate of frequency than people without schizophrenia, whose overactive immune systems tend to be indiscriminately rejecting

   O Miscarriages are more common among people with schizophrenia than among people without schizophrenia, being that their overactive immune systems tend to indiscriminately reject

   O Miscarriages are more common between people with schizophrenia than they are between people without schizophrenia because the overactive immune systems of people with schizophrenia tend to be indiscriminately rejecting

   O The miscarriage rate of people with schizophrenia is higher than the rate for people without schizophrenia because the former's overactive immune systems tend to reject

   O People with schizophrenia have more common miscarriages than do people without schizophrenia, because their immune systems tend to indiscriminately reject

65. Working with musician Stevie Wonder as a musical adviser, Ray Kurzweil developed what is now the preferred medium for creating nearly all music for today's commercial albums, films, and television: a computer-based instrument capable of <u>reproducing musical sounds of a quality once thought to be</u> possible only on grand pianos and other acoustic instruments.

   O reproducing musical sounds of a quality once thought to be

   O reproducing musical sounds with a quality as were once thought to be

   O reproducing in musical sounds a quality that was once thought to be

   O reproduction of musical sounds whose quality is the same as what were once thought to be

   O reproduction of musical sounds at a quality once thought of as

66. Twenty years ago, only 6 percent of students at Dunmore College who intended to major in chemistry were women; today that figure is <u>at least as high as 40 percent</u>.

   O at least as high as 40 percent

   O higher than at least 40 percent

   O higher by 40 percent at the least

   O 40 percent high or more

   O more higher than 40 percent

ANSWERS AND EXPLANATIONS

1. E	18. D	35. E	52. D
2. D	19. A	36. A	53. D
3. C	20. E	37. C	54. C
4. A	21. C	38. D	55. E
5. A	22. C	39. C	56. C
6. D	23. D	40. E	57. B
7. C	24. C	41. E	58. B
8. A	25. B	42. E	59. C
9. D	26. E	43. A	60. C
10. D	27. C	44. A	61. A
11. B	28. B	45. C	62. E
12. C	29. A	46. E	63. A
13. C	30. E	47. D	64. D
14. D	31. B	48. C	65. A
15. B	32. A	49. D	66. A
16. D	33. C	50. C	
17. E	34. D	51. A	

1. **(E)**

The rise in the number of new housing starts in the final two quarters of last year <u>suggest that the sluggish economy should continue its recovery into the first quarter of this year, but</u> weak job growth in the private sector continues to worry some economists.

- ○ suggest that the sluggish economy should continue its recovery into the first quarter of this year, but
- ○ suggest that the sluggish economy will continue to recover in the first quarter of this year, but that
- ○ suggest that the sluggish economy is continuing to recover in the first quarter of this year, but
- ○ suggests that the sluggish economy should continue its recovery into the first quarter of this year, but that
- ○ suggests that the sluggish economy will continue to recover in the first quarter of this year, but

Step 1: Read the Original Sentence Carefully, Looking for Errors

Whenever the subject or predicate verb of a sentence is underlined, we need to check for subject-verb agreement. In this sentence, the predicate verb, "suggest," is underlined. The subject of that verb is "rise," which is singular, so we need a singular verb. However, "suggest" is plural. We've discovered a subject-verb agreement error, and the right answer will correct it.

Step 2: Scan and Group the Answer Choices

(A), **(B)**, and **(C)** retain the error; all use "suggest." **(D)** and **(E)** change the verb to "suggests."

Step 3: Eliminate Choices Until Only One Remains

Because **(A)**, **(B)**, and **(C)** all make the same subject-verb agreement mistake, we can eliminate them. The answer will be either **(D)** or **(E)**. Choice **(D)** adds the word "that" to the end of the underlined part of the sentence, which changes the meaning. According to the original sentence, the only thing suggested by the rise in housing starts is that the sluggish economy will continue to recover. Adding the word "that" makes it sound as if the rise in housing starts also suggests that weak job growth continues to worry some economists, which is not what the original sentence implied. Because the correct choice will retain the meaning of the original sentence, **(D)** is incorrect, and **(E)** is the correct answer.

2. **(D)**

The green flash, an atmospheric refractive phenomenon whereby the top edge of a setting sun will momentarily turn green, rarely is seen by the naked eye, primarily <u>on account of requiring</u> specific favorable conditions to occur.

- O   on account of requiring
- O   on account of their requiring
- O   because they require
- O   because it requires
- O   because of requiring

Step 1: Read the Original Sentence Carefully, Looking for Errors

The GMAT prefers concise constructions. This underlined piece sounds awkward. Moreover, *-ing* constructions such as "of requiring" are generally suspect on the GMAT. We'll seek an answer choice that is less wordy and that removes the phrase "of requiring."

Step 2: Scan and Group the Answer Choices

(A) and **(B)** keep "on account of." **(C)**, **(D)**, and **(E)** all use "because."

Step 3: Eliminate Choices Until Only One Remains

"Because" is certainly shorter and more concise than "on account of," so we'll eliminate **(A)** and **(B)**. Choice **(C)** uses the pronoun "they," but it refers to the "green flash," so the pronoun should be singular. Hence, **(C)** cannot be correct. **(D)** uses the pronoun "it," which agrees with its antecedent, the "green flash." This choice is concise and grammatically correct and is thus the correct answer. **(E)** is incorrect because it uses the phrase "of requiring," which we found awkward in the original sentence. Choice **(D)** is the correct answer.

3. **(C)**

A new study has found that college students <u>had been more involved in on-campus political activities during the last few years than at any time</u> in the past two decades.

O   had been more involved in on-campus political activities during the last few years than at any time

O   had been more involved in on-campus political activities during the last few years than at any other time

O   have been more involved in on-campus political activities during the last few years than at any other time

O   have been more involved in on-campus political activities during the last few years than at any time

O   are more involved in on-campus political activities during the last few years as compared to any other time

Step 1: Read the Original Sentence Carefully, Looking for Errors

This sentence contains an underlined verb, so that's where we'll start our investigation. There is no difference between the singular and plural forms of "had been," so there is no subject-verb agreement error. However, the verb tense does not match the meaning of the sentence. The past perfect tense, indicated by the use of the helping verb "had," is only appropriate when there are two past events, with one having occurred before the other. In that situation, the past perfect would be used for the earlier of the two events. In the underlined clause of this sentence, though, there is only a single, continuous action—involvement in on-campus political activities. So there should be no use of the past perfect, and the use of the word "had" needs to be corrected.

Step 2: Scan and Group the Answer Choices

(A) and **(B)** retain the verb "had been involved." **(C)** and **(D)** both use "have been involved," while **(E)** uses "are involved."

Step 3: Eliminate Choices Until Only One Remains

We know that "had been involved" is an incorrect verb tense, so we can eliminate **(A)** and **(B)**. Choice **(E)** uses the present tense, but the action being described has been happening "during the last few years," so we have another inappropriate tense and can eliminate **(E)** as well. That leaves **(C)** and **(D)**. Both use the correct tense, the present perfect, to describe an action that occurred in the past over the course of several years. The only difference between them is that **(C)** adds the word "other" to the phrase "at any time," while **(D)** does not. We'll need to look carefully at the intended meaning of the original sentence to see which is correct. The "last few years" are included in the "past two decades," so the author of the sentence is really trying to compare the "last few years" to any "other" time during the past two decades. **(C)** adds this subtle but proper comparative adjective and is therefore the correct answer.

4. **(A)**

Depending on which scholar you consult, Christopher Columbus, Leif Ericson, or the Chinese eunuch Zheng Ho <u>is credited with being the first explorer from the Eurasian continent to have traveled to the New World by ship</u>.

- ○ is credited with being the first explorer from the Eurasian continent to have traveled to the New World by ship
- ○ is credited to be the first explorer from the Eurasian continent to have traveled to the New World by ship
- ○ is credited to have been the first explorer from the Eurasian continent to have traveled to the New World by ship
- ○ are credited with being the first explorers from the Eurasian continent to have traveled to the New World by ship
- ○ are credited to be the first explorers from the Eurasian continent to have traveled to the New World by ship

Step 1: Read the Original Sentence Carefully, Looking for Errors

Whenever a sentence contains an underlined verb, we need to make sure that it agrees with its subject; if it does not, there is an error. In this sentence, the predicate verb phrase "is credited" is singular. The subject of the sentence is composed of the names of three different explorers, connected by the conjunction "or," which means that the verb must agree with that part of the subject that is nearest to the verb. That's the third explorer, Zheng Ho. Because he's just one person, we need a singular verb, so "is credited" is correct.

Step 2: Scan and Group the Answer Choices

(A), **(B)**, and **(C)** keep the verb "is credited." **(D)** and **(E)** both substitute "are credited."

Step 3: Eliminate Choices Until Only One Remains

Because we know that "is credited" is correct, we can eliminate **(D)** and **(E)**. Of the remaining choices, **(B)** changes "with being" to "to be," and **(C)** changes "with being" to "to have been." However, only the original sentence is idiomatically correct: One credits someone "with" doing something. That leaves choice **(A)** as the correct answer.

5. **(A)**

Noting that <u>its revenues had fallen due to a recent</u> prolonged slump in CD sales, the music-store chain announced that it would be forced to raise prices at all of its outlets.

- ○ its revenues had fallen due to a recent
- ○ its revenues have fallen due to a recently
- ○ its revenues are falling due to a recently
- ○ their revenues are falling due to a recent
- ○ their revenues had fallen due to a recent

Step 1: Read the Original Sentence Carefully, Looking for Errors

This sentence contains an underlined verb and a pronoun; we should check both. The verb, "had fallen," agrees with its plural subject, "revenues." It is in the past perfect tense, which is appropriate because the revenues fell before the announcement was made. Whenever there are two past events, with one occurring before the other, the chronologically earlier event should be in the past perfect tense. The verb "had fallen," then, is correct. The singular pronoun "its" refers unambiguously to "the music-store chain," which is also singular, so the pronoun is correct as well. Chances are that the answer will be **(A)**, but we'll check the other choices as well to make sure we haven't overlooked anything.

Step 2: Scan and Group the Answer Choices

(A), **(B)**, and **(C)** retain the pronoun "its." **(D)** and **(E)** change the pronoun to "their." There is a second 3-2 split: **(A)**, **(D)**, and **(E)** keep the adjective "recent," while **(B)** and **(C)** change "recent" to "recently."

Step 3: Eliminate Choices Until Only One Remains

(D) and **(E)** can be eliminated because they use a plural pronoun, "their," to refer to a singular subject, "the music-store chain." Of the remaining choices, **(B)** and **(C)** change the last underlined word from "recent" to "recently." The original sentence referred to a "prolonged slump" that happened in a "recent" time frame. If the adjective "recent" is changed to the adverb "recently," this word can no longer describe the noun "slump" (only adjectives can describe nouns). Instead, the adverb "recently" must describe the adjective "prolonged" (i.e., the slump was "recently prolonged"), thereby changing the meaning of the sentence. The correct answer to a Sentence Correction question must match the intended meaning of the original sentence. We can thus throw out **(B)** and **(C)**. The correct answer remains choice **(A)**.

6. **(D)**

After all the research that has been conducted in the last 30 years, it is readily apparent that <u>there are, without question, a wealth of good reasons to do aerobic exercise regularly.</u>

- O there are, without question, a wealth of good reasons to do aerobic exercise regularly
- O there are, without question, a wealth of good reasons to exercise aerobically regularly
- O there are, without question, a wealth of good reasons to engage regularly in aerobic exercise
- O there is, without question, a wealth of good reasons to engage regularly in aerobic exercise
- O there is, without question, a wealth of good reasons to do regular aerobic exercises

Step 1: Read the Original Sentence Carefully, Looking for Errors

Sometimes the subject of a clause will appear after the verb, as is the case in this sentence. In the underlined subordinate clause, the subject is "a wealth" and the verb is "are"—and both are underlined, so we must check for agreement. (The noun "reasons" cannot be the subject because it is part of the prepositional phrase "of good reasons," which modifies the subject.) "Wealth" is a singular noun, so we need a singular verb; "are" is plural, so we have a subject-verb agreement error.

Step 2: Scan and Group the Answer Choices

(A), **(B)**, and **(C)** retain the verb "are." **(D)** and **(E)** both change the verb to "is."

Step 3: Eliminate Choices Until Only One Remains

We know that "are" is incorrect, so we can eliminate **(A)**, **(B)**, and **(C)**. Choice **(E)** changes "do aerobic exercise regularly" to "do regular aerobic exercises," which alters the meaning of the sentence in an illogical way. Here we want the adverb "regularly," which modifies how often a person should engage in exercise, not the adjective "regular," which modifies the noun "exercises," indicating that the exercises themselves should be "regular" or "normal." Because the correct answer must fix any existing errors without changing the meaning of the original sentence, **(E)** is incorrect, and **(D)** is the correct answer.

7. **(C)**

As state governments <u>become less and less able to support higher education in the coming years, universities have been becoming</u> more and more dependent on alumni networks, corporate sponsorships, and philanthropists.

- O become less and less able to support higher education in the coming years, universities have been becoming
- O are becoming less and less able to support higher education in the coming years, universities have become
- O become less and less able to support higher education in the coming years, universities will become
- O become less and less able to support higher education in the coming years, universities have become
- O are becoming less and less able to support higher education in the coming years, universities will become

Step 1: Read the Original Sentence Carefully, Looking for Errors

This sentence contains two underlined verbs. The first, "become," is plural, and agrees with its subject, "state governments," which is also plural. The second verb, "have been becoming," also agrees with its subject, "universities." However, universities' increasing dependence on alumni networks will take place "in the coming years," so we need the future tense, "will become." We can instantly rule out **(A)**.

Step 2: Scan and Group the Answer Choices

Because we have identified a tense error in the second verb, we'll use that verb to split the answer choices. **(C)** and **(E)** use the future tense, "will become." **(A)**, **(B)**, and **(D)** retain some version of a past tense.

Step 3: Eliminate Choices Until Only One Remains

We definitely need the second verb to be in the future tense, so we can throw out **(A)**, **(B)**, and **(D)**. Of the remaining choices, **(C)** keeps the first verb, "become," while **(E)** changes the first verb to "are becoming." In general, the GMAT testmakers prefer the simplest and most concise constructions. "As state governments become less and less able ... in the coming years" makes sense, so there is no need to complicate the verb tense. Choice **(C)** is the correct answer.

8. **(A)**

The most common breed of rabbit, *Oryctolagus cuniculus,* <u>is native to Europe but was accidentally introduced into the Australian continent in the 1850s, causing</u> decades of habitat destruction and crop devastation before its numbers were finally brought under control by bounty hunters.

- ○ is native to Europe but was accidentally introduced into the Australian continent in the 1850s, causing
- ○ is a native of Europe but was accidentally introduced into the Australian continent in the 1850s, which caused
- ○ was a native of Europe but was accidentally introduced into the Australian continent in the 1850s, causing
- ○ had been native to Europe but was accidentally introduced into the Australian continent in the 1850s, which caused
- ○ had been a native of Europe but was accidentally introduced into the Australian continent in the 1850s, causing

Step 1: Read the Original Sentence Carefully, Looking for Errors

Note the verbs "is" and "was accidentally introduced," as well as "causing" at the end of the underlined portion. Always pay attention to verbs in the underlined portion of a GMAT Sentence Correction question. Also pay attention to how the underlined portion ends, because that will likely be a source of variation among the answer choices.

Step 2: Scan and Group the Answer Choices

Conducting a quick survey of the beginnings and ends of the answer choices, note the 2-2-1 split among "is," "had been," and "was." Also, **(A)**, **(C)**, and **(E)** all end with "causing," while **(B)** and **(D)** end with "which caused."

Step 3: Eliminate Choices Until Only One Remains

First, let's tackle the verb issue. The rabbit breed *is* native to Europe; the status of its origins is immutable and does not change because it was introduced into the Australian continent in the 1850s. Therefore, the present tense is correct, making **(C)**, **(D)**, and **(E)** wrong. And **(B)** is wrong because the correct idiom to describe a species is "native to" rather than "a native of." My uncle is *a native of* Australia; the kangaroo is *native to* Australia. The sentence is correct as written, making **(A)** our answer. The author's use of "causing" is just fine here.

9. **(D)**

A recent spate of news reports questioning the long-term health benefits of high-fat diets <u>have done little to convince its practitioners that they should follow more traditional weight-loss plans</u>.

○ have done little to convince its practitioners that they should follow more traditional weight-loss plans

○ have done little to convince their practitioners to follow more traditional weight-loss plans

○ has done little to convince its practitioners to follow more traditional weight-loss plans

○ has done little to convince practitioners of these diets to follow more traditional weight-loss plans

○ has done little to convince practitioners of these diets they should follow more traditional weight-loss plans

Step 1: Read the Original Sentence Carefully, Looking for Errors

Note the verb in the beginning of the underlined portion. Here the GMAT is testing a common error in a classic way: The test is assessing your ability to determine correct subject-verb agreement by placing the subject as far as possible from the verb to disguise the error. The singular subject of the sentence, "spate," does not agree with the plural verb "have."

Step 2: Scan and Group the Answer Choices

Even if you didn't notice the subject-verb error, seeing the 3-2 split between "has" and "have," you should get the sense that subject-verb agreement is at issue here.

Step 3: Eliminate Choices Until Only One Remains

The actual subject of the sentence is "spate," which is singular, so **(A)** and **(B)** are out. Reading further, **(C)** is wrong because "its" is singular while the pronoun's antecedent, "diets," is plural. **(D)** is the correct answer because "convince practitioners ... to follow" is idiomatically correct, whereas "convince practitioners ... they should follow" is not. If **(D)** sounded better to you than **(E)**, you should learn to trust your ear on GMAT Sentence Correction questions.

EXPLANATIONS

10. (D)

Some economists contend that the way markets react to financial news <u>are based as much on irrational fears and expectations than on</u> sound fiscal analyses.

○   are based as much on irrational fears and expectations than on

○   are based as much on their irrational fears and expectations as they are on

○   is based as much on irrational fears and expectations than on

○   is based as much on irrational fears and expectations as on

○   has been based on irrational fears and expectations as much as

Step 1: Read the Original Sentence Carefully, Looking for Errors

Whenever a sentence contains an underlined verb, we must be sure to check whether it agrees with its subject. In this sentence, the verb "are based" is plural, but its subject, "way," is singular, so we have a subject-verb agreement error. Moreover, the words "as much" are part of the idiomatic phrase "as much ... as," but this sentence instead uses "as much ... than." The correct answer will fix both mistakes without introducing any new errors.

Step 2: Scan and Group the Answer Choices

(A) and **(B)** retain the plural verb phrase "are based." **(C)** and **(D)** instead use the singular "is based." **(E)** uses "has been based."

Step 3: Eliminate Choices Until Only One Remains

We can eliminate **(A)** and **(B)** because we know that the plural verb is incorrect. **(E)** has a singular verb, but it changes the tense and therefore the meaning of the sentence, so we can rule out **(E)** as well. **(C)** and **(D)** both correctly use the present tense singular "is based." However, choice **(C)** does not correct the "as much ... than" error. The correct answer is **(D)**, which corrects "as much ... than" to "as much ... as" and also uses the correct verb form.

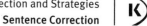

11. (B)

The newspaper reported that <u>some homes that were destroyed and severely damaged in the hurricane last year were</u> built too close to the coastline.

- ○ some homes that were destroyed and severely damaged in the hurricane last year were
- ○ some homes that were destroyed or severely damaged in the hurricane last year had been
- ○ some homes the hurricane destroyed and severely damaged last year have been
- ○ last year the hurricane destroyed or severely damaged some homes that have been
- ○ last year some of the homes that were destroyed or severely damaged in the hurricane have been

Step 1: Read the Original Sentence Carefully, Looking for Errors

This underlined portion contains a lot of verbs. The homes "were destroyed and severely damaged" and "were built" too close to the coast. Did you notice the erroneous "and" in the underlined portion? It's actually not possible for homes to be destroyed and severely damaged. Homes are either destroyed *or* severely damaged, not both.

Step 2: Scan and Group the Answer Choices

(A) and **(C)** use "and," while the remaining choices use "or." Note also that the ends of the answer choices present a variety of verb tenses: "were," "had been," and "have been."

Step 3: Eliminate Choices Until Only One Remains

Because "and" is an inappropriate conjunction to use, **(A)** is out, as is **(C)**, which repeats the error. Since the homes were built first and then destroyed or damaged, the past perfect tense, "had been built," is appropriate to use here, making **(B)** the correct answer. **(D)** and **(E)** use the present perfect tense, "have been built," which doesn't make sense given the sequence of events in the sentence.

12. (C)

The activism of state citizens, who have demanded safer road conditions as well as stiffer penalties for intoxicated drivers, <u>have led to a significant decrease in the number</u> of traffic accidents.

○ have led to a significant decrease in the number
○ have led to significant decreases in the amount
○ has led to a significant decrease in the number
○ has been significant in the decrease in the number
○ has significantly decreased the amount

Step 1: Read the Original Sentence Carefully, Looking for Errors

The GMAT will often insert long intervening phrases between commas in order to put distance between a subject and a verb that don't agree. This sentence is no different. The actual subject of the sentence is "activism," which is singular, but the underlined portion uses "have led," a plural verb phrase.

Step 2: Scan and Group the Answer Choices

The answer choices present a choice between "have," in **(A)** and **(B)**, and "has," in **(C)**, **(D)**, and **(E)**, so even if you didn't notice the error, you could have guessed that subject-verb agreement was an issue here.

Step 3: Eliminate Choices Until Only One Remains

Ignoring the long modifying phrase set off between commas, we see that the subject of this sentence is "activism," making the singular verb "has" correct, so **(A)** and **(B)** are out. There's also a choice between "number" and "amount" at the ends of the answer choices. Because traffic accidents are countable, the correct word to use is "number," so **(E)** is out. Finally, **(D)** is wordy and a bit awkward ("has been significant in the decrease in"), and it changes the meaning of the sentence. **(C)** is therefore the correct answer.

13. (C)

The government <u>has imposed sanctions and restricted foreign aid to a renegade nation last month after it violated</u> the terms of a worldwide arms control treaty.

- ○ has imposed sanctions and restricted foreign aid to a renegade nation last month after it violated
- ○ has imposed sanctions on and restricted foreign aid to a renegade nation last month after it violated
- ○ imposed sanctions on and restricted foreign aid to a renegade nation last month after that nation violated
- ○ imposed sanctions and restricted foreign aid to a renegade nation last month after violating
- ○ had imposed sanctions and restricted foreign aid to a renegade nation last month after it had violated

Step 1: Read the Original Sentence Carefully, Looking for Errors

This sentence contains three errors. First, the underlined pronoun "it" is ambiguous; it is unclear whether it refers to the "government" or to the "renegade nation," though logically it should refer to the latter. Second, while the predicate verb "has imposed" agrees with its subject, "the government," the verb tense is incorrect. It makes no sense to say that "the government has imposed sanctions last month." When we are describing a single past event that occurred at a specific time point, we need the simple past tense: "The government imposed sanctions last month." Third, the phrase "imposed sanctions" must be followed by the preposition "on" instead of "to" as written. The correct answer must fix the ambiguous pronoun, the faulty verb tense, and the idiomatic phrase "imposed sanctions on" without introducing any new errors.

Step 2: Scan and Group the Answer Choices

(A), **(B)**, and **(E)** retain the pronoun ambiguity. **(C)** changes "it" to "that nation," while **(D)** removes the pronoun altogether. We have the same 3-2 split for the verb error: **(A)**, **(B)**, and **(E)** use "has imposed," while **(C)** and **(D)** use "imposed." There is also a 3-2 split following "imposed sanctions": **(B)** and **(C)** add the word "on," while **(A)**, **(D)**, and **(E)** do not.

Step 3: Eliminate Choices Until Only One Remains

We can eliminate **(A)**, **(B)**, and **(E)** because all three commit the pronoun and verb tense errors we spotted in the original sentence. Of the remaining choices, **(D)** attempts to fix the ambiguous pronoun by simply leaving it out: "The government imposed sanctions ... after violating ..." This construction makes it sound as if the same government that imposed the sanctions violated the treaty, which doesn't make much logical sense. **(C)** fixes the pronoun ambiguity and also conveys the more logical meaning: "That nation" (i.e., the renegade nation) violated the treaty. Because **(C)** also fixes the verb tense error by changing "has imposed" to "imposed" and adds the preposition "on" after "imposed sanctions," it is the correct answer.

14. **(D)**

Every one of the police reports <u>have been filed so that they can be located by their case number, the date they were created, or the victim's last name</u>.

O   have been filed so that they can be located by their case number, the date they were created, or the victim's last name

O   have been filed so that they can be located by their case numbers, the dates they were created, or by the victims' last names

O   has been filed so that they can be located by their case number, the date they were created, or the victim's last name

O   has been filed so that it can be located by its case number, the date it was created, or the victim's last name

O   has been filed so that it can be located by its case number, the date it was created, or by the victim's last name

Step 1: Read the Original Sentence Carefully, Looking for Errors

The subject of this sentence, "Every one," is singular. However, the verbs and pronouns in the underlined segment are all plural, so there are multiple errors: "Have" should be "has," "they" and "their" should be "it" and "its," and "were" should be "was." Note that the testmaker is trying to trick us into thinking that the subject is "the police reports." We always need to remember to mentally bracket out prepositional phrases when searching for the subject of a sentence. The "police reports" are, in fact, the object of the preposition "of" and therefore cannot be the subject of the sentence.

Step 2: Scan and Group the Answer Choices

(A), **(B)**, and **(C)** keep the plural pronouns, while **(D)** and **(E)** change "they" and "their" to "it" and "its." There is a second split among the answer choices with regard to the predicate verb. **(A)** and **(B)** retain the plural form "have been," while **(C)**, **(D)**, and **(E)** change the predicate verb to the singular "has been."

Step 3: Eliminate Choices Until Only One Remains

We can throw out **(A)**, **(B)**, and **(C)** because all three use the incorrect plural pronouns. **(D)** and **(E)** both use the singular verb and singular pronouns, so we need to look for some other difference between them. **(E)** introduces the word "by" into the last phrase: "or by the victim's last name." This addition creates a parallelism error. The original sentence contains a list of three different ways to locate a report, and the word "by" is used only once, before the first item in the list. Introducing "by" before the third term makes the second and third terms structurally different from each other so that the items in the list are no longer parallel. Because **(D)** is the only choice that fixes the errors in the original sentence without introducing any new mistakes, it is the correct answer.

15. **(B)**

<u>Although swimming can cause cramps in a swimmer's legs or feet, they</u> can usually be avoided if the swimmer avoids overexertion and performs stretching exercises before entering the pool.

○   Although swimming can cause cramps in a swimmer's legs or feet, they

○   Cramps in a swimmer's legs or feet caused by swimming

○   Swimming can cause cramps in a swimmer's legs or feet, which

○   The fact that swimming can cause cramps in a swimmer's legs or feet

○   Swimming can cause cramps in a swimmer's legs or feet, although they

Step 1: Read the Original Sentence Carefully, Looking for Errors

It's not enough to have a good sense of which noun an underlined pronoun refers back to; the sentence has to be 100 percent clear about it. As you were reading, you might have instinctively assumed that "they" refers back to "cramps," but this isn't good enough on the GMAT. Because "they" could also refer to "legs" or "feet," its use here is wrong.

Step 2: Scan and Group the Answer Choices

An initial scan doesn't yield much in the way of splits, but it's important to scan for the ways in which the answer choices will deal with the all too common "they" problem.

Step 3: Eliminate Choices Until Only One Remains

(A) is incorrect because the pronoun "they" here is ambiguous; "they" could refer to "cramps," "legs," or "feet." Likewise, **(E)** is wrong, as is **(C)**, although here the ambiguous pronoun is "which." What does "which" refer to in choice **(C)**: the legs or feet, the cramps, or the entire preceding clause? **(D)** is also wrong; a *fact* cannot be avoided. "The fact that" is another phrase that almost always signals a wrong answer choice on GMAT Sentence Corrections. Finally, **(B)** is correct because it avoids pronoun reference problems and makes it clear that "cramps" can be avoided.

16. (D)

Some mathematicians argue that <u>to permit a candidate to win an election because they have won a plurality vote is like ranking a student</u> who earned three As and two Fs higher than one who got two As and three Bs.

- ○ to permit a candidate to win an election because they have won a plurality vote is like ranking a student
- ○ permitting a candidate to win an election because they have won a plurality of votes is like ranking a student
- ○ permitting candidates to win elections because they have won a plurality of votes is like to rank a student
- ○ permitting candidates to win elections because they have won a plurality of votes is like ranking a student
- ○ to permit candidates to win elections because they have won a plurality of votes is like ranking students

Step 1: Read the Original Sentence Carefully, Looking for Errors

This sentence, like many others on the GMAT, contains the underlined pronoun "they." But here, the plural pronoun "they" refers to "a candidate," which is singular, so the pronoun agreement is wrong.

Step 2: Scan and Group the Answer Choices

Note that all the answer choices contain "they," so in order to make the pronoun and antecedent agree, you'll probably have to change the antecedent to something plural, such as "candidates."

Step 3: Eliminate Choices Until Only One Remains

You can eliminate **(A)**, as well as **(B)**, because these choices contain the same pronoun agreement error. Examining the remaining choices, note that comparisons require parallel structure, which means that ultimately **(C)** and **(E)** must be eliminated in favor of **(D)**: "*Permitting* … is like *ranking* …" is correct, whereas comparing a gerund ("permitting" or "ranking") to an infinitive ("to rank" or "to permit") is not. Choice **(D)** is the correct answer.

17. **(E)**

According to a recently enacted law, any organization that engages in lobbying activities is required either to notify <u>their members about the percentage of dues that are used for lobbying activities or</u> pay a proxy tax.

- ○ their members about the percentage of dues that are used for lobbying activities or
- ○ their members about the percentage of dues they use for lobbying activities or to
- ○ their members about the percentage of dues that are used for lobbying activities or they should
- ○ its members about the percentage of dues that are used for lobbying activities or it should
- ○ its members about the percentage of dues that is used for lobbying activities or to

Step 1: Read the Original Sentence Carefully, Looking for Errors

This sentence contains several errors. For one thing, the plural pronoun "their" refers to the singular noun "organization." Pronouns must agree with their antecedents in number, so we need the singular pronoun "its." There is also a subject-verb agreement issue: "Percentage" is a collective noun referring to a sum of money being spent as a single unit, so it needs a singular verb. However, the verb phrase "are used" is plural. Finally, there is a parallelism error. The word "either" signals a list of two actions, "to notify" and "to pay." Both actions should be in parallel structure, but the sentence omits the second "to."

Step 2: Scan and Group the Answer Choices

Let's use the pronoun at the beginning of the underlined segment to split the choices because it's the easiest split to see. **(A)**, **(B)**, and **(C)** retain the plural pronoun "their." **(D)** and **(E)** use the singular pronoun "its."

Step 3: Eliminate Choices Until Only One Remains

(A), **(B)**, and **(C)** are out because they use the plural pronoun, which we know to be incorrect. We can also eliminate **(D)**, which does not correct the subject-verb agreement error. That leaves **(E)**, which corrects "are used" to "is used." Moreover, **(E)** fixes the parallelism error by inserting the word "to," so that we now have the correct construction "either to notify ... or to pay." Choice **(E)** is the correct answer.

18. (D)

The chief executive officer met with the board of directors to consider the possibility of a hostile takeover attempt by a competitor and <u>how they would have to respond to deal with them</u>.

- ○ how they would have to respond to deal with them
- ○ how to deal with them if action would become necessary
- ○ what action would be required for dealing with such an event
- ○ what action would be necessary to deal with such an event
- ○ the necessity of taking action in order to deal with it

Step 1: Read the Original Sentence Carefully, Looking for Errors

The sentence as written is wrong because "they" and "them" have no clear antecedent nouns. On the GMAT, any hint of pronoun ambiguity indicates an incorrect answer choice.

Step 2: Scan and Group the Answer Choices

Sniff out pronouns in the choices. **(A)** and **(B)** use "them," and **(E)** uses "it."

Step 3: Eliminate Choices Until Only One Remains

Because of their ambiguous use of "them," **(A)** and **(B)** are wrong. **(C)** contains the unidiomatic construction "required for dealing," and likewise **(E)** contains the unidiomatic construction "necessity of taking." Only **(D)** is idiomatically correct and avoids misused pronouns.

EXPLANATIONS

19. (A)

Arguing that the dominance of an economic theory has more to do with the persuasive skills of <u>its expositors than with its</u> accuracy in predicting economic events, Professor McCloskey examines the rhetorical practices of economists.

- ○ its expositors than with its
- ○ these expositors than its
- ○ its expositors compared to its
- ○ the theory's expositors than their
- ○ its expositors than with their

Step 1: Read the Original Sentence Carefully, Looking for Errors

There are no obvious problems with the original sentence. The underlined portion uses the pronoun "its" twice, though, so you should ensure that the pronouns agree in number with their antecedents and are not being used ambiguously.

Step 2: Scan and Group the Answer Choices

(A), (B), and (C) use "its" exclusively, while (D) and (E) introduce "their."

Step 3: Eliminate Choices Until Only One Remains

The sentence is correct as written. Here the pronoun "its" clearly refers to "theory," so the use is correct. Eliminate (D) and (E), which use "their." Also, (A) is the only choice that maintains correct parallel structure in the two-part construction "more to do with ... than with ..." Thus, choice (A) is the correct answer. Eliminate (B) and (C) because they violate the parallel structure.

20. (E)

In an effort to determine whether changes in diet and exercise can reverse coronary heart disease, <u>1,800 elderly heart patients will participate in a Medicare program costing $12,960,000 over the next three years to reduce lifestyle-related risk factors.</u>

○ 1,800 elderly heart patients will participate in a Medicare program costing $12,960,000 over the next three years to reduce lifestyle-related risk factors

○ $12,960,000 will be spent by Medicare over the next three years in a program to reduce lifestyle-related risk factors in 1,800 elderly patients

○ over the next three years $12,960,000 will be spent on 1,800 patients by Medicare on a program to reduce lifestyle-related risk factors

○ Medicare is to spend $12,960,000 over the next three years on a program for reducing lifestyle-related risk factors in 1,800 elderly heart patients

○ Medicare will spend $12,960,000 over the next three years on a program to reduce lifestyle-related risk factors in 1,800 elderly heart patients

Step 1: Read the Original Sentence Carefully, Looking for Errors

The intended meaning of this sentence is clear enough: Medicare is making an effort to determine whether lifestyle changes can reverse coronary heart disease. However, the modifying phrase at the beginning of the sentence that describes this effort is followed by the subject of the sentence, "1,800 elderly heart patients." Grammatically, a modifying phrase modifies whatever is nearest to it in the sentence. So, according to the grammar of this sentence as written, it is the heart patients who are trying to figure out whether lifestyle changes can reverse coronary heart disease—but that's not the intended meaning. The correct answer would have to either place "Medicare" next to the opening modifying phrase or use a different construction.

Step 2: Scan and Group the Answer Choices

(A), (B), and (C) place something other than "Medicare" next to the opening modifying phrase. (D) and (E) start with "Medicare."

Step 3: Eliminate Choices Until Only One Remains

(A), (B), and (C) can be eliminated because none of them fixes the misplaced modifier. The only difference between (D) and (E) is the verb phrase: "is to spend" versus "will spend." Because the program will occur over "the next three years," we need the future tense, and "will spend" is correct. That makes (E) the correct answer.

21. (C)

Children often pick up on gender norms very early in life, as many parents discover when <u>their toddlers recoil at toys that have only been designed to appeal to toddlers of the opposite sex</u>.

- ○ their toddlers recoil at toys that have only been designed to appeal to toddlers of the opposite sex
- ○ only their toddlers recoil at toys that have been designed to appeal to toddlers of the opposite sex
- ○ their toddlers recoil at toys that have been designed to appeal to toddlers of the opposite sex only
- ○ toys that have only been designed to appeal to toddlers of the opposite sex cause their toddlers to recoil
- ○ only toys that have been designed to appeal to toddlers of the opposite sex cause their toddlers to recoil

Step 1: Read the Original Sentence Carefully, Looking for Errors

As written, this sentence is illogical. No toy would be designed "only ... to appeal to toddlers of the opposite sex." Toys are designed with lots of functions in mind—entertainment, safety, etc. The modifier "only" is in the wrong place. It should be modifying "toddlers of the opposite sex." The correct answer will place it properly.

Step 2: Scan and Group the Answer Choices

The choices place the word "only" in a variety of different places. Because this is the only error we've spotted, and "only" should go toward the end of the sentence, we expect that the correct answer will still start the same way as the underlined part of the original sentence, so let's split the choices along these lines. **(A)** and **(C)** retain "their toddlers" at the beginning of the underlined segment; choices **(B)**, **(D)**, and **(E)** do not.

Step 3: Eliminate Choices Until Only One Remains

We know that **(A)** is incorrect, and chances are that **(B)**, **(D)**, and **(E)** make erroneous changes, so let's start by checking choice **(C)**. Here, "only" falls at the very end of the sentence and correctly modifies "toddlers of the opposite sex." This is the correct answer. For the record: **(B)** uses "only" to modify "their toddlers," so that the sentence now excludes any other toddlers. That's not the intended meaning of the original sentence, so **(B)** is incorrect. **(D)** rephrases the underlined segment, but the word "only" still modifies the verb "designed," so the original error is preserved. **(E)** uses "only" to modify "toys," so that the sentence now indicates that nothing besides toys can cause toddlers to recoil. This is again not the intended meaning of the original sentence, so it is also incorrect. Choice **(C)** is the correct answer.

22. (C)

Based on the candidates' performances in the televised debates, many pundits predicted that the rival was likely to score an upset defeat over the incumbent senator.

- ○ Based on the candidates' performances in the televised debates
- ○ Basing it on the candidates' performances in the televised debates
- ○ Basing their assessments on the candidates' performances in the televised debates
- ○ With the candidates' performances in the televised debates used as a basis
- ○ By the assessments of the candidates' performances in the televised debates that they made

Step 1: Read the Original Sentence Carefully, Looking for Errors

When a modifying phrase at the beginning of the sentence is underlined, your job is to make sure that the subject of the phrase is what follows the comma. If you read this sentence aloud, you might not have noticed anything because this is a very common error in spoken English. But the subject following the comma is "pundits," and the modifying phrase "Based on the candidates' performances in the televised debates" refers not to the pundits but to their predictions. This is a big error.

Step 2: Scan and Group the Answer Choices

There aren't many obvious splits here, but the opening phrase followed by a comma tells you to eliminate choices based on how they handle the modification error.

Step 3: Eliminate Choices Until Only One Remains

(A) should be eliminated because of the modification error just mentioned. **(B)** is wrong because the pronoun "it" is misused here, as the reference is unclear and the number should be plural. **(D)** and **(E)** are awkward and unidiomatic. **(E)** is also wrong because it is not clear what "they" refers to. Only **(C)** is correct, because the subject of the phrase is "pundits," as it should be, and this choice also avoids pronoun reference problems.

23. (D)

Hoping to avert another situation in which the candidate who won the popular vote could lose the electoral vote, <u>it was proposed by Congress</u> that the Electoral College be abolished.

- ○ it was proposed by Congress
- ○ there was a proposal by Congress
- ○ a proposal was made by Congress
- ○ Congress proposed
- ○ Congress will have proposed

Step 1: Read the Original Sentence Carefully, Looking for Errors

See that opening phrase followed by a comma? Since that phrase is not underlined, you cannot change it. Instead, you need to make the rest of the sentence align with it. So ask yourself, "Who in the sentence was hoping to avert the situation?" The answer, Congress, should come right after that comma. Anything else is wrong.

Step 2: Scan and Group the Answer Choices

(A), **(B)**, and **(C)** all begin by talking about the proposal, whereas **(D)** and **(E)** begin by talking about Congress.

Step 3: Eliminate Choices Until Only One Remains

Since Congress hoped to avert the situation in the sentence, Congress needs to be placed at the beginning of the underlined portion. This eliminates **(A)**, **(B)**, and **(C)**. Between **(D)** and **(E)**, the difference lies in verb tense. **(E)**'s "will have proposed" doesn't make sense; we would need specific clues in the sentence that require the use of the future perfect tense, and no such clues exist. The simple past, "proposed," works perfectly well, making **(D)** the correct answer.

24. (C)

Cheered by better-than-expected opening week box office returns, <u>it was decided by the movie's producer to give bonuses to the entire cast</u>.

- ○ it was decided by the movie's producer to give bonuses to the entire cast
- ○ the entire cast was given bonuses by the movie's producer
- ○ the movie's producer decided to give the entire cast bonuses
- ○ the decision of the movie's producer was to give the entire cast bonuses
- ○ bonuses to the entire cast were given by the movie's producer

Step 1: Read the Original Sentence Carefully, Looking for Errors

When a sentence starts with a modifying phrase, as this one does, we should be on the alert for misplaced modifiers. The modifying phrase should be placed right next to whatever it logically modifies. In this case, the logic of the sentence dictates that it is the producer who felt "cheered" by the great box office returns. Therefore, "the movie's producer" should immediately follow the comma. **(A)** cannot be the correct answer.

Step 2: Scan and Group the Answer Choices

Only **(C)** places "the movie's producer" immediately after the comma that follows the modifying phrase. In **(B)**, "the entire cast" follows the comma, while **(D)** and **(E)** start out with "the decision" and "bonuses," respectively.

Step 3: Eliminate Choices Until Only One Remains

We cannot change anything in the part of the sentence that is not underlined, so the opening phrase has to stay where it is. Because we can only rearrange the underlined segment, the only way to fix the modification error is to place "the movie's producer" right at the beginning of the answer choice. **(C)** is therefore the correct answer. For the record: **(D)** and **(E)** place inanimate things after the comma, which makes no logical sense. A "decision" cannot feel "cheered," nor can "bonuses." As for **(B)**, while it may be true that the "entire cast" felt happy about the box office returns, the logical cause-and-effect relationship indicated by the sentence needs to be reflected in its grammar. The producer feels "cheered" and therefore awards the cast bonuses. No matter how the cast feels about the box office returns, the sentence's initial phrase logically refers to "the movie's producer." Choice **(C)** is correct.

25. (B)

States now have an incentive to lower the blood alcohol level <u>that constitutes drunk driving by a federal law that withholds</u> highway funds from those states that don't enforce the applicable standard.

- O   that constitutes drunk driving by a federal law that withholds
- O   that constitutes drunk driving, because a federal law withholds
- O   that constitutes drunk driving, because a federal law withheld
- O   which constitutes drunk driving by a federal law that withholds
- O   which constitutes drunk driving, because a federal law withholds

Step 1: Read the Original Sentence Carefully, Looking for Errors

The sentence as written is wrong, because the phrase "drunk driving by a federal law" makes it sound as if the federal law was driving drunk, when the federal law is actually providing an incentive for states to lower their drunk-driving blood alcohol threshold.

Step 2: Scan and Group the Answer Choices

Note that **(A)**, **(B)**, and **(C)** begin with "that," while **(D)** and **(E)** begin with "which."

Step 3: Eliminate Choices Until Only One Remains

The original "by a federal law" error disqualifies **(A)** and **(D)**. On the GMAT, "that" is a restrictive pronoun to be used when the information following "that" is necessary to the sentence. If someone says, "read the book *that* is on the shelf," you are presumably in a room that contains multiple books in various locations, so "on the shelf" is necessary information if you want to read the right book. However, if someone says "read the book, *which* is on the shelf," you are in a room where there is only one book and that book just so happens to be on the shelf. In this case, "on the shelf" is not necessary information. Back to our sentence. Since the sentence is specifically interested in the blood alcohol level that indicates drunk driving, and not just any old blood alcohol level, "that" is correct because the information is necessary. This eliminates **(D)** and **(E)**. Finally, **(C)** can be eliminated because "withheld" is the wrong tense given that the rest of the sentence is in the present tense. Thus, **(B)** is the correct answer.

26. (E)

<u>Using a seismic survey, hydrocarbons can be located even though they are buried far beneath Earth's surface</u>.

- O Using a seismic survey, hydrocarbons can be located even though they are buried far beneath Earth's surface
- O Hydrocarbons can be located even though they are buried far beneath Earth's surface, using a seismic survey
- O Locating hydrocarbons that are buried far beneath Earth's surface, a geophysicist can use a seismic survey
- O Buried far beneath Earth's surface, hydrocarbons can be detected using a seismic survey
- O Using a seismic survey, a geophysicist can locate hydrocarbons even though they are buried far beneath Earth's surface

Step 1: Read the Original Sentence Carefully, Looking for Errors

The original sentence is wrong because it begins with the modifying phrase "using a seismic survey," so what follows the phrase should be its subject, which is definitely not "hydrocarbons" (it wouldn't make any sense for hydrocarbons to use a seismic survey).

Step 2: Scan and Group the Answer Choices

These choices don't scan easily, but since we know that we are dealing with an error with the modifying phrase "using a seismic survey," we can group choices based on what subject that phrase modifies. **(C)** and **(E)** both have the subject "a geophysicist," which makes sense. **(B)** and **(D)** are both vague at best about the subject. In any case, it's not someone who'd use a seismic survey.

Step 3: Eliminate Choices Until Only One Remains

The modification error disqualifies **(A)**. Choice **(B)** likewise contains the same misplaced modifying phrase, although here it can be found at the end of the sentence rather than the beginning. **(C)** sounds awkward and changes the meaning of the sentence, because the seismic survey is precisely what the geophysicist uses to locate the hydrocarbons in the first place. **(D)** uses a passive verb and never explains who is using the seismic survey. Only **(E)** correctly places the phrase "Using a seismic survey" next to the subject of the phrase, "a geophysicist." Thus, choice **(E)** is the correct answer.

27. (C)

The creation of an independent treasury, establishing lower tariffs, and purchasing the Oregon Territory, all credited to the presidency of James Knox Polk, are among the significant accomplishments that persuade historians to rank this former governor of Tennessee as an above-average president.

- ○ The creation of an independent treasury, establishing lower tariffs, and purchasing
- ○ The creation of an independent treasury, establishing lower tariffs, as well as purchasing
- ○ The creation of an independent treasury, the establishment of lower tariffs, and the purchase of
- ○ Creating an independent treasury, the establishment of lower tariffs, and purchasing
- ○ Creating an independent treasury, the establishing of lower tariffs, and the purchasing of

Step 1: Read the Original Sentence Carefully, Looking for Errors

The underlined segment of this sentence contains a list of three accomplishments of Polk's presidency. Items in a list must have parallel form, but these do not: The first term in the list is a noun, "creation," but the second and third terms are -*ing* verb forms. The correct answer will either change "The creation of" to "Creating," or it will change "establishing" and "purchasing" to "the establishment of" and "the purchase of," respectively.

Step 2: Scan and Group the Answer Choices

(A), (B), and (C) keep the noun "creation" at the beginning of the sentence, while (D) and (E) change "creation" to "creating."

Step 3: Eliminate Choices Until Only One Remains

(A) is definitely incorrect due to the parallelism issue. We'll need to check each of the other choices for proper parallel structure. (B) and (C) begin with the word "creation," so the remaining two items on the list should both be nouns. (B) still has the two gerund forms, "establishing" and "purchasing," so it does not have the correct parallel structure and cannot be correct. Choice (C), though, gets it right; the three items here are "creation," "establishment," and "purchase." This is the correct answer. A quick look at (D) and (E) reveals that neither has parallel structure. In (D), the middle term is different from the first and third. Choice (E) uses three gerund forms, but there is still a parallelism error. The second and third terms are in the same form, "the establishing of" and "the purchasing of," but the first term lacks the words "the" and "of." Choice (C) is correct.

28. (B)

The rapid-rail lines that were recently introduced in southern California have had positive effects: <u>not only have they lowered pollution levels, they have helped in decongesting</u> the region's freeway system, which had been operating far above its capacity.

- ○ not only have they lowered pollution levels, they have helped in decongesting
- ○ the lines have not only lowered pollution levels, but also helped to decongest
- ○ not only have pollution levels been lowered, but they have helped to decongest
- ○ lines have lowered pollution levels, as well as helped in decongesting
- ○ not only have they lowered pollution levels, but also have they helped decongest

Step 1: Read the Original Sentence Carefully, Looking for Errors

The underlined part of this sentence contains the phrase "not only." That means that we expect to see the words "but also" elsewhere in the sentence, but those words are absent. Additionally, the sentence includes the phrase "helped in decongesting" where "helped to decongest" would be more idiomatic. We can therefore eliminate **(A)**. The correct answer will fix these problems without introducing any new errors.

Step 2: Scan and Group the Answer Choices

(B) and **(E)** add the "but also" construction; the remaining choices do not, though **(C)** adds the word "but," and **(D)** adds "as well as."

Step 3: Eliminate Choices Until Only One Remains

(C) adds "but," but it leaves out "also." **(E)** has both halves of the proper construction, but the verb phrase at the end, "have they helped decongest," sounds like a question and is awkward at best. **(D)** avoids the "not only ... but also" problem by deleting the first half of the construction, but it retains the awkward phrase "helped in decongesting." More seriously, **(D)** omits the article "the" at the beginning, such that the second half of the sentence now seems to refer to "lines" generally, rather than to the new Californian rapid rail lines specifically. That leaves **(B)**, which provides both parts of the "not only ... but also" construction. Additionally, **(B)** uses the idiomatically correct form "helped to decongest." Choice **(B)** is the correct answer.

29. (A)

A national study evaluating the need for gun control is currently attempting to document where criminals purchase guns, how gun owners are trained in the use of firearms, and <u>what character traits are common to persons who are liable to turn</u> to violence to resolve problems.

O   what character traits are common to persons who are liable to turn

O   what are the character traits common to persons who are liable to turning

O   the common character traits of persons who are liable to turn

O   the traits of character common to persons who are liable to turn

O   the traits of character that are common to persons who are liable to turn

Step 1: Read the Original Sentence Carefully, Looking for Errors

Because this sentence has a list, you have to check for parallel structure. The parallel list is "where criminals purchase ... how gun owners are trained ... and what character traits are common ..."

Step 2: Scan and Group the Answer Choices

(A) and **(B)** begin with "what," which is parallel to "where" and "how," whereas the remaining choices begin with elements that are not parallel.

Step 3: Eliminate Choices Until Only One Remains

(C), **(D)**, and **(E)** are incorrect because they do not begin the third element in the sequence with "what." Finally, **(B)** is wrong because it replaces the correct form "to turn" with the incorrect "to turning." The sentence here is correct as written, so select **(A)**.

30. (E)

Hearing Kenneth Branagh deliver the "St. Crispin's Day" speech in *Henry V* is to be mesmerized by a great performer, with seemingly boundless emotional energy.

○ Hearing Kenneth Branagh deliver the "St. Crispin's Day" speech in *Henry V* is to be mesmerized by a great performer, with seemingly

○ Hearing Kenneth Branagh deliver the "St. Crispin's Day" speech in *Henry V* is to be mesmerized by a great performer, one with seeming

○ Hearing Kenneth Branagh deliver the "St. Crispin's Day" speech in *Henry V* is being mesmerized by a great performer, one with seeming

○ To hear Kenneth Branagh deliver the "St. Crispin's Day" speech in *Henry V* is being mesmerized by a great performer, with seemingly

○ To hear Kenneth Branagh deliver the "St. Crispin's Day" speech in *Henry V* is to be mesmerized by a great performer, one with seemingly

Step 1: Read the Original Sentence Carefully, Looking for Errors

Elements in a comparison or analogy, like items in a list, must exhibit parallel structure. Here, the original sentence is incorrect because the analogy states that "Hearing ... is to be mesmerized ..." The two ideas compared should both be either gerunds ending in *-ing* or infinitives. Because the GMAT is not particularly fond of gerunds, expect the right answer to change "hearing" to "to hear."

Step 2: Scan and Group the Answer Choices

The first three answer choices all begin with "hearing," while the last two begin with "to hear."

Step 3: Eliminate Choices Until Only One Remains

Because the elements in the comparison in the original sentence are not parallel, eliminate **(A)**. Choice **(B)** should be eliminated because it contains the same parallel structure error. Choice **(D)** also contains a parallel structure error: "To hear ... is being mesmerized ..." Choice **(C)** may seem a bit more parallel, but it still sounds awkward: "Hearing is being mesmerized ..." (You should usually try to avoid answer choices that contain "being" on GMAT Sentence Corrections.) Moreover, **(C)** contains an adverb/adjective error: The adjective form "seeming" is incorrect because it modifies the adjective "boundless," and thus the correct form is the adverb "seemingly." Finally, **(E)** is correct because it exhibits parallel structure and uses the correct adverbial form, "seemingly."

31. (B)

By the time they completed their journey, the young explorers had overcome their fears, sharpened their survival <u>skills, and had developed a healthy respect</u> for nature's potential destructiveness.

- ○ skills, and had developed a healthy respect
- ○ skills, and developed a healthy respect
- ○ skills and a healthy respect developed
- ○ skills, developing a healthy respect
- ○ skills, all the while developing a healthy respect

Step 1: Read the Original Sentence Carefully, Looking for Errors

This sentence contains an underlined verb, which means that we must check for subject-verb agreement and correct tense. The verb phrase "had developed" agrees with its subject, "the young explorers." Because the young explorers' actions precede the completion of their journey, the use of the past perfect tense is correct. However, the phrase "had developed a healthy respect" is part of a list of three things the young explorers did during their journey, and we must therefore also check for parallel structure. Here there is an error, as the second and third items on the list do not have the same structure. The second verb on the list, "sharpened," does not repeat the helping verb, "had," that is used at the beginning of the list to indicate the past perfect tense. But the third verb, "had developed," does repeat the word "had." We can rule out **(A)**.

Step 2: Scan and Group the Answer Choices

Of the remaining choices, **(B)** simply removes "had" but leaves the rest of the underlined segment alone, while **(D)** and **(E)** change the verb to "developing." Like **(B)**, choice **(C)** uses "developed," but changes the word order.

Step 3: Eliminate Choices Until Only One Remains

Because we cannot change anything in the sentence except the underlined part, we cannot correct the parallelism error by changing "sharpened" to "had sharpened." Our only recourse is to change "had developed" to "developed." **(B)** does just that without changing anything else, and this will likely turn out to be the correct answer. A quick look at **(C)** reveals that in changing the word order, it destroys the parallelism of the list of three actions completely. As for **(D)** and **(E)**, changing "developed" to "developing" changes the tense and again destroys the list's parallel structure. Choice **(B)** remains the correct answer.

32. (A)

<u>However much Americans may agree that</u> the financing of elections with special interest money undermines democracy and that campaign finance reform would produce better government, it has been very difficult to push such measures through a Congress that has been elected using the old financing system.

- ○ However much Americans may agree that
- ○ Despite agreement among Americans to the fact
- ○ Although Americans agree
- ○ Even though Americans may agree
- ○ There is agreement among Americans that

Step 1: Read the Original Sentence Carefully, Looking for Errors

The sentence as written may sound a little unusual, so look for the grammatical issues present before turning to style. The sentence sets up a two-part parallel structure: "that the financing of elections with special interest money undermines ... and that campaign finance reform would produce ..."

Step 2: Scan and Group the Answer Choices

Only **(A)** and **(E)** contain the required first "that." If you don't read **(B)** into the rest of the sentence, your brain might fill in the word "that," but it actually isn't present in the answer choice.

Step 3: Eliminate Choices Until Only One Remains

Because only **(A)** and **(E)** contain the "that" necessary for the parallel structure, eliminate **(B)**, **(C)**, and **(D)**. Choice **(E)** is wrong because there is no connector between the two clauses in the sentence, save for a measly comma. (Also note that "There is" sentences are usually wrong on the GMAT.) So even though the construction in **(A)** is not an obviously correct stylistic choice, there's no better alternative in the other answer choices. This shows us that we don't have to be in love with the correct answer; it just has to be grammatically and stylistically correct and more concise than any other answer choice. Thus, **(A)** is the correct answer.

33. (C)

South Pacific Vacations has a package tour to Sydney, Australia, for $999 per person, including airfare from Los Angeles, <u>spending five nights at the Mega Hotel, and to take a harbor cruise, and round-trip airfare from New York is</u> an additional $400.

- ○ spending five nights at the Mega Hotel, and to take a harbor cruise, and round-trip airfare from New York is
- ○ spending five nights at the Mega Hotel, and taking a harbor cruise; and in addition round-trip airfare from New York is
- ○ five nights at the Mega Hotel, and a harbor cruise; round-trip airfare from New York is
- ○ with five nights at the Mega Hotel, and a harbor cruise, with round-trip airfare from New York being
- ○ to spend five nights at the Mega Hotel, and to take a harbor cruise; round-trip airfare from New York is

Step 1: Read the Original Sentence Carefully, Looking for Errors

Note that the sentence makes a list of items included in the package tour, so that list should be in parallel form. But each of the three items is in a different form: "Airfare," "spending five nights," and "to take a harbor cruise" are about as far from parallel as you can get. Expect the right answer to rectify this by making the other items parallel to "airfare," since that's the one item we can't change.

Step 2: Scan and Group the Answer Choices

(A) and **(B)** don't change the form of the second item in the list ("spending five nights"), while **(C)**, **(D)**, and **(E)** change it in various ways.

Step 3: Eliminate Choices Until Only One Remains

Since the noun "airfare," the first item in the list, is not underlined, the other items in the list must be changed to agree with this form. The only choice that turns the second item, "spending five nights," into a simple noun is **(C)**. Each of the other choices fails to exhibit truly parallel structure and should be eliminated on that basis. As a side note, **(C)** also changes the conjunction "and" before "round-trip airfare" to a semicolon, which is preferable because this part of the sentence starts a new thought.

34. (D)

Recent surveys indicate that, contrary to popular belief, total abstinence from alcohol does not correlate <u>as strongly with good health as with moderate drinking</u>.

- ○ as strongly with good health as with moderate drinking
- ○ strongly with good health, like moderate drinking does
- ○ as strongly with good health as does moderately drinking
- ○ as strongly with good health as does moderate drinking
- ○ as strongly with good health as moderate drinking

Step 1: Read the Original Sentence Carefully, Looking for Errors

This sentence contains an illogical comparison. The sentence is trying to say that abstinence does not correlate as strongly with good health as moderate drinking does. In other words, it is trying to compare abstinence to moderate drinking in terms of health impact. However, the word "with" before "moderate drinking" creates the rather bizarre comparison between good health and moderate drinking; what the sentence actually says is that abstinence correlates better with moderate drinking than it does with good health, which makes no logical sense. We rule out **(A)** and proceed to split the remaining choices.

Step 2: Scan and Group the Answer Choices

(C), **(D)**, and **(E)** retain the comparison, "as strongly," while **(B)** uses the comparison word "like" instead of "as."

Step 3: Eliminate Choices Until Only One Remains

We can eliminate **(B)** because it uses the wrong word, "like," to make a comparison between clauses (subject + verb), whereas "like" should be used only to compare nouns. **(B)** also alters the meaning of the sentence: Rather than comparing how strongly total abstinence and moderate drinking correlate with good health, **(B)** states that only one of the two behaviors correlates strongly with good health. **(C)** corrects the comparison, but "drinking" is a gerund—a verb being used as a noun—and should therefore be modified by an adjective, not the adverb "moderately." While **(E)** leaves out the word "with," it still commits the same illogical comparison as does the original sentence. Choice **(D)**, like **(C)**, fixes the comparison, this time without introducing any new mistakes. **(D)** is the correct answer.

35. **(E)**

Unlike <u>its fellow Baltic nations, Latvia and Lithuania, the economy of Estonia grew at an astonishing rate in the late 1990s, and at the end of the decade it was placed</u> on the fast track to join the European Union.

- ○ its fellow Baltic nations, Latvia and Lithuania, the economy of Estonia grew at an astonishing rate in the late 1990s, and at the end of the decade it was placed

- ○ its fellow Baltic nations, Latvia and Lithuania, Estonia grew at an astonishing rate economically in the late 1990s, and at the end of the decade earned itself a place

- ○ its fellow Baltic nations, Latvia and Lithuania, Estonia's economy grew at an astonishing rate in the late 1990s, and at the end of the decade they were placed

- ○ Latvia and Lithuania, its fellow Baltic nations, the economy of Estonia grew at an astonishing rate in the late 1990s, and at the end of the decade it was placed

- ○ its fellow Baltic nations, Latvia and Lithuania, Estonia experienced economic growth at an astonishing rate in the late 1990s, and at the end of the decade it earned a place

Step 1: Read the Original Sentence Carefully, Looking for Errors

"Unlike" signals that this sentence will contain a comparison, so we'll need to check whether that comparison is logical. In this sentence, it is not: Latvia and Lithuania are being compared to Estonia's economy. Countries can only be compared to other countries, not to economies. The correct answer will fix this illogical comparison.

Step 2: Scan and Group the Answer Choices

(A) and **(D)** compare Latvia and Lithuania to "the economy of Estonia." **(C)** compares Latvia and Lithuania to "Estonia's economy." **(B)** and **(E)** compare Latvia and Lithuania to "Estonia."

Step 3: Eliminate Choices Until Only One Remains

(A), **(C)**, and **(D)** all commit the error of comparing a country to a country's economy, so all are incorrect. **(B)** correctly compares Latvia and Lithuania to Estonia, but it unnecessarily employs a reflexive pronoun, "itself," and its use of the word "economically" sounds rather awkward. **(E)** also correctly compares Latvia and Lithuania to Estonia, this time without resorting to unnecessary or awkward constructions. Choice **(E)** is the correct answer.

EXPLANATIONS

36. **(A)**

<u>No less significant than</u> international pressures are the constraints that domestic culture and ideology impose on decision making by national political figures.

○ No less significant than

○ The things that are just as significant as

○ Just like the significant

○ Not lesser than the significance of

○ What are as significant as

Step 1: Read the Original Sentence Carefully, Looking for Errors

The original sentence contains a slightly unusual construction but is nonetheless correct. Because a comparison is made in this sentence, you should see whether the comparison is valid.

Step 2: Scan and Group the Answer Choices

There are no splits here, but be on the lookout for answer choices that alter the comparison in any way.

Step 3: Eliminate Choices Until Only One Remains

The original sentence appears to make a valid comparison between "international pressures" and "constraints," so **(A)** is correct. Eliminate **(B)** and **(E)** for being unnecessarily wordy. Eliminate **(C)** because it changes the meaning of the sentence slightly by leaving out the idea that the constraints are equally significant. Finally, eliminate **(D)** because it compares "significance" with "constraints."

37. (C)

Golden and Labrador Retrievers have enjoyed wide popularity as guide dogs because their dispositions are more suited to companion work <u>than</u> most other breeds.

○   than

○   than is true of

○   than are those of

○   in comparison to

○   as compared to

Step 1: Read the Original Sentence Carefully, Looking for Errors

Even though your ear may not catch the error in this sentence the first time you read it, the comparison in the sentence needs to compare two logically comparable things in order to be correct. Here, "dispositions" are being compared to "breeds," which is an illogical comparison.

Step 2: Scan and Group the Answer Choices

(A), **(B)**, and **(C)** begin with "than," while **(D)** and **(E)** use lengthier constructions. Note that the only way one of these can be correct is if one of them corrects the error, and none of the shorter answer choices does.

Step 3: Eliminate Choices Until Only One Remains

Because the sentence needs to compare the dispositions of Golden Retrievers and Labradors with the dispositions of other breeds, you can eliminate **(A)**, **(B)**, **(D)**, and **(E)** as none of them makes the proper comparison. Only the correct answer, **(C)**, offers a logical comparison.

EXPLANATIONS

38. (D)

Unlike other primates, which are born with <u>fully formed craniums, a newborn human baby's cranium</u> consists of eight bones that take years to fuse together fully, allowing the brain to grow much larger during those early years.

- ○ fully formed craniums, a newborn human baby's cranium
- ○ fully formed craniums, newborn human babies have craniums that
- ○ a fully formed craniums, a human baby's cranium
- ○ fully formed craniums, a human is born with a cranium that
- ○ a fully formed cranium, the cranium of a newborn human baby

Step 1: Read the Original Sentence Carefully, Looking for Errors

The word "Unlike" at the beginning of the sentence signals a comparison, which we must check for logic. To do this, we can leave out the distracting phrase between the commas: "Unlike other primates, a newborn human baby's cranium ...." Whenever we see a comparison on the GMAT, we need to make certain that the sentence compares classes of things that yield meaningful information when placed side by side. In this sentence, it would be logical to compare other primates to humans or other primates' craniums to humans' craniums. But as written, the sentence compares other primates to a human baby's cranium, which makes no logical sense. We have an error and can rule out **(A)**.

Step 2: Scan and Group the Answer Choices

(C) and **(E)** retain the comparison between other primates and a human cranium. **(B)** compares "other primates" to "newborn human babies," and **(D)** compares "other primates" to "a human."

Step 3: Eliminate Choices Until Only One Remains

We already know that **(A)** is incorrect. We can eliminate **(C)** and **(E)** because they commit the same illogical comparison as the original sentence. **(B)** logically compares "other primates" to "newborn human babies." However, reading **(B)** back into the original sentence reveals a new error: "newborn babies have craniums that consists ...." The verb "consists" is singular, so "craniums" should be singular as well. A choice that introduces a new error is incorrect, so we can rule out **(B)**. Finally, **(D)** makes a logical comparison between "other primates" and "a human," and this time, "cranium" is singular and agrees with "consists." Because **(D)** fixes the error in the original sentence without introducing any new mistakes, it is the correct answer.

39. (C)

The legal considerations that have forced some universities to revise their affirmative action admissions programs are similar to <u>the revisions that certain large businesses have recently made to their affirmative action hiring practices</u>.

- ○ the revisions that certain large businesses have recently made to their affirmative action hiring practices
- ○ the affirmative action hiring practices that certain large business recently have revised
- ○ those that have recently forced certain large businesses to revise their affirmative action hiring practices
- ○ those recent revisions that have been made by certain large businesses to their affirmative action hiring practices
- ○ what certain large businesses have done to their affirmative action hiring practices in the recent past

Step 1: Read the Original Sentence Carefully, Looking for Errors

"Are similar to" in the original sentence indicates a comparison, so you have to make sure that similar elements are being compared. Whenever you recognize a comparison, cut through the filler until you've assessed whether the elements being compared are logically and grammatically similar. This sentence begins with "legal considerations … are similar to …," so what follows should also be "legal considerations."

Step 2: Scan and Group the Answer Choices

(A) begins with "revisions." **(B)** begins with " … hiring practices." **(C)** and **(D)** begin with "those," a word that could refer to "legal considerations." **(E)** begins with "what certain large businesses have done."

Step 3: Eliminate Choices Until Only One Remains

"Revisions" and "practices" aren't comparable to "legal considerations," so eliminate **(A)** and **(B)**. Choice **(D)** begins with "those," but if you read further, you'll notice that **(D)** uses "those recent revisions," which are not comparable to "legal considerations," so eliminate **(D)**. Finally, **(E)** is unclear and doesn't provide a specific noun to compare to "legal considerations." Only **(C)** make logical sense and corrects the comparison error.

40. (E)

During the Civil War, nearly three times as many Americans lost their lives from infections that could have been prevented with antiseptic techniques <u>than</u> were killed on the battlefield.

- ○ than
- ○ than those who
- ○ than the number who
- ○ as the number who
- ○ as

Step 1: Read the Original Sentence Carefully, Looking for Errors

The underlined portion here is only one word: "than." Note that in the beginning of the sentence, the phrase "nearly three times as many" indicates a comparison. Comparisons require parallel construction. If you remove the intervening words "Americans … antiseptic techniques," the sentence would read, "nearly three times as many than." That's an incorrect construction.

Step 2: Scan and Group the Answer Choices

One choice here is between "than" in **(A)**, **(B)**, and **(C)** and "as" in **(D)** and **(E)**, so you would have to decide which one is correct even if you didn't spot the error while completing Step 1 of the Kaplan Method.

Step 3: Eliminate Choices Until Only One Remains

The correct word is "as," to complete the construction "as many … as … ." Thus **(A)**, **(B)**, and **(C)** are all out. But the comparison also requires parallel structure to "Americans lost their lives …" "The number" is not parallel to "Americans." So **(D)** needs to be eliminated in favor of **(E)**. Choice **(E)** is the correct answer.

41. (E)

When a product costs more, be it a bottle of wine or a handbag, the more likely it is to be esteemed by consumers.

- ○ When a product costs more, be it
- ○ When a product costs more, whether it is
- ○ As a product becomes more and more costly, like
- ○ The more a product costs, like
- ○ The more a product costs, whether it is

Step 1: Read the Original Sentence Carefully, Looking for Errors

The underlined segment of this sentence gives us the first half of a comparison: "A product costs more" than something. Unfortunately, the sentence fails to state what the product is being compared to. It costs more than … what? Half a comparison is definitely an error that the correct answer will have to fix. We get a clue as to the proper construction we need from the second half of the sentence. The construction "the more likely" is part of a two-part construction, similar to "not only … but also." The correct construction is "the more … the more." This sentence should read, "The more a product costs, … the more likely it is to be esteemed by consumers."

Step 2: Scan and Group the Answer Choices

(A) and **(B)** retain the partial comparison. **(C)** gets rid of the comparison with the phrase, "more and more costly." **(D)** and **(E)** use the construction we're looking for: "The more a product costs … ."

Step 3: Eliminate Choices Until Only One Remains

(A) and **(B)** are incorrect because both contain the partial comparison that we flagged as an error. We can eliminate **(C)** because while it attempts a statement of proportionality, it does not use the correct grammatical construction; the sentence needs to start with the phrase "The more." Both remaining choices use "The more," so one of them will be the correct answer. **(D)** uses "like" in place of the original "be it." The original meaning of the sentence is that it doesn't matter whether the product in question is a bottle of wine or a handbag (or something else). The use of the word "like" in **(D)** changes the meaning of the sentence. On the GMAT, "like" is used to mean "similar to," so this answer choice causes the sentence to refer only to items that are similar to wine and handbags. An answer choice that changes the meaning of the sentence cannot be correct, so the answer must be **(E)**. Indeed, **(E)** substitutes "whether it is" for "be it," so that the idea that the identity of the product makes no difference is preserved. Choice **(E)** is the correct answer.

42. (E)

Mary Shelley is widely credited <u>for the invention of a new literary genre; many scholars consider her first and only novel, *Frankenstein*, to be</u> the first science fiction story.

○　for the invention of a new literary genre; many scholars consider her first and only novel, *Frankenstein*, to be

○　for inventing a new literary genre; many scholars consider her first and only novel, *Frankenstein*, as being

○　to have invented a new literary genre; many scholars regard her first and only novel, *Frankenstein*, to be

○　with the invention of a new literary genre; many scholars regard her first and only novel, *Frankenstein*, to be

○　with the invention of a new literary genre; many scholars consider her first and only novel, *Frankenstein*,

Step 1: Read the Original Sentence Carefully, Looking for Errors

The original sentence contains an idiom error—two, in fact. The sentence says Shelley is "credited for" inventing a genre and that her book is "consider(ed) … to be" the first science fiction book.

Step 2: Scan and Group the Answer Choices

The choices have a 2-2-1 split: **(A)** and **(B)** begin with "for," **(C)** begins with "to have," and **(D)** and **(E)** begin with "with."

Step 3: Eliminate Choices Until Only One Remains

The correct idiomatic expression is "credited *with*," so **(A)**, **(B)**, and **(C)** are all wrong. Also, you should note that, although many grammarians have no problem using "consider" with "to be," on the GMAT the correct answer choice will always use "consider" without the "to be." **(D)** is wrong because the correct idiomatic expression is "regard *as*," not "regard *to be*." Only **(E)** is idiomatically correct.

EXPLANATIONS

43. **(A)**

The percentage of people aged 25–44 living alone increased abruptly between 1990 and 1995 and continued to rise more slowly over the next five years.

- O The percentage of people aged 25–44 living alone increased abruptly between 1990 and 1995 and
- O There was an abruptly increased percentage of people aged 25–44 who lived alone between 1990 and 1995 and they
- O The percentage of people aged 25–44 who lived alone increased abruptly between 1990 and 1995 and has
- O There has been an abrupt increase in the percentage of people aged 25–44 living alone between 1990 and 1995 and it
- O Between 1990 and 1995, there was an abrupt increase in the percentage of people aged 25–44 who lived alone which

Step 1: Read the Original Sentence Carefully, Looking for Errors

The original sentence sounds correct and exhibits parallel structure: "increased abruptly … and continued to rise more slowly … ." But you should check out the other choices to see whether you may have missed something.

Step 2: Scan and Group the Answer Choices

Note that **(B)**, **(D)**, and **(E)** contain "there was" or "there has been." This type of construction is rarely correct on the GMAT. Unless the other choices commit grievous errors, be prepared to eliminate these.

Step 3: Eliminate Choices Until Only One Remains

You can eliminate **(B)**, **(D)**, and **(E)** because "there" constructions ("there was," "there has been," etc.) should generally be avoided; these constructions are wordy and often turn verbs into passive voice. **(C)** is wrong here because the present perfect tense, "has continued," indicates that the action began in the past but continues into the present. Because the sentence is discussing what happened between 1995 and 2000, the simple past tense is correct. Therefore, **(A)** is in fact correct.

44. (A)

The macabre nature of *Macbeth*, together with the widespread belief that real-life tragedies have accompanied many productions, <u>has made the name of the play so dreaded that not even the least superstitious members of most casts dare</u> utter it.

- O has made the name of the play so dreaded that not even the least superstitious members of most casts dare
- O have made the name of the play so dreaded, even the least superstitious members of most casts will not dare to
- O have made the play's name sufficiently dreaded, so that even the less superstitious members of most casts will not dare to
- O have made the name of the play sufficiently dreaded, so that not even the least superstitious members of most casts dare
- O has made the name of the play is dreaded, so that even the least superstitious members of most casts dare not

Step 1: Read the Original Sentence Carefully, Looking for Errors

You should learn to ignore long phrases between commas when you first read the sentence. If you do that you'll see that the subject of the sentence, "nature," is singular, so the verb should be singular too, and "has made" fits that bill.

Step 2: Scan and Group the Answer Choices

One split here is between "has" in **(A)** and **(E)** and "have" in **(B)**, **(C)**, and **(D)**. Use that split to begin eliminating answer choices.

Step 3: Eliminate Choices Until Only One Remains

Because "has made" is the correct verb for a singular subject, eliminate **(B)**, **(C)**, and **(D)**. Eliminate **(E)** because it contains an extra verb, "is," that makes the sentence unclear. **(A)** is the only choice left, which means the sentence must be correct as written. Note that **(A)** also contains the correct construction "so dreaded … that."

45. (C)

The university's board of trustees, <u>being worried over declining student enrollments and their failing</u> to secure additional funding from the state, has formed a committee to determine what cuts need to be made to staff and programs.

- ○ being worried over declining student enrollments and their failing
- ○ worrying over declining student enrollments and also the failure
- ○ worried about declining student enrollments and the failure
- ○ in that they are worried about the decline in student enrollments and the failure
- ○ because of its worry concerning the decline of student enrollments and, as well as concerning the failure

Step 1: Read the Original Sentence Carefully, Looking for Errors

The sentence as written is wrong because the underlined portion begins with the suspicious and unnecessary "being," which is rarely correct on the GMAT. Another thing to notice is that the underlined portion contains a two-part list, so you should check for parallel structure. As written, the board is worried over (1) "declining student enrollments" and (2) "their failing to secure ..." This is not parallel. Finally, notice the original sentence's improper use of the pronoun "their." The antecedent is "board," and the members of the board are acting as a unit, so the correct pronoun would be "its." (And notice, by the way, that the non-underlined part of the sentence includes the singular verb "has." This alerts us that the plural pronoun "their" is not correct here.)

Step 2: Scan and Group the Answer Choices

All four of the viable answer choices, **(B)**, **(C)**, **(D)**, and **(E)**, correct the pronoun error and the parallel structure error—the original sentence's "their failing" is replaced in each of these choices by "the failure"—so we can turn our focus to the first part of each choice. The options are "worrying," "worried," "in that they are worried," and "because of its worry." **(D)**'s "in that they are worried" is verbose and introduces another *it/they* pronoun error, so we can eliminate it right away. Now we must decide which of the three remaining choices, **(B)**, **(C)**, and **(E)**, is the most economical and idiomatic.

Step 3: Eliminate Choices Until Only One Remains

(E)'s phrase "because of its worry" is needlessly wordy, so we can strike it out. **(B)**'s phrase "worrying over" is not idiomatic. Notice, too, that **(B)** adds a superfluous word: "also." **(C)** contains the correct idiom "worried about" and does not add any excess verbiage. **(C)** is the correct answer.

46. (E)

The United States' trade deficit with China rose in 2003 to $123 billion, <u>which is 17 percent more than the previous year</u> and more than 10 times the U.S.-China trade deficit in 1998.

- ○ which is 17 percent more than the previous year
- ○ which is 17 percent higher than it was the previous year
- ○ 17 percent higher than the previous year's figure was
- ○ an amount that is 17 percent more than the previous year was
- ○ an amount that is 17 percent higher than the previous year's figure

Step 1: Read the Original Sentence Carefully, Looking for Errors

Because the relative pronoun "which" refers to the noun that comes immediately before it, this means the underlined segment illogically compares a sum of money, "$123 billion," to "the previous year." The correct answer must compare a sum and a sum, not a sum and a year.

Step 2: Scan and Group the Answer Choices

(A) and **(B)** both start with "which." **(C)** leaves out "which," while **(D)** and **(E)** substitute "an amount that" for "which."

Step 3: Eliminate Choices Until Only One Remains

We can eliminate **(A)** because of its illogical comparison. **(B)** also screws up the comparison, thanks to its careless use of the slippery pronoun "it." Because "which" refers to "123 billion," **(B)** seems to say, nonsensically, that $123 billion is 17 percent higher than $123 billion was the previous year. **(D)** also fails to fix the illogical comparison; it compares "an amount" to "the previous year." That leaves only **(C)** and **(E)**. Both of these choices correctly compare two amounts of money. However, **(C)** adds "was" at the end, which is unnecessary and not parallel with the last part of the sentence, which does not use the verb. **(E)**, which introduces no new errors, is the correct answer.

47. (D)

The two-party political system is one <u>where the electorate gives its votes largely to only two major parties and where</u> one or the other party can usually win a majority in the legislature.

- O where the electorate gives its votes largely to only two major parties and where
- O in which the electorate largely gives only its votes to two major parties and where
- O where the electorate gives largely its votes to only two major parties and in which
- O in which the electorate gives its votes largely to only two major parties and in which
- O in which the electorate largely gives only its votes to two major parties and in which

Step 1: Read the Original Sentence Carefully, Looking for Errors

The underlined part of this sentence contains two incorrect uses of "where." On the GMAT, "where" is used correctly only if it refers to location. (For instance, "this is the café where we had lunch last week.") In the original sentence, "where" refers, both times, to the "two-party political system." A system is not a location, so we have an error, and we know that **(A)** is incorrect.

Step 2: Scan and Group the Answer Choices

Of the remaining choices, **(B)** substitutes "in which" for the first "where," but it retains the second "where." **(C)** keeps the first "where" and substitutes "in which" for the second. **(D)** and **(E)** substitute "in which" for both uses of "where" in the original sentence.

Step 3: Eliminate Choices Until Only One Remains

We can eliminate **(B)** and **(C)** because each still contains an incorrect usage of "where" to refer to something other than a location. That leaves **(D)** and **(E)** as the remaining contestants. The difference between them is that **(E)** moves the placement of "only," so instead of "gives its votes largely to only two major parties," the sentence now reads, "gives only its votes to two major parties." It's a small change, but it alters the meaning of the sentence dramatically. **(E)** makes it sound as if the electorate had other things besides its votes to give to the parties, which is not a meaning implied by the original sentence. We're left with **(D)** as the correct answer, since it fixes the original mistake without introducing any new errors and without changing the meaning of the original sentence.

48. (C)

Most financial advisers <u>recommend that stock portfolios should be reviewed</u> at least once a year, if only to make sure that changes do not need to be made.

- ○ recommend that stock portfolios should be reviewed
- ○ recommend you to review your stock portfolio
- ○ recommend that stock portfolios be reviewed
- ○ are recommending that stock portfolios are reviewed
- ○ have a recommendation to review stock portfolios

Step 1: Read the Original Sentence Carefully, Looking for Errors

Underlined verbs demand our attention. The subject of "recommend" is "advisers." Subject and verb are both plural, so there is no subject-verb agreement error. However, verbs describing orders and recommendations must be followed by "that," a new subject, and another verb in the infinitive, but without the "to." In this sentence, the phrase that follows "recommend" contains the extra, unnecessary word "should." Choice **(A)** will not be the correct answer.

Step 2: Scan and Group the Answer Choices

Of the remaining choices, **(C)** and **(D)** preserve "that," while **(B)** and **(E)** leave it out.

Step 3: Eliminate Choices Until Only One Remains

We can eliminate **(B)** and **(E)** because orders and recommendations must be followed by "that." Moreover, "have a recommendation" in **(E)** is wordy and awkward. **(D)** uses "that," but it introduces a new error: Instead of "be," it uses "are." Only **(C)** remains and must be correct. Indeed, **(C)** has exactly the right grammatical structure for a recommendation: "that ... be reviewed." Choice **(C)** is the correct answer.

49. (D)

The United States <u>would achieve a 10 percent reduction in gasoline consumption, if Congress will raise</u> fuel economy standards to 31.3 miles per gallon for passenger cars and to 24.5 mpg for light trucks.

- ○ would achieve a 10 percent reduction in gasoline consumption, if Congress will raise
- ○ will achieve a 10 percent reduction in gasoline consumption, if Congress were to raise
- ○ will have achieved a 10 percent reduction in gasoline consumption, if Congress will raise
- ○ would achieve a 10 percent reduction in gasoline consumption, if Congress were to raise
- ○ would achieve a 10 percent reduction in gasoline consumption, if Congress were raising

Step 1: Read the Original Sentence Carefully, Looking for Errors

The word "if" in the underlined part of this sentence signals a hypothetical situation, so we need the subjunctive mood; we must use "were" and "would." "Would achieve" is correct, but "will raise" is not. We can rule out **(A)**.

Step 2: Scan and Group the Answer Choices

(B) and **(C)** start with "will." **(D)** and **(E)** start with "would."

Step 3: Eliminate Choices Until Only One Remains

(B) is incorrect because "will achieve" is ordinary future tense, not subjunctive. Similarly, **(C)** is incorrect because "will have achieved" is also not subjunctive. **(D)** and **(E)** both use "would achieve," which is the proper subjunctive mood. The difference between them comes at the end. **(D)** uses "if Congress were to raise," while **(E)** has "if Congress were raising." The final phrase in **(E)** sounds a bit odd and is in fact grammatically incorrect. The proper subjunctive construction calls for the verb that follows "were" to be in the infinitive, not the *-ing* form. Choice **(E)** is thus incorrect, and **(D)**, which contains the proper "were"-plus-infinitive construction, is the correct answer.

EXPLANATIONS

50. (C)

Because the moon's distance from Earth varies, <u>so the gravitational pull between the two bodies differ</u>, as do the size and times of oceanic tides.

- ○ so the gravitational pull between the two bodies differ
- ○ so the gravitational pull between the two bodies differs
- ○ the gravitational pull between the two bodies differs
- ○ therefore the gravitational pull between the two bodies differ
- ○ therefore the gravitational pull between the two bodies differs

Step 1: Read the Original Sentence Carefully, Looking for Errors

Two clauses need to be connected by one, and only one, conjunction. This sentence connects its introductory clause to its main clause with two conjunctions, "because" and "so." That's one conjunction too many. Moreover, this sentence contains a subject-verb agreement error. The subject of "differ" is "gravitational pull," which is singular. The verb should be "differs." The correct answer will fix both these mistakes without introducing any new ones.

Step 2: Scan and Group the Answer Choices

The choices group naturally with respect to the conjunction. **(A)** and **(B)** retain "so." **(D)** and **(E)** substitute "therefore," while **(C)** eliminates the conjunction entirely.

Step 3: Eliminate Choices Until Only One Remains

We've already determined that "Because" at the beginning of the sentence is the only conjunction we need to connect the first and second clauses of this sentence. **(A)**, **(B)**, **(D)**, and **(E)** all have an extra conjunction and are therefore all incorrect. Only **(C)** eliminates the superfluous conjunction. It also changes "differ" to "differs," so it fixes both mistakes and is the correct answer.

51. (A)

With a boiling temperature of –195.8 degrees Celsius, <u>nitrogen composes approximately 78 percent of the volume of the atmosphere</u>.

○ nitrogen composes approximately 78 percent of the volume of the atmosphere

○ nitrogen is composing the volume of 78 percent of the atmosphere

○ the atmosphere is approximately 78 percent nitrogen, as measured by volume

○ nitrogen is composed of 78 percent of the atmosphere's volume

○ the atmosphere is composed, in terms of volume, of 78 percent nitrogen

Step 1: Read the Original Sentence Carefully, Looking for Errors

The introductory phrase followed by a comma indicates that this question is testing modifiers. So you need to be sure that the subject being modified is in the right position relative to the modifier. Since the modifier in this case is "With a boiling temperature of … ," the subject being modified must be something that has a boiling point, and it must come right after the comma. "Nitrogen" has a boiling point and is the logical subject of the modifier. The rest of the underlined portion is correct as well, but scan the choices just in case another choice somehow expresses this idea more concisely.

Step 2: Scan and Group the Answer Choices

(A), **(B)**, and **(D)** begin with "nitrogen," while **(C)** and **(E)** begin with "the atmosphere."

Step 3: Eliminate Choices Until Only One Remains

Based on the opening modifier, eliminate **(C)** and **(E)**, since it doesn't make sense for the atmosphere to have a boiling point. **(B)** has a strange construction ("is composing the volume of") and should be eliminated on that basis. Also eliminate **(D)**, which makes it sound as though nitrogen itself contains 78 percent of the atmosphere's volume (how is that possible?), when the sentence intends to communicate that 78 percent of the volume of the atmosphere is *made up of* nitrogen. Since no other choice expresses the main idea of the sentence more clearly and more correctly than the original, **(A)** is correct.

52. (D)

At more than 800 pages in length, the <u>novelist's life stands revealed in the new biography, which sets the standard for research</u>.

- ○ novelist's life stands revealed in the new biography, which sets the standard for research
- ○ new biography is setting standards of research on the novelist's life
- ○ standard for research has been set by a new biography on the novelist
- ○ new biography about the novelist sets the standard for research
- ○ novelist's life is revealed in a standard-setting new biography

Step 1: Read the Original Sentence Carefully, Looking for Errors

The opening phrase of this sentence is a modifier, and modifiers on the GMAT always need to be placed as close to what they modify as possible. When you see such opening phrases, ask yourself, "what in the sentence is this phrase describing?" Here, the only thing in the sentence that could be more than 800 pages in length is "the new biography," so that should come right after the comma.

Step 2: Scan and Group the Answer Choices

In GMAT sentences that open with a modifying phrase set off by a comma, what comes after the comma is crucial. **(A)** and **(E)** begin with the "novelist's life," **(B)** and **(D)** begin with the "new biography," and **(C)** begins with the "standard for research …."

Step 3: Eliminate Choices Until Only One Remains

Get rid of **(A)**, **(C)**, and **(E)**, because none of them has the correct subject for the modifier. Only **(B)** and **(D)** use the correct subject after the phrase. But the verb tense in **(B)** changes the original sense of the sentence ("is setting" would indicate that the process of setting the standard hasn't yet been completed, which doesn't make sense). Only **(D)** has the correct subject and the correct tense.

53. (D)

Because women buy approximately 80 percent of ties sold in the United States, <u>they are often displayed</u> near perfume or women's clothing departments.

- ○ they are often displayed
- ○ ties are often being displayed
- ○ the displaying of ties is often
- ○ ties are often displayed
- ○ they often can be found

Step 1: Read the Original Sentence Carefully, Looking for Errors

As you read more and more GMAT Sentence Correction questions, you'll develop a keen sense of the words that are the biggest "troublemakers." One of them is the pronoun "they," a pronoun that is often used ambiguously in everyday speech but must have a clear antecedent on the GMAT. The problem with this sentence is that it's unclear whether the pronoun "they" refers to "women" or "ties." Of course, logic dictates that it must refer to the ties, but the structure of the sentence doesn't make this explicit.

Step 2: Scan and Group the Answer Choices

(A) and **(E)** use "they." **(B)**, **(C)**, and **(D)** don't contain pronouns, but these choices contain largely the same words in very different arrangements.

Step 3: Eliminate Choices Until Only One Remains

Once you spot a pronoun ambiguity error, keep in mind that the right answer may very well dispense with pronouns altogether. Because "they" is being used so ambiguously here, eliminate **(A)** and **(E)**. Eliminate **(C)** because of its awkward construction ("the displaying of ties" turns the verb "display" into a gerund, which the GMAT is not fond of). **(B)** is out because it needlessly uses another problematic GMAT word—"being." Only **(D)** clears up the ambiguous pronoun in a correct, concise way.

54. (C)

Although the British were responsible for the early European settlement <u>of both Australia and the United States, Australia is having much closer political and cultural links with Britain than the United States is having</u>.

- ○ of both Australia and the United States, Australia is having much closer political and cultural links with Britain than the United States is having
- ○ in both Australia and the United States, they are closer in their political and cultural links in Australia than in the United States
- ○ of both nations, Australia has much closer political and cultural links to Britain than the United States has
- ○ in both nations, Australia is politically and culturally linked to Britain in a much closer fashion than the United States
- ○ of both Australia and the United States, they have much closer political and cultural links to it than the United States has

Step 1: Read the Original Sentence Carefully, Looking for Errors

Note the strange verb tense—present progressive—used in the underlined portion. The *-ing* tense is usually wrong on the GMAT and is certainly not correct if the intention is to express a permanent state of affairs, as is the case here. Also, in most cases, the present progressive can be ditched in favor of the more concise present tense. (Why use "is having" when you can use "has"?) The only time that the GMAT tends to use the progressive tense in the correct answer is when doing so changes a misplaced modifier to a verb. (Example: "The dog walked down the street, which was carrying a stick" should actually be "the dog walked down the street, carrying a stick.") Here, there's no good reason for the verb construction "is having," so it's incorrect.

Step 2: Scan and Group the Answer Choices

As you scan, you might notice that the sentence is also testing an idiom issue. **(A)**, **(C)**, and **(E)** all begin with "of," while **(B)** and **(D)** begin with "in." This difference forces you to decide which one is correct, even if you hadn't thought of it while reading the original sentence.

Step 3: Eliminate Choices Until Only One Remains

The correct idiom is "settlement of," not "settlement in," so eliminate **(B)** and **(D)**. The odd choice of verb tense in the original sentence disqualifies **(A)**. Finally, **(E)** can be eliminated because it includes the pronouns "it" and "they," which make the sentence ambiguous. Only **(C)** corrects the verb tense and does so in a clear, concise manner.

55. (E)

Each of the major setbacks the Germans suffered in June 1944—the fall of Rome, the collapse of Army Group Center on the Eastern Front, and the breaching of the Atlantic Wall at Normandy—were powerful shocks signaling the inability of the German war machine to compete on multiple fronts.

- ○ Each of the major setbacks the Germans suffered in June 1944—the fall of Rome, the collapse of Army Group Center on the Eastern Front, and the breaching of the Atlantic Wall at Normandy—were powerful shocks

- ○ The fall of Rome, the collapse of Army Group Center on the Eastern Front, and the breaching of the Atlantic Wall at Normandy—each of them major setbacks the Germans suffered in June 1944—were powerful shocks

- ○ Powerful shocks—the fall of Rome, the collapse of Army Group Center on the Eastern Front, and the breaching of the Atlantic Wall at Normandy—each a major setback for the Germans in June 1944, was such

- ○ The major setbacks suffered by the Germans in June 1944—the fall of Rome, the collapse of Army Group Center on the Eastern Front, and the breaching of the Atlantic Wall at Normandy—each were powerful shocks

- ○ Each of the major setbacks the Germans suffered in June 1944—the fall of Rome, the collapse of Army Group Center on the Eastern Front, and the breach of the Atlantic Wall at Normandy—was a powerful shock

Step 1: Read the Original Sentence Carefully, Looking for Errors

Note that this question is testing two classic GMAT Sentence Correction concepts. The first, parallel structure, was probably easier to spot since the sentence uses dashes to set off a list of the setbacks that the Germans faced. Those elements—(1) "the fall," (2) "the collapse," and (3) "the breaching"—are not parallel, since "breaching" is a gerund. Also, the use of a lengthy phrase between dashes should signal this sentence's attempt to disguise a subject-verb agreement error. The subject of the sentence is not "setbacks" but "each," which is singular, so the verb "were" doesn't agree in number with this subject. (The subject of a sentence will never appear in a prepositional phrase, as "setbacks" does.)

Step 2: Scan and Group the Answer Choices

Because of the verb issue, see if you can scan the choices quickly to note the verb each uses. **(B)** and **(D)**, like the original sentence, use "were," so unless one of these choices changes the subject of the sentence to something plural, these can probably be eliminated.

Step 3: Eliminate Choices Until Only One Remains

Get rid of **(A)** right away because of both errors present there. **(B)**, **(C)**, and **(D)** all fail to correct the parallelism error, so they can all be eliminated. Only **(E)** has parallel structure and uses the singular verb "was." (Note that **(D)** also continues to use "each ... were" and **(C)** is incredibly confusing and poorly constructed. Often the GMAT will put multiple errors in an underlined portion to give you more than one opportunity to eliminate wrong answers.) Thus, choice **(E)** is the correct answer.

56. (C)

Adult pelicans store fish in a deep, expandable pouch below the lower mandible, <u>of which the young feed</u>.

- ○ of which the young feed
- ○ being for the feeding of the young
- ○ from which the young feed
- ○ that it feeds the young from
- ○ young feed from

Step 1: Read the Original Sentence Carefully, Looking for Errors

This underlined portion is quite short, but a quick reading indicates that this question is testing idiomatic usage. Young pelicans do not feed "of" something, as the original sentence says. They feed "from" something.

Step 2: Scan and Group the Answer Choices

As you scan the choices, try to spot constructions and individual words that are not likely to be correct, such as "being" in **(B)**.

Step 3: Eliminate Choices Until Only One Remains

To "feed of" something is incorrect, so **(A)** is out. Eliminate **(B)** because it is way too wordy and uses the disfavored "being" construction. Eliminate **(D)** and **(E)** because "from" is left dangling at the end of the sentence, and it is considered poor form on the GMAT to end a sentence with a preposition. Furthermore, **(D)** uses the singular pronoun "it" to stand in for plural "pelicans," and **(E)** hardly makes sense as written; it merely tacks on a separate clause with no conjunction to connect it to the rest of the sentence. Only **(C)** is both idiomatically and grammatically correct.

57. (B)

Anthony Trollope, one of the most famous English novelists of the nineteenth century, also <u>wrote travel books, some based on his undertaking of journeys</u> while an employee of the postal service.

- ○ wrote travel books, some based on his undertaking of journeys
- ○ wrote travel books, some based on journeys he undertook
- ○ undertook journeys, having based travel books on them
- ○ based travel books on journeys undertaken
- ○ wrote travel books, some based on journeys which he was to undertake

Step 1: Read the Original Sentence Carefully, Looking for Errors

The beginning of the underlined portion contains the verb "wrote," which is correct here given the appropriateness of the simple past tense. The problem with this sentence is one of usage and style. As we have seen, the GMAT disfavors *-ing* constructions. The phrase "based on his undertaking" is needlessly awkward.

Step 2: Scan and Group the Answer Choices

There are no discernible splits here. Since "wrote" is correct, though, be suspicious of **(C)** and **(D)**, which change the verb to something different.

Step 3: Eliminate Choices Until Only One Remains

Because of the awkward construction in the original sentence, eliminate **(A)**. Eliminate **(C)**, which makes it sound as though Trollope based the travel books on the journeys before he took the journeys. Similarly, eliminate **(E)** because the travel books were based on journeys he had already undertaken, not on journeys he would undertake in the future. Eliminate **(D)**, which makes it unclear who is actually undertaking the journeys. Only **(B)** keeps the meaning of the sentence intact while adhering to GMAT style. Thus, choice **(B)** is the correct answer.

EXPLANATIONS

58. (B)

A federal government survey taken in 1997 showed that during the 12 months preceding the survey, 36 percent of the United States population had tried marijuana, cocaine, or other illicit drugs, 71 percent of the population <u>were smoking cigarettes, and 82 percent</u> tried alcoholic beverages.

- ○ were smoking cigarettes, and 82 percent
- ○ had smoked cigarettes, and 82 percent had
- ○ smoked cigarettes, and that 82 percent
- ○ smoked cigarettes, and 82 percent had
- ○ will be smoking cigarettes, and 82 percent

Step 1: Read the Original Sentence Carefully, Looking for Errors

This question is testing parallel structure: Similar elements must be in a similar form. Here you have three statistics being compared, and the one that is not underlined reads "36 percent … had … ." Therefore, the other two statistics must be in the same form.

Step 2: Scan and Group the Answer Choices

Note the variety of verb tenses: **(A)** uses "were smoking," **(B)** uses "had smoked," **(C)** and **(D)** use "smoked," and **(E)** uses "will be smoking."

Step 3: Eliminate Choices Until Only One Remains

"Had smoked" is correct for two reasons. First of all, it's the past perfect tense, which should always be used to describe actions occurring before other actions in the past. Here, before the survey was *taken* in 1997, people *had used* drugs, cigarettes, and alcohol. Second, "had smoked" is parallel to the elements of the sentence that are not underlined and that therefore cannot be changed. Eliminate **(A)**, **(C)**, **(D)**, and **(E)** because they use tenses that don't make sense given the sequence of events in the sentence and because they do not put similar elements in a similar form. Only choice **(B)** corrects both problems.

EXPLANATIONS

59. (C)

Like Art Nouveau jewelry designers, the <u>Art Deco movement used art materials suitable for expressing</u> the new stylistic language of the 1920s, one dominated by an interplay of geometric forms.

- ○ Art Deco movement used art materials suitable for expressing
- ○ Art Deco movement was expressed through the use of materials suitable for the
- ○ artists of the Art Deco movement used materials suitable for expressing
- ○ Art Deco movement's materials were used by artists to suitably express
- ○ artists of the Art Deco movement also used suitable materials for the expression of

Step 1: Read the Original Sentence Carefully, Looking for Errors

As soon as you see "like" at the beginning of the sentence, know that a comparison is being made. The GMAT is fond of testing your ability to distinguish between logical and illogical comparisons. As written, the sentence compares "Art Nouveau jewelry designers" to "the Art Deco movement," which is an illogical comparison. The beginning of the underlined portion will need to be changed to something more comparable to "jewelry designers."

Step 2: Scan and Group the Answer Choices

(A) and **(B)** begin with "Art Deco movement," **(C)** and **(E)** begin with "artists of the Art Deco movement," and **(D)** begins with "Art Deco movement's materials." Only one of these beginnings will be correct.

Step 3: Eliminate Choices Until Only One Remains

"Artists of the Art Deco movement" is correct, since "artists" can properly be compared to "jewelry designers" in the beginning of the sentence. Therefore, eliminate **(A)**, **(B)**, and **(D)**. Then eliminate **(E)** because "also" here is redundant (since the sentence already begins with "like") and because it is less concise than **(C)**, which is the only choice that remains.

EXPLANATIONS

60. (C)

Amtrak, a government-owned corporation, schedules passenger rail service, <u>payments to privately owned firms to run trains, and bears all administrative costs, such as</u> those incurred by the purchase of new equipment and by the sale of tickets.

- ○ payments to privately owned firms to run trains, and bears all administrative costs, such as
- ○ pays privately owned firms to run trains, and is bearing all administrative costs, such as
- ○ pays privately owned firms to run trains, and bears all administrative costs, such as
- ○ pays privately owned firms to run trains, and bears all administrative costs, being inclusive of
- ○ pays privately owned firms to run trains, and the bearer of all costs of administration, for example

Step 1: Read the Original Sentence Carefully, Looking for Errors

The sentence presents a list of Amtrak's responsibilities. The first one is a verb in the present tense, "schedules," and this verb isn't underlined, so the other two elements in the list must be parallel to this form. As it stands, "payments" is not parallel with "schedules" and "bears."

Step 2: Scan and Group the Answer Choices

Every choice except for **(A)** uses "pays." Furthermore, **(A)**, **(C)**, and **(D)** use "bears," while **(B)** uses "is bearing" and **(E)** uses "the bearer."

Step 3: Eliminate Choices Until Only One Remains

Because of the original parallelism error, eliminate **(A)**. Eliminate **(B)** and **(E)** because they change the verb tense in the second part of the clause from "bears" to a non-parallel construction. Finally, eliminate **(D)** because "being inclusive of" is wordy and awkward and contains the oft-incorrect "being." Choice **(C)** has all elements parallel and, thus, is the correct answer.

61. (A)

In feudal Korea, <u>cattle were traditionally used as beasts of burden, rather than as a food source, and fish were</u> the primary source of protein in the typical diet.

- ○ cattle were traditionally used as beasts of burden, rather than as a food source, and fish were
- ○ cattle were being used as beasts of burden, rather than as a food source, and fish were providing
- ○ cattle were traditionally used as beasts of burden, rather than a food source, with fish being
- ○ the traditional use of cattle was as beasts of burden, rather than for the provision of food, and fish were
- ○ cattle were traditionally used for beasts of burden, rather than for a food source, and fish were

Step 1: Read the Original Sentence Carefully, Looking for Errors

When reading the sentence, you may have noticed that the sentence uses passive voice in the beginning of the underlined portion ("cattle were ... used"). Normally, the GMAT does not prefer to use passive voice because it is wordier and takes the focus off the person/thing completing the action of the sentence. In order to select a better alternative, though, you'll need to pinpoint the specific people who used the cattle as beasts of burden.

Step 2: Scan and Group the Answer Choices

(A), **(B)**, **(C)**, and **(E)** all continue to use passive voice in the beginning of the underlined portion. **(D)** avoids this in favor of the wordy "the traditional use of cattle was as ... ." None of the sentences actually make clear who is completing the action described. Without a clear way to eliminate using passive voice to group the answer choices, we must evaluate them one by one, eliminating those that contain identifiable flaws.

Step 3: Eliminate Choices Until Only One Remains

Because the sentence discusses traditional uses, all verbs should be in the past tense. Eliminate **(B)** and **(C)** because they use the incorrect *-ing* verb tense in the second part of the sentence; **(B)** uses "were providing" at the end, which is awkward, and **(C)** contains "being," which is rarely correct on the GMAT. Eliminate **(D)** because it is overly wordy; whenever there is some other answer choice that expresses the same idea just as correctly but with fewer words, select that answer. Eliminate **(E)** because it incorrectly substitutes "used for" for "used as." The sentence is correct as written, making **(A)** the answer.

62. (E)

The term "support staff" is often used to describe employees <u>that perform lower-level tasks but also are providing</u> essential administrative duties for executive-level managers.

- ○ that perform lower-level tasks but also are providing
- ○ performing lower-level tasks but also providing
- ○ who perform lower-level tasks, but are also providing
- ○ that performs lower-level tasks but also provide
- ○ who perform lower-level tasks but also provide

Step 1: Read the Original Sentence Carefully, Looking for Errors

Always pay close attention to the beginnings of underlined portions—these beginnings are not chosen at random. The underlined portion of this sentence begins with "that." Looking at what comes before, you should notice that the previous word, "employees," requires the pronoun "who" on the GMAT, since the noun "employees" refers to people. Also, the verb tenses of the elements that are being compared should be the same, and here, "perform" doesn't match "are providing."

Step 2: Scan and Group the Answer Choices

(A) and (D) begin with "that." (C) and (E) begin with "who." (B) gets rid of the pronoun altogether and begins with "performing."

Step 3: Eliminate Choices Until Only One Remains

The modifier should begin with "who" rather than "that," so (A) and (D) should be eliminated. Get rid of (B) because there is no need to use the progressive verb tense ("performing" and "providing") when the simple present tense conveys the idea clearly. Eliminate (C) because the verb forms are not parallel. Choice (E) is correct because it uses the pronoun "who" and the verbs are parallel, both using the simple present tense.

EXPLANATIONS

63. **(A)**

National Women's History Month <u>began as a single week and as a local event when, in 1978, Sonoma County, California, sponsored</u> a women's history week to promote the teaching of women's history—a neglected subject in elementary and high school curricula at that time.

- O   began as a single week and as a local event when, in 1978, Sonoma County, California, sponsored
- O   began as a single week local event sponsoring, in Sonoma County, California,
- O   begins with a single week in 1978 sponsoring the local Sonoma County, California of
- O   will have began in 1978 as a single week local event when Sonoma County, California was in sponsorship of
- O   was begun in 1978 when, in Sonoma County, California, there was to be a sponsorship of

Step 1: Read the Original Sentence Carefully, Looking for Errors

From the beginning of the underlined portion, you can tell that this question tests verb tenses and clarity. Since the sentence discusses something that happened in 1978, all verbs should be in the past tense, and the structure of the sentence should reflect the facts that National Women's History Month was both a single week and a local event and that it was sponsored by Sonoma County. All of that information is clearly reflected in the question stem, so it is most likely correct. However, it is important to check all the answer choices to make sure that none of them are more concise, especially in such a long sentence.

Step 2: Scan and Group the Answer Choices

The most obvious difference in the answer choices is in their beginnings. **(A)** and **(B)** use "began," while the remaining choices use a variety of tenses ranging from present in **(C)** to future perfect in **(D)** to a passive construction in **(E)**.

Step 3: Eliminate Choices Until Only One Remains

Eliminate **(B)** because it does not make it clear that Sonoma County sponsored the event. Eliminate **(C)** both because it uses the incorrect verb tense and because it suggests that the single week sponsors Sonoma County. Eliminate **(D)** because it uses the incorrect verb tense. Eliminate **(E)** because "there was to be a sponsorship" is awkward and wordy. This leaves choice **(A)** as the correct answer.

64. **(D)**

People with schizophrenia experience miscarriages at a higher rate of frequency than people without schizophrenia, whose overactive immune systems tend to be indiscriminately rejecting the foreign DNA of the fetus.

- ○ People with schizophrenia experience miscarriages at a higher rate of frequency than people without schizophrenia, whose overactive immune systems tend to be indiscriminately rejecting

- ○ Miscarriages are more common among people with schizophrenia than among people without schizophrenia, being that their overactive immune systems tend to indiscriminately reject

- ○ Miscarriages are more common between people with schizophrenia than they are between people without schizophrenia because the overactive immune systems of people with schizophrenia tend to be indiscriminately rejecting

- ○ The miscarriage rate of people with schizophrenia is higher than the rate for people without schizophrenia because the former's overactive immune systems tend to reject

- ○ People with schizophrenia have more common miscarriages than do people without schizophrenia, because their immune systems tend to indiscriminately reject

Step 1: Read the Original Sentence Carefully, Looking for Errors

The original sentence uses the pronoun "whose" next to "people without schizophrenia," but read closely: Are they the ones who have the overactive immune systems? No, that would be the people with schizophrenia, because their overactive immune systems are causing them to miscarry more frequently. Therefore, the original sentence doesn't make sense and will need to be changed.

Step 2: Scan and Group the Answer Choices

It's hard to find splits here, and the choices are long, but watch for whether the answer choices will continue to use "whose" and where they will place that pronoun. There is one noticeable split: **(A)** and **(C)** end with "rejecting" while **(B)**, **(D)**, and **(E)** all end with "reject."

Step 3: Eliminate Choices Until Only One Remains

The sentence as written does not properly express its meaning, so **(A)** is out. Eliminate **(C)** because of its misuse of the word "between" and its use of the wordy "tend to be indiscriminately rejecting." Eliminate **(B)** because of the awkward "being that" construction and its ambiguous use of the pronoun "their." Eliminate **(E)** because the pronoun "their" is ambiguous and could refer to either group. Only **(D)** expresses the sentence's meaning clearly and concisely.

65. (A)

Working with musician Stevie Wonder as a musical adviser, Ray Kurzweil developed what is now the preferred medium for creating nearly all music for today's commercial albums, films, and television: a computer-based instrument capable of <u>reproducing musical sounds of a quality once thought to be</u> possible only on grand pianos and other acoustic instruments.

- ○ reproducing musical sounds of a quality once thought to be
- ○ reproducing musical sounds with a quality as were once thought to be
- ○ reproducing in musical sounds a quality that was once thought to be
- ○ reproduction of musical sounds whose quality is the same as what were once thought to be
- ○ reproduction of musical sounds at a quality once thought of as

Step 1: Read the Original Sentence Carefully, Looking for Errors

This is a long sentence, but the colon indicates that what comes after the colon is simply going to explain more about what comes before the colon, so let's just focus on what comes after the colon, since that's where the underlined portion is. The original sentence may have sounded just fine to you. Before selecting **(A)**, though, make sure none of the other choices expresses the idea more clearly and concisely.

Step 2: Scan and Group the Answer Choices

(A) and **(B)** begin with "reproducing musical sounds," **(C)** begins with "reproducing in musical sounds," and **(D)** and **(E)** begin with "reproduction of musical sounds." It appears that this sentence is testing idiomatic constructions.

Step 3: Eliminate Choices Until Only One Remains

The original sentence is correct as written, making **(A)** the correct answer. It contains the correct constructions: "capable of reproducing ... sounds of a quality once thought to be possible ... ." In **(B)**, "with a quality" changes the sentence to mean that the instrument possesses the "quality," when it's the quality of the *sounds* that's discussed here; furthermore, "as were once" is unidiomatic in the sentence. **(C)** unnecessarily introduces "in" and "that was." Extraneous words are a sign of an incorrect answer in GMAT Sentence Correction questions. **(D)** and **(E)** introduce the awkward construction "capable of reproduction of." **(D)** is also extremely wordy, and **(E)** also includes the unidiomatic "at a quality" and "once thought of as."

66. (A)

Twenty years ago, only 6 percent of students at Dunmore College who intended to major in chemistry were women; today that figure is <u>at least as high as 40 percent</u>.

- ○ at least as high as 40 percent
- ○ higher than at least 40 percent
- ○ higher by 40 percent at the least
- ○ 40 percent high or more
- ○ more higher than 40 percent

Step 1: Read the Original Sentence Carefully, Looking for Errors

Comparisons are being tested in this sentence (your hint is the use of the words "at least as high" and the words "higher" and "more" throughout the answer choices). Here you are looking for the construction that makes the comparison as clear and correct as possible. This sentence compares the previous figure, or "6 percent," with today's figure, so you want something that is as similar in structure as possible to "6 percent."

Step 2: Scan and Group the Answer Choices

The comparison sounds good as is, but scan the choices for the ways in which the choices use other comparative words like "higher" (as in **(B)**, **(C)**, and **(E)**) and "more" (as in **(D)** and **(E)**).

Step 3: Eliminate Choices Until Only One Remains

(B) is awkward and redundant; it doesn't make sense to have both "higher than" and "at least" next to each other. **(C)** changes the meaning of the sentence by saying "higher *by* 40 percent," which means something different from "higher *than* 40 percent." **(D)** introduces the awkward and confusing "40 percent high," which is hard to decipher. Finally, **(E)** uses the egregious construction "more higher." The best choice is **(A)**, "at least as high as 40 percent."

GMAT BY THE NUMBERS: SENTENCE CORRECTION

Now that you've learned how to approach Sentence Correction questions on the GMAT, let's add one more dimension to your understanding of how they work.

Take a moment to try the following question. The next page features performance data from thousands of people who have studied with Kaplan over the decades. Through analyzing this data, we will show you how to approach questions like this one most effectively and how to avoid similarly tempting wrong answer choice types on Test Day.

The European Union announced that cod and mackerel are the only fish that <u>exceeds their new requirements for dioxin level and that they allow</u> fishermen to catch.

- O exceeds their new requirements for dioxin level and that they allow
- O exceed its new requirements for dioxin level and that they allow
- O exceeds its new requirements for dioxin level and that it allows
- O exceed its new requirements for dioxin level and that it allows
- O exceed their new requirements for dioxin level and that they allow

EXPLANATION

Attention to the Right Detail and Pattern Recognition are both essential to success on Sentence Correction questions. You want to check the sentence very carefully for errors, giving special consideration to the recurring patterns that the GMAT testmaker is so fond of. In this sentence, there are two underlined pronouns plus an underlined verb. Both underlined pronouns, "their" and "they," refer to the European Union, which is a singular noun. These pronouns are therefore incorrect; the sentence should use "its" and "it," respectively. Only **(C)** and **(D)** get both pronouns right, so one of these choices has to be the correct answer. The difference between **(C)** and **(D)** is the use of "exceeds" versus "exceed." Since there are two kinds of fish, "cod and mackerel," you need the plural verb. Choice **(D)** is correct.

QUESTION STATISTICS

2% of test takers choose **(A)**

6% of test takers choose **(B)**

14% of test takers choose **(C)**

56% of test takers choose **(D)**

22% of test takers choose **(E)**

Sample size = 4,437

Note that the two most popular wrong answer choices, **(C)** and **(E)**, each correct one of the two errors in the sentence but not both. Many test takers will spot an answer choice that fixes the one mistake they were scanning for and think, "Aha—that's the answer!" and move on without actually reading the answer choice back into the sentence. The testmaker is aware of this tendency. So beware of trap answers that correct just one of two or more errors, as well as trap answers that fix one mistake but introduce another. Always read your choice back into the sentence. It only takes a few seconds and prevents careless mistakes.

MORE GMAT BY THE NUMBERS ...

To see more questions with answer choice statistics, be sure to review the full-length CATs in your Online Center.

PART FOUR

Quantitative Section and Strategies

CHAPTER 9

Quantitative Section Overview

- Composition of the Quantitative Section
- What the Quantitative Section Tests
- Pacing on the Quantitative Section
- How the Quantitative Section Is Scored
- Core Competencies on the Quantitative Section

COMPOSITION OF THE QUANTITATIVE SECTION

Slightly fewer than half of the multiple-choice questions that count toward your overall score appear in the Quantitative (math) section. You'll have 75 minutes to answer 37 Quantitative questions in two formats: Problem Solving and Data Sufficiency. These two types of questions are mingled throughout the Quantitative section, so you never know what's coming next. Here's what you can expect to see:

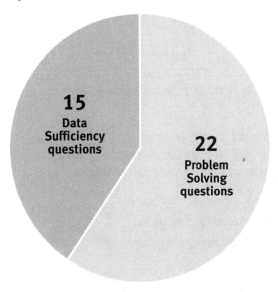

The Approximate Mix of Questions on the GMAT Quantitative Section:
22 Problem Solving Questions and 15 Data Sufficiency Questions

You may see more of one question type and fewer of the other. Don't worry. It's likely just a slight difference in the types of "experimental" questions you get.

WHAT THE QUANTITATIVE SECTION TESTS

MATH CONTENT KNOWLEDGE

Of course, the GMAT tests your math skills. So you will have to work with concepts that you may not have used for the last few years. Even if you use math all the time, it's probably been a while since you were unable to use a calculator or computer to perform computations. So refreshing your fundamental math skills is definitely a crucial part of your prep.

But the range of math topics tested is actually fairly limited. The GMAT covers only the math that U.S. students usually see during or before their first two years of high school. No trigonometry, no advanced algebra, no calculus. As you progress in your GMAT prep, you'll see that the same concepts are tested again and again in remarkably similar ways.

Areas of math content tested on the GMAT include the following: algebra, arithmetic, number properties, proportions, basic statistics, certain specific math formulas, and geometry. Algebra and arithmetic are the most commonly tested topics—they are tested either directly or indirectly on a majority of GMAT Quantitative questions. Geometry questions account for fewer than one-sixth of all GMAT math questions, but they can often be among the most challenging for test takers, so you may benefit from thorough review and practice with these concepts.

A large part of what makes the GMAT Quantitative section so challenging, however, is not the math content itself, but rather how the testmakers combine the different areas of math to make questions more challenging. Rare is the question that tests a single concept; more commonly, you will be asked to integrate multiple skills to solve a question. For instance, a question that asks you about triangles could also require you to solve a formula algebraically and apply your understanding of ratios to find the correct answer.

QUANTITATIVE ANALYSIS

Most of the math tests you've taken before—even other standardized tests like the SAT and the ACT—ask questions in a fairly straightforward way. You know pretty quickly how you should solve the problem, and the only thing holding you back is how quickly or accurately you can do the math.

But the GMAT is a little different. Often the most difficult part of a GMAT Quantitative problem is figuring out which math skills to use in the first place. In fact, the GMAT's hardest Quantitative problems are about 95 percent analysis, 5 percent calculation. You'll have to do the following:

- Understand complicated or awkward phrasing.
- Process information presented out of order.
- Analyze incomplete information.
- Simplify complicated information.

In the next few chapters, we'll show you how to approach Quant problems strategically so you can do the analysis that will lead you to efficient solutions, correct answers, and a high score. But first, let's look at some techniques for managing the Quantitative section as a whole.

PACING ON THE QUANTITATIVE SECTION

The best way to attack the computer-adaptive GMAT is to exploit the way it determines your score. Here's what you're dealing with:

- **Penalties:** If you run out of time at the end of the section, you receive a penalty that's about twice what you'd have received if you got all those answers wrong. *And* there's an extra penalty for long strings of wrong answers at the end.

- **No review:** There is no going back to check your work. You cannot move backward to double-check your earlier answers or skip past a question that's puzzling and return to try it again later. So if you finish early, you won't be able to use that remaining time.

- **Difficulty level adjustment:** Questions get harder or easier, depending on your performance. Difficult questions raise your score more when you get them right and hurt your score less when you get them wrong. Easier questions are the opposite—getting them right helps your score less, and getting them wrong hurts your score more.

Obviously, the best of both worlds is being able to get the early questions mostly right, while taking less than *two minutes per question on average* so that you have a little extra time to think about those harder questions later on. To achieve that goal, you need to do three things:

1. **Know your math basics cold.** Don't waste valuable time on Test Day sweating over how to add fractions, reverse-FOIL quadratic equations, or use the rate formula. When you do math, you want to feel right at home.

2. **Look for strategic approaches.** Most GMAT problems are susceptible to multiple possible approaches. So the testmakers deliberately build in shortcuts to reward critical thinkers by allowing them to move quickly through the question, leaving them with extra time. We'll show you how to find these most efficient approaches.

3. **Practice, practice, practice.** Do lots of practice problems so that you get as familiar as possible with the GMAT's most common analytical puzzles. That way you can handle them quickly (and correctly!) when you see them on Test Day. We've got tons in the upcoming chapters.

If you follow this advice, you'll do more than just set yourself up to manage your pacing well. You'll also ensure that most of the questions fall into a difficulty range that's right for you. If you struggle on a few hard questions and are sent back down to the midrange questions, that's OK! You'll get them correct, which will send you right back up to the high-value hard questions again.

During the test, do your best not to fall behind early on. Don't rush, but don't linger. Those first 5 questions shouldn't take more than 10 minutes total, and the first 10 questions shouldn't take more than 20 minutes. Pay attention to your timing as you move through the section. If you notice that you are falling behind, try to solve some questions more quickly (or if you're stuck, make strategic guesses) to catch up.

STRATEGIC GUESSING

Since missing hard questions doesn't hurt your score very much but not finishing definitely does, making a few guesses on the hardest questions will give you the chance to finish on time and earn your highest possible score.

Occasionally, you'll find that you have to make a guess, but don't guess at random. Narrowing down the answer choices first is imperative. Otherwise, your odds of getting the right answer will be pretty slim. Follow this plan when you guess:

1. **Eliminate answer choices you know are wrong.** You can often identify wrong answer choices after a little calculation. For instance, on Data Sufficiency questions, you can eliminate at least two answer choices by determining the sufficiency of just one statement.

2. **Avoid answer choices that make you suspicious.** You can get rid of these without doing any work on the problem! These answer choices either don't make logical sense with the problem, or they conform to common wrong-answer types. For example, if only one of the answer choices in a Problem Solving question is negative, chances are that it will be incorrect.

3. **Choose one of the remaining answer choices.** The fewer options you have to choose from, the higher your chances of selecting the right answer. You can often identify the correct answer using estimation, especially if the answer choices are spaced widely apart.

EXPERIMENTAL QUESTIONS

Some questions on the GMAT are experimental. These questions are not factored into your score. They are questions that the testmaker is evaluating for possible use on future tests. To get good data, the testmakers have to test each question against the whole range of test takers—that is, high and low scorers. Therefore, you could be on your way to an 800 and suddenly come across a question that feels out of line with how you think you are doing.

Don't panic; just do your best and keep on going. The difficulty level of the experimental questions you see has little to do with how you're currently scoring. Remember, there is no way for you to know for sure whether a question is experimental or not, so approach every question as if it were scored.

Keep in mind that it's hard to judge the true difficulty level of a question. A question that seems easy to you may simply be playing to your personal strengths and be very difficult for other test takers. So treat every question as if it counts. Don't waste time trying to speculate about the difficulty of the questions you're seeing and what that implies about your performance. Rather, focus your energy on answering the question in front of you as efficiently as possible.

HOW THE QUANTITATIVE SECTION IS SCORED

The Quantitative section of the GMAT is quite different from the math sections of paper-and-pencil tests you may have taken. The major difference between the test formats is that the GMAT computer-adaptive test (CAT) adapts to your performance. Each test taker is given a different mix of questions, depending on how well he or she is doing on the test. In other words, the questions get harder or easier depending on whether you answer them correctly or incorrectly. Your GMAT score is not determined by the number of questions you get right but rather by the difficulty level of the questions you get right.

When you begin a section, the computer

- assumes you have an average score (500), and
- gives you a medium-difficulty question. About half the people who take the test will get this question right, and half will get it wrong. What happens next depends on whether you answer the question correctly.

If you answer the question correctly,

- your score goes up, and
- you are given a slightly harder question.

If you answer the question incorrectly,

- your score goes down, and
- you are given a slightly easier question.

This pattern continues for the rest of the section. As you get questions right, the computer raises your score and gives you harder questions. As you get questions wrong, the computer lowers your score and gives you easier questions. In this way, the computer homes in on your score.

If you feel like you're struggling at the end of the section, don't worry! Because the CAT adapts to find the outer edge of your abilities, the test will feel hard; it's designed to be difficult for everyone, even the highest scorers.

CORE COMPETENCIES ON THE QUANTITATIVE SECTION

Unlike most subject-specific tests you have taken throughout your academic career, the scope of knowledge that the GMAT requires of you is fairly limited. In fact, you don't need any background knowledge or expertise beyond fundamental math and verbal skills. While mastering those fundamentals is essential to your success on the GMAT—and this book is concerned in part with helping you develop or refresh those skills—the GMAT does *not* primarily seek to reward test takers for content-specific knowledge. Rather, the GMAT is a test of high-level thinking and reasoning abilities; it uses math and verbal subject matter as a platform to build questions that test your critical thinking and problem solving capabilities. As you prepare for the GMAT, you will notice that similar analytical skills come into play across the various question types and sections of the test.

Kaplan has adopted the term "Core Competencies" to refer to the four bedrock thinking skills rewarded by the GMAT: Critical Thinking, Pattern Recognition, Paraphrasing, and Attention to the Right Detail. The Kaplan Methods and strategies presented throughout this book will help you demonstrate these all-important skills. Let's dig into each of the Core Competencies in turn and discuss how each applies to the Quantitative section.

CRITICAL THINKING

Most potential MBA students are adept at creative problem solving, and the GMAT offers many opportunities to demonstrate this skill. You probably already have experience assessing situations to see when data are inadequate; synthesizing information into valid deductions; finding creative solutions to complex problems; and avoiding unnecessary, redundant labor.

In GMAT terms, a critical thinker is a creative problem solver who engages in critical inquiry. One of the traits of successful test takers is their skill at asking the right questions. GMAT critical thinkers first consider what they're being asked to do, then study the given information and ask the right questions, especially, "How can I get the answer in the most direct way?" and "How can I use the question format to my advantage?"

For instance, the answer choices in a GMAT Problem Solving question often give clues to the solution. Use them. As you examine a Problem Solving question, you'll ask the testmaker: "What are you really looking for in this math problem?" or "Why have you set things up in this way?" You might even discover opportunities to find the answer to a difficult question by plugging the answer choices into the information in the question—a strategy Kaplan calls "Backsolving."

Likewise, as you examine a Data Sufficiency question, you'll learn to ask: "What information will I need to answer this question?" or "How can I determine whether more than one solution is possible?"

Those test takers who learn to ask the right questions become creative problem solvers—and GMAT champs. Let's see how to apply the GMAT Core Competency of Critical Thinking to a sample Problem Solving question:

1. If the perimeter of a rectangular property is 46 meters, and the area of the property is 76 square meters, what is the length of each of the shorter sides?

   ○ 4
   ○ 6
   ○ 9
   ○ 18
   ○ 23

This question is a perfect example of one that can be answered with minimal calculations, provided the test taker understands how to use the test format to his advantage.

Here you are asked for the shorter sides of a rectangle. Recalling the formula for the area of a rectangle (*area = length × width*) may help you see a shorter path to the solution here. Rather than set up a complicated system of equations, remember that the property is 76 square meters in size. Since you're looking for the shorter side, you're looking for the smaller number that, when multiplied by a larger number, yields 76. You can immediately eliminate 9, 18, and 23 as possible answers, since multiplying any of those numbers by something larger than itself will give a result bigger than 76. Out of the two remaining choices, 4 divides evenly into 76. If the shorter sides measure 4, the larger sides would measure 19. And if the dimensions of the rectangle are 4 and 19, then the perimeter does equal 46. Therefore, choice **(A)** is correct.

This isn't to say that all questions are amenable to such amazing "shortcuts." But it is true that almost every question on the Quantitative section of the GMAT could be solved using more than one approach. The time constraints on the GMAT are designed to reward those test takers who, through Critical Thinking and practice, have honed their ability to identify and execute the most efficient approach to every problem they might see on Test Day.

PATTERN RECOGNITION

Most people fail to appreciate the level of constraint standardization places on testmakers. Because the testmakers must give reliable, valid, and comparable scores to many thousands of students each year, they're forced to reward the same skills on every test. They do so by repeating the same kinds of questions with the same traps and pitfalls, which are susceptible to the same strategic solutions.

Inexperienced test takers treat every problem as if it were a brand-new task, whereas the GMAT rewards those who spot the patterns and use them to their advantage. Of course Pattern Recognition is a key business skill in its own right: Executives who recognize familiar situations and apply proven solutions to them will outperform those who reinvent the wheel every time.

Even the smartest test taker will struggle if she approaches each GMAT question as a novel exercise. But the GMAT features nothing novel—just repeated patterns. Kaplan knows this test inside and out, and we'll show you which patterns you will encounter on Test Day. You will know the test better than your competition does. Let's see how to apply the GMAT Core Competency of Pattern Recognition to a sample Problem Solving question:

2. If $x > 7$, which of the following is equal to $\dfrac{x^2 + 8x + 16}{x^2 - 16}$?

   ○ $\dfrac{x+4}{4(x-4)}$

   ○ $\dfrac{x-4}{x+4}$

   ○ $\dfrac{x-2}{x+4}$

   ○ $\dfrac{x+4}{x-4}$

   ○ $\dfrac{x-8}{x-4}$

This question features one of the many patterns that is repeated over and over in the Quantitative section. The Kaplan-trained test taker looks at this problem and sees two "classic quadratics": the square of a binomial in the numerator and the difference of squares in the denominator. Factoring these expressions allows you to rewrite them as follows:

$$\frac{(x+4)(x+4)}{(x+4)(x-4)}$$

You can then cancel an $(x + 4)$ on the top and bottom and choose the correct answer, choice **(D)**. As you practice with more and more GMAT questions, stay attuned to patterns you see; certain math concepts appear regularly enough on the GMAT to warrant memorization.

PARAPHRASING

The third Core Competency is Paraphrasing: The GMAT rewards those who can reduce difficult, abstract, or polysyllabic prose to simple terms. Paraphrasing is, of course, an essential business skill: Executives must be able to define clear tasks based on complicated requirements and accurately summarize mountains of detail.

In the Quantitative section of the GMAT, you will often be asked to paraphrase English as "math" or to simplify complicated equations using arithmetic or algebraic properties. Let's see how to apply the GMAT Core Competency of Paraphrasing to a sample Problem Solving question:

3. A basketball team plays games only against the other five teams in its league and always in the following order: Croton, Darby, Englewood, Fiennes, and Garvin. If the team's final game of the season is against Fiennes, which of the following could be the number of games in the team's schedule?

    O   18
    O   24
    O   56
    O   72
    O   81

Rather than become intimidated by the complicated wording of this question, a smart test taker will ask, "How might I rephrase this question more simply?" A good paraphrase looks something like this: A team plays five other teams over and over in the same order, but the season stops at Fiennes. This is the fourth game of the sequence; what could the total number of games be?

With this paraphrase in hand, it's time to employ some Critical Thinking. Suppose the team plays a full round, and the next round is interrupted after the fourth game—what will the total number of games be? 5 + 4 = 9. Suppose there are two full rounds before the interruption? 5 + 5 + 4 = 14. Three rounds? 5 + 5 + 5 + 4 = 19. Thinking through these scenarios causes the pattern to emerge: The answer must end in 4 or 9. The correct choice is **(B)**, which represents four full rounds plus a set of four games ending with Fiennes.

Notice how this convoluted word problem becomes manageable once paraphrased. Putting GMAT prose into your own words helps you get a handle on the situation being described and know what to do next.

ATTENTION TO THE RIGHT DETAIL

Details present a dilemma: Missing them can cost you points. But if you try to absorb every fact in a complicated word problem all at once, you may find yourself swamped, delayed, and still unable to determine the best approach, because you haven't sorted through the information to determine what's most important. Throughout this book, you will learn how to discern the essential details from those that can slow you down or confuse you. The GMAT testmakers reward examinees for paying attention to "the right details"—the ones that make the difference between right and wrong answers.

Attention to the Right Detail distinguishes great administrators from poor ones in the business world as well. Just ask anyone who's had a boss who had the wrong priorities or who was so bogged down in minutiae that the department stopped functioning.

Not all details are created equal, and there are mountains of them on the test. Learn to target only what will turn into correct answers. Let's see how to apply the GMAT Core Competency of Attention to the Right Detail to a sample Problem Solving question:

4. A drought decreased the amount of water in city X's reservoirs from 118 million gallons to 96 million gallons. If the reservoirs were at 79 percent of total capacity before the drought began, approximately how many million gallons were the reservoirs below total capacity after the drought?

   ○   67
   ○   58
   ○   54
   ○   46
   ○   32

There are a lot of words in this problem, but there's one that's more important than all the others. Recognizing the word "approximately" is crucial to being able to take a strategic approach to this question.

Attention to the Right Detail on the Quantitative section also means defining precisely what the question is asking you to solve for. Here you need the current (post-drought) difference between capacity and holdings. Identifying up front what you need to solve for is important on the GMAT because the answer choices will often include options that represent "the right answer to the wrong question": the value you might come up with if you did all the math correctly but solved accidentally for a different unknown in the problem (for instance, the number of gallons below capacity the reservoir was *before* the drought).

This question gives information on the pre- and post-drought holdings, as well as on the pre-drought percentage of capacity. Use that info to approximate the current shortage. To start, figure out the total capacity before the drought. You know that 118 million was 79 percent of capacity. Because approximation is perfectly fine in this case, you can round these numbers to 120 million and 80 percent, respectively, to make the math easier. Then use the percent formula:

$$120 = 0.80(\text{total capacity})$$
$$120 = \frac{4}{5}(\text{total capacity})$$
$$120\left(\frac{5}{4}\right) = \text{total capacity}$$
$$150 = \text{total capacity}$$

The question states that the current volume is 96 million gallons, which is 54 million gallons under capacity. Choice **(C)** is correct.

Think of how much time you saved by noticing that the question asked for an approximate value, thereby allowing you to avoid precise calculation with unwieldy numbers. Moreover, Attention to the Right Detail ensured that you did not select a trap answer choice: If you had accidentally solved for the total capacity and then subtracted 118 (the amount of water originally in the reservoir), you would have selected incorrect choice **(E)**.

CHAPTER 10

Problem Solving

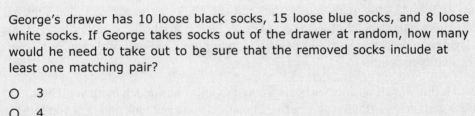

George's drawer has 10 loose black socks, 15 loose blue socks, and 8 loose white socks. If George takes socks out of the drawer at random, how many would he need to take out to be sure that the removed socks include at least one matching pair?

- ○ 3
- ○ 4
- ○ 9
- ○ 15
- ○ 31

Above is a typical Problem Solving question. In this chapter, we'll look at how to apply the Kaplan Method to this question, discuss the math concepts being tested, and go over the basic principles and strategies that you want to keep in mind on every Problem Solving question. But before you move on, take a minute to think about what you see in this question and answer some questions about how you think it works:

- What mathematical concepts are being tested in this question?

- How is this different from a typical math question you may have seen in high school?

- How can you use the answer choices to your advantage?

- What GMAT Core Competencies are most essential to success on this question?

PREVIEWING PROBLEM SOLVING

WHAT MATHEMATICAL CONCEPTS ARE BEING TESTED IN THIS QUESTION?

At first this question appears to be setting up a situation involving probability. George is randomly selecting socks from a drawer whose contents are described in the question. But then the question takes an unexpected turn—rather than asking for the probability of choosing a certain combination of socks, it instead asks for the minimum number of socks George would need to draw in order to be sure of having a matching pair. There's no formula to follow here or algebraic equation to solve. This question is testing your ability to reason through the situation and choose the correct answer.

Problem Solving questions test basic math skills and an understanding of some elementary mathematical concepts—ones such as algebra, arithmetic, and geometry that most U.S. students have learned by 10th grade. Most importantly, they test the ability to reason quantitatively. All GMAT Quantitative questions depend at least as much on logical analysis as on math skills. Most rely more on logic than on math. Some, like this one, rely purely on logic and require no math skills beyond the ability to count.

Think about it this way: If business schools wanted to know how much math you knew, they could easily look at your college transcript to see what math classes you took and how you fared in them. So why require the GMAT? Because they want to look at something else. In business school, you will be given *a lot* of information, especially in the form of case studies. One of the biggest challenges you'll face will be figuring out how to think about all that information—deciding how it fits together, what deductions you can make from it, and how it pertains to business challenges.

So the Quantitative section presents you with microcosms of that task—mathematical puzzles in which the data are often presented in a confusing or misleading way, demanding that you first figure out how you can solve the puzzles before beginning any calculations. Hence the name "Problem Solving" instead of just "Math."

The most advanced questions rarely involve math that is much more difficult than the math used in intermediate-range questions. Rather, the task of analyzing the problem to figure out what math to use becomes harder.

HOW IS THIS DIFFERENT FROM A TYPICAL MATH QUESTION YOU MAY HAVE SEEN IN HIGH SCHOOL?

Besides the emphasis on logic mentioned above, there's another important characteristic of GMAT Problem Solving that distinguishes it from the math you have likely been required to do on exams throughout your educational career: All that the GMAT requires is that you choose the correct answer. There's no math teacher looking over your shoulder to verify that you are completing each step precisely and showing your work fully. There is no extra or partial credit for finding a mathematically elegant solution. It may seem obvious, but it bears emphasizing: The sole goal on a Problem Solving question is getting the question correct and earning your points.

What that means for the savvy test taker is that a range of paths to the solution are available. Of course, you can do the straightforward math, but you can also use other strategies such as the ones you will learn in this chapter. The value of a strategic approach is that you can often get to the answer more quickly and accurately than if you had relied on classroom math.

The challenge is that the classroom math approach has probably been so impressed upon you throughout school that you are likely to favor that approach automatically, even when it's not the best way to a solution. So as you practice, one of the best things you can do for your ultimate success on Test Day is get into the habit of Critical Thinking: Always ask yourself what approaches are available to you and which one will work best on that particular question. Since the GMAT is a timed test and the adaptive format ensures that you will see questions you will find difficult, finding opportunities to increase your efficiency is of paramount importance to your score.

How Can You Use the Answer Choices to Your Advantage?

One of the big advantages you have on Problem Solving questions is the presence of the five answer choices, one of which *must* be correct. Especially when those answers are simple numbers, as they are in this question, you can often find your way to the correct answer by plugging the answer choices back into the situation described in the problem to see which one works. This is a strategy called Backsolving, and you will learn later in this chapter how to apply it.

In this question, you can't literally substitute the answer choices back into the problem, since there's very little math to do here. But in this case, you can use the answer choices to help think through the basic scenario you are given. For instance, try choice **(A)** on for size: If George has three types of sock, is he guaranteed to pull out a matching pair when he draws only three socks? No, of course not; he could end up drawing one sock of each color. At the other end of the spectrum, what about choice **(E)**? If he pulls out 31 of his 33 socks, will he end up with a matching pair? Surely he will; in fact, he'll have many matching pairs. So the correct answer will be smaller than 31. If you aren't sure at first how to approach a question, thinking through the answer choices you are given will often guide you toward a game plan.

What GMAT Core Competencies Are Most Essential to Success on This Question?

The first step of the Kaplan Method for Problem Solving is to analyze the question. This analysis up front helps you find the most efficient approach to the question.

Attention to the Right Detail comes into play in Step 2 of the Method when you identify the task that the question requires of you. It's all too easy to be in a hurry and solve for a value other than what the question asks for. The GMAT testmakers know this and include such trap answers among the answer choices.

Pattern Recognition is essential to determining what math topic a question is testing and recognizing what formulas or rules will get you to the answer. Since the GMAT structures questions similarly from test to test, you'll become familiar with the common tasks and traps as you practice. Remember that the goal of your practice is never simply to find the correct answer. You won't see your practice questions on Test Day, but you will likely see questions very similar to them; if you keep your eyes open to patterns, you will feel prepared for any question the GMAT can throw at you.

Finally, you will benefit from Paraphrasing the information given to you by Problem Solving questions. Sometimes the given information is complicated or presented in a less-than-helpful order. Other times, the information is in the form of a word problem that must be "translated" into math. In all cases, you will distill the given information into scratchwork, which should be simple, accurate, and well organized.

Here are the main topics we'll cover in this chapter:

- Question Format and Structure
- The Kaplan Method for Problem Solving
- The Basic Principles of Problem Solving
- Problem Solving Strategy
  - Picking Numbers
  - Backsolving
  - Strategic Guessing

QUESTION FORMAT AND STRUCTURE

The instructions for the Problem Solving questions look like this:

Directions: Solve the problems and choose the best answer.

Note: Unless otherwise indicated, the figures accompanying questions have been drawn as accurately as possible and may be used as sources of information for answering the questions.

All figures lie in a plane except where noted.

All numbers used are real numbers.

There are about 22 Problem Solving questions on each GMAT Quantitative section. Happily, the format of the questions is simple enough: Each Problem Solving question consists of the question stem—which gives you information and defines your task—and five answer choices. To answer a question, select the choice that correctly answers the question.

The directions indicate that some diagrams on the GMAT are drawn to scale, which means that you can use them to estimate measurements and size relationships. Other diagrams are labeled "Not drawn to scale," so you can't eyeball them. In fact, when a diagram says "Not drawn to scale," working past the confusing picture is often the key to the problem.

The directions also let you know that you won't have to deal with imaginary numbers, such as $\sqrt{-1}$, and that you'll be dealing with flat figures, such as squares and circles, unless a particular question says otherwise.

THE KAPLAN METHOD FOR PROBLEM SOLVING

Now that you've seen how Problem Solving questions are constructed, let's look at how to handle them. Kaplan has developed a Method for Problem Solving that you can use to attack each and every question of this type.

The Kaplan Method for Problem Solving

1. **Analyze the question.**

2. **State the task.**

3. **Approach strategically.**

4. **Confirm your answer.**

STEP 1: ANALYZE THE QUESTION

Begin your analysis of the problem by getting an overview. If it's a word problem, what's the basic situation? Or is this an algebra problem? An overlapping sets problem? A permutations problem? Getting a general idea of what's going on will help you to organize your thinking and know which rules or formulas you'll have to use.

If there's anything that can be quickly simplified, do so—but don't start solving yet. For example, if a question stem gives you the classic quadratic $x^2 - y^2 = 64$, it would be fine to rewrite it immediately in your scratchwork as $(x + y)(x - y) = 64$. But you wouldn't want to start solving for values just yet; doing so would likely cause you to miss an important aspect of the problem or to overlook an efficient alternative solution.

Also, make sure to glance at the answer choices. Can they help you choose an approach? If they are variable expressions, you can use Picking Numbers (a strategy we'll cover later in this chapter). If they are widely spread, you can estimate. If they are numerical values, you might be able to plug them back into the question, a strategy we call Backsolving. Looking at the choices may trigger an important strategic insight for you.

STEP 2: STATE THE TASK

Before you choose your approach, make sure you know what you're solving for. The most common wrong answer trap in Problem Solving is the right answer—but to the wrong question. And perhaps you won't have to do as much work as you might think—you may be able to solve for what you need without calculating the value of every single variable involved in the problem.

STEP 3: APPROACH STRATEGICALLY

The operative word here is *strategically*. Resist the temptation to hammer away at the problem, hoping for something to work. Use your analysis from Steps 1 and 2 to find the most straightforward approach that allows you to make sense of the problem.

There is rarely a single "right approach." Choose the easiest for you given the current problem. Broadly speaking, there are three basic approaches.

Approach 1: A Kaplan Strategy

Frequently there will be a more efficient strategic approach to the math for those who analyze the problem carefully. Consider Picking Numbers or Backsolving, which you will learn about later in this chapter. These approaches can simplify some tough problems and should always be on your mind as possible alternatives.

Approach 2: Straightforward Math

Sometimes simply doing the math is the most efficient approach. But remember, only do math that feels *straightforward*. To be sure, the hardest problems will make you sweat during the *analysis*, but you should never find yourself performing extremely complicated calculations.

Remember, the only thing that matters is that you select the correct answer. There is no human GMAT grader out there who's going to give you extra points for working out a math problem the hard way.

Approach 3: Guess Strategically

If you notice that estimation or simple logic will get you the answer, use those guessing techniques. They will often be faster than doing the math. If you have spent 60 to 90 seconds analyzing the problem and still haven't found a straightforward path to a solution, make a guess. You only have an average of two minutes per question, so you need to keep moving.

And if you have fallen behind pace, you need to guess strategically to get back on track. Hunt actively for good guessing situations and guess quickly on them (within 20–30 seconds). Don't wait until you fall so far behind that you are forced into random guesses or forced to guess on questions that you could otherwise have easily solved. Never try to make up time by rushing!

STEP 4: CONFIRM YOUR ANSWER

Because the GMAT is adaptive, you aren't able to return to questions you've already seen to check your work, so you need to build that step into your process on each question. The most efficient way to do this is to reread the question stem as you select your answer. If you notice a wrinkle in the problem that you missed earlier, you should redo the problem (if you have time) or change your answer. If you got everything right the first time, move on to the next problem with confidence.

Now, let's apply the Kaplan Method for Problem Solving to the question you saw at the beginning of this chapter:

> George's drawer has 10 loose black socks, 15 loose blue socks, and 8 loose white socks. If George takes socks out of the drawer at random, how many would he need to take out to be sure that the removed socks include at least one matching pair?
>
> ○ 3
> ○ 4
> ○ 9
> ○ 15
> ○ 31

Step 1: Analyze the Question

George has a bunch of unpaired socks and is pulling them out at random. This doesn't sound like the best way to get dressed, but that's the situation the question gives you.

Step 2: State the Task

What's the smallest number of socks George has to remove to be sure of getting a matching pair? In other words, how many socks does George need to pick before he is guaranteed to have 2 matching socks? The question doesn't specify which color, so any matching color will do.

Step 3: Approach Strategically

There's no equation to set up here. Despite the fact that the question starts off sounding like a probability question, you're not asked to calculate probabilities directly.

So think logically. Obviously George can't have a matching pair of socks if he only removes 1 sock. You need at least 2 for a pair. So what if George removes 2 socks? He *could* get a pair, of course; there's nothing stopping him from randomly drawing, for example, 2 blue socks. But he also *could* get an unmatched pair—1 blue and 1 black, perhaps—so removing 2 socks doesn't *guarantee* a matching pair.

What if he takes 3 socks? Again, he *could* match a color—1 blue and 2 whites, for example. But could he still have no match with 3 socks? Yes, as it's possible (and happily you are not asked to calculate exactly *how* possible) for him to get 1 of each color—1 white, 1 blue, and 1 black.

But after that, he's guaranteed to match 1 of the colors. After all, there are only 3 colors. So even if he didn't have a match after taking out 3 (1 white, 1 blue, and 1 black), he's guaranteed to have a pair when he selects a fourth. You can't know whether that pair will be white, blue, or black, but the question didn't ask you to get a specific color ... any one will do. The correct answer is **(B)**.

Step 4: Confirm Your Answer

Reread the question stem, making sure that you didn't miss anything about the problem or give the right answer to the wrong question—a common GMAT trap. For example, **(E)** is what you would have selected if you solved for the total number of socks minus one pair.

TAKEAWAYS: THE KAPLAN METHOD FOR PROBLEM SOLVING

- The Kaplan Method is a tested, proven way to approach Problem Solving questions consistently, efficiently, and confidently.
- Through practice, the Kaplan Method will become second nature by Test Day.
- Always be on the lookout for the most strategic approach; some Problem Solving questions require more logical analysis than mathematical calculation.

PRACTICE SET: THE KAPLAN METHOD FOR PROBLEM SOLVING

Answers and explanations at end of chapter

1. Youssef lives x blocks from his office. It takes him 1 minute per block to walk to work and 20 seconds per block to ride his bicycle to work. If it takes him exactly 10 minutes more to walk to work than to ride his bicycle, then x equals

   ○ 4
   ○ 7
   ○ 10
   ○ 15
   ○ 20

2. A book club rented the party room of a local restaurant to meet and discuss its current novel over dinner. The total charge, including food and service, was $867.50. If each member of the club paid at least $42, then what is the greatest possible number of members in the club?

   ○ 19
   ○ 20
   ○ 21
   ○ 23
   ○ 25

3. A machine manufactures notebooks in a series of five colors: red, blue, black, white, and yellow. After producing a notebook of one color from that series, it produces a notebook of the next color. Once five are produced, the machine repeats the same pattern. If the machine began a day producing a red notebook and completed the day by producing a black notebook, how many notebooks could have been produced that day?

   ○ 27
   ○ 34
   ○ 50
   ○ 61
   ○ 78

THE BASIC PRINCIPLES OF PROBLEM SOLVING

By adopting a methodical approach to Problem Solving, you will have a clear, strategic way to think through your way to a response. You won't waste time by attacking a question in a tentative or haphazard manner, nor will you get stuck doing inefficient math. A systematic approach will ensure that you find the most efficient solution to the problem and that you make as few careless and unnecessary errors as possible. Here are some ways you can optimize your Problem Solving performance by employing the Method in conjunction with the Core Competencies.

ANALYZE AND SIMPLIFY BEFORE SOLVING

The biggest mistake test takers make on GMAT Problem Solving is doing the math right after reading the problem (or even more dangerously, *while* still reading the problem). Problem Solving questions are written to be confusing, and the approach that the question might seem to be talking you into may not be the most efficient. Consider this problem:

> At a certain diner, Joe ordered 3 doughnuts and a cup of coffee and was charged $2.25. Stella ordered 2 doughnuts and a cup of coffee and was charged $1.70. What is the price of 2 doughnuts?
>
> ○ $0.55
> ○ $1.00
> ○ $1.10
> ○ $1.30
> ○ $1.80

If you started doing math right away, you might immediately jot down something like $J = 3d + c$, thereby making the problem a lot tougher by introducing a variable, J, that really doesn't need to be part of the solution. If you used x and y instead of d and c, you would make your job even harder, as a part of your brain that could be used to solve the problem would be taken up remembering whether x stood for doughnuts or coffee.

However, if you analyzed the question before getting into math, you would realize that the orders are very similar. In fact, they differ by only one doughnut. So the price of a doughnut could be calculated simply by subtracting the prices of the orders. Instead of wasting time writing out $S = 2d + c$, you have almost completely solved the problem. Time invested in analysis usually pays off in a much more efficient solution and in less time spent on the question overall.

Here's another example of the benefit of analysis and simplification:

> What is the product of all the possible values of x if $x^2(x + 2) + 7x(x + 2) + 6(x + 2) = 0$?
>
> ○   −29
> ○   −12
> ○   12
> ○   29
> ○   168

If you did math before any analysis, you'd distribute the multiplication and get $x^3 + 9x^2 + 20x + 12 = 0$. You might then be stuck not knowing what to do next to simplify this equation.

But if you analyzed first, you'd realize that distribution would lead to a complicated cubic equation. Looking for an easier way, you might notice that if the multiple occurrences of $(x + 2)$ were gone, you'd have a normal quadratic. You could factor out the occurrences of $(x + 2)$ and be on your way to solving:

$$x^2(x + 2) + 7x(x + 2) + 6(x + 2) = 0$$

Factor: $\quad\quad\quad\quad\quad (x + 2)(x^2 + 7x + 6) = 0$

Reverse-FOIL: $\quad\quad\quad (x + 2)(x + 6)(x + 1) = 0$

Solve for x: $\quad\quad\quad\quad\quad\quad\quad\quad x = -2 \text{ or } -6 \text{ or } -1$

Multiply: $\quad\quad\quad\quad\quad\quad -2 \times -6 \times -1 = -12$

Focus on What's Asked

Go back to the problem with the doughnuts and the coffee. Did you spot the trap? The question doesn't ask for the price of a doughnut but rather for the price of *two* doughnuts. Sure enough, one of the answer choices gives the cost of only one.

Focusing on what's asked will also help you to choose an efficient approach. Consider this question:

If $4x + y = 8$ and $y - 3x = 7$, then what is the value of $x + 2y$?

○ $\dfrac{1}{7}$

○ 3

○ 15

○ $\dfrac{52}{7}$

○ $\dfrac{60}{7}$

You might just rush into solving for x and y and then plug them in, but focus on what you are being asked for: not x or y individually but rather $x + 2y$. How could you solve for *that*? Looking at the equations, you might notice that one equation has $4x$ and the other $-3x$, and together, that's x. Each has one y, so together you have $2y$. You can add the equations together.

Rearrange $y - 3x = 7$ to $-3x + y = 7$ so things line up nicely. Then combine the equations:

$$
\begin{array}{r}
4x + y = 8 \\
+[-3x + y = 7] \\
\hline
x + 2y = 15
\end{array}
$$

In the end, the math was quick because you focused on what the question asked.

Note that in this question, answer choices **(A)** and **(D)** represent the values of the individual variables. Right answers to the wrong questions are the most common wrong answer type in Problem Solving, so it pays to define the task in Step 2 of the Kaplan Method.

CONSIDER ALTERNATIVE APPROACHES

You just saw three questions that were all most easily solved in a manner other than the math that might first occur to you. You added equations in the $x + 2y$ problem, factored instead of multiplied in the $(x + 2)$ problem, and realized that all you needed to do on the diner problem was find the difference in cost between the two orders.

The takeaway from these examples: It pays to *think* about what you're doing before diving into math. Most problems can be solved many different ways, some easy and some not so easy. The GMAT testmaker writes the questions in such a way that the first approaches that occur to you are usually of the not-so-easy variety. So turn the problem over in your mind until you find an approach that will work. Trust your intuition—if you're thinking of a solution that involves lots of difficult math, then look for a different approach.

Here's how you might approach a more difficult question, considering different approaches until you find one that works:

$$\begin{array}{r} AB \\ +BA \\ \hline 121 \end{array}$$

In the addition problem above, A and B represent digits in two different two-digit numbers. What is the sum of A and B?

- ○ 6
- ○ 8
- ○ 9
- ○ 11
- ○ 14

This question may seem intimidating, so approach it calmly and methodically. Start as always by analyzing the question stem. You are told that A and B represent digits in two different two-digit numbers. Recall that a digit is any of the integers 0 through 9 and that a two-digit number is a number that has digits in the tens place and the units place, like 42, or 11. This means that AB is a two-digit number with A in the tens place and B in the units place. For example, if A is 3 and B is 5, then AB is 35.

Now, how do you solve for A and B? You could just experiment with different possibilities, plugging different combinations of digits in until you get $AB + BA = 121$. But since there are 10 digits, there'd be something like 100 different possible combinations. You don't have time for that. And, you know that when you find yourself beginning a drawn-out, tedious process like this, there's usually an easier way to solve the problem.

This is where Critical Thinking can help. You know that you can sometimes solve for an expression without figuring out the individual variables. The sum of A and B is $A + B$, and that is in fact what you are being asked to solve for. Look back at the question stem, and see if you can find $A + B$:

$$
\begin{array}{r}
AB \\
+BA \\
\hline
121
\end{array}
$$

$A + B$ is the sum of the digits in the tens place. Is the answer 12? You know that it can't be, because 12 isn't an answer choice. It's possible that the $A + B$ in the tens column is getting spillover from the $B + A$ in the units column, which would mean $A + B$ is less than 12, but you can't know the amount. At the very least, though, you've established that answer **(E)** is too large, since the answer is either 12 or something less.

By now, or before now, you've realized that $B + A$ is the same as $A + B$. So the answer is also the sum of the digits in the units places:

$$
\begin{array}{r}
AB \\
+BA \\
\hline
121
\end{array}
$$

So the units digit of the answer has to be 1. Having recognized this pattern, you can look at the answer choices and see that only **(D)** has a 1 in the units place. The answer has to be **(D)**.

Note that you didn't need the exact values of A and B to solve this problem. In fact, many different pairs of digits would satisfy this equation.

Don't be put off by the challenging presentation of a problem, even when you're not sure at first how you're going to solve it. As with this problem, separate what you know from what you don't, so you don't feel overwhelmed. Always consider multiple possible approaches, reevaluating them if they get too hard to follow or seem not to be working. Use what you know about the GMAT to help you, and look everywhere for clues to the solution—both in the question stem and in the answer choices.

APPLYING THE KAPLAN METHOD: THE BASIC PRINCIPLES OF PROBLEM SOLVING

Now let's use the Kaplan Method and the strategic principles of Problem Solving to answer a sample question:

> In a certain town, there are four times as many people who were born in the town's state as there are people who were born in another state or country. The ratio of those residents born in the town's state to the town's total population is
>
> O   1 to 4
> O   1 to 3
> O   1 to 2
> O   3 to 4
> O   4 to 5

Step 1: Analyze the Question

The phrase "total population" near the end of the question stem should stand out as key. One of the classic tricks used by the GMAT testmakers is to give you a part-to-part ratio and ask for an answer expressed as a part-to-whole ratio.

Step 2: State the Task

You need to use the ratio of those born in state to those born out of state to determine the ratio of those born in state to the total population.

Step 3: Approach Strategically

Having four times as many people born in state as out of state means a ratio of 4:1. You are looking for the ratio of those born in the state to the total. You are told that 4 is the part of the ratio for those who were born in the state. You can find the total by adding the two parts, in state (4) and out of state (1), getting 5. The part-to-whole ratio is then 4:5, choice **(E)**.

Step 4: Confirm Your Answer

A good natural-language paraphrase of the information is "Four of every five residents were born in-state." That matches choice **(E)**. You need to avoid traps that restate or distort the part-to-part information. Be wary of answer choice **(A)**, which is just a distortion of the original ratio.

TAKEAWAY: THE BASIC PRINCIPLES OF PROBLEM SOLVING

- Most GMAT word problems do not present the information in the most straightforward way. You will need to read strategically to understand the problem.
- Focusing on the question first
  - helps you understand what to look for in the problem.
  - allows you to avoid solving for "the right answer to the wrong question"—a common GMAT mistake.

PRACTICE SET: THE BASIC PRINCIPLES OF PROBLEM SOLVING

Answers and explanations at end of chapter

4. A team won 50 percent of its first 60 games in a particular season, and 80 percent of its remaining games. If the team won a total of 60 percent of its games that season, what was the total number of games that the team played?

   - ○ 180
   - ○ 120
   - ○ 90
   - ○ 85
   - ○ 30

5. A local restaurant recently renovated its dining space, purchasing new tables and chairs to use in addition to the original tables and chairs. The new tables each seat six customers, while the original tables each seat four customers. Altogether, the restaurant now has 40 tables and is capable of seating 220 customers. How many more new tables than original tables does the restaurant have?

   - ○ 10
   - ○ 20
   - ○ 30
   - ○ 34
   - ○ 36

PROBLEM SOLVING STRATEGY

In the previous section, you learned about the attitude that all great GMAT test takers share: that there must be a straightforward way to solve and there's no need to panic if you don't find it right away. And even if you don't use the algebra-based approach that your high school math teacher would have preferred, you will get the right answer and you will raise your score.

Identifying a more efficient alternative approach involves staying open to possibilities that might not occur to you immediately. Two such approaches—Picking Numbers and Backsolving—are so straightforward, can eliminate so much math, and can be used so often that they deserve special mention.

PICKING NUMBERS

Picking Numbers is a powerful alternative to solving problems by brute force. Rather than trying to work with unknown variables, you pick concrete values for the variables. In essence, you're transforming algebra or abstract math rules into basic arithmetic, giving yourself a much simpler task. Pick Numbers to stand in for the variables or unknowns.

How does Picking Numbers work?

- Pick **permissible** numbers. Some problems have explicit rules such as "x is odd." Other problems have implicit rules. For example, if a word problem says, "Betty is five years older than Tim," don't pick $b = -2$ and $t = -7$; these numbers wouldn't work in the problem.
- Pick **manageable** numbers. Some numbers are simply easier to work with than others. $d = 2$ will probably be a more successful choice than will $d = 492\sqrt{\pi}$, for example. The problems themselves will tell you what's manageable. For instance, $d = 2$ wouldn't be a great pick if an answer choice were $\frac{d}{12}$. (The number 12, 24, or even 120 would be much better in that case, since each is divisible by 12.)
- Once you've picked numbers to substitute for unknowns, approach the problem as basic arithmetic instead of algebra or number properties.
- Test every answer choice—sometimes certain numbers will yield a "false positive" in which a wrong answer looks right. If you get more than one "right answer," just pick a new set of numbers. The truly correct answer must work for all permissible numbers.

Note that it's just fine to pick the numbers 0 or 1 for most questions. True, the special properties of 0 and 1 do sometimes cause "false positives," but so do other numbers. The GMAT sometimes writes questions based on those special properties, so if you aren't considering 0 and 1, you won't get the right answer to those questions. Furthermore, they are the most manageable numbers in all of math. Imagine Picking Numbers for the following problem with anything other than $b = 0$ or $b = 1$:

$7^b + 7^b + 7^b + 7^b + 7^b + 7^b + 7^b =$

- ○ 7^b
- ○ 7^{b+1}
- ○ 7^{7b}
- ○ 8^b
- ○ 49^b

The occasional inconvenience of repicking numbers is far outweighed by the advantages that 0 and 1 provide.

Picking $b = 1$:

$$= 7^b + 7^b + 7^b + 7^b + 7^b + 7^b + 7^b$$

$$= 7^1 + 7^1 + 7^1 + 7^1 + 7^1 + 7^1 + 7^1$$

$$= 7 + 7 + 7 + 7 + 7 + 7 + 7$$

$$= 49$$

Plugging $b = 1$ into the answer choices yields

(A) $7^b = 7^1 = 7$

(B) $7^{b+1} = 7^{1+1} = 7^2 = 49$

(C) $7^{7b} = 7^7$—Whatever that is, it's a lot bigger than 49.

(D) $8^b = 8^1 = 8$

(E) $49^b = 49^1 = 49$

Two answer choices match the desired result of 49, so you need to pick a new number. Try $b = 0$. First, plug it into the stem.

$$= 7^b + 7^b + 7^b + 7^b + 7^b + 7^b + 7^b$$

$$= 7^0 + 7^0 + 7^0 + 7^0 + 7^0 + 7^0 + 7^0$$

$$= 1 + 1 + 1 + 1 + 1 + 1 + 1$$

$$= 7$$

Now you only need to plug $b = 0$ into **(B)** and **(E)**, the only two answer choices that worked when $b = 1$. Doing so yields

(B) $7^{b+1} = 7^{0+1} = 7^1 = 7$

(E) $49^b = 49^0 = 1$

The answer is **(B)**.

PICKING NUMBERS

There are four signals that Picking Numbers will be a possible approach to the problem:

1. Variables in the Question Stem
2. Percents in the Answer Choices
3. Variables in the Answer Choices
4. Must Be/Could Be/Cannot Be

These aren't in any particular order. You'll see many instances of each case on Test Day. We'll start with the first.

PICKING NUMBERS WITH VARIABLES IN THE QUESTION STEM

If you see a question that has variables in the question stem or asks about a fraction of an unknown whole, pick numbers to represent the unknown(s) in the question stem and walk through the arithmetic of the problem. Look in the question stem and the answer choices for clues about what the most manageable numbers might be.

Example:

Carol spends $\frac{1}{4}$ of her savings on a stereo and $\frac{1}{3}$ less than she spent on the stereo for a television. What fraction of her savings did she spend on the stereo and television?

○ $\frac{1}{4}$

○ $\frac{2}{7}$

○ $\frac{5}{12}$

○ $\frac{1}{2}$

○ $\frac{7}{12}$

Lowest common denominators of fractions in the question stem are good choices for numbers to pick. So are numbers that appear frequently as denominators in the answer choices. In this case, the common denominator of the fractions in the stem is 12, so let the number 12 represent Carol's total savings (12 dollars).

That means she spends $\frac{1}{4} \times 12$ dollars, or 3 dollars, on her stereo, and $\frac{2}{3} \times 3$ dollars, or 2 dollars, on her television. That comes out to be 3 + 2 = 5 dollars; that's how much she spent on the stereo and television combined. You're asked what *fraction* of her savings she spent. Because her total savings was 12 dollars, she spent $\frac{5}{12}$ of her savings; **(C)** is correct. Notice how picking a common denominator for the variable (Carol's savings) made it easy to convert each of the fractions $\left(\frac{1}{4} \text{ and } \frac{2}{3} \times \frac{1}{4} \text{ of her savings} \right)$ to a simple integer.

A tricky part of this question is understanding how to determine the price of the television. The television does not cost $\frac{1}{3}$ of her savings. It costs $\frac{1}{3}$ *less* than the stereo; that is, it costs $\frac{2}{3}$ as much as the stereo.

By the way, some of these answers could have been eliminated quickly using basic logic. **(A)** is too small; the stereo alone costs $\frac{1}{4}$ of her savings. **(D)** and **(E)** are too large. The television costs *less* than the stereo, so the two together must cost less than $2 \times \frac{1}{4}$, or half, of Carol's savings. We'll look more at using logic to eliminate answers later in this chapter.

APPLYING THE KAPLAN METHOD: PICKING NUMBERS WITH VARIABLES IN THE QUESTION STEM

Now let's use the Kaplan Method on a Problem Solving question that involves Picking Numbers with variables in the question stem:

> If $w > x > y > z$ on the number line, y is halfway between x and z, and x is halfway between w and z, then $\frac{y-x}{y-w} =$

- ○ $\frac{1}{4}$
- ○ $\frac{1}{3}$
- ○ $\frac{1}{2}$
- ○ $\frac{3}{4}$
- ○ 1

Step 1: Analyze the Question

This question presents a very complicated relationship among four variables. Since there are multiple variables in the problem, Picking Numbers is a possible approach. The answer choices are all numbers, so you won't have to test each answer choice—you'd just plug numbers into the question. Since the phrase *number line* appears, you may want to consider drawing a number line to help visualize the situation:

Step 2: State the Task

The question asks you to evaluate a rather complicated fraction: $\frac{y-x}{y-w}$. The question stem gives you no actual values for the variables, but the answer choices are numbers. This means that the value of the fractional expression must always be the same, as long as the values of the variables follow the rules described in the question stem.

Step 3: Approach Strategically

The math seems like it would be difficult and time-consuming. You'd have to translate each rule that states a relationship between variables into a separate algebraic equation and then somehow combine them to solve for the fraction in the stem. Picking Numbers, on the other hand, will be much more straightforward.

The rules are pretty complicated, so pick numbers one at a time, making sure the numbers you pick are permissible (follow the rules in the stem) and manageable (easy to work with). x and z each appear twice in the rules, so starting with those two numbers would seem to make sense.

Let's go with $z = 1$ and $x = 3$ to leave room for y.

y is halfway between 3 and 1, so $y = 2$.

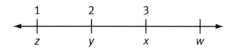

x, or 3, is halfway between w and 1, so $w = 5$.

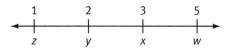

Once you've picked a set of permissible numbers, it's time to plug these numbers into the expression in the stem:

$$\frac{y-x}{y-w} = \frac{2-3}{2-5} = \frac{-1}{-3} = \frac{1}{3}$$

The answer is **(B)**. Picking Numbers can often take you to the correct answer much more directly than algebra.

Step 4: Confirm Your Answer

Look back at the question stem and make sure you understood all the rules and picked permissible numbers. "y is halfway between x and z." Check. "x is halfway between w and z." Check. Another potential error would have been to make w the smallest variable instead of the largest. (Did you notice how the question stem puts w on the left of the inequality statement, even though it belongs on the right-hand side of the number line?) That's another potential mistake you could catch in this step.

TAKEAWAYS: PICKING NUMBERS WITH VARIABLES IN THE QUESTION STEM

- Most people find it easier to perform calculations with numbers than to perform calculations with variables.
- Variables may be letters (n, x, t, etc.) or unspecified values (e.g., "a factory produces some number of units of a product each month").
- When Picking Numbers, be sure that the numbers are permissible and manageable.

PRACTICE SET: PICKING NUMBERS WITH VARIABLES IN THE QUESTION STEM

Answers and explanations at end of chapter

6. If $\dfrac{c-a}{c-b} = 2$, then $\dfrac{5b-5a}{c-a} =$

    ○   0.5

    ○   1

    ○   1.5

    ○   2

    ○   2.5

7. Company Z spent $\frac{1}{4}$ of its revenues last year on marketing and $\frac{1}{7}$ of the remainder on maintenance of its facilities. What fraction of last year's original revenues did company Z have left after its marketing and maintenance expenditures?

    ○ $\dfrac{5}{14}$

    ○ $\dfrac{1}{2}$

    ○ $\dfrac{17}{28}$

    ○ $\dfrac{9}{14}$

    ○ $\dfrac{9}{11}$

8. During a sale, a store sells 20 percent of its remaining stock each day, without replenishment. After four days, what fraction of its original stock has it sold?

    ○ $\dfrac{1}{625}$

    ○ $\dfrac{256}{625}$

    ○ $\dfrac{61}{125}$

    ○ $\dfrac{64}{125}$

    ○ $\dfrac{369}{625}$

PICKING NUMBERS WITH PERCENTS IN THE ANSWER CHOICES

Picking Numbers also works well on Problem Solving questions for which the answer choices are given in percents. When the answers are in percents, 100 will almost always be the most manageable number to pick. Using 100 not only makes your calculations easier, but it also simplifies the task of expressing the final value as a percent of the original.

Example:

> The manufacturer of Sleep-EZ mattresses is offering a 10% discount on the price of its king-size mattress. Some retailers are offering additional discounts. If a retailer offers an additional 20% discount, then what is the total discount available at that retailer?
>
> O   10%
> O   25%
> O   28%
> O   30%
> O   35%

Since the answers are in percents, pick $100 as the original price of the mattress. (Remember, realism is irrelevant—only permissibility and manageability matter.) The manufacturer offers a 10% discount: 10% of $100 is $10. So now the mattress costs $90.

Then the retailer offers an additional 20% discount. Since the price has fallen to $90, that 20% is taken off the $90 price. A 20% discount is now a reduction of $18. The final price of the mattress is $90 – $18, or $72.

The mattress has been reduced to $72 from an original price of $100. That's a $28 reduction. Since you started with $100, you can easily calculate that $28 is 28% of the original price. Choice **(C)** is correct.

Notice that choice **(D)** commits the error of simply adding the two percents given in the question stem. An answer choice like **(D)** will never be correct on a question that gives you information about multiple percent changes.

APPLYING THE KAPLAN METHOD: PICKING NUMBERS WITH PERCENTS IN THE ANSWER CHOICES

Now let's use the Kaplan Method on a Problem Solving question that involves Picking Numbers with percents in the answer choices:

> In 1998 the profits of company N were 10 percent of revenues. In 1999, the revenues of company N fell by 20 percent, but profits were 15 percent of revenues. The profits in 1999 were what percent of the profits in 1998?
>
> O   80%
> O   105%
> O   120%
> O   124.2%
> O   138%

Step 1: Analyze the Question

Profits and revenues are both changing over time. Since the answer choices are percents, picking 100 is a good idea.

Step 2: State the Task

The profits in 1999 were what percent of the profits in 1998?

You'll have to compare the profits of the two years. The year 1998 is the basis of the comparison. You're not solving for the increase or decrease, just the relative amount.

In other words, you want this fraction, $\dfrac{1999 \text{ profits}}{1998 \text{ profits}}$, expressed as a percent.

Step 3: Approach Strategically

You should start with the original profits, since the question presents its 1999 information as a change from the 1998 information. You read this about 1998 profits: "In 1998 the profits of company N were 10 percent of revenues." So you'll know profits if you know revenues. You're given no information about revenue at all. So just pick a number. Given the percents in the answer choices, pick $100. That makes profits in 1998 equal to $10.

Now, what about 1999 profits? You read "In 1999 ... profits were 15% of revenues." So you have to know revenues in 1999 to know profits. What does the question say about 1999's revenues? "In 1999, the revenues of company N fell by 20 percent." Revenues were $100, so they fell $20 to $80. Profits, then, were 15% of $80, or 0.15($80) = $12.

By the way, you don't have to calculate that directly. You can use Critical Thinking and say:

15% of 80 = 10% of 80 + 5% of 80

15% of 80 = 10% of 80 + half of (10% of 80)

15% of 80 = 8 + half of 8

15% of 80 = 8 + 4

15% of 80 = 12

Plugging your results back into our question yields $\dfrac{1999 \text{ profits}}{1998 \text{ profits}} = \dfrac{12}{10} = 1.2$

Just multiply by 100% to convert to percent: 1.2 × 100% = 120%. Choice **(C)** is correct.

Step 4: Confirm Your Answer

Make sure to reread the question stem to confirm that you interpreted the relationships correctly.

TAKEAWAYS: PICKING NUMBERS WITH PERCENTS IN THE ANSWER CHOICES

- On a question involving multiple changes in percent, one of the trap answers will most likely involve simply adding or subtracting the percents.
- When you see a percent question with unspecified values, pick 100 for the unknown value. Doing so will make the calculations much easier.

PRACTICE SET: PICKING NUMBERS WITH PERCENTS IN THE ANSWER CHOICES

Answers and explanations at end of chapter

9. If a bicyclist in motion increases his speed by 30 percent and then increases this speed by 10 percent, what percent of the original speed is the total increase in speed?

○ 10%
○ 40%
○ 43%
○ 64%
○ 140%

10. Jane makes toy bears. When she works with an assistant, she makes 80 percent more bears per week and works 10 percent fewer hours each week. Having an assistant increases Jane's output of toy bears per hour by what percent?

○ 20%
○ 80%
○ 100%
○ 180%
○ 200%

11. John spent 40 percent of his earnings last month on rent and 30 percent less than what he spent on rent to purchase a new dishwasher. What percent of last month's earnings did John have left over?

○ 30%
○ 32%
○ 45%
○ 68%
○ 70%

PICKING NUMBERS WITH VARIABLES IN THE ANSWER CHOICES

Whenever the answer choices contain variables, you should consider Picking Numbers. The correct answer choice is the one that yields the result that you got when you plugged the same number(s) into the question stem. Make sure that you test each answer choice, just in case more than one answer choice produces the desired result. In such a case, you will need to pick a new set of numbers and repeat the process only for the answer choices that worked out the first time.

Example:

If $a > 1$, which of the following is equal to $\dfrac{2a + 6}{a^2 + 2a - 3}$?

- ○ a
- ○ $a + 3$
- ○ $\dfrac{2}{a - 1}$
- ○ $\dfrac{2a}{a - 3}$
- ○ $\dfrac{a - 1}{2}$

The question says that $a > 1$, so the most manageable permissible number will probably be 2. Then $\dfrac{2(2)+6}{2^2+2(2)-3} = \dfrac{4+6}{4+4-3} = \dfrac{10}{5} = 2$.

Now substitute 2 for a in each answer choice, looking for choices that equal 2 when $a = 2$. Eliminate choices that do not equal 2 when $a = 2$.

Choice **(A)**: $a = 2$. Choice **(A)** is possibly correct.

Choice **(B)**: $a + 3 = 2 + 3 = 5$. This is not 2. Discard.

Choice **(C)**: $\dfrac{2}{a-1} = \dfrac{2}{2-1} = \dfrac{2}{1} = 2$. Possibly correct.

Choice **(D)**: $\dfrac{2a}{a-3} = \dfrac{2(2)}{2-3} = \dfrac{4}{-1} = -4$. This is not 2. Discard.

Choice **(E)**: $\dfrac{a-1}{2} = \dfrac{2-1}{2} = \dfrac{1}{2}$. This is not 2. Discard.

You're down to **(A)** and **(C)**. When more than one answer choice remains, you must pick another number. Try $a = 3$. Then $\dfrac{2(3)+6}{3^2+2(3)-3} = \dfrac{6+6}{9+6-3} = \dfrac{12}{12} = 1$.

Now work with the remaining answer choices.

Choice **(A)**: $a = 3$. This is not 1. Discard.

Now that all four incorrect answer choices have been eliminated, you know that **(C)** must be correct. Check to see whether it equals 1 when $a = 3$.

Choice **(C)**: $\dfrac{2}{a-1} = \dfrac{2}{3-1} = \dfrac{2}{2} = 1$. Choice **(C)** does equal 1 when $a = 3$.

This approach to Picking Numbers also applies to many confusing word problems on the GMAT. Picking Numbers can resolve a lot of that confusion. The key to Picking Numbers in word problems is to reread the question stem after you've picked numbers, substituting the numbers in place of the variables.

Example:

A car rental company charges for mileage as follows: x dollars per mile for the first n miles and $x + 1$ dollars per mile for each mile over n miles. How much will the mileage charge be, in dollars, for a journey of d miles, where $d > n$?

O $d(x + 1) - n$
O $xn + d$
O $xn + d(x + 1)$
O $x(n + d) - d$
O $(x + 1)(d - n)$

Suppose that you pick $x = 4$, $n = 3$, and $d = 5$. Now the problem would read like this:

A car rental company charges for mileage as follows: $4 per mile for each of the first 3 miles and $5 per mile for each mile over 3 miles. How much will the mileage charge be, in dollars, for a journey of 5 miles?

All of a sudden, the problem has gotten much more straightforward. The first 3 miles are charged at $4/mile. So that's $4 + $4 + $4, or $12. There are 2 miles remaining, and each one costs $5. So that's $5 + $5, for a total of $10. If the first 3 miles cost $12 and the next 2 cost $10, then the total charge is $12 + $10, which is $22.

Plugging $x = 4$, $n = 3$, and $d = 5$ into the answer choices, you get

(A) $d(x + 1) - n = 5(4 + 1) - 3 = 22$

(B) $xn + d = 4 \times 3 + 5 = 17$

(C) $xn + d(x + 1) = 4 \times 3 + 5(4 + 1) = 37$

(D) $x(n + d) - d = 4(3 + 5) - 5 = 27$

(E) $(x + 1)(d - n) = (4 + 1)(5 - 3) = 10$

Only **(A)** yields the same number you got when you plugged these numbers into the question stem, so **(A)** is the answer. No need for algebra at all.

APPLYING THE KAPLAN METHOD: PICKING NUMBERS WITH VARIABLES IN THE ANSWER CHOICES

Now let's use the Kaplan Method on a Problem Solving question that involves Picking Numbers with variables in the answer choices:

> Cindy paddles her kayak upstream at m kilometers per hour, and then returns downstream the same distance at n kilometers per hour. How many kilometers upstream did she travel if she spent a total of p hours for the round trip?

○ mnp

○ $\dfrac{mn}{p}$

○ $\dfrac{m+n}{p}$

○ $\dfrac{mnp}{m+n}$

○ $\dfrac{pm}{n} - \dfrac{pn}{m}$

Step 1: Analyze the Question

Cindy is going upstream and then the same distance back downstream. Notice that the answer choices contain variables. Whenever the answer choices have variable(s), consider Picking Numbers as an approach.

Step 2: State the Task

The question asks, "How many kilometers upstream did she travel if she spent a total p hours for the round trip?" You're solving not for the total distance of her round trip, just one leg of it.

Step 3: Approach Strategically

It will be hard to pick all the variables at once, so don't try to do so. You can always go one variable at a time. It's often easiest to start with the variable that appears most often, as that value often has the greatest influence over what numbers will be manageable. In this problem, that's the distance upstream (it appears twice, since she goes the same distance downstream). So if you picked that distance to be, say 6 kilometers, you could then easily pick manageable numbers for m and n.

But for the sake of argument, let's say you didn't see that you needed to pick distance. That's OK. If you start by picking two manageable numbers for m and n—for example, $m = 2$ and $n = 3$—then the question becomes this:

> Cindy paddles her kayak upstream at 2 kilometers per hour, and then returns downstream the same distance at 3 kilometers per hour. How many kilometers upstream did she travel if she spent a total of p hours for the round trip?

To figure out the time, you'd need the distance. As none is given, you can pick one. If the speeds are 2 kph and 3 kph, a distance of 6 kilometers works nicely. Now the question is this:

> Cindy paddles her kayak 6 kilometers upstream at 2 kilometers per hour, and then returns downstream 6 kilometers at 3 kilometers per hour. How many kilometers upstream did she travel if she spent a total of p hours for the round trip?

Now time is very straightforward to calculate. Six kilometers upstream at 2 kilometers per hour means a total of 3 hours. Six kilometers downstream at 3 kilometers per hour means a total of 2 hours. That's 3 + 2 = 5 hours for the round trip.

Now plug $m = 2$, $n = 3$, and $p = 5$ into the answer choices to see which yields 6 for the number of kilometers traveled upstream.

(A) $mnp = 2 \times 3 \times 5 = 30$. Eliminate.

(B) $\dfrac{mn}{p} = \dfrac{(2\times3)}{5} = \dfrac{6}{5}$. Eliminate.

(C) $\dfrac{m+n}{p} = \dfrac{(3+2)}{5} = \dfrac{5}{5} = 1$. Eliminate.

(D) $\dfrac{mnp}{m+n} = \dfrac{(2\times3\times5)}{(2+3)} = \dfrac{(2\times3\times5)}{5} = 2\times3 = 6$. **(D)** could be right, but you need to test **(E)** to make sure.

(E) $\dfrac{pm}{n} - \dfrac{pn}{m} = \dfrac{5\times2}{3} - \dfrac{5\times3}{2} = \dfrac{10}{3} - \dfrac{15}{2} = \dfrac{20}{6} - \dfrac{45}{6} = -\dfrac{25}{6}$. Eliminate.

Only choice **(D)** remains, so it is correct.

Step 4: Confirm Your Answer

Make sure to reread the question stem to confirm that you interpreted the information correctly.

Picking Numbers can make word problems much easier to understand, so it's important that you don't hastily start writing down equations. Were you to immediately start writing down algebraic equations for this question, you'd wind up with six variables: speed upstream, speed downstream, time upstream, time downstream, distance for each leg of the trip, and total time. That's a lot to deal with. See how Picking Numbers simplifies things.

TAKEAWAYS: PICKING NUMBERS WITH VARIABLES IN THE ANSWER CHOICES

- Questions with variables in the answer choices comprise the majority of situations in which test takers should consider Picking Numbers.
- After Picking Numbers, reread the question stem, substituting your number(s) for the variable(s).
- When Picking Numbers with variables in the answer choices, check each answer choice to make sure the numbers you picked don't happen to work for more than one choice.
  - Exception: For "could be" questions (e.g., "Which of the following could be odd?"), you can safely choose the first answer choice that works.

PRACTICE SET: PICKING NUMBERS WITH VARIABLES IN THE ANSWER CHOICES

Answers and explanations at end of chapter

12. Each writer for the local newspaper is paid as follows: a dollars for each of the first n stories each month, and $a + b$ dollars for each story thereafter, where $a > b$. How many more dollars will a writer who submits $n + a$ stories in a month earn than a writer who submits $n + b$ stories?

    ○ $(a - b)(a + b + n)$

    ○ $a - b$

    ○ $a^2 - b^2$

    ○ $n(a - b)$

    ○ $an + bn - an$

13. The positive difference between Sam and Lucy's ages is a, and the sum of their ages is z. If Lucy is older than Sam, then which of the following represents Lucy's age?

    ○ $\dfrac{z - a}{2}$

    ○ $a - \dfrac{z}{2}$

    ○ $2a + z$

    ○ $\dfrac{z + a}{2}$

    ○ $\dfrac{a - z}{2}$

14. In order to fulfill a local school's request for x cakes, B parents agreed to each bake an equal number of cakes. If p of the parents did not bake any cakes, which of the following represents the additional number of cakes that each of the other parents had to bake in order for the school's request for x cakes to be fulfilled?

    ○ $\dfrac{px}{B}$

    ○ $\dfrac{px}{B(B - p)}$

    ○ $\dfrac{x}{B - p}$

    ○ $\dfrac{p}{B - px}$

    ○ $\dfrac{p}{B(B - p)}$

PICKING NUMBERS ON MUST BE/COULD BE/CANNOT BE QUESTIONS

This is a slightly different style of question that asks things like "Which of the following must be an even integer?" or "Which of the following CANNOT be true?" These questions are usually based not on algebra or arithmetic but rather on the properties of the numbers themselves. Some of these questions can be very abstract, so Picking Numbers really helps. Just as with word problems, making a number properties question concrete helps you to understand it.

Example:

If *a* and *b* are odd integers, which of the following must be an even integer?

○ $a(b - 2)$
○ $ab + 4$
○ $(a + 2)(b - 4)$
○ $3a + 5b$
○ $a(a + 6)$

You can run through the answer choices quite quickly using the Picking Numbers strategy. Try $a = 1$, $b = 3$. Only **(D)**, $3 + 15 = 18$, is even.

Another approach that works well for many "must be"/"could be"/"cannot be" problems is to pick different numbers for each answer choice, looking to eliminate the wrong answers. The principle of focusing on what's asked is particularly important here, as you need a clear idea of what you're looking for in a wrong answer. Always characterize what you're looking for among the answer choices before you dive in and start testing them. For instance, in the example you just saw, any expression that comes back even may be the correct answer, but any expression that comes back odd must certainly be incorrect and should be eliminated.

Knowing how to test the answer choices on "must be"/"could be"/"cannot be" questions is essential to your success on these questions. As you just saw, on a "must be" question, it's not enough to stop when you reach the first answer choice that works with the numbers you picked. If an answer choice works, that only proves that it *could* be true, not that it *must* be true every time. To be sure you're choosing the right answer to a "must be" or "cannot be" question, pick numbers to eliminate all four incorrect answers. However, for a "could be" question (e.g., "Which of the following could be odd?"), you can safely choose the first answer choice that works. If none of the answer choices work using the numbers you picked, you will need to pick another set of numbers and test the choices again. Always think critically about what the question stem is asking and *how* to pick numbers to find the answer most efficiently.

Roman numeral questions often feature "must be"/"could be"/"cannot be" language in their question stems. Let's look at how to handle one of these questions.

Example:

If integers *x* and *y* are distinct factors of 24, then which of the following CANNOT be a factor of 24?

    I. $(x + y)^2$

    II. $x^2 - y^2$

    III. $xy + y^2$

○   I only
○   I and II
○   II and III
○   II only
○   III only

Roman numeral questions are rare but can be big time wasters if you don't work strategically. Evaluate statements one at a time, eliminating answer choices as you go. Usually you should start with the statement that appears most frequently in the answer choices.

This question asks you to figure out which statement or statements can never be a factor of 24. That means you can eliminate a statement if it could ever possibly equal a factor of 24. If you pick some numbers that don't yield a factor of 24, all that means is that the statement *might* be part of the right answer. But if you pick numbers that do yield a factor of 24, you know that any answer choice that includes that statement can be eliminated. It's much more straightforward, therefore, to prove answers wrong rather than to prove them right.

Since the question involves factors of 24, it's a good idea to list these factors out. Anytime a question deals with a small set of specific numbers, write them down. You'll find keeping track of the options to be much easier:

$$1, 2, 3, 4, 6, 8, 12, 24$$

Statement II appears three times among the answer choices, so if you can eliminate it, you'll be down to two choices right away. Squaring something large like 24 or 12 is going to produce a large number, which wouldn't be a factor of 24. So choose smaller numbers instead: $x = 4$ and $y = 2$, perhaps. Then $x^2 - y^2$ would equal 16 – 4, or 12. 12 is a factor of 24, so you can eliminate any answer choice containing statement II. That leaves only **(A)** and **(E)**.

Look at statement III next. Not only are you squaring and multiplying, but you're also adding, so this number is going to get big fast. To keep it in your target range, pick the smallest numbers on your list, $x = 1$ and $y = 2$. Then $xy + y^2$ would equal 1(2) + 4, or 6. That's a factor of 24, so **(E)** is eliminated. You know that **(A)** is the right answer without ever having to evaluate statement I.

APPLYING THE KAPLAN METHOD: PICKING NUMBERS ON MUST BE/COULD BE/CANNOT BE QUESTIONS

Now let's use the Kaplan Method on a Problem Solving question that involves Picking Numbers with "must be"/"could be"/"cannot be" questions:

If j and k are integers, and $2j + k = 15$, which of the following must be true?

○ $j + k$ is odd.
○ $j + k$ is even.
○ j is odd.
○ k is odd.
○ $k > j$

Step 1: Analyze the Question

You're given the equation $2j + k = 15$ and told that j and k are integers. Those two variables also show up in the answer choices. Whenever the answer choices contain variables, consider Picking Numbers.

Step 2: State the Task

You're looking for an answer that MUST be true. Since you know to characterize the answer choices on "must be"/"could be"/"cannot be" problems, you know to remind yourself that if an answer choice could be false, even in one case, it can be eliminated.

Step 3: Approach Strategically

Pretend for a moment that you weren't able to confidently pick different numbers, trying to see whether each answer could be false and thus eliminated. You'd have to pick one set of numbers and plug them into all the choices.

Let's say that you start with $j = 4$ and $k = 7$.

(A) $4 + 7$ is odd. True. Can't be eliminated.

(B) $4 + 7$ is even. False. Eliminate.

(C) 4 is odd. False. Eliminate.

(D) 7 is odd. True. Can't be eliminated.

(E) $7 > 4$. True. Can't be eliminated.

Now you'd have to try a different set of numbers, hoping to eliminate some more. **(E)** looks like the easiest one to target, as you just have to think of a j that's greater than or equal to k. You could choose $j = 5$ and $k = 5$. There's no need to test **(C)** or **(B)**, as they've already been eliminated.

(A) $5 + 5$ is odd. False. Eliminate.

(D) 5 is odd. True. Can't be eliminated.

(E) $5 > 5$. False. Eliminate.

Only **(D)** wasn't eliminated, so it must be the correct answer.

Step 4: Confirm Your Answer

Make sure to reread the question stem to confirm that you interpreted the stem correctly.

TAKEAWAYS: PICKING NUMBERS ON MUST BE/COULD BE/CANNOT BE QUESTIONS

- On these questions, you can pick numbers and plug them into every answer choice ...
- ... or you can pick different numbers for each answer choice, trying either to eliminate it or to confirm it.
- Characterizing what you're looking for in the answer choices will help you to pick numbers.
- On Roman numeral questions, test the options that appear most often in the available choices, and try to eliminate answer choices.

PRACTICE SET: PICKING NUMBERS ON MUST BE/ COULD BE/CANNOT BE QUESTIONS

Answers and explanations at end of chapter

15. If integers a and b are distinct factors of 30, which of the following CANNOT be a factor of 30?

      I. $ab + b^2$

      II. $(a + b)^2$

      III. $a + b$

   ○ I only

   ○ II only

   ○ III only

   ○ I and II only

   ○ I, II, and III

16. If q and r are both odd numbers, which of the following must also be odd?

   ○ $q - r$

   ○ $(q + r)^2$

   ○ $q(q + r)$

   ○ $(qr)^2$

   ○ $\dfrac{q}{r}$

17. If a, b, and c are positive integers such that a is divisible by b, and c is divisible by a, which of the following is NOT necessarily an integer?

   ○ $\dfrac{a + c}{b}$

   ○ $\dfrac{c - a}{b}$

   ○ $\dfrac{ca}{b}$

   ○ $\dfrac{c + b}{a}$

   ○ $\dfrac{cb}{a}$

BACKSOLVING

Backsolving is just like Picking Numbers, except instead of coming up with the number yourself, you use the numbers in the answer choices. You'll literally work backward through the problem, looking for the answer choice that agrees with the information in the question stem. This is a good approach whenever the task of plugging a choice into the question would allow you to confirm its details in a straightforward way.

You want to Backsolve systematically, not randomly. Start with either **(B)** or **(D)**. If the choice you pick isn't correct, you'll often be able to figure out whether you need to try a number that's larger or one that's smaller. Since numerical answer choices will always be in ascending or descending order, you'll be able to eliminate several choices at once.

Backsolving can save you a great deal of time. It is also an exceptional approach when you have no idea how to begin a problem.

Example:

> Ron begins reading a book at 4:30 p.m. and reads at a steady pace of 30 pages per hour. Michelle begins reading a copy of the same book at 6:00 p.m. If Michelle started 5 pages behind the page that Ron started on and reads at an average pace of 50 pages per hour, at what time would Ron and Michelle be reading the same page?

- O   7:00 p.m.
- O   7:30 p.m.
- O   7:45 p.m.
- O   8:00 p.m.
- O   8:30 p.m.

You could perhaps set up a complex system of equations to solve this problem. Even if you knew exactly what those equations would be and how to solve them, that's not a very efficient use of your time. Backsolving will work better here. Pick an answer choice and see whether Michelle and Ron are on the same page at that time. There's no compelling reason to prefer one choice to another. So just quickly choose **(B)** or **(D)**.

Let's say you choose **(B)**. On what page is Ron at 7:30 p.m.? He started reading at 4:30 p.m., so he's been reading for 3 hours. His pace is 30 pages per hour. So he's read 30 × 3, or 90 pages. Since Michelle started 5 pages behind Ron, she'd need to read 95 pages to be at the same place. She's been reading since 6:00 p.m., so she's read for 1.5 hours. At 50 pages per hour, she's read 75 pages. That's 20 short of what she needs. So **(B)** is not the right answer.

Since Michelle is reading faster than Ron, she'll catch up to him with more time. Therefore, they'll be on the same page sometime later than 7:30 p.m., so you should try an answer choice that gives a later time. The most strategic answer choice to turn to at this point is choice **(D)**. If **(D)** ends up being correct, you can choose it and move on. If **(D)** is too late, then **(C)** must be the answer. If **(D)** is too early, then the correct choice must be **(E)**.

Let's try out **(D)**. At 8:00 p.m. Ron has read for 3.5 hours. At a pace of 30 pages per hour he's read 30 × 3.5, or 105 pages. Since Michelle started 5 pages behind, she'd need to read 110 pages to be at the same place. She's been reading for 2 hours at this point; at 50 pages per hour, she's read 100 pages. That's still 10 short of what she needs to catch up. So **(D)** is also not the right answer, and you need a later time than 8:00 p.m.—choice **(E)** must be correct.

When you start with either **(B)** or **(D)**, you'll have picked the right answer 20 percent of the time. Another 20 percent of the time, you'll know the right answer by process of elimination without ever having to test another choice.

Sometimes you may have to test more than one choice. But as you saw above, you should never have to test more than two answer choices. Stick to **(B)** or **(D)**, and you'll save valuable time and worry.

Example:

A crate of apples contains 1 bruised apple for every 30 apples in the crate. Three out of every 4 bruised apples are considered not fit to sell, and every apple that is not fit to sell is bruised. If there are 12 apples not fit to sell in the crate, how many apples are there in the crate?

O   270
O   360
O   480
O   600
O   840

Start Backsolving with choice **(B)**. Suppose that there are 360 apples in the crate. Then $\frac{360}{30}$ apples, or 12 apples, are bruised. Then $\frac{3}{4}$ of those 12 apples, or 9 apples, are unsalable. This is too few unsalable apples. So **(B)** is too small. The answer must be larger than 360, so **(A)** and **(B)** are eliminated. Regardless of what you might suspect the answer to be, you should next test **(D)**. If **(D)** is not right, you'll know whether it's too large—in which case **(C)** would be correct—or too small—in which case **(E)** would be correct. No matter what, you'll only have to test one more choice.

Testing **(D)**, suppose that there are 600 apples in the crate. Then $\frac{600}{30}$ apples, or 20 apples, are bruised. Of those 20, $\frac{3}{4}$, or 15, are unsalable. That's too many. So **(D)** and **(E)** are both out, proving that **(C)** is correct.

Backsolving works for more than just word problems. You can use it whenever you're solving for a single variable in the question stem.

Example:

What is the value of x if $\dfrac{x+1}{x-3} - \dfrac{x+2}{x-4} = 0$?

O   −2
O   −1
O   0
O   1
O   2

Since **(D)** looks easier to work with than **(B)**, start with that choice.

$$\frac{1+1}{1-3} - \frac{1+2}{1-4} = \frac{2}{-2} - \frac{3}{-3} = -1 - (-1) = 0$$

Therefore, **(D)** is correct, and you don't have to test any more choices.

APPLYING THE KAPLAN METHOD: BACKSOLVING

Now let's use the Kaplan Method on a Problem Solving question that lends itself to Backsolving:

> At a certain zoo, the ratio of sea lions to penguins is 4 to 11. If there are 84 more penguins than sea lions at the zoo, how many sea lions are there?
>
> ○ 24
> ○ 36
> ○ 48
> ○ 72
> ○ 132

Step 1: Analyze the Question

A zoo has more penguins than sea lions, and you're given both a ratio and a numerical difference between them.

Step 2: State the Task

You need to figure out the number of sea lions. You should jot this down in your scratchwork to help you keep track of the task.

Step 3: Approach Strategically

Backsolving is an option whenever you can manageably plug an answer choice into the question stem. After doing so, you merely confirm whether that value is consistent with the other values given in the stem.

Let's say you start by Backsolving answer choice **(B)**. You're pretending that there are, in fact, 36 sea lions. So "the ratio of sea lions to penguins is 4 to 11" becomes "the ratio of 36 to penguins is 4 to 11," or 36:*penguins* is 4:11. If you don't see the number of penguins right away, consider rewriting the ratio vertically:

sea lions : penguins

4 : 11

36 : penguins

You multiply the proportional value (4) by 9 to get the actual value (36). So the actual number of penguins is $11 \times 9 = 99$.

Is that consistent with the rest of the information? There should be 84 more penguins than sea lions, but $99 - 36 = 63$. If **(B)** were correct, there would be only 63 more penguins. You can eliminate **(B)**. Do you need more or fewer sea lions? Well, you need to increase the difference between them. Since the animals are in a ratio of 4:11, every time you remove 4 sea lions, you'd remove 11 penguins, *shrinking* the difference between them by 7. So you definitely need *more* sea lions—every time you add 4 sea lions, you add 11 penguins, increasing the difference by 7. Eliminate **(A)** as well and test **(D)**.

sea lions : penguins

4 : 11

72 : penguins

You multiply the proportional value (4) by 18 to get the actual value (72). So the actual number of penguins is 11 × 18 = 198. (Or you could more simply say that since you've doubled the number of sea lions from what you had in choice **(B)**, you must double the number of penguins as well.)

Is that consistent with the rest of the information? There should be 84 more penguins than sea lions. But 198 − 72 = 126. If **(D)** were correct, there would be 126 more penguins. That's too many more, so **(D)** is eliminated. You need a smaller difference, which means you need a smaller number of sea lions. The answer must be **(C)**.

Step 4: Confirm Your Answer

If you had accidentally answered **(E)**, which is the number of penguins, this step would save you from a wrong answer.

Did you start this problem by adding 84 to the number of sea lions in one of the answer choices and then checking whether it was consistent with the given ratio? That's fine too. If you had trouble figuring out whether you needed to increase or decrease the number of sea lions, you could have either checked all five answer choices, stopping when you found the right ratio, or changed your approach to the question.

TAKEAWAYS: BACKSOLVING

- Like Picking Numbers, Backsolving allows you to plug numbers into the problem. In this case, the numbers are those in the answer choices.
- To Backsolve, plug in a value from an answer choice and solve the problem arithmetically. If your calculations are consistent with the question stem, then the answer is correct.
- The most efficient way to Backsolve is to plug in either **(B)** or **(D)** first. If your first choice isn't correct, consider whether the correct answer is larger or smaller.
- Testing the answer choices strategically allows you to find the answer after testing, at most, two answer choices.

Practice Set: Backsolving

Answers and explanations at end of chapter

18. A teacher grades students' tests by subtracting twice the number of incorrect responses from the number of correct responses. If Student A answers each of the 100 questions on her test and receives a score of 73, how many questions did Student A answer correctly?

   ○ 55
   ○ 60
   ○ 73
   ○ 82
   ○ 91

19. If $2 + \dfrac{2}{x} = 3 - \dfrac{3}{x}$, then $x =$

   ○ −5
   ○ $\dfrac{2}{3}$
   ○ 1
   ○ $\dfrac{3}{2}$
   ○ 5

20. One used-car salesperson receives a commission of $200 plus 4 percent of $1,000 less than the car's final sale price. Another car salesperson earns a straight commission of 6 percent of the car's final sale price. What is the final sale price of a car if both salespeople would earn the same commission for selling it?

   ○ $5,000
   ○ $6,000
   ○ $8,000
   ○ $10,000
   ○ $12,000

STRATEGIC GUESSING

A well-placed guess can sometimes be the best thing you can do on a problem. Because of the severe penalty exacted on those who fail to finish a section, you need to stay on a steady pace. If you fall behind, it's a good idea to guess on the hardest problems. That way you'll get back lost time instead of falling further behind. And while you shouldn't be afraid to guess, you *should* be afraid to rush! The GMAT builds in twists and writes problems in complicated ways; rushing almost always leads to a misperception of the problem. The testmakers base many wrong answers on the most common misperceptions. So rushing through a problem virtually guarantees a wrong answer. It's far better to guess as needed than to rush through an entire section.

Sometimes you just have no idea how to approach a problem. Instead of throwing away three or four minutes getting frustrated, make a guess. If you didn't know how to approach the problem, you weren't likely to choose the right answer in any case, and you can use the time you save to solve other problems that you stand a better chance of answering correctly.

Lastly, there are some problems that are *best* solved using guessing techniques. The two keys to good guessing are (1) elimination of likely wrong answers by using your knowledge of the problem and of the GMAT's tendencies and (2) maintaining your focus on the "big picture" —remembering that your performance on the section as a whole matters much more than your performance on two or three questions. Better to make a guess in one minute and be done with a hard problem than spend six minutes before guessing; the extra time will pay off.

Also keep in mind that the hardest questions are the ones you'll be most likely to need to guess on—and are also the ones that will hurt your score the *least* when you get them wrong. So don't be afraid to guess!

There are six guessing strategies that you can apply to Problem Solving:

1. Use Critical Thinking
2. Estimate the Answer
3. Eliminate Numbers Appearing in the Question Stem
4. Eliminate the Oddball
5. Eliminate Uncritical Solutions
6. On "Which of the Following" Questions, Favor **(D)** and **(E)**

You won't be able to use all of these strategies on every problem. But if you run through the "check-list" and eliminate what you can, you'll make your best possible guess in the least possible amount of time. Let's look at the strategies.

Use Critical Thinking

Some answers are simply logically impossible. By analyzing and simplifying before attempting to solve, you may learn enough about the problem to eliminate many wrong answer choices. Consider this problem:

> A container holding 12 ounces of a solution that is 1 part alcohol to 2 parts water is added to a container holding 8 ounces of a solution that is 1 part alcohol to 3 parts water. What is the ratio of alcohol to water in the resulting solution?
>
> ○   2:5
> ○   3:7
> ○   3:5
> ○   4:7
> ○   7:3

It seems a challenging problem at first glance. But the simplified version of the problem is that you're adding a 1:2 solution to a 1:3 solution. So logically, the right answer has to be between 1:3 (or $\frac{1}{3}$, or 0.333 ...) and 1:2 (or $\frac{1}{2}$, or 0.5). **(A)** and **(B)** are both in that range, but all the others are above 1:2. So you can make a guess—with 50 percent odds of being right—just by analyzing the problem logically.

In case you were curious, the answer is **(B)**. The 12-ounce solution has 4 oz alcohol and 8 oz water. The 8 oz solution has 2 oz alcohol and 6 oz water. Add the amounts of alcohol and water to get 6 oz alcohol and 14 oz water for a ratio of 3:7 alcohol to water.

Also, note that Roman numeral questions are good candidates for logic-based guessing. If you can evaluate only one statement, you can still logically eliminate several answers.

Estimate the Answer

The GMAT asks some questions that are intended to be solved via estimation. When a question stem includes a word like *approximately*, that's a clear signal that estimation is the best approach you can take.

Example:

> The product of all positive even numbers less than or equal to 20 is closest to which of the following?
>
> ○ 10^6
> ○ 10^7
> ○ 10^8
> ○ 10^9
> ○ 10^{10}

If you had a calculator on the Quant section, you could quickly figure out that the product in question is 3,715,891,200. But with no calculator, what can you do? The keys to the solution are the word *closest* and the big spread of values in the answer choices—each is 10 times the nearest value. This problem has "estimation" written all over it.

Jot down the numbers in question:

$$2 \times 4 \times 6 \times 8 \times 10 \times 12 \times 14 \times 16 \times 18 \times 20$$

Now, how to estimate these values? Since each answer is a power of 10, you should estimate each value in a way that easily relates to 10:

$$2 \times 4 \times 6 \times 8 \times 10 \times 12 \times 14 \times 16 \times 18 \times 20$$

$$2 \times 4 \times 6 \times 10 \times 10 \times 10 \times 10 \times 20 \times 20 \times 20$$

What about the small ones? $2 \times 4 \times 6 = 48$, which is very close to 50.

$$50 \times 10 \times 10 \times 10 \times 10 \times 20 \times 20 \times 20$$

Continuing to look for tens:

$$(5 \times 10) \times 10 \times 10 \times 10 \times 10 \times (2 \times 10) \times (2 \times 10) \times (2 \times 10)$$

That's eight 10s, one 5, and three 2s:

$$2 \times 2 \times 2 \times 5 \times 10^8$$

$$(2 \times 2) \times (2 \times 5) \times 10^8$$

$$4 \times 10 \times 10^8$$

$$4 \times 10^9$$

That's closer to 10^9 than to 10^{10}, so **(D)** is the correct answer. No calculator needed, just the willingness to estimate!

Eliminate Numbers Appearing in the Question Stem

The testmakers lay psychological traps as well as mathematical ones, and this guessing principle helps you to stay out of them. It's part of human psychology to deal with being lost by looking for familiar things. When you get lost in a problem, you tend to grab hold of familiar numbers, such as those you've just seen in the question stem. The GMAT doesn't like to reward people who get lost with right answers, so such numbers tend to be wrong.

Eliminate the Oddball

This is psychology again. Our eyes are attracted to difference. (Next time you watch a movie or a TV show, notice how often no one else is dressed in the same color as the main character—it's a subtle trick to keep your attention where the director wants it.) Random guessers, then, will be attracted to uniqueness. As the GMAT does not like to reward random guessing, the "oddballs" should be eliminated.

A word of warning about this technique: The GMAT also uses a little reverse psychology. The testmakers know that people tend to be afraid of answers that seem *too* out of line with the others. These outlying values, then, will sometimes be *correct*. What Kaplan means by an "oddball," then, is *not* a number that's notably bigger or smaller but an answer choice that is structurally unique—the only fraction or the only negative number, for example.

Look at these five answer choices, for example:

- $\sqrt{2}$
- 2
- 4
- 16
- 2,056

In this case, the answer choice 2,056 is *not* an oddball and should not be eliminated. But $\sqrt{2}$ is and should be.

Eliminate Uncritical Solutions

Because the GMAT is a test of critical thinking, answers that you'd get just by mashing numbers together are usually wrong. Consider this question:

> A bag holds 2 red marbles and 3 green marbles. If you removed two randomly selected marbles from the bag, without replacement, what is the probability that both would be red?

- $\frac{1}{10}$
- $\frac{1}{5}$
- $\frac{3}{10}$
- $\frac{2}{5}$
- $\frac{1}{2}$

It's true that you want two of the five marbles in the bag. But GMAT questions usually require a little more math than just that, so $\frac{2}{5}$ isn't likely to be correct. (In fact, it's the odds of getting *one* red marble when selecting one; the probability of getting two red when selecting two is actually $\frac{1}{10}$.)

On "Which of the Following" Questions, Favor (D) and (E)

When Problem Solving questions include the phrase "which of the following," the answer is about 60 percent likely to be either **(D)** or **(E)**. The reason for this is that questions that ask "which of the following" are generally set up in such a way that the only way to solve for the answer is to test the answer choices one by one. On such questions, the testmakers "hide" the correct answers at the end of the set of choices disproportionately often. So if you haven't eliminated both **(D)** and **(E)** for other reasons, the odds are in your favor if you guess one of those two choices. (Note that this is only true for Problem Solving in the Quantitative section, not for any questions in the Verbal section.)

Furthermore, if you do plan to solve the question rather than take a strategic guess, it's a good idea to start by testing choice **(E)** and work your way up through the answer choices, since doing so will often enable you to find the correct answer sooner and avoid spending time testing more choices than necessary.

Stay Alert for Guessing Opportunities

Believe it or not, there are some GMAT problems for which a guessing strategy—most notably Logic or Estimation—is the best approach you could take. Remember that the testmakers aren't trying to judge your math skills alone; they are also testing your ability to find efficient solutions to problems. Every so often, they give you a set of choices with only one logically possible answer. Make sure to look at the answer choices before you choose your approach. Otherwise, you might not realize that you can estimate.

Example:

If a store owner increases a product's price by 20 percent and then increases this price by another 15 percent, what percent of the original price is the total price increase?

    O   20%
    O   35%
    O   38%
    O   65%
    O   135%

It's true that you could pick the original price to be $100, but you can do better here by thinking logically about the question and the answer choices. The price goes up 20% and then up another 15%. That 15% increase is being applied not to the original price but to the price after the first increase. If it were 15% of the original, then the total increase would be 20% + 15% = 35% (that's the "uncritical solution"). But since the second increase is based on a higher starting price, the total increase will be a little more than 35%. Only one answer, choice **(C)**, fits the bill, so it must be correct.

If applied strategically, guessing will be a great tool for you on Test Day. It will help keep you out of time management trouble, help you to feel confident and in charge of the test, and occasionally reward you with a very quick right answer.

ANSWERS AND EXPLANATIONS

1.	D	8.	E	15.	B
2.	B	9.	C	16.	D
3.	E	10.	C	17.	D
4.	C	11.	B	18.	E
5.	B	12.	C	19.	E
6.	E	13.	D	20.	C
7.	D	14.	B		

1. **(D)**

Youssef lives *x* blocks from his office. It takes him 1 minute per block to walk to work and 20 seconds per block to ride his bicycle to work. If it takes him exactly 10 minutes more to walk to work than to ride his bicycle, then *x* equals

- ○ 4
- ○ 7
- ○ 10
- ○ 15
- ○ 20

Step 1: Analyze the Question

Youssef walks a block in 1 minute and bikes a block in 20 seconds. As the answer choices are all in minutes, we can convert the bike rate to 3 blocks per minute. It takes Youssef 10 minutes longer to walk *x* blocks than to bike *x* blocks. Such a setup implies the need for algebra, but that might not be the best way to solve.

Step 2: State the Task

This question asks us to find the value of *x*.

Step 3: Approach Strategically

Setting up the algebra will get complicated quickly, but the answer choices are whole numbers that represent the number of blocks Youssef might have traveled to work, so Backsolving is the best approach. Backsolving is an option whenever you can manageably plug an answer choice into the question stem.

As it takes Youssef 10 more minutes to walk than bike, let's start with **(D)**. If Youssef lives 15 blocks from his office, it would take him 15 minutes to walk (at 1 block per minute) and 5 minutes to bike (at 3 blocks per minute). That's a difference of 15 − 5 = 10 minutes. A 10-minute difference is exactly what we were looking for, so **(D)** is the correct answer.

Step 4: Confirm Your Answer

Walking takes Youssef 10 minutes longer than biking. Since it takes Youssef a minute to walk each block, the correct answer must be greater than 10. That allows us to quickly eliminate choices **(A)**, **(B)**, and **(C)**. Choice **(E)** results in a biking time that isn't a whole number of minutes, which would lead to an answer choice that isn't a whole number. We can therefore confirm that choice **(D)** is correct.

2. **(B)**

A book club rented the party room of a local restaurant to meet and discuss its current novel over dinner. The total charge, including food and service, was $867.50. If each member of the club paid at least $42, then what is the greatest possible number of members in the club?

- ○ 19
- ○ 20
- ○ 21
- ○ 23
- ○ 25

Step 1: Analyze the Question

For word problems, we need to get a logical sense of the situation so that we can understand how the information fits together. This question tells us that some unknown number of people split a bill of $867.50 and that each person paid at least $42—meaning that some could have paid more than $42 but no one could have paid less.

Step 2: State the Task

We have to figure out the greatest possible number of club members. This tells us that there's probably no way to calculate the exact number, but there is some way to set an upper limit on the number.

Step 3: Approach Strategically

Since we're asked about the number of club members, see what the question stem tells us about club members. We're only told that each one paid a minimum of $42. So we'll know something about the total number of members if we learn something about the total amount paid. The question tells us that the total paid was $867.50.

There's no way to figure out the exact number of members—perhaps there are 2 members, each of whom paid $433.75, or perhaps there are 10 members, each of whom paid $86.75. But we know from Step 2 that we don't have to find the exact number, just the biggest number possible. The bigger the number of members, the less each one would have to pay to cover the tab (e.g., if there were 868 members, each would pay a little less than $1). The least each member can pay is $42. So if we split the total of $867.50 into portions of $42, we'll figure out how many members we need to have to cover those portions.

We don't have a calculator, so let's not do $867.50 ÷ $42 through long division. We can get there quickly doing a few easy steps: $42 × 10 is a quick calculation, yielding $420. Twice that is $42 × 20 = $840. One more $42, or $42 × 21, yields $882. That's too much money. If there were 21 members, and each one paid no less than the minimum of $42, then they'd have paid more than the question stem says they did. So there can be at most 20 members (some will have to pay a little more than $42 to meet the bill, but the question allows for that).

Since we have numbers in the answer choices, Backsolving is also a great strategy to use here. Start with **(B)**, since 20 is a nice round number. We have 20 members, each of whom pays a minimum of $42, and in total they pay a minimum of $42 × 20 = $840. The question stem tells us that they paid $867.50, so $840 might be too low a minimum. Eliminate **(A)** and test **(C)**: $42 × 21 = $882, which is too high a minimum. Eliminate **(C)**, **(D)**, and **(E)**. Finally we have a minimum that permits the group to pay $867.50, so **(B)** is the right answer.

Step 4: Confirm Your Answer

Reread the question stem, making sure that you didn't miss anything about the problem. For example, if you misread the question stem to think that each member paid exactly $42, you may not have selected **(B)**. But then when you reread, you'd see the "at least" and realize that you had to rethink your answer choice.

3. **(E)**

A machine manufactures notebooks in a series of five colors: red, blue, black, white, and yellow. After producing a notebook of one color from that series, it produces a notebook of the next color. Once five are produced, the machine repeats the same pattern. If the machine began a day producing a red notebook and completed the day by producing a black notebook, how many notebooks could have been produced that day?

- ○ 27
- ○ 34
- ○ 50
- ○ 61
- ○ 78

Step 1: Analyze the Question

A machine makes notebooks in five colors, following a repeating pattern: red, blue, black, white, and yellow. We can abbreviate this in our scratchwork as: R, Blu, Bla, W, Y. The machine starts on R and ends on Bla.

Step 2: State the Task

How many notebooks could the machine have made? The question makes it clear that there's more than one possible number of notebooks produced, but since this is a multiple-choice question, we know that the answer choices contain only one possible value and four impossible values.

Step 3: Approach Strategically

So, what do we know about what's possible or impossible for this machine?

The numerical answers are so high that it will probably take a long time to count each notebook one by one. Let's see whether there's a way to deduce some sort of pattern or rule that we could apply to know what kinds of numbers are possible or impossible answers.

The machine always follows the same pattern: R, Blu, Bla, W, Y. Since it starts on R, the third notebook will be Bla. Sadly, 3 is not an answer. The machine will make 2 more (W and Y) before the pattern is set to repeat. Then, as before, 3 new notebooks are made before we get Bla. So after the first 3, we needed to make 5 more to get another Bla. Since the pattern repeats, we do the same thing over and over again. So while we don't know exactly how many times the pattern repeats, we know that each time it does, 5 notebooks get made.

In other words, we've reconceptualized the pattern from "repeat {R, Blu, Bla, W, Y}" to "R, Blu, Bla + repeat {W, Y, R, Blu, Bla}."

To get a Bla notebook, then, we make 3 notebooks and then any repetition of 5 notebooks. So the correct answer will be "some multiple of 5" + 3. This means the correct answer will end in either a 3 or an 8. Only **(E)**, 78, which is 75 + 3, is possible.

Step 4: Confirm Your Answer

Reread the question stem, making sure that you didn't miss anything about the problem. For example, if the machine had started on a W notebook, then the answer would have been "some multiple of 5" without the "plus 3."

4. **(C)**

A team won 50 percent of its first 60 games in. a particular season, and 80 percent of its remaining games. If the team won a total of 60 percent of its games that season, what was the total number of games that the team played?

- O   180
- O   120
- O   90
- O   85
- O   30

Step 1: Analyze the Question

We are given many different pieces of information about a team. First, the team won 50% of its first 60 games, for a total of 30 wins. Then we are told that the team won 80% of the remaining games after the initial 60. Finally, we know that the team won 60% of its games overall.

Step 2: State the Task

What was the total number of games the team played throughout the entire season?

Step 3: Approach Strategically

The quickest way to solve this problem is to use Backsolving. We'll start with **(B)**. If the total number of games is equal to 120, we know that the team played 60 more games after the initial 60. They won 80% of the latter 60 games, for a total of 48 games. Adding the initial 30 games won to the 48 games won in the second part of the season, we get 78 games won out of a total of 120 games. We are told the winning percentage is 60% overall, but $\frac{78}{120} = 0.65$, or 65%. This number is too high, so we can eliminate **(B)**.

We must think strategically about which answer choice to try next. The first portion of games has a 50% winning average, while the second portion has an 80% winning average. Since the percentage we calculated for **(B)** was too high and the second portion of games has the higher winning percentage, **(B)** has too much weight on the later portion of games. We need fewer games in the second portion and therefore fewer games total. We can eliminate both **(A)** and **(B)**.

(D) gives a total number of games equaling 85. We have already accounted for the first 60 games, so let's focus on the remaining 25. If the team won 80% of those games, they won 20 more games. In total, the team would have won $\frac{50}{85} \approx 0.59$, or 59%. Since **(D)** is too small (less than 60%) and **(B)** is too big (greater than 60%), we know without calculating that the correct answer is **(C)**.

Step 4: Confirm Your Answer

To confirm our answer, we can Backsolve for **(C)**. If there are 90 total games, then there are 30 games in the second portion of the season. The team won 80% of those games, or 24 games. In total, the team would have won $\frac{54}{90} = 0.6$ or 60%.

5. **(B)**

A local restaurant recently renovated its dining space, purchasing new tables and chairs to use in addition to the original tables and chairs. The new tables each seat six customers, while the original tables each seat four customers. Altogether, the restaurant now has 40 tables and is capable of seating 220 customers. How many more new tables than original tables does the restaurant have?

- ○ 10
- ○ 20
- ○ 30
- ○ 34
- ○ 36

Step 1: Analyze the Question

This is an algebra word problem with two variables. We should also note that we are told that the restaurant has more new tables than old and that the correct answer will represent the difference between those two numbers.

Step 2: State the Task

Our task is to determine the difference between the number of new tables and the number of old tables. We will need to find the number of each and then subtract.

Step 3: Approach Strategically

We could solve this problem by translating the information directly into equations and then combining or substituting the variables to determine the number of each type of table. But Backsolving provides a more efficient route to the correct answer here. When Backsolving, begin with **(B)** or **(D)**, since this will require checking at most two answers. Remembering that we have a total of 40 tables, begin with **(D)**. A difference of 34 would mean that the restaurant has 37 new tables and 3 old tables. With 37 tables seating six diners each (37 × 6 = 222) we are already over our seating capacity of 220. That means we need fewer of the new tables in our mix. Try **(B)**. A difference of 20 means 30 new tables and 10 original tables: 30 × 6 = 180 and 10 × 4 = 40. Adding 180 and 40 gives us 220, the seating capacity indicated in the question stem. Choice **(B)** is correct.

Step 4: Confirm Your Answer

The easiest way to go wrong in a problem like this one is to solve for the wrong thing. Both the number of new tables (30) and the number of old tables (10) are present in an answer choice. A quick check of the question to confirm that the correct answer represents the *difference* between the table types is worthwhile before selecting the answer and moving on.

6. (E)

If $\dfrac{c-a}{c-b} = 2$, then $\dfrac{5b-5a}{c-a} =$

○   0.5

○   1

○   1.5

○   2

○   2.5

Step 1: Analyze the Question

There isn't much to analyze here, as we are given one algebraic expression set equal to 2 and asked to solve for another.

Step 2: State the Task

What is the value of the second expression?

Step 3: Approach Strategically

We are given an initial equation with three variables and asked to solve for a second expression that uses the same variables. Rather than trying to isolate variables or use substitution (which could get complicated with three variables), let's try Picking Numbers. We need to make sure that they are permissible, meaning that they fit the given equation.

Let's start by choosing a value for c, since it appears twice in the initial equation. By setting $c = 4$ and $a = 2$, the numerator becomes 2. Since the numerator is 2 and the entire expression must be equal to 2, the denominator must be equal to 1. We need to choose $b = 3$. Once we have chosen our numbers, we need to plug them into the second expression. Once we do so, the expression becomes $\dfrac{5b-5a}{c-a} = \dfrac{5(3)-5(2)}{4-2} = \dfrac{5}{2} = 2.5$. This corresponds to answer choice **(E)**.

Step 4: Confirm Your Answer

To confirm our answer, we should go back through our math. Check that when the numbers are substituted into the initial equation, we get 2, and that when they are substituted into the second equation, we get 2.5. Since both of these are true, the answer is confirmed.

7. **(D)**

Company Z spent $\frac{1}{4}$ of its revenues last year on marketing and $\frac{1}{7}$ of the remainder on maintenance of its facilities. What fraction of last year's original revenues did company Z have left after its marketing and maintenance expenditures?

- ○ $\frac{5}{14}$

- ○ $\frac{1}{2}$

- ○ $\frac{17}{28}$

- ○ $\frac{9}{14}$

- ○ $\frac{9}{11}$

Step 1: Analyze the Question

Company Z spends portions of its revenues on two things. It's also important to note that the answer choices are fractions, not dollar values and not variable expressions.

Step 2: State the Task

What fraction of last year's revenues did company Z have left after the expenses?

Notice that we are given absolutely no way to know how much revenue company Z received last year. But the answer choices don't contain any variables at all. Somehow, then, the variable that would represent the unknown revenue gets canceled out along the way.

Step 3: Approach Strategically

Whenever variables cancel, leaving only numbers in the answer choices, Picking Numbers is an approach you should consider. Be sure to pick a permissible and manageable number for company Z's revenue. Since we have to take $\frac{1}{4}$ and $\frac{1}{7}$ of the revenue, a number divisible by both 4 and 7 will be most manageable. Let's make the calculations even easier by picking the smallest such number, 28.

Now, "Company Z spent $\frac{1}{4}$ of its revenues last year on marketing," becomes "Company Z spent \$7 last year on marketing."

The next sentence mentions "the remainder," so we need to know what that is. Because \$28 − \$7 = \$21, "Company Z spent ... $\frac{1}{7}$ of the remainder on maintenance," means "Company Z spent ... \$3 on maintenance."

What's left from \$28 after company Z spent \$7 and then \$3 is \$18. So the answer is $\frac{18}{28}$. A common factor of 2 can be canceled from both the numerator and the denominator, leaving $\frac{9}{14}$. Choice **(D)** is correct.

Step 4: Confirm Your Answer

Had you accidentally answered how much company Z spent, which is **(A)**, this step would save you from a wrong answer.

8. **(E)**

During a sale, a store sells 20 percent of its remaining stock each day, without replenishment. After four days, what fraction of its original stock has it sold?

○ $\dfrac{1}{625}$

○ $\dfrac{256}{625}$

○ $\dfrac{61}{125}$

○ $\dfrac{64}{125}$

○ $\dfrac{369}{625}$

Step 1: Analyze the Question

For four days, a store sells the same percentage of its remaining stock each day. In other words, it's not selling the same amount each day but the same proportion of each day's stock.

We're given no way to know exactly how much stock the store starts with. But the answer choices don't have any variables. Whenever variables cancel, leaving only numbers in the answer choices, Picking Numbers is an approach you should consider. Note that the answers are fractions. So despite the word "percent" in the question stem, 100 might not be as safe a choice when Picking Numbers as would a common denominator.

Step 2: State the Task

What fraction of its original stock has the store sold after four days?

Step 3: Approach Strategically

Instead of picking 100 for the stock, pick a common denominator. A good choice seems to be 625. Not only is it the denominator of three of the answer choices, but the number in the other two denominators (125) is a factor of 625.

There's a lot to keep track of—starting stock, stock sold, stock remaining for the next day, all on four different days—so jotting down a chart on your scratch paper would not be a bad idea:

Day	Start	Sold	Remains
1	625	125	500
2	500	100	400
3	400	80	320
4	320	64	256

You can calculate the total amount sold either by adding 125 + 100 + 80 + 64 or by subtracting the eventual remains from the original amount (625 − 256). Whichever approach you take, 369 is the result.

The store sold $\frac{369}{625}$ of its original stock, so choice **(E)** is correct.

Step 4: Confirm Your Answer

Had you accidentally answered **(B)**, which is how much stock remained, or **(D)**, which resembles how much was sold on the fourth day, this step would save you from a wrong answer.

9. **(C)**

If a bicyclist in motion increases his speed by 30 percent and then increases this speed by 10 percent, what percent of the original speed is the total increase in speed?

- ○ 10%
- ○ 40%
- ○ 43%
- ○ 64%
- ○ 140%

Step 1: Analyze the Question

The question gives us information about two increases to the speed of a bicyclist.

Step 2: State the Task

What is the total percent increase?

Step 3: Approach Strategically

When faced with percentages in the question stem and in the answer choices, we should use the strategy of Picking Numbers and pick 100. If the bicyclist is initially riding at 100 (the units aren't mentioned in this problem, and in any case, our numbers don't need to be realistic—just permissible and manageable) and then increases his speed by 30%, he is now riding at 130. To increase 130 by 10%, we can find 10% of 130, which is 13, and add it to 130, making his final speed 143. That is an increase of 43 over his original speed of 100. Since we chose 100 as our initial number, 43 is simply 43% of the original, answer choice **(C)**.

Step 4: Confirm Your Answer

When confirming the answer for questions that ask about multiple percent changes, make sure that you calculated the percent changes appropriately and didn't simply add the percentages given in the question, as **(B)** does. Also, check to make sure that you solved for the correct value, the increase in speed as a percentage of the original speed. **(E)** is a trap answer because it makes the same mistake as **(B)** but is close to the final speed of 143.

10. (C)

Jane makes toy bears. When she works with an assistant, she makes 80 percent more bears per week and works 10 percent fewer hours each week. Having an assistant increases Jane's output of toy bears per hour by what percent?

○ 20%
○ 80%
○ 100%
○ 180%
○ 200%

Step 1: Analyze the Question

Jane seems to work faster with an assistant. Since the answer choices are percents, picking 100 is a good idea.

It's also worth noting that the answer choices are widely spaced—**(A)** has no answer close to it, and **(B)** and **(C)** are much smaller than **(D)** and **(E)**. When answers are spread out, estimation and logic are also great approaches.

Step 2: State the Task

How much does having an assistant increase Jane's output of toy bears per hour?

"Percent increase" is not the same thing as "what percent of the old value is the new value." We need to make sure we solve for the *increase*, not just for the new value.

Step 3: Approach Strategically

Search the question stem for information about "output of toy bears" or "hours." For the former, we read this: "When she works with an assistant, she makes 80% more bears per week." To make things easy, let's say that Jane alone makes 100 bears. With the assistant, she makes 180.

Looking for hours, we read this: "When she works with an assistant, she ... works 10 percent fewer hours each week." So let's say that she initially works 100 hours per week by herself. With an assistant, she works 10 fewer hours, or 90 in total.

Our task is to find the increase in bears/hour. Her rate used to be $\frac{100\,\text{bears}}{100\,\text{hours}}$, or 1 bear per hour. With an assistant, it's $\frac{180\,\text{bears}}{90\,\text{hours}}$, or 2 bears per hour. She has increased from 1 bear per hour to 2 bears per hour. We're solving for the increase, which is 2 − 1, or 1. That's 100% of the original value.

However, look at how our work could have been simpler had we started just by thinking logically about the answers: An 80% increase in bears produced in the same number of hours would mean an 80% increase in bears per hour. But the number of hours does change—it is reduced by 10%. So 80% more bears are made in a little less time than before, so her per-hour output must be a little higher than 80%. Only one answer choice, **(C)**, is a little higher than 80%. So **(C)** must be correct.

Step 4: Confirm Your Answer

Had you chosen **(E)**, which is Jane's new output rate as a percentage of her old rate, confirming your answer would have uncovered that error.

EXPLANATIONS

11. (B)

John spent 40 percent of his earnings last month on rent and 30 percent less than what he spent on rent to purchase a new dishwasher. What percent of last month's earnings did John have left over?

- ○ 30%
- ○ 32%
- ○ 45%
- ○ 68%
- ○ 70%

Step 1: Analyze the Question

John spends 40% on one thing and 30% less than that on another. Since the answer choices are percents, picking 100 is a good idea.

Some answer choices are widely spread out. When choices are spread out, estimation and logic are also great approaches.

Step 2: State the Task

What percent of last month's earnings did John have left over?

We now know that we'd pick $100 as his earnings. (We care much more about picking manageable numbers than about giving imaginary people a living wage.) It's also important to focus on the fact that we are solving for what he has left after paying for rent and the dishwasher, not what he spent on those things.

Step 3: Approach Strategically

Some answer choices could be logically eliminated right away. After spending 40% of his earnings on rent, he'd have 60% left. Then he spends some more. Therefore, no answer 60% or greater could be possible. That eliminates (D) and (E) very quickly. And since simple combinations of percents are rarely the right answer, the odds of the right answer being "subtract 40% and then subtract 30%" are very small. That makes 100% − 40% − 30% = 30%, choice (A), a safe elimination as well. We could make a 50/50 guess very quickly on this problem, which is sometimes a good thing to do if you are falling behind pace.

But let's say that you had the time to solve. Picking $100 for his earnings, we see that John spends $40 on rent. He spends 30% less than $40 on a dishwasher; "30% less than something" is the same as "70% of that something." So John spent 0.7($40), or $28, on a dishwasher. Taking $40 and $28, or $68, away from $100, John is left with $32. That's 32% of his original earnings, so choice (B) is correct.

Step 4: Confirm Your Answer

If you misread "30% less than his rent" as "30% of his earnings," and chosen (A) as a result, this step would save you from a wrong answer. Also, (D) is another trap answer that represents the total percentage of this earnings that John spent.

12. **(C)**

Each writer for the local newspaper is paid as follows: a dollars for each of the first n stories each month, and $a + b$ dollars for each story thereafter, where $a > b$. How many more dollars will a writer who submits $n + a$ stories in a month earn than a writer who submits $n + b$ stories?

○ $(a - b)(a + b + n)$

○ $a - b$

○ $a^2 - b^2$

○ $n(a - b)$

○ $an + bn - an$

Step 1: Analyze the Question

We are given information about the amount reporters are paid for writing newspaper stories. They are paid at one rate for each of a certain number of stories and another rate for each remaining story after that. We are also given information about two specific writers and the number of stories that they write.

Step 2: State the Task

How much more will the first writer earn than the second?

Step 3: Approach Strategically

Since there are variables in the question stem and the answer choices, we will try Picking Numbers. The only rule given in the stimulus is that $a > b$. We can pick $a = 3$ and $b = 2$. The remaining variable is n; for this we should pick a number that is easy to work with, such as 10.

Once we have chosen our numbers, it is helpful to reread the question stem with the new numbers replacing the variables, as this can help the problem make more sense. We want to know how much more a writer who writes $n + a = 10 + 3 = 13$ stories will make than will a writer who writes $n + b = 10 + 2 = 12$ stories.

Let's start with the writer who writes 13 stories. She makes \$3 for each of the first 10 stories, or \$30 total. Then, she makes $a + b = 3 + 2 = \$5$ for each story after that. She wrote 3 more stories, so she earned \$15 more for the additional stories. In total, the writer earned \$45.

Next, look at the writer who wrote 12 stories. She too will make \$3 for each of the first 10 stories, or \$30 total. Then she will make \$5 for each of the remaining 2 stories, another \$10. In total, the second writer earns \$40. Therefore, the difference in the two writers' earnings is \$5, but we're not done yet. Next, we have to plug our variables into the answer choices to find one that gives us \$5.

(A) $(3 - 2)(3 + 2 + 10) = (1)(15) = 15$. Eliminate.

(B) $3 - 2 = 1$. Eliminate.

(C) $3^2 - 2^2 = 9 - 4 = 5$. This could be the correct answer, but we need to keep checking to make sure no other answer choices also calculate to 5.

(D) $10(3 - 2) = 10(1) = 10$. Eliminate.

(E) $3(10) + 2(10) - 3(10) = 30 + 20 - 30 = 20$. Eliminate.

The correct answer is **(C)**. Note that if more than one answer choice were to yield the number 5, we would simply pick new numbers and retry only the answer choices that worked the first time.

Step 4: Confirm Your Answer

Check again to be sure that you correctly substituted the numbers in for the variables in every equation.

13. (D)

The positive difference between Sam and Lucy's ages is a, and the sum of their ages is z. If Lucy is older than Sam, then which of the following represents Lucy's age?

○ $\dfrac{z-a}{2}$

○ $a - \dfrac{z}{2}$

○ $2a + z$

○ $\dfrac{z+a}{2}$

○ $\dfrac{a-z}{2}$

Step 1: Analyze the Question

There are two people—Sam and Lucy—whose ages are related in some way. We don't need to translate to algebra in this step. We don't have to do any math to know that Lucy is the eldest.

Notice that the answer choices contain variables. Whenever this is the case, consider Picking Numbers.

Step 2: State the Task

We're solving for Lucy's age. We'll be careful not to answer with Sam's age, as that's likely to be one of the wrong answers.

Step 3: Approach Strategically

It's easy enough to pick two numbers for a and z. But then you still have to backtrack from those to calculate the two ages. So you still have to do algebra. If this happens, consider reevaluating your approach. Are there other variables you could pick first that would make things easier?

If you pick numbers for Lucy's and Sam's ages, then all you need to do to figure out the values of a and z is simple arithmetic. Let's say that Lucy is 5 years old and Sam is 3 years old. That makes a, their difference, equal to 2. And z, their sum, is equal to 8.

Plug in $a = 2$ and $z = 8$ to see which choices yield Lucy's age of 5.

(A) is $\dfrac{8-2}{2} = \dfrac{6}{2} = 3$. Eliminate.

(B) is $2 - \dfrac{8}{2} = 2 - 4 = -2$. Eliminate.

(C) is $2(2) + 8 = 4 + 8 = 12$. Eliminate.

(D) is $\dfrac{8+2}{2} = \dfrac{10}{2} = 5$. Possibly right.

(E) is $\dfrac{2-8}{2} = \dfrac{-6}{2} = -3$. Eliminate.

As the only possible answer, **(D)** is correct.

Step 4: Confirm Your Answer

Make sure to reread the question stem to confirm that you interpreted the information correctly.

14. (B)

In order to fulfill a local school's request for x cakes, B parents agreed to each bake an equal number of cakes. If p of the parents did not bake any cakes, which of the following represents the additional number of cakes that each of the other parents had to bake in order for the school's request for x cakes to be fulfilled?

○ $\dfrac{px}{B}$

○ $\dfrac{px}{B(B - p)}$

○ $\dfrac{x}{B - p}$

○ $\dfrac{p}{B - px}$

○ $\dfrac{p}{B(B - p)}$

Step 1: Analyze the Question

Remember, don't translate word problems into algebra right away—focus on the logic of the situation first. Some parents are baking cakes for a school, but a couple of them don't follow through, leaving the other parents to pick up the slack.

Notice that the answer choices contain variables. Whenever this is the case, consider Picking Numbers.

Step 2: State the Task

We're solving for the number of extra cakes to be baked by each of the parents who didn't abandon the project.

Step 3: Approach Strategically

Let's pick some numbers for x, B, and p, making sure that the numbers we pick are manageable and permissible (if p is bigger than B, we'll be left with a negative number of parents trying to bake cakes!).

Let's say that we started with 10 parents, so $B = 10$. Now let's say that 4 don't bake any, so $p = 4$. That leaves 6 parents left to bake the cakes. We're going to want to pick x so that it can be divided evenly both by 10 (the original parents) and 6 (the ones who stay on the project). $x = 30$ will do nicely.

Now the question reads:

In order to fulfill a local school's request for *30 cakes, 10 parents* agreed to each bake an equal number of cakes. If *4 of the parents did not bake any cakes,* which of the following represents the additional number of cakes that each of the *6 other parents* had to bake in order for the school's request for *30 cakes* to be fulfilled?

Now the math is much easier to see. If 10 parents agreed to bake an equal number of cakes, totaling 30 cakes, that's 3 cakes for each parent. When 4 of the parents drop out, that leaves 6 parents baking an equal number of cakes, totaling 30 cakes. That's 5 cakes for each parent.

The extra number of cakes each parent needs to bake is 2. Now plug $x = 30$, $B = 10$, and $p = 4$ into the answer choices and see which ones equal 2:

(A) is $\dfrac{4 \times 30}{10} = \dfrac{120}{10} = 12$. Eliminate.

(B) is $\dfrac{4 \times 30}{10(10-4)} = \dfrac{120}{10 \times 6} = \dfrac{120}{60} = 2$. Possibly correct.

(C) is $\dfrac{30}{10-4} = \dfrac{30}{6} = 5$. Eliminate.

(D) is $\dfrac{4}{10-(4 \times 30)} = \dfrac{4}{10-120} = \dfrac{4}{-110} =$ definitely not 2. Eliminate.

(E) is $\dfrac{4}{10(10-4)} = \dfrac{4}{10 \times 6} = \dfrac{4}{60} =$ definitely not 2. Eliminate.

Only **(B)** remains as a possible answer, and it must therefore be correct.

Step 4: Confirm Your Answer

Make sure to reread the question stem to confirm that you interpreted the information correctly.

15. **(B)**

If integers *a* and *b* are distinct factors of 30, which of the following CANNOT be a factor of 30?

> I. $ab + b^2$
>
> II. $(a + b)^2$
>
> III. $a + b$

- ○ I only
- ○ II only
- ○ III only
- ○ I and II only
- ○ I, II, and III

Step 1: Analyze the Question

We are given two integers, *a* and *b*, and are then told that they are distinct factors of 30. This means that *a* cannot equal *b*. Before working out the problem, we should jot down the factors of 30: 1, 2, 3, 5, 6, 10, 15, 30.

Step 2: State the Task

Which of the Roman numeral expressions cannot be a factor of 30?

Step 3: Approach Strategically

We will start with Roman numeral I, not because it is first but because it appears in the most answer choices. Since variables in the expression are multiplied together or squared, the value could get quite large; we should therefore pick small numbers for *a* and *b*. Let's choose *a* = 1 and *b* = 2. Substituting into the equation, we get $1(2) + 2^2 = 2 + 4 = 6$. Since 6 is a factor of 30, Roman numeral I can be a factor of 30. Because we are looking for the choice that CANNOT be a factor of 30, we can eliminate any answer choice containing Roman numeral I: **(A)**, **(D)**, and **(E)** cannot be correct.

Since Roman numerals II and III each appear once in the remaining answer choices, pick the easier expression to evaluate, Roman numeral III. If we again pick *a* = 1 and *b* = 2, we will get 1 + 2 = 3. Because 3 is a factor of 30, we can eliminate **(C)**. Without even needing to evaluate Roman numeral II, we know the correct answer is **(B)**.

Step 4: Confirm Your Answer

We can check our answer by reviewing our substitutions and checking that all expressions were solved correctly.

Alternatively, we can verify that Roman numeral II CANNOT be a factor of 30 by Picking Numbers. If *a* = 1 and *b* = 2, we get $(1 + 2)^2 = 3^2 = 9$, which is not a factor of 30. However, one instance of not being a factor of 30 doesn't mean this expression can never equal a factor of 30. Let's try the next smallest possible set of numbers that would produce a distinct result: *a* = 1 and *b* = 3. Plugging these in, we get $(1 + 3)^2 = 4^2 = 16$, also not a factor of 30. Trying a third set, *a* = 2 and *b* = 3, we get $(2 + 3)^2 = 5^2 = 25$. Again, this is not a factor of 30. One more set is all we need here; if *a* = 1 and *b* = 5, we get $(1 + 5)^2 = 6^2 = 36$. Since this is higher than 30, any other number combination we plug in will also be higher than 30 and therefore not a factor. We have confirmed that **(B)** is correct.

16. (D)

If q and r are both odd numbers, which of the following must also be odd?

- ○ $q - r$
- ○ $(q + r)^2$
- ○ $q(q + r)$
- ○ $(qr)^2$
- ○ $\dfrac{q}{r}$

Step 1: Analyze the Question

Seeing the word "odd" show up in the question stem, we know that this question is about the properties of odd numbers—that is to say, of integers that are not divisible by 2.

We're given two variables that must each be odd. The answer choices are made up of those variables. Whenever the answer choices contain variables, consider Picking Numbers.

Step 2: State the Task

Our task is to find the one answer choice that MUST be odd.

On "must be"/"could be"/"cannot be" problems, it's worthwhile to characterize the answer choices. Thinking a bit about what characterizes the right and wrong answers will help us find the correct solution.

The right answer has to be true, no matter what permissible values are picked for q and r. If an answer choice might not be odd, even if for just one unique set of numbers, then that answer choice can be eliminated. The most efficient approach on these problems is to pick a different set of numbers for each answer choice, trying to eliminate it.

Step 3: Approach Strategically

If you are comfortable with the rules of odd and even numbers, you might well be able to spot the right answer to this problem without Picking Numbers at all. However, the purpose of these questions is to help train your skill at Picking Numbers, so let's continue along those lines.

Since the question says "which of the following," we might save time by starting with **(E)** and working our way up.

(E) Can we pick numbers to make $\frac{q}{r}$ not odd? Sure. Since odd numbers are integers, we'll just pick values for q and r that yield a fraction. If $q = 1$ and $r = 3$, then $\frac{q}{r} = \frac{1}{3}$. Eliminate.

(D) Can we pick numbers to make $(qr)^2$ not odd? Since we're multiplying and squaring, these numbers will get pretty big. Let's start small, with $q = 1$ and $r = 3$ again. $(qr)^2 = 3^2 = 9$. This is odd, so we can't eliminate this choice yet. What if the variables were the same? Let's use $q = 3$ and $r = 3$. $(qr)^2 = 9^2 = 81$. We still can't eliminate. Let's not waste time trying more numbers. Instead, let's work on the other choices. If we eliminate **(C)**, **(B)**, and **(A)**, that'll confirm that **(D)** is correct.

(C) Could $q(q + r)$ not be odd? Using $q = 1$ and $r = 1$ yields $1(1 + 1) = 1(2) = 2$. Eliminate.

(B) Using $q = 1$ and $r = 1$ makes quick work of $(q + r)^2$, which becomes 2^2, or 4. Eliminate.

(A) Using $q = 5$ and $r = 1$ yields $5 - 1 = 4$. Eliminate.

Only one answer, **(D)**, was not eliminated and is therefore correct.

Step 4: Confirm Your Answer

Make sure to reread the question stem to confirm that you interpreted the stem correctly. If we were solving for "which of the following *could* be odd," you might have thought **(E)** was the answer.

17. (D)

If a, b, and c are positive integers such that a is divisible by b, and c is divisible by a, which of the following is NOT necessarily an integer?

○ $\dfrac{a+c}{b}$

○ $\dfrac{c-a}{b}$

○ $\dfrac{ca}{b}$

○ $\dfrac{c+b}{a}$

○ $\dfrac{cb}{a}$

Step 1: Analyze the Question

This question gives us plenty of variables and relationships involving divisibility—a is divisible by b, which means that $\frac{a}{b}$ will be a whole number (and that a is a multiple of b, and that b is a factor of a—these four statements are all equivalent). We also learn that $\frac{c}{a}$ will be a whole number.

We also see that the answer choices are made up of variables. Whenever the answer choices contain variables, consider Picking Numbers.

Step 2: State the Task

Our task is to find the one answer choice that is "not necessarily" an integer. What that means is that all the wrong answers will necessarily be integers—in other words, they *must* be whole numbers. The correct answer is *the only one that could possibly be* a non-integer.

Step 3: Approach Strategically

Characterizing the answer choices can be especially valuable on "could be" questions—we might not have to test all the choices. Since only the right answer could yield a non-integer value, we can try to pick numbers to make each answer a non-integer. As soon as we find one for which we can, we can stop our work—we'll know it's right.

When you're looking for numbers to produce an unusual result—such as what *could* be in a "must be"/"could be"/"cannot be" question, or a different answer to a Data Sufficiency question—it's often helpful to think about the numbers that have unique properties. Fractions, negatives, 0, and 1 all behave differently than other numbers in many situations. This question identifies a, b, and c as positive integers, so negatives, fractions, and 0 are not permitted. But there's no reason that one or more of these variables couldn't equal 1.

We know that $\frac{a}{b}$ and $\frac{c}{a}$ are whole numbers. *Any* integer divided by 1 yields a whole number (the original integer itself), so it would be very easy to pick $b = 1$ and look for the unusual result. (We could pick $a = 1$ as well, if we chose.)

Since the question says "which of the following," let's start with **(E)** and work up.

(E) Can we pick numbers to make $\frac{cb}{a}$ not an integer? Hard to make that happen, even using $b = 1$. Let's pick $b = 1$, $a = 2$, and $c = 4$. Then $\frac{cb}{a} = \frac{4(1)}{2} = 2$. Since c is divisible by a, c times another integer will also be divisible by a. We can't select **(E)** as correct.

(D) Can we pick numbers to make $\frac{(c+b)}{a}$ not an integer? Considering $b = 1$ as a value likely to produce the unusual result really pays off here. If we use $b = 1$, $a = 2$, and $c = 4$ (the same values as before), we get $\frac{(4+1)}{2} = \frac{5}{2} = 2.5$, which is not an integer.

Since only the correct answer could yield a non-integer value, we know that **(D)** is right without testing the others.

Step 4: Confirm Your Answer

Make sure to reread the question stem to confirm that you interpreted the stem correctly.

18. (E)

A teacher grades students' tests by subtracting twice the number of incorrect responses from the number of correct responses. If Student A answers each of the 100 questions on her test and receives a score of 73, how many questions did Student A answer correctly?

- ○ 55
- ○ 60
- ○ 73
- ○ 82
- ○ 91

Step 1: Analyze the Question

Student A received a score of 73 for answering 100 questions. Her score is computed by subtracting twice the number of incorrect answers from the number of correct answers.

Step 2: State the Task

Find the number of questions Student A answered correctly.

Step 3: Approach Strategically

We could solve this problem algebraically, but seeing whole numbers in the answer choices is a clue that it might be easier to Backsolve this one instead. Backsolving is an option whenever you can manageably plug an answer choice into the question stem.

A penalty equal to twice the number of incorrect answers is rather harsh, so a student would have to answer many questions correctly to receive a decent score. Therefore, let's begin by testing **(D)**. If Student A answered 82 questions out of 100 correctly, she must have gotten $100 - 82 = 18$ incorrect. On Test Day, do not actually calculate $82 - 2(18) = 82 - 36 = 46$. Instead, get into the habit of realizing that 82 minus such a large penalty will definitely result in a number that's smaller than 73. As **(D)** is too small, the correct answer choice must be **(E)**.

Step 4: Confirm Your Answer

If Student A got 91 questions right, she would have gotten $100 - 91 = 9$ questions wrong. That would result in a score of $91 - 2(9) = 91 - 18 = 73$, the exact score we are looking for. The astute test taker will notice that a score of 73 on such a punishing scale allows us to eliminate choices **(A)**, **(B)**, and **(C)** before we even begin; this student must have answered more than 73 questions correctly to receive that score.

19. (E)

If $2 + \dfrac{2}{x} = 3 - \dfrac{3}{x}$, then $x =$

○ -5

○ $\dfrac{2}{3}$

○ 1

○ $\dfrac{3}{2}$

○ 5

Step 1: Analyze the Question

This question gives us a complicated-looking equation with one variable. The answer choices are just numbers.

Step 2: State the Task

Our task is to solve for the value of x.

Step 3: Approach Strategically

Since the answer choices are potential values for the variable in the equation, we could just plug those values back in to see which value makes the equation true. Backsolving is an option whenever you can manageably plug an answer choice into the question stem.

Let's say that you started with **(D)**, $x = \dfrac{3}{2}$. That makes the equation

$$2 + \frac{2}{\dfrac{3}{2}} = 3 - \frac{3}{\dfrac{3}{2}}$$

$$2 + \left(2 \times \frac{2}{3}\right) = 3 - \left(3 \times \frac{2}{3}\right)$$

$$2 + \frac{4}{3} = 3 - 2$$

$$\frac{10}{3} = 1$$

That's not a true statement. So we need to try other values. It's very hard to see whether you needed a larger or smaller x, so it's perfectly fine to try different answer choices. **(C)** is a sensible choice to test next, as it's the most manageable. It would leave you with $2 + 2 = 3 - 3$, which is also false.

(E) is the next most manageable. Plugging 5 in for x makes the equation

$$2 + \frac{2}{5} = 3 - \frac{3}{5}$$

$$\frac{12}{5} = \frac{12}{5}$$

That's true, so **(E)** is correct.

Step 4: Confirm Your Answer

Reread the original equation, making sure you didn't make a careless error such as switching the plus and minus signs.

20. (C)

One used-car salesperson receives a commission of $200 plus 4 percent of $1,000 less than the car's final sale price. Another car salesperson earns a straight commission of 6 percent of the car's final sale price. What is the final sale price of a car if both salespeople would earn the same commission for selling it?

- ○ $5,000
- ○ $6,000
- ○ $8,000
- ○ $10,000
- ○ $12,000

Step 1: Analyze the Question

This question presents us with two salespeople, each with different commission rules. Don't jump to translating the information algebraically, as that might not be the most strategic solution.

Step 2: State the Task

Our task is to find the price of a car for which the two salespeople would earn an equal commission.

Step 3: Approach Strategically

Since we could just pick a price from the answer choices and see whether the salespeople earn the same commission, Backsolving is a good choice. Backsolving is an option whenever you can manageably plug an answer choice into the question stem.

Let's say that you started with **(D)**, the $10,000 car. Salesperson 1 earns $200 + 4% of $9,000. That's $200 + $360 = $560. Salesperson 2 earns 6% of $10,000, or $600. They aren't earning the same commission, so we can eliminate **(D)**.

How does the price of the car need to change? If you have trouble figuring out abstractly whether you need a larger or smaller value, consider what would happen with extremely large or extremely small values. With a $10,000 car, we saw that Salesperson 2 earns just $40 more. But if the car cost $10 billion, then that extra 2% earned by Salesperson 2 would be so large as to make the extra $200 earned by Salesperson 1 meaningless. So, as the car gets more expensive, Salesperson 2 gets more money relative to Salesperson 1. Therefore, the correct answer must be less than $10,000. Eliminate **(E)** and test **(B)**.

If the car were $6,000, then Salesperson 1 would earn $200 + 4% of $5,000. That's $200 + $200 = $400. Salesperson 2 would earn 6% of $6,000, or $360. Now the car is too cheap. So **(C)** must be the answer.

Step 4: Confirm Your Answer

Reread the question, making sure you didn't miss anything. For example, if you overlooked the "$1,000 less than" phrase, you'd have selected **(D)**. This step would save you from the wrong answer.

GMAT BY THE NUMBERS: PROBLEM SOLVING

Now that you've learned how to approach Problem Solving questions on the GMAT, let's add one more dimension to your understanding of how they work.

Take a moment to try the following question. The next page features performance data from thousands of people who have studied with Kaplan over the decades. Through analyzing this data, we will show you how to approach questions like this one most effectively and how to avoid similarly tempting wrong answer choice types on Test Day.

The number x of cars sold each week varies with the price y in dollars according to the equation $x = 800{,}000 - 50y$. What would be the total weekly revenue, in dollars, from the sale of cars priced at $15,000?

- ○ 50,000
- ○ 750,000
- ○ 850,000
- ○ 7,500,000
- ○ 750,000,000

EXPLANATION

The first—and in many ways most important—step in Problem Solving is to understand what you're solving for. This problem gives you an equation: $x = 800,000 - 50y$, with x representing the number of cars sold and y representing their price. You're given the price, so $y = 15,000$. But you aren't solving for x. Rather, you're solving for the total revenue. You'll therefore find the number of cars sold (x), then multiply by their price ($\$15,000$).

Substituting 15,000 for y in the equation, you get:

$$x = 800,000 - 50y$$

$$x = 800,000 - 50(15,000)$$

$$x = 800,000 - 750,000$$

$$x = 50,000$$

Multiplying 50,000 cars by $\$15,000$ yields a total revenue of $\$750,000,000$. Answer choice **(E)** is correct.

QUESTION STATISTICS

30% of test takers choose **(A)**

18% of test takers choose **(B)**

3% of test takers choose **(C)**

5% of test takers choose **(D)**

44% of test takers choose **(E)**

Sample size = 4,464

Notice that the actual math involved here is not extremely challenging, yet fewer than half of test takers select the right answer. That's because two wrong answers are actually right answers—but to the wrong questions. **(A)**, the most popular incorrect answer choice, is actually the value of x. It's easy to assume that you're solving for a variable given to you by the problem, but often you won't be. **(B)**, the other commonly selected wrong answer, is the value of $50y$. These "intermediate values" that you generate on your way to the right answer make for very tempting wrong answers—so tempting in this problem that more test takers choose them than the right answer! Be clear about what you need to solve for, and you'll avoid the biggest Problem Solving pitfall.

MORE GMAT BY THE NUMBERS ...

To see more questions with answer choice statistics, be sure to review the full-length CATs in your Online Center.

CHAPTER 11

Data Sufficiency

Is the product of *x*, *y*, and *z* equal to 1?

(1) $x + y + z = 3$

(2) *x*, *y*, and *z* are each greater than 0.

○   Statement (1) ALONE is sufficient, but statement (2) is not sufficient.

○   Statement (2) ALONE is sufficient, but statement (1) is not sufficient.

○   BOTH statements TOGETHER are sufficient, but NEITHER statement ALONE is sufficient.

○   EACH statement ALONE is sufficient.

○   Statements (1) and (2) TOGETHER are NOT sufficient.

Above is a typical Data Sufficiency question. In this chapter, we'll look at how to apply the Kaplan Method to this question, discuss how to tackle this question type, and go over the basic principles and strategies that you want to keep in mind on every Data Sufficiency question. But before you move on, take a minute to think about what you see in this question and answer some questions about how you think it works:

- How is the structure of this question different from that of a typical "math" question?

- What mathematical concepts are tested in this question?

- How can you use the answer choices to your advantage?

- What GMAT Core Competencies are most essential to success on this question?

PREVIEWING DATA SUFFICIENCY

How Is the Structure of This Question Different from That of a Typical "Math" Question?

The problem starts off with the question stem, which asks whether the product of *x*, *y*, and *z* equals the value of 1. But then there's no other information in the question stem. So how are you supposed to answer the question? A Data Sufficiency question stem will never give you enough information to solve for an answer, which is very different from typical math problems. You're probably used to having a lot of information presented up front, followed by the actual question. But Data Sufficiency works differently: The other data are presented *after* the initial question; these are called the "statements." Your goal in a Data Sufficiency question is to determine whether the data in the statements are enough to allow you to answer the question.

Sound unusual? Absolutely. Data Sufficiency is unique to the GMAT—no other standardized test presents questions in this format. Confusing? It doesn't have to be. As just noted, all you need to do is determine whether the data are sufficient to be able to answer the question. What is *not* your goal? To do a lot of time-consuming calculations. Business schools don't care about how many advanced math classes you took. They care about something else: They want to know that you're able to assimilate a lot of information and make deductions from that information. Many Data Sufficiency questions can be solved without finding the specific answer to the question presented in the stem.

What Mathematical Concepts Are Tested in This Question?

At first, it appears that this question tests only some fairly basic arithmetic concepts: namely, multiplication (in the question stem), addition (in the first statement), and inequalities (in the second statement). But as is often the case on GMAT Quantitative questions, what's *not* stated is also important. This is not merely an arithmetic question. It's testing number properties: how numbers with certain characteristics behave in predictable ways. A careless test taker might take for granted that *x*, *y*, and *z* are integers. But unless the question stem says so, never assume that variables must be integers—or even positive numbers, for that matter. Training your mind to think like this on the GMAT will take time and practice, but using the Kaplan Method for Data Sufficiency and remembering how to apply the Core Competencies will help you through even the toughest Data Sufficiency questions.

How Can You Use the Answer Choices to Your Advantage?

Earlier you read that Data Sufficiency questions don't necessarily require you to solve the problem. This is because the answer choices are in a fixed format. All five of the answer choices have to do with the "sufficiency" or "insufficiency" of the statements. In other words, does one of the statements alone provide enough information to answer the question? Do both of them? Do both of them, but only when combined? Or is there just not enough information? Again, the answer choices will never give you actual values or expressions, such as "35,612" or "$4x^3 - 15y$." We'll show you how to use this fixed format to your advantage.

What GMAT Core Competencies Are Most Essential to Success on This Question?

For all Data Sufficiency questions, Critical Thinking is crucial. Mastering the format and structure will put you at an advantage over your competition, since Data Sufficiency is notoriously one of the greatest challenges for most GMAT test takers. By understanding how these questions are constructed and what the potential traps are, you will know how to get at the heart of what the testmakers are asking you to do.

Attention to the Right Detail is also key to your success on Data Sufficiency. Most importantly, don't fail to consider the details that *aren't* mentioned or the restrictions that *don't* exist. Never assume anything in a Data Sufficiency question.

Here are the main topics we'll cover in this chapter:

- Question Format and Structure
- The Kaplan Method for Data Sufficiency
- The Basic Principles of Data Sufficiency
- Data Sufficiency Strategy
  - Picking Numbers in Data Sufficiency
  - Combining Statements
  - Strategic Guessing

QUESTION FORMAT AND STRUCTURE

The instructions for the Data Sufficiency section on the GMAT look like this:

Directions: In each of the problems, a question is followed by two statements containing certain data. You are to determine whether the data provided by the statements are sufficient to answer the question. Choose the correct answer based upon the statements' data, your knowledge of mathematics, and your familiarity with everyday facts (such as the number of minutes in an hour or cents in a dollar). You must indicate whether

O   Statement (1) ALONE is sufficient, but statement (2) is not sufficient.

O   Statement (2) ALONE is sufficient, but statement (1) is not sufficient.

O   BOTH statements TOGETHER are sufficient, but NEITHER statement ALONE is sufficient.

O   EACH statement ALONE is sufficient.

O   Statements (1) and (2) TOGETHER are NOT sufficient.

Note: Diagrams accompanying problems agree with information given in the question but may not agree with additional information given in statements (1) and (2).

All numbers used are real numbers.

The GMAT is the only test featuring Data Sufficiency questions, and beginners often misunderstand the format. On the Quantitative section, you'll see about 15 Data Sufficiency questions, which ask you to assess whether certain statements provide enough information to answer a question. Often the question requires little or no mathematical work. The key to solving the question is understanding how the question type is structured and using that knowledge to work efficiently.

The directions may seem confusing at first, but they become clear with use. Let's walk through a simple example:

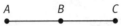

What is the length of segment *AC*?

(1) *B* is the midpoint of *AC*.

(2) *AB* = 5

○   Statement (1) ALONE is sufficient, but statement (2) is not sufficient.

○   Statement (2) ALONE is sufficient, but statement (1) is not sufficient.

○   BOTH statements TOGETHER are sufficient, but NEITHER statement ALONE is sufficient.

○   EACH statement ALONE is sufficient.

○   Statements (1) and (2) TOGETHER are NOT sufficient.

The diagram tells you that there is a line segment *AC* with point *B* somewhere between *A* and *C*. You're asked to figure out the length of *AC*.

Statement (1) tells you that *B* is the midpoint of *AC*, so $AB = BC$ and $AC = 2AB = 2BC$. Since Statement (1) does not give an actual value for *AB* or *BC*, you cannot answer the question using Statement (1) alone.

Statement (2) says that $AB = 5$. Since Statement (2) does not give you any information about *BC*, the question cannot be answered using Statement (2) alone.

Using both of the statements together, you can find a value for both *AB* and *BC*; therefore you can solve for the length of *AC*, and the answer to the question is choice **(C)**.

THE KAPLAN METHOD FOR DATA SUFFICIENCY

This Method is the essential systematic approach to mastering Data Sufficiency. Use this approach for every Data Sufficiency question. It will allow you to answer questions quickly and will guarantee that you avoid the common Data Sufficiency mistake of subconsciously combining the statements instead of considering them separately at first.

The Kaplan Method for Data Sufficiency
1. Analyze the question stem.   • Determine Value or Yes/No.   • Simplify.   • Identify what is needed to answer the question.   **2. Evaluate the statements using 12TEN.**

STEP 1: ANALYZE THE QUESTION STEM

There are three things you should accomplish in this step:

- **Determine Value or Yes/No.** Which type of Data Sufficiency question is this? Depending on whether the question is a Value question or a Yes/No question, the rules for sufficiency are a little different. If you treat the two types the same way, you probably won't get the right answer. Later in this chapter, you'll learn the critical differences between these two types.

- **Simplify.** If the given information is an equation that can be simplified, you should do so up front. Likewise, any word problems should be translated into math or otherwise paraphrased in your scratchwork. When a question asks for the value of a specific variable and gives you a multi-variable equation, isolate the variable being asked for so you can more clearly see what kind of information you need in order to solve.

- **Identify What Is Needed to Answer the Question.** What kind of information would get you the answer to the question? The more you think up front about what information would be sufficient, the better you'll be able to evaluate the statements.

Don't rush through this step, even for seemingly simple questions. The more you glean from the question stem, the easier it will be to find the right answer.

STEP 2: EVALUATE THE STATEMENTS USING 12TEN

Since the answer choices depend on considering each statement alone, don't let the information you learn from one statement carry over into your analysis of the other. Consider each statement separately, in conjunction with the question stem. Remember that each statement is always true. Don't waste time verifying the statements; just evaluate whether this information lets you answer the question.

On Test Day, you don't want to spend even a second reading the answer choices or thinking about which answer choice is which. They will never change, so you will save yourself much time and confusion by memorizing what the answer choices mean and working with them until you've fully internalized them.

A helpful way to remember how the answer choices are structured is to use the acronym **1-2-TEN**.

1	Only Statement **(1)** is sufficient.
2	Only Statement **(2)** is sufficient.
T	You must put the statements **together** for them to be sufficient.
E	**Either** statement alone is sufficient.
N	**Neither** separately nor together are the statements sufficient.

In fact, it's so important to memorize the answer choices that after this initial sample question, we will no longer print the choices along with the questions. For each practice question, you should follow the routine you will use on Test Day: Write 12TEN in your scratchwork for each question and cross out the incorrect answer choices as you eliminate them. We'll teach you patterns for eliminating answer choices later in this chapter.

Now, let's apply the Kaplan Method for Data Sufficiency to the question you saw at the beginning of this chapter:

Is the product of x, y, and z equal to 1?

(1) $x + y + z = 3$

(2) x, y, and z are each greater than 0.

○ Statement (1) ALONE is sufficient, but statement (2) is not sufficient.
○ Statement (2) ALONE is sufficient, but statement (1) is not sufficient.
○ BOTH statements TOGETHER are sufficient, but NEITHER statement ALONE is sufficient.
○ EACH statement ALONE is sufficient.
○ Statements (1) and (2) TOGETHER are NOT sufficient.

Step 1: Analyze the Question Stem

This is a Yes/No question. If $xyz = 1$, then the answer is "yes." If $xyz \neq 1$, then the answer is "no." Either answer—"yes" or "no"—would be sufficient. There's nothing that needs to be simplified in this step; all variables are in their simplest terms, and there are no common variables to combine. It's often worth thinking about how you could get the "yes" or "no" that you're looking for. For instance, if x, y, and z all equal 1, you would get an answer of "yes." But is this the only way? This question is short but definitely not simple, since there may be many other possibilities to consider.

Step 2: Evaluate the Statements Using 12TEN

Picking Numbers for Statement (1), you can readily see how to get a "yes": $x = 1$, $y = 1$, and $z = 1$. Can you Pick Numbers in such a way that the sum is 3 but the product is not 1? Not if you only consider positive integers. But if you consider different kinds of numbers, you can easily find some. Zero doesn't alter a sum, but it forces a product to be 0. So $x = 3$, $y = 0$, and $z = 0$, while they follow the restrictions given in Statement (1), will give you an answer of "no" to the original question. Since you can get both a "yes" and a "no," Statement (1) is insufficient. Eliminate **(A)** and **(D)**—or choices "1" and "E," if you've written 12TEN in your scratchwork.

Now that you've reached a verdict on Statement (1) on its own, completely put Statement (1) out of your mind as you evaluate Statement (2) independently. Statement (2) rules out the possibility of using 0 but not the possibility of using fractions or decimals. So $x = 1$, $y = 1$, and $z = 1$ is also permissible here, but so is something like $x = 100$, $y = 100$, and $z = 100$. So xyz could equal 1, but it could also equal 1,000,000. So you can get both a "yes" and a "no" here, as well. Statement (2) is also insufficient, so you can eliminate **(B)**—which is the "2" of 12TEN.

Since each statement is insufficient on its own, you need to consider them together. Can you pick numbers that add to 3 and are all positive? Again, $x = 1$, $y = 1$, and $z = 1$ makes the cut and answers the question with a "yes." Can you think of numbers that *don't* multiply to 1 that also are consistent with both statements? Once again, you have to expand your thinking to include other types of numbers besides positive integers. Fractions and decimals make things bigger when added but smaller when multiplied. For example, $x = 2.8$, $y = 0.1$, and $z = 0.1$ fit the bill. They are all positive and sum to 3. Their product is $2.8(0.1)(0.1) = 0.028$; this answers the question with a "no." Since you can get both a "yes" and a "no" answer, the statements are insufficient to answer the question even when combined. The answer is **(E)**—which corresponds to the "N" of 12TEN.

Now take a few minutes and answer the questions in the following practice set. Don't worry if they're challenging at first; you're only getting started working with this unique question type. For now, do not concentrate on speed—or even on getting the correct answer in the end—but rather on building your technique for approaching Data Sufficiency questions systematically using the Method. You'll get much more practice with these questions throughout the chapter.

PRACTICE SET: THE KAPLAN METHOD FOR DATA SUFFICIENCY

Answers and explanations at end of chapter

1. If $x > 0$, what is the value of x?

   (1) $x > 5$
   (2) $40 - x^2 = 4$

2. If $a > 0$, $b > 0$, and $2c = \sqrt{\dfrac{a}{b}}$, what is the value of b?

   (1) $a = 8$ and $c = 2$
   (2) $\dfrac{c^2}{a} = \dfrac{1}{2}$

3. Team X won 40 basketball games. What percent of its basketball games did Team X win?

   (1) Team X played the same number of basketball games as Team Y.
   (2) Team Y won 45 games, representing 2.5 percent of the basketball games it played.

4. If $2b - a^2 = 18$, what is the value of b?

   (1) $a^2 = 1,156$

   (2) $a > 0$

5. A certain company produces exactly three products: X, Y, and Z. In 1990, what was the total income for the company from the sale of its products?

   (1) In 1990, the company sold 8,000 units of product X, 10,000 units of product Y, and 16,000 units of product Z.

   (2) In 1990, the company charged $28 per unit for product X and twice as much for product Z.

THE BASIC PRINCIPLES OF DATA SUFFICIENCY

Especially because this question type is more abstract than Problem Solving, it's essential to have a strategic approach to every Data Sufficiency question. Don't waste time or mental energy doing unnecessary calculations. A systematic approach will ensure that you find the most efficient solution to the problem and that you make as few careless and avoidable errors as possible. Here are some ways you can optimize your Data Sufficiency performance by using the Kaplan Method.

KNOW HOW TO ELIMINATE DATA SUFFICIENCY ANSWER CHOICES

As you've already learned, the directions and answer choices for Data Sufficiency questions never change, so it's to your advantage to memorize them. But you can take this approach one step further by learning how to eliminate answer choices as you work through Data Sufficiency problems.

As you evaluate the two statements, use your noteboard to keep track of which answer choices you have ruled out as incorrect. Use the following patterns to guide your elimination:

> If Statement (1) is sufficient, the answer could only be **(A)** or **(D)**. *Eliminate* **(B)**, **(C)**, *and* **(E)**.
>
> If Statement (1) is insufficient, the answer could only be **(B)**, **(C)**, or **(E)**. *Eliminate* **(A)** *and* **(D)**.
>
> If Statement (2) is sufficient, the answer could only be **(B)** or **(D)**. *Eliminate* **(A)**, **(C)**, *and* **(E)**.
>
> If Statement (2) is insufficient, the answer could only be **(A)**, **(C)**, or **(E)**. *Eliminate* **(B)** *and* **(D)**.

Using the mnemonic device 12TEN will help you keep track of these answer choices, allowing you to attack the question more efficiently and avoid considering an answer choice you've already ruled out.

You also want to avoid a common mistake on Data Sufficiency: choosing **(C)** when the answer is actually **(A)**, **(B)**, or **(D)**. Remember: If either statement *by itself* is sufficient, then of course the two statements *together* will also be sufficient, since the statements are always true and never contradict each other. But **(C)** can be correct *only* when each statement alone is insufficient and combining the statements is necessary to obtain sufficiency.

You should consider the statements together only if each is insufficient on its own. When you evaluate the statements together, keep in mind that each statement is true. So if you're Picking Numbers to evaluate the statements combined, you must choose values that are permitted by *both* statements.

KNOW THE TWO TYPES OF DATA SUFFICIENCY QUESTIONS

There are two broad types of Data Sufficiency questions, and they play by slightly different rules. The two types are Value questions and Yes/No questions. During Step 1 of the Kaplan Method for Data Sufficiency, you need to determine which type of question you're dealing with, since this will determine your approach.

Value Questions

A Value question will ask you for the exact value of something. If a statement narrows the possibilities down to exactly one number, then it is sufficient. Otherwise, it is not. Of the Data Sufficiency questions you'll see on Test Day, approximately two-thirds will be Value questions.

Let's take a closer look at how this question type functions using a sample question:

Example:

What is the value of x?

(1) $x^2 - 7x + 6 = 0$
(2) $5x = 30$

Step 1: Analyze the Question Stem

This is a Value question, meaning you need to find the value of x to obtain sufficiency. There's nothing that needs to be simplified in this step, since there's just one variable: x. Before you evaluate the statements, remember that sufficiency is obtained when you can identify one, and *only* one, possible value for x.

Step 2: Evaluate the Statements Using 12TEN

Statement (1) can be reverse-FOILed to $(x - 1)(x - 6) = 0$, which means that there are two possible values for x, either 1 or 6. But you don't even need to calculate these two values; once you know there is more than one possible value, you know that Statement (1) must be insufficient.

Statement (2) is a linear equation, containing a single variable. Therefore, there can only be one possible result (in this case, $x = 6$), and it is sufficient.

Since Statement (1) is insufficient and Statement (2) is sufficient by itself, the answer is **(B)**.

PRACTICE SET: VALUE QUESTIONS

Answers and explanations at end of chapter

6. What is the value of $4n - 5m$?

    (1) $\dfrac{n}{5} = \dfrac{m}{4}$

    (2) $\dfrac{n}{4} = \dfrac{m}{5}$

7. What is the value of $\dfrac{st}{u}$?

    (1) $s = \dfrac{3t}{4}$ and $u = 2t$.

    (2) $s = u - 10$ and $u = s + t + 2$.

8. If z is an integer, what is the units digit of z^3?

    (1) z is a multiple of 5.

    (2) $\sqrt{z}$ is an integer.

9. What is the value of the integer p?

    (1) p is a prime number.

    (2) $88 \leq p \leq 95$

Yes/No Questions

Yes/No questions are, simply put, questions that call for a "yes" or a "no" answer. A key difference between Value questions and Yes/No questions is that a range of values can establish sufficiency for Yes/No questions. For example, if a question asks "Is $x > 10$?" a statement saying $x < 9$ will be sufficient.

Note that in this example, the answer to the question in the stem is, "No, x is never greater than 10." Don't confuse a "yes" to the question "Is Statement (1) sufficient?" with a "yes" to the question in the stem; they are not the same. This mistake is the most common pitfall test takers face on Yes/No questions. You can avoid this pitfall by remembering that any answer of "ALWAYS yes" or "ALWAYS no" is sufficient; only "sometimes yes, sometimes no" answers are insufficient. The definitiveness of your answer to the stem question is more important in determining sufficiency than whether the answer itself happens to be "yes" or "no."

Sometimes Yes/No questions don't appear to call for a "yes" or "no" answer. Suppose a Data Sufficiency question asks which employee, Jane or Sam, earned more in 2009. Ask yourself, "Do I absolutely need to know the specific values for Jane and Sam?" As it turns out, you don't. You should handle this question the same way as you would a Yes/No question that asked, "Did Jane earn more than Sam last year?" In both cases you have sufficient information when you determine that only one answer is possible—Jane or Sam—even if you don't know a precise value for either Jane's earnings or Sam's earnings. Again, you can determine sufficiency knowing only ranges of values (for example, it's sufficient to know that Jane earned more than $20,000 and that Sam earned less than $16,000).

Let's take a closer look at how this question type functions using a sample question:

Example:

> If x is an integer, and $0 < x < 4$, is x prime?
>
> (1) $x > 1$
> (2) x is even.

Step 1: Analyze the Question Stem

This is a Yes/No question, meaning you need to determine whether x is prime or not. According to the question stem, x could be 1, 2, or 3. You know that 2 and 3 are prime but 1 is not. In order to attain a definite "yes" answer, x must be either 2 or 3, and to obtain a definite "no" answer, x must be equal to 1. In other words, you could restate the question as "Does x equal 2 or 3?"

Step 2: Evaluate the Statements Using 12TEN

Start with Statement (1). Knowing that x is greater than 1 rules out 1, leaving only 2 and 3 as possible values of x. Since both 2 and 3 are prime, you have an answer: definitely "yes." This statement is sufficient. Notice that you don't know which of those two values x equals, but for a Yes/No question, knowing a precise value is irrelevant; you can still have sufficiency as long as you know the answer is "always yes" or "always no." Eliminate choices **(B)**, **(C)**, and **(E)**.

Now set aside Statement (1) and move on to Statement (2). Of the possible values of x—1, 2, and 3—only one of them is even. You've determined that x must be 2. Because 2 is prime, the statement gives you a definite "yes." Statement (2) is also sufficient, so the answer is **(D)**.

PRACTICE SET: YES/NO QUESTIONS

Answers and explanations at end of chapter

10. Is $4 + \dfrac{n}{6}$ an integer?

    (1) n is a multiple of 3.

    (2) n divided by 6 has a remainder of 0.

11. If x and y are prime numbers, is $y(x - 3)$ odd?

    (1) $x > 10$

    (2) $y < 3$

12. Is $0 < \dfrac{a}{b} < 1$?

    (1) $ab > 1$

    (2) $a - b < 1$

13. If $y > 0$, is x less than 0?

    (1) $xy = 16$

    (2) $x - y = 6$

THE STATEMENTS ARE ALWAYS TRUE

The statements are new pieces of data that apply to the problem and are always true. Don't waste time trying to verify a statement.

The fact that the statements are always true has an important corollary that will help you catch careless errors: The statements will never contradict each other. Although they won't always be sufficient to answer the question, they'll never be mutually exclusive. If it appears that two statements are in disagreement with each other, you should recheck your work, because you have made an error.

Example:

> What is the value of t?
>
> (1) $t^2 = t$
> (2) $t + 6 = 6$

This is a straightforward Value question for which you need a value of t. Let's say that you made an error in your analysis of Statement (1) and thought that t had to equal 1. You'd think that Statement (1) was sufficient.

Then you'd look at Statement (2). Simplifying, you'd learn that t equals 0. That's also sufficient. So you'd think that the answer would be **(D)**. However, according to your analysis, the statements contradict each other:

> (1) $t = 1$
> (2) $t = 0$

That isn't possible. So you'd know to go back and recheck your work. Statement (2) pretty obviously says that $t = 0$, so you would recheck your work on Statement (1). Is 1 the only number that equals itself when squared? Substitute the 0 from Statement (2) and you get $0^2 = 0 \times 0 = 0$. So Statement (1) actually permits *two* values and is therefore insufficient.

> (1) $t = 0$ or 1
> (2) $t = 0$

The correct answer is **(B)**, not **(D)**.

IT'S ALL ABOUT THE QUESTION STEM

On Data Sufficiency questions, if you rush past the question and dive into the statements, you risk doing a whole bunch of unnecessary—and possibly misleading—math. It's essential that you understand the question stem before you analyze the statements. For one thing, there's a huge difference between a Value question and a Yes/No question. Consider this identical pair of statements:

(1) $x^3 = x$	(1) $x^3 = x$
(2) $x^2 = x$	(2) $x^2 = x$

Here's how they evaluate:

(1) $x = -1$, 0, or 1	(1) $x = -1$, 0, or 1
(2) $x = 0$ or 1	(2) $x = 0$ or 1

But you still have no idea what the answers are without seeing the question stems:

What is the value of x?   Is $x < -1$?

(1) $x = -1$, 0, or 1   (1) $x = -1$, 0, or 1
(2) $x = 0$ or 1   (2) $x = 0$ or 1

For the question on the left, a Value question, Statement (1) is insufficient because there are three possible values of x. Statement (2) is also insufficient because it permits two possible values. Even when the statements are considered together, x could be either 0 or 1. That's two values, which is insufficient for a Value question. The answer is **(E)**.

But the question on the right is a Yes/No question, so you will need to evaluate it differently. This question asks whether x is less than -1. First, look at Statement (1). Is $-1 < -1$? No. Is $0 < -1$? No. Is $1 < -1$? No. Always "no": This statement is sufficient. The same for Statement (2): Both values answer the question with a "no," so it's sufficient, as well. The answer is **(D)**.

That's as different as two Data Sufficiency answers can be, and it had *nothing* to do with the statements, which were identical. It's all about the question stem.

But during Step 1 of the Kaplan Method, you want to look for more than just whether the question is a Value or a Yes/No question. You saw how Problem Solving questions get much easier with some analysis and simplification before an approach is chosen. So too with Data Sufficiency.

Example:

If $w \neq x, w \neq z$, and $x \neq y$, is $\dfrac{(x-y)^3(w-z)^3}{(w-z)^2(x-y)(w-x)^2} > 0$?

(1) $x > y$
(2) $w > z$

This is a Yes/No question that asks about a fraction containing multiple variable expressions as factors. At first glance, this may look like a scary question stem. But take a closer look at that fraction. There are a lot of shared terms in the numerator and the denominator. Using the laws of exponents, you can cancel the $(w-z)^2$ and the $(x-y)$ in the denominator:

If $w \neq x, w \neq z$, and $x \neq y$, is $\dfrac{(x-y)^{\cancel{3}^2}(w-z)^{\cancel{3}^1}}{\cancel{(w-z)^2}\ \cancel{(x-y)}(w-x)^2} > 0$?

That simplifies the question to this:

If $w \neq x, w \neq z$, and $x \neq y$, is $\dfrac{(x-y)^2(w-z)}{(w-x)^2} > 0$?

This is looking better already. You can simplify even further by thinking logically about the question. You aren't asked for the value of anything, just whether this complicated fraction is positive. Without knowing anything about the values of w, x, y, and z, what can you already know about the answer to this question stem? Well, for one thing, you know that a squared term cannot be negative. So there's no way that $(x-y)^2$ or $(w-x)^2$ is negative. In fact, since $w \neq x$ and $x \neq y$, they can't be zero, either. So those two terms are both positive, which is the only thing that matters to the question. You can simplify the question even further, to this:

$$\text{Is } \frac{(\text{Positive})(w-z)}{(\text{Positive})} > 0?$$

Since multiplying and/or dividing $(w - z)$ by anything positive will not change its sign, you have this:

Is $w - z > 0$?

Now *that's* a much simpler question. Look at how much easier the statements have become to evaluate:

(1) $x > y$
(2) $w > z$

Statement (1) is totally irrelevant to whether $w - z > 0$. This statement is insufficient.

Statement (2) tells you that w is bigger than z, so $w - z$ must be positive. (Subtract z from both sides of the inequality, and you get $w - z > 0$.) That's a definite "yes." This is sufficient, so the answer is **(B)**.

The more analysis and simplification you do with the question stem, the easier dealing with the statements will become.

THINK ABOUT SUFFICIENCY, NOT CALCULATION

Get into the habit of thinking about what's needed for *sufficiency*, rather than doing arithmetic calculations. One of the ways that the GMAT makes a Data Sufficiency question harder is to make the numbers scarier. But if you aren't worrying about arithmetic, you won't be fazed by this. Let's take a look at two important math concepts that can help you avoid number crunching in Data Sufficiency.

The "*N*-Variables, *N*-Equations" Rule

Perhaps one of the most powerful tools to evaluate sufficiency is the *n*-variables, *n*-equations rule. If you have at least as many distinct, linear equations as you have variables, you will be able to solve for the unique numerical values of all the variables. If there are two variables, you need at least two equations to solve for all the values. If you have three variables, you need at least three equations. If you have four variables, you need at least four equations, and so on.

Note that when you apply the *n*-variables, *n*-equations rule, you must be alert to the exact definition of the word "distinct": each equation must provide new, different information. For instance, even though the equations $x + 3y = 5$ and $2x + 6y = 10$ look different, they are not in fact distinct—the second equation is merely the first equation multiplied by 2. Another example is the following system of equations: $x + 2y - 3z = 8$; $2y + 6z = 2$; and $x + 4y + 3z = 10$. These may also initially seem to be distinct, but a closer look reveals that the third equation is merely the sum of the first two. It therefore adds no new information, so this system of equations cannot be solved for unique numerical values for each variable.

Example:

A souvenir shop made $2,400 in revenue selling postcards. If a large postcard costs twice as much as a small postcard, the shop sold 950 large postcards, and it sold no other type of postcard besides these two sizes, then how many small postcards did it sell?

(1) A large postcard costs $2.
(2) If the shop had sold 20% fewer small postcards, its revenue would have been reduced by $4\frac{1}{6}\%$.

There are four factors that affect the outcome of this problem: (1) the price of a small postcard, (2) the price of a large postcard, (3) the number of small postcards sold, and (4) the number of large postcards sold. That's four variables, so four distinct, linear equations would enable you to solve for any of the variables. How many equations do you have already? Well, something-or-other equals $2,400 (that's one), there's a relationship between the prices (that's two), and you get the number of large postcards (that's three). With three equations for four variables, *any new equation* will be sufficient, as long as it is distinct and it doesn't introduce a new variable.

Statement (1) is a new equation and is therefore sufficient. Statement (2) is a more complicated equation, and it would likely be time-consuming to calculate. But it is still a new, distinct equation, and it is therefore sufficient. The answer is **(D)**.

Imagine how much time it would take to work through these equations. Using the *n*-variables, *n*-equations rule, it need take no longer than a minute.

One word of caution, though: Having the same number of distinct, linear equations guarantees sufficiency, but having fewer does *not* guarantee insufficiency. The GMAT will set up equations so that you can sometimes solve for what's asked even though you can't solve for every variable individually.

Example:

> A fruit stand sells apples, pears, and oranges. If oranges cost $0.50 each, then what is the cost of 5 oranges, 4 apples, and 3 pears?
>
> (1) The cost of 1 apple is $0.30.
> (2) The cost of 8 apples and 6 pears is $3.90.

There are three variables in this problem (the cost of an orange, the cost of an apple, and the cost of a pear), so three distinct equations could solve for everything. You're given only one (the exact price of an orange). So two additional distinct equations will guarantee sufficiency. But you should keep your eyes open for a way to answer your question with fewer. Since you already know the price of an orange, the only thing you'd need to answer your question is the price of 4 apples and 3 pears.

Statement (1) is insufficient, as you still do not know anything about the price of a pear. Statement (2) is only one equation, but if you divided it by 2, you'd get the cost of 4 apples and 3 pears, which is exactly what you need. This statement is sufficient, so the correct answer is **(B)**.

Proportions

Another common way that the GMAT allows you to get sufficiency without knowing all the individual values is to ask questions based on proportions (ratios, percents, averages, rates/speed, etc.). The goal of the following exercise is to get you to think about what kind of information can be sufficient to answer a question, even though you can't calculate the exact value of every variable involved. Read the question stem and each of the following statements, asking yourself whether it gives you enough information to answer. Don't waste time trying to come up with the actual value.

What was the percent increase in profits for Company X between 1991 and 1993?

Do the following statements provide sufficient information?

(1) The company earned 20 percent less profit in 1991 than in 1993.

(2) The average annual profit from 1991 to 1993 was 12.5% higher than the profit in 1991.

(3) The average of the annual profits of 1991 and 1993 was 12.5% higher than the profit in 1991.

(4) In 1991, the profit was $4.5 million less than in 1993.

Let's evaluate each statement on its own:

Statement (1) is sufficient. You could "reverse" the math and figure out percent increase from the given decrease. Let the 1993 profit equal P_{1993} and the 1991 profit equal P_{1991}. The statement can be translated to $P_{1991} = 0.8\ (P_{1993})$, which is $P_{1991} = \frac{4}{5}(P_{1993})$. That means $P_{1993} = \frac{5}{4} P_{1991} = 1.25\ (P_{1991})$. That's 125% of 1991, or a 25% increase.

Statement (2) is insufficient because you don't know anything about the profit in 1992, and this information would be necessary to set up the calculation.

Statement (3) is sufficient because you are given a proportional relationship between the two years' profits: $\left(\frac{P_{1991} + P_{1993}}{2} = 1.125(P_{1991}) \right)$. The question asks you for a proportional relationship, so this is exactly what you need.

Statement (4) is insufficient because you aren't given the total; you don't know what percentage a $4.5 million difference represents.

TAKEAWAYS: THE BASIC PRINCIPLES OF DATA SUFFICIENCY

The basic principles of Data Sufficiency are the following:

- Know the Data Sufficiency answer choices cold.
- Know the two types of Data Sufficiency questions.
- The statements are always true.
- It's all about the question stem.
- Think about sufficiency, not calculation.

DATA SUFFICIENCY STRATEGY

Now that you're familiar with how Data Sufficiency questions are constructed, let's look at two important strategic approaches to these questions. The first you're already familiar with from the Problem Solving chapter: We'll start by looking at how to effectively utilize the Picking Numbers strategy. After that, we'll discuss in greater detail how to most effectively combine statements.

PICKING NUMBERS IN DATA SUFFICIENCY

You've already seen the power of the Kaplan strategy of Picking Numbers for Problem Solving questions. You can also use this strategy for many Data Sufficiency questions that contain variables, unknown quantities, or percents of an unknown whole. When using this strategy, you always pick at least two different sets of numbers, trying to prove that the statements are *insufficient* by producing two different results. It's usually easier to prove insufficiency than sufficiency. But as you practice this strategy, the Core Competency of Pattern Recognition will also come into play. You will become adept at recognizing the types of numbers that can produce different results: positives vs. negatives, fractions vs. integers, odds vs. evens, and so on. Also, don't hesitate to use the numbers 0 and 1, as they have unique properties that make them great candidates for the Picking Numbers strategy.

APPLYING THE KAPLAN METHOD: PICKING NUMBERS IN DATA SUFFICIENCY

Now let's use the Kaplan Method on a Data Sufficiency question that involves Picking Numbers:

If $a + b = 20$, then what is the value of $c - d$?

(1) $ac - bd + bc - ad = 60$
(2) $d = 4$

Step 1: Analyze the Question Stem

Here's a Value question, so you need one, and *only* one, value for the expression $c - d$. There's nothing much to simplify here, but keep in mind that you are given a value for another expression, $a + b$. To obtain sufficiency, you'll need values for both c and d or a way to relate the equation $a + b = 20$ to the expression $c - d$.

Step 2: Evaluate the Statements Using 12TEN

As always, think strategically. Since the GMAT doesn't present the statements in any particular order, it's sometimes wise to start by evaluating Statement (2) if it looks easier to evaluate than Statement (1). Here, Statement (2) gives you a value for d but not for c. There's also no way to relate the equation $a + b = 20$ to the expression $c - d$. Eliminate **(B)** and **(D)**. Notice that you've eliminated 50 percent of the wrong answer choices very quickly.

Now let's tackle Statement (1), remembering to use the information it provides in conjunction with the question stem. You're given $a + b = 20$, so let's use Picking Numbers here. Pick $a = 10$ and $b = 10$.

Now, Statement (1) reads: $10c - 10d + 10c - 10d = 60$

Combine the like terms: $20c - 20d = 60$

Factor out the 20: $20(c - d) = 60$

Divide out the 20: $c - d = 3$

So, the expression $c - d$ can equal 3. But you're not finished yet. You have to pick a different set of numbers to see whether you can produce a different answer.

What permissible numbers might be likely to produce a different answer? Since Statement (1) involves subtraction, try negative numbers. Try $a = 25$ and $b = -5$.

Now Statement (1) reads:	$25c - (-5)d + (-5)c - 25d = 60$
Move the common terms next to each other:	$25c + (-5)c - (-5)d - 25d = 60$
Simplify the positive and negative signs:	$25c - 5c + 5d - 25d = 60$
Combine like terms:	$20c - 20d = 60$
Factor out the 20:	$20(c - d) = 60$
Divide out the 20:	$c - d = 3$

After picking two sets of numbers that have different properties and receiving the same result, you can say with reasonable confidence that Statement (1) is sufficient. Eliminate **(C)** and **(E)**. The correct answer is **(A)**.

TAKEAWAYS: PICKING NUMBERS IN DATA SUFFICIENCY

- To evaluate a statement (or the statements combined), you must pick at least two sets of numbers.
- When picking the second set of numbers, try to produce a different answer than that given by the first set.

PRACTICE SET: PICKING NUMBERS IN DATA SUFFICIENCY

Answers and explanations at end of chapter

14. If x is an integer with n distinct prime factors, is n greater than or equal to 3?

   (1) x is divisible by 6.
   (2) x is divisible by 10.

15. If $x^3 < x$, is $x > x^2$?

   (1) $x > -5$
   (2) $x < -2$

16. Is $|15 - m| + |m - 15| > 15$?

   (1) $m > 6$
   (2) $m < 7$

COMBINING STATEMENTS

If—and *only* if—each statement on its own is insufficient, you must then consider the statements together. The best way to do this is to think of the statements as one long sentence. At this stage, you can essentially approach the question as you would a Problem Solving question, using all the information you're given to answer the question. The main difference is that, since this is still Data Sufficiency, you will stop solving as soon as you know that you *can* solve. The time saved by avoiding unnecessary calculations is better spent on questions later in the section.

As you've learned earlier in this chapter, information is always consistent between the statements. The statements never contradict each other. For example, you'll never see a question in which Statement (1) says that x must be negative and Statement (2) says that x is positive. You might, however, learn from Statement (1) that x is greater than −5 and learn from Statement (2) that it's positive. Learning to recognize how one statement does or does not limit the information in the other is the key in deciding between choices **(C)** and **(E)**.

Combining Statements Exercise

Answers on the following page

The following exercise contains a single question stem—"What is the value of x?"— and many sets of sample statements, which have already been simplified and evaluated for you. Imagine that you had analyzed the statements and gotten the possible values for x listed below: Which statements, either separately or combined, are sufficient to answer the question? Choose the appropriate Data Sufficiency answer choice—**(A)**, **(B)**, **(C)**, **(D)**, or **(E)**—for each pair of statements.

What is the value of x?

1. (1) $x = -1, 0, 1$
   (2) $x = 0, 1$

2. (1) $x < 3$
   (2) $x > 1$

3. (1) $x = -1, 0$
   (2) $x < 0$

4. (1) $x = -1, 1$
   (2) $x = 1, 2$

5. (1) $x < 4$
   (2) $x < 2$

6. (1) $x = -1, 0$
   (2) $x = -1, 0$

7. (1) $x = -1, 1$
   (2) $x = -1$

8. (1) $x \geq 2$
   (2) $x \leq 2$

9. (1) x is even.
   (2) x is prime.

Combining Statements Exercise: Answers

1. **(E)**; x could be 0 or 1.
2. **(E)**; x could be any number between (but not including) 1 and 3. Don't assume that variables are integers.
3. **(C)**; $x = -1$.
4. **(C)**; $x = 1$.
5. **(E)**; x could be any number smaller than 2.
6. **(E)**; x could be 0 or -1. Statements that give redundant information are never sufficient when combined.
7. **(B)**; Statement (2) is sufficient. Note that you would never combine statements in this case.
8. **(C)**; $x = 2$.
9. **(C)**; $x = 2$.

APPLYING THE KAPLAN METHOD: COMBINING STATEMENTS

Now let's use the Kaplan Method on a Data Sufficiency question that involves Picking Numbers:

If x and y are positive integers, is $\frac{2x}{y}$ an integer?

(1) Some factors of y are also factors of x.
(2) All distinct prime factors of y are also prime factors of x.

Step 1: Analyze the Question Stem

First, this is a Yes/No question. Any statement that gives you a "sometimes yes; sometimes no" answer is insufficient. Now, how can you paraphrase the question in the stem? You can say either, "Is $2x$ a multiple of y?" or "Does $2x$ divide evenly by y?"

Step 2: Evaluate the Statements Using 12TEN

Use the Kaplan strategy of Picking Numbers. Pick permissible, manageable numbers. If you pick $x = 5$ and $y = 5$, that will give you a "yes" to the original question, since $2x$, or 10, divided by y, or 5, will yield an integer. But if you pick a different set of numbers, say $x = 2$ and $y = 42$, that will yield a fraction. Statement (1) is insufficient; eliminate **(A)** and **(D)**.

Pick numbers for Statement (2), making sure they're permissible. For example, 36 and 6 have the same distinct prime factors: 2 and 3. Picking the numbers $x = 36$ and $y = 6$ gives you an integer; choosing $x = 6$ and $y = 36$, on the other hand, gives you a fraction. Therefore, Statement (2) is insufficient; eliminate **(B)**.

Now, combining the statements, you will notice something interesting. Statement (2) is more restrictive than Statement (1). So as you combine the statements, ask yourself, "Will any numbers that satisfy Statement (2) also satisfy Statement (1)?" Yes, they will. For instance, $x = 36$ and $y = 6$, which you picked for Statement (2), also works for Statement (1): These numbers will again yield a "yes" answer. And $x = 6$ and $y = 36$ also works for Statement (1), yielding a "no" answer. Since combining the statements didn't add any new information and the information presented was insufficient, the answer must be **(E)**. Even combined, you get a "sometimes yes, sometimes no" answer to the question in the stem.

TAKEAWAYS: COMBINING STATEMENTS

- Each data statement is true. Therefore, when combining statements, look for values that are permitted by both statements.
- Treat combined statements as one long statement.
- Never combine statements unless each statement is insufficient on its own.

Practice Set: Combining Statements

Answers and explanations at end of chapter

17. What is the value of x?

   (1) $x^2 - 9 = 16$
   (2) $3x(x - 5) = 0$

18. Is $y^2 < 1$?

   (1) $y > -1$
   (2) $y < 1$

19. If a coffee shop sold 600 cups of coffee, some of which were large cups and the remainder of which were small cups, what was the revenue that the coffee shop earned from the sale of coffee?

   (1) The number of large cups sold was $\frac{3}{5}$ the total number of small cups sold.
   (2) The price of a small cup of coffee was $1.50.

STRATEGIC GUESSING

When you run into a very complicated question, like the following, don't forget to use a sound Data Sufficiency guessing strategy. That means perhaps skipping a statement that looks too daunting and trying to eliminate some answer choices by looking at the easier statement. Try your hand at the difficult question below. Don't try to solve it; instead, see if you can narrow down the possibilities quickly.

Example:

What was the maximum temperature in City A on Saturday, May 14?

(1) The average (arithmetic mean) of the maximum daily temperatures in City A from Sunday, May 8, to Saturday, May 14, was 72 degrees, which was 2 degrees less than the average (arithmetic mean) of the maximum daily temperatures in City A from Monday, May 9, to Friday, May 13.

(2) The maximum temperature in City A on Saturday, May 14, was 5 degrees greater than the maximum temperature in City A on Sunday, May 8.

Step 1: Analyze the Question Stem

This is a Value question. To obtain sufficiency, you need an exact maximum temperature.

Step 2: Evaluate the Statements Using 12TEN

Statement (1) is long and complicated. Skip it and go straight to Statement (2); it's much easier.

Statement (2) tells you that the value you're looking for is 5 degrees more than the temperature on some other day. Without knowing the temperature on that other day, you don't have the information you need. This statement is insufficient. You can eliminate **(B)** and **(D)** and give yourself a one-in-three chance to get the right answer without even evaluating Statement (1).

Perhaps you feel comfortable evaluating Statement (1). Perhaps you don't. But let's pretend for a moment that you aren't sure how to evaluate Statement (1). Keep in mind that on the GMAT, complicated or hard-to-evaluate statements are more likely to be sufficient than insufficient. For this reason, you should avoid **(E)** and lean toward **(A)**, unless you have a logical reason to suspect that Statement (1) alone is insufficient. Of course, this doesn't guarantee you a correct answer, but if you're falling behind on time, it will help you move through the Quantitative section most efficiently. Remember, no one particular question will make or break your GMAT score, but spending too much time on one question and having to rush through several others just to make up for the lost time will hurt your score. As it turns out, **(C)** is the right answer to this particular problem.

Fortunately, you're unlikely to run into anything as complicated as Statement (1) on Test Day. The point of this exercise is to show you that even if you do encounter something this difficult, you're still in control. If you work the odds and look for the strategic approach, you will increase your likelihood of picking up the points even for questions you're not sure how to solve.

For the record, let's analyze Statement (1). If the average maximum temperature from May 8 to May 14 was 72 degrees, then the sum of the maximum temperatures of those days is $7 \times 72 = 504$ degrees. If the average maximum temperature from May 9 to May 13 was 72 + 2, or 74 degrees, then the sum of the maximum temperatures of those days was $5 \times 74 = 370$ degrees.

The difference between those two sums is simply the sum of the maximum temperature on May 8, which you can call x, and the maximum temperature on May 14, which you can call y (since these two days were left out of the second time period). So $x + y = 504 - 370 = 134$. Statement (1) by itself is insufficient. But Statement (2) tells you that $y - x = 5$. You have the two distinct linear equations, $x + y = 134$ and $y - x = 5$. These equations can be solved for a single value for y, so the statements taken together are sufficient: choice **(C)**.

This example demonstrates how guessing can be a good alternative approach for certain questions. By looking at only one statement, you can narrow down the possibilities to two or three choices. This can be a great help, particularly on difficult or time-consuming problems for which you think you might have to guess. But you must be sure you know the rules for eliminating answer choices absolutely cold by Test Day.

ANSWERS AND EXPLANATIONS

1. B
2. D
3. C
4. A
5. E
6. A
7. C
8. E
9. C
10. B
11. D
12. E
13. D
14. C
15. B
16. B
17. C
18. C
19. E

1. **(B)**

If $x > 0$, what is the value of x?

(1) $x > 5$
(2) $40 - x^2 = 4$

Step 1: Analyze the Question Stem

In this Value question, sufficiency means finding one and only one value for x. We are told that x must be greater than 0.

Step 2: Evaluate the Statements Using 12TEN

Statement (1) tells us that $x > 5$. While that certainly narrows down the options for x, there is no way to figure out one and only one value for x from that information alone, so this statement is insufficient. Eliminate **(A)** and **(D)**.

Statement (2) provides an equation that allows us to determine the value of x^2. Every positive number has two square roots, one positive and one negative, so this statement narrows the options down to two values for x. This would normally not be sufficient. However, the question stem states that $x > 0$, which eliminates the negative square root, leaving one and only one value for x. Statement (2) alone is sufficient, so **(B)** is correct.

2. **(D)**

If $a > 0$, $b > 0$, and $2c = \sqrt{\dfrac{a}{b}}$, what is the value of b?

(1) $a = 8$ and $c = 2$

(2) $\dfrac{c^2}{a} = \dfrac{1}{2}$

Step 1: Analyze the Question Stem

In this Value question, sufficiency means finding one and only one value for b. We are told that a and b are both positive and are given an equation. Let's simplify the equation before proceeding to the statements.

$$(2c)^2 = \left(\sqrt{\dfrac{a}{b}}\right)^2$$

$$4c^2 = \dfrac{a}{b}$$

$$4c^2 b = a$$

$$b = \dfrac{a}{4c^2}$$

Solving for b means having either the values for both a and c or the value of $\dfrac{a}{4c^2}$.

Step 2: Evaluate the Statements Using 12TEN

Statement (1) provides the values of a and c. By plugging these provided values into the expression $\dfrac{a}{4c^2}$, we can solve for b, so Statement (1) is sufficient. Eliminate **(B)**, **(C)**, and **(E)**.

Statement (2) may not look sufficient at first glance, but we can actually change the left side of the equation to $\dfrac{a}{4c^2}$:

$$\dfrac{c^2}{a} = \dfrac{1}{2}$$

$$a = 2c^2$$

$$\dfrac{a}{c^2} = 2$$

$$\dfrac{a}{4c^2} = \dfrac{2}{4}$$

$$\dfrac{a}{4c^2} = \dfrac{1}{2}$$

Since $\dfrac{a}{4c^2}$ is also the value of b, this statement is sufficient. Eliminate **(A)**.

Each statement alone is sufficient to answer the question, so **(D)** is the correct answer.

3. **(C)**

Team X won 40 basketball games. What percent of its basketball games did Team X win?

(1) Team X played the same number of basketball games as Team Y.

(2) Team Y won 45 games, representing 2.5 percent of the basketball games it played.

Step 1: Analyze the Question Stem

In this Value question, the stem gives us the number of games won by Team X and asks for the percentage of games the team won. For sufficiency, we need to be able to determine the number of games Team X played. From that, we can determine Team X's winning percentage.

Step 2: Evaluate the Statements Using 12TEN

Statement (1) tells us that Team X played the same number of games as Team Y, but we know nothing of Team Y. This statement is insufficient, so we can eliminate **(A)** and **(D)**.

Statement (2) tells us how many games Team Y won and gives us enough information to calculate how many total games Team Y played. Because we do not know the relevance of Team Y's performance from this statement (remember not to combine the statements yet), the statement is insufficient. We can eliminate **(B)**.

Because each of the statements is insufficient alone, we now combine the statements. From Statement (2), we could determine the number of games that Team Y played, and from Statement (1), we know that this is equal to the number of games that Team X played. Together, the statements are sufficient, so the correct answer choice is **(C)**.

EXPLANATIONS

4. **(A)**

    If $2b - a^2 = 18$, what is the value of b?

    (1) $a^2 = 1{,}156$

    (2) $a > 0$

Step 1: Analyze the Question Stem

This is a Value question, which means that sufficiency requires one and only one value for b. We need a value for a or a^2 in order to solve for b.

Step 2: Evaluate the Statements Using 12TEN

Statement (1) gives a value for a^2. Therefore, it is sufficient, thus eliminating **(B)**, **(C)**, and **(E)**.

Statement (2) gives a range of values for a. This is insufficient, eliminating **(D)**.

Therefore, the correct answer is **(A)**; Statement (1) alone is sufficient.

Note that using the Kaplan Method will keep you from falling into a trap laid by the testmaker. If you thought from the first statement that having two possible values—one positive and one negative—for a meant that the information was insufficient to get one value, you might have thought you needed the information in Statement (2) to get one value for a. However, by determining what you need for sufficiency before looking at the statements, you realized that it does not matter whether we have the positive or negative value of a, as long as we can solve for one and only one value for b.

5. **(E)**

    A certain company produces exactly three products: X, Y, and Z. In 1990, what was the total income for the company from the sale of its products?

    (1) In 1990, the company sold 8,000 units of product X, 10,000 units of product Y, and 16,000 units of product Z.

    (2) In 1990, the company charged $28 per unit for product X and twice as much for product Z.

Step 1: Analyze the Question Stem

In this Value question, we are told that a company makes three products and are asked to find the total income from the sale of these products. For sufficiency, we need to be able to determine the quantities and prices of all three products.

Step 2: Evaluate the Statements Using 12TEN

Statement (1) gives us quantity information, by product, for each of the three products. Because it has no pricing information, the statement is insufficient. Eliminate **(A)** and **(D)**.

Statement (2) gives us pricing information for one product and information to calculate the price of a second product. However, it has no quantity information and nothing about the pricing of the third product. The statement is therefore insufficient, and you can eliminate **(B)**.

Because each of the statements is insufficient, we now combine the statements. When combined, we have quantity information for all three products but only have pricing information for two of them. Therefore, the two statements combined are insufficient to answer the question. Answer choice **(E)** is correct.

6.   **(A)**

What is the value of $4n - 5m$?

(1) $\dfrac{n}{5} = \dfrac{m}{4}$

(2) $\dfrac{n}{4} = \dfrac{m}{5}$

Step 1: Analyze the Question Stem

This Value question requires one and only one value for the expression $4n - 5m$. We will either need to find the value for that expression or find the values of n and m individually.

Step 2: Evaluate the Statements Using 12TEN

Statement (1) may not look like much help at first, but cross-multiplying results in the equation $4n = 5m$. Subtract $5m$ from both sides to find that $4n - 5m = 0$. This is one and only one value for the expression in the question stem, so this statement is sufficient. Eliminate **(B)**, **(C)**, and **(E)**.

Statement (2) looks very similar to Statement (1), but cross-multiplying here results in the equation $5n = 4m$. From this, there is no way to figure out the values of n or m (we would need two distinct equations to do that, given that there are two variables) and no way to isolate $4n - 5m$. Statement (2) is therefore insufficient, so we can eliminate **(D)**.

Statement (1) alone is sufficient, so the correct answer is **(A)**.

7. **(C)**

What is the value of $\dfrac{st}{u}$?

(1) $s = \dfrac{3t}{4}$ and $u = 2t$.

(2) $s = u - 10$ and $u = s + t + 2$.

Step 1: Analyze the Question Stem

This is a Value question. The stem for this item includes three variables. Specific values for each of the variables would be sufficient to get one value for the entire expression.

Step 2: Evaluate the Statements Using 12TEN

Statement (1) gives us restatements of two of the variables—s and u—in terms of the third variable, t. If we take the expression in the stem and replace s and u with the expressions given in the statement, we can see that the variable t is not eliminated:

$$\frac{st}{u} = \frac{\left(\dfrac{3t}{4}\right)t}{2t} = \frac{\dfrac{3t^2}{4}}{2t} = \frac{3t^2}{4} \times \frac{1}{2t} = \frac{3t^2}{8t} = \frac{3}{8}t$$

Therefore, Statement (1) is insufficient, and we can eliminate **(A)** and **(D)**.

At first glance, Statement (2) appears to invite a similar conclusion to the one for Statement (1). However, further analysis of the information is worth a try. We are told that $s = u - 10$ and also that $u = s + t + 2$. Substituting $u - 10$ for s in the second equation, we find that

$$u = u - 10 + t + 2$$

$$8 = t$$

Substituting the value of 8 for t and substituting $u - 10$ for s,

$$\frac{st}{u} = \frac{(u-10)(8)}{u} = \frac{8u-80}{u}$$

Unfortunately, this still doesn't eliminate the variable u, so Statement (2) is insufficient and we can further eliminate **(B)**.

Combining the statements, we determined from Statement (1) that the expression $\dfrac{st}{u} = \dfrac{3}{8}t$. If we substitute the value of 8 for the variable t—from Statement (2)—we see that we can get one value even without actually solving the math.

Therefore, the correct answer is **(C)**: Neither statement alone is sufficient, but the statements combined are sufficient.

8. **(E)**

    If z is an integer, what is the units digit of z^3?

    (1) z is a multiple of 5.
    (2) $\sqrt{z}$ is an integer.

Step 1: Analyze the Question Stem

In this Value question, to have sufficiency, we need to know either the value of integer z or something about z that would enable us to determine the units digit of its cube.

Step 2: Evaluate the Statements Using 12TEN

Statement (1) tells us that z is a multiple of 5. Multiples of 5 have units digits of either 0 or 5. Cubes of numbers with units digits of 0 or 5 keep the same units digit (e.g., the cube of 10 is 1,000; the cube of 5 is 125). The statement is insufficient because it gives us two possible answers to the question stem. Eliminate **(A)** and **(D)**.

Statement (2) tells us that the square root of z is an integer. This means that z is a perfect square. The statement is insufficient because there are perfect squares with many different units values. Eliminate **(B)**.

Because each of the statements is insufficient on its own, we now combine the statements. Combined, we know that z is both a multiple of 5 and a perfect square. If we can find examples for z that are perfect squares ending in each of the values from Statement (1), then the combined statements are insufficient. If $z = 25$, it is a multiple of 5 and its square root is an integer, and the answer to the question stem is 5. If $z = 100$, then both statements are true, and the answer to the question is 0. Since more than one answer to the question is possible, the two statements taken together are insufficient. Eliminate **(C)**. **(E)** is the correct answer.

EXPLANATIONS

9. (C)

What is the value of the integer *p*?

(1) *p* is a prime number.

(2) 88 ≤ *p* ≤ 95

Step 1: Analyze the Question Stem

This is a Value question, so we'll need one exact value for *p*. There's nothing to simplify in the question stem, but it's worth noting that *p* is an integer—we won't need to consider decimal values. So what we need is very clear—one specific numeric value for *p*.

Step 2: Evaluate the Statements Using 12TEN

Statement (1) doesn't give us one exact value, as there are many prime numbers. Eliminate **(A)** and **(D)**.

Likewise, Statement (2) doesn't give us one exact value, only a range with eight possibilities. Eliminate **(B)**.

To choose between **(C)** and **(E)**, we must consider these statements in combination. Treating (1) and (2) as one long statement, we know that *p* is between 88 and 95, inclusive, and that it's prime. If you happen to have all the primes through 100 memorized, then you know right away that *p* can only equal 89 and that the answer is **(C)**.

But what if you don't have all those primes memorized? When evaluating a reasonably short list of numbers, it's often beneficial to write out the possibilities on your noteboard. Then, instead of the abstract "88 ≤ *p* ≤ 95," we have *p* = 88, 89, 90, 91, 92, 93, 94, or 95. A prime number is a number that is divisible only by 1 and itself. So any of these that are divisible by any other number can be crossed off the list. If we can cross off seven of these eight numbers, we'll know *p*.

Any even number is divisible by 2, so that eliminates 88, 90, 92, and 94. Any number that ends in a 0 or a 5 is divisible by 5, so that eliminates 95 (and 90, if it weren't already gone). We know that 93 is divisible by 3. (The divisibility test for 3 is to check whether the digits of a number sum to a multiple of 3; if so, that number is itself divisible by 3. The digits of 93 are 9 and 3. Since 9 + 3 = 12 and 12 is a multiple of 3, 93 is a multiple of 3.)

Now we've narrowed the possibilities down to *p* = 89 or 91. We've checked for divisibility by the primes 2, 3, and 5. What about the next prime, 7? There is a little-known way to test divisibility by 7. But the GMAT often rewards test takers who think about numbers in creative ways, so even if you don't know the divisibility rule, you can still try to break 91 into multiples of 7 that you know. Because 91 is also 70 + 21, it's 7(10) + 7(3), or 7(10 + 3), or 7(13). So, it's definitely a multiple of 7 and can be eliminated. We have now determined that *p* must equal 89. The statements together are sufficient, so the answer is **(C)**.

(Incidentally, that little-known divisibility test for 7 is this: Separate the units digit from the rest of the number, then multiply that units digit by 2. Subtract that from what's left of the original number. If the result is a multiple of 7, the original number is a multiple of 7. Here's how that works for 91. Separate 91 into the digits 9 and 1. Multiply 1 by 2: 1 × 2 = 2. Subtract: 9 − 2 = 7. 7 is obviously a multiple of 7, so 91 is a multiple of 7. Try it out on other multiples of 7, and you'll see that it works every time.)

10. (B)

Is $4 + \dfrac{n}{6}$ an integer?

(1) n is a multiple of 3.

(2) n divided by 6 has a remainder of 0.

Step 1: Analyze the Question Stem

This Yes/No question asks whether $4 + \dfrac{n}{6}$ is an integer. Sufficiency means showing that the value of the expression is definitely an integer or definitely not an integer. As 4 is an integer and will therefore have no effect on whether the entire expression is equal to an integer, we simply need to consider whether $\dfrac{n}{6}$ is definitely an integer.

Step 2: Evaluate the Statements Using 12TEN

Statement (1) narrows the value of n to multiples of 3. Picking Numbers can illustrate for us: If $n = 6$, $\dfrac{n}{6}$ is an integer, but if $n = 9$, $\dfrac{n}{6}$ is not an integer. There is no definite "yes" or "no" outcome for the given expression, so this statement is insufficient. Eliminate **(A)** and **(D)**.

Statement (2) restricts n to values that leave a remainder of 0 when divided by 6. These are, by definition, multiples of 6, and any multiple of 6 for n will always make $\dfrac{n}{6}$ an integer. This statement provides a definite "yes" answer, so it is sufficient. Eliminate **(C)** and **(E)**.

Statement (2) alone is sufficient, so the correct answer is **(B)**.

EXPLANATIONS

11. (D)

If x and y are prime numbers, is $y(x - 3)$ odd?

(1) $x > 10$

(2) $y < 3$

Step 1: Analyze the Question Stem

This is a Yes/No question. We are asked whether a particular expression is odd. For sufficiency, we need to be able to determine whether the solution to the expression is definitely odd or definitely even. Here, we should consider the rules of odds and evens: (odd × odd) = odd, (even × even) = even, and (odd × even) = even; (odd + odd) = even, (odd + even) = odd, and (even + even) = even. So if either y is even or if x is odd (making $x - 3$ even), we will be able to answer the question with a "no." Note also that we're told that x and y are prime numbers. Seeing that we're asked about odd numbers, and seeing that we're dealing with primes, we should expect that the question involves the fact that 2 is the only even prime number.

Step 2: Evaluate the Statements Using 12TEN

Statement (1): If x is a prime number greater than 10, then it must be odd. Therefore, $x - 3$ must be even. The statement is sufficient to answer the question stem with a "no," which eliminates **(B)**, **(C)**, and **(E)**.

Statement (2): If y is a prime number less than 3, y must equal 2, which is even. The statement is sufficient to answer the question stem with a "no." That eliminates **(A)** and tells us that **(D)** is the correct answer.

Because at least one of the statements alone is sufficient to answer the question, we do not evaluate the statements combined.

EXPLANATIONS

12. (E)

Is $0 < \dfrac{a}{b} < 1$?

(1) $ab > 1$

(2) $a - b < 1$

Step 1: Analyze the Question Stem

This is a Yes/No question. For sufficiency, a definite "yes" would show that $\frac{a}{b}$ is always a positive fraction less than 1, or a definite "no" would show that $\frac{a}{b}$ is always something other than a positive fraction less than 1. Picking Numbers will help simplify this.

Step 2: Evaluate the Statements Using 12TEN

Statement (1) tells us that ab is greater than 1. That means either that a and b are both positive or that they are both negative. Let's pick some numbers to test out the possibilities:

Case 1:	a = –3, b = –2	(–3)(–2) > 1	Stem question: No
Case 2:	a = 2, b = 3	(2)(3) > 1	Stem question: Yes

Because we can pick numbers that follow the rules of the statement without giving a clear "yes" or "no" answer to the question stem, the statement is insufficient. We can eliminate **(A)** and **(D)**.

Statement (2) tells us that $a - b$ is less than 1. The same pairs of numbers we tested for Statement (1) apply here as well, making the statement insufficient.

Case 1:	a = –3, b = –2	(–3) – (–2) < 1	Stem question: No
Case 2:	a = 2, b = 3	2 – 3 < 1	Stem question: Yes

We can eliminate **(B)**.

Because each of the statements is insufficient on its own, we now combine the statements. Since the same cases applied to both statements, combining the statements adds no new information to the analysis, and the combined statements are therefore insufficient. The answer must be **(E)**.

EXPLANATIONS

13. **(D)**

If $y > 0$, is x less than 0?

(1) $xy = 16$

(2) $x - y = 6$

Step 1: Analyze the Question Stem

This is a Yes/No question. What can we learn from the stem? It tells us that y is positive and asks us whether x is negative. What would constitute sufficiency? Learning that x is definitely negative or that x is definitely not negative. (Keep in mind that the number 0 is neither positive nor negative.)

Step 2: Evaluate the Statements Using 12TEN

Statement (1) tells us that $xy = 16$. To get a positive outcome when multiplying two variables, we need to have either two positive numbers or two negative numbers. Because the question stem tells us that y is positive, that means that x also has to be positive. Therefore, this statement is sufficient to answer the question with a "no" (x cannot be negative in this case), and we can eliminate **(B)**, **(C)**, and **(E)**.

Statement (2) tells us that $x - y = 6$. Adding y to both sides of this equation shows that x is 6 greater than y. Since we already know that y is positive, Statement (2) is sufficient to answer the question with a "no," and we can eliminate **(A)**.

The correct answer is **(D)**: Either statement alone is sufficient to answer the question.

14. (C)

If x is an integer with n distinct prime factors, is n greater than or equal to 3?

(1) x is divisible by 6.

(2) x is divisible by 10.

Step 1: Analyze the Question Stem

This is a Yes/No question, so we don't need to know the exact value of n, just whether $n \geq 3$.

There's nothing to simplify, but it's important to note the relationship between the variables: n is the number of distinct prime factors of x. (Every non-prime number can be rewritten as a series of prime numbers multiplied together; those are the number's prime factors.)

To answer the question, we'll need to know whether or not x has at least three distinct prime factors.

Step 2: Evaluate the Statements Using 12TEN

Let's say that you weren't sure how to evaluate the statements abstractly. Picking Numbers allows you to evaluate a Data Sufficiency statement when you aren't comfortable with a more rules-based approach.

Statement (1): Let's pick the simplest number that's divisible by 6, namely $x = 6$ itself. We get $6 = 2 \times 3$. Since there are two prime factors, $n = 2$. Now test that number in the question: "Is $2 \geq 3$?" No, it isn't.

But our work on Statement (1) isn't done. We only know that Statement (1) *can* yield the answer "no." We have no idea yet whether the answer is "definitely no," because other permissible numbers might yield different results. Always test at least two sets of numbers when Picking Numbers in Data Sufficiency so that you can differentiate between the *definite* answers and the *maybe* answers.

Since we already got a "no" answer, our task is to see whether we can get a "yes," thus proving that Statement (1) does not provide one definite answer. Could we think of a value for x that has three or more prime factors? Since 2 and 3 showed up as prime factors already, we can think of a value for x that has a different prime factor: 5, perhaps. So let's pick x to be a multiple of 5 that is also divisible by 6 (otherwise it won't be permissible). $x = 30$ fits the bill: $30 = 2 \times 3 \times 5$. That's three prime factors, so $n = 3$. Put that into the question: "Is $3 \geq 3$?" Yes, it is.

Because we've found both a "yes" and a "no" answer, Statement (1) answers the question "maybe yes, maybe no." That's not a definite answer, so Statement (1) is insufficient. Eliminate **(A)** and **(D)**.

Statement (2): Now let's pick the simplest number that's divisible by 10, namely $x = 10$ itself. We get $10 = 2 \times 5$. Since there are two prime factors, $n = 2$. Now test that number in the question: "Is $2 \geq 3$?" No, it isn't. Let's see whether we can pick a number that yields a different answer. We've already seen a number that has three prime factors: 30. And it's divisible by 10, so it's permitted by Statement (2). We get $30 = 2 \times 3 \times 5$. That's three prime factors, so $n = 3$. Put that into the question: "Is $3 \geq 3$?" Yes, it is. As with Statement (1), we've produced a "maybe" answer, so Statement (2) is insufficient. Eliminate **(B)**.

(C) and **(E)** still remain, so now we have to consider the statements together. We have to pick values for x that are divisible both by 6 and by 10. Happily, we already know one from our earlier work. If $x = 30$, then the answer to our question is "yes." Can we find a number that's divisible both by 6 and by 10 but has fewer than three prime factors? Let's try $x = 6 \times 10$, or $x = 60$. We get $60 = 6 \times 10 = 2 \times 3 \times 2 \times 5 = 2^2 \times 3 \times 5$. That's also three distinct prime factors. If you weren't at this point confident that any number that's divisible both by 6 and by 10 would have to have 2, 3, and 5 as prime factors (that's at least three!), quickly testing one or two other possibilities (e.g., $x = 90$, $x = 120$) would confirm it. No matter what permissible numbers we pick, we get the same answer: "yes." So considering the statements together, the answer is "definitely yes." **(C)** is correct.

15. (B)

If $x^3 < x$, is $x > x^2$?

(1) $x > -5$

(2) $x < -2$

Step 1: Analyze the Question Stem

This is a Yes/No question, so we don't need to know the exact value of x, just whether x is definitely greater than x^2 or definitely *not* greater than x^2.

Is it possible to simplify the question? We're told that $x^3 < x$. When would a number be *greater* than its cube? Picking Numbers can help us understand the question. If $x = 2$, then $x^3 = 8$; 8 is not less than 2, so $x = 2$ is not a permissible number according to the question stem. Neither is $x = 1$ nor $x = 0$, as in both cases $x^3 = x$. What about other kinds of numbers, like fractions or negatives?

If $x = \frac{1}{2}$, then $x^3 = \left(\frac{1}{2}\right)^3 = \frac{1}{8}$. Because $\frac{1}{8}$ is less than $\frac{1}{2}$, x could be a fraction between 0 and 1. And if $x = -2$, then $x^3 = -8$; -8 is less than -2, so x could be a negative number less than -1.

How would these different possible values affect the question "Is $x > x^2$?" If $x = \frac{1}{2}$, then $x^2 = \left(\frac{1}{2}\right)^2 = \frac{1}{4}$; $\frac{1}{2}$ is greater than $\frac{1}{4}$. So if x is a fraction between 0 and 1, the answer to the question is "yes." And if $x = -2$, then $x^2 = 4$; -2 is not greater than 4, so if x is negative, then the answer to our question is "no."

To answer the question, we'll need to know definitely which of the two permitted types of number x is—a positive fraction or a number less than -1.

Step 2: Evaluate the Statements Using 12TEN

Statement (1) permits any number greater than -5. Certainly x could be negative. And since there's no upper limit provided on x, it could also be a positive fraction. We haven't gotten a definite "yes" or "no" answer to our question, so Statement (1) is insufficient. Eliminate **(A)** and **(D)**.

Statement (2) permits only negative numbers and excludes positive fractions. So the answer to our question is "definitely no." Statement (2) is sufficient, so **(B)** is correct.

16. (B)

Is $|15 - m| + |m - 15| > 15$?

(1) $m > 6$

(2) $m < 7$

Step 1: Analyze the Question Stem

In this Yes/No question, sufficiency means proving that $|15 - m| + |m - 15|$ is either definitely greater than 15 or definitely less than or equal to 15. As the question stem is dealing with a range, Picking Numbers will help in evaluating the statements.

Step 2: Evaluate the Statements Using 12TEN

Statement (1) restricts m to values greater than 6. When Picking Numbers to evaluate statements, remember to always pick at least two sets of numbers to see if you can get more than one possible answer to the question—in this case, let's pick one number near the start of the range and one much farther away. Let's first try $m = 7$.

$$|15 - m| + |m - 15| = |15 - 7| + |7 - 15|$$
$$= |8| + |-8|$$
$$= 8 + 8$$
$$= 16$$

Since 16 is greater than 15, $m = 7$ results in a "yes" answer to the question. Let's now try $m = 15$.

$$|15 - m| + |m - 15| = |15 - 15| + |15 - 15|$$
$$= |0| + |0|$$
$$= 0 + 0$$
$$= 0$$

Since 0 is less than 15, $m = 15$ results in a "no." As $m > 6$ sometimes means "yes" and sometimes means "no," this statement is insufficient. Eliminate **(A)** and **(D)**.

Statement (2) restricts m to values less than 7. We'll need to pick at least two values once again, so let's start with $m = 6$.

$$|15 - m| + |m - 15| = |15 - 6| + |6 - 15|$$
$$= |9| + |-9|$$
$$= 9 + 9$$
$$= 18$$

Because 18 is greater than 15, that's a "yes." Let's try $m = 0$.

$$|15 - m| + |m - 15| = |15 - 0| + |0 - 15|$$
$$= |15| + |-15|$$
$$= 15 + 15$$
$$= 30$$

Not only is that also a "yes," but the value is actually getting larger as m gets smaller, so this statement will always return an answer of "yes" to the question. Eliminate **(C)** and **(E)**.

Statement (2) alone is sufficient, so the correct answer is **(B)**.

17. (C)

What is the value of x?

(1) $x^2 - 9 = 16$

(2) $3x(x - 5) = 0$

Step 1: Analyze the Question Stem

In this Value question, we must find one and only one value for x to have sufficiency.

Step 2: Evaluate the Statements Using 12TEN

Statement (1) provides an equation that allows us to determine the value of x^2. Every positive number has two square roots, one positive and one negative, so this statement narrows things down to two values for x: 5 and -5 Without further information, we cannot determine one and only one value for x, so this statement is insufficient. Eliminate **(A)** and **(D)**.

Statement (2) provides an equation in which at least one of the expressions $3x$ or $(x - 5)$ is equal to 0. That translates into two possible values for x: 0 and 5. We need one and only one value for sufficiency, so this statement is insufficient. Eliminate **(B)**.

Combining the statements tells us that x is either 5 or -5 and either 0 or 5. The only way to satisfy both statements is for x to be 5. That is the one and only one possible value for x, so combining the statements leads to sufficiency, and the correct answer is **(C)**.

18. (C)

Is $y^2 < 1$?

(1) $y > -1$

(2) $y < 1$

Step 1: Analyze the Question Stem

In this Yes/No question, sufficiency means determining that y^2 is either definitely less than 1 or definitely greater than or equal to 1. All squares are nonnegative—so how could it be that y^2 is less than 1? The only way this could happen is if y fell somewhere between 1 and −1 on the number line. The square of $\frac{1}{2}$, for instance, is $\frac{1}{4}$; the square of $-\frac{1}{2}$ is also $\frac{1}{4}$. Likewise, the square of 0 is 0. So the question stem can be simplified to "Is y less than 1 and greater than −1?"

Step 2: Evaluate the Statements Using 12TEN

Statement (1) states that $y > -1$. Picking Numbers will make this easier: $y = 0$ leads to a "yes" answer, as y^2 would be less than 1. However, $y = 2$ leads to a "no" answer, as y^2 would be greater than 1. This statement is insufficient, so we can eliminate **(A)** and **(D)**.

Statement (2) states that $y < 1$. As we saw above, $y = 0$ leads to a "yes" answer. However, $y = -2$ would lead to a "no" answer, as y^2 would be greater than 1. This statement is insufficient, so we can eliminate **(B)**.

Combining the statements results in the inequality $-1 < y < 1$. That effectively limits the range of values for y to 0 and fractions whose absolute value is less than 1. Squaring any fraction whose absolute value is less than 1 will always result in a positive fraction less than 1, which produces a "yes" answer, and we've already seen that $y = 0$ produces a "yes" answer. Therefore, combining the statements will produce a definite "yes" to the question and the correct answer is **(C)**.

EXPLANATIONS

19. **(E)**

If a coffee shop sold 600 cups of coffee, some of which were large cups and the remainder of which were small cups, what was the revenue that the coffee shop earned from the sale of coffee?

(1) The number of large cups sold was $\frac{3}{5}$ the total number of small cups sold.

(2) The price of a small cup of coffee was $1.50.

Step 1: Analyze the Question Stem

This is a Value question. Simplifying a word problem essentially entails understanding the situation, allowing us to figure out what variables would need to be calculated in order to answer the question. This coffee shop sells two sizes of coffee, and we are asked to determine its revenue. To answer this question, we need to ascertain both how many cups of each size were sold and the price of each size of cup.

Step 2: Evaluate the Statements Using 12TEN

Statement (1) has no pricing information at all. We can eliminate **(A)** and **(D)** as potential answers. Even though we could create an equation that, when combined with the stimulus, would tell us the number of cups of each size that were sold, doing so would be a waste of time—we already know that Statement (1) is insufficient, so there's no point in working further.

Statement (2) tells us the price of one size—small. This is insufficient because it tells us nothing about the price of the large cup or about the number of cups sold. We can now eliminate **(B)**.

Because each statement alone is insufficient, we now combine both statements to determine whether they are sufficient together. Combined, we still know nothing about the price of a large cup. A crucial piece of data is missing, so the two statements combined are insufficient to answer the question. Eliminate **(C)**. The correct answer is **(E)**.

GMAT BY THE NUMBERS: DATA SUFFICIENCY

Now that you've learned how to approach Data Sufficiency questions on the GMAT, let's add one more dimension to your understanding of how they work.

Take a moment to try the following question. The next page features performance data from thousands of people who have studied with Kaplan over the decades. Through analyzing this data, we will show you how to approach questions like this one most effectively and how to avoid similarly tempting wrong answer choice types on Test Day.

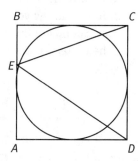

In the figure above, a circle is inscribed in square ABCD. What is the area of △CDE?

(1) The circle has a radius of length 3.

(2) CDE is isosceles.

○ Statement (1) ALONE is sufficient, but statement (2) is not sufficient.

○ Statement (2) ALONE is sufficient, but statement (1) is not sufficient.

○ BOTH statements TOGETHER are sufficient, but NEITHER statement ALONE is sufficient.

○ EACH statement ALONE is sufficient.

○ Statements (1) and (2) TOGETHER are NOT sufficient.

EXPLANATION

You're asked to find the area of triangle *CDE*. The area of a triangle is equal to $\frac{1}{2}$ base × height. You can use *CD* as a base, and the height would be the length of a perpendicular drawn from point *E* to *CD*. Since that perpendicular line would be equal in length to *BC*, you only need to learn the length of the sides of square *ABCD* to know the length of both the base (*CD*) and the height (equal to *BC*) of triangle *CDE*.

Statement (1) says that the radius of the inscribed circle is 3, so you know that its diameter is 6. That diameter will equal the length of the sides of the square, which is what you need to answer the question. So Statement (1) is sufficient. Statement (2), however, gives you no measurements to work with at all. It does allow you to figure out that point *E* bisects *AB*, but that's irrelevant to the question. Statement (2) is insufficient. Since Statement (1) is sufficient but Statement (2) is not, the correct answer is **(A)**.

QUESTION STATISTICS

44% of test takers choose **(A)**

2% of test takers choose **(B)**

32% of test takers choose **(C)**

1% of test takers choose **(D)**

21% of test takers choose **(E)**

Sample size = 4,069

The question statistics reveal two very common habits that lead to wrong answers. Many test takers select **(C)**, believing that the statements are sufficient only when combined. Statement (1) alone does not tell you the exact placement of point *E*. But you don't need that information to know the triangle's height, and therefore its area. You don't always need to know *everything* to be able to answer the question that's asked.

Also, some people struggle to relate the data about the circle to the square and then to the triangle. They look at Statement (1) and think, "I don't know how to solve with this," so they treat the statement as insufficient, leading in this question to choice **(E)**. But to do so is to equate "I don't know how to solve this" with "This can't be solved"—not the same thing at all! You can see from the question statistics that this is a common line of thinking—and not one that the GMAT likes to reward. Be wary of guessing that a statement is insufficient unless you can see exactly why it doesn't lead to a clear answer. If you don't know how to deal with a statement, guessing that it's sufficient is often the better strategy.

MORE GMAT BY THE NUMBERS ...

To see more questions with answer choice statistics, be sure to review the full-length CATs in your Online Center.

CHAPTER 12

GMAT Math Fundamentals

ARITHMETIC

TERMS

Consecutive numbers: Numbers of a certain type, following one another without interruption. Numbers may be consecutive in ascending or descending direction. The GMAT prefers to test consecutive integers (e.g., –2, –1, 0, 1, 2, 3 . . .), but you may encounter other types of consecutive numbers. For example:

–4, –2, 0, 2, 4, 6, . . . is a series of consecutive even numbers.

–3, 0, 3, 6, 9, . . . is a series of consecutive multiples of 3.

2, 3, 5, 7, 11, . . . is a series of consecutive prime numbers.

Cube: A number raised to the 3rd power. For example $4^3 = (4)(4)(4) = 64$, and 64 is the cube of 4.

Decimal: A fraction written in decimal system format. For example, 0.6 is a decimal. To convert a fraction to a decimal, divide the numerator by the denominator.

Decimal system: A numbering system based on the powers of 10. The decimal system is the only numbering system used on the GMAT. Each figure, or digit, in a decimal number occupies a particular position, from which it derives its place value.

Denominator: The quantity in the bottom of a fraction, representing the whole.

Difference: The result of subtraction.

Digit: One of the numerals 0, 1, 2, 3, 4, 5, 6, 7, 8, or 9. A number can have several digits. For example, the number 542 has three digits: a 5, a 4, and a 2. The number 321,321,000 has nine digits, but only four distinct (different) digits: 3, 2, 1, and 0.

Element: One of the members of a set.

Exponent: The number that denotes the power to which another number or variable is raised. The exponent is typically written as a superscript to a number. For example, 5^3 equals $(5)(5)(5)$. The exponent is also occasionally referred to as a "power." For example, 5^3 can be described as "5 to the 3rd power." The product, 125, is "the 3rd power of 5."

Fraction: The division of a part by a whole. $\dfrac{\text{Part}}{\text{Whole}}$ = Fraction. For example, $\dfrac{3}{5}$ is a fraction.

Integer: A number without fractional or decimal parts, including negative whole numbers and zero. All integers are multiples of 1. The following are examples of integers: $-5, -4, -3, -2, -1, 0, 1, 2, 3, 4, 5$.

Number line: A straight line, extending infinitely in either direction, on which numbers are represented as points. The number line below shows the integers from -3 to 4. Decimals and fractions can also be depicted on a number line, as can irrational numbers, such as $\sqrt{2}$.

The values of numbers get larger as you move to the right along the number line. Numbers to the right of zero are *positive*; numbers to the left of zero are *negative*. **Zero is neither positive nor negative.** Any positive number is larger than any negative number. For example, $-300 < 4$.

Numerator: The quantity in the top of the fraction, representing the part.

Operation: A function or process performed on one or more numbers. The four basic arithmetic operations are addition, subtraction, multiplication, and division.

Part: A specified number of the equal sections that compose a whole.

Product: The result of multiplication.

Set: A well-defined collection of items, typically numbers, objects, or events. The bracket symbols { } are normally used to define sets of numbers. For example, {2, 4, 6, 8} is a set of numbers.

Square: The product of a number multiplied by itself. A squared number has been raised to the 2nd power. For example, $4^2 = (4)(4) = 16$, and 16 is the square of 4.

Sum: The result of addition.

Whole: A quantity that is regarded as a complete unit.

SYMBOLS

=	is equal to
≠	is not equal to
<	is less than
>	is greater than
≤	is less than or equal to
≥	is greater than or equal to
÷	divided by
π	pi (the ratio of the circumference of a circle to the diameter)
±	plus or minus
√	square root
∠	angle

RULES OF OPERATION

There are certain mathematical laws governing the results of the four basic operations: addition, subtraction, multiplication, and division. Although you won't need to know the names of these laws for the GMAT, you'll benefit from understanding them.

PEMDAS

A string of operations must be performed in proper order. The acronym PEMDAS stands for the correct order of operations:

Parentheses

Exponents

Multiplication

Division
} simultaneously from left to right

Addition

Subtraction
} simultaneously from left to right

If you have trouble remembering PEMDAS, you can think of the mnemonic "Please Excuse My Dear Aunt Sally."

Example:

$$66 (3 - 2) \div 11$$

If you were to perform all the operations sequentially from left to right, without using PEMDAS, you would arrive at an answer of $\frac{196}{11}$. But if you perform the operation within the parentheses first, you get $66(1) \div 11 = 66 \div 11 = 6$, which is the correct answer.

Example:

$$30 - 5(4) + \frac{(7-3)^2}{8}$$

$$= 30 - 5(4) + \frac{4^2}{8}$$

$$= 30 - 5(4) + \frac{16}{8}$$

$$= 30 - 20 + 2$$

$$= 10 + 2$$

$$= 12$$

Commutative Laws of Addition and Multiplication

Addition and multiplication are both commutative; switching the order of any two numbers being added or multiplied together does not affect the result.

Example:

$$5 + 8 = 8 + 5$$

$$(2)(3)(6) = (6)(3)(2)$$

$$a + b = b + a$$

$$ab = ba$$

Division and subtraction are not commutative; switching the order of the numbers changes the result. For instance, $3 - 2 \neq 2 - 3$; the left side yields a difference of 1, while the right side yields a difference of –1. Similarly, $\frac{6}{2} \neq \frac{2}{6}$; the left side equals 3, while the right side equals $\frac{1}{3}$.

Associative Laws of Addition and Multiplication

Addition and multiplication are also associative; regrouping the numbers does not affect the result.

Example:

$$(3 + 5) + 8 = 3 + (5 + 8) \qquad (a + b) + c = a + (b + c)$$

$$8 + 8 = 3 + 13 \qquad\qquad\qquad (ab)c = a(bc)$$

$$16 = 16$$

The Distributive Law

In multiplication, the distributive law of multiplication allows you to "distribute" a factor over numbers that are added or subtracted. You do this by multiplying that factor by each number in the group.

Example:

$$4(3 + 7) = (4)(3) + (4)(7) \qquad a(b + c) = ab + ac$$

$$4(10) = 12 + 28$$

$$40 = 40$$

The law works for the numerator in division as well.

$$\frac{a + b}{c} = \frac{a}{c} + \frac{b}{c}$$

However, when the sum or difference is in the denominator—that is, when you're dividing by a sum or difference—no distribution is possible.

$\frac{9}{4+5}$ is *not* equal to $\frac{9}{4} + \frac{9}{5}$.

NUMBER PROPERTIES

ADDING AND SUBTRACTING

Numbers can be treated as though they have two parts: a positive or negative sign and a number. Numbers without any sign are understood to be positive.

To add two numbers that have the same sign, add the number parts and keep the sign. Example: To add $(-6) + (-3)$, add 6 and 3 and then attach the negative sign from the original numbers to the sum: $(-6) + (-3) = -9$.

To add two numbers that have different signs, find the difference between the number parts and keep the sign of the number whose number part is larger. Example: To add $(-7) + (+4)$, subtract 4 from 7 to get 3. Because $7 > 4$ (the number part of -7 is greater than the number part of 4), the final sum will be negative: $(-7) + (+4) = -3$.

Subtraction is the opposite of addition. You can rephrase any subtraction problem as an addition problem by changing the operation sign from a minus to a plus and switching the sign on the second number. Example: $8 - 5 = 8 + (-5)$. There's no real advantage to rephrasing if you are subtracting a smaller positive number from a larger positive number. But the concept comes in very handy when you are subtracting a negative number from any other number, a positive number from a negative number, or a larger positive number from a smaller positive number.

To subtract a negative number, rephrase as an addition problem and follow the rules for addition of signed numbers. For instance, $9 - (-10) = 9 + 10 = 19$.

To subtract a positive number from a negative number, or from a smaller positive number, change the sign of the number that you are subtracting from positive to negative and follow the rules for addition of signed numbers. For example, $(-4) - 1 = (-4) + (-1) = -5$.

MULTIPLICATION AND DIVISION OF SIGNED NUMBERS

Multiplying or dividing two numbers with the same sign gives a positive result.

Examples:

$(-4)(-7) = +28$

$(-50) \div (-5) = +10$

Multiplying or dividing two numbers with different signs gives a negative result.

Examples:

$(-2)(+3) = -6$

$8 \div (-4) = -2$

ABSOLUTE VALUE

The absolute value of a number is the value of a number without its sign. It is written as two vertical lines, one on either side of the number and its sign.

Example:

$|-3| = |+3| = 3$

The absolute value of a number can be thought of as the number's distance from zero on the number line. Since both 3 and −3 are 3 units from 0, each has an absolute value of 3. If you are told that $|x| = 5$, x could equal 5 or −5.

PROPERTIES OF ZERO

Adding zero to or subtracting zero from a number does not change the number.

$$x + 0 = x$$

$$0 + x = x$$

$$x - 0 = x$$

Examples:

$5 + 0 = 5$

$0 + (-3) = -3$

$4 - 0 = 4$

Notice, however, that subtracting a number from zero changes the number's sign. It's easy to see why if you rephrase the problem as an addition problem.

Example:

Subtract 5 from 0.

$0 - 5 = -5$. That's because $0 - 5 = 0 + (-5)$, and according to the rules for addition with signed numbers, $0 + (-5) = -5$.

The product of zero and any number is zero.

Examples:

$(0)(z) = 0$

$(z)(0) = 0$

$(0)(12) = 0$

Division by zero is undefined. For GMAT purposes, that translates as "it can't be done." Since fractions are essentially division (that is, $\frac{1}{4}$ means $1 \div 4$), any fraction with zero in the denominator is also undefined. So when you are given a fraction that has an algebraic expression in the denominator, be sure that the expression cannot equal zero.

PROPERTIES OF 1 AND −1

Multiplying or dividing a number by 1 does not change the number.

$$(a)(1) = a$$

$$(1)(a) = a$$

$$a \div 1 = a$$

Examples:

$$(4)(1) = 4$$

$$(1)(-5) = -5$$

$$(-7) \div 1 = -7$$

Multiplying or dividing a nonzero number by −1 changes the sign of the number.

$$(a)(-1) = -a$$

$$(-1)(a) = -a$$

$$a \div (-1) = -a$$

Examples:

$$(6)(-1) = -6$$

$$(-3)(-1) = 3$$

$$(-8) \div (-1) = 8$$

FACTORS, MULTIPLES, AND REMAINDERS

Multiples and Divisibility

A multiple is the product of a specified number and an integer. For example, 3, 12, and 90 are all multiples of 3: 3 = (3)(1); 12 = (3)(4); and 90 = (3)(30). The number 4 is not a multiple of 3, because there is no integer that can be multiplied by 3 and yield 4.

The concepts of multiples and factors are tied together by the idea of divisibility. A number is said to be evenly divisible by another number if the result of the division is an integer with no remainder. A number that is evenly divisible by a second number is also a multiple of the second number.

For example, 52 ÷ 4 = 13, which is an integer. So 52 is evenly divisible by 4, and it's also a multiple of 4.

On some GMAT math problems, you will find yourself trying to assess whether one number is evenly divisible by another. You can use several simple rules to save time.

- An integer is divisible by 2 if its last digit is divisible by 2.
- An integer is divisible by 3 if its digits add up to a multiple of 3.
- An integer is divisible by 4 if its last two digits are a multiple of 4.
- An integer is divisible by 5 if its last digit is 0 or 5.
- An integer is divisible by 6 if it is divisible by 2 and 3.
- An integer is divisible by 9 if its digits add up to a multiple of 9.

Example:

6,930 is a multiple of 2, since 0 is even.

... a multiple of 3, since 6 + 9 + 3 + 0 = 18, which is a multiple of 3.

... not a multiple of 4, since 30 is not a multiple of 4.

... a multiple of 5, since it ends in zero.

... a multiple of 6, since it is a multiple of 2 and 3.

... a multiple of 9, since 6 + 9 + 3 + 0 = 18, a multiple of 9.

Properties of Odd/Even Numbers

Even numbers are integers that are evenly divisible by 2; *odd* numbers are integers that are not evenly divisible by 2. Integers whose last digit is 0, 2, 4, 6, or 8 are even; integers whose last digit is 1, 3, 5, 7, or 9 are odd. The terms *odd* and *even* apply only to integers, but they may be used for either positive or negative integers. 0 is considered even.

Rules for Odds and Evens

Odd + Odd = Even

Even + Even = Even

Odd + Even = Odd

Odd × Odd = Odd

Even × Even = Even

Odd × Even = Even

Note that multiplying any even number by *any* integer always produces another even number.

It may be easier to pick numbers in problems that ask you to decide whether some unknown will be odd or even.

Example:

Is the sum of two odd numbers odd or even?

Pick any two odd numbers, for example, 3 and 5. 3 + 5 = 8. Since the sum of the two odd numbers that you picked is an even number, 8, it's safe to say that the sum of any two odd numbers is even.

Picking Numbers will work in any odds/evens problem, no matter how complicated. The only time you have to be careful is when division is involved, especially if the problem is in Data Sufficiency format; different numbers may yield different results.

Example:

Integer x is evenly divisible by 2. Is $\frac{x}{2}$ even?

By definition, any multiple of 2 is even, so integer x is even. And $\frac{x}{2}$ must be an integer. But is $\frac{x}{2}$ even or odd? In this case, picking two different even numbers for x can yield two different results. If you let $x = 4$, then $\frac{x}{2} = \frac{4}{2} = 2$ which is even. But if you let $x = 6$, then $\frac{x}{2} = \frac{6}{2} = 3$, which is odd. So $\frac{x}{2}$ could be even or odd—and you wouldn't know that if you picked only one number.

Factors and Primes

The *factors*, or *divisors*, of an integer are the positive integers by which it is evenly divisible (leaving no remainder).

Example:

What are the factors of 36?

36 has nine factors: 1, 2, 3, 4, 6, 9, 12, 18, and 36. We can group these factors in pairs: (1)(36) = (2)(18) = (3)(12) = (4)(9) = (6)(6).

The *greatest common factor*, or greatest common divisor, of a pair of integers is the largest factor that they share.

To find the greatest common factor, break down both integers into their prime factorizations and multiply all the prime factors they have in common: 36 = (2)(2)(3)(3), and 48 = (2)(2)(2)(2)(3). What they have in common is two 2s and one 3, so the GCF is (2)(2)(3) = 12.

A prime number is an integer greater than 1 that has only two factors: itself and 1. The number 1 is not considered a prime, because it is divisible only by itself. The number 2 is the smallest prime number and the only even prime. (Any other even number must have 2 as a factor and therefore cannot be prime.)

Prime Factors

The prime factorization of a number is the expression of the number as the product of its prime factors (the factors that are prime numbers).

There are two common ways to determine a number's prime factorization. The rules given above for determining divisibility by certain numbers come in handy in both methods.

Method #1: Work your way up through the prime numbers, starting with 2. (You'll save time in this process, especially when you're starting with a large number, by knowing the first ten prime numbers by heart: 2, 3, 5, 7, 11, 13, 17, 19, 23, and 29.)

Example:

What is the prime factorization of 210?

$$210 = (2)(105)$$

Since 105 is odd, it can't contain another factor of 2. The next smallest prime number is 3. The digits of 105 add up to 6, which is a multiple of 3, so 3 is a factor of 105.

$$210 = (2)(3)(35)$$

The digits of 35 add up to 8, which is not a multiple of 3. But 35 ends in 5, so it is a multiple of the next largest prime number, 5.

$$210 = (2)(3)(5)(7)$$

Since 7 is a prime number, this equation expresses the complete prime factorization of 210.

Method #2: Figure out one pair of factors, and then determine their factors, continuing the process until you're left with only prime numbers. Those primes will be the prime factorization.

Example:

What is the prime factorization of 1,050?

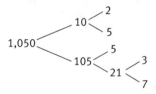

The discrete prime factors of 1,050 are therefore 2, 5, 3, and 7, with the prime number 5 occurring twice in the prime factorization. We usually write out the prime factorization by putting the prime numbers in increasing order. Here, that would be (2)(3)(5)(5)(7). The prime factorization can also be expressed in exponential form: $(2)(3)(5^2)(7)$.

The Least Common Multiple

The *least common multiple* of two or more integers is the smallest number that is a multiple of each of the integers. Here's one quick way to find it:

(1) Determine the prime factorization of each integer.
(2) Write out each prime number the maximum number of times that it appears in any one of the prime factorizations.
(3) Multiply those prime numbers together to get the least common multiple of the original integers.

Example:

What is the least common multiple of 6 and 8?

Start by finding the prime factors of 6 and 8.

$$6 = (2)(3)$$

$$8 = (2)(2)(2)$$

The factor 2 appears three times in the prime factorization of 8, while 3 appears as only a single factor of 6. So the least common multiple of 6 and 8 will be (2)(2)(2)(3), or 24.

Note that the least common multiple of two integers is smaller than their product if they have any factors in common. For instance, the product of 6 and 8 is 48, but their least common multiple is only 24.

Although you won't see the term *least common multiple* very often on the GMAT, you'll find the concept useful whenever you're adding or subtracting fractions with different denominators.

Remainders

The remainder is what is "left over" in a division problem. A remainder is always smaller than the number you are dividing by. For instance, 17 divided by 3 is 5, with a remainder of 2. Likewise, 12 divided by 6 is 2, with a remainder of 0 (since 12 is evenly divisible by 6).

GMAT writers often disguise remainder problems. For instance, a problem might state that the slats of a fence are painted in three colors, which appear in a fixed order, such as red, yellow, blue, red, yellow, blue. You would then be asked something like, "If the first slat is red, what color is the 301st slat?" Since 3 goes into 300 evenly, the whole pattern must finish on the 300th slat and start all over again on the 301st. Therefore, the 301st would be red.

EXPONENTS AND ROOTS

Rules of Operations with Exponents

To multiply two powers with the same base, keep the base and add the exponents together.

Example:

$$2^2 \times 2^3 = (2 \times 2)(2 \times 2 \times 2) = 2^5$$

or

$$2^2 \times 2^3 = 2^{2+3} = 2^5$$

To divide two powers with the same base, keep the base and subtract the exponent of the denominator from the exponent of the numerator.

Example:

$$4^5 \div 4^2 = \frac{(4)(4)(4)(4)(4)}{(4)(4)} = 4^3$$

or

$$4^5 \div 4^2 = 4^{5-2} = 4^3$$

To raise a power to another power, multiply the exponents.

Example:

$$(3^2)^4 = (3 \times 3)^4$$

or

$$(3^2)^4 = (3 \times 3)(3 \times 3)(3 \times 3)(3 \times 3)$$

or

$$(3^2)^4 = 3^{2 \times 4} = 3^8$$

Commonly Tested Properties of Powers

Many Data Sufficiency problems test your understanding of what happens when negative numbers and fractions are raised to a power.

Raising a fraction between zero and one to a power produces a smaller result.

Example:

$$\left(\frac{1}{2}\right)^2 = \left(\frac{1}{2}\right)\left(\frac{1}{2}\right) = \frac{1}{4}$$

Raising a negative number to an even power produces a positive result.

Example:

$$(-2)^2 = 4$$

Raising a negative number to an odd power gives a negative result.

Example:

$$(-2)^3 = -8$$

Powers of 10

When 10 is raised to an exponent that is a positive integer, that exponent tells how many zeros the number would contain if it were written out.

Example:

Write 10^6 in ordinary notation.

The exponent 6 indicates that you will need six zeros after the 1: 1,000,000. That's because 10^6 means six factors of 10, that is, $(10)(10)(10)(10)(10)(10)$.

To multiply a number by a power of 10, move the decimal point the same number of places to the right as the exponent (or as the number of zeros in that power of 10).

Example:

Multiply 0.029 by 10^3

The exponent is 3, so move the decimal point three places to the right.

$$(0.029)10^3 = 0029. = 29$$

If you had been told to multiply 0.029 by 1,000, you could have counted the number of zeros in 1,000 and done exactly the same thing.

Sometimes you'll have to add zeros as placeholders.

Example:

Multiply 0.029 by 10^6.

Add zeros until you can move the decimal point six places to the right:

$$0.029 \times 10^6 = 0029000. = 29,000$$

To divide by a power of 10, move the decimal point the corresponding number of places to the left, inserting zeros as placeholders if necessary.

Example:

Divide 416.03 by 10,000

There are four zeros in 10,000, but only three places to the left of the decimal point. You'll have to insert another zero:

$$416.03 \div 10,000 = .041603 = 0.041603$$

By convention, one zero is usually written to the left of the decimal point on the GMAT. It's a place-holder and doesn't change the value of the number.

Scientific Notation

Very large numbers (and very small decimals) take up a lot of space and are difficult to work with. So in some scientific texts, they are expressed in a shorter, more convenient form, called scientific notation.

For example, 123,000,000,000 would be written in scientific notation as $(1.23)(10^{11})$, and 0.000000003 would be written as $(3.0)(10^{-9})$. (If you're already familiar with the concept of negative exponents, you'll know that multiplying by 10^{-9} is equivalent to dividing by 10^9.)

To express a number in scientific notation, rewrite it as a product of two factors. The first factor must be greater than or equal to 1 but less than 10. The second factor must be a power of 10.

To translate a number from scientific notation to ordinary notation, use the rules for multiplying and dividing by powers of 10.

Example:

$5.6 \times 10^6 = 5,600,000$, or 5.6 million

Rules of Operations with Roots and Radicals

A square root of any nonnegative number x is a number that, when multiplied by itself, yields x. Every positive number has two square roots, one positive and one negative. For instance, the positive square root of 25 is 5, because $5^2 = 25$. The negative square root of 25 is -5, because $(-5)^2$ also equals 25.

By convention, the radical symbol $\sqrt{}$ stands for the positive square root only. Therefore, $\sqrt{9} = 3$ only, even though both 3^2 and $(-3)^2$ equal 9. This has important implications in Data Sufficiency.

Example:

What is the value of x?

(1) $x = \sqrt{16}$
(2) $x^2 = 16$

The first statement is sufficient, since there is only one possible value for $\sqrt{16}$, positive 4. The second statement is insufficient since x could be 4 or -4.

When applying the four basic arithmetic operations, radicals (roots written with the radical symbol) are treated in much the same way as variables.

Addition and Subtraction of Radicals

Only like radicals can be added to or subtracted from one another.

Example:

$$2\sqrt{3} + 4\sqrt{2} - \sqrt{2} - 3\sqrt{3} =$$
$$(4\sqrt{2} - \sqrt{2}) + (2\sqrt{3} - 3\sqrt{3}) =$$
$$3\sqrt{2} + (-\sqrt{3}) =$$
$$3\sqrt{2} - \sqrt{3}$$

This expression cannot be simplified any further.

Multiplication and Division of Radicals

To multiply or divide one radical by another, multiply or divide the numbers outside the radical signs, then the numbers inside the radical signs.

Example:

$$(6\sqrt{3})2\sqrt{5} = (6)(2)(\sqrt{3})(\sqrt{5}) = 12\sqrt{15}$$

Example:

$$12\sqrt{15} \div 2\sqrt{5} = \left(\frac{12}{2}\right)\left(\frac{\sqrt{15}}{\sqrt{5}}\right) = 6\sqrt{\frac{15}{5}} = 6\sqrt{3}$$

Simplifying Radicals

If the number inside the radical is a multiple of a perfect square, the expression can be simplified by factoring out the perfect square.

Example:

$$\sqrt{72} = (\sqrt{36})\sqrt{2} = 6\sqrt{2}$$

PROPORTIONS AND MATH FORMULAS

FRACTIONS

The simplest way to understand the meaning of a fraction is to picture the denominator as the number of equal parts into which a whole unit is divided. The numerator represents a certain number of those equal parts.

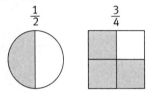

On the left, the shaded portion is one of two equal parts that make up the whole. On the right, the shaded portion is three of four equal parts that make up the whole.

The fraction bar is interchangeable with a division sign. You can divide the numerator of a fraction by the denominator to get an equivalent decimal. However, the numerator and denominator must each be treated as a single quantity.

Example:

Evaluate $\dfrac{5 + 2}{7 - 3}$

You can't just rewrite the fraction as $5 + 2 \div 7 - 3$, because the numerator and the denominator are each considered distinct quantities. Instead, you would rewrite the fraction as $(5 + 2) \div (7 - 3)$. The order of operations (remember PEMDAS?) tells us that operations in parentheses must be performed first. That gives you $7 \div 4$. Your final answer would be $\dfrac{7}{4}$, $1\dfrac{3}{4}$, or 1.75, depending on the form of the answer choices.

Equivalent Fractions

Since multiplying or dividing a number by 1 does not change the number, multiplying the numerator and denominator of a fraction by the same nonzero number doesn't change the value of the fraction—it's the same as multiplying the entire fraction by 1.

Example:

Change $\dfrac{1}{2}$ into an equivalent fraction with a denominator of 4.

To change the denominator from 2 to 4, you'll have to multiply it by 2. But to keep the value of the fraction the same, you'll also have to multiply the numerator by 2.

$$\frac{1}{2} = \frac{1}{2}\left(\frac{2}{2}\right) = \frac{2}{4}$$

Similarly, dividing the numerator and denominator by the same nonzero number leaves the value of the fraction unchanged.

Example:

Change $\dfrac{16}{20}$ into an equivalent fraction with a denominator of 10.

To change the denominator from 20 to 10, you'll have to divide it by 2. But to keep the value of the fraction the same, you'll have to divide the numerator by the same number.

$$\frac{16}{20} = \frac{16 \div 2}{20 \div 2} = \frac{8}{10}$$

Reducing (Canceling)

Most fractions on the GMAT are in lowest terms. That means that the numerator and denominator have no common factor greater than 1.

For example, the final answer of $\frac{8}{10}$ that we obtained in the previous example was not in lowest terms, because both 8 and 10 are divisible by 2. In contrast, the fraction $\frac{7}{10}$ is in lowest terms, because there is no factor greater than 1 that 7 and 10 have in common. To convert a fraction to its lowest terms, we use a method called reducing, or canceling. To reduce, simply divide any common factors out of both the numerator and the denominator.

Example:

Reduce $\dfrac{15}{35}$ to lowest terms.

$\dfrac{15}{35} = \dfrac{15 \div 5}{35 \div 5} = \dfrac{3}{7}$ (because a 5 cancels out, top and bottom)

The fastest way to reduce a fraction that has very large numbers in both the numerator and denominator is to find the greatest common factor and divide it out of both the top and the bottom.

Example:

Reduce $\dfrac{1040}{1080}$ to lowest terms.

$$\frac{1040}{1080} = \frac{104}{108} = \frac{52}{54} = \frac{26}{27}$$

Adding and Subtracting Fractions

You cannot add or subtract fractions unless they have the same denominator. If they don't, you'll have to convert each fraction to an equivalent fraction with the least common denominator. Then add or subtract the numerators (not the denominators!) and, if necessary, reduce the resulting fraction to its lowest terms.

Given two fractions with different denominators, the least common denominator is the least common multiple of the two denominators, that is, the smallest number that is evenly divisible by both denominators.

Example:

What is the least common denominator of $\dfrac{2}{15}$ and $\dfrac{3}{10}$?

The least common denominator of the two fractions will be the least common multiple of 15 and 10.

Because $15 = (5)(3)$ and $10 = (5)(2)$, the least common multiple of the two numbers is $(5)(3)(2)$, or 30. That makes 30 the least common denominator of $\dfrac{2}{15}$ and $\dfrac{3}{10}$.

Example:

$\dfrac{2}{15} + \dfrac{3}{10} = ?$

As we saw in the previous example, the least common denominator of the two fractions is 30. Change each fraction to an equivalent fraction with a denominator of 30.

$$\frac{2}{15}\left(\frac{2}{2}\right) = \frac{4}{30}$$

$$\frac{3}{10}\left(\frac{3}{3}\right) = \frac{9}{30}$$

Then add:

$$\frac{4}{30} + \frac{9}{30} = \frac{13}{30}$$

Since 13 and 30 have no common factor greater than 1, $\dfrac{13}{30}$ is in lowest terms. You can't reduce it further.

Multiplying Fractions

To multiply fractions, multiply the numerators and multiply the denominators.

$$\frac{5}{7}\left(\frac{3}{4}\right) = \frac{15}{28}$$

Multiplying numerator by numerator and denominator by denominator is simple. But it's easy to make careless errors if you have to multiply a string of fractions or work with large numbers. You can minimize those errors by reducing before you multiply.

Example:

Multiply $\left(\dfrac{10}{9}\right)\left(\dfrac{3}{4}\right)\left(\dfrac{8}{15}\right)$.

First, cancel a 5 out of the 10 and the 15, a 3 out of the 3 and the 9, and a 4 out of the 8 and the 4:

$$\left(\frac{\cancel{10}^{2}}{\cancel{9}_{3}}\right)\left(\frac{\cancel{3}^{1}}{\cancel{4}_{1}}\right)\left(\frac{\cancel{8}^{2}}{\cancel{15}_{3}}\right)$$

Then multiply numerators together and denominators together:

$$\left(\frac{2}{3}\right)\left(\frac{1}{1}\right)\left(\frac{2}{3}\right) = \frac{4}{9}$$

Reciprocals

To get the reciprocal of a common fraction, turn the fraction upside-down so that the numerator becomes the denominator, and vice versa. If a fraction has a numerator of 1, the fraction's reciprocal will be equivalent to an integer.

Example:

What is the reciprocal of $\frac{1}{25}$?

Inverting the fraction gives you the reciprocal, $\frac{25}{1}$. But dividing a number by 1 doesn't change the value of the number.

Since $\frac{25}{1} = 25$, the reciprocal of $\frac{1}{25}$ equals 25.

Dividing Common Fractions

To divide fractions, multiply by the reciprocal of the number or fraction that follows the division sign.

$$\frac{1}{2} \div \frac{3}{5} = \frac{1}{2}\left(\frac{5}{3}\right) = \frac{5}{6}$$

(The operation of division produces the same result as multiplication by the inverse.)

Example:

$$\frac{4}{3} \div \frac{4}{9} = \frac{4}{3}\left(\frac{9}{4}\right) = \frac{36}{12} = 3$$

Comparing Positive Fractions

Given two positive fractions with the same denominator, the fraction with the larger numerator will have the larger value.

Example:

Which is greater, $\frac{3}{8}$ or $\frac{5}{8}$?

$$\frac{3}{8} < \frac{5}{8}$$

But if you're given two positive fractions with the same numerator but different denominators, the fraction with the smaller denominator will have the larger value.

Example:

Which is greater, $\frac{3}{4}$ or $\frac{3}{8}$?

The diagrams below show two wholes of equal size. The one on the left is divided into 4 equal parts, 3 of which are shaded. The one on the right is divided into 8 equal parts, 3 of which are shaded.

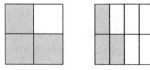

$\frac{3}{4}$ is clearly greater than $\frac{3}{8}$

If neither the numerators nor the denominators are the same, you have three options. You can turn both fractions into their decimal equivalents. Or you can express both fractions in terms of some common denominator and then see which new equivalent fraction has the largest numerator. Or you can cross multiply the numerator of each fraction by the denominator of the other. The greater result will wind up next to the greater fraction.

Example:

Which is greater, $\frac{5}{6}$ or $\frac{7}{9}$?

$$45 \frac{5}{6} \times \frac{7}{9} 42$$

Since $45 > 42$, $\frac{5}{6} > \frac{7}{9}$.

Mixed Numbers and Improper Fractions

A *mixed number* consists of an integer and a fraction.

An improper fraction is a fraction whose numerator is greater than its denominator. To convert an improper fraction to a mixed number, divide the numerator by the denominator. The number of "whole" times that the denominator goes into the numerator will be the integer portion of the improper fraction; the remainder will be the numerator of the fractional portion.

Example:

Convert $\frac{23}{4}$ to a mixed number.

Dividing 23 by 4 gives you 5 with a remainder of 3, so $\frac{23}{4} = 5\frac{3}{4}$.

To change a mixed number to a fraction, multiply the integer portion of the mixed number by the denominator and add the numerator. This new number is your numerator. The denominator will not change.

Example:

Convert $2\frac{3}{7}$ to a fraction.

$$2\frac{3}{7} = \frac{7(2)+3}{7} = \frac{17}{7}$$

Properties of Fractions Between −1 and +1

The reciprocal of a fraction between 0 and 1 is greater than both the original fraction and 1.

Example:

The reciprocal of $\dfrac{2}{3}$ is $\dfrac{3}{2}$, which is greater than both 1 and $\dfrac{2}{3}$.

The reciprocal of a fraction between –1 and 0 is less than both the original fraction and –1.

Example:

The reciprocal of $-\dfrac{2}{3}$ is $-\dfrac{3}{2}$, or $-1\dfrac{1}{2}$, which is less than both –1 and $-\dfrac{2}{3}$.

The square of a fraction between 0 and 1 is less than the original fraction.

Example:

$$\left(\frac{1}{2}\right)^2 = \left(\frac{1}{2}\right)\left(\frac{1}{2}\right) = \frac{1}{4}$$

But the square of any fraction between 0 and –1 is greater than the original fraction, because multiplying two negative numbers gives you a positive product, and any positive number is greater than any negative number.

Example:

$$\left(-\frac{1}{2}\right)^2 = \left(-\frac{1}{2}\right)\left(-\frac{1}{2}\right) = \frac{1}{4}$$

Multiplying any positive number by a fraction between 0 and 1 gives a product smaller than the original number.

Example:

$$6\left(\frac{1}{4}\right) = \frac{6}{4} = \frac{3}{2}$$

Multiplying any negative number by a fraction between 0 and 1 gives a product greater than the original number.

Example:

$$(-3)\left(\frac{1}{2}\right) = -\frac{3}{2}$$

DECIMALS

Converting Decimals

It's easy to convert decimals to common fractions, and vice versa. Any decimal fraction is equivalent to some common fraction with a power of 10 in the denominator.

To convert a decimal between 0 and 1 to a fraction, determine the place value of the last nonzero digit, and set this as the denominator. Then use all the digits of the decimal number as the numerator, ignoring the decimal point. Finally, if necessary, reduce the fraction to its lowest terms.

Example:

Convert 0.875 to a fraction in lowest terms.

The last nonzero digit is the 5, which is in the thousandths place. So the denominator of the common fraction will be 1,000. The numerator will be 875: $\frac{875}{1000}$.

(You can ignore the zero to the left of the decimal point, since there are no nonzero digits to its left; it's just a "placeholder.")

Both 875 and 1,000 contain a factor of 25. Canceling it out leaves you with $\frac{35}{40}$. Reducing that further by a factor of 5 gives you $\frac{7}{8}$, which is in lowest terms.

To convert a fraction to a decimal, simply divide the numerator by the denominator.

Example:

What is the decimal equivalent of $\frac{4}{5}$?

$$4 \div 5 = 0.8$$

Comparing Decimals

Knowing place values allows you to assess the relative values of decimals.

Example:

Which is greater, 0.254 or 0.3?

Of course, 254 is greater than 3. But $0.3 = \frac{3}{10}$, which is equivalent to $\frac{300}{1000}$, while 0.254 is equivalent to only $\frac{254}{1000}$. Since $\frac{300}{1000} > \frac{254}{1000}$, 0.3 is greater than 0.254.

Here's the simplest way to compare decimals: Add zeros after the last digit to the right of the decimal point in each decimal fraction until all the decimals you're comparing have the same number of digits. Essentially, what you're doing is giving all the fractions the same denominator so that you can just compare their numerators.

Example:

Arrange in order from smallest to largest: 0.7, 0.77, 0.07, 0.707, and 0.077.

The numbers 0.707 and 0.077 end at the third place to the right of the decimal point—the thousandths place. Add zeros after the last digit to the right of the decimal point in each of the other fractions until you reach the thousandths place:

$$0.7 = 0.700 = \frac{700}{1000}$$

$$0.77 = 0.770 = \frac{770}{1000}$$

$$0.07 = 0.070 = \frac{70}{1000}$$

$$0.707 = \frac{707}{1000}$$

$$0.077 = \frac{77}{1000}$$

$$\frac{70}{1000} < \frac{77}{1000} < \frac{700}{1000} < \frac{707}{1000} < \frac{770}{1000}$$

Therefore, $0.07 < 0.077 < 0.7 < 0.707 < 0.77$.

Estimation and Rounding on the GMAT

You should be familiar and comfortable with the practice of "rounding off" numbers. To round off a number to a particular place, look at the digit immediately to the right of that place. If the digit is 0, 1, 2, 3, or 4, don't change the digit that is in the place to which you are rounding. If it is 5, 6, 7, 8, or 9, change the digit in the place to which you are rounding to the next higher digit. Replace all digits to the right of the place to which you are rounding with zeros.

For example, to round off 235 to the tens place, look at the units place. Since it is occupied by a 5, you'll round the 3 in the tens place up to a 4, giving you 240. If you had been rounding off 234, you would have rounded down to the existing 3 in the tens place; that would have given you 230.

Example:

Round off 675,978 to the hundreds place.

The 7 in the tens place means that you will have to round the hundreds place up. Since there is a 9 in the hundreds place, you'll have to change the thousands place as well. Rounding 675,978 to the hundreds place gives you 676,000.

Rounding off large numbers before calculation will allow you quickly to estimate the correct answer.

Estimating can save you valuable time on many GMAT problems. But before you estimate, check the answer choices to see how close they are. If they are relatively close together, you'll have to be more accurate than if they are farther apart.

Percents

The word *percent* means "hundredths," and the percent sign, %, means $\frac{1}{100}$. For example, 25% means $25\left(\frac{1}{100}\right) = \frac{25}{100}$. (Like the division sign, the percent sign evolved from the fractional relationship; the slanted bar in a percent sign represents a fraction bar.)

Percents measure a part-to-whole relationship with an assumed whole equal to 100. The percent relationship can be expressed as $\frac{\text{Part}}{\text{Whole}}$ (100%). For example, if $\frac{1}{4}$ of a rectangle is shaded, the percent of the rectangle that is shaded is $\frac{1}{4}$ (100%) = 25%.

Like fractions, percents express the relationship between a specified part and a whole. In fact, by plugging the part and whole from the shaded rectangle problem into the fraction and decimal versions of the part-whole equation, you can verify that 25%, $\frac{25}{100}$, and 0.25 are simply different names for the same part-whole relationship.

Translating English to Math in Part-Whole Problems

On the GMAT, many fractions and percents appear in word problems. You'll solve the problems by plugging the numbers you're given into some variation of one of the three basic formulas:

$$\frac{Part}{Whole} = Fraction$$

$$\frac{Part}{Whole} = Decimal$$

$$\frac{Part}{Whole}(100) = Percent$$

To avoid careless errors, look for the key words *is* and *of*. *Is* (or *are*) often introduces the part, while *of* almost invariably introduces the whole.

Properties of 100%

Since the percent sign means $\frac{1}{100}$, 100% means $\frac{100}{100}$, or one whole. The key to solving some GMAT percent problems is to recognize that all the parts add up to one whole: 100%.

Example:

All 1,000 registered voters in Smithtown are Democrats, Republicans, or independents. If 75% of the registered voters are Democrats, and 5% are independents, how many are Republicans?

We calculate that 75% + 5%, or 80% of the 1,000 registered voters are either Democrats or independents. The three party affiliations together must account for 100% of the voters; thus, the percentage of Republicans must be 100% – 80%, or 20%. Therefore, the number of Republicans must be 20% of 1,000, which is 20% (1,000), or 200.

Multiplying or dividing a number by 100% is just like multiplying or dividing by 1; it doesn't change the value of the original number.

Converting Percents

To change a fraction to its percent equivalent, multiply by 100%.

Example:

What is the percent equivalent of $\frac{5}{8}$?

$$\frac{5}{8}(100\%) = \frac{500}{8}\% = 62\frac{1}{2}\%$$

To change a decimal fraction to a percent, you can use the rules for multiplying by powers of 10. Move the decimal point two places to the right and insert a percent sign.

Example:

What is the percent equivalent of 0.17?

$$0.17 = 0.17\,(100\%) = 17\%$$

To change a percent to its fractional equivalent, divide by 100%.

Example:

What is the common fraction equivalent of 32%?

$$32\% = \frac{32\%}{100\%} = \frac{8}{25}$$

To convert a percent to its decimal equivalent, use the rules for dividing by powers of 10—just move the decimal point two places to the left.

Example:

What is the decimal equivalent of 32%?

$$32\% = \frac{32\%}{100\%} = \frac{32}{100} = 0.32$$

When you divide a percent by another percent, the percent sign "drops out," just as you would cancel out a common factor.

Example:

$$\frac{100\%}{5\%} = \frac{100}{5} = 20$$

Translation: There are 20 groups of 5% in 100%.

But when you divide a percent by a regular number (not by another percent), the percent sign remains.

Example:

$$\frac{100\%}{5} = 20\%$$

Translation: One-fifth of 100% is 20%.

Common Percent Equivalents

As you can see, changing percents to fractions, or vice versa, is pretty straightforward. But it does take a second or two that you might spend more profitably doing other computations or setting up another GMAT math problem. Familiarity with the following common equivalents will save you time.

$$\frac{1}{20} = 5\%$$ $$\frac{1}{2} = 50\%$$

$$\frac{1}{12} = 8\frac{1}{3}\%$$ $$\frac{3}{5} = 60\%$$

$$\frac{1}{10} = 10\%$$ $$\frac{5}{8} = 62\frac{1}{2}\%$$

$$\frac{1}{8} = 12\frac{1}{2}\%$$ $$\frac{2}{3} = 66\frac{2}{3}\%$$

$$\frac{1}{6} = 16\frac{2}{3}\%$$

$$\frac{1}{5} = 20\%$$

$$\frac{1}{4} = 25\%$$

$$\frac{3}{10} = 30\%$$

$$\frac{1}{3} = 33\frac{1}{3}\%$$

$$\frac{3}{8} = 37\frac{1}{2}\%$$

$$\frac{2}{5} = 40\%$$

$$\frac{7}{10} = 70\%$$

$$\frac{3}{4} = 75\%$$

$$\frac{4}{5} = 80\%$$

$$\frac{5}{6} = 83\frac{1}{3}\%$$

$$\frac{7}{8} = 87\frac{1}{2}\%$$

$$\frac{9}{10} = 90\%$$

$$\frac{11}{12} = 91\frac{2}{3}\%$$

Using the Percent Formula to Solve Percent Problems

You can solve most percent problems by plugging the given data into the percent formula:

$$\frac{\text{Part}}{\text{Whole}}(100\%) = \text{Percent}$$

Most percent problems give you two of the three variables and ask for the third.

Example:

Ben spends $30 of his annual gardening budget on seed. If his total annual gardening budget is $150, what percentage of his budget does he spend on seed?

This problem specifies the whole ($150) and the part ($30) and asks for the percentage. Plugging those numbers into the percent formula gives you this:

$$\text{Percent} = \frac{30}{150}(100\%) = \frac{1}{5}(100\%) = 20$$

Ben spends 20% of his annual gardening budget on seed.

Percent Increase and Decrease

When the GMAT tests percent increase or decrease, use the formulas: Percent increase $= \frac{\text{Increase}(100\%)}{\text{Original}}$ or Percent decrease $= \frac{\text{Decrease}(100\%)}{\text{Original}}$. To find the increase or decrease, just take the difference between the original and the new. Note that the "original" is the base from which change occurs. It may or may not be the first number mentioned in the problem.

Example:

Two years ago, 450 seniors graduated from Inman High School. Last year, 600 seniors graduated. By what percentage did the number of graduating seniors increase?

The original is the figure from the earlier time (two years ago): 450. The increase is 600 − 450, or 150. So the percentage increase is $\frac{150}{450}(100\%) = 33\frac{1}{3}\%$.

Example:

If the price of a $120 dress is increased by 25%, what is the new selling price?

To find the new whole, you'll first have to find the amount of increase. The original whole is $120, and the percent increase is 25%. Plugging in, we find that

$$\frac{\text{increase}}{120}(100\%) = 25\%$$

$$\frac{\text{increase}}{120} = \frac{25}{100}$$

$$\frac{\text{increase}}{120} = \frac{1}{4}$$

$$\text{increase} = \frac{120}{4}$$

$$\text{increase} = 30$$

The amount of increase is $30, so the new selling price is $120 + $30, or $150.

Multistep Percent Problems

On some difficult problems, you'll be asked to find more than one percent, or to find a percent of a percent. Be careful: You can't add percents of different wholes.

Example:

The price of an antique is reduced by 20 percent, and then this price is reduced by 10 percent. If the antique originally cost $200, what is its final price?

The most common mistake in this kind of problem is to reduce the original price by a total of 20% + 10%, or 30%. That would make the final price 70 percent of the original, or 70% ($200) = $140. This is not the correct answer. In this example, the second (10%) price reduction is taken off of the first sale price—the new whole, not the original whole.

To get the correct answer, first find the new whole. You can find it by calculating either $200 − (20% of $200) or 80% ($200). Either way, you will find that the first sale price is $160. That price then has to be reduced by 10%. Either calculate $160 − (10% ($160)) or 90%($160). In either case, the final price of the antique is $144.

Picking Numbers with Percents

Certain types of percent problems lend themselves readily to the alternative technique of Picking Numbers. These include problems in which no actual values are mentioned, just percents. If you assign values to the percents you are working with, you'll find the problem less abstract.

You should almost always pick 100 in percent problems, because it's relatively easy to find percentages of 100.

Example:

The price of a share of company A's stock fell by 20 percent two weeks ago and by another 25 percent last week to its current price. By what percent of the current price does the share price need to rise in order to return to its original price?

○　　45%

○　　55%

○　　$66\frac{2}{3}\%$

○　　75%

○　　82%

Pick a value for the original price of the stock. Since it is a percent question, picking $100 will make the math easy. The first change in the price of the stock was by 20% of $100, or $20, making the new price $100 − $20 = $80. The price then fell by another 25%.

25% is the same as $\frac{1}{4}$, and $\frac{1}{4}$ of $80 is $20. Therefore, the current price is $80 − $20 = $60. To return to its original price, the stock needs to rise from $60 to $100, that is, by $100 − $60 = $40. Then $40 is what percent of the current price, $60?

$$\frac{40}{60}(100\%) = \frac{2}{3}(100\%) = 66\frac{2}{3}\%$$

Percent Word Problems

Percent problems are often presented as word problems. We have already seen how to identify the percent, the part, and the whole in simple percent word problems. Here are some other terms that you are likely to encounter in more complicated percent word problems:

Profit made on an item is the seller's price minus the costs to the seller. If a seller buys an item for $10 and sells it for $12, he or she has made $2 profit. The percent of the selling price that is profit is $\frac{\text{Profit}}{\text{Original selling price}}(100\%) = \frac{\$2}{\$12}(100\%) = 16\frac{2}{3}\%$.

A *discount* on an item is the original price minus the reduced price. If an item that usually sells for $20 is sold for $15, the discount is $5. Discount is often represented as a percentage of the original price. In this case, the percentage discount $= \frac{\text{Discount}}{\text{Original price}}(100\%) = \frac{\$5}{\$20} = 25\%$.

The *sale price* is the final price after discount or decrease.

Occasionally, percent problems will involve *interest*. Interest is given as a percent per unit time, such as 5% per month. The sum of money invested is the *principal*. The most common type of interest you will see is *simple interest*. In simple interest, the interest payments received are kept separate from the principal.

Example:

If an investor invests $100 at 20 percent simple annual interest, how much does he or she have at the end of 3 years?

The principal of $100 yields 20% interest every year. Because 20% of $100 is $20, after three years the investor will have 3 years of interest, or $60, plus the principal, for a total of $160.

In *compound interest*, the money earned as interest is reinvested. The principal grows after every interest payment received.

Example:

If an investor invests $100 at 20% compounded annually, how much does he or she have at the end of 3 years?

The first year the investor earns 20% of $100 = $20. So, after one year he or she has $100 + $20 = $120.

The second year the investor earns 20% of $120 = $24. So, after two years he or she has $120 + $24 = $144.

The third year the investor earns 20% of $144 = $28.80. So, after 3 years he or she has $144 + $28.80 = $172.80.

Percents and Data Sufficiency

Data Sufficiency questions (covered in Session 2) test your knowledge of percents in a different way. The crux of these problems, as a rule, is finding all the pieces of the percent formula. You can use the percent formula to pinpoint exactly what you need to achieve sufficiency.

Example:

By what percent did the price of stock X increase?

(1) The price after the increase was $12.

(2) The stock increased in price by $1.50.

To prove sufficiency, you would have to be capable of filling in all parts of the equation. Statement (1) informs you of the price after the increase. This does not give you either the amount of increase or the original price, so it is not sufficient. Statement (2) informs you of the increase in price, but not the original price, so it, too, is not sufficient. Combining the statements, however, gives you the increase in price, $1.50, and the original price, $12.00 − $1.50 = $10.50. So the correct answer is choice **(C)**.

RATIOS

A ratio is the proportional relationship between two quantities. The ratio, or relationship, between two numbers, for example, 10 and 15, may be expressed with a colon between the two numbers (10:15), in words ("the ratio of 10 to 15"), or as a common fraction $\left(\frac{10}{15}\right)$.

To translate a ratio in words to numbers separated by a colon, replace *to* with a colon.

To translate a ratio in words to a fractional ratio, use whatever follows the word *of* as the numerator and whatever follows the word *to* as the denominator. For example, if we had to express the ratio of glazed doughnuts *to* chocolate doughnuts in a box of doughnuts that contained 5 glazed and 7 chocolate doughnuts, we would do so as $\frac{5}{7}$.

Note that the fraction $\frac{5}{7}$ does not mean that $\frac{5}{7}$ of all the doughnuts are glazed doughnuts. There are 5 + 7, or 12 doughnuts all together, so of the doughnuts, $\frac{5}{12}$ are glazed. The $\frac{5}{7}$ ratio merely indicates the proportion of glazed to chocolate doughnuts. For every five glazed doughnuts, there are seven chocolate doughnuts.

Treating ratios as fractions usually makes computation easier. Like fractions, ratios often require division. And, like fractions, ratios can be reduced to lowest terms.

Example:

Joe is 16 years old, and Mary is 12 years old. Express the ratio of Joe's age to Mary's age in lowest terms.

The ratio of Joe's age to Mary's age is $\frac{16}{12} = \frac{4}{3}$, or 4:3.

Part:Whole Ratios

In a part:whole ratio, the "whole" is the entire set (for instance, all the workers in a factory), while the "part" is a certain subset of the whole (for instance, all the female workers in the factory).

In GMAT ratio question stems, the word *fraction* generally indicates a part:whole ratio. "What fraction of the workers are female?" means "What is the ratio of the number of female workers to the total number of workers?"

Example:

The sophomore class at Milford Academy consists of 15 boys and 20 girls. What fraction of the sophomore class is female?

The following three statements are equivalent:

1. $\frac{4}{7}$ of the sophomores are female.

2. 4 out of every 7 sophomores are female.

3. The ratio of female sophomores to total sophomores is 4:7.

Ratio vs. Actual Number

Ratios are usually reduced to their simplest form (that is, to lowest terms). If the ratio of men to women in a room is 5:3, you cannot necessarily infer that there are exactly five men and three women.

If you knew the total number of people in the room, in addition to the male to female ratio, you could determine the number of men and the number of women in the room. For example, suppose you know that there are 32 people in the room. If the male to female ratio is 5 to 3, then the ratio of males to the total is 5:(5 + 3), which is 5:8. You can set up an equation as $\frac{5}{8} = \frac{\#\,of\,males\,in\,room}{32}$. Solving, you will find that the number of males in the room is 20.

Example:

The ratio of domestic sales revenues to foreign sales revenues of a certain product is 3:5. What fraction of the total sales revenues comes from domestic sales?

At first, this question may look more complicated than the previous example. You have to convert from a part:part ratio to a part:whole ratio (the ratio of domestic sales revenues to total sales revenues). And you're not given actual dollar figures for domestic or foreign sales. But since all sales are either foreign or domestic, "total sales revenues" must be the sum of the revenues from domestic and foreign sales. You can convert the given ratio to a part:whole ratio, because the sum of the parts equals the whole.

Although it's impossible to determine dollar amounts for the domestic, foreign, or total sales revenues from the given information, the 3:5 ratio tells you that of every $8 in sales revenues, $3 come from domestic sales and $5 from foreign sales. Therefore, the ratio of domestic sales revenues to total sales revenues is 3:8, or $\frac{3}{8}$.

You can convert a part:part ratio to a part:whole ratio (or vice versa) only if there are no missing parts and no overlap among the parts; that is, if the whole is equal to the sum of the parts.

This concept is often tested in Data Sufficiency.

Example:

In a certain bag, what is the ratio of the number of red marbles to the total number of marbles?

(1) The ratio of the number of red marbles to the number of blue marbles in the bag is 3:5.

(2) There are only red and blue marbles in the bag.

In this case, Statement (1), by itself, is insufficient. You cannot convert a part-to-part ratio (red marbles to blue marbles) to a part-to-whole ratio (red marbles to all marbles) because you don't know whether there were any other colored marbles in the bag. Only when you combine the two statements do you have enough information to answer the question, so the answer is **(C)**.

Example:

Of the 25 people in Fran's apartment building, what is the ratio of people who use the roof to total residents?

(1) There are 9 residents who use the roof for tanning and 8 residents who use the roof for gardening.

(2) The roof is only used by tanners and gardeners.

In this question, we do not know if there is any overlap between tanners and gardeners. How many, if any, residents do both? Since we don't know, the answer is **(E)**.

Ratios of More Than Two Terms

Most of the ratios that you'll see on the GMAT have two terms. But it is possible to set up ratios with more than two terms. These ratios express more relationships, and therefore convey more information, than two-term ratios. However, most of the principles discussed so far with respect to two-term ratios are just as applicable to ratios of more than two terms.

Example:

The ratio of x to y is 5:4. The ratio of y to z is 1:2. What is the ratio of x to z?

We want the y's in the two ratios to equal each other, because then we can combine the x:y ratio and the y:z ratio to form the x:y:z ratio that we need to answer this question. To make the y's equal, we can multiply the second ratio by 4. When we do so, we must perform the multiplication on both components of the ratio. Since a ratio is a constant proportion, it can be multiplied or divided by any number without losing its meaning, as long as the multiplication and division are applied to all the components of the ratio. In this case, we find that the new ratio for y to z is 4:8. We can combine this with the first ratio to find a new x to y to z ratio of 5:4:8. Therefore, the ratio of x to z is 5:8.

RATES

A rate is a special type of ratio. Instead of relating a part to the whole, or to another part, a rate relates one kind of quantity to a completely different kind. When we talk about rates, we usually use the word *per*, as in "miles per hour," "cost per item," etc. Since *per* means "for one" or "for each," we express the rates as ratios reduced to a denominator of 1.

Speed

The most commonly tested rate on the GMAT is speed. This is usually expressed in miles or kilometers per hour. The relationship between speed, distance, and time is given by the formula Speed $= \frac{\text{Distance}}{\text{Time}}$ which can be rewritten two ways: Time $= \frac{\text{Distance}}{\text{Speed}}$, and Distance = (Speed)(Time).

Any time you can find two out of the three elements in this equation, you can find the third.

For example, if a car travels 300 miles in 5 hours, it has averaged $\frac{300 \text{ miles}}{5 \text{ hours}} = 60$ miles per hour. (Note that speeds are usually expressed as averages because they are not necessarily constant. For instance, in the previous example, the car traveled 300 miles in 5 hours. It moved at an "average speed" of 60 miles per hour, but probably not at a constant speed of 60 miles per hour.)

Likewise, a rearranged version of the formula can be used to solve for missing speed or time.

Example:

How far do you drive if you travel for 5 hours at 60 miles per hour?

$$\text{Distance} = (\text{Speed})(\text{Time})$$

$$\text{Distance} = (60 \text{ mph})(5 \text{ hours})$$

$$\text{Distance} = 300 \text{ miles}$$

Example:

How much time does it take to drive 300 miles at 60 miles per hour?

$$\text{Time} = \frac{\text{Distance}}{\text{Speed}}$$

$$\text{Time} = \frac{300 \text{ miles}}{60 \text{ mph}}$$

$$\text{Time} = 5 \text{ hours}$$

Other Rates

Speed is not the only rate that appears on the GMAT. For instance, you might get a word problem involving liters per minute or cost per unit. All rate problems, however, can be solved using the speed formula and its variants by conceiving of "speed" as "rate," and "distance" as "quantity."

Example:

How many hours will it take to fill a 500-liter tank at a rate of 2 liters per minute?

Plug the numbers into our rate formula:

$$\text{Time} = \frac{\text{Quantity}}{\text{Rate}}$$

$$\text{Time} = \frac{500\,\text{liters}}{2\,\text{liters per minute}}$$

$$\text{Time} = 250\ \text{minutes}$$

Now convert 250 minutes to hours: 250 minutes $\div$ 60 minutes per hour = $4\frac{1}{6}$ hours to fill the pool. (As you can see from this problem, GMAT Problem Solving questions test your ability to convert minutes into hours and vice versa. Pay close attention to what units the answer choice must use.)

In some cases, you should use proportions to answer rate questions.

Example:

If 350 widgets cost $20, how much will 1,400 widgets cost at the same rate?

Set up a proportion:

$$\frac{\text{Number of widgets}}{\text{Cost}} = \frac{350\,\text{widgets}}{\$20} = \frac{1400\,\text{widgets}}{\$x}$$

Solving, you will find that $x = 80$.

So, 1,400 widgets will cost $80 at that rate.

Combined Rate Problems

Rates can be added.

Example:

Nelson can mow 200 square meters of lawn per hour. John can mow 100 square meters of lawn per hour. Working simultaneously but independently, how many hours will it take Nelson and John to mow 1,800 square meters of lawn?

Add Nelson's rate to John's rate to find the combined rate.

200 meters per hour + 100 meters per hour = 300 meters per hour.

Divide the total lawn area, 1,800 square meters, by the combined rate, 300 square meters per hour, to find the number of required hours, 6.

Work Problems (Given Hours per Unit of Work)

The work formula can be used to find out how long it takes a number of people working together to complete a task. Let's say we have three people. The first takes a units of time to complete the job, the second b units of time to complete the job, and the third c units of time. If the time it takes all three working together to complete the job is T, then $\frac{1}{a} + \frac{1}{b} + \frac{1}{c} = \frac{1}{T}$.

Example:

John can weed the garden in 3 hours. If Mary can weed the garden in 2 hours, how long will it take them to weed the garden at this rate, working independently?

Set John's time per unit of work as a and Mary's time per unit of work as b. (There is no need for the variable c, since there are only two people.) Plugging in, you find that

$$\frac{1}{3} + \frac{1}{2} = \frac{1}{T}$$

$$\frac{2}{6} + \frac{3}{6} = \frac{1}{T}$$

$$\frac{5}{6} = \frac{1}{T}$$

$$T = \frac{6}{5} \text{ hours}$$

WORK FORMULA

We can use the above equation, $\frac{1}{a} + \frac{1}{b} = \frac{1}{T}$, to derive the work formula, a convenient formula to use on Test Day.

$$\frac{1}{a} + \frac{1}{b} = \frac{1}{T}$$

$$(ab)\left(\frac{1}{a} + \frac{1}{b}\right) = \left(\frac{1}{T}\right)(ab)$$

$$\frac{ab}{a} + \frac{ab}{b} = \frac{ab}{T}$$

$$b + a = \frac{ab}{T}$$

$$T(b + a) = \left(\frac{ab}{T}\right)T$$

$$T(b + a) = ab$$

$$T = \frac{ab}{a+b}$$

This last equation is the work formula.

Here, a = the amount of time is takes person a to complete the job and b = the amount of time it takes person b to complete the job.

Example:

Let's use the same example from above: John takes 3 hours to weed the garden, and Mary takes 2 hours to weed the same garden. How long will it take them to weed the garden together?

$$\text{Work formula} = \frac{a \times b}{a + b} = \frac{3 \times 2}{3 + 2} = \frac{6}{5} \text{ hours}$$

AVERAGES

The average of a group of numbers is defined as the sum of the terms divided by the number of terms.

$$\text{Average} = \frac{\text{Sum of terms}}{\text{Number of terms}}$$

This equation can be rewritten two ways:

$$\text{Number of terms} = \frac{\text{Sum of terms}}{\text{Average}}$$

$$\text{Sum of terms} = (\text{Number of terms})(\text{Average})$$

Thus, any time you have two out of the three values (average, sum of terms, number of terms), you can find the third.

Example:

Henry buys three items costing \$2.00, \$1.75, and \$1.05. What is the average price (arithmetic mean) of the three items? (Don't let the phrase *arithmetic mean* throw you; it's just another term for *average*.)

$$\text{Average} = \frac{\text{Sum of terms}}{\text{Number of terms}}$$

$$\text{Average} = \frac{\$2.0 + \$1.75 + \$1.05}{3}$$

$$\text{Average} = \frac{\$4.80}{3}$$

$$\text{Average} = \$1.60$$

Example:

June pays an average price of \$14.50 for 6 articles of clothing. What is the total price of all 6 articles?

$$\text{Sum of terms} = (\text{Average})(\text{Number of terms})$$

$$\text{Sum of terms} = (\$14.50)(6)$$

$$\text{Sum of terms} = \$87.00$$

Example:

The total weight of the licorice sticks in a jar is 30 ounces. If the average weight of each licorice stick is 2 ounces, how many licorice sticks are there in the jar?

$$\text{Number of terms} = \frac{\text{Sum of terms}}{\text{Average}}$$

$$\text{Number of terms} = \frac{30 \text{ ounces}}{2 \text{ ounces}}$$

$$\text{Number of terms} = 15$$

Using the Average to Find a Missing Number

If you're given the average, the total number of terms, and all but one of the actual numbers, you can find the missing number.

Example:

The average annual rainfall in Boynton for 1976–1979 was 26 inches per year. Boynton received 24 inches of rain in 1976, 30 inches in 1977, and 19 inches in 1978. How many inches of rainfall did Boynton receive in 1979?

You know that total rainfall equals 24 + 30 + 19 + (number of inches of rain in 1979).

You know that the average rainfall was 26 inches per year.

You know that there were 4 years.

So, plug these numbers into any of the three expressions of the average formula to find that Sum of terms = (Average)(Number of terms)

$$24 + 30 + 19 + \text{inches in 1979} = (26)(4)$$
$$73 + \text{inches in 1979} = (26)(4)$$
$$73 + \text{inches in 1979} = 104$$
$$\text{inches in 1979} = 31$$

Another Way to Find a Missing Number: The Concept of "Balanced Value"

Another way to find a missing number is to understand that the *sum of the differences between each term and the mean of the set must equal zero*. Plugging in the numbers from the previous problem, for example, we find that

$$(24 - 26) + (30 - 26) + (19 - 26) + (\text{inches in 1979} - 26) = 0$$
$$(-2) + (4) + (-7) + (\text{inches in 1979} - 26) = 0$$
$$-5 + (\text{inches in 1979} - 26) = 0$$
$$\text{inches in 1979} = 31$$

It may be easier to comprehend why this is true by visualizing a balancing, or weighting, process. The combined distance of the numbers above the average from the mean must be balanced with the combined distance of the numbers below the average from the mean.

Example:

The average of 63, 64, 85, and x is 80. What is the value of x?

Think of each value in terms of its position relative to the average, 80.

63 is 17 less than 80.

64 is 16 less than 80.

85 is 5 greater than 80.

So these three terms are a total of 17 + 16 − 5, or 28, less than the average. Therefore, x must be 28 greater than the average to restore the balance at 80. So $x = 28 + 80 = 108$.

Average of Consecutive, Evenly Spaced Numbers

When consecutive numbers are evenly spaced, the average is the middle value. For example, the average of consecutive integers 6, 7, and 8 is 7.

If there is an even number of evenly spaced numbers, there is no single middle value. In that case, the average is midway between (that is, the average of) the middle two values. For example, the average of 5, 10, 15, and 20 is 12.5, midway between the middle values 10 and 15.

Note that not all consecutive numbers are evenly spaced. For instance, consecutive prime numbers arranged in increasing order are not evenly spaced. But you can use the handy technique of finding the middle value whenever you have consecutive integers, consecutive odd or even numbers, consecutive multiples of an integer, or any other consecutive numbers that are evenly spaced.

Combining Averages

When there is an equal number of terms in each set, and *only when there is an equal number of terms in each set*, you can average averages.

For example, suppose there are two bowlers, and you must find their average score per game. One has an average score per game of 100, and the other has an average score per game of 200. If both bowlers bowled the same number of games, you can average their averages to find their combined average. Suppose they both bowled 4 games. Their combined average will be equally influenced by both bowlers. Hence, their combined average will be the average of 100 and 200. We can find this quickly by remembering that the quantity above the average and the quantity below the average must be equal. Therefore, the average will be halfway between 100 and 200, which is 150. Or, we could solve using our average formula:

$$\text{Average} = \frac{\text{Sum of terms}}{\text{Number of terms}} = \frac{4(100) + 4(200)}{8} = 150$$

However, if the bowler with the average score of 100 had bowled 4 games, and the bowler with the 200 average had bowled 16 games, the combined average would be weighted further toward 200 than toward 100, to reflect the greater influence of the 200 bowler than the 100 bowler upon the total. This is known as a *weighted average*.

Again, you can solve this by using the concept of a balanced average or by using the average formula.

Since the bowler bowling an average score of 200 bowled $\frac{4}{5}$ of the games, the combined average will be $\frac{4}{5}$ of the distance along the number line between 100 and 200, which is 180. Or, you can plug numbers into an average formula to find that

$$\text{Average} = \frac{\text{Sum of terms}}{\text{Number of terms}}$$

$$\text{Average} = \frac{4(100) + 16(200)}{20}$$

$$\text{Average} = \frac{400 + 3200}{20}$$

$$\text{Average} = 180$$

Averages and Data Sufficiency

For Data Sufficiency average questions, you will have to scan the statements for any two elements of the average formula, from which you will know that you can find the third.

Example:

> If the receipts for a matinee performance at the Granada Theater totaled $2,400, how many tickets were sold for that performance?
>
> (1) The average price of a ticket sold was $7.50.
> (2) All tickets sold cost either $10.00 or $6.00.

Use the average formula: Average $= \frac{\text{Sum of terms}}{\text{Number of terms}}$. In this case, you already know the sum of terms (total receipts = $2,400). All that you need to find the number of terms (number of tickets sold) is the other part of the equation: the average price of a ticket sold. Statement (1) gives you this information; so it is sufficient. Since you don't know how many $10.00 versus $6.00 tickets were sold, Statement (2) does not give you the number of tickets sold and so is not sufficient. The answer then is choice **(A)**.

ALGEBRA

ALGEBRAIC TERMS

Variable: A letter or symbol representing an unknown quantity.

Constant (term): A number not multiplied by any variable(s).

Term: A numerical constant; also, the product of a numerical constant and one or more variables.

Coefficient: The numerical constant by which one or more variables are multiplied. The coefficient of $3x^2$ is 3. A variable (or product of variables) without a numerical coefficient, such as z or xy^3, is understood to have a coefficient of 1.

Algebraic expression: An expression containing one or more variables, one or more constants, and possibly one or more operation symbols. In the case of the expression x, there is an implied coefficient of 1. An expression does not contain an equals sign. x, $3x^2 + 2x$, and $\frac{7x+1}{3x^2-14}$ are all algebraic expressions.

Monomial: An algebraic expression with only one term. To *multiply monomials*, multiply the coefficients and the variables separately: $2a \times 3a = (2 \times 3)(a \times a) = 6a^2$.

Polynomial: The general name for an algebraic expression with more than one term.

Algebraic equation: Two algebraic expressions separated by an equals sign, or one algebraic expression separated from a number by an equals sign.

BASIC OPERATIONS

Combining Like Terms

The process of simplifying an expression by adding together or subtracting terms that have the same variable factors is called *combining like terms*.

Example:

Simplify the expression $2x - 5y - x + 7y$.

$2x - 5y - x + 7y = (2x - x) + (7y - 5y) = x + 2y$

Notice that the commutative, associative, and distributive laws that govern arithmetic operations with ordinary numbers also apply to algebraic terms and polynomials.

Adding and Subtracting Polynomials

To *add or subtract polynomials*, combine like terms.

$$(3x^2 + 5x + 7) - (x^2 + 12) = (3x^2 - x^2) + 5x + (7 - 12) = 2x^2 + 5x - 5$$

Factoring Algebraic Expressions

Factoring a polynomial means expressing it as a product of two or more simpler expressions. Common factors can be factored out by using the distributive law.

Example:

Factor the expression $2a + 6ac$.

The greatest common factor of $2a + 6ac$ is $2a$. Using the distributive law, you can factor out $2a$ so that the expression becomes $2a(1 + 3c)$.

Example:

All three terms in the polynomial $3x^3 + 12x^2 - 6x$ contain a factor of $3x$. Pulling out the common factor yields $3x(x^2 + 4x - 2)$.

ADVANCED OPERATIONS

Substitution

Substitution, a process of plugging values into equations, is used to evaluate an algebraic expression or to express it in terms of other variables.

Replace every variable in the expression with the number or quantity you are told is its equivalent. Then carry out the designated operations, remembering to follow the order of operations (PEMDAS).

Example:

Express $\dfrac{a - b^2}{b - a}$ in terms of x if $a = 2x$ and $b = 3$.

Replace every a with $2x$ and every b with 3:

$$\frac{a - b^2}{b - a} = \frac{2x - 9}{3 - 2x}$$

Without more information, you can't simplify or evaluate this expression further.

Solving Equations

When you manipulate any equation, *always do the same thing on both sides of the equals sign.* Otherwise, the two sides of the equation will no longer be equal.

To solve an algebraic equation without exponents for a particular variable, you have to manipulate the equation until that variable is on one side of the equals sign with all numbers or other variables on the other side. You can perform addition, subtraction, or multiplication; you can also perform division, as long as the quantity by which you are dividing does not equal zero.

Typically, at each step of the process, you'll try to isolate the variable by using the reverse of whatever operation has been applied to the variable. For example, in solving the equation $n + 6 = 10$ for n, you have to get rid of the 6 that has been added to the n. You do that by subtracting 6 from both sides of the equation: $n + 6 - 6 = 10 - 6$, so $n = 4$.

Example:

If $4x - 7 = 2x + 5$, what is the value of x?

Start by adding 7 to both sides. This gives us $4x = 2x + 12$. Now subtract $2x$ from both sides. This gives us $2x = 12$. Finally, let's divide both sides by 2. This gives us $x = 6$.

Inequalities

There are two differences between solving an inequality (such as $2x < 5$) and solving an equation (such as $2x - 5 = 0$).

First, the solution to an inequality is almost always a range of possible values, rather than a single value. You can see the range easily by expressing it visually on a number line.

The shaded portion of the number line above shows the set of all numbers between -4 and 0 excluding the endpoints -4 and 0; this range would be expressed algebraically by the inequality $-4 < x < 0$.

The shaded portion of the number line above shows the set of all numbers greater than -1, up to and including 3; this range would be expressed algebraically by the inequality $-1 < x \leq 3$.

The other difference when solving an inequality—and the only thing you really have to remember—is that if you multiply or divide the inequality by a negative number, you have to reverse the direction of the inequality. For example, when you multiply both sides of the inequality $-3x < 2$ by -1, you get $3x > -2$.

Example:

Solve for x: $3 - \dfrac{x}{4} \geq 2$

Multiply both sides of the inequality by 4: $12 - x \geq 8$

Subtract 12 from both sides: $-x \geq -4$

Multiply (or divide) both sides by –1 and change the direction of the inequality sign: $x \leq 4$

As you can see from the number line, the range of values that satisfies this inequality includes 4 and all numbers less than 4.

Solving for One Unknown in Terms of Another

In general, in order to solve for the value of an unknown, you need as many distinct equations as you have variables. If there are two variables, for instance, you need two distinct equations.

However, some GMAT problems do not require you to solve for the numerical value of an unknown. Instead you are asked to solve for one variable in terms of the other(s). To do so, isolate the desired variable on one side of the equation and move all the constants and other variables to the other side.

Example:

In the formula $z = \dfrac{xy}{a+yb}$, solve for y in terms of x, z, a, and b.

Clear the denominator by multiplying both sides by $a + yb$: $(a + yb)z = xy$

Remove parentheses by distributing: $az + ybz = xy$

Put all terms containing y on one side and all other terms on the other side: $az = xy - ybz$

Factor out the common factor, y: $az = y(x - bz)$

Divide by the coefficient of y to get y alone: $\dfrac{az}{x - bz} = y$

Simultaneous Equations

We've already discovered that you need as many different equations as you have variables to solve for the actual value of a variable. When a single equation contains more than one variable, you can only solve for one variable in terms of the others.

This has important implications for Data Sufficiency. For sufficiency, you usually must have at least as many equations as you have variables.

On the GMAT, you will often have to solve two simultaneous equations, that is, equations that give you different information about the same two variables. There are two methods for solving simultaneous equations.

Method 1—Substitution

Step 1: Solve one equation for one variable in terms of the second.

Step 2: Substitute the result back into the other equation and solve.

Example:

If $x - 15 = 2y$ and $6y + 2x = -10$, what is the value of y?

Solve the first equation for x by adding 15 to both sides.

$$x = 2y + 15$$

Substitute $2y + 15$ for x in the second equation:

$$6y + 2(2y + 15) = -10$$
$$6y + 4y + 30 = -10$$
$$10y = -40$$
$$y = -4$$

Method 2—Adding to Cancel

Combine the equations in such a way that one of the variables cancels out. To solve the two equations $4x + 3y = 8$ and $x + y = 3$, multiply both sides of the second equation by -3 to get $-3x - 3y = -9$. Now add the two equations; the $3y$ and the $-3y$ cancel out, leaving: $x = -1$.

Before you use either method, make sure you really do have two distinct equations. For example, $2x + 3y = 8$ and $4x + 6y = 16$ are really the same equation in different forms; multiply the first equation by 2, and you'll get the second.

Whichever method you use, you can check the result by plugging both values back into both equations and making sure they fit.

Example:

If $m = 4n + 2$, and $3m + 2n = 16$, find the values of m and n.

Since the first equation already expresses m in terms of n, this problem is best approached by substitution.

Substitute $4n + 2$ for m into $3m + 2n = 16$, and solve for n.

$$3(4n + 2) + 2n = 16$$
$$12n + 6 + 2n = 16$$
$$14n = 10$$
$$n = \frac{5}{7}$$

Now solve either equation for m by plugging in for n.

$$m = 4n + 2$$
$$m = 4\left(\frac{5}{7}\right) + 2$$
$$m = \frac{20}{7} + 2$$
$$m = \frac{20}{7} + \frac{14}{7}$$
$$m = \frac{34}{7}$$

So $m = \frac{34}{7}$ and $n = \frac{5}{7}$.

Example:

If $3x + 3y = 18$ and $x - y = 10$, find the values of x and y.

You could solve this problem by the substitution method. But look what happens if you multiply the second equation by 3 and add it to the first:

$$3x + 3y = 18$$
$$+(3x - 3y = 30)$$
$$\overline{6x = 48}$$

If $6x = 48$, then $x = 8$. Now you can just plug 8 into either equation in place of x and solve for y. Your calculations will be simpler if you use the second equation: $8 - y = 10$; $-y = 2$; $y = -2$.

Simultaneous Equations in Data Sufficiency

Data Sufficiency questions will sometimes test your understanding of how many equations you need to solve for a variable.

Example:

What is the value of x?

(1) $x - 6y = 24$
(2) $4x + 2y = 16$

Neither statement alone is sufficient, since each equation allows you only to solve for x in terms of *another variable*. However, both statements together give two different equations with two unknowns—enough information to find the value of x. The answer is **(C)**.

Example:

What is the value of $x + y$?

(1) $x + 4y = -12$
(2) $5x + 5y = 18$

We don't need the value of either variable by itself, but their sum. The second statement gives us enough information. If we divided both sides by 5, we could find the value of $x + y$. The answer is **(B)**.

Symbolism

Don't panic if you see strange symbols like ★, ✧, and ♦ in a GMAT problem.

Problems of this type usually require nothing more than substitution. Read the question stem carefully for a definition of the symbols and for any examples of how to use them. Then, just follow the given model, substituting the numbers that are in the question stem.

Example:

An operation symbolized by ✴ is defined by the equation $x ✴ y = x - \dfrac{1}{y}$. What is the value of $2 ✴ 7$?

The ✴ symbol is defined as a two-stage operation performed on two quantities, which are symbolized in the equation as x and y. The two steps are (1) find the reciprocal of the second quantity and (2) subtract the reciprocal from the first quantity. To find the value of $2 ✴ 7$, substitute the numbers 2 and 7 into the equation, replacing the x (the first quantity given in the equation) with the 2 (the first number given) and the y (the second quantity given in the equation) with the 7 (the second number given). The reciprocal of 7 is $\frac{1}{7}$, and subtracting $\frac{1}{7}$ from 2 gives you

$$2 - \frac{1}{7} = \frac{14}{7} - \frac{1}{7} = \frac{13}{7}$$

When a symbolism problem involves only one quantity, the operations are usually a little more complicated. Nonetheless, you can follow the same steps to find the correct answer.

Example:

Let $x★$ be defined by the equation: $x★ = \dfrac{x^2}{1-x^2}$. Evaluate $\left(\dfrac{1}{2}\right)★$.

$$\left(\frac{1}{2}\right)★ = \frac{\left(\frac{1}{2}\right)^2}{1-\left(\frac{1}{2}\right)^2} = \frac{\frac{1}{4}}{1-\frac{1}{4}} = \frac{\frac{1}{4}}{\frac{3}{4}} = \frac{1}{4} \times \frac{4}{3} = \frac{1}{3}$$

Every once in a while, you'll see a symbolism problem that doesn't even include an equation. The definitions in this type of problem usually test your understanding of number properties.

Example:

✴x is defined as the largest even number that is less than the negative square root of x. What is the value of ✴81?

- ○ −82
- ○ −80
- ○ −10
- ○ −8
- ○ 8

Plug in 81 for x and work backward logically. The negative square root of 81 is −9 because $(-9)(-9) = 81$. The largest even number that is less than −9 is −10. (The number part of −8 is smaller than the number part of −9; however, you're dealing with negative numbers, so you have to look for the even number that would be just to the *left* of −9 along the number line.) Thus, the correct answer choice is **(C)**, −10.

Sequences

Sequences are lists of numbers. The value of a number in a sequence is related to its position in the list. Sequences are often represented on the GMAT as follows:

$$s_1, s_2, s_3, \ldots s_n, \ldots$$

The subscript part of each number gives you the position of each element in the series. s_1 is the first number in the list. s_2 is the second number in the list, and so on.

You will be given a formula that defines each element. For example, if you are told that $s_n = 2n + 1$, then the sequence would be $(2 \times 1) + 1$, $(2 \times 2) + 1$, $(2 \times 3) + 1$, ..., or 3, 5, 7, ...

POLYNOMIALS AND QUADRATICS

The FOIL Method

When two binomials are multiplied, each term is multiplied by each term in the other binomial. This process is often called the FOIL method, because it involves adding the products of the First, Outer, Inner, and Last terms. Using the FOIL method to multiply out $(x + 5)(x - 2)$, the product of the first terms is x^2, the product of the outer terms is $-2x$, the product of the inner terms is $5x$, and the product of the last terms is −10. Adding, the answer is $x^2 + 3x - 10$.

Factoring the Product of Binomials

Many of the polynomials that you'll see on the GMAT can be factored into a product of two binomials by using the FOIL method backwards.

Example:

Factor the polynomial $x^2 - 3x + 2$.

You can factor this into two binomials, each containing an x term. Start by writing down what you know:

$$x^2 - 3x + 2 = (x \quad)(x \quad)$$

You'll need to fill in the missing term in each binomial factor. The product of the two missing terms will be the last term in the original polynomial: 2. The sum of the two missing terms will be the coefficient of the second term of the polynomial: −3. Find the factors of 2 that add up to −3. Since $(-1) + (-2) = -3$, you can fill the empty spaces with −1 and −2.

Thus, $x^2 - 3x + 2 = (x - 1)(x - 2)$.

Note: Whenever you factor a polynomial, you can check your answer by using FOIL to multiply the factors and obtain the original polynomial.

Factoring the Difference of Two Squares

A common factorable expression on the GMAT is the difference of two squares (for example, $a^2 - b^2$). Once you recognize a polynomial as the difference of two squares, you'll be able to factor it automatically, since any polynomial of the form $a^2 - b^2$ can be factored into a product of the form $(a + b)(a - b)$.

Example:

Factor the expression $9x^2 - 1$.

$9x^2 = (3x)^2$ and $1 = 1^2$, so $9x^2 - 1$ is the difference of two squares.

Therefore, $9x^2 - 1 = (3x + 1)(3x - 1)$.

Factoring Polynomials of the Form $a^2 + 2ab + b^2$

Any polynomial of this form is the square of a binomial expression, as you can see by using the FOIL method to multiply $(a + b)(a + b)$ or $(a - b)(a - b)$.

To factor a polynomial of this form, check the sign in front of the $2ab$ term. If it's a *plus* sign, the polynomial is equal to $(a + b)^2$. If it's a *minus* sign, the polynomial is equal to $(a - b)^2$.

Example:

Factor the polynomial $x^2 + 6x + 9$.

x^2 and 9 are both perfect squares, and $6x$ is $2(3x)$, which is twice the product of x and 3, so this polynomial is of the form $a^2 + 2ab + b^2$ with $a = x$ and $b = 3$. Since there is a plus sign in front of the $6x$, $x^2 + 6x + 9 = (a + 3)^2$.

Quadratic Equations

A quadratic equation is an equation of the form $ax^2 + bx + c = 0$. Many quadratic equations have two solutions. In other words, the equation will be true for two different values of x.

When you see a quadratic equation on the GMAT, you'll generally be able to solve it by factoring the algebraic expression, setting each of the factors equal to zero, and solving the resulting equations.

Example:

$x^2 - 3x + 2 = 0$. Solve for x.

To find the solutions, or roots, start by factoring $x^2 - 3x + 2 = 0$ into $(x - 2)(x - 1) = 0$.

The product of two quantities equals zero only if one (or both) of the quantities equals zero. So if you set each of the factors equal to zero, you will be able to solve the resulting equations for the solutions of the original quadratic equation. Setting the two binomials equal to zero gives you

$$x - 2 = 0 \quad \text{or} \quad x - 1 = 0$$

That means that x can equal 2 or 1. As a check, you can plug each of those values in turn into $x^2 - 3x + 2 = 0$, and you'll see that either value makes the equation work.

ALTERNATIVE STRATEGIES FOR MULTIPLE-CHOICE ALGEBRA

Backsolving

On GMAT Problem Solving questions, you may find it easier to attack algebra problems by Backsolving.

To backsolve, substitute each answer choice into the equation until you find the one that satisfies the equation.

Example:

If $x^2 + 10x + 25 = 0$, what is the value of x?

○   25

○   10

○   5

○   −5

○   −10

The textbook approach to solve this problem would be to recognize the polynomial expression as the square of the binomial $(x + 5)$ and set $x + 5 = 0$. That's the fastest way to arrive at the correct answer of −5.

But you could also plug each answer choice into the equation until you found the one that makes the equation true. Backsolving can be pretty quick if the correct answer is the first choice you plug in, but here, you have to get all the way down to choice **(D)** before you find that $(-5)^2 + 10(-5) + 25 = 0$.

Example:

If $\dfrac{5x}{3} + 9 = \dfrac{x}{6} + 18$, $x =$

○   12

○   8

○   6

○   5

○   4

To avoid having to try all five answer choices, look at the equation and decide which choice(s), if plugged in for x, would make your calculations easiest. Since x is in the numerators of the two fractions in this equation, and the denominators are 3 and 6, try plugging in a choice that is divisible by both 3 and 6. Choices **(A)** and **(C)** are divisible by both numbers, so start with one of them.

Choice **(A)**:

$$20 + 9 = 2 + 18$$

$$29 \neq 20$$

This is not true, so x cannot equal 12.

Choice **(C)**:

$$10 + 9 = 1 + 18$$

$$19 = 19$$

This is correct, so x must equal 6. Therefore, choice **(C)** is correct.

Backsolving may not be the fastest method for a multiple-choice algebra problem, but it's useful if you don't think you'll be able to solve the problem in the conventional way.

Picking Numbers

On other types of multiple-choice algebra problems, especially where the answer choices consist of variables or algebraic expressions, you may want to pick numbers to make the problem less abstract. Evaluate the answer choices and the information in the question stem by picking a number and substituting it for the variable wherever the variable appears.

Example:

If $a > 1$, the ratio of $2a + 6$ to $a^2 + 2a - 3$ is

- $2a$
- $a + 3$
- $\dfrac{2}{a - 1}$
- $\dfrac{2a}{3(3 - a)}$
- $\dfrac{a - 1}{2}$

You can simplify the process by replacing the variable a with a number in each algebraic expression. Since a has to be greater than 1, why not pick 2? Then the expression $2a + 6$ becomes $2(2) + 6$, or 10. The expression $a^2 + 2a - 3$ becomes $2^2 + 2(2) - 3 = 4 + 4 - 3 = 5$.

So now the question reads, "the ratio of 10 to 5 is what?" That's easy enough to answer: 10:5 is the same as $\dfrac{10}{5}$, or 2. Now you can just eliminate any answer choice that doesn't give a result of 2 when you substitute 2 for a. Choice **(A)** gives you 2(2), or 4, so discard it. Choice **(B)** results in 5—also not what you want. Choice **(C)** yields $\dfrac{2}{1}$ or 2. That looks good, but you can't stop here.

If another answer choice gives you a result of 2, you will have to pick another number for a and reevaluate the expressions in the question stem and the choices that worked when you let $a = 2$.

Choice **(D)** gives you $\dfrac{2(2)}{3(3-2)}$ or $\dfrac{4}{3}$, so eliminate choice **(D)**.

Choice **(E)** gives you $\dfrac{2-1}{2}$ or $\dfrac{1}{2}$, so discard choice **(E)**.

Fortunately, in this case, only choice **(C)** works out equal to 2, so it is the correct answer. But remember: When Picking Numbers, always check every answer choice to make sure you haven't chosen a number that works for more than one answer choice.

Using Picking Numbers to Solve for One Unknown in Terms of Another

It is also possible to solve for one unknown in terms of another by Picking Numbers. If the first number you pick doesn't lead to a single correct answer, be prepared to either pick a new number (and spend more time on the problem) or settle for guessing strategically among the answers that you haven't eliminated.

Example:

If $\dfrac{x^2 - 16}{x^2 + 6x + 8} = y$ and $x > -2$, which of the following is an expression for x in terms of y?

○ $\dfrac{1 + y}{2 - y}$

○ $\dfrac{2y + 4}{1 - y}$

○ $\dfrac{4y - 4}{y + 1}$

○ $\dfrac{2y - 4}{2 + y}$

○ $\dfrac{y + 4}{y + 1}$

Pick a value for x that will simplify your calculations. If you let x equal 4, then $x^2 - 16 = 4^2 - 16 = 0$, and so the entire fraction on the left side of the equation is equal to zero.

Now, substitute 0 for y in each answer choice in turn. Each choice is an expression for x in terms of y, and since $y = 0$ when $x = 4$, the correct answer will have to give a value of 4 when $y = 0$. Just remember to evaluate all the answer choices, because you might find more than one that gives a result of 4.

Substituting 0 for y in choices **(A)**, **(C)**, and **(D)** yields $\dfrac{1}{2}$, $-\dfrac{4}{1}$, and $-\dfrac{4}{2}$, respectively, so none of those choices can be right. But both **(B)** and **(E)** give results of 4 when you make the substitution; choosing between them will require picking another number.

Again, pick a number that will make calculations easy. If $x = 0$, then $y =$

$$\frac{x^2 - 16}{x^2 + 6x + 8} = \frac{0 - 16}{0 + 0 + 8} = \frac{-16}{8} = -2$$

Therefore, $y = -2$ when $x = 0$. You don't have to try the new value of y in all the answer choices, just in **(B)** and **(E)**. When you substitute -2 for y in choice **(B)**, you get 0. That's what you're looking for, but again, you have to make sure it doesn't work in choice **(E)**. Plugging -2 in for y in **(E)** yields -2 for x, so **(B)** was correct.

STATISTICS

MEDIAN, MODE, AND RANGE

Median: The middle term in a group of terms that are arranged in numerical order. To find the median of a group of terms, first arrange the terms in numerical order. If there is an odd number of terms in the group, then the median is the middle term.

Example:

Bob's test scores in Spanish are 84, 81, 88, 70, and 87. What is his median score?

In increasing order, his scores are 70, 81, 84, 87, and 88. The median test score is the middle one: 84.

If there is an even number of terms in the group, the median is the average of the two middle terms.

Example:

John's test scores in biology are 92, 98, 82, 94, 85, 97. What is his median score?

In numerical order, his scores are 82, 85, 92, 94, 97, and 98. The median test score is the average of the two middle terms, or $\frac{92+94}{2} = 93$.

The median of a group of numbers is often different from its average.

Example:

Caitlin's test scores in math are 92, 96, 90, 85, and 82. Find the difference between Caitlin's median score and the average (arithmetic mean) of her scores.

In ascending order, Caitlin's scores are 82, 85, 90, 92, and 96. The median score is the middle one: 90. Her average score is $\frac{82+85+90+92+96}{5} = \frac{445}{5} = 89$.

As you can see, Caitlin's median score and average score are not the same. The difference between them is $90 - 89$, or 1.

Mode: The term that appears most frequently in a set.

Example:

The daily temperatures in city Q for one week were 25°, 33°, 26°, 25°, 27°, 31°, and 22°. What was the mode of the daily temperatures in city Q for that week?

Each of the temperatures occurs once on the list, except for 25°, which occurs twice. Since 25° appears more frequently than any other temperature, it is the mode.

A set may have more than one mode if two or more terms appear an equal number of times within the set and each appears more times than any other term.

Example:

The table below represents the score distribution for a class of 20 students on a recent chemistry test. Which score, or scores, are the mode?

Score	# of Students Receiving That Score
100	2
91	1
87	5
86	2
85	1
84	5
80	1
78	2
56	1

The largest number in the second column is 5, which occurs twice. Therefore, there were two mode scores on this test: 87 and 84. Equal numbers of students received those scores, and more students received those scores than any other score.

If every element in the set occurs an equal number of times, then the set has no mode.

COMBINATION

A combination question asks you how many unordered subgroups can be formed from a larger group.

Some combination questions on the GMAT can be solved without any computation just by counting or listing possible combinations.

Example:

Allen, Betty, and Claire must wash the dishes. They decide to work in shifts of two people. How many shifts will it take before all possible combinations have been used?

It is possible, and not time-consuming, to solve this problem by writing a list. Call Allen "*A*," Betty "*B*," and Claire "*C*." There are three (*AB*, *AC*, *BC*) possible combinations.

The Combination Formula

Some combination questions use numbers that make quick, noncomputational solving difficult. In these cases, use the combination formula $\frac{n!}{k!(n-k)!}$, where n is the number of items in the group as a whole and k is the number of items in each subgroup formed. The ! symbol means factorial (for example, $5! = (5)(4)(3)(2)(1) = 120$).

Example:

The 4 finalists in a spelling contest win commemorative plaques. If there are 7 entrants in the spelling contest, how many possible groups of winners are there?

Plug the numbers into the combination formula, such that n is 7 (the number in the large group) and k is 4 (the number of people in each subgroup formed).

$$\frac{7!}{4!(7-4)!}$$

$$\frac{7!}{4!3!}$$

At this stage, it is helpful to reduce these terms. Since 7 factorial contains all the factors of 4 factorial, we can write 7! as (7)(6)(5)(4!) and then cancel the 4! in the numerator and denominator.

$$\frac{(7)(6)(5)}{(3)(2)(1)} = ?$$

We can reduce further by crossing off the 6 in the numerator and the (3)(2) in the denominator.

$$\frac{(7)(5)}{1} = 35$$

There are 35 potential groups of spelling contest finalists.

When you are asked to find potential combinations from multiple groups, multiply the potential combinations from each group.

Example:

How many groups can be formed consisting of 2 people from room A and 3 people from room B if there are 5 people in room A and 6 people in room B?

Insert the appropriate numbers into the combination formula for each room and then multiply the results. For room A, the number of combinations of 2 in a set of 5 is

$\frac{n!}{k!(n-k)!} = \frac{5!}{2!3!} = \frac{(5)(4)(3)(2)(1)}{(2)(1)(3)(2)(1)}$. Reducing this you get $\frac{(5)(4)}{(2)} = 10$. For room B, the number of combinations of 3 in a set of 6 is $\frac{n!}{k!(n-k)!} = \frac{6!}{3!3!} = \frac{(6)(5)(4)(3)(2)(1)}{(3)(2)(1)(3)(2)(1)}$. Reducing this you get $\frac{(6)(5)(4)}{(3)(2)} = 20$.

Multiply these to find that there are (10)(20) = 200 possible groups consisting of 2 people from room A and 3 people from room B.

Sometimes the GMAT will ask you to find the number of possible subgroups when choosing one item from a set. In this case, the number of possible subgroups will always equal the number of items in the set.

Example:

> Restaurant A has 5 appetizers, 20 main courses, and 4 desserts. If a meal consists of 1 appetizer, 1 main course, and 1 dessert, how many different meals can be ordered at restaurant A?
>
> The number of possible outcomes from each set is the number of items in the set. So there are 5 possible appetizers, 20 possible main courses, and 4 possible desserts. The number of different meals that can be ordered is (5)(20)(4) = 400.

PERMUTATION

Within any group of items or people, there are multiple arrangements, or permutations, possible. For instance, within a group of three items (for example: *A*, *B*, *C*), there are six permutations (*ABC*, *ACB*, *BAC*, *BCA*, *CAB*, and *CBA*).

Permutations differ from combinations in that permutations are ordered. By definition, each combination larger than 1 has multiple permutations. On the GMAT, a question asking "How many ways/arrangements/orders/schedules are possible?" generally indicates a permutation problem.

To find permutations, think of each place that needs to be filled in a particular arrangement as a blank space. The first place can be filled with any of the items in the larger group. The second place can be filled with any of the items in the larger group except for the one used to fill the first place. The third place can be filled with any of the items in the group except for the two used to fill the first two places, etc.

Example:

> In a spelling contest, the winner will receive a gold medal, the second-place finisher will receive a silver medal, the third-place finisher will receive a bronze medal, and the fourth-place finisher will receive a blue ribbon. If there are 7 entrants in the contest, how many different arrangements of award winners are there?
>
> The gold medal can be won by any of 7 people. The silver medal can be won by any of the remaining (6) people. The bronze medal can be won by any of the remaining (5) people. And the blue ribbon can be won by any of the remaining (4) people. Thus, the number of possible arrangements is (7)(6)(5)(4) = 840.

PROBABILITY

Probability is the numerical representation of the likelihood of an event or combination of events. This is expressed as a ratio of the number of desired outcomes to the total number of possible outcomes. Probability is usually expressed as a fraction (for example "the probability of event A occurring is $\frac{1}{3}$), but it can also be expressed in words ("the probability of event *A* occurring is 1 in 3"). The probability of any event occurring cannot exceed 1 (a probability of 1 represents a 100% chance of an event occurring), and it cannot be less than 0 (a probability of 0 represents a 0% chance of an event occurring).

Example:

If you flip a fair coin, what is the probability that it will fall with the "heads" side facing up?

The probability of the coin landing heads up is $\frac{1}{2}$, since there is one outcome you are interested in (landing heads up) and two possible outcomes (heads up or tails up).

Example:

What is the probability of rolling a 5 or a 6 on a six-sided die numbered 1 through 6?

The probability of rolling a 5 or a 6 on a six-sided die numbered 1 through 6 is $\frac{2}{6}=\frac{1}{3}$, since there are 2 desired outcomes (rolling a 5 or a 6) and 6 possible outcomes (rolling a 1, 2, 3, 4, 5, or 6).

The sum of all possible outcomes, desired or otherwise, must equal 1. In other words, if there is a 25% chance that event *A* will occur, then there is a 75% chance that it will not occur. So, to find the probability that an event *does not* occur, subtract the probability that it *does* occur from 1. In the previous example, the probability of not throwing a 5 or a 6 on the die is $1-\frac{1}{3}=\frac{2}{3}$.

When events are independent, that is, the events do not depend on the other event or events, the probability that several events all occur is the product of the probability of each event occurring individually.

Example:

A fair coin is flipped twice. What is the probability of its landing with the heads side facing up on both flips?

Multiply the probability for each flip: $\left(\frac{1}{2}\right)\left(\frac{1}{2}\right)=\frac{1}{4}$.

PROBABILITY OF DEPENDENT EVENTS

In some situations, the probability of a later event occurring varies according to the results of an earlier event. In this case, the probability fraction for the later event must be adjusted accordingly.

Example:

A bag contains 10 marbles, 4 of which are blue, and 6 of which are red. If 2 marbles are removed without replacement, what is the probability that both marbles removed are red?

The probability that the first marble removed will be red is $\frac{6}{10}=\frac{3}{5}$. The probability that the second marble removed will be red will not be the same, however. There will be fewer marbles overall, so the denominator will be one less. There will also be one fewer red marble. (Note that since we are asking about the odds of picking two red marbles, we are only interested in choosing a second marble if the first was red. Don't concern yourself with situations in which a blue marble is chosen first.) If the first marble removed is red, the probability that the second marble removed will also be red is $\frac{5}{9}$. So the probability that both marbles removed will be red is $\left(\frac{3}{5}\right)\left(\frac{5}{9}\right)=\frac{15}{45}=\frac{1}{3}$.

GEOMETRY

LINES AND ANGLES

A **line** is a one-dimensional geometrical abstraction—infinitely long, with no width. A straight line is the shortest distance between any two points. There is exactly one straight line that passes through any two points.

Example:

In the figure above, $AC = 9$, $BD = 11$, and $AD = 15$. What is the length of BC?

When points are in a line and the order is known, you can add or subtract lengths. Since $AC = 9$ and $AD = 15$, $CD = AD - AC = 15 - 9 = 6$. Now, since $BD = 11$ and $CD = 6$, $BC = BD - CD = 11 - 6 = 5$.

A **line segment** is a section of a straight line, of finite length, with two endpoints. A line segment is named for its endpoints, as in segment AB.

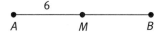

Example:

In the figure above, A and B are the endpoints of the line segment AB, and M is the midpoint ($AM = MB$). What is the length of AB?

Since AM is 6, MB is also 6, and so AB is $6 + 6$, or 12.

Two lines are **parallel** if they lie in the same plane and never intersect regardless of how far they are extended. If line ℓ_1 is parallel to line ℓ_2, we write $\ell_1 \parallel \ell_2$. If two lines are both parallel to a third line, then they are parallel to each other as well.

A **vertex** is the point at which two lines or line segments intersect to form an **angle**. Angles are measured in **degrees** (°).

Angles may be named according to their vertices. Sometimes, especially when two or more angles share a common vertex, an angle is named according to three points: a point along one of the lines or line segments that form the angle, the vertex point, and another point along the other line or line segment. A diagram will sometimes show a letter inside the angle; this letter may also be used to name the angle.

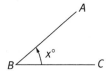

The angle shown in the diagram above could be called $\angle x$, $\angle ABC$, or $\angle B$. (We use a lowercase x because x is not a point.)

Sum of Angles Around a Point

The sum of the measures of the angles around a point is 360°.

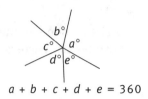

$$a + b + c + d + e = 360$$

Sum of Angles Along a Straight Line

The sum of the measures of the angles on one side of a straight line is 180°. Two angles are *supplementary* to each other if their measures sum to 180°.

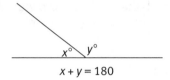

$$x + y = 180$$

Perpendicularity and Right Angles

Two lines are perpendicular if they intersect at a 90° angle (a right angle). If line ℓ_1 is perpendicular to line ℓ_2, we write $\ell_1 \perp \ell_2$. If lines ℓ_1, ℓ_2, and ℓ_3 all lie in the same plane, and $\ell_1 \perp \ell_2$ and $\ell_2 \perp \ell_3$, then $\ell_1 \parallel \ell_3$, as shown in the diagram below.

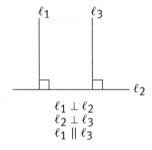

To find the shortest distance from a point to a line, draw a line segment from the point to the line such that the line segment is perpendicular to the line. Then, measure the length of that segment.

Example:

$\angle A$ of triangle ABC is a right angle. Is side BC longer or shorter than side AB?

This question seems very abstract, until you draw a diagram of a right triangle, labeling the vertex with the 90° angle as point A.

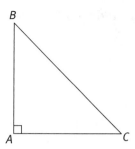

Line segment *AB* has to be the shortest route between point *B* and side *AC*, since side *AB* is perpendicular to side *AC*. If *AB* is the shortest line segment that can join point *B* to side *AC*, *BC* must be longer than *AB*. **Note:** The side opposite the 90° angle, called the *hypotenuse*, is always the longest side of a right triangle.

Two angles are *complementary* to each other if their measures sum to 90°. An *acute angle* measures less than 90°, and an *obtuse angle* measures between 90° and 180°. Two angles are *supplementary* if their measures sum to 180°.

Angle Bisectors

A line or line segment bisects an angle if it splits the angle into two smaller, equal angles. Line segment *BD* below bisects ∠*ABC*, and ∠*ABD* has the same measure as ∠*DBC*. The two smaller angles are each half the size of ∠*ABC*.

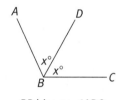

BD bisects ∠*ABC*
∠*ABD* + ∠*DBC* = ∠*ABC*

Adjacent and Vertical Angles

Two intersecting lines form four angles. The angles that are adjacent (next) to each other are *supplementary* because they lie along a straight line. The two angles that are not adjacent to each other are *opposite*, or *vertical*. Opposite angles are equal in measure because each of them is supplementary to the same adjacent angle.

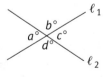

In the diagram above, ℓ_1 intersects ℓ_2 to form angles *a*, *b*, *c*, and *d*. Angles *a* and *c* are opposite, as are angles *b* and *d*. So the measures of angles *a* and *c* are equal to each other, and the measures of angles *b* and *d* are equal to each other. And each angle is supplementary to each of its two adjacent angles.

Angles Around Parallel Lines Intersected by a Transversal

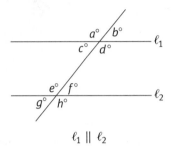

$$\ell_1 \parallel \ell_2$$

A line that intersects two parallel lines is called a *transversal*. Each of the parallel lines intersects the third line at the same angle. In the figure above, $a = e$. Since a and e are equal, and since $a = d$ and $e = h$ (because they are opposite angles), $a = d = e = h$. By similar reasoning, $b = c = f = g$.

In short, when two (or more) parallel lines are cut by a transversal: all acute angles formed are equal; all obtuse angles formed are equal; and any acute angle formed is supplementary to any obtuse angle formed.

Example:

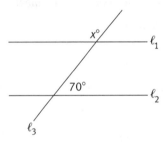

In the diagram above, line ℓ_1 is parallel to line ℓ_2. What is the value of x?

The angle marked $x°$ and the angle adjacent and to the left of the 70° angle on line ℓ_2 are corresponding angles. Therefore, the angle marked $x°$ must be supplementary to the 70° angle. If $70° + x° = 180°$, x must equal 110.

POLYGONS

Important Terms

Polygon: A closed figure whose sides are straight line segments. Families or classes of polygons are named according to the number of sides. A triangle has three sides; a quadrilateral has four sides; a pentagon has five sides; and a hexagon has six sides. Triangles and quadrilaterals are by far the most important polygons on the GMAT; other polygons appear only occasionally.

Perimeter: The distance around a polygon; the sum of the lengths of its sides.

Vertex of a polygon: A point where two sides intersect; *pl.* vertices. Polygons are named by assigning each vertex a letter and listing them in order, as in pentagon *ABCDE* below.

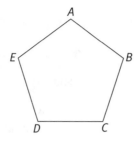

Diagonal of a polygon: A line segment connecting any two nonadjacent vertices.

Regular polygon: A polygon with sides of equal length and interior angles of equal measure.

Small slash marks can provide important information in diagrams of polygons. Sides with the same number of slash marks are equal in length, while angles with the same number of slash marks through circular arcs have the same measure. In the triangle below, for example, $a = b$, and angles X and Z are equal in measure.

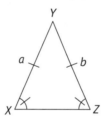

You can figure out the sum of the interior angles of a polygon by dividing the polygon into triangles. Draw diagonals from any vertex to all the nonadjacent vertices. Then, multiply the number of triangles by 180° to get the sum of the interior angles of the polygon. This works because the sum of the interior angles of any triangle is always 180°.

Example:

What is the sum of the interior angles of a pentagon?

Draw a pentagon (a five-sided polygon) and divide it into triangles, as discussed above.

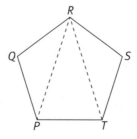

No matter how you've drawn the pentagon, you'll be able to form three triangles. Therefore, the sum of the interior angles of a pentagon is 3 × 180° = 540°.

TRIANGLES

Important Terms

Triangle: A polygon with three straight sides and three interior angles.

Right triangle: A triangle with one interior angle of 90° (a right angle).

Hypotenuse: The longest side of a right triangle. The hypotenuse is always opposite the right angle.

Isosceles triangle: A triangle with two equal sides, which are opposite two equal angles. In the figure below, the sides opposite the two 70° angles are equal, so $x = 7$.

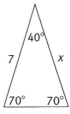

Legs: The two equal sides of an isosceles triangle, or the two shorter sides of a right triangle (the ones forming the right angle). **Note:** The third, unequal side of an isosceles triangle is called the *base*.

Equilateral triangle: A triangle whose three sides are all equal in length and whose three interior angles each measure 60°.

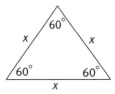

The **altitude,** or **height,** of a triangle is the perpendicular distance from a vertex to the side opposite the vertex. The altitude may fall inside or outside the triangle, or it may coincide with one of the sides.

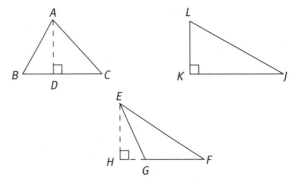

In the diagrams above, *AD*, *EH*, and *LK* are altitudes.

Interior and Exterior Angles of a Triangle

The sum of the interior angles of any triangle is 180°. Therefore, in the figure below, $a + b + c = 180$.

An *exterior angle of a triangle* is equal to the sum of the remote interior angles. The exterior angle labeled $x°$ is equal to the sum of the remote angles: $x = 50 + 100 = 150$.

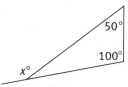

The three exterior angles of any triangle add up to 360°.

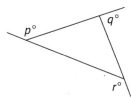

In the figure above, $p + q + r = 360$.

Sides and Angles

The sum of the lengths of any two sides of a triangle is greater than the length of the third side. In the triangle below, $b + c > a$, $a + b > c$, and $a + c > b$.

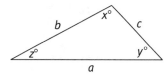

If the lengths of two sides of a triangle are unequal, the greater angle lies opposite the longer side, and vice versa. In the figure above, if $x > y > z$, then $a > b > c$.

Since the two legs of an isosceles triangle have the same length, the two angles opposite the legs must have the same measure. In the figure below, $PQ = PR$, and $\angle Q = \angle R$.

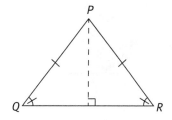

Perimeter and Area of Triangles

There is no special formula for the perimeter of a triangle; it is just the sum of the lengths of the sides.

Example:

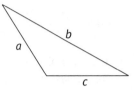

If $b = 2a$ and $c = \dfrac{b}{2}$, find the perimeter of the triangle above in terms of a.

Perimeter $= a + b + c = a + 2a + \dfrac{2a}{2} = 3a + \dfrac{2a}{2} = 3a + a = 4a$.

Incidentally, this is really an isosceles triangle, since $c = \dfrac{b}{2} = \dfrac{2a}{2} = a$.

The area of a triangle is $\left(\dfrac{1}{2}\right)$ (Base)(Height).

Example:

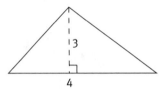

In the diagram above, the base has length 4 and the altitude has length 3. What is the area of the triangle?

$$\text{Area} = \frac{1}{2}bh$$

$$= \frac{bh}{2}$$

$$= \frac{4 \times 3}{2}$$

$$= 6$$

Since the lengths of the base and altitude were not given in specific units, such as centimeters or feet, the area of the triangle is simply said to be 6 square units.

The area of a right triangle is easy to find. Think of one leg as the base and the other as the height. Then the area is one-half the product of the legs, or $\frac{1}{2} \times \text{Leg}_1 \times \text{Leg}_2$.

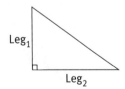

RIGHT TRIANGLES

The right angle is always the largest angle in a right triangle; therefore, the hypotenuse, which lies opposite the right angle, is always the longest side.

Pythagorean Theorem

The Pythagorean theorem, which holds for all right triangles and for no other triangles, states that the square of the hypotenuse is equal to the sum of the squares of the legs.

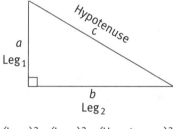

$$(\text{Leg}_1)^2 + (\text{Leg}_2)^2 = (\text{Hypotenuse})^2$$
$$\textbf{or } a^2 + b^2 = c^2$$

The Pythagorean theorem is very useful whenever you're given the lengths of any two sides of a right triangle; as long as you know whether the remaining side is a leg or the hypotenuse, you can find its length by using the Pythagorean theorem.

Example:

What is the length of the hypotenuse of a right triangle with legs of lengths 9 and 10?

$$(\text{Hypotenuse})^2 = (\text{Leg}_1)^2 + (\text{Leg}_2)^2$$
$$= 9^2 + 10^2$$
$$= 81 + 100$$
$$= 181$$

If the square of the hypotenuse equals 181, then the hypotenuse itself must be the square root of 181, or $\sqrt{181}$.

Pythagorean Triples

Certain ratios of integers always satisfy the Pythagorean theorem. You might like to think of them as "Pythagorean triples." One such ratio is 3, 4, and 5. A right triangle with legs of lengths 3 and 4 and hypotenuse of length 5 is probably the most common kind of right triangle on the GMAT. Whenever you see a right triangle with legs of 3 and 4, with a leg of 3 and a hypotenuse of 5, or with a leg of 4 and a hypotenuse of 5, you immediately know the length of the remaining side. In addition, any multiple of these lengths makes another Pythagorean triple; for instance, $6^2 + 8^2 = 10^2$, so a triangle with sides of lengths 6, 8, and 10 is also a right triangle.

The other triple that commonly appears on the GMAT is 5, 12, and 13.

Special Right Triangles

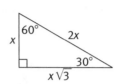

There are two more special kinds of right triangles for which you won't have to use the Pythagorean theorem to find the lengths of the sides. There are special ratios between the lengths of the sides in isosceles right triangles (45°/45°/90° right triangles) and 30°/60°/90° right triangles (right triangles with acute angles of 30° and 60°). As you can see in the first drawing above, the sides of an isosceles right triangle are in a ratio of $x:x:x\sqrt{2}$, with the $x\sqrt{2}$ in the ratio representing the hypotenuse. The sides of a 30°/60°/90° right triangle are in a ratio of $x:x\sqrt{3}:2x$, where $2x$ represents the hypotenuse and x represents the side opposite the 30° angle. (Remember: The longest side has to be opposite the greatest angle.)

Example:

What is the length of the hypotenuse of an isosceles right triangle with legs of length 4?

You can use the Pythagorean theorem to find the hypotenuse, but it's quicker to use the special right triangle ratios. In an isosceles right triangle, the ratio of a leg to the hypotenuse is $x:x\sqrt{2}$. Since the length of a leg is 4, the length of the hypotenuse must be $4\sqrt{2}$.

Triangles and Data Sufficiency

In all Data Sufficiency questions, the approach is to focus on the information you need to answer the question. In geometry, that's often a matter of knowing the correct definition or formula (but not using it!). With triangles, keep in mind the following:

- If you know two angles, you know the third.
- To find the area, you need the base and the height.
- In a right triangle, if you have two sides you can find the third. And if you have two sides, you can find the area.
- In isosceles right triangles and 30°/60°/90° triangles, if you know one side, you can find everything.

Be careful though! Be sure you know as much as you think you do.

Example:

What is the area of right triangle *ABC*?

(1) *AB* = 5

(2) *BC* = 4

Clearly, neither statement alone is sufficient. You may think at first that both together are enough, since it looks like ABC is a 3:4:5 right triangle. Not so fast! We're given two sides, but we don't know which sides they are. If AB is the hypotenuse, then it is a 3:4:5 triangle, and the area is $\frac{1}{2}(3 \times 4) = 6$, but it's also possible that AC, the missing side, is the hypotenuse. In that case, the area would be $\frac{1}{2}(4 \times 5) = 10$. Both statements together are insufficient, and the answer is **(E)**.

QUADRILATERALS

A **quadrilateral** is a four-sided polygon. Regardless of a quadrilateral's shape, the four interior angles sum to 360°.

A **parallelogram** is a quadrilateral with two pairs of parallel sides. Opposite sides are equal in length; opposite angles are equal in measure; angles that are not opposite are supplementary to each other (measure of $\angle A$ + measure of $\angle D$ = 180° in the figure below).

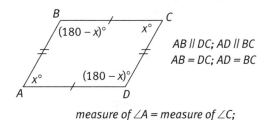

$AB \parallel DC; AD \parallel BC$
$AB = DC; AD = BC$

measure of $\angle A$ = measure of $\angle C$;
measure of $\angle B$ = measure of $\angle D$

A **rectangle** is a parallelogram with four right angles. Opposite sides are equal; diagonals are equal.

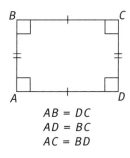

$AB = DC$
$AD = BC$
$AC = BD$

A **square** is a rectangle with equal sides.

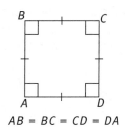

$AB = BC = CD = DA$

Perimeters of Quadrilaterals

To find the perimeter of any polygon, you can simply add the lengths of its sides. However, the properties of rectangles and squares lead to simple formulas that may speed up your calculations.

Because the opposite sides are equal, the *perimeter of a rectangle* is twice the sum of the length and the width:

$$\text{Perimeter} = 2(\text{Length} + \text{Width})$$

The perimeter of a 5 by 2 rectangle is 2(5 + 2) = 14.

The *perimeter of a square* is equal to the sum of the lengths of the 4 sides. Because all 4 sides are the same length, Perimeter = 4 (Side). If the length of one side of a square is 3, the perimeter is 4 × 3 = 12.

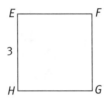

Areas of Quadrilaterals

Area formulas always involve multiplication, and the results are always stated in "square" units. You can see why if you look at the drawing below:

The rectangle is composed of six squares, all equal in size. Let's say that the side of a single small square is 1 unit. Then, we would say that a single square measures "1 by 1." That translates into math as 1 × 1, or 1^2—in other words, "one square unit."

As you can see from the drawing, there are 6 such square units in the rectangle. That's its area: 6 square units. But you could also find the area by multiplying the number of squares in a row by the number of squares in a column: 3 × 2, or 6. And since we've defined the length of the side of a square as 1 unit, that's also equivalent to multiplying the length of a horizontal side by the length of a vertical side: again, 3 × 2 = 6.

Formulas for Area

To find the area of a rectangle, multiply the **length** by the **width**.

Area of rectangle = ℓw

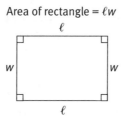

Since the length and width of a square are equal, the area formula for a square just uses the length of a **side:**

Area of square = $(\text{Side})^2 = s^2$

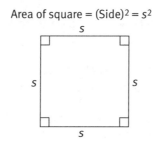

If you're working with a parallelogram, designate one side as the **base**. Then, draw a line segment from one of the vertices opposite the base down to the base so that it intersects the base at a right angle. That line segment will be called the **height**. To find the area of the parallelogram, multiply the length of the base by the length of the height:

Area of parallelogram = (Base)(Height), or $A = bh$

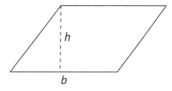

Quadrilaterals and Data Sufficiency

Remember the following:

- In a parallelogram, if you know two adjacent sides, you know all of them; and if you know two adjacent angles, you know all of them.
- In a rectangle, if you know two adjacent sides, you know the area.
- In a square, if you're given virtually any measurement (area, length of a side, length of a diagonal), you can figure out the other measurements.

CIRCLES

Important Terms

Circle: The set of all points in a plane at the same distance from a certain point. This point is called the center of the circle. A circle is labeled by its center point; circle O means the circle with center point O.

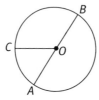

Diameter: A line segment that connects two points on the circle and passes through the center of the circle. AB is a diameter of circle O above.

Radius: A line segment that connects the center of the circle with any point on the circle; *pl.* radii. The radius of a circle is one-half the length of the diameter. In circle O above, OA, OB, and OC are radii.

Central angle: An angle formed by two radii. In circle O above, AOC is a central angle. COB and BOA are also central angles. (The measure of BOA happens to be 180°.) The total degree measure of a circle is 360°.

Chord: A line segment that joins two points on the circle. The longest chord of a circle is its diameter. AT is a chord of circle P below.

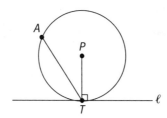

Tangent: A line that touches only one point on the circumference of a circle. A line drawn tangent to a circle is perpendicular to the radius at the point of tangency. In the diagram above, line ℓ is tangent to circle P at point T.

Circumference and Arc Length

The distance around a polygon is called its **perimeter**; the distance around a circle is called its **circumference**.

The ratio of the circumference of any circle to its diameter is a constant, called **pi** (π). For GMAT purposes, the value of π is usually approximated as 3.14.

Since π equals the ratio of the circumference, C, to the diameter, d, we can say that
$$\pi = \frac{\text{Circumference}}{\text{Diameter}} = \frac{C}{d}.$$
The formula for the circumference of a circle is $C = \pi d$.

The circumference formula can also be stated in terms of the radius, r. Since the diameter is twice the length of the radius, that is, $d = 2r$, then $C = 2\pi r$.

An **arc** is a section of the circumference of a circle. Any arc can be thought of as the portion of a circle cut off by a particular central angle. For example, in circle Q, arc ABC is the portion of the circle that is cut off by central angle AQC. Since arcs are associated with central angles, they can be measured in degrees. The degree measure of an arc is equal to that of the central angle that cuts it off. So in circle Q, arc ABC and central angle AQC would have the same degree measure.

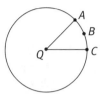

An arc that is exactly half the circumference of its circle is called a **semicircle**.

The length of an arc is the same fraction of a circle's circumference as its degree measure is of 360° (the degree measure of a whole circle). For an arc with a central angle measuring $n°$,

$$\text{Arc length} = \frac{n}{360}(\text{Circumference})$$

$$= \frac{n}{360} \times 2\pi r$$

Example:

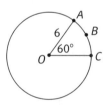

What is the length of arc ABC of circle O above?

$C = 2\pi r$; therefore, if $r = 6$, $C = 2 \times \pi \times 6 = 12\pi$. Since AOC measures 60°, arc ABC is $\frac{60}{360}$, or $\frac{1}{6}$ of the circumference. Thus, the length of arc ABC is $\frac{1}{6} \times 12\pi$, or 2π.

Area and Sector Area Formulas

The area of a circle is πr^2.

A sector is a portion of a circle's area that is bounded by two radii and an arc. The shaded area of circle X is sector AXB.

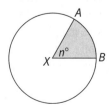

Like arcs, sectors are associated with central angles. And the process and formula used to find the area of a sector are similar to those used to determine arc length. First, find the degree measure of the sector's central angle and figure out what fraction that degree measure is of 360°. Then, multiply the area of the whole circle by that fraction. In a sector whose central angle measures $n°$,

$$\text{Area of sector} = \frac{n}{360} \text{ (Area of circle)}$$

$$= \frac{n}{360} \pi r^2$$

Example:

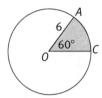

In circle O above, what is the area of sector AOC?

Since $\angle AOC$ measures 60°, a 60° "slice" of the circle is $\frac{60°}{360°}$, or $\frac{1}{6}$ of the total area of the circle. Therefore, the area of the sector is $\frac{1}{6}\pi r^2 = \frac{1}{6}(36\pi) = 6\pi$.

Circles and Data Sufficiency

A circle is a regular shape whose area and perimeter can be determined through the use of formulas. If you're given virtually any measurement (radius, diameter, circumference, area), you can determine all the other measurements.

Example:

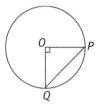

What is the circumference of the circle with center O?

(1) The length of chord $PQ = 4\sqrt{2}$.

(2) The area of sector OPQ is 4π.

To find the circumference, we need the radius, which is either OP or OQ in this circle. Statement (1) gives us the length of PQ. PQ is a chord of the circle (it connects two points on the circle), but it's also the hypotenuse of right triangle OPQ. Do we know anything else about that triangle? Since OP and OQ are both radii of the circle, they must have the same length, so the triangle is an isosceles right triangle. That means that knowing the hypotenuse tells us the length of each leg, which gives us the radius, and is enough to tell us the circumference. Statement (1) is sufficient.

Statement (2) gives us the area of the sector. Since the angle at O is a right angle, we know that the sector must be one-quarter of the whole circle. Therefore, knowing the area of the sector can give us the area of the whole circle, and from that we can find the radius, and then the circumference. Statement (2) is also sufficient, and the correct answer is **(D)**.

Coordinate Geometry

In coordinate geometry, the locations of points in a plane are indicated by ordered pairs of real numbers.

Important Terms and Concepts

Plane: A flat surface that extends indefinitely in any direction.

x-axis and y-axis: The horizontal (x) and vertical (y) lines that intersect perpendicularly to indicate location on a coordinate plane. Each axis is a number line.

Ordered pair: Two numbers or quantities separated by a comma and enclosed in parentheses. An example would be (8, 7). All the ordered pairs that you'll see in GMAT coordinate geometry problems will be in the form (x, y), where the first quantity, x, tells you how far the point is to the left or right of the y-axis, and the second quantity, y, tells you how far the point is above or below the x-axis.

Coordinates: The numbers that designate distance from an axis in coordinate geometry. The first number is the x-coordinate; the second is the y-coordinate. In the ordered pair (8, 7), 8 is the x-coordinate and 7 is the y-coordinate.

Origin: The point where the x- and y-axes intersect; its coordinates are (0, 0).

Plotting Points

Here's what a coordinate plane looks like:

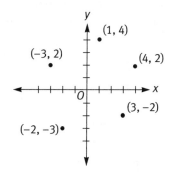

Any point in a coordinate plane can be identified by an ordered pair consisting of its x-coordinate and its y-coordinate. Every point that lies on the x-axis has a y-coordinate of 0, and every point that lies on the y-axis has an x-coordinate of 0.

When you start at the origin and move:

to the right	x is positive
to the left	x is negative
up	y is positive
down	y is negative

Therefore, the coordinate plane can be divided into four quadrants, as shown below.

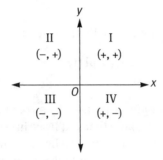

Distances on the Coordinate Plane

The distance between two points is equal to the length of the straight-line segment that has those two points as endpoints.

If a line segment is parallel to the x-axis, the y-coordinate of every point on the line segment will be the same. Similarly, if a line segment is parallel to the y-axis, the x-coordinate of every point on the line segment will be the same.

Therefore, to find the length of a line segment parallel to one of the axes, all you have to do is find the difference between the endpoint coordinates that do change. In the diagram below, the length of AB equals $x_2 - x_1$.

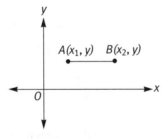

You can find the length of a line segment that is not parallel to one of the axes by treating the line segment as the hypotenuse of a right triangle. Simply draw in the legs of the triangle parallel to the two axes. The length of each leg will be the difference between the x- or y-coordinates of its endpoints. Once you've found the lengths of the legs, you can use the Pythagorean theorem to find the length of the hypotenuse (the original line segment).

In the diagram below, $(DE)^2 = (EF)^2 + (DF)^2$.

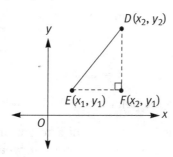

Example:

If the coordinates of point A are (3, 4), and the coordinates of point B are (6, 8), what is the distance between points A and B?

You don't have to draw a diagram to use the method just described, but drawing one may help you to visualize the problem. Plot points A and B and draw in line segment AB. The length of AB is the distance between the two points. Now draw a right triangle, with AB as its hypotenuse. The missing vertex will be the intersection of a line segment drawn through point A parallel to the x-axis and a line segment drawn through point B parallel to the y-axis. Label the point of intersection C. Since the x- and y-axes are perpendicular to each other, AC and BC will also be perpendicular to each other.

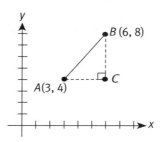

Point C will also have the same x-coordinate as point B and the same y-coordinate as point A. That means that point C has coordinates (6, 4).

To use the Pythagorean theorem, you'll need the lengths of AC and BC. The distance between points A and C is simply the difference between their x-coordinates, while the distance between points B and C is the difference between their y-coordinates. So $AC = 6 - 3 = 3$, and $BC = 8 - 4 = 4$. If you recognize these as the legs of a 3:4:5 right triangle, you'll know immediately that the distance between points A and B must be 5. Otherwise, you'll have to use the Pythagorean theorem to come to the same conclusion.

Equations of Lines

Straight lines can be described by linear equations.

Commonly:

$$y = mx + b,$$

where m is the slope $\left(\dfrac{\Delta y}{\Delta x}\right)$ and b is the point where the line intercepts the y-axis.

Lines that are parallel to the x-axis have a slope of zero and therefore have the equation $y = b$. Lines that are parallel to the y-axis have the equation $x = a$, where a is the x-intercept of that line.

If you're comfortable with linear equations, you'll sometimes want to use them to find the slope of a line or the coordinates of a point on a line. However, many such questions can be answered without determining or manipulating equations. Check the answer choices to see if you can eliminate any by common sense.

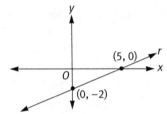

Example:

Line r is a straight line as shown above. Which of the following points lies on line r?

- ○ (6, 6)
- ○ (7, 3)
- ○ (8, 2)
- ○ (9, 3)
- ○ (10, 2)

Line r intercepts the y-axis at $(0, -2)$, so you can plug -2 in for b in the slope-intercept form of a linear equation. Line r has a rise (Δy) of 2 and a run (Δx) of 5, so its slope is $\frac{2}{5}$. That makes the slope-intercept form $y = \frac{2}{5}x - 2$.

The easiest way to proceed from here is to substitute the coordinates of each answer choice into the equation in place of x and y; only the coordinates that satisfy the equation can lie on the line. Choice **(E)** is the best answer to start with, because 10 is the only x-coordinate that will not create a fraction on the right side of the equals sign. Plugging in $(10, 2)$ for x and y in the slope-intercept equation gives you $2 = \frac{2}{5}(10) - 2$ which simplifies to $2 = 4 - 2$.

That's true, so the correct answer choice is **(E)**.

SOLIDS

Important Terms

Solid: A three-dimensional figure. The dimensions are usually called length, width, and height (ℓ, w, and h) or height, width, and depth (h, w, and d). There are only two types of solids that appear with any frequency on the GMAT: rectangular solids (including cubes) and cylinders.

Uniform solid: A solid that could be cut into congruent cross sections (parallel "slices" of equal size and shape) along a given axis. Solids you see on the GMAT will almost certainly be uniform solids.

Face: The surface of a solid that lies in a particular plane. Hexagon *ABCDEF* is one face of the solid pictured below.

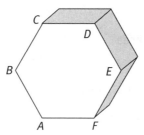

Edge: A line segment that connects adjacent faces of a solid. The sides of hexagon *ABCDEF* are also edges of the solid pictured above.

Base: The "bottom" face of a solid as oriented in any given diagram.

Rectangular solid: A solid with six rectangular faces. All edges meet at right angles. Examples of rectangular solids are cereal boxes, bricks, etc.

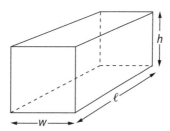

Cube: A special rectangular solid in which all edges are of equal length, *e*, and therefore all faces are squares. Sugar cubes and dice without rounded corners are examples of cubes.

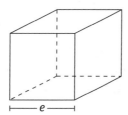

Cylinder: A uniform solid whose horizontal cross section is a circle—for example, a soup can or a pipe that is closed at both ends. A cylinder's measurements are generally given in terms of its radius, *r*, and its height, *h*.

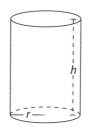

Lateral surface of a cylinder: The "pipe" surface, as opposed to the circular "ends." The lateral surface of a cylinder is unlike most other surfaces of solids that you'll see on the GMAT, first because it does not lie in a plane and second because it forms a closed loop. Think of it as the label around a soup can. If you could remove it from the can in one piece, you would have an open tube. If you then cut the label and unrolled it, it would form a rectangle with a length equal to the circumference of the circular base of the can and a height equal to that of the can.

Formulas for Volume and Surface Area

Volume of a rectangular solid = (Area of base)(Height) = (Length × Width)(Height) = lwh

Surface area of a rectangular solid = Sum of areas of faces = $2lw + 2lh + 2hw$

Since a cube is a rectangular solid for which $l = w = h$, the formula for its volume can be stated in terms of any edge:

- Volume of a cube = lwh = (Edge)(Edge)(Edge) = e^3
- Surface area of a cube = Sum of areas of faces = $6e^2$

To find the volume or surface area of a cylinder, you'll need two pieces of information: the height of the cylinder and the radius of the base.

- Volume of a cylinder = (Area of base)(Height) = $\pi r^2 h$
- Lateral surface area of a cylinder = (Circumference of base)(Height) = $2\pi rh$
- Total surface area of a cylinder = Areas of circular ends + Lateral surface area = $2\pi r^2 + 2\pi rh$

MULTIPLE FIGURES

Some GMAT geometry problems involve combinations of different types of figures. Besides the basic rules and formulas that you would use on normal geometry problems, you'll need an intuitive understanding of how various geometrical concepts relate to each other to answer these "multiple figures" questions correctly. For example, you may have to revisualize the side of a rectangle as the hypotenuse of a neighboring right triangle, or as the diameter of a circumscribed circle. Keep looking for the relationships between the different figures until you find one that leads you to the answer.

Area of Shaded Regions

A common multiple figures question involves a diagram of a geometrical figure that has been broken up into different, irregularly shaped areas, often with one region shaded. You'll usually be asked to find the area of the shaded (or unshaded) portion of the diagram. Your best bet will be to take one of the following two approaches:

1. Break the area into smaller pieces whose separate areas you can find; add those areas together.
2. Find the area of the whole figure; find the area of the region(s) that you're *not* looking for; subtract the latter from the former.

Example:

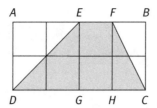

Rectangle *ABCD* above has an area of 72 and is composed of 8 equal squares. What is the area of the shaded region?

The first thing you have to realize is that, for the 8 equal squares to form a total area of 72, each square must have an area of 72 ÷ 8, or 9. Since the area of a square equals the square of the length of a side, each side of a square in the diagram must have a length of $\sqrt{9}$ or 3.

At this point, you choose your approach. Either one will work:

Approach 1:

Break up the shaded area into right triangle *DEG*, rectangle *EFHG*, and right triangle *FHC*. The area of triangle *DEG* is $\frac{1}{2}$ (6)(6) = 18. The area of rectangle *EFHG* is (3)(6), or 18. The area of triangle *FHC* is $\frac{1}{2}$(3)(6), or 9. The total shaded area is 18 + 18 + 9, or 45.

Approach 2:

The area of unshaded right triangle *AED* is $\frac{1}{2}$(6)(6), or 18. The area of unshaded right triangle *FBC* is $\frac{1}{2}$(3)(6), or 9. Therefore, the total unshaded area is 18 + 9 = 27. Subtract the total unshaded area from the total area of rectangle *ABCD*: 72 − 27 = 45.

Inscribed/Circumscribed Figures

A polygon is inscribed in a circle if all the vertices of the polygon lie on the circle. A polygon is circumscribed about a circle if all the sides of the polygon are tangent to the circle.

Square *ABCD* is inscribed in circle *O*. We can also say that circle *O* is circumscribed about square *ABCD*.

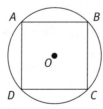

Square *PQRS* is circumscribed about circle *O*. We can also say that circle *O* is inscribed in square *PQRS*.

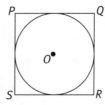

When a triangle is inscribed in a semicircle in such a way that one side of the triangle coincides with the diameter of the semicircle, the triangle is a right triangle.

Example:

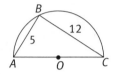

What is the diameter of semicircle *O* above?

AC is a diameter of semicircle *O*, because it passes through center point *O*. So triangle *ABC* fits the description given above of a right triangle. Moreover, triangle *ABC* is a special 5:12:13 right triangle with a hypotenuse of 13. Therefore, the length of diameter *AC* is 13.

OTHER TOPICS

DEALING WITH WORD PROBLEMS

The key to solving word problems is translation: turning English into math. Rather than having an equation set up for you, *you* have to decide what arithmetic or algebraic operations to perform on which numbers.

For example, suppose the core of a problem involves working with the equation $3j = s - 4$.

In a word problem, this might be presented as "If John had three times as many macaroons as he has now, he would have four fewer macaroons than Susan would."

Your job is to translate the problem from English into math. A phrase like "three times as many as John has" can be translated as $3j$; the phrase "four fewer than Susan" can be translated as "$s - 4$."

Many people dislike word problems. But on the GMAT, the math involved is often easier than in other math problems. Once you've translated the language, most word problems boil down to rather simple mathematical concepts and processes—probably because the testmakers figure that the extra step of translation makes the problem difficult enough.

Here's a general approach to any word problem:

1. Read through the whole question once, without lingering over details, to get a sense of the overall problem.
2. Identify and label the variables or unknowns in a way that makes it easy to remember what they stand for.
3. Translate the problem into one or more equations, sentence by sentence. Be careful of the order in which you translate the terms. For example, consider the phrase "5 less than $4x$ equals 9." The *correct* way to translate it is "$4x - 5 = 9$." But many students make the mistake of writing the terms in the order in which they appear in words: "$5 - 4x = 9$."
4. Solve the equation(s).
5. Check your work, if time permits.

Translation Table

This table contains common phrases used in GMAT math problems. The left column lists words and phrases that occur frequently; the right column lists the corresponding algebraic symbols.

Equals, is, was, will be, has, costs, adds up to, is the same as	=
Times, of, multiplied by, product of, twice, double, half, triple	×
Divided by, per, out of, each, ratio of _ to _	÷
Plus, added to, sum, combined, and, total	+
Minus, subtracted from, less than, decreased by, difference between	−
What, how much, how many, a number	Variable (x, n, etc.)

Example:

Beatrice has three dollars more than twice the number of dollars Allan has.

Translate into $B = 3 + 2A$.

For Word Problems:

Add ...

- when you are given the amounts of individual quantities and asked to find the total.

Example:

If the sales tax on a $12.00 lunch is $1.20, what is the total amount of the check?

$$\$12.00 + \$1.20 = \$13.20$$

- when you are given an original amount and an increase, and then asked to find the new amount.

Example:

The bus fare used to be 55 cents. If the fare increased by 35 cents, what is the new fare?

$$55 \text{ cents} + 35 \text{ cents} = 90 \text{ cents}$$

Subtract ...

- when you are given the total and one part of the total, and you want to find the remaining part or parts.

Example:

If 32 out of 50 children are girls, what is the number of boys?

50 children − 32 girls = 18 boys

- when you are given two numbers and asked *how much more* or *how much less* one number is than the other. The amount is called the **difference**.

Example:

How much larger than 30 is 38?

38 (larger) − 30 (smaller) = 8

Multiply ...

- when you are given an amount for one item and asked for the total amount of *many* of these items.

Example:

If 1 book costs $6.50, what is the cost of 12 copies of the same book?

12 ($6.50) = $78.00

Divide ...

- when you are given a total amount for *many* items and asked for the amount for *one* item.

Example:

If 5 pounds of apples cost $6.75, what is the price of 1 pound of apples?

$6.75 ÷ 5 = $1.35

- when you are given the size of one group and the total size for many such identical groups and asked how many of the small groups fit into the larger one.

Example:

How many groups of 30 students can be formed from a total of 240 students?

240 ÷ 30 = 8 groups of 30 students

Special Word Problems Tip #1
Don't try to combine several sentences into one equation; each sentence usually translates into a separate equation.

Special Word Problems Tip #2
Pay attention to what the question asks for and make a note to yourself if it is not one of the unknowns in the equation(s). Otherwise, you may stop working on the problem too early.

LOGIC PROBLEMS

You won't always have to set up an equation to solve a word problem. Some of the word problems you'll encounter on the GMAT won't fall into recognizable textbook categories. Many of these problems are designed to test your analytical and deductive logic. You can solve them with common sense and a little basic arithmetic. Ask yourself how it would be helpful to arrange the information, such as by drawing a diagram or making a table.

In these problems, the issue is not so much translating English into math as simply using your head. The problem may call for nonmath skills, including the ability to organize and keep track of different possibilities, the ability to visualize something (for instance, the reverse side of a symmetrical shape), the ability to think of the exception that changes the answer to a problem, or the ability to deal with overlapping groups.

Example:

If ! and ∫ are digits, and $(! \, !)(\int \int) = 60\int$, what is the value of $\int$?

Since the symbols used each represent a digit 0 through 9, we know that the product of the multiplication equals a value from 600 to 609. We know that the two quantities multiplied each consist of a two-digit integer in which both digits are the same. So list the relevant two-digit integers (00, 11, 22, 33, 44, 55, 66, 77, 88, and 99), and see which two of them can be multiplied evenly into the 600 to 609 range. Only (11)(55) satisfies this requirement. The ∫ symbol equals 5.

TABLES, GRAPHS, AND CHARTS

Some questions combine numbers and text with visual formats. Different formats are suitable for organizing different types of information. The formats that appear most frequently on GMAT math questions are tables, bar graphs, line graphs, and pie charts.

Questions involving tables, graphs, and charts may *look* different from other GMAT math questions, but the ideas and principles are the same. The problems are unusual only in the way that they present information, not in what they ask you to do with that information. Typically, they test your ability to work with percents and averages and your ability to solve for unknowns.

Tables

The most basic way to organize information is to create a table. Tables are in some ways the most accurate graphic presentation format—the only way you can misunderstand a number is to read it from the wrong row or column—but they don't allow the reader to spot trends or extremes very readily.

Here's an example of a very simple table.

John's Income: 2007–2011	
YEAR	INCOME
2007	$20,000
2008	$22,000
2009	$18,000
2010	$15,000
2011	$28,000

An easy question might ask for John's income in a particular year or for the difference in his income between two years. To find the difference, you would simply look up the amount for both years and subtract the smaller income from the larger income. A harder question might ask for John's average annual income over the five-year period shown; to determine the average, you would have to find the sum of the five annual incomes and divide it by 5.

Bar Graphs

Here's the same information that you saw previously in a table. This time, it's presented as a bar graph.

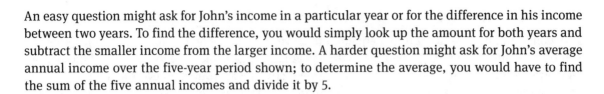

Bar graphs can be used to visually show information that would otherwise appear as numbers in a table. Bar graphs are somewhat less accurate than tables, but that's not necessarily a bad attribute, especially on the GMAT, where estimating often saves time on calculations.

What's handy about a bar graph is that you can see which values are larger or smaller without reading actual numbers. Just a glance at this graph shows that John's 2011 income was almost double his 2010 income. Numbers are represented on a bar graph by the heights or lengths of the bars. To find the height of a vertical bar, look for the point where a line drawn across the top of the bar parallel to the horizontal axis would intersect the vertical axis. To find the length of a horizontal bar, look for the point where a line drawn across the end of the bar parallel to the vertical axis would intersect the horizontal axis.

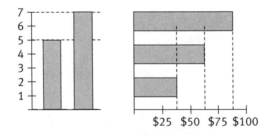

If the height or length of the bar falls in between two numbers on the axis, you will have to estimate.

Line Graphs

Line graphs follow the same general principle as bar graphs, except that instead of using the lengths of bars to represent numbers, they use points connected by lines. The lines further emphasize the relative values of the numbers.

John's Income, 2007–2011

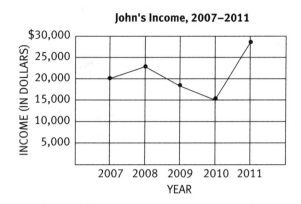

To read John's income for any particular year from this line graph, determine where a line drawn from the appropriate point would intersect the vertical axis.

Pie Charts

Pie charts show how things are distributed. The fraction of a circle occupied by each piece of the "pie" indicates what fraction of the whole that piece represents. In most pie charts, the percentage of the pie occupied by each "slice" will be shown on the slice itself or, for very narrow slices, outside the circle with an arrow or a line pointing to the appropriate slice.

The total size of the whole pie is usually given at the top or bottom of the graph, either as "TOTAL = xxx" or as "100% = xxx." To find the approximate amount represented by a particular piece of the pie, just multiply the whole by the appropriate percent.

John's Expenditures, 2007
Total = $20,000

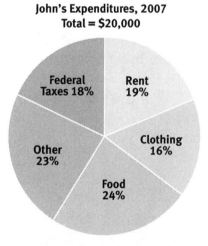

For instance, to find the total tax that John paid to the federal government in 2007, look at the slice of this chart labeled "Federal Tax." It represents 18% of John's 2007 expenditures. Since his total 2007 expenditures were $20,000, he paid 0.18($20,000) = $3,600 in federal taxes in 2007.

One important note about pie charts: If you're not given the whole, and you don't know both the percentage and the actual number that at least one slice represents, you won't be able to find the whole. Pie charts are ideal for presenting the kind of information that ratio problems present in words.

PART FIVE

Analytical Writing and Integrated Reasoning Sections

CHAPTER 13

Analytical Writing Assessment

- **Essay Format and Structure**
- **The Basic Principles of Analytical Writing**
- **How the AWA Is Scored**
- **The Kaplan Method for Analytical Writing**
- **Breakdown: Analysis of an Argument**
- **GMAT Style Checklist**
- **Practice Essays**

The Analytical Writing Assessment (AWA) is the first task on the GMAT. After you are situated at your computer workstation, you will be presented with the Analysis of an Argument essay assignment. You will have 30 minutes to complete it.

For the essay, you will analyze a given topic and then type your essay into a simple word processing program. It allows you to do only the following basic functions:

- Insert text
- Delete text
- Cut and paste
- Undo the previous action
- Scroll up and down on the screen

Spell check and grammar check functions are not available in the program, so you will have to check those things carefully yourself. One or two spelling errors or a few minor grammatical errors will not lower your score. But many spelling errors can hurt your score, as can errors that are serious enough to obscure your intended meaning.

Thirty minutes is not enough time to produce the same kind of essay you've written for college classes. Nor is it enough time to do a lot of trial and error as you type. It is, however, enough time to write a "strong first draft" if you plan carefully, and that's what the essay graders are looking for.

After the AWA, you will move directly into the Integrated Reasoning section.

ESSAY FORMAT AND STRUCTURE

At the start of the AWA, you'll be given a brief tutorial on how to use the word processor. If you are concerned that you do not type very fast, you should practice giving yourself 30 minutes to brainstorm and type AWA essays between now and Test Day. By doing so, you will get an idea of how much you can type in the time allotted; your typing speed might also improve with practice.

Your task for the Argument essay is to assess the logic and use of evidence in an argument. It doesn't matter whether you agree or disagree with the argument's conclusion. Rather, you need to explain the ways in which the author has failed to fully support that conclusion.

Let's take a look at a sample prompt:

> The following appeared in a memo from the CEO of Hula Burger, a chain of hamburger restaurants.
>
> "Officials in the film industry report that over 60% of the films released last year targeted an age 8–12 audience. Moreover, sales data indicate that, nationally, hamburgers are the favorite food among this age group. Since a branch store of Whiz Vid Video Store opened in town last year, hamburger sales at our restaurant next door have been higher than at any other restaurant in our chain. Because the rental of movies seems to stimulate hamburger sales, the best way to increase our profits is to open new Hula Burger restaurants right nearby every Whiz Vid Video Store."
>
> Consider how logical you find this argument. In your essay, be sure to discuss the line of reasoning and the use of evidence in the argument. For example, you may need to consider what questionable assumptions underlie the thinking and what alternative explanations or counterpoints might weaken the conclusion. You may also discuss what types of evidence would strengthen or refute the argument, what changes in the argument would make it more logically sound, and what, if anything, would help you better evaluate its conclusion.

Where are the holes in the argument? In what ways does it fail to be completely convincing? Why might the plan fail? Not only do you have to identify its major weaknesses, you must also explain them.

THE BASIC PRINCIPLES OF ANALYTICAL WRITING

You aren't being evaluated solely on the strength of your ideas. Your score will also depend on how well you express them. If your writing style isn't clear, your ideas won't come across, no matter how brilliant they are.

Good essay writing isn't just grammatically correct. It is also clear and concise. The following principles will help you express your ideas in good GMAT style.

YOUR CONTROL OF LANGUAGE IS IMPORTANT

Writing that is grammatical, concise, direct, and persuasive displays the "superior control of language" (as the testmaker terms it) that earns top GMAT Analytical Writing scores. To achieve effective GMAT style in your essays, you should pay attention to the following points.

Grammar

Your writing must follow the same general rules of standard written English that are tested by Sentence Correction questions. If you're not confident of your mastery of grammar, review the Sentence Correction chapter of this book.

Diction

Diction means word choice. Do you use the words *affect* and *effect* correctly? What about *its* and *it's*, *there* and *their*, *precede* and *proceed*, *principal* and *principle*, and *whose* and *who's*? In addition to avoiding errors of usage, you will need to demonstrate your ability to use language precisely and employ a formal, professional tone.

Syntax

Syntax refers to sentence structure. Do you construct your sentences so that your ideas are clear and understandable? Do you vary the length and structure of your sentences?

KEEP THINGS SIMPLE

Perhaps the single most important piece of advice to bear in mind when writing a GMAT essay is to keep everything simple. This rule applies to word choice, sentence structure, and organization. If you obsess about how to use or spell an unusual word, you can lose your way. The more complicated your sentences are, the more likely they'll be plagued by errors. The more complex your organization becomes, the more likely your argument will get bogged down in convoluted sentences that obscure your point.

Keep in mind that simple does not mean *simplistic*. A clear, straightforward approach can still be sophisticated and convey perceptive insights.

MINOR GRAMMATICAL FLAWS WON'T HARM YOUR SCORE

Many test takers mistakenly believe they'll lose points over a few mechanical errors. That's not the case. GMAT essays should be final first drafts. This means that a couple of misplaced commas, misspellings, or other minor glitches aren't going to affect your score. Occasional mistakes of this type are acceptable and inevitable, given that you have only 30 minutes to construct your essay. In fact, according to the scoring rubric, a top-scoring essay may well have a few minor grammatical flaws.

But if your essays are littered with misspellings and grammar mistakes, the graders may conclude that you have a serious communication problem. Keep in mind that sentence fragments are not acceptable, nor are informal structures such as bullet points or numerical enumeration (e.g., "(1)" instead of "first"). So be concise, forceful, and correct. An effective essay wastes no words; makes its point in a clear, direct way; and conforms to the generally accepted rules of grammar and style.

USE A LOGICAL STRUCTURE

Good essays have a straightforward, linear structure. The problem is that we rarely think in a straightforward, linear way. That's why it's so important to plan your response before you begin typing. If you type *while* planning, your essay will likely loop back on itself, contain redundancies, or fail to follow through on what it sets up.

Logical structure consists of three things:

Paragraph Unity

Paragraph unity means each paragraph discusses one thing and all the discussion of that one thing happens in that paragraph. Let's say that you're responding to the essay prompt we just saw and one of your points is that there may have been reasons for the success of the Hula Burger restaurant other than its proximity to the Whiz Vid Video store. Your next paragraph should move on to another idea—perhaps something about the expense of opening a new Hula Burger restaurant near every Whiz Vid Video Store. If, in the middle of that next paragraph, you went back to your point about other possible reasons for the success of the Hula Burger restaurant, you'd be violating paragraph unity.

Train of Thought

This is similar to paragraph unity, but it applies to the whole essay. It's confusing to the reader when an essay keeps jumping back and forth between the different weaknesses of an argument. Discuss one point fully, and then address the next. Don't write another paragraph about a topic you've already discussed.

Flow

The basic idea of flow is that you should deliver on what you promise and not radically change the subject. If your introductory paragraph says that you will mention reasons why Hula burgers might be less popular among the 8- to 12-year-old demographic than regular hamburgers are, you need to make sure that you actually do so. Similarly, avoid suddenly expanding the scope of the essay in the last sentence.

TAKEAWAYS: THE BASIC PRINCIPLES OF ANALYTICAL WRITING

- Your control of language is important.
- Keep things simple.
- Minor grammatical flaws won't harm your score.
- Use a logical structure.

HOW THE AWA IS SCORED

Your essays will be graded on a scale from 0 to 6 (highest). You'll receive one score, which will be an average of the scores that you receive from each of the two graders, rounded up to the nearest half point. Your essay will be graded by a human grader as well as a computerized essay grader (the IntelliMetric™ system). The two grade completely independently of each other—IntelliMetric™ isn't told the human's score, nor is the human told the computer's.

If the two scores are identical, then that's your score. If the scores differ by one point, those scores are averaged. If they differ by more than one point, a second human will grade the essay to resolve any differences. IntelliMetric™ and the human grader agree on the same grade about 55 percent of the time and agree on identical or adjacent grades 97 percent of the time. (Only 3 percent of essays need rereading.) These figures are equivalent to how often two trained human graders agree.

IntelliMetric™ was designed to make the same judgments that a good human grader would. In fact, part of the Graduate Management Admission Council's (GMAC's) argument for the validity of IntelliMetric™ is that its performance is statistically indistinguishable from a human's. Still, you should remember that it is *not* a human and write accordingly.

IntelliMetric's™ grading algorithm was designed using 400 officially graded essays for each prompt. That's a huge sample of responses, so don't worry about whether IntelliMetric™ will understand your ideas—it's highly likely that someone out of those 400 responses made a similar point.

Before you begin to write, outline your essay. Good organization always counts, but with a computer grader, it's more important than ever. Use transitional phrases like *first*, *therefore*, *since*, and *for example* so that the computer can recognize structured arguments. The length of your essay is not a factor; the computer does not count the number of words in your response.

Furthermore, computers are not good judges of humor or creativity. (The human judges don't reward those either. The standard is business writing, and you shouldn't be making overly witty or irreverent remarks in, say, an email to a CEO.)

Though IntelliMetric™ doesn't grade spelling per se, it could give you a lower score if it can't understand you or thinks you used the wrong words.

Here's what your essay will be graded on:

- **Structure.** Does your essay have good paragraph unity, organization, and flow?
- **Evidence.** It's not enough simply to assert good points. Do you develop them well? How strong are the examples you provide?
- **Depth of Logic.** Did you take apart the argument and analyze its major weaknesses effectively?
- **Style.** The GMAC calls this "control of the elements of standard written English." How well do you express your ideas?

Now let's take a more in-depth look at the scoring scale so you get a sense of what to aim for. The following rubric shows how the GMAC will grade your essay based on the four categories of Structure, Evidence, Depth of Logic, and Style:

	1 Seriously Deficient	2 Substantially Flawed	3 Inadequate	4 Satisfactory	5 Good	6 Excellent
Structure	Lacks length and organization; *does not adhere* to topic.	Lacks length and organization; *unclear understanding* of topic.	Lacks length enough for real analysis; *strays from topic* or is partially unfocused.	Has *good basic organization* and sufficient paragraphing.	Has *well-developed paragraphs* and structure; stays on topic.	Has well-developed paragraphs and structure; *paragraphing works with examples*.
Evidence	Provides *few, if any, examples* to back up claims.	Provides *very sparse examples* to back up claims.	Provides *insufficient examples* to back up claims.	Provides *sufficient examples* to back up claims.	Provides *strong examples* to back up claims.	Provides *very strong examples* to back up claims.
Depth of Logic	Shows *very little understanding of the argument* and gives no analysis of/takes no position on it.	Presents the writer's views, but *fails to give any analytical critique*.	Analyzes somewhat, but *fails to show some key parts of the argument*.	Shows key parts of the argument adequately with *some analysis*.	Shows key parts of the argument and *analyzes them thoughtfully*.	Shows key parts of the argument and *analyzes them with great clarity*.
Style	Has *severe and persistent errors* in sentence structure and use of language; meaning is lost.	*Frequently uses language incorrectly* and sentence structure, grammar, and usage errors inhibit meaning.	*Uses language imprecisely* and is deficient in variety; some major errors or a number of small errors.	*Controls language adequately*, including syntax and diction; a few flaws.	*Controls language with clarity*, including variety of syntax and diction; may have a flaw here and there.	*Controls language extremely well*, including variety of syntax and diction; may have a small flaw here and there.

GMAC will grade your essay holistically based on the above rubric to arrive at your final score:

- **6: Excellent.** Essays that earn the top score must be insightful, well supported by evidence, logically organized, and skillfully written. A 6 need not be "perfect," just very good.
- **5: Good.** A 5 essay is well written and well supported but may not be as compellingly argued as a 6. There may also be more frequent or more serious writing errors than in a 6.
- **4: Satisfactory.** The important elements of the argument are addressed but not explained robustly. The organization is good, and the evidence provided is adequate. The writing may have some flaws but is generally acceptable.
- **3: Inadequate.** A 3 response misses important elements of the argument, has little or no evidence to support its ideas, and doesn't clearly express its meaning.
- **2: Substantially Flawed.** An essay scoring a 2 has some serious problems. It may not use any examples whatsoever or support its ideas in any way. Its writing will have many errors that interfere with the meaning of the sentences.

- **1: Seriously Deficient.** These essays are rare. A 1 score is reserved for essays that provide little or no evidence of the ability to analyze an argument or to develop ideas in any way. A 1 essay will have so many writing errors that the essay may be unintelligible.
- **0: No Score.** A score of 0 signifies an attempt to avoid addressing the prompt at all, either by writing only random or repeating characters or by copying the prompt. You could also score a 0 by not writing in English or by addressing a completely different topic.
- **NR: Blank.** This speaks for itself. This is what you get if you write no essay at all. Some schools will not consider your GMAT score if your essay receives an NR. By skipping the essay, you give yourself an unfair advantage—everyone else wrote an essay for 30 minutes *before* the other sections!

TAKEAWAYS: HOW THE AWA IS SCORED

- Your AWA score does not count toward the 200–800 score for the rest of the test.
- Business schools receive the text of your essay along with your score report.
- The essay grading is almost pass/fail in nature: There's a clear line between 1–3 (bad) and 4–6 (good).
- A writer with a solid plan should earn a score of 4 or higher on the AWA.

THE KAPLAN METHOD FOR ANALYTICAL WRITING

You have a limited amount of time to show the business school admissions officers that you can think logically and express yourself in clearly written English. They don't care how many syllables you can cram into a sentence or how fancy your phrases are. They care that you make sense. Whatever you do, don't hide beneath a lot of hefty words and abstract language. Make sure that everything you say is clearly written and relevant to the topic. Get in there, state your main points, back them up, and get out. The Kaplan Method for Analytical Writing—along with Kaplan's recommendations for how much time you should devote to each step of the Method—will help you produce the best essay you're capable of writing in 30 minutes.

The Kaplan Method for Analytical Writing

1. Take apart the argument.

2. Select the points you will make.

3. Organize using Kaplan's essay template.

4. Write your essay.

5. Proofread your work.

STEP 1: TAKE APART THE ARGUMENT

- Read through the prompt to get a sense of its scope.
- Identify the author's conclusion and the evidence used to support it.
- You can take about 2 minutes on this step.

STEP 2: SELECT THE POINTS YOU WILL MAKE

- Identify all the important gaps (assumptions) between the evidence and the conclusion.
- Think of how you'll explain or illustrate those gaps and under what circumstances the author's assumptions would not hold true.
- Think about how the author could remedy these weaknesses. This part of the Kaplan Method is very much like predicting the answer to a Critical Reasoning Strengthen or Weaken question.
- Step 2 should take about 5 minutes.

STEP 3: ORGANIZE USING KAPLAN'S ESSAY TEMPLATE

- Outline your essay.
- Lead with your best arguments.
- If you practice with the Kaplan template for the Argument essay before Test Day, organizing the essay will go smoothly and predictably. Using the Kaplan template will help you turn vague thoughts about the prompt into organized, developed paragraphs.
- The organization process should take less than 1 minute.

ORGANIZING THE ARGUMENT ESSAY: THE KAPLAN TEMPLATE

PARAGRAPH 1:
SHOW that you understand the argument by putting it in your own words.

PARAGRAPH 2:
POINT OUT one flawed assumption in the author's reasoning; explain why it is questionable.

PARAGRAPH 3:
IDENTIFY another source of the author's faulty reasoning; explain why it is questionable.

ADDITIONAL PARAGRAPHS AS APPROPRIATE:
CONTINUE to bring in points of fault in the argument, as time permits.

        Time Valve #1:
        Skip to the next paragraph without adding any additional flaws.

SECOND-TO-LAST PARAGRAPH:
DESCRIBE evidence that would—if it were provided—strengthen the argument.

        Time Valve #2:
        Combine this paragraph with the last paragraph.

LAST PARAGRAPH:
CONCLUDE that without such evidence, you're not persuaded.

STEP 4: WRITE YOUR ESSAY

- Be direct.
- Use paragraph breaks to make your essay easier to read.
- Use transitions and structural keywords to link related ideas; they will help your writing flow.
- Finish strongly.
- You can afford no more than 20 minutes of typing. The other 10 minutes should be dedicated to planning and correcting.

STEP 5: PROOFREAD YOUR WORK

- Save enough time to read through the entire essay—2 minutes at minimum.
- Fix any spelling, grammar, syntax, or diction errors.
- Add any needed keywords to improve the flow of your ideas.
- Don't add any new ideas or change the structure of your essay. There just isn't time.

BREAKDOWN: ANALYSIS OF AN ARGUMENT

THE INSTRUCTIONS

Screen 1: General Instructions

The general instructions for the Argument essay will look like this:

**Analytical Writing Assessment Instructions
Analysis of an Argument Essay**

Time: 30 Minutes

In this part of the test, you will be asked to write a critical analysis of the argument in the prompt. You are not being asked to give your own views on the topic.

COMPOSING YOUR ESSAY: Before you begin to type, take a little time to look at the argument and plan your essay. Make sure your ideas are organized and clearly stated. Leave some time to read over your essay and make any changes you think are necessary. You will have 30 minutes to write your essay.

ESSAY ASSESSMENT: Qualified graders with varied backgrounds, including experience in business subject areas, will assess the overall quality of your analysis and composition. They will look at how well you:

- identify key elements of the argument and examine them;
- arrange your analysis of the argument presented;
- give appropriate examples and reasons for support; and
- master the components of written English.

The instructions on Screen 1 tell you to read the argument, plan your essay before writing it, and leave a little time at the end for review. Sound familiar? The Kaplan Method mirrors these steps. While the prompts for the essay vary, the general directions are always the same. Become familiar with the essay directions now so you don't waste valuable time reading them on Test Day.

Screen 2: Specific Prompt

The next screen you go to will contain the specific essay prompt.

> Read the argument and the directions that follow it, and write down any ideas that will be helpful in mapping out your essay. Begin writing your essay in the box at the bottom of this screen.
>
> "The problem of poorly trained teachers that has plagued the state public school system is bound to become a good deal less serious in the future. The state has initiated comprehensive guidelines that oblige state teachers to complete a number of required credits in education and educational psychology at the graduate level before being certified."
>
> Consider how logical you find this argument. In your essay, be sure to discuss the line of reasoning and the use of evidence in the argument. For example, you may need to consider what questionable assumptions underlie the thinking and what alternative explanations or counterpoints might weaken the conclusion. You may also discuss what types of evidence would strengthen or refute the argument, what changes in the argument would make it more logically sound, and what, if anything, would help you better evaluate its conclusion.

The only part of Screen 2 that will change is the specific prompt, which is in quotation marks. The instructions above and below it will stay the same. Again, practicing with these directions now will mean that you won't waste time reading them on Test Day.

THE STIMULUS

Analysis of an Argument topics will probably remind you of Critical Reasoning questions. The basic idea is similar. Just as in Critical Reasoning, the writer tries to persuade you of something—her conclusion—by citing some evidence. So look for these two basic components of an argument: a conclusion and supporting evidence. You should read the argument in the Analysis of an Argument topic in much the same way you read Critical Reasoning stimuli; be on the lookout for assumptions—the ways the writer makes the leap from evidence to conclusion.

THE QUESTION STEM

The question stem instructs you to decide how convincing you find the argument, explain why, and discuss what might improve the argument. Note that there is a right answer here: The argument *always* has some problems. You want to focus your efforts on finding them, explaining them, and fixing them.

Exactly what are you being asked to do here? Paraphrase the following sentences of the question stem.

> Consider how logical you find this argument. In your essay, be sure to discuss the line of reasoning and the use of evidence in the argument.

Translation: Critique the argument. Discuss the ways in which it is not convincing. How and why might the evidence not fully support the conclusion?

> For example, you may need to consider what questionable assumptions underlie the thinking and what alternative explanations or counterpoints might weaken the conclusion. You may also discuss what types of evidence would strengthen or refute the argument, what changes in the argument would make it more logically sound, and what, if anything, would help you better evaluate its conclusion.

Translation: Spot weak links in the argument and offer constructive modifications that would strengthen them.

Let's use the Kaplan Method for Analytical Writing on the Analysis of an Argument topic we saw before:

> "The problem of poorly trained teachers that has plagued the state public school system is bound to become a good deal less serious in the future. The state has initiated comprehensive guidelines that oblige state teachers to complete a number of required credits in education and educational psychology at the graduate level before being certified."

> Consider how logical you find this argument. In your essay, be sure to discuss the line of reasoning and the use of evidence in the argument. For example, you may need to consider what questionable assumptions underlie the thinking and what alternative explanations or counterpoints might weaken the conclusion. You may also discuss what types of evidence would strengthen or refute the argument, what changes in the argument would make it more logically sound, and what, if anything, would help you better evaluate its conclusion.

STEP 1: TAKE APART THE ARGUMENT

First, identify the conclusion—the point the argument is trying to make. Here, the conclusion is the first sentence:

> The problem of poorly trained teachers that has plagued the state public school system is bound to become a good deal less serious in the future.

Next, identify the evidence—the basis for the conclusion. Here, the evidence is the second sentence of the argument:

> The state has initiated comprehensive guidelines that oblige state teachers to complete a number of required credits in education and educational psychology at the graduate level before being certified.

Finally, paraphrase the argument in your own words: The problem of badly trained teachers will become less serious because new teachers will be required to take a certain number of graduate level classes.

If you aren't able to put the argument in your own words, you don't yet understand it well enough to analyze it sufficiently. Don't rush this step; you can afford a full two minutes if you need it.

STEP 2: SELECT THE POINTS YOU WILL MAKE

Now that you've found the conclusion and evidence, think about what assumptions the author is making or any reasoning flaws she commits. Also, think about any unaddressed questions that you feel would be relevant.

- She assumes that the courses will improve teachers' classroom performance.
- What about bad teachers who are already certified? Would they also be required to retrain?
- Have currently poor-performing teachers already had this training?
- Will this plan have any unintended negative consequences?

You also will need to explain how these assumptions could be false or how the questions reveal weaknesses in the author's argument. Add to your notes:

- She assumes that the courses will improve teachers' classroom performance. What if the problem is cultural? Or if it's a language barrier? Or if the teacher doesn't know the subject?
- What about bad teachers who are already certified? Would they also be required to retrain? If not, those bad teachers would still be in the system.
- Have currently poor-performing teachers already had this training? If so, this fact demonstrates that this training won't solve the problems.
- Will this plan have any unintended negative consequences? What does this training cost? If the state has to pay for it, will that mean there is less money available for other uses? If teachers have to pay for it, will good teachers leave the system?

Then think about evidence that would make the argument stronger or more logically sound:

- Evidence verifying that the training will make teachers better
- Evidence that currently bad teachers have not already received this training and that they either will soon receive it or will be removed from the classroom
- Evidence that the cost of the training is not prohibitive

STEP 3: ORGANIZE USING KAPLAN'S ESSAY TEMPLATE

Look over the notes you've jotted down. Select the strongest point to be first, the next-strongest to be second, and so on. Two criteria determine whether a point is strong. One is how well you can explain it. If, for example, you aren't sure how to explain potential negative consequences of an expensive training program, you should use that idea last—if at all. The other is how severe a problem the weakness poses to the argument's persuasiveness. If the training doesn't work, for example, the argument is in serious trouble.

Then decide how you'll arrange your points. Follow the Kaplan template. The following is an example of an effective shorthand outline like the one you will create on Test Day:

¶ Restate argument (conc: solve problem of poorly trained teachers; evid: courses in education and ed. psychology)

¶ Assump: courses = better performance. Culture? Language? Subject matter? Need: evid. of relevance

¶ Assump: current bad teachers not already trained. If they have, training doesn't work. Need: evid. of no training

¶ Assump: bad teachers will go if not trained. If not, will be bad until they retire. Need: everyone to be trained or leave

¶ Assump: not too $. If too $, other priorities suffer. Need: evid. of low $

¶ ways to strengthen arg. (needed evid.)

Remember, you may not have time to use all your points. Leaving your weakest for last means that if you run short on time, you'll leave out your weakest point instead of your best.

STEP 4: WRITE YOUR ESSAY

Begin typing your essay now. Keep in mind the basic principles of writing that we discussed earlier.

Keep your writing simple and clear. Choose words that you know how to use well. Avoid the temptation to make your writing "sound smarter" with overly complicated sentences or vocabulary that feels awkward.

Keep your eye on the clock and make sure that you don't run out of time to proofread. If you need to, leave out your last point or two. (Make sure that you include at least two main points.) Let's pretend that the writer of the following essay had only six minutes left on the clock after the third paragraph. She wisely chooses neither to rush through her final paragraph nor to skip proofreading. Instead, she leaves out her point about cost and uses the time valve in the template of combining the next-to-last and last paragraphs.

> The author concludes that the present problem of poorly trained teachers will become less severe in the future because of required credits in education and psychology. However, the conclusion relies on assumptions for which the author does not supply clear evidence.
>
> The author assumes that the required courses will produce better teachers. In fact, the courses might be entirely irrelevant to the teachers' failings. If, for example, the prevalent problem is cultural or linguistic gaps between teacher and student, graduate-level courses that do not address these specific issues probably won't do much good. The courses also would not be heplful for a teacher who does not know their subject matter.
>
> In addition, the author assumes that currently poor teachers have not already had this training. In fact, the author doesn't mention whether some or all of the poor teachers have had similar training. If they have, then the training seems not to have been effective and the plan should be rethought.
>
> Finally, the author assumes that poor teachers currently working will either stop teaching in the future or will receive training. The author provides no evidence, though, to indicate that this is the case. As the argument stands, it's highly possible that only brand-new teachers will be receiving the training and the bright future to which the author refers is decades away.
>
> To strengthen the argument, the author must provide several pieces of evidence to support his assumptions. First of all, the author's implicit claim that the courses will improve teachers could be strengthened by providing evidence that the training will be relevant to teachers' problems. The author could also make a stronger case by showing that currently poor teachers have not already had training comparable to the new requirements. Finally, the author's argument can only hold in the presence of evidence that all teachers in the system will receive the training—and will then change there teaching methods accordingly. In its current state, the argument relies too heavily on unsupported assumptions to be convincing.

STEP 5: PROOFREAD YOUR WORK

Save a few minutes to go back over your essay and catch any obvious errors. Look over the essay above. It has at least four grammatical errors and is missing at least one keyword. By leaving herself ample proofreading time, our author will be able to find them.

- **Paragraph 1:**
  - The phrase "because of required credits" is awkward and unclear. Change to "because the state will require teachers to complete credits."

- **Paragraph 2:**
  - Add a keyword to the beginning of the paragraph. Since it is the first assumption discussed, "The author assumes ..." should be changed to "First, the author assumes...."
  - The last sentence could be improved: "The courses also would not be heplful for a teacher who does not know their subject matter." For one thing, "heplful" should be "helpful." For another, "a teacher" is singular, but "their" is plural. Change "their" to "his" or "her."

- **Paragraph 3:** no errors
- **Paragraph 4:**
  - There's an awkward phrase about halfway through: "only brand-new teachers will be receiving the training." There's no need for anything but simple future tense: "only brand-new teachers will receive the training."

- **Paragraph 5:**
  - In the next-to-last sentence, "there teaching methods" should be "their teaching methods."

The best way to improve your writing and proofreading skills is practice. When you practice responding to AWA prompts, do so on a computer—but to mimic test conditions, don't use the automatic spell check or grammar check. Write practice essays using the prompts at the end of this chapter, those provided by the testmaker at **mba.com**, or those in the *Official Guide for GMAT Review*. The pool of prompts provided by the testmaker contains the actual prompts from which the GMAT will select your essay topic on Test Day.

GMAT STYLE CHECKLIST

On the GMAT, there are three rules of thumb for successful writing: Be concise, be forceful, and be correct. Following these rules is a sure way to improve your writing style—and your score. Let's look at each one in more depth.

BE CONCISE

- Cut out words, phrases, and sentences that don't add any information or serve a necessary purpose.
- Watch out for repetitive phrases such as "refer back" or "absolutely essential."
- Don't use conjunctions to join sentences that would be more effective as separate sentences.
- Don't use needless qualifiers such as "really" or "kind of."

Examples

Wordy: The agency is not prepared to undertake expansion at this point in time.
Concise: The agency is not ready to expand.

Redundant: All of these problems have combined together to create a serious crisis.
Concise: Combined, these problems create a crisis.

Too many qualifiers: Ferrara seems to be sort of a slow worker.
Concise: Ferrara works slowly.

BE FORCEFUL

- Don't refer to yourself needlessly. Avoid pointless phrases like "in my personal opinion"; even phrases such as "I agree" or "I think" are considered stylistically weak.
- Avoid jargon and pompous language; it won't impress anybody. For example, "a waste of time and money" is better than "a pointless expenditure of temporal and financial resources."
- Don't use the passive voice. Use active verbs whenever possible.
- Avoid clichés and overused terms or phrases (for example, "beyond the shadow of a doubt").
- Don't be vague. Avoid generalizations and abstractions when more specific words would be clearer.
- Don't use weak sentence openings. Be wary of sentences that begin with "there is" or "there are." For example, "There are several ways in which this sentence is awkward," should be rewritten as "This sentence is awkward in several ways."
- Don't be monotonous; vary sentence length and style.
- Use transitions to connect sentences and make your essay easy to follow.

Examples

Needlessly references self: Although I am no expert, I do not think privacy should be valued more than social concerns.
Speaks confidently: Privacy should not be valued more than social concerns.

Uses passive voice: The report was compiled by a number of field anthropologists and marriage experts.
Uses active voice: A number of field anthropologists and marriage experts compiled the report.

Opens weakly: It would be of no use to fight a drug war without waging a battle against demand for illicit substances.
Opens strongly: The government cannot fight a drug war effectively without waging a battle against the demand for illicit substances.

Uses cliché: A ballpark estimate of the number of fans in the stadium would be 120,000.
Employs plain English: About 120,000 fans were in the stadium.

BE CORRECT

- Observe the rules of standard written English. The most important rules are covered in the Sentence Correction chapter of this book.

Examples

Subject and verb disagree: Meredith, along with her associates, expect the sustainable energy proposal to pass.
Subject and verb agree: Meredith, along with her associates, expects the sustainable energy proposal to pass.

Uses faulty modification: Having worked in publishing for 10 years, Stokely's résumé shows that he is well qualified.
Uses correct modification: Stokely, who has worked in publishing for 10 years, appears from his résumé to be well qualified.

Uses pronouns incorrectly: A retirement community offers more activities than a private dwelling does, but it is cheaper.

Uses pronouns correctly: A retirement community offers more activities than a private dwelling does, but a private dwelling is cheaper.

Has unparallel structure: The dancer taught her understudy how to move, how to dress, and how to work with choreographers and deal with professional competition.

Has parallel structure: The dancer taught her understudy how to move, dress, work with choreographers, and deal with professional competition.

Fragmented sentence: There is time to invest in property. After one has established oneself in the business world, however.

Complete sentence: There is time to invest in property, but only after one has established oneself in the business world.

Run-on sentence: Antonio just joined the athletic club staff this year, however, because Barry has been with us since 1975, we would expect Barry to be more skilled with the weight-lifting equipment.

Correct sentence: Antonio joined the athletic club staff this year. However, because Barry has been with us since 1975, we would expect him to be more skilled with the weight-lifting equipment.

PRACTICE ESSAYS

Directions: Write an essay on each of the three topics below. The writing should be concise, forceful, and grammatically correct. After you have finished, proofread to catch any errors. Allow yourself 30 minutes to complete each essay. Practice writing under timed conditions so that you get a feel for how much you can afford to write while leaving enough time to proofread.

ESSAY 1

The following appeared in a memo from a staff member of a local health care clinic.

"Many lives might be saved if inoculations against cow flu were routinely administered to all people in areas where the disease is detected. However, since there is a small possibility that a person will die as a result of the inoculations, we cannot permit inoculations against cow flu to be routinely administered."

Consider how logical you find this argument. In your essay, be sure to discuss the line of reasoning and the use of evidence in the argument. For example, you may need to consider what questionable assumptions underlie the thinking and what alternative explanations or counterpoints might weaken the conclusion. You may also discuss what types of evidence would strengthen or refute the argument, what changes in the argument would make it more logically sound, and what, if anything, would help you better evaluate its conclusion.

After writing your essay, compare it to the sample responses that follow. Don't focus on length, as word count is not part of the grading criteria. Rather, focus on how logical the structure is and whether the essay makes its points in a clear and straightforward style.

Student Response 1 (as written, including original errors):

The writer argues that innoculations against cow flu shouldn't be administered because there is a possibility of a person dying from the innoculation. The flaw in this argument is suggested by the writer's use of the phrases "many lives" and "small possibility." These are vague words, but, they imply, that cow flu itself poses a greater risk to people in an area where the disease is present than the prevention against it. If this is the case, then the writer's argument is greatly weakened.

The writer could make the argument better by showing that the overall death rate from cow flu among those who haven't been innoculated in an area where cow flu has been detected is lower than the death rate from the vaccine among individuals who have been given the innoculation. This would show that the vaccine poses a greater risk than the disease itself. Also, it would be good to know whether some people are more likely to die from the innoculation than others and whether these people can be located. It's possible that those people who are most at risk from the innoculation are also most at risk from the disease itself, in which case the innoculation might do no greater harm than the disease would, and would also save the lives of many who were not in this high risk group. On the other hand, if those people who are most at risk from the vaccine are not at a very high risk from the disease, then maybe we can exempt them from the vaccine, but continue to administer it to those people who it will help.

Analysis 1:
Structure: The writer gives his evaluation of the argument in paragraph 1. However, the organization breaks down in paragraph 2, where the writer tries to cover too much. In this paragraph, the writer discusses ways of strengthening the argument, the need for more information, and alternative possibilities for the scenario. A better-written essay might have split paragraph 2 into several different paragraphs, each covering one topic.

Evidence: The writer does not fully support his position with specific examples. Rather, he writes vaguely of different possibilities. While this is not completely wrong, it's also not the type of concrete support that is needed here.

Depth of Logic: This is probably the weakest area in the essay. The writer fails to fully develop his ideas. He looks at the problem only through a cost-benefit lens—which way saves more lives?—as opposed to questioning whether any risk of death means that we shouldn't routinely inoculate.

Style: The writing style is flat and the first sentence in paragraph 2 is long and convoluted. The ideas in paragraph 2 seem strung together.

This essay would earn a score of 3. While the writer has some decent ideas and shows adequate writing ability, the structure of the essay is poor, the logic fails to show some parts of the author's argument, and the writer inadequately develops support for his own points. Had this student used the same ideas, but developed and organized them according to the Kaplan template, he would almost assuredly have earned a score of 4 or better.

Student Response 2 (as written, including original errors):
The argument above states that inoculations against cow flu could be useful in combating the disease, but, due to the risk of death from the inoculations themselves, the vaccines should not be widely administered. This argument relies on several unsupported assumptions and therefore fails to be persuasive.

The argument against widespread inoculations is rooted in the assumption that the risk of death from the inoculations is greater than the risk of death from cow flu. However, the author provides no evidence to support this key assumption. Without specific statistics regarding the death rates from inoculations and cow flu, we cannot assume that one outweighs the other: cow flu and the inoculations may be equally risky, or cow flu may in fact be riskier than the inoculations. In addition, the language of the argument appears to contradict its primary assumption. The author states that "many lives" could be saved by inoculations, but there is a "small possibility" of death from the inoculations. These terms suggest that the risk from cow flu is greater than that of the inoculations, further weakening the author's position that inoculations should not be routinely administered.

Additionally, the author takes an "all or nothing" position, suggesting that inoculations must be widely administered or not administered at all. This position ignores the possibility of variation in rates of infection and effects of the inoculation in different environments. The vaccine may pose a serious risk to those relatively unaffected by cow flu, while posing little risk to those most impacted by cow flu. In this case, vaccines administered to select portions of the population might save the most lives while putting the fewest lives in danger.

To make this argument persuasive, the author needs to present specific evidence to support the argument's assumptions. For instance, details regarding the number of deaths caused by cow flu and the vaccine would clarify the relative risks of the flu and the inoculations, allowing an accurate evaluation of the merits and risks of the vaccine. Also, a less extreme stance on inoculations—one that allowed for selective administration of the inoculations based upon an area's risk for the disease—would provide a more realistic solution to the challenge of balancing the dangers of cow flu and inoculations. Without such changes, the conclusion of this argument remains unconvincing.

Analysis 2:

Structure: The writer of this essay has clearly used the Kaplan template to her benefit. She frames the argument succinctly in the first paragraph. In each of the middle paragraphs, she lays out one major problem in the argument's reasoning and explains with clear support why it is a problem. In the final paragraph, the writer introduces evidence that would strengthen the argument and then draws her conclusion.

Evidence: The evidence is solid. The writer could have brought in counterexamples to support criticisms of the argument, but this is not a fatal flaw.

Depth of Logic: The logic in this essay is much stronger than in the last. The organization of the essay leaves few gaps in the reasoning.

Style: The writing style is superior, with fewer (although not zero) grammatical mistakes and much stronger flow.

This essay would receive a score of 6 from the GMAT graders. It is not perfect, but the graders do not expect perfection. The conclusion is somewhat clunky, and the writer missed one or two opportunities to strengthen her point. However, it is still a very strong essay in all four categories of evaluation, and it is a vast improvement over the earlier effort.

ESSAY 2

The following appeared in a memo from the regional manager of Luxe Spa, a chain of high-end salons.

"Over 75% of households in Parksboro have Jacuzzi bathtubs. In addition, the average family income in Parksboro is 50% higher than the national average, and a local store reports record-high sales of the most costly brands of hair and body care products. With so much being spent on personal care, Parksboro will be a profitable location for a new Luxe Spa—a salon that offers premium services at prices that are above average."

Consider how logical you find this argument. In your essay, be sure to discuss the line of reasoning and the use of evidence in the argument. For example, you may need to consider what questionable assumptions underlie the thinking and what alternative explanations or counterpoints might weaken the conclusion. You may also discuss what types of evidence would strengthen or refute the argument, what changes in the argument would make it more logically sound, and what, if anything, would help you better evaluate its conclusion.

After writing your essay, compare it to the sample response that follows.

Student Response (as written, including original errors):

Though it might seem at first glance that the regional manager of Luxe Spa has good reasons for suggesting that Parksboro would be a profitable location for a new spa, a closer examination of the arguments presented reveals numerous examples of leaps of faith, poor reasoning, and ill-defined terminology. In order to better support her claim, the manager would need to show a correlation between the figures she cites in reference to Parksboro's residents and a willingness to spend money at a spa with high prices.

The manager quotes specific statistics about the percentage of residents with Jacuzzis and the average income in Parksboro. She then uses these figures as evidence to support her argument. However, neither of these statistics as presented does much to bolster her claim. Just because 75% of homes have Jacuzzis doesn't mean those homeowners are more likely to go to a pricey spa. For instance, the presence of Jacuzzis in their houses may indicate a preference for pampering themselves at home. Parksboro could also be a planned development in the suburbs where all the houses are designed with Jacuzzis. If this is the case, than the mere ownership of a certain kind of bathtub should hardly be taken as a clear indication of a person's inclination to go to a spa. In addition, the fact that Parksboro's average family income is 50% higher than the national average is not enough on its own to predict the success or failure of a spa in the region. Parksboro may have a very small population, for instance, or a small number of wealthy people counterbalanced by a number of medium- to low-income families. We simply cannot tell from the information provided. In addition, the failure of the manager to provide the national average family income for comparison makes it unclear if earning 50% more would allow for a luxurious lifestyle or not.

The mention of a local store's record-high sales of expensive personal care items similarly provides scant evidence to support the manager's assertions. We are given no indication of what constitutes "record-high" sales for this particular store or what "most costly" means in this context. Perhaps this store usually sells very few personal care products and had one unusual month. Even if this one store sold a high volume of hair- and body-care products, it may not be representative of the Parksboro market as a whole. And perhaps "most costly" refers only to the most costly brands available in Parksboro, not to the most costly brands nationwide. The manager needs to provide much more specific information about residents' spending habits in order to provide compelling evidence that personal care ranks high among their priorities.

To make the case that Parksboro would be a profitable location for Luxe Spa, the regional manager should try to show that people there have a surplus of income and a tendency to spend it on indulging in spa treatments. Although an attempt is made to make this very argument, the lack of supporting information provided weakens rather than strengthens the memo. Information such as whether there are other high-end spas in the area and the presence of tourism in the town could also have been introduced as reinforcement. As it stands, Luxe Spa would be ill-advised to open a location in Parksboro based solely on the evidence provided here.

Analysis:

Structure: The use of the Kaplan template is evident here. In the first paragraph, the writer demonstrates his understanding of the argument and gives a summary of its flaws. Each paragraph that follows elaborates on one flaw in the author's reasoning. The final paragraph introduces evidence that, if provided, would strengthen the argument.

Evidence: The evidence is strong. The writer develops his points by providing examples to explain why the author's reasoning is questionable. Some minor flaws are evident, as in the second paragraph, when the writer misses an opportunity to point out that a small population might not be enough to support a spa.

Depth of Logic: Once again, the organization of the essay enhances its depth of logic. The writer takes apart the argument methodically and provides clear analysis of each part.

Style: The writing style is smooth and controlled, and grammar and syntax errors are minimal to nonexistent.

This essay would score a 6. The writer makes a very strong showing in all four categories of the grading rubric.

ESSAY 3

The following appeared in a document released by a community's arts bureau:

"In a recent county survey, 20 percent more county residents indicated that they watch TV programs dedicated to the arts than was reported eight years ago. The number of visitors to our county's museums and galleries over the past eight years has gone up by a comparable proportion. Now that the commercial funding public TV relies on is facing severe cuts, which will consequently limit arts programming, it is likely that attendance at our county's art museums will also go down. Therefore, public funds that are currently dedicated to the arts should be partially shifted to public television."

Consider how logical you find this argument. In your essay, be sure to discuss the line of reasoning and the use of evidence in the argument. For example, you may need to consider what questionable assumptions underlie the thinking and what alternative explanations or counterpoints might weaken the conclusion. You may also discuss what types of evidence would strengthen or refute the argument, what changes in the argument would make it more logically sound, and what, if anything, would help you better evaluate its conclusion.

After writing your essay, compare it to the sample response that follows.

Student Response (as written, including original errors):

In a time of threatened scarcity of funding, a community arts organization is asking to shift public arts funds partly to public television. The organization cites a recent survey of county residents that shows a 20 percent self-reported increase in arts TV-watching over the last eight years concomitant with a similar, documented increase in local museum and art gallery attendance. This earnest plea is understandable, but the underlying rationale for shifting funding is flawed and lacks sufficient substantiation.

First, the author may be confusing correlation with causation. Does the survey—even if we accept its findings as valid—really indicate that people went to museums as a result of seeing arts programming on television? Its quite possible that there are alternate reasons for the increase in attendance at museums, such as partnerships with schools, discount programs for senior citizens, introduction of IMAX theaters, or popular traveling exhibits. Alternatively, people may be watching more arts programming on television as a direct result of being lured into museum attendance for reasons that have nothing to do with television.

A second reason to be hesitant to adopt the recommended funding shift is that it assumes that there are only two viable sources of funding for public television: commercial and public. Before it resorts to diverting public funds from other arts organizations, public television has the option to pursue direct fundraising from viewers; these newly enthusiastic television arts program viewers may be delighted to support such programming directly. Public television has a unique opportunity to reach its audience in a way that is more elusive to smaller art museums. It is potentially in a superior position to recover from reduced corporate funding without needing to rely more heavily on public funds.

Conversely, it is possible that the author knows more than he has shared about a connection between public television watching and local museum attendance. For instance, there may have been some specific partnerships in the last eight years between local museums and local public television stations, including specific programming designed to tie in with current museum exhibitions. The recent survey to which the author alluded may have referenced direct ties between the television programming and museum attendance. Such data would make it more likely that increasing the public funding for public television would also directly benefit local museums.

Until more information is provided to us, however, we cannot accept the authors' argument for a shift in public funds to local public television as a way to support local art museums.

Analysis:

Structure: This essay is very well organized. The essayist's use of transitions is particularly strong here, as she leads the reader through the points of fault in the argument and describes evidence that could potentially strengthen the argument.

Evidence: The essayist provides multiple, strong examples that strengthen her major points.

Depth of Logic: The essayist accurately identifies the assumptions inherent in the argument and develops her points by proposing plausible alternative explanations for the evidence the argument's author cites.

Style: The essayist has a few problems with misplaced apostrophes; otherwise, the grammar and syntax are strong.

This essay would score a 6. It is an excellent example of how following the Kaplan template will help you organize your ideas into a convincing essay. After the introduction, two paragraphs develop and support the author's two main points, followed by a paragraph describing how the argument could be strengthened and a clear conclusion.

CHAPTER 14

Integrated Reasoning

- Section Format and Structure
- The Integrated Reasoning Question Types
  - Graphics Interpretation
  - Multi-Source Reasoning
  - Table Analysis
  - Two-Part Analysis
- Conclusion

The Integrated Reasoning section is the second section of GMAT. It appears immediately after the AWA, and you'll have 30 minutes to complete the 12 questions it contains. After the Integrated Reasoning section, you'll receive an optional 8-minute break before advancing to the Quantitative section.

The Integrated Reasoning section consists of four unique question types. They are as follows:

- **Graphics Interpretation** questions contain two statements that must be completed using drop-down menus. The statements pertain to a graph, scatter plot, or other form of visual information.
- **Multi-Source Reasoning** questions provide given information in the form of text, charts, or tables spread across two or three tabbed pages. Some of the questions are traditional, 5-answer multiple choice, while others consist of three true/false–style statements that must all be answered correctly in order to receive credit for the question.
- **Table Analysis** questions present information in the form of a sortable spreadsheet. Table Analysis questions feature the same question formats as Multi-Source Reasoning questions.
- **Two-Part Analysis** questions start out like an ordinary Quant or Verbal question, but instead of selecting one answer from five choices, you must select answers to two related questions from a common pool of six choices. The two answers can be the same.

SECTION FORMAT AND STRUCTURE

SCORING

The Integrated Reasoning section does not contribute to the total 200 to 800 GMAT score, and is therefore less important than the Quantitative and Verbal sections. Instead, it's scored on its own scale from 1 to 8, in whole-point increments.

With the exception of the occasional traditional multiple choice question, every question in an Integrated Reasoning section requires two or three selections. There is no partial credit. Thus, getting two questions right and one question wrong on a three-part question in Table Analysis or

Multi-Source Reasoning is exactly the same as getting all three questions wrong. For more information about scoring, see Chapter 1: Introduction to the GMAT.

FORM AND CONTENT

Integrated Reasoning questions are designed to resemble the types of problems you will encounter in business school and in your business and management career. These questions focus on your ability to solve complex problems using data from multiple sources in a variety of formats.

In the Integrated Reasoning section, you must analyze different types of data (presented in graphs, tables, and passages, among other formats), synthesize data in verbal and graphical formats, and evaluate outcomes and tradeoffs. Some of the data are presented in interactive formats, such as spreadsheets. You may need to sort data within columns to determine the answer or click on multiple tabbed pages to view additional information.

There are 12 questions in the Integrated Reasoning section, nearly all of which include multiple parts. For example, a single graph, discussion, or chart will be used as the basis for several parts of one question, and each question may measure a different skill set.

In this chapter, you will find two to three examples of each type of question set. You can practice with additional Integrated Reasoning questions, complete with answers and explanations, in the quizzes and practice tests in your Online Center.

Because the questions in the Integrated Reasoning section vary greatly in form and content, flexibility will be key to success. Since Integrated Reasoning questions draw on many of the same skills you need for the Verbal and Quantitative sections, thorough practice with GMAT questions of all types is the best way to prepare for Integrated Reasoning.

LENGTH AND NAVIGATION

The new Integrated Reasoning section is 30 minutes long. Navigation on the Integrated Reasoning section, as on the rest of the GMAT, moves forward only. You may not skip questions and go back to them later, and you may not return to questions you have already answered. If you are unsure of the answer, you need to take your best guess and keep going.

Unlike the Quantitative and Verbal sections of the GMAT, the Integrated Reasoning section is not computer adaptive. Your performance on one question will not determine the difficulty of the one that follows.

USER INTERFACE

The Integrated Reasoning section looks very different from the rest of the GMAT. Because hands-on experience is the best way to learn the user interface, it is recommended that you practice with these question types in your Kaplan Online Center.

In the Integrated Reasoning section, you will see question formats other than multiple-choice. You may be required to select your answer from drop-down menus or true/false options. The new formats are straightforward and easy to use but look very different from the multiple-choice questions used in the Quantitative and Verbal sections and require some different techniques.

You will also need to understand how to navigate through spreadsheets and tabbed pages. Table Analysis questions present you with a table of data that can be sorted using a drop-down menu. Pay close attention to how the drop-down menu operates and make sure to consider all your sorting options. Multi-Source Reasoning questions require you to integrate information from several tabbed pages.

You have the use of an onscreen calculator for the Integrated Reasoning section *only*. You are not allowed to bring your own calculator into the exam. The calculator performs basic functions and can be accessed by clicking an icon on the screen. A calculator screen will then pop up over the question. The calculator looks like this:

Use caution when using the calculator. You run the risk of entering information incorrectly, resulting in a wrong answer; moreover, rounding and estimation are often much faster than the time-consuming process of entering multiple large numbers. Use the calculator only when necessary.

THE INTEGRATED REASONING QUESTION TYPES

Now that you have an idea of what to expect in the Integrated Reasoning section, let's examine each of the four question types.

GRAPHICS INTERPRETATION

Graphics Interpretation questions test your ability to interpret and analyze data presented visually in graphs or graphical images. For each question, you will see a graph with accompanying text and two questions.

As with a Reading Comprehension passage, you do not need to absorb every bit of information on the graph to answer the questions. What you *do* need to do is get the gist of the graph and what it contains so that you can efficiently find the information you need. You will then read the question stem, view the answer choices, and use the information in the graph to select the correct answer.

Graphics Interpretation questions feature many different types of graphs, including line graphs, scatter plots, Venn diagrams, and even geological timelines. Both examples in this chapter happen to focus on scatter plots, but don't take this as a sign that scatter plots are more important than any other type of graphic you may see on Test Day. We chose these for our examples because you're probably less familiar with scatter plots than with the other types of graphs commonly seen on the Integrated Reasoning section.

All graphics are accompanied by two incomplete sentences. Test takers must use a drop-down menu to select a word or phrase that completes the sentence according to the information presented in the graphic. The sample graphs in this book are accompanied by more than two sentences in order to give you a better sense of the variety of questions you may be asked. The drop-down menus in this chapter are represented in multiple-choice format for ease of reading.

Let's take a look at some Graphics Interpretation questions.

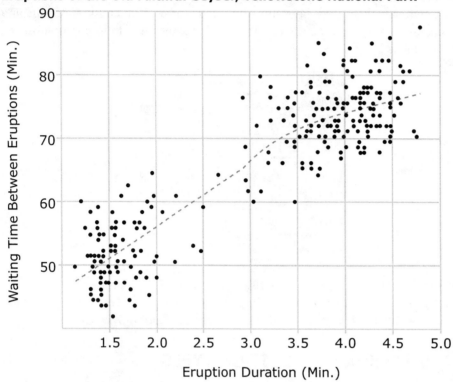

Eruptions of the Old Faithful Geyser, Yellowstone National Park

The graph above is a scatter plot with each point representing the duration of an eruption of Old Faithful, a geyser in Yellowstone National Park, and the time in minutes until the following eruption occurred. The dotted line represents a regression line. For each blank, select the answer choice that correctly completes the statement according to the information in the graph.

1a. The relationship between the duration of eruptions and the waiting time between eruptions is _____.

  O   linear and positive

  O   nonlinear and positive

  O   linear and negative

  O   nonlinear and negative

1b. The graph suggests that Old Faithful has _____ of eruption.

  O   one type

  O   two distinct types

  O   more than two distinct types

1c. For an eruption of less than two minutes, the maximum recorded wait time is _____ the minimum recorded wait time of an eruption of more than four minutes.

    O   greater than

    O   equal to

    O   less than

Get the Gist of the Graph

Your first step with a question of this type should be to read the text that accompanies the graph. You may see only a single sentence, or you may see (as in this case) a full paragraph. This text is important. Although most Graphics Interpretation questions can be answered without reference to the text, reading will give you an overview of the information the graph contains and how it is presented. On Test Day, taking a moment to paraphrase the written information will improve your understanding of the image, speeding up your analysis and reducing your chances of committing a careless error.

Here, the paragraph tells you that the graph shows the behavior of a single geyser, Old Faithful. The graph presents two types of information: how long the eruptions of Old Faithful last and how long it then takes before the next eruption happens. Each point on the graph represents an eruption.

Next, look at the graph itself. Get a bird's-eye view of the graph by reading the title and the labels of the axes and notice how the information from the paragraph is represented in the graph. Here, you'll notice that the duration, or length, of the eruption is measured against the waiting time that follows it before the next eruption. Now look at the units of measurement that correspond to each axis and determine whether the scales are similar. In this case, both axes are measured in minutes, but the scales are very different: The x-axis is measured in 0.5-minute increments, while the y-axis is measured in 10-minute increments. Furthermore, the x-axis starts at 1.0 and ends at 5.0, while the y-axis starts at 40 and goes to 90. Then notice if there are any specific features mentioned in the accompanying paragraph that you see represented on the graph, such as a regression line.

The final step before answering the questions is to look at the data to see if they fall into a general pattern. On this scatter plot, most of the data points separate into two distinct groups. With a pattern this clear, you can anticipate that this observation will be key to answering one or more of the accompanying questions. Making these observations before analyzing the questions will help you answer each question more effectively.

Answer the Questions

Question 1a: First, read and paraphrase the question. It asks about the relationship between the duration of eruptions and the waiting time between eruptions, which means that you are looking for a pattern in how the data points are arrayed on the graph. Before attempting to predict an answer, scan the answer choices. Here, you see the words *linear, nonlinear, positive,* and *negative,* which indicate that the pattern may take the shape and slope of a line. The regression line will help you here. There is more than one type of regression line, and in this case, the exact type of regression line has not been specified. But you should know that a regression line, however it is calculated, represents the overall trend of the points as a group. The regression line slopes upward—meaning the waiting time gets longer as the explosion duration gets longer. This is a positive relationship—both variables tend to increase and decrease together—so you can narrow the answer down to choices **(A)** and **(B)**. Next you need to determine whether the relationship is linear or nonlinear by looking at the shape of the regression line. You'll notice that the regression "line" isn't really a line, because its slope changes as the amounts of time get longer. Since the relationship isn't linear through the entire data set, the answer is choice **(B)**.

Question 1b: This question might seem a little tricky at first, since the way it's worded might make you think you need to know something qualitative about the types of eruptions the geyser experiences—perhaps something about their magnitude or geological characteristics. But the GMAT will never require you to have outside knowledge beyond high school math and general knowledge of grammar and logic. All the information you need to answer this question is contained in the graph. Begin by paraphrasing the question for yourself: Does Old Faithful have one, two, or more than two distinct types of eruption? As you noticed before, the data points separate themselves into two main clusters. There are a few stray data points scattered outside these clusters, but their number is not significant. Therefore, you can infer from the graph that Old Faithful has two types of eruptions, choice **(B)**.

Question 1c: For this question, you need to examine the data in the graph more closely. This statement contains a comparison between two data points: the maximum wait time for an eruption that lasts less than two minutes and the minimum wait time for an eruption that lasts more than four minutes. Note that you're asked to compare the wait times of these two points—that's their height along the *y*-axis. So this question asks you to find these two points and compare their heights. The first point is the highest point to the left of the two-minute line on the *x*-axis, which looks to be just below 65 on the *y*-axis. Now find the second point, the lowest point to the right of the four-minute line on the *x*-axis. The lowest point to the right of that line appears to be just below the 70-minute mark on the *y*-axis. The first point is therefore lower than the second, so you would choose "less than," choice **(C)**.

We've discussed how, before attacking any Graphics Interpretation question, you need to understand what the graph contains and how it is constructed. You can then target your research to answer each question correctly and efficiently. Try using these techniques on the next set of questions.

Public Elementary and High Schools, by State: 2008–2009

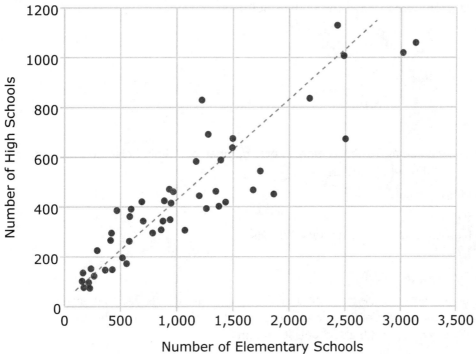

The graph above is a scatter plot with 49 points. The 49 points represent the number of elementary and high schools in 48 U.S. states and the District of Columbia (the numbers of schools in California and Texas are too large to appear on a graph of this scale). The dotted line represents a regression line. For each blank, select the answer choice that correctly completes the statement according to the information in the graph.

2a. The slope of the regression line is _____.

○ greater than 1
○ approximately 1
○ less than 1

2b. Approximately _____ percent of the 49 states (including the District of Columbia) represented in the graph have fewer than 500 elementary schools.

○ 10
○ 25
○ 50
○ 75
○ 90

2c. Approximately _____ percent of the 49 states (including the District of Columbia) represented in the graph have fewer than 500 high schools.

- ○ 10
- ○ 25
- ○ 50
- ○ 75
- ○ 90

2d. The point corresponding to the greatest total number of schools also corresponds to the greatest number of _____.

- ○ elementary schools
- ○ high schools
- ○ both high schools and elementary schools

Get the Gist of the Graph

First, familiarize yourself with the text that describes the graph. It tells you that each data point represents a state (or the District of Columbia) and that each state is plotted on the graph according to the number of elementary and high schools it contains.

Now take a look at the graph to get the big picture. You see that elementary schools are plotted along the *x*-axis and high schools along the *y*-axis. In this case, both axes begin at zero, but again the scales of the two axes are different. The axis for elementary schools increases in increments of 500, while the axis for high schools moves up more slowly, in increments of 200. Looking at the points with these increments in mind, you can see that the states generally have more elementary schools than high schools. Again, you see a pattern in the graph; the data points and the regression line trend upward. That pattern makes sense—states that have more kids or higher populations are generally going to need more schools of both types.

Answer the Questions

Question 2a: First read the question; then glance at the answer choices. Again, as a Kaplan-trained test taker, you'll see how important it is to look at the answer choices before predicting an answer; this important step will save you time on Test Day. You'll notice that your only choices are a slope greater than, equal to, or less than 1. Think about what it means for a line to have a slope of 1. It rises at the same rate that it moves to the right. A line with a slope of 1 usually makes a 45-degree angle with the *x*- and *y*-axes. The line on this graph looks to be about 45 degrees, so does it have a slope of 1? If you said "no," you just avoided an important trap in this question. A line with a slope of 1 makes a 45-degree angle with the *x*- and *y*-axes only when the scales of both axes are the same. But here, the scales are not the same; the numbers on the *y*-axis move upward much more slowly than the numbers on the *x*-axis. Remember the formula for the slope of a line:

$$\text{Slope} = \frac{\text{Change in } y}{\text{Change in } x}, \text{ or to put it another way, Slope} = \frac{\text{Rise}}{\text{Run}}$$

On this graph, the change in *y* is a lot less than the corresponding change in *x*. So the slope will be less than 1. You can test this out quickly using some approximate points from the graph. The regression line is close to the points (500, 200) and (1,000, 400). As the line moves up by 200, it moves to the right by 500. Plugging these points into the slope formula above, you get $\frac{400-200}{1000-500}$, which reduces to $\frac{2}{5}$, a positive fraction less than 1. Choice **(C)** is correct.

Question 2b: This question asks about elementary schools only, so focus on the x-axis and count the number of points that fall to the left of the 500 mark on that axis. This number appears to be about 13 points. (The exact number does not matter, as the question is asking for an approximate percentage.) Since you want to know what percentage these states represent out of all the states on the graph, you can set up a fraction: 13 over the total number of data points, which the paragraph accompanying the graph tells you is 49. Using estimation, $\frac{13}{49} \approx \frac{13}{50}$, which when converted to a percentage is equal to 26 percent. The closest answer is choice **(B)**.

Question 2c: This question looks similar to the previous question, except it is asking about high schools, which are measured on the y-axis. This time, you need to estimate the percentage of schools that are below 500 on the y-axis. Rather than counting up all the points below 500, which would be a time-consuming task, count the points *above* 500, find the percentage that those points represent, and subtract that percentage from 100. In this case, you have about 13 points above 500, representing approximately 25 percent of the total (you might recall this same calculation from the previous question). Subtracting this percentage from 100 percent leaves you with 75 percent, or choice **(D)**.

Question 2d: Read the question and notice that you are looking for a particular point: the state with the greatest total number of schools. There are two points in the upper right portion of the graph that look like they could be the answer: the point highest on the y-axis and the point farthest to the right on the x-axis. Also, recall that the axes are scaled differently and the increments on the x-axis increase much more quickly than those on the y-axis. The point farthest to the right, then, will have the greatest number of schools. The state represented by this point has the greatest total number of elementary schools, but it does not have the greatest number of high schools. The answer is choice **(A)**.

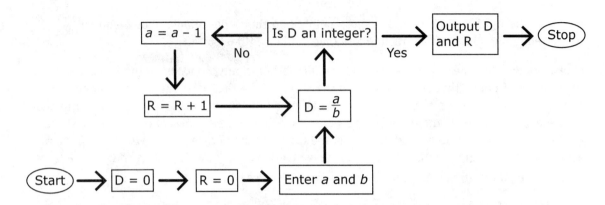

The flowchart represents a computer algorithm that takes two positive integers as the input and is intended to return two integers as the output. Each process is symbolized by an equation, such as $a = a - 1$. In this particular process, 1 is subtracted from the current value of the variable a, and the difference then becomes the value of a. For example, if the value of a is 5 before the process $a = a - 1$ is completed, then the value of a will be 4 after the process is completed. Algorithms that are incorrectly formed may sometimes get stuck in an infinite loop. An infinite loop is a sequence of instructions that never terminates. Complete the following statements by making selections from the drop-down menus in accordance with the algorithm represented by the flowchart.

3a. If 58 and 11 are entered as the values for a and b, respectively, then one of the outputs of the function will be _____.

   O   D = 0
   O   D = 4
   O   D = 55
   O   R = 3
   O   R = 4

3b. The algorithm will get stuck in an infinite loop

   O   if $a > b$
   O   if $a = b$
   O   if $a < b$
   O   never

Get the Gist of the Flowchart

Paraphrase what the algorithm does. First, D is set to $\frac{a}{b}$. Then, if D is an integer, the algorithm outputs D and R and stops. If D is not an integer, then a is decreased by 1 and R is increased by 1, and the process repeats. Thus, the loop will keep repeating until $\frac{a}{b}$ is an integer, at which point it will output the value of D (which is $\frac{a}{b}$) and R (which is the number of times the algorithm divided a by b and didn't get an integer).

If you try a few examples, you might notice that this algorithm isn't just a random sequence of steps: the outputs are the integer part (D) and the remainder (R) when a is divided by b. R also acts as a "counter" of the number of times the algorithm loops before stopping. For example, given

$a = 13$ and $b = 5$, the outputs are D = 2 and R = 3, because $\frac{13}{5}$ equals 2 with a remainder of 3, and the algorithm will loop 3 times before it stops.

Answer the Questions

Question 3a: The first time through the loop, D will be set to $\frac{58}{11}$, a will be set to 58 − 1 = 57, and R will be set to 0 + 1 = 1. The second time through the loop, D will be set to $\frac{57}{11}$, a will be set to 57 − 1 = 56, and R will be set to 1 + 1 = 2. The third time through the loop, D will be set to $\frac{56}{11}$, a will be set to 56 − 1 = 55, and R will be set to 2 + 1 = 3. On the fourth time through the loop, D will be set to $\frac{55}{11}$ = 5, which is an integer, so the algorithm will stop and the values of a and R will not be changed. Thus, the outputs are D = 5 and R = 3. D = 5 is not present among the selections, but R = 3 is. The correct answer is choice **(D)**.

Question 3b: If $a > b$, then you've already seen that the algorithm will stop. If $a = b$, then the algorithm will also stop, because a number divided by itself always equals 1 with a remainder of 0. If $a < b$, it may seem that the algorithm will get stuck because D will keep getting set to a fraction. For example, if $a = 9$ and $b = 10$, D will get set to $\frac{9}{10}$, then $\frac{8}{10}$, then $\frac{7}{10}$, and so on. However, a will eventually be reduced to 0, at which point $\frac{a}{b}$ will equal 0 (which is an integer) and the algorithm will stop. Thus, no matter the values of a and b, the algorithm's termination condition is always triggered. This mean that it will never not stop, which is choice **(D)**.

MULTI-SOURCE REASONING

As its name suggests, Multi-Source Reasoning tests your ability to take information from multiple sources and synthesize it to answer questions. The information will be presented on two to three tabbed pages. You will have to click through the tabs to find the information you need. The data can be in the form of text, charts, or tables and may be presented in a combination of all three.

The information on the tabs may seem overwhelming, so you'll need to approach it similarly to how you approach Reading Comprehension. Get the gist of what the tabs contain and take brief notes highlighting the main points of each tab. Don't try to absorb all of the information at first, but make sure you scan all of the information on each tab so that you'll know where to find it when you answer the questions.

The tabbed pages are on the left side of the screen, and the questions are on the right. There may be more than one page of questions associated with a prompt, in which case you must click on the Next button to advance to the next page of questions. You can get hands-on experience with tabbed pages in your Online Center. Take a few minutes to become familiar with the navigation of this section. Doing so will save you valuable time when answering the questions.

Some of the questions about the tabbed information will be in the standard multiple-choice format that you're familiar with from the Verbal and Quantitative sections. Others, called multiple–dichotomous choice questions, will require you to evaluate multiple statements individually; you may be required to figure out whether statements are true or whether certain expenditures are within a given budget. On the actual test, each of these yes/no or true/false questions will require you to evaluate three separate statements. This book presents four or five statements per question to provide additional practice.

American Pets	Table #1	Table #2

78.4 million dogs and 86.4 million cats are owned as pets in the U.S. Though some pets come from breeders, many others are adopted from shelters and pounds. Even though 78 percent of pet dogs and 88 percent of pet cats are spayed or neutered, there has never been a shortage of animals available for adoption. The result of these staggering numbers of animals is a booming industry of pet supplies, services, and medical care.

Tables 1 and 2, respectively, indicate the average one-time adoption costs and average annual expenses associated with pet ownership. However, dogs vary significantly in size; small dogs such as chihuahuas cost on average 25 percent less than the values shown in the adoption and ownership cost tables, while larger canines such as mastiffs often cost 50 percent more.

American Pets	Table #1	Table #2

Average Per-Animal Adoption Expenses in America

	Dog	Cat
Spay/neuter	$100	$75
Collar/leash	$30	$10
Litter box	—	$20
Carrier	$40	$30
Sleeper crate	$80	—

American Pets	Table #1	Table #2

Average Per-Animal Annual Ownership Expenses in America

	Dog	Cat
Food	$250	$215
Veterinary	$240	$210
Litter	—	$150
Toys/treats	$60	$40
License	$25	—
House cleaning	$50	$50

4. Consider each of the following statements. Does the information in the passage and tables support the inference as stated? Choose *Yes* if the statement can be accurately inferred; otherwise choose *No*.

Yes	No	
○	○	Americans spend over $10 billion annually on toys and treats for their cats and dogs.
○	○	Not counting spaying and neutering, more money is spent every year in America on the veterinary expenses of cats than on the veterinary expenses of dogs.
○	○	The average cost of adopting an average small dog and keeping it for a year is less than the cost of doing so for an average cat.
○	○	The number of categories of expenses unique to cats is the same as the number of categories unique to dogs.

5. Based on the information in the passage and tables, the total cost of spaying or neutering all unspayed and non-neutered pet cats and dogs in America would be closest to

- ○ $2.5 billion
- ○ $4.0 billion
- ○ $12 billion
- ○ $14.5 billion
- ○ $27.5 billion

Get the Gist of the Tabbed Pages

We approached Graphics Interpretation by first getting a general sense of how the graph works. Similarly, you need to know what is on each tabbed page before you begin answering Multi-Source Reasoning questions. Take brief notes on the content of each tab as you examine it. In the first tab, the text gives you data about the number of American pets and the frequency of spaying and neutering. It then goes on to describe the tables in the next two tabs. More specifically, the first table will show the one-time costs of adopting an animal in the United States, and the second table will focus on yearly expenses. Finally, it gives us an important warning: The data in the tabs are averages, and some dogs will require very different expenses according to their size.

Next, move to the second tab. Here, you are given a table with rows indicating several adoption expenses, separated into a column for dogs and a column for cats. Notice that not all expenses apply to both types of animal. The total cost of adoption isn't calculated for you, but you could find it with simple addition if necessary.

Switch to the third tab to view another table. This one also shows expenses for dogs and cats. Rather than listing one-time expenses, this lists the repeating yearly costs of those pets. Other than that, it's similar in structure to Table 1.

Answer the Questions

Question 4a: You can expect two things on a yes/no question like this. First, the answer will require you to look at two or three tabs. Second, the question will reward estimation.

Table 2 in the third tab gives the annual cost of toys and treats, but that cost is per animal. Calculating the total expenditure for all pets requires knowing the total number of pets. To look for that data you should check your notes, which will send you to the first tab. According to the combined data from Tabs 1 and 3, there are approximately 80 million (rounded from 78.4 million) dogs in America, and their treats and toys cost an average of $60 per dog, meaning the total toy and treat expense for dogs would be about $4.8 billion. The same tabs tell you that there are approximately 90 million (rounded from 86.4 million) cats and their owners spend an average of $40 for toys and treats per cat, meaning owners spend about $3.6 billion annually on toys and treats for cats. The combined total for money spent on cat and dog treats and toys is therefore only a little over $8 billion. Even though this is a high estimate (since both of the values above were estimated by rounding up), it's still less than $10 billion, so the answer is "No."

Question 4b: You might remember seeing veterinary expenses on the tables, but even if you don't, you can probably deduce that visits to the veterinarian are a yearly expense—that means Table 2 in the third tab. And just as in the previous question, calculating the total expenditure for all pets requires you to know how many pets there are. Refer to the first tab for that information—or better yet, refer to your scratchwork from the previous question, which used the same numbers.

The table says that Americans spend on average $240 per year on veterinary expenses for dogs and $210 per year on veterinary expenses for cats. But even though dogs cost more, there are a greater number of cats. You can figure out which total is greater by multiplying $240/dog by 78 million dogs and $210/cat by 86 million cats. But it's even more effective to think proportionally; the ratio $240:$210 can be reduced, resulting in a ratio of dog costs to cat costs of 8:7. Now you can multiply each of the numbers in this simplified ratio by the corresponding number of pets: $8 \times 78 = 624$, and $7 \times 86 = 602$, meaning that more money is spent on the veterinary expenses of dogs each year than is spent on cats. The answer is "No."

Question 4c: This problem requires you to total the adoption and annual ownership costs. You will need information from the tables in the second and third tabs. You'll also need to do some addition, if you haven't already, to total up the costs in each column.

If you add all of the expenses for cats, the total comes out to $800 for adopting and owning a cat for a year. For a dog the same costs $875, although if you were rounding to speed up the addition, you might have ended up with $850 or $900. Regardless, at first glance it seems clear-cut that the dog will cost more than the cat.

But something should have caught your eye: This question specifies a "small" dog. When you paraphrased the tabs, you noticed that size is mentioned briefly in Tab 1. Researching that tab will reveal that small dogs average 25% less money to adopt and keep. Because 25% (or one-fourth) of $875 is well over $200 ($875 × 0.25 = $218.75, but it's probably not worth calculating exactly), the cost reduction of having a small dog easily offsets the initial $75 difference you calculated between the cost of a dog and that of a cat. A small dog is therefore cheaper than a cat, so the answer is "Yes."

Question 4d: This question requires only simple counting, but you need to know what you're looking for. "Categories of expenses unique to cats" means expenses that are paid only for cats, not for dogs. Since this doesn't specify which expenses, look in both tabs that list expenses, Tables 1 and 2.

Litter box and litter are the two categories unique to cats. Sleeper crate and license are the two categories unique to dogs. Both animals have two unique categories, the same number, so the answer to this question is "Yes."

Question 5: This question asks you for the cost of spaying or neutering all unspayed and non-neutered dogs and cats in America. A glance at the answer choices can provide an important hint, as many of the answer choices are quite far apart. With numbers this big and this spread out in the answer choices, it's usually best to estimate.

Spaying and neutering statistics, as well as numbers of pets, are in the first tab. Researching this background information reveals that 22% of 78.4 million dogs and 12% of 86.4 million cats are unspayed or non-neutered. To estimate, instead say 20% of 80 million = 16 million dogs and 10% of 90 million = 9 million cats are unspayed or non-neutered.

Spaying and neutering are one-time expenditures, so the second tab contains the price. At $100 each, it will cost about $1.6 billion to spay or neuter 16 million dogs. At $75 per cat, it will cost $675 million, or about $0.68 billion, to spay or neuter 9 million cats.

The combined cost of spaying or neutering all unspayed and non-neutered dogs and cats is therefore about $2.3 billion. Although the estimate above rounds both percentages significantly down, it rounds the number of animals of both types up to compensate, so the resulting estimate is likely close to the real solution; regardless, the next closest answer choice ($4 billion) can't be correct unless the above estimation is off by more than 50%. Verify that you calculated the number of decimal places correctly and didn't confuse millions with billions. Once you've double-checked the accuracy of your estimations and calculations, you can see that $2.5 billion is closest and confidently choose **(A)** as the correct answer.

You've learned from working through this set of Multi-Source Reasoning questions that it's crucial to get the gist of each tabbed page and take brief notes highlighting the main points before attempting to answer any questions. Now apply these techniques to the next set of Multi-Source Reasoning questions.

| Email #1 | Email #2 | Email #3 |

*Email from **project manager** to financial officer*

August 3, 9:43 a.m.

Did all three bids arrive on time last night? We need to minimize delays on construction, so if the contractors have submitted their estimates and our research team has compiled reports on the contractors' histories, we should make a decision on which firm to hire by the end of the day.

| Email #1 | Email #2 | Email #3 |

*Email from **financial officer** in response to the project manager's August 3, 9:43 a.m. email*

August 3, 10:12 a.m.

Appaloosa Construction sent us a bid of $1.35 million. Its bid is the highest of the three, but its track record is spotless; none of the past 10 major projects it has worked on has gone over budget by more than 4%. Breton Construction did manage to underbid them—its representative claims that it can do the project for $1.25 million. However, in the past two years, Breton oversaw two different projects that went over budget by a full 25%. If our project were to exceed Breton's estimate by a comparable percentage, we would run out of funds before completion. Finally, Campolina Construction presented a $1.1 million plan, and its track record is as good as Appaloosa's. Unfortunately, although Appaloosa and Breton can both start tomorrow, Campolina would be unable to begin work until August 25, so we cannot accept Campolina's low bid.

| Email #1 | Email #2 | Email #3 |

*Email from **project manager** in response to the financial officer's August 3, 10:12 a.m. email*

August 3, 10:38 a.m.

Even though Breton's work could potentially cost less than either of the other two, that savings does not justify the risk of being unable to complete the project. But as far as Campolina is concerned, you're not considering the actual cost of a delay. It's true that we are losing money at a constant rate each day we don't start building. But even after factoring in the losses of waiting until August 25, the estimated cost of working with Campolina still ends up $50,000 below Appaloosa's bid.

6. Consider each of the following statements. Does the information in the three emails support the inferences as stated? Choose *Yes* if the statement can be accurately inferred; otherwise choose *No*.

Yes	No	
○	○	The total budget for the project is between $1.4 million and $1.5 million.
○	○	The project manager and the financial officer agree in their evaluation of Appaloosa's bid.
○	○	In making their decision, the project manager and the financial officer considered how much time the contractors would spend on construction.
○	○	The project manager and the financial officer disagree about the best choice of contractors for completing the project.
○	○	The project manager is willing to wait a few days before deciding on Campolina's bid.

7. The amount of money lost each day that construction is delayed is closest to

- ○ $2,500
- ○ $10,000
- ○ $20,000
- ○ $55,000
- ○ $65,000

Get the Gist of the Tabbed Pages

First, look through the tabbed pages and notice the basics: You have three emails, sent minutes apart, between a project manager and a financial officer. Use your Reading Comprehension Passage Mapping skills to create a brief synopsis of each email in your scratchwork:

Email 1—project manager to financial officer:

- Asking about the bids
- Start construction as soon as possible
- Make a decision by the end of the day

Email 2—financial officer to project manager:

- Appaloosa—$1.35 million—great track record
- Breton—$1.25 million—usually over budget—would run out of funds before completion
- Campolina—$1.1 million—can't begin work until August 25—can't accept

Think strategically here: Although the financial officer never draws an explicit conclusion about which company should be hired, his opinion is clear. Breton could cause the company to run out of money for the project, and Campolina's delayed start date is unacceptable, so the financial officer must be in favor of Appaloosa.

Email 3—project manager to financial officer:

- Breton—not worth the risk
- Reminder about the cost of delay
- Campolina is still cheaper, even with the delay

It is not necessary to jot down all of the figures and calculations from the email. Just as with Reading Comprehension, if you need the details, they will be there for you to refer to later.

Answer the Questions

Question 6: Notice that you have another set of yes/no questions. As always, you'll want to read the introductory sentences very carefully. Your task is to consider whether the inferences in the questions are supported by the information in the three emails. Critical Reasoning skills will help you here; you must use *only* the evidence in the three emails to determine your answers.

Question 6a: This question asks whether the construction budget falls within a range of $1.4 million to $1.5 million. Notice that the specific amount of the budget is never stated in the emails. We know, however, that the company is able to spend $1.35 million, since the financial officer describes Appaloosa's bid as acceptable. The only reference to the budget's upper limit comes in the second email. This email states that Breton bid $1.25 million and that if this bid were exceeded by 25 percent, the project would go over budget. $1.25 million × 125% ≈ $1.56 million. The total construction budget must therefore fall somewhere between $1.35 million and $1.56 million. We don't have enough information to conclude that the budget falls within the narrower range of $1.4 million to $1.5 million, so the answer is "No."

Question 6b: This question refers to Appaloosa's bid and the opinions of the two writers. Look at your notes: The financial officer is in favor of accepting Appaloosa's bid, while the project manager is in favor of accepting Campolina's instead. The two do not agree on their assessment of Appaloosa's bid, making the answer to this question "No."

Question 6c: Read carefully here. Time is discussed, but it is discussed in reference to when the construction can begin, not how long it will take. There isn't any mention of the length of construction in your notes, and if you glance through the three emails, there isn't any information there either. The answer is "No."

Question 6d: This question is very similar to the one asking about Appaloosa's bid. This time, the question is asking whether the two people disagree about the best contractor to hire. The answer to this question, as seen in your notes on the emails, is "Yes." The project manager thinks Campolina is the best choice, and the financial officer is in favor of Appaloosa.

Question 6e: The wording of this statement is tricky, so answer it by doing some careful research in the emails. Here, the question asks whether the project manager is willing to wait a few days to decide. Glance at your notes to find relevant keywords: "decide" is mentioned in the first email, and "delay," or waiting, is mentioned in the third. Going to the first email, you see that the project manager wants to reach a decision by the end of the day. This seems to contradict the inference given in the question, but don't stop just yet. Check the third email to see whether the project manager changed her mind. In the third email, the project manager discusses waiting, stating that it might be acceptable to wait to begin construction with Campolina—but there is nothing in this email about waiting to make a decision. Thus, you cannot infer that the project manager is willing to wait a few days, and the answer here is "No."

Question 7: By now, you can expect that you'll need to find information in multiple emails to answer this question. Looking at your notes, you see that the delay costs are discussed in the third email. The email states that a constant amount is lost every day that construction is delayed. From the second email, you find that the other two companies can start the next day, August 4, but Campolina can't start until August 25, a delay of 21 days. Next, use the information given to determine how much money is lost in those 21 days.

The third email says that even with the delay, Campolina would cost $50,000 less than Appaloosa's $1.35 million bid, or $1.3 million. That means the cost caused by the delay would be $1.3 million − $1.1 million, or $200,000. To determine the cost per day, calculate $\frac{\$200,000}{21} \approx \$9,524$. However, since the question asks for the number that's "closest to" the amount lost per day, you can save time by estimating. Round 21 to 20 and calculate much more easily that $200,000 divided by 20 is $10,000, or answer choice **(B)**.

| Email #1 | Email #2 | Email #3 |

*Text from **CEO** to store manager*

April 10, 2:53 a.m.

I just got a call from the police. Our store on Thompson street was robbed again. This is the third time in exactly seven months. After the first robbery, you said you would heighten security, but the measures you took had no effect; 60 days later the same store was robbed. Then you said you'd install an alarm system, but I guess you never got around to that. After the second robbery, the insurance company threatened to cancel our account if the store was robbed again and we hadn't done anything to increase the security of the premises. What am I supposed to tell them?

| Email #1 | Email #2 | Email #3 |

*Email from **store manager** in response to the CEO's April 10, 2:53 a.m. text*

April 10, 3:38 a.m.

I had an alarm system installed within a week after the second robbery. It took the police exactly four minutes to get to the store after the alarm was triggered; the robber was in and out in three. The alarm company called me after calling the police, and I still beat the police to the scene. I've told the alarm company to call me first next time—I missed the robber by no more than thirty seconds.

You can tell the insurance company that the measures I undertook after the first robbery did have a major impact. We started moving inventory from the shelves to the back room before closing the store each day. This cut our losses in the second robbery by nearly 70 percent as compared to the first robbery. I've attached the exact numbers for your perusal. After the second robbery, we began leaving even less inventory on the shelves. It's too soon to tell exactly how much money we lost in this morning's robbery, but my survey indicates that the losses are about another 40 percent smaller than those of the second robbery.

| Email #1 | Email #2 | Email #3 |

*Attachment to the **store manager's** April 10, 3:38 a.m. email*

Value of Stolen Inventory

Robbery	Cameras	Tripods	Lenses	Accessories
First	$45,652	$9,834	$2,119	$589
Second	$11,000	$4,832	$1,003	$672

8. If the manager's estimates are correct and if the tripods stolen in the third robbery account for 15 percent of the value of the stolen inventory, then the value of the stolen tripods is closest to

   O $800
   O $1,100
   O $1,600
   O $2,100
   O $4,800

9. For each of the following statements, select *True* if the statement can be verified to be true assuming that the information in the emails (but not necessarily the attachment) is accurate. Otherwise, select *False*.

True	False	
O	O	An alarm system was installed at the store in November.
O	O	Upon being reached by phone, the store manager can make it to the store in under 5 minutes.
O	O	The attachment contradicts the store manager.

10. For each of the following statements, select *Yes* if the statement can be reasonably inferred from the emails and the attachment. Otherwise, select *No*.

Yes	No	
O	O	The robbery could have been prevented if the store manager had installed shatterproof windows.
O	O	The alarm company's phone call to the police lasted less than 45 seconds.
O	O	The value of the lenses stolen in the third robbery is less than that of the second robbery.

Answers and Explanations:

Question 8: The store manager's email states that there was an estimated 40% reduction in losses from the second robbery to the third. The total losses of the second robbery were $17,507, so the losses of the third robbery were $17,507 × 60%, or $10,504. Fifteen percent of that is $10,504 × 15%, or $1,575, which is closest to choice (C). Note that you could also arrive at this answer via approximation: 60% of $18,000 is about $11,000, and 15% of that is about $1,650, which is also closest to choice **(C)**.

Question 9a: The CEO's text message states that the first robbery was exactly seven months ago and that the second robbery happened 60 days later. The current day is April 10, so the first robbery happened around September 10 and the second on November 10. The store manager's email states that the alarm was installed within a week of the second robbery, so there was indeed an alarm installed in November. The answer is "true".

Question 9b: According to the second email, the store manager missed the robber by 30 seconds. Since the robber was in and out in 3 minutes, the maximum time it could have taken for the store manager to reach the store was 3 minutes and 30 seconds. We actually know it was less than this because the alarm company called the police first. If the store manager made the trip in less than 3.5 minutes, then he or she certainly made it in less than 5. The answer is "true".

Question 9c: The total losses of the first robbery were $58,194. The total losses of the second robbery were $17,507. This is a percent change of $\frac{58,194 - 17,507}{58,194}$, or 69.9%, which confirms the store manager's claim that the reduction in losses was "nearly 70 percent." The answer is "False"

Question 10a: There's no information in the tabs about how the robber broke into the store. For all we know, the robber could have broken a window, kicked down the door, crawled through an air vent, or any of the above. Thus, there's no way to tell whether shatterproof windows would have made any difference. The answer is "no".

Question 10b: The store manager's email states that he or she missed the robber by 30 seconds. This means that the alarm company's phone call to the police (whom they called first) lasted at least 30 seconds, but there's no way to tell whether that call was longer or shorter than 45 seconds. The answer is "no".

Question 10c: According to the store manager, the total losses of the third robbery are 40% less than those of the second robbery. However, the store manager doesn't say that the losses are proportional in all categories. It's possible that decreases in losses for other goods compensated for an increases in losses for lenses. The answer is "no"

TABLE ANALYSIS

Table Analysis questions measure your ability to interpret and analyze information presented in a sortable table similar to a spreadsheet. You will see a table, a paragraph of text that describes it, and the same kinds of questions as you saw for Multi-Source Reasoning: traditional multiple choice, and three-part multiple–dichotomous choice questions (i.e., yes/no, true/false, etc.). Again, please note that, in the name of extra practice, we've included more than three statements for the multiple–dichotomous choice questions that appear in this book, whereas you will see exactly three parts to these questions on Test Day.

Directly above the table, you will see a Sort button that, when clicked, opens a drop-down menu of options that correspond to the column headers in the table. When you select a category from the drop-down menu, the entire chart will be sorted in order based on the category you select. If the information in that column is numerical, it will be sorted from lowest to highest. If the information in that column is text, it will be sorted in alphabetical order. In this book, a working Sort button is obviously not an option, so use the column headings to determine how the tables can be sorted. While working through the questions in this book, decide how you would sort the information before answering each question. To gain experience sorting tables in the test interface, use the questions in your Online Center.

The key to understanding the table is the paragraph of text that accompanies it. Read this first to get a general overview of the table's content. Then look at the table itself, paying special attention to the table headings and the drop-down menu.

Now let's look at some Table Analysis questions.

Total Fall Enrollment in Private Degree-Granting Institutions: 2008

Sort By [Select...   ▼]

| | Undergraduate | | | | | Postbaccalaureate | | |
| | 4-year | | 2-year | | | | | |
	Total	Not-for-profit	For-profit	Not-for-profit	For-profit	Total	Not-for-profit	For-profit
Alabama	58,558	23,229	34,000	0	1,329	7,343	4,128	3,215
Arizona	291,869	3,539	275,530	0	12,800	81,066	4,507	76,559
California	264,775	136,304	76,356	2,375	49,740	147,979	129,522	18,457
Colorado	69,460	18,375	40,733	165	10,187	20,507	13,586	6,921
District of Columbia	71,465	37,967	33,498	0	0	49,061	36,575	12,486
Florida	206,477	106,089	79,732	152	20,504	56,629	48,067	8,562
Georgia	76,356	47,701	23,670	1,057	3,928	23,757	17,940	5,817
Illinois	200,263	134,075	56,676	1,126	8,386	98,568	86,235	12,333
Indiana	88,896	68,677	13,020	495	6,704	16,110	15,652	458
Iowa	113,385	45,397	67,601	151	236	16,487	10,919	5,568
Massachusetts	173,897	166,873	2,800	1,737	2,487	97,339	97,203	136
Michigan	101,252	93,562	4,649	0	3,041	23,507	22,870	637
Minnesota	78,855	50,793	25,723	106	2,233	75,567	21,232	54,335
Missouri	117,735	95,299	12,510	2,275	7,651	49,937	49,298	639
New York	390,435	341,205	24,241	6,575	18,414	168,531	166,449	2,082
North Carolina	75,228	68,524	4,635	572	1,497	18,773	18,039	734
Ohio	146,395	107,277	7,044	1,272	30,802	31,669	30,621	1,048
Pennsylvania	251,369	195,359	17,783	7,492	30,735	83,943	83,372	571
Tennessee	75,283	54,023	8,373	278	12,609	18,187	17,097	1,090
Texas	127,359	92,495	12,935	867	21,062	36,657	33,996	2,661
Virginia	90,439	59,959	24,416	0	6,064	27,236	24,789	2,447

The table above gives the 2008 enrollment in private degree-granting institutions for the 20 states with the highest total enrollment, as well as for the District of Columbia. These statistics do not include state-funded and federally funded public institutions. The data include both for-profit and not-for-profit institutions; enrollment for both of these categories is provided in addition to the total enrollment.

11. Consider the following statements about enrollment in the 21 states (including the District of Columbia) shown in the table. For each statement, indicate whether the statement is *True* or *False*, based on the information provided in the table.

True	False	
○	○	The state with the largest number of students enrolled in for-profit four-year undergraduate programs has the smallest number of students enrolled in not-for-profit four-year undergraduate programs.
○	○	Combined, the two states with the lowest nonzero enrollment in for-profit two-year undergraduate programs have more students enrolled in not-for-profit than in for-profit programs.
○	○	The state with the median number of students enrolled in not-for-profit four-year undergraduate programs also has the median number of students enrolled in not-for-profit two-year undergraduate programs.
○	○	More than half of the students enrolled in degree-granting programs in Minnesota attend for-profit schools.

12. The state with the median number of postbaccalaureate enrollments has approximately how many more students enrolled in not-for-profit postbaccalaureate programs than in for-profit ones?

- ○ 24,000
- ○ 29,500
- ○ 31,500
- ○ 34,000
- ○ 45,000

Get the Gist of the Table

As with Graphics Interpretation questions, your first step should be to read the text accompanying the table. Here, the text explains that the table shows the private school enrollment numbers for various states, as well as for the District of Columbia, in 2008. It also tells you that the table distinguishes between for-profit and not-for-profit institutions.

Next, look at the table itself and read the column headings. The private institutions are split into two main categories, undergraduate and postbaccalaureate, which are further broken down into for-profit and not-for-profit schools. The undergraduate schools are also divided into two- and four-year programs. Total enrollment numbers for undergraduate and postbaccalaureate programs are also provided. This is a lot of information, and you will need to pay attention to how it is organized in order to answer the questions.

Answer the Questions

Question 11a: Many Table Analysis questions ask you to compare pieces of information. Take each question one piece at a time. For this question, you first need to find the state with the largest enrollment in for-profit four-year undergraduate schools. Look at your table and find the column that contains that information. Here, it's easy to see that Arizona has the highest enrollment, with 275,530 students. If you weren't able to see that at a glance, you could sort the table by the for-profit four-year undergraduate column. Now that you have the first piece of information, it's time to find the second. You now know that you're looking for information about Arizona. Sort the table by the not-for-profit four-year undergraduate column, and you'll see that Arizona is by far the lowest, at 3,539 students. Arizona, the state with the largest for-profit four-year undergraduate enrollment, does in fact have the smallest not-for-profit four-year undergraduate enrollment, so the answer is "True."

Question 11b: Notice the keyword "combined" in the question. This means that you will find more than one number and add them together. You are looking for the two states with the lowest nonzero enrollment in for-profit two-year undergraduate colleges. First, sort the table by for-profit two-year undergraduate colleges:

Sort By [Undergraduate 2-year For-profit | ▼]

| | Undergraduate | | | | | Postbaccalaureate | | |
| | | 4-year | | 2-year | | | | |
	Total	Not-for-profit	For-profit	Not-for-profit	For-profit	Total	Not-for-profit	For-profit
District of Columbia	71,465	37,967	33,498	0	0	49,061	36,575	12,486
Iowa	113,385	45,397	67,601	151	236	16,487	10,919	5,568
Alabama	58,558	23,229	34,000	0	1,329	7,343	4,128	3,215
North Carolina	75,228	68,524	4,635	572	1,497	18,773	18,039	734
Minnesota	78,855	50,793	25,723	106	2,233	75,567	21,232	54,335
Massachusetts	173,897	166,873	2,800	1,737	2,487	97,339	97,203	136
Michigan	101,252	93,562	4,649	0	3,041	23,507	22,870	637
Georgia	76,356	47,701	23,670	1,057	3,928	23,757	17,940	5,817
Virginia	90,439	59,959	24,416	0	6,064	27,236	24,789	2,447
Indiana	88,896	68,677	13,020	495	6,704	16,110	15,652	458
Missouri	117,735	95,299	12,510	2,275	7,651	49,937	49,298	639
Illinois	200,263	134,075	56,676	1,126	8,386	98,568	86,235	12,333
Colorado	69,460	18,375	40,733	165	10,187	20,507	13,586	6,921
Tennessee	75,283	54,023	8,373	278	12,609	18,187	17,097	1,090
Arizona	291,869	3,539	275,530	0	12,800	81,066	4,507	76,559
New York	390,435	341,205	24,241	6,575	18,414	168,531	166,449	2,082
Florida	206,477	106,089	79,732	152	20,504	56,629	48,067	8,562
Texas	127,359	92,495	12,935	867	21,062	36,657	33,996	2,661
Pennsylvania	251,369	195,359	17,783	7,492	30,735	83,943	83,372	571
Ohio	146,395	107,277	7,044	1,272	30,802	31,669	30,621	1,048
California	264,775	136,304	76,356	2,375	49,740	147,979	129,522	18,457

The two lowest nonzero enrollment states are Iowa and Alabama. Now that you've identified the two relevant states, determine what the question is asking: Do these states have more students enrolled in not-for-profit than in for-profit programs? In the table, each state has three categories of for-profit and three categories of not-for-profit schools. You will need to combine these somehow.

With the onscreen calculator, it may seem tempting to plug everything in and get an exact value. But the calculation process uses up precious time, and it is easy to introduce errors when you enter so many numbers under time pressure. The testmakers know this, so they design problems that are best solved strategically. In this case, you can accurately estimate the answer just by looking at the four-year undergraduate institutions.

In Iowa, the for-profit enrollment exceeds the not-for-profit enrollment by about 22,000 students. In Alabama, the difference is about 11,000, leading to a combined difference of about 33,000 in favor of the for-profit side. The two-year undergraduate institutions also have more for-profit students, so the trend continues. On the postbaccalaureate side, there are more enrollments in not-for-profit schools, but given how small the numbers are, there is no way they will balance out the 33,000-student difference you already calculated. Through strategic estimation, you can determine which category has more students in much less time than it would take to calculate precisely.

If you really want to calculate—perhaps you're not confident, or maybe you have some extra time from answering earlier questions efficiently—you could do so. First, calculate the not-for-profit enrollments in each state. Use your onscreen calculator:

Iowa:	$45{,}397 + 151 + 10{,}919 = 56{,}467$
Alabama:	$23{,}229 + 0 + 4{,}128 = 27{,}357$

Make sure you note these values in your scratchwork, because if you forget one of them, you're in trouble! Once you've finished the math, take the numbers from your notes and add the two totals together:

Combined:	$56{,}467 + 27{,}357 = 83{,}824$ students

Next, calculate the for-profit enrollments:

Iowa:	$67{,}601 + 236 + 5{,}568 = 73{,}405$
Alabama:	$34{,}000 + 1{,}329 + 3{,}215 = 38{,}544$
Combined:	$73{,}405 + 38{,}544 = 111{,}949$ students

Whichever way you solve, it's clear that there are more students enrolled in for-profit institutions than in not-for-profit institutions, making the answer to this question "False."

Question 11c: Here, you are asked again to compare two pieces of information. By now, you should be zeroing in on the keywords in the statement that will tell you how to sort the table. In this case, you are looking for the "not-for-profit four-year undergraduate" column and the "not-for-profit two-year undergraduate" column. Also notice the keyword "median," which appears twice. You need to sort two columns and compare the median numbers. The median number of each set will appear exactly in the middle of the set when all the terms are placed in ascending or descending order. You won't be able to eyeball the median number, so get ready to use the Sort function. First, sort by not-for-profit four-year undergraduate institutions:

Sort By [Undergraduate 4-year Not-for-profit | ▼]

		Undergraduate				Postbaccalaureate		
		4-year		2-year				
	Total	Not-for-profit	For-profit	Not-for-profit	For-profit	Total	Not-for-profit	For-profit
Arizona	291,869	3,539	275,530	0	12,800	81,066	4,507	76,559
Colorado	69,460	18,375	40,733	165	10,187	20,507	13,586	6,921
Alabama	58,558	23,229	34,000	0	1,329	7,343	4,128	3,215
District of Columbia	71,465	37,967	33,498	0	0	49,061	36,575	12,486
Iowa	113,385	45,397	67,601	151	236	16,487	10,919	5,568
Georgia	76,356	47,701	23,670	1,057	3,928	23,757	17,940	5,817
Minnesota	78,855	50,793	25,723	106	2,233	75,567	21,232	54,335
Tennessee	75,283	54,023	8,373	278	12,609	18,187	17,097	1,090
Virginia	90,439	59,959	24,416	0	6,064	27,236	24,789	2,447
North Carolina	75,228	68,524	4,635	572	1,497	18,773	18,039	734
Indiana	88,896	68,677	13,020	495	6,704	16,110	15,652	458
Texas	127,359	92,495	12,935	867	21,062	36,657	33,996	2,661
Michigan	101,252	93,562	4,649	0	3,041	23,507	22,870	637
Missouri	117,735	95,299	12,510	2,275	7,651	49,937	49,298	639
Florida	206,477	106,089	79,732	152	20,504	56,629	48,067	8,562
Ohio	146,395	107,277	7,044	1,272	30,802	31,669	30,621	1,048
Illinois	200,263	134,075	56,676	1,126	8,386	98,568	86,235	12,333
California	264,775	136,304	76,356	2,375	49,740	147,979	129,522	18,457
Massachusetts	173,897	166,873	2,800	1,737	2,487	97,339	97,203	136
Pennsylvania	251,369	195,359	17,783	7,492	30,735	83,943	83,372	571
New York	390,435	341,205	24,241	6,575	18,414	168,531	166,449	2,082

There are 21 states in this table, so you will be looking for the 11th state. To calculate which line you're looking for in a table with an odd number of lines, you can always use the following formula: Median = $\frac{Total-1}{2}$ + 1.

In this example, $\frac{21-1}{2}$ + 1 = 10 + 1 = 11. According to the sorted chart, the 11th state is Indiana. Once you know to focus on Indiana, sort the table by not-for-profit two-year undergraduate institutions:

Sort By [Undergraduate 2-year Not-for-profit ▾]

		Undergraduate				Postbaccalaureate		
		4-year		**2-year**				
	Total	Not-for-profit	For-profit	Not-for-profit	For-profit	Total	Not-for-profit	For-profit
Arizona	291,869	3,539	275,530	0	12,800	81,066	4,507	76,559
Michigan	101,252	93,562	4,649	0	3,041	23,507	22,870	637
Virginia	90,439	59,959	24,416	0	6,064	27,236	24,789	2,447
District of Columbia	71,465	37,967	33,498	0	0	49,061	36,575	12,486
Alabama	58,558	23,229	34,000	0	1,329	7,343	4,128	3,215
Minnesota	78,855	50,793	25,723	106	2,233	75,567	21,232	54,335
Iowa	113,385	45,397	67,601	151	236	16,487	10,919	5,568
Florida	206,477	106,089	79,732	152	20,504	56,629	48,067	8,562
Colorado	69,460	18,375	40,733	165	10,187	20,507	13,586	6,921
Tennessee	75,283	54,023	8,373	278	12,609	18,187	17,097	1,090
Indiana	88,896	68,677	13,020	495	6,704	16,110	15,652	458
North Carolina	75,228	68,524	4,635	572	1,497	18,773	18,039	734
Texas	127,359	92,495	12,935	867	21,062	36,657	33,996	2,661
Georgia	76,356	47,701	23,670	1,057	3,928	23,757	17,940	5,817
Illinois	200,263	134,075	56,676	1,126	8,386	98,568	86,235	12,333
Ohio	146,395	107,277	7,044	1,272	30,802	31,669	30,621	1,048
Massachusetts	173,897	166,873	2,800	1,737	2,487	97,339	97,203	136
Missouri	117,735	95,299	12,510	2,275	7,651	49,937	49,298	639
California	264,775	136,304	76,356	2,375	49,740	147,979	129,522	18,457
New York	390,435	341,205	24,241	6,575	18,414	168,531	166,449	2,082
Pennsylvania	251,369	195,359	17,783	7,492	30,735	83,943	83,372	571

Again, Indiana is the median (the 11th state), so the answer to this question is "True."

Question 11d: For this question, you'll be looking for information about Minnesota. Specifically, you'll need to find the number of students in that state who attend for-profit schools and then determine whether that number is more than half of Minnesota's total enrollment.

Again, approach strategically here—rather than add all the numbers, do some comparisons. In the four-year undergraduate programs, there are approximately 25,000 more students in not-for-profit schools. Look next at the two-year undergraduate enrollments. These numbers are probably too low to significantly affect the total, so turn your attention to the postbaccalaureate column: Here there are approximately 33,000 more students enrolled in for-profit schools. Because 33,000 is significantly higher than 25,000, you know that there are more students enrolled in the for-profit schools, making the answer to this question "True."

Of course, if you have time to check your work, straight math works here, as well:

For-profit: 25,723 + 2,233 + 54,335 = 82,291

Not-for-profit: 50,793 + 106 + 21,232 = 72,131

More than half the enrollments in Minnesota are in for-profit institutions, confirming our answer of "True."

Question 12: Here, you first need to find the state with the median number of postbaccalaureate enrollments. Begin by sorting the "Total" column in this category:

Sort By [Postbaccalaureate Total | ▾]

| | Undergraduate | | | | | Postbaccalaureate | | |
| | 4-year | | 2-year | | | | | |
	Total	Not-for-profit	For-profit	Not-for-profit	For-profit	Total	Not-for-profit	For-profit
Alabama	58,558	23,229	34,000	0	1,329	7,343	4,128	3,215
Indiana	88,896	68,677	13,020	495	6,704	16,110	15,652	458
Iowa	113,385	45,397	67,601	151	236	16,487	10,919	5,568
Tennessee	75,283	54,023	8,373	278	12,609	18,187	17,097	1,090
North Carolina	75,228	68,524	4,635	572	1,497	18,773	18,039	734
Colorado	69,460	18,375	40,733	165	10,187	20,507	13,586	6,921
Michigan	101,252	93,562	4,649	0	3,041	23,507	22,870	637
Georgia	76,356	47,701	23,670	1,057	3,928	23,757	17,940	5,817
Virginia	90,439	59,959	24,416	0	6,064	27,236	24,789	2,447
Ohio	146,395	107,277	7,044	1,272	30,802	31,669	30,621	1,048
Texas	127,359	92,495	12,935	867	21,062	36,657	33,996	2,661
District of Columbia	71,465	37,967	33,498	0	0	49,061	36,575	12,486
Missouri	117,735	95,299	12,510	2,275	7,651	49,937	49,298	639
Florida	206,477	106,089	79,732	152	20,504	56,629	48,067	8,562
Minnesota	78,855	50,793	25,723	106	2,233	75,567	21,232	54,335
Arizona	291,869	3,539	275,530	0	12,800	81,066	4,507	76,559
Pennsylvania	251,369	195,359	17,783	7,492	30,735	83,943	83,372	571
Massachusetts	173,897	166,873	2,800	1,737	2,487	97,339	97,203	136
Illinois	200,263	134,075	56,676	1,126	8,386	98,568	86,235	12,333
California	264,775	136,304	76,356	2,375	49,740	147,979	129,522	18,457
New York	390,435	341,205	24,241	6,575	18,414	168,531	166,449	2,082

The median state here is Texas. The question asks you to find the difference in enrollments between for-profit and not-for-profit postbaccalaureate institutions in Texas. Additionally, the question is asking for an approximate value, so you can round when calculating the answer. Look at the not-for-profit and for-profit columns in the postbaccalaureate category. Texas has approximately 34,000 students enrolled in not-for-profit postbaccalaureate programs and 2,500 enrolled in for-profit postbaccalaureate programs. That is an approximate difference of 31,500 students. The correct answer is **(C)**.

Remember, for success in Table Analysis, you need to understand what information the table contains and how it is organized before attacking the questions. Pay close attention to the column headings and use the Sort function whenever possible, especially when finding the median. Apply this strategic approach to the next set of Table Analysis questions.

Household Size: Occupied Housing Units by State, 2010 Census

Sort By [Select... | ▼]

	1-person households	2-person households	3-person households	4-person households	5-person households	6-person households	7-or-more-person households	Total households
Connecticut	373,648	443,095	226,658	197,116	84,916	29,348	16,306	1,371,087
Maine	159,533	213,695	84,340	64,010	23,840	7,854	3,947	557,219
Massachusetts	732,263	813,166	417,216	353,676	150,842	51,409	28,503	2,547,075
New Hampshire	133,057	188,923	85,046	70,835	27,365	9,286	4,461	518,973
Vermont	72,233	96,889	39,695	31,210	11,107	3,480	1,828	256,442

The above data are drawn from 2010 census data for New England (excluding Rhode Island, whose data is not available). The table provides the total number of households in each state and the distribution of households of various sizes within each state.

13. Based on the information in the table above, the population of Vermont is approximately

   O   194,000
   O   256,000
   O   440,000
   O   510,000
   O   600,000

14. Consider the following statements about these states. For each statement, evaluate whether that statement is *True* or *False*, according to the information in the table.

True   False

O   O   New Hampshire has the largest percent difference between the number of two-person households and the number of three-person households.

O   O   The median household size of all households in the five states combined is two people.

O   O   Of the seven categories of household size, Maine has the median number of households in exactly three.

O   O   In each of the seven categories of household size, Massachusetts has more households than the next highest two states combined.

Get the Gist of the Table

This table has fewer rows, but don't assume that means you're in for an easy time—the questions are likely to compensate for the graph's simplicity. They may require abstract reasoning, challenging math, or both. Begin as always by reading the paragraph of text that accompanies the table. It tells you that the table provides data about the number of households and the size of those households in several New England states.

Now look at the table itself. Note the column headings, which are broken down into households of seven different sizes, plus the total number of households, for each of the five states. Take note of the outliers in the data sets; a quick glance at the "Total" column shows you that Massachusetts has an overwhelmingly large number of households compared to the other states.

Answer the Questions

Question 13: This question asks for the approximate population of Vermont, but be careful: The answer is *not* 256,000, the approximate number in the "Total" column. The GMAT is very unlikely to ask you a question that can be answered with a number directly from the table. In this case, 256,000 is the approximate number of households, not the approximate number of people. To determine population, you must multiply the number of households by the number of people in each household. If you actually plug the exact numbers into the onscreen calculator, it will work out like this:

$$1(72,233) + 2(96,889) + 3(39,695) + 4(31,210) + 5(11,107) + 6(3,480) + 7(1,828) =$$

$$72,233 + 193,778 + 119,085 + 124,840 + 55,535 + 20,880 + 12,796 =$$

$$599,147$$

But the answer choices are far enough apart that you could estimate by rounding the numbers to the nearest thousand and get

$$1,000 \times [1(72) + 2(97) + 3(40) + 4(31) + 5(11) + 6(3) + 7(2)] = 597,000$$

in a fraction of the time. Either way, this answer is approximately 600,000, answer choice **(E)**.

Note that here you multiplied the number in the category "7-or-more" simply by 7; in reality, there are likely some households with more than seven members, but since the number of households in this "7-or-more" category is so small compared to those in the other categories, the difference isn't likely to matter much.

Question 14a: Here, you are presented with another series of true/false statements. The first one asks you to find the percent difference between two-person and three-person households in New Hampshire and compare that to the percent difference between two-person and three-person households in each other state. Recall that percent difference can be calculated by finding the difference between the two numbers and then dividing that difference by the original. For New Hampshire, that is $\frac{188,923 - 85,046}{188,923} = 0.5498$, or approximately 55 percent. In order for New Hampshire to be the largest, all other states must have a smaller percent difference.

You've got four more states, so think strategically. New Hampshire has more than a 50 percent difference, so if you can determine that a given state has less than a 50 percent difference, there is no need to do the actual calculation for that state. In this way, you know that you can eliminate Connecticut and Massachusetts, since you can look at them and see that there's slightly less than a 50 percent difference (the three-person-household number is slightly more than half of the two-person-household number in each state). To prove this statement false, you only need to find one state that has a difference larger than 55 percent. Let's start with Maine: $\frac{213,695 - 84,340}{213,695} = 0.6053$, or approximately 60 percent. Maine has a higher percentage difference than New Hampshire does, making this statement "False."

The GMAT is very unlikely to ask you a question for which the exact values matter down to the decimal place. If you were pressed for time, you could have rounded the values from the table to the nearest thousand and calculated the correct answer more quickly.

Question 14b: Now you're being asked to determine the median household size for all states combined. To do this, first sum up the total number of households for all five states (the far right column). Rounding to the nearest thousand, you get $1000 \times (1,371 + 557 + 2,547 + 519 + 256) = 5,250,000$. That means that if you were to place all these households in order according to their size, the median household would be roughly the $\frac{5,250,000}{2} = 2,625,000$th household. The household size of the 2,625,000th household is therefore the median household size.

To determine the size of that particular household, you need to total the number of households of each size until you hit the 2.6-million mark. Starting at either end of the table will eventually get you to the middle, but because there are bigger numbers of smaller households, you'll reach the threshold faster if you start on the left with the one-person households. Rounding to the thousands place gets you $1,000 \times (374 + 160 + 732 + 133 + 72) = 1,471,000$, so you're a little over halfway to the 2,625,000th house.

Careful observation saves even more work on the next step of finding this solution. Every state has more two-person households than one-person households. If you actually tallied up the exact number of one- and two-person households, you'd end up with a number well above 2,900,000 (twice the previous total). Therefore, the 2,625,000th household must be a two-person household, so this statement can be marked "True."

Question 14c: This is another question about medians. You need to find the median number for each of the seven categories and determine whether Maine has the median for exactly three of them. It's time to use the Sort function again.

One-person households:

Sort By [1-person households ‎ | ▾]

	1-person households	2-person households	3-person households	4-person households	5-person households	6-person households	7-or-more-person households	Total households
Vermont	72,233	96,889	39,695	31,210	11,107	3,480	1,828	256,442
New Hampshire	133,057	188,923	85,046	70,835	27,365	9,286	4,461	518,973
Maine	159,533	213,695	84,340	64,010	23,840	7,854	3,947	557,219
Connecticut	373,648	443,095	226,658	197,116	84,916	29,348	16,306	1,371,087
Massachusetts	732,263	813,166	417,216	353,676	150,842	51,409	28,503	2,547,075

Maine is the median for one-person households. That's one instance so far.

Two-person households:

Sort By [2-person households ▾]

	1-person households	2-person households	3-person households	4-person households	5-person households	6-person households	7-or-more-person households	Total households
Vermont	72,233	96,889	39,695	31,210	11,107	3,480	1,828	256,442
New Hampshire	133,057	188,923	85,046	70,835	27,365	9,286	4,461	518,973
Maine	159,533	213,695	84,340	64,010	23,840	7,854	3,947	557,219
Connecticut	373,648	443,095	226,658	197,116	84,916	29,348	16,306	1,371,087
Massachusetts	732,263	813,166	417,216	353,676	150,842	51,409	28,503	2,547,075

Maine is again the median; that makes two instances.

Three-person households:

Sort By [3-person households ▾]

	1-person households	2-person households	3-person households	4-person households	5-person households	6-person households	7-or-more-person households	Total households
Vermont	72,233	96,889	39,695	31,210	11,107	3,480	1,828	256,442
Maine	159,533	213,695	84,340	64,010	23,840	7,854	3,947	557,219
New Hampshire	133,057	188,923	85,046	70,835	27,365	9,286	4,461	518,973
Connecticut	373,648	443,095	226,658	197,116	84,916	29,348	16,306	1,371,087
Massachusetts	732,263	813,166	417,216	353,676	150,842	51,409	28,503	2,547,075

New Hampshire is the median; keep going.

Four-person households:

Sort By [4-person households ▾]

	1-person households	2-person households	3-person households	4-person households	5-person households	6-person households	7-or-more-person households	Total households
Vermont	72,233	96,889	39,695	31,210	11,107	3,480	1,828	256,442
Maine	159,533	213,695	84,340	64,010	23,840	7,854	3,947	557,219
New Hampshire	133,057	188,923	85,046	70,835	27,365	9,286	4,461	518,973
Connecticut	373,648	443,095	226,658	197,116	84,916	29,348	16,306	1,371,087
Massachusetts	732,263	813,166	417,216	353,676	150,842	51,409	28,503	2,547,075

New Hampshire again; not what you're looking for.

Five-person households:

Sort By [5-person households ▼]

	1-person households	2-person households	3-person households	4-person households	5-person households	6-person households	7-or-more-person households	Total households
Vermont	72,233	96,889	39,695	31,210	11,107	3,480	1,828	256,442
Maine	159,533	213,695	84,340	64,010	23,840	7,854	3,947	557,219
New Hampshire	133,057	188,923	85,046	70,835	27,365	9,286	4,461	518,973
Connecticut	373,648	443,095	226,658	197,116	84,916	29,348	16,306	1,371,087
Massachusetts	732,263	813,166	417,216	353,676	150,842	51,409	28,503	2,547,075

Still New Hampshire.

Six-person households:

Sort By [6-person households ▼]

	1-person households	2-person households	3-person households	4-person households	5-person households	6-person households	7-or-more-person households	Total households
Vermont	72,233	96,889	39,695	31,210	11,107	3,480	1,828	256,442
Maine	159,533	213,695	84,340	64,010	23,840	7,854	3,947	557,219
New Hampshire	133,057	188,923	85,046	70,835	27,365	9,286	4,461	518,973
Connecticut	373,648	443,095	226,658	197,116	84,916	29,348	16,306	1,371,087
Massachusetts	732,263	813,166	417,216	353,676	150,842	51,409	28,503	2,547,075

New Hampshire is the median frequently in this table. There's only one more chance to find a third instance of Maine being the median.

Seven-or-more-person households:

Sort By [7-or-more-person households ▼]

	1-person households	2-person households	3-person households	4-person households	5-person households	6-person households	7-or-more-person households	Total households
Vermont	72,233	96,889	39,695	31,210	11,107	3,480	1,828	256,442
Maine	159,533	213,695	84,340	64,010	23,840	7,854	3,947	557,219
New Hampshire	133,057	188,923	85,046	70,835	27,365	9,286	4,461	518,973
Connecticut	373,648	443,095	226,658	197,116	84,916	29,348	16,306	1,371,087
Massachusetts	732,263	813,166	417,216	353,676	150,842	51,409	28,503	2,547,075

No luck. The median is once again New Hampshire.

Maine is the median in exactly two of the seven categories, making the answer to this statement "False." Note that Maine is the median of the "Total" column, so there are actually three instances in the table in which Maine is the median. However, this question asks only for the seven categories, not all columns. Pay close attention to each column heading as you work through Table Analysis questions.

Question 14d: From your first glance at the table, you noticed that Massachusetts has by far the largest total number of households. So you can guess that Massachusetts might be the greatest in every subcategory. You can sort the tables as before to determine the rankings of the states in each column. For each one, you need to determine whether the number of households in Massachusetts is greater than the second-highest state plus the third-highest state. Perform the calculation for each household-size category and, where possible, use approximation instead of calculation:

One-person households: Is 732,263 > 373,648 + 159,533? Yes

Two-person households: Is 813,166 > 443,095 + 213,695? Yes

Three-person households: Is 417,216 > 226,658 + 85,046? Yes

Four-person households: Is 353,676 > 197,116 + 70,835? Yes

Five-person households: Is 150,842 > 84,916 + 27,365? Yes

Six-person households: Is 51,409 > 29,348 + 9,286? Yes

Seven-or-more-person households: Is 28,503 > 16,306 + 4,461? Yes

Since Massachusetts is higher than the next highest two states combined in each category, the answer here is "True." Note that you did not need to perform the exact calculations for any of those comparisons; once you identified the correct values to compare, you could estimate the sum of the second-highest state plus the third-highest state and see that in each case, it is less than the number of households in Massachusetts.

Sort By [Select... ▾]

Manager	Employee satisfaction rating (%)	Yearly sales (thousands of dollars)	Percent change in sales over previous year	Underground parking	Free shipping	Size of sales force
L. Jenkins	32.3	58.4	+5.3	no	no	5
P. Parsons	44.4	92.0	–7.8	yes	yes	11
A. Yangzou	65.7	105.2	–1.2	no	yes	10
D. Xin	55.7	85.1	+10.8	yes	yes	15
M. Stover	18.0	116.9	+15.5	no	yes	12
Z. Szymes	50.1	64.7	+4.8	no	no	8
T. Emerald	64.2	77.4	+0.3	yes	no	11
O. McDonough	75.5	79.6	+31.2	no	yes	8
K. Eriksson	46.9	58.9	–20.0	no	no	13
B. Stripley	48.7	101.7	–9.4	yes	yes	16

A small furniture store chain conducted performance reviews of its 10 branch managers. The managers' performance in several metrics over the last year has been compiled in the table. The table also lists some relevant features of each manager's branch.

15. For each of the following statements, select *True* if the statement can be verified to be true based on the given information. Otherwise, select *False*.

True   False

○   ○   A majority of the managers who oversaw an increase in sales over the previous year have an employee satisfaction rating higher than the median.

○   ○   There is a positive correlation between the size of a branch's sales force and that branch's change in year-over-year sales.

○   ○   The branch that had the highest sales in the previous year has underground parking.

16. The employee satisfaction rating of the manager of the branch that has the largest sales force but not underground parking is what percent of that of the manager of the branch with the smallest sales force and free shipping?

○   46.9%

○   62.1%

○   66.3%

○   75.5%

○   161.0%

Answers and Explanations:

Question 15a: Sort the data by employee satisfaction rating to quickly find the median; it's about 49%. Six managers saw positive sales growth. Of these, four have an employee rating above 49% —Emerald, Xin, Szymes, and McDonough—and two have an employee rating below 49%—Jenkins and Stover. Four out of six is a majority. The correct answer is "True".

Question 15b:. The second statement asserts that as the size of a branch's sales force increases, so too does its change in year-over-year sales. This is untrue: the three smallest branches saw positive growth, while the two biggest branches saw negative growth. There is in fact no correlation between sales force and change in sales, and the second statement is "False".

Question 15c: For the third statement, locate the branch that had the highest sales in the previous year. While Stover's branch had the highest sales this year, that's up 15.5% over the previous year, so Stover's sales in the previous year were under $100,000. The branch with the highest sales the previous year was Stripley's. $101,700 in sales this year with a 9.4 percent decrease over the previous year puts the previous year's sales at around $112,000. Stripley's branch does have underground parking, so this statement is "True".

Question 16: The branch with the largest sales force but not underground parking is Eriksson's. The branch with the smallest sales force and free shipping is McDonough's. Eriksson's employee satisfaction rating is 46.9%; McDonough's is 75.5%. The question asks for the answer as a percent: $\frac{0.469}{0.755} = 0.621 = 62.1\%$ which is choice (**B**).

TWO-PART ANALYSIS

Simply put, Two-Part Analysis questions have solutions in two parts. Two-Part Analysis questions consist of a few lines of text and instructions to select choices in a table based on the given information.

Solving an algebraic Two-Part Analysis usually necessitates setting up an algebraic equation with two variables. You'll want to begin by first reading the text and identifying the two unknowns, which may be provided or may need to be assigned variables. Then, you'll create one or more equations that relate the two values or variables. Once you've set up your equations, you can simplify them and look for a match (if the answer choices are algebraic equations or expressions) or start plugging in answer choices from the table until you find two corresponding values that work together.

Other Two-Part Analysis questions test your verbal skills. For example, after reading about a type of dwelling used by a certain species of animal, you might identify from among the choices a characteristic that must be true of all dwellings of that type and a characteristic that can never be true. Such questions draw on many of the same logical reasoning skills, such as drawing supported inferences, that you use on the Verbal section of the GMAT.

Two-Part Analysis can be hard to visualize, so let's take a look at some questions to see how this question type works.

17. At University X there are 146 students who are taking economics and 97 students who are taking history.

In the table below, pick two numbers that are consistent with the information that is given. In the first column, select the row that shows the number of students at University X who are taking at least one of economics and history, and in the second column, select the row that shows the number of students at University X who are taking both economics and history.

Taking at Least One of Economics and History	Taking Both Economics and History	Possible Answers
○	○	78
○	○	83
○	○	104
○	○	154
○	○	160
○	○	164

Get the Gist of the Information

The text in Two-Part Analysis questions is likely to be brief, so read it thoroughly before doing anything else. Here, you are given information about students at University X: the number of students who are taking economics, 146, and the number of students who are taking history, 97. The question asks you to find two numbers: first, the number of students taking at least one of these two subjects and, second, the number of students taking both.

Answer the Questions

Start by solving for the number of students taking at least one subject. The most efficient way to determine this number is to think critically. If you add together the numbers of students taking each subject, you get: 146 + 97 = 243. However, you know from the question stem and the column header that some students are taking both; if you rely on simple addition, you end up counting those students twice. Instead, set up an equation that relates the number of students in *at least* one subject, a, to the number of students in *both*, b.

Initial formula: # in at least one = # in Group 1 + # in Group 2 – # in both

Fill in what you know: $a = 146 + 97 - b$

Simplify: $a = 243 - b$

Before you start plugging in the answer choices to find two values that satisfy this equation, think critically: Which number will be bigger? In this case, it has to be a. With that in mind, move to the answer choices.

Because your equation is $a = 243 - b$, start by plugging b into the equation to determine if there is a corresponding value for a in the chart. b must be the smaller of the two numbers, so start testing at the top of the column with $b = 78$. Your equation is now $a = 243 - 78 = 165$. Do you see 165 in the possible answer choices? Nope. The closest they get is 164, so this is not the correct answer. Once you know that 78 is not a possible answer for b, move on to 83. Plugging it into the formula, you have $a = 243 - 83 = 160$. Do you see 160 among the possible answer choices? Yes. This question format always has a single solution, so you don't need to test any further answer choices. You have your answer: $a = 160$ and $b = 83$.

Before submitting your answers, make sure that you enter each of your choices in the correct column. It would be unfortunate to do all of the work correctly, get the correct answers, and then not receive credit simply because you selected the numbers in the opposite columns. Look back at your scratchwork and remember that a represents the number of students in at least one subject and b represents the number of students in both subjects. You can now be sure that 160 belongs in the first column and 83 belongs in the second column.

Take what you've learned about solving for unknowns by using the given information to set up an equation and apply it to the next Two-Part Analysis question.

18. When car P travels at a constant speed of x miles per hour for 84 minutes, and car Q travels at an average speed of y miles per hour for 168 minutes, car P travels 21 miles more than car Q.

    In the table below, select a value for x and a value for y that together are consistent with the given information. In the first column, select the row that corresponds to the value of x, and in the second column, select the row that corresponds to the value of y.

Value of *x*	Value of *y*	Possible Answers
○	○	8
○	○	14
○	○	17
○	○	29
○	○	42
○	○	49

Get the Gist of the Information

When reading the information, remember that your goal is to use it to create an equation that relates the two unknowns, x and y. The text gives information about two cars and states one definitive relationship between them: Car P travels 21 more miles than car Q. That is enough to indicate that your equation will focus on distance traveled. Go back to the beginning of the question stem to determine what you can about the distance the two cars travel.

Answer the Questions

Since the time traveled is given in terms of minutes, and speed in terms of miles per hour, you need to convert to get all of the times expressed in the same units.

$$\text{Car P time traveled} = 84 \text{ minutes} \times \left(\frac{1 \text{ hour}}{60 \text{ minutes}} \right) = 1.4 \text{ hours}$$

$$\text{Car Q time traveled} = 168 \text{ minutes} \times \left(\frac{1 \text{ hour}}{60 \text{ minutes}} \right) = 2.8 \text{ hours}$$

Since *distance = speed × time*, the distance each car traveled, in terms of x and y, is as follows:

$$\text{Car P distance traveled} = \left(\frac{x \text{ miles}}{\text{hour}} \right) \times 1.4 \text{ hours} = 1.4x \text{ miles}$$

$$\text{Car Q distance traveled} = \left(\frac{y \text{ miles}}{\text{hour}} \right) \times 2.8 \text{ hours} = 2.8y \text{ miles}$$

Once you have determined the distance traveled by each car, use the information that car P travels 21 miles farther to set up the following equation: $1.4x = 2.8y + 21$. Before moving to the answer choices, be sure to get one variable entirely by itself. In this case, you can divide both sides by 1.4 to get $x = 2y + 15$. You can now plug possible values for y into this equation to see what value for x would result.

To simplify the process of plugging in answer choices, first determine which value is going to be bigger. Since all of the answer choices are positive (as they would have to be, since they represent the speed a car travels), you know that x must be greater than y. This makes sense when you think about the logic of the problem, which specifies that car P travels a greater distance than car Q in a shorter amount of time.

Use the possible answer choices to start testing for y. As before, since you are starting with the smaller value, y, you will start plugging in numbers from the top of the list and work down. Start with $y = 8$. Substituting into the equation, you get $x = 2(8) + 15 = 31$. Since 31 is not an option in the table, you know that 8 is not the value of y. Next, try $y = 14$. In this case, the calculation would be $x = 2(14) + 15 = 43$. Again, 43 is not one of the available choices, so keep going. If $y = 17$, then $x = 2(17) + 15 = 49$. Since 49 is among the answer choices, it must be the value for x. Again, be very careful when filling in the answer choices. Your answers are $x = 49$ and $y = 17$.

Now that you are familiar with the basic format and structure of Two-Part Analysis questions, try your hand at the following question, which focuses on your reasoning skills rather than on math.

19. A publisher has traditionally printed 10 abridged editions of Victorian or Edwardian writing each spring. In order to cut production costs, the publisher has decided to print only five of these books this spring and to offer the remaining five as e-books. The publisher wishes to print at least four abridged Victorian books. Moreover, the publisher has decided to include no single author more than twice in total and to offer at least three e-books that are detective fiction. Finally, in keeping with the strong British influence on Victorian and Edwardian literature in English-speaking countries everywhere, the publisher wants at least four e-books to be by British authors.

Four printed books and four e-books have already been chosen for publication:

Printed:

Dickens, *David Copperfield* (British Victorian autobiographical novel)

Thoreau, *Walden* (American Victorian nature writing)

Doyle, *The Hound of the Baskervilles* (British Edwardian detective fiction)

Collins, *The Woman in White* (British Victorian epistolary novel)

E-Books:

Doyle, *The Valley of Fear* (British Edwardian detective fiction)

Stoker, *Dracula* (British Victorian gothic novel)

Allen, *The Great Taboo* (Canadian Victorian adventure novel)

Freeman, *The Red Thumb Mark* (British Edwardian detective fiction)

Select a title that could be published as either a printed book or an e-book. Then select a title that could not be published as a printed book or as an e-book. Make only two selections, one in each column.

Either Printed or E-Book	Neither Printed nor E-Book	Possible Titles
○	○	Cooper, *Rural Hours* (American Victorian nature writing)
○	○	Doyle, *A Study in Scarlet* (British Victorian detective fiction)
○	○	Collins, *The Moonstone* (British Victorian detective fiction)
○	○	Freeman, *The Eye of Osiris* (British Edwardian detective fiction)
○	○	Orczy, *The Old Man in the Corner* (British Edwardian detective fiction)
○	○	Wells, *The Invisible Man* (British Victorian science fiction)

Get the Gist of the Information

You are given two lists of four book titles each; the fifth in each list is missing. The question asks you to find a book that would work on either list and to find a book that would work for neither list, given the publisher's selection criteria for printed books and e-books. In other words, the question wants one answer that "could be true" for either list and one that "must be false" for both lists.

Answer the Questions

You don't need to set up an equation to solve this problem, but you do need to use the GMAT Core Competency of Attention to the Right Detail as you consider the rules governing each set of books. Start by thinking about how to complete the list of printed books, which has only a single rule: There must be at least four Victorian titles. The list of printed books currently has only three Victorian titles, so you need a fourth. On Test Day, you would write, "Printed: need Victorian," on your scratchwork.

The list of e-books is governed by two rules: There must be at least three works of detective fiction and at least four books by British authors. The list already includes two detective titles and three titles by British authors. It follows that you need a work of detective fiction by a British author to complete the list of e-books. Your scratchwork might read, "E-books: need British detective fiction."

A book permissible for either list must have all the qualities that the rules for both lists require. The title that "could be true" for either list, therefore, must be a work of British Victorian detective fiction. There are two such books available among the answer choices—those by Doyle and Collins. If you have paid Attention to the Right Details, however, you know that another rule from the question states that no author may be included more than twice on both lists combined. Doyle shows up on both lists already, so it follows that the Collins book, *The Moonstone*, is the only one that would satisfy the requirements of either list.

Moreover, since Doyle has already appeared twice, he cannot appear again. So among the answer choices, the Doyle book is the "must be false" answer, the one that may not appear on either list.

Pay close attention to the column headings when filling in the answer choices. The correct answer for the first column (either printed or e-book) is *The Moonstone* by Collins, and the correct answer for the second column (neither printed nor e-book) is Doyle's *A Study in Scarlet*.

20. In the coordinate plane, $f(x) = \frac{-x}{4} - 13$, $g(x) = x^2 + 14x - 26$, and $h(x)$ is perpendicular to $f(x)$ and passes through the point $(-2, -10)$. Functions $g(x)$ and $h(x)$ intersect at the point (r, s).

    In the table below, select a value for r and a value for s that together are consistent with the given information. Make only two selections, one in each column.

r	s	Possible Answers
○	○	−18
○	○	−12
○	○	−4
○	○	2
○	○	4
○	○	6

Answer and Explanation:

Start by finding the equation for h(x). You know that h(x) is perpendicular to f(x), which has a slope of $\frac{-1}{4}$. Since perpendicular lines have negative reciprocal slopes, the slope of h(x) must be 4. Thus, in slope-intercept form, h(x) = 4x + b. To find the y-intercept b, plug in the known point on h(x), (−2, −10): −10 = 4(−2) + b, −10 = −8 + b, and b = −2. Thus, h(x) = 4x − 2. To find (r, s), the point where g(x) and h(x) intersect, set the two functions equal to each other and factor to solve for x:

$$x^2 + 14x - 26 = 4x - 2$$

$$x^2 + 10x - 24 = 0$$

$$(x - 2)(x + 12) = 0$$

The possible values of x are therefore 2 and −12. Plug these x-values into h(x) to find the corresponding y-values:

$$4(-12) - 2 = -48 - 2 = -50$$

$$4(2) - 2 = 8 - 2 = 6$$

Thus, the two points of intersection for h(x) and g(x) are (−12, −50) and (2, 6). Although −12 is one of the values in the table, it is incorrect because −50 is not available. Therefore, **(r, s) = (2, 6)**. Always take a few extra seconds on Test Day to make sure you select the right value for the right column!

CONCLUSION

As you've seen from the examples in this chapter, Integrated Reasoning questions measure many of the same skills that you use for the Quantitative and Verbal sections of the test, such as paraphrasing information, finding keywords, determining whether an inference is supported, and using estimation instead of calculation. Regular review of the questions in this chapter, as well as those found in the quizzes and practice tests in your Online Center, will help you get the best score you possibly can on Integrated Reasoning.

PART SIX

Test Day and Business School

CHAPTER 15

Take Control of Test Day

- Mental Conditioning
- Stress Management
- The Week Before Test Day
- On Test Day
- Cancellation and Multiple Scores Policy

In the earlier parts of this book, we looked at the content covered on the various sections of the GMAT. We also discussed the test expertise you'll need to move through those sections. Now we turn to the often overlooked topic of test mentality: that is, how to get into peak mental condition for the GMAT.

MENTAL CONDITIONING

Your frame of mind has a lot to do with the level of success you achieve. Here's what's involved in developing your best mindset for the GMAT.

TEST AWARENESS

To do your best on the GMAT, you must always keep in mind that the test is unlike other tests that you've taken, in terms of both the content and the scoring system. If you took a test in high school or college and got a quarter of the questions wrong, you'd probably receive a pretty lousy grade. But due to the adaptive nature of the GMAT, missing only a quarter of the questions would give you a very high score. The test is designed to push test takers to their limits, so people rarely get every question right. In fact, you can get a handful of questions wrong and still score in the 99th percentile.

In other words, don't let what you consider to be a subpar performance on a handful of questions ruin your performance on the rest. A couple of missed questions won't, by themselves, spoil your score. But if you allow the frustration of those questions to unnerve you, you could end up compromising your performance on other questions or on the section as a whole. Missing a few points won't ruin your score, but losing your head will.

The test is designed to find your limits, so it should feel challenging. If you feel you've done poorly on a section, don't worry—you may have done just fine. Keep in mind that the questions that you are likely to struggle on most will be the hardest ones—the ones that hurt your score *least* if you miss them. To reach your highest potential score, you must remain calm and focused. Simply do your best on each question, and once a question or section is over, forget about it and move on.

Moreover, don't try to guess which questions are unscored (experimental questions). This kind of speculation has gotten countless test takers into trouble. They have a hunch that a certain question is one that doesn't count and then don't take it seriously. You cannot know which questions are experimental, so treat each one as if it counts. That way, you're covered no matter what. Likewise, don't worry if a question you get seems "too easy." This doesn't necessarily mean that you're doing poorly; it might be experimental. Or it might happen to align well with your individual strengths. Or perhaps you are just well prepared, have great strategies, and are beating the test! Do your best, get it right, and move on with confidence.

STAMINA

The GMAT is a grueling experience, and some test takers simply run out of gas when they reach the final questions. To avoid this, you must prepare by taking several full-length practice tests (not skipping over any sections) in the week or two before the test so that on Test Day, that four-hour test will seem like a breeze—or at least not a hurricane.

Your Online Center includes full-length CATs for just this purpose. If you finish the tests included with this book, a further option is to download the testmaker's GMATPrep™ software, which contains full-length exams and is available free from **mba.com**. One drawback to the software is that it does not include explanations, so you will want to rely on your Kaplan materials, which include thorough explanations, for the bulk of your study. However, the GMATPrep™ CATs should give you a good indication of your score range.

CONFIDENCE

Confidence in your ability leads to quick, sure answers and a sense of poise that translates into more points. Confidence builds on itself, but unfortunately, so does self-doubt. If you lack confidence, you end up reading sentences and answer choices two, three, or four times until you confuse yourself and get off track. This uncertainty ruins your timing, only perpetuating a downward spiral.

If you cultivate a positive GMAT mindset, however, you'll gear your practice toward taking control of the test. And when you have achieved that goal—armed with the techniques and strategies explained in this book—you'll be ready to face the GMAT with supreme confidence.

POSITIVE ATTITUDE

Those who approach the GMAT as an obstacle and who rail against the necessity of taking it usually don't fare as well as those who see the GMAT as an opportunity. Those who look forward to doing battle with the GMAT—or, at least, who enjoy the opportunity to distinguish themselves from the rest of the applicant pack—tend to score better than do those who resent or dread it.

Take our word for it: Developing a positive attitude is a proven test-taking technique. Here are a few steps you can take to make sure you develop the right GMAT attitude:

- Look at the GMAT as a challenge but try not to obsess over it; you certainly don't want to psych yourself out of the game.

- Remember that, yes, the GMAT is obviously important, but contrary to popular belief, this one test will not single-handedly determine the outcome of your life—or even of your business school admissions.

- Try to have fun with the test. Learning how to match your wits against those of the testmakers can be a very satisfying experience, and the critical thinking skills you'll acquire will benefit you in business school, as well as in your future career.

- Remember that you're more prepared than most people. You've trained with Kaplan. You have the tools you need, plus the ability to use those tools.

STRESS MANAGEMENT

The countdown has begun. Your date with the test is looming on the horizon. Anxiety is on the rise. You have butterflies in your stomach, and your thinking is getting cloudy. Maybe you think you won't be ready. Maybe you already know your stuff, but you're going into panic mode anyway. Don't worry! It's possible to tame that anxiety and stress—before *and* during the test.

Remember, some stress is normal and good. Anxiety is a motivation to study. The adrenaline that gets pumped into your bloodstream when you're stressed helps you stay alert and think more clearly. But if you feel that the tension is so great that it's preventing you from using your study time effectively, here are some things you can do to get it under control.

TAKE CONTROL

Lack of control is a prime cause of stress. Research shows that if you don't have a sense of control over what's happening in your life, you can easily end up feeling helpless and hopeless. Try to identify the sources of the stress you feel. Which ones can you do something about? Can you find ways to reduce the stress you're feeling from any of these sources?

MAKE A STUDY SCHEDULE

Often the mere realization that you're procrastinating on your GMAT study can cause stress. To help you gain control over your preparation process, make study appointments with yourself on your calendar—and then keep these appointments with yourself! Without setting aside time to study for the GMAT, it's easy to keep putting it off due to looming work deadlines, business school applications, or other commitments on your calendar. The hardest part of studying is getting started, so get started soon and start small. Even committing to working on five problems a day will produce a pleasant feeling of accomplishment and momentum, leading you to be able to make longer and longer commitments to your Test Day success.

FOCUS ON YOUR STRENGTHS

Make a list of areas of strength you have that will help you do well on the test. We all have strengths, and recognizing your own is like having reserves of solid gold in the bank. You'll be able to draw on your reserves as you need them, helping you solve difficult questions, maintain confidence, and keep test stress and anxiety at a distance. And every time you recognize a new area of strength, solve a challenging problem, or score well on a practice test, congratulate yourself—you'll only increase your reserves.

IMAGINE YOURSELF SUCCEEDING

Close your eyes and imagine yourself in a relaxing situation. Breathe easily and naturally. Now think of a real-life situation in which you did well on an assignment. Focus on this success. Now turn your thoughts to the GMAT and keep your thoughts and feelings in line with that successful experience. Don't make comparisons between them; just imagine yourself taking the upcoming test with the same feelings of confidence and relaxed control.

SET REALISTIC GOALS

Facing your problem areas gives you some distinct advantages. What do you want to accomplish in the study time remaining? Make a list of realistic goals. You can't help feeling more confident when you know you're actively improving your chances of earning a higher GMAT score.

EXERCISE REGULARLY

Whether it's jogging, biking, push-ups, or a pickup basketball game, physical exercise will stimulate your mind and body and improve your ability to think and concentrate. A surprising number of test takers fall out of the habit of regular exercise, ironically because they're spending so much time prepping for the exam. A little physical exertion will help you to keep your mind and body in sync and to sleep better at night.

EAT WELL

Good nutrition will help you focus and think clearly. Eat plenty of fruits and vegetables; low-fat protein such as fish, skinless poultry, beans, and legumes; and whole grains such as brown rice, whole-wheat bread, and pastas. Don't eat a lot of sugary and high-fat snacks or salty foods. Note that on Test Day, you can't bring food or drink into the testing room. But you can keep a healthy snack in your locker to recharge you between sections.

SLEEP WELL

Every GMAT problem requires careful critical thinking. Unfortunately, that's the first mental skill to go away when you are sleep deprived. Get a full night's sleep as often as you can during your preparation, especially as Test Day approaches.

KEEP BREATHING

Conscious attention to breathing is an excellent way to manage stress while you're taking the test. Most of the people who get into trouble during the GMAT take shallow breaths; they breathe using only their upper chests and shoulder muscles and may even hold their breath for long periods of time. Conversely, test takers who breathe deeply in a slow, relaxed manner are likely to be in better control during the session.

STRETCH

If you find yourself getting spaced out or burned out as you're studying or taking the test, stop for a brief moment and stretch. Even though you'll be pausing for a moment, it's a moment well spent. Stretching will help to refresh you and refocus your thoughts.

STRESS MANAGEMENT QUIZ

Don't be alarmed: This is not a GMAT quiz. It is important to your score, though. Imagine that there are two people with equal GMAT knowledge, skill, and practice. Why might one still outperform the other? The biggest difference will likely be that one manages stress and anxiety better than the other.

This quiz is a chance to reinforce and expand upon the ideas and advice you've read so far in this chapter. Have fun with it and think about how to apply the correct answers to your own life and study schedule.

1. What is Test Day stress?

   O   A feeling of anxiety felt only by those aiming for a top score

   O   Any factor, physical or psychological, that impedes my performance on the GMAT

   O   A consequence of poor preparation

   O   A constant fear of not getting into my first-choice school

   O   Something that only poor test takers experience

2. It is most helpful to my Test Day success when my friends and family

   O   push me to study more.

   O   tell me how much more I have to learn.

   O   compete with me over test scores.

   O   have positive attitudes about my ability to achieve my best score, and help me get my mind off the test whenever I am not studying.

   O   care little about my performance and prevent me from getting sufficient time to prep.

3. In the weeks leading up to the exam, how can I reduce stress?

   O   List my weaknesses and create a study schedule to overcome them, one topic at a time

   O   Get some exercise

   O   Limit self-deprecating humor and keep a positive attitude

   O   Get sufficient sleep

   O   All of the above

4. In the final days before my exam, I should worry about all of the topics that I still have trouble with or haven't hit, rather than congratulate myself on how far I've come.

   O   True
   O   False

5. The night before the exam, what can I do to reduce stress?

   O   Try to learn topics that I have not mastered yet
   O   Go to my local bar with my friends, drink a few pitchers of beer, and try to get my mind off the exam
   O   Briefly review the topics that I mastered but haven't looked at in a while, and get a good night's sleep
   O   Stay up all night, memorizing the grammar and math concepts
   O   Panic

6. On Test Day, what can I do to reduce stress?

   O   Make sure I know where the testing center is and allow plenty of time to get there early
   O   Eat a nutritious breakfast
   O   Dress in layers to be ready for any temperature in the testing room
   O   Expect a lot of paperwork before the test begins
   O   All of the above

7. During the exam, if I don't know how to answer a question and I begin to panic, I should

   O   keep rereading the question until I determine the correct approach, no matter how long it takes.

   O   bite my fingernails and moan.

   O   keep breathing, take a moment to get my bearings, and determine whether I should take a strategic guess or give the question another minute or two.

   O   remind myself that if I miss the question, I will not get into business school, I will fail in life, and I will be forced to live with my parents forever.

   O   choose an answer choice that I haven't chosen much so far in that section.

8. During the GMAT, I should avoid worrying about questions that I have already answered.

   O   True

   O   False

9. What should I do next to make sure that I am prepared to overcome the natural stress that comes with taking a standardized test?

   O   Find a good psychiatrist

   O   Take control of my preparation by following a study schedule and cultivating a positive attitude

   O   Forget about Test Day stress until Test Day, and then figure out how to deal with it

   O   Decide not to take the GMAT

   O   Nothing. This exercise has taught me all I need to know about Test Day stress management.

ANSWER KEY

1. B
2. D
3. E
4. False
5. C
6. E
7. C
8. True
9. B

THE WEEK BEFORE TEST DAY

Is it starting to feel like your whole life is a buildup to the GMAT? You've known about it for years, worried about it for months and have now spent at least a few weeks in solid preparation for it. As Test Day approaches, you may find your anxiety is on the rise. You shouldn't worry. After the preparation you've received from this book, you're in good shape for the test. To calm any jitters you may have, though, let's go over a few strategies for the couple of days before the test.

In the week or so leading up to Test Day, you should do the following:

- Visit the testing center. Sometimes seeing the actual room where your test will be administered and taking notice of little things—such as the kind of desk you'll be working on, whether the room is likely to be hot or cold, etc.—may help to calm your nerves. And if you've never been to the testing center, visiting beforehand is a good way to ensure that you don't get lost on Test Day. If you can go on the same day of the week and at the same time of day as your actual test, so much the better; you'll be able to scope out traffic patterns and parking. Remember, you must be on time—the computers at the testing centers are booked all day long.
- Practice working on test material, preferably a full-length test, at the same time of day that your test is scheduled for as if it were the real Test Day.
- Time yourself while practicing so you don't feel as though you are rushing on Test Day.
- Evaluate thoroughly where you stand. Use the time remaining before the test to shore up your weak points, rereading the appropriate sections of this book. But make sure not to neglect your strong areas; after all, those are where you'll rack up most of your points.

THE DAY BEFORE TEST DAY

This advice might seem counterintuitive, but try to avoid intensive studying the day before the test. There's little you can do to improve your score at this late date, and you may just wind up exhausting yourself and burning out. Our advice is to review a few key concepts, get together everything you'll need for Test Day (acceptable photo identification, the names of schools to which you'd like to send your GMAT scores, directions to the testing center, a healthy snack for the break), and then take the night off entirely. Go to see a movie, rent a video, or watch some TV. Try not to think too much about the test; just relax and store up some energy for the big day.

ON TEST DAY

Test Day should contain no surprises. Test takers who feel in control of the events leading up to the test take that confidence with them into the testing center.

Leave early for the testing center, giving yourself plenty of time. Read something to warm up your brain; you don't want the GMAT to be the first written material your brain tries to assimilate that day. Dress in layers for maximum comfort. That way, you'll be able to adjust to the testing room's temperature. In traveling to the testing center, leave yourself enough time for traffic or mass transit delays.

Be ready for a long day. Total testing time, remember, is three and a half hours. When you add the administrative paperwork before and after, and the two 8-minute breaks, you're looking at an experience of four hours or more.

You will feel most prepared and confident if you have an understanding of how the logistics of Test Day will play out. Taking the full-length practice CATs in your Online Center and those from **mba. com** will help you get the feel for the GMAT itself, but certain events are unique to the experience in the testing center. Here's what to expect:

At the testing center, you will...

- Check in.
- Place your belongings in a locker.
- Receive a noteboard and pen for your scratch work.
- Go to the assigned computer. (Note that you will be videotaped as you take the test. Don't be disturbed by any video cameras facing you; this is just a tool that enables the test administrators to maintain a fair testing environment.)
- Select your score recipients. The computer will ask you where to send your results. You may send your scores to up to five schools free of charge. You should take advantage of this free service, as waiting until later has no advantage. If you specify your score recipients after the test or choose more than five schools, you will have to pay $28 per school (as this book goes to press) to send results.
- Complete a brief tutorial on the computer interface. The computer will ask whether you want to take a brief tutorial. It's not tremendously informative, but you should take it and use the time to make sure your environment is set up correctly—that your monitor is adjusted so as not to glare, that your chair is the right height, that your mouse and keyboard work.
- Complete the Analytical Writing section, using the Kaplan Method for Analytical Writing.
- Complete the Integrated Reasoning section, using Kaplan's Integrated Reasoning strategies.
- Take an 8-minute break.
- Complete the Quantitative section, using the Kaplan Methods for Problem Solving and Data Sufficiency.
- Take an 8-minute break.
- Complete the Verbal section, using the Kaplan Methods for Critical Reasoning, Sentence Correction, and Reading Comprehension.
- Complete a brief optional survey.
- Choose whether to cancel your scores.
- See your unofficial Quantitative and Verbal scores.
- Check out.
- Remove your belongings from the locker and leave the testing facility.

Here are some strategic reminders to help guide your work on Test Day:

- Read each question stem carefully and reread it before making your final selection.
- Don't get bogged down in the middle of any section. You may find later questions more to your liking. So don't panic. Eliminate answer choices, guess, and move on.
- Don't fall behind early. Even if you get most of the first 10 questions right, you'll wind up rushing yourself into enough errors that you cancel out your early success. Keep a steady pace throughout the test and finish each section strong, avoiding the penalty for not completing all the questions.

- Don't bother trying to figure out which questions are unscored. It can't help you, and you might very well be wrong. Instead, just resolve to do your best on every question.
- Confidence is key. Accentuate the positives and don't dwell on the negatives. Your attitude and outlook are crucial to your performance on Test Day.
- During the exam, try not to speculate about how you're scoring. Imagine a baseball player who's focusing on the crowd's cheers and the sportswriters and his contract as he steps up to the plate: There's no surer way to strike out. Instead, focus on the question-by-question task of picking an answer choice. The correct answer is there. You don't have to come up with it; it's sitting right there in front of you!

What should you do if you...

- **Start to lose confidence?** If questions seem to be getting hard, don't lose confidence; since the GMAT is adaptive, it is practically guaranteed to feel like a struggle—for everyone! Trust in your preparation and in the skills and strategies you have practiced.
- **Start to lose concentration?** If you lose your concentration, pause, take a deep breath, exhale, and go back to the test. This will help you refocus and settle back in.
- **Take too long at the break?** If you take too long at the break, the test will continue without you. When the 8-minute countdown timer hits zero, the next section of the test—and its clock—will start.
- **Find the test environment too distracting?** If the test environment is too distracting, tell the proctor. If the proctor can't—or won't—do anything about it, mention the problem in the exit survey.

After Test Day, you should...

- Congratulate yourself for all the hard work you've put in. Make sure you celebrate afterward—and start thinking about all of the great times you'll be having at the business school of your choice!
- Plan your approach to business school applications, including references and essays.
- Go to **KaplanGMAT.com/businessadmissions/** to investigate options for admissions consulting programs through Kaplan's partner for business school admissions, mbaMission. Also, see the chapter of this book dealing with business school admissions for advice from mbaMission's founder and president, Jeremy Shinewald.
- Expect to wait approximately 20 days for your Official Score Report (which includes your Analytical Writing and Integrated Reasoning scores) to be posted online.

CANCELLATION AND MULTIPLE SCORES POLICY

Unlike many things in life, the GMAT allows you a second chance. If you finish the test feeling that you've not done as well as you can, you have the option to cancel your scores—before you see the scores, of course. Immediately after you complete the test—but before you view your scores—a message will appear, asking if you want to cancel your scores. You cannot cancel your scores after they are displayed or reported to you.

Canceling a test means that it won't be scored. It will just appear on your score report as a canceled test. No one will know how well or poorly you actually did—not even you.

If you cancel your scores...

- They cannot be reinstated.
- You will not receive a refund for the test.
- A score cancellation notice will be sent to you and the schools you selected as score recipients.
- The score cancellation will remain a part of your permanent record and will be reported on all future score reports.

If you do not cancel your scores ...

- You can choose to see and print a copy of your unofficial Quantitative, Verbal, and total scores.
- An official score report, including scores for the AWA and Integrated Reasoning sections, will be available online and sent to your designated schools 20 days after you take the test.

When deciding whether to cancel your score, a good rule of thumb is to make an honest assessment of whether you'll do better on the next test. Wishful thinking doesn't count; you need to have a valid reason to believe that the next time will be different. Remember, no test experience is going to be perfect, and the test is designed to find the limits of your ability. Two legitimate reasons to cancel your test are illness and personal circumstances that cause you to perform unusually poorly on that particular day. Also, if you feel that you didn't prepare sufficiently, then it may be advisable to cancel your score and approach your test preparation more seriously the next time.

But keep in mind that test takers historically underestimate their performance, especially immediately following the test. They tend to forget about all of the things that went right and focus on everything that went wrong. So unless your performance is terribly marred by unforeseen circumstances, don't cancel your test. Just remember, cancellations are permanent. Once you hit that button, you can't change your mind.

If you take the GMAT multiple times, your score report sent to business schools will contain all of your scores from the past five years. Most business schools consider only your highest GMAT score, but a few may average your scores. Check with individual schools for their policies on multiple scores.

CHAPTER 16

Business School Admissions Myths Destroyed (Before They Destroy You!)

By Jeremy Shinewald

Founder/President of mbaMission, Kaplan's Recommended Admissions Consulting Partner

ABOUT mbaMISSION

Your business school application is your ticket to a new and exciting phase of your life and career, so of course you want it to be the best it can be, and you might benefit from the advice of someone who is uniquely knowledgeable. But who? Someone with professional writing experience, perhaps? Someone with profound knowledge of the MBA application process? Maybe someone with an MBA who has been through the process? With mbaMission, you will work with a consultant who not only has all of these attributes and more, but who will also ensure that your business school application helps set you apart from the crowd. Our senior consultants are all published authors with elite MBA experience who will get to know you intimately and work one-on-one with you to discover, select, and articulate the unique stories that will force admissions committees to take notice. Your consultant will work with you on all aspects of your application, reducing your stress level and maximizing your chances of being admitted to the business school of your dreams.

Applicant blogs. Student tweets. Message board chatter. Competitive peers (some with agendas that run contrary to yours!). So many people try to influence you as you apply to business school, and these people frequently offer conflicting opinions and sources of information. In addition to managing your busy professional, community, and personal lives, you are suddenly attempting to process a seemingly infinite influx of application information. Welcome to the world of the MBA applicant! You'll need to find your way through an intensely competitive process whose rules are not clear and where questions sometimes seem unwelcome.

Given that the admissions process is not completely transparent—after all, decisions are still made behind closed doors—some armchair experts try to make sense of the process by simplifying it.

So, for example, a successful candidate may extrapolate from her own results and assume, "I had an alumni recommendation and I got in. So I'll tell my friend that she needs to have an alumni rec!" Similarly, an unsuccessful applicant might examine his results and conclude, "I submitted my application in Round 2, but my friend who got in submitted in Round 1. I am going to tell my colleagues that they'd better apply early if they want to be accepted!"

Can we really tell that much from the experiences of a single individual? After all, MBA candidates are not evaluated like data, their info run through a scanner that spits out a simple pass or fail determination. Rather, business school applicants are sophisticated human beings with interesting lives that cannot be measured quantitatively but can be understood subjectively. As candidates make snap judgments about the reasons behind their successful or unsuccessful applications and broadcast these simplifications to the world, and as these opinions are then retweeted and blogged about, opinions begin to propagate, and admissions myths start to develop. And once a myth develops, trying to change it—or to dissuade anxious business school applicants from believing it—is a real challenge. Yet these myths regularly cause candidates like you to inadvertently misdirect their energies and waste their time. So, here we present you with ten myths and their opposing realities to help ensure that you stay on the right path and apply your energies appropriately.

MYTH #1: THE ADMISSIONS COMMITTEE WANTS A SPECIFIC TYPE

Many MBA candidates believe that admissions committees have narrowed down their criteria for selecting applicants over the years and that each school has one distinct "type" that it seeks. So, in this world of stereotypes, Harvard Business School (HBS) is looking only for leaders, Kellogg is looking only for marketing students, Chicago Booth is looking only for finance students, and MIT Sloan is looking only for "eggheads." Of course, these stereotypes—like most stereotypes—are not accurate. Chicago Booth wants far more than one-dimensional finance students in its classes, and it provides its MBA students with training in far more than just finance (offering, to the surprise of some, an excellent marketing program). HBS is not a school just for "generals"; among the 950 students in each of its classes, HBS has a wide variety of personalities, including some excellent "foot soldiers." So, we strongly suggest that you eschew these stereotypes, because pandering to them can sink your applications.

For example, imagine that you have worked in operations at a manufacturing company. You have profound experience managing and motivating dozens of different types of people, at different levels, in both good and bad economic times. Even though your exposure to finance has been minimal, you erroneously determine that in order to get into New York University's Stern School of Business, you have to convince the school that you are a "finance guy." So in your application essays, you tell your best—but nonetheless weak—finance stories. What happens is that you are now competing in the Stern applicant pool with elite finance candidates whose stories are far more impressive. What if you had instead told your unique operations/management stories and stood out from the other applicants, rather than trying to compete in the school's most overrepresented pool?

We believe that defying stereotypes and truly being yourself is the best course of action. But if you are still not convinced, consider this nugget of advice offered on Stanford's admissions website:

> Because we want to discover who you are, resist the urge to "package" yourself in order
> to come across in a way you think Stanford wants. Such attempts simply blur our under-
> standing of who you are and what you can accomplish. We want to hear your genuine

voice throughout the essays that you write, and this is the time to think carefully about your values, your passions, your hopes and dreams.

Kind of makes sense, doesn't it?

MYTH #2: MY HIGH GMAT SCORE WILL GET ME IN

So you have taken the GMAT and exceeded even your highest expectations, scoring at the very top of the scale. Congratulations! But please, do not assume that earning a high score means you can pay less attention the other components of your application. Every year, applicants who have scored 750 or even higher are rejected from their target business schools—even when their GMAT score falls within the top 10 percent of the schools' range. And many of these candidates were rejected because of a fatal, but ultimately avoidable, mistake: They got overconfident and assumed their GMAT score alone would get them in.

"I joke sometimes that I relish nothing more than rejecting people that have a 780 on the GMAT," Jonathan Fuller, senior associate director of admissions at the University of Michigan's Ross School of Business, said in an online chat, "because they come with the 780 GMAT and think they're golden, and they don't have to worry about anything else on the application. Well, you do. There are all these other pieces of information that we ask for, and you have to make sure that you are strong across the board." Similarly, candidates need not worry that a lower score will sink their candidacy entirely. We would never lie to you and tell you that being accepted with a lower GMAT score will be easy, but every year we see a few particularly accomplished individuals with scores in the 500s get into top-ten programs. It can be done!

Business schools want to learn a lot more about you than your GMAT score alone can convey. MBA programs are interested in hearing about your ambitions, accomplishments, leadership skills, teamwork experience, perseverance, motivation, integrity, compassion ... and the list goes on. Fundamentally, admissions committees need to be able to determine whether you will be a vital and contributing member of their school's community, and your GMAT score, while important, is only one piece of that puzzle.

Whether you have a 780 or a 580, heed our advice and commit yourself wholeheartedly to all the elements of your application. No single data point will result in a decision to admit or reject!

MYTH #3: MY SUPERVISOR GRADUATED FROM HBS—HE KNOWS

We know of a now 70-year-old man who graduated from a virtually unknown Canadian undergraduate school in 1963 and who, with no work experience at all, applied to HBS, the Wharton School of the University of Pennsylvania, and the Stanford Graduate School of Business (GSB), gaining acceptances at all three (though the GSB deferred his entry for one year so he could earn a little more experience first). He ultimately studied at HBS and now runs a small grain-trading business. You could not meet a nicer man, and although he is certainly wise in many respects, one thing he knows nothing about is MBA admissions. "I attended so long ago, things must have changed since then," he says. "I did not have any work experience at all. I had studied four years of commerce, and that was it!"

Why are we telling you this? Many candidates each year tell us that their bosses, who applied to business school during far different times, have given them "sage" advice about applying and that they feel they should follow it—after all, what worked for their boss in 1964, 1974, 1984, 1994, or even 2004 must still be applicable today, right? Wrong.

For a long time, the MBA was actually not all that desirable a degree, so admissions were not very competitive. To give you an idea of the relative popularity, Duke University (Fuqua) did not even start its MBA program until 1970, but its law school was founded in 1868. Yale University was founded in 1701, but it did not have an MBA program until 1976. So, the MBA is a relatively new degree that has only recently (in the late 1990s) reached its current level of popularity and prestige.

What does all of this mean with regard to your boss's advice? Although your supervisor may have gotten into one of your target schools, he or she likely did so years ago and therefore may not have had to contend with the steep competition you now face. Your boss may also not know anything about what the admissions process is like today and could—however inadvertently—be leading you astray. If your supervisor starts any bit of well-intended advice with the phrase "when I applied," you should view this guidance with tremendous caution.

MYTH #4: IF I DID NOT GO TO AN IVY, I'M NOT GETTING IN

Have you ever heard of Ateneo de Manila University in the Philippines? What about Universidad Metropolitana in Venezuela? Do you know anyone at New College of Florida or Carleton College? Why do we ask? HBS posted profiles of 33 students in its Class of 2012, and you might be surprised to learn that not all of them got their undergraduate degrees at Harvard. In fact, only a few among this group did. You may say, "Yes, but the school selectively released information on these students." True, but the school also offers a full list of the 500 undergraduate institutions represented in its previous three classes of 900 to 950 students each and notes that 243 different institutions are represented in the Class of 2013 alone. Meanwhile, the Stanford admissions office states that 156 schools were represented among the 397 students in its Class of 2013. And the list goes on ...

Although Harvard graduates are certainly well represented in each HBS class, most business schools attract a high number of applicants from among their undergrad alumni. Still, being an alumnus or alumna of an MBA program's undergraduate institution is neither a prerequisite nor a hindrance. The admissions committees are more interested in your performance—academic, professional, volunteer, personal—than your pedigree. The committees are also interested in diversity. We don't feel we are going out on a limb by stating that Wharton does not want—and indeed cannot have—a class made up of 850 UPenn undergrads; the school wants the best potential business leaders and thus must select from a much deeper pool.

So, if you graduated from a school that has no international profile or even a limited national profile, you should not worry. Your performance at your academic institution is far more important than your institution's name. Furthermore, you represent much more than your undergraduate institution. You should not be an apologist for your school but an advocate of your skills.

MYTH #5: IF I HAVE A GAP IN MY HISTORY, I'M NOT GETTING IN

The perfect MBA applicant simply does not exist. However, the perception of the perfect applicant certainly does: an individual who is on a very narrow course, scaling greater and greater academic, personal, community, and professional peaks (all of which are related to each other) unabated until he or she finally applies to business school. As a result, those who have taken some time off at any point in their professional lives tend to perceive themselves as being at a disadvantage in the business school application process. They worry that admissions committees will see these gaps and dismiss them outright. After all, don't the schools have many more determined individuals in the applicant pool whom they can choose to admit instead?

It's true that time off can potentially be detrimental to your application. If you spent a year on your couch watching reality TV, you are likely going to have difficulty presenting this in a positive way to the admissions committee. However, if you have a strong professional history overall and once spent a month between jobs sitting on your couch watching reality TV, your record should still speak favorably for itself. But even if you have taken an extended leave, as long as you were productive during that time and grew personally, you should be just fine. In fact, if you had some kind of an adventure during your break, this may even add to your story and help you differentiate yourself.

For example, if you spent six months or a year travelling before you started your professional career, you are certainly still eligible for a spot in a top MBA program. Similarly, if you took a personal leave to care for a family member in need, to do charity work, or even to pursue a personal passion (an art form, for example), an admissions officer should still see your merits as long as you can show purpose and reveal a broad record of competency.

Admissions officers are actual human beings. They understand that applicants are not robots and that they have interests, passions, and personal lives outside the workplace. If you have generally made good use of your time, they will not condemn you. In fact, they just might envy you.

MYTH #6: IF I HAVE NO MANAGERIAL EXPERIENCE, I'M NOT GETTING IN

It might seem ironic that having formal management experience is not a prerequisite for getting into a top MBA program. But keep in mind that an MBA education is meant for those who aspire to become managers—not only those who already *are* managers. So if you are fretting that you have not had any subordinates to date and feel that having supervised a staff is a requirement for getting into a top business school, you are actually adhering to a myth and can stop worrying. Instead, focus on the ways in which you have excelled in your positions thus far and made the most of the leadership opportunities that have presented themselves.

For example, consider the many investment banking analysts who apply to MBA programs each year. While analysts are at the bottom of most banks' organizational charts and therefore do not have staffs to manage, they still have demanding jobs and have to perform at a high level each day to succeed. Most analysts can therefore talk about thriving in an ultracompetitive environment and can reveal their professional excellence via their resumes, essays, and recommendations. And even if most analysts do not have a staff of their own, second-year analysts still have ample opportunity to train and mentor first-year analysts, and third-year analysts can mentor and train first- and second-year analysts. So, even without direct subordinates, investment banking analysts can demonstrate strong leadership and de facto management skills.

Of course, there are ways other than through conventional professional management to show evidence of your leadership traits. If you have not yet had the opportunity in your professional life to demonstrate that you have the interpersonal skills necessary to lead others, you can look to your community activities and even personal leadership experiences to positively illustrate your potential in this capacity. The bottom line is that business schools are not looking exclusively for managers but for individuals who display true promise for their future careers. After all, an MBA program is designed to teach you management!

MYTH #7: I MUST SUBMIT IN ROUND 1

Many MBA admissions officers will tell candidates that if they can complete their applications in time to submit them in Round 1, then they should do so. Most programs will also tell applicants that they should try to avoid Round 3, because most of the places in the class will have been filled by then. So, what does that say about Round 2?

We have noticed a strange trend lately: Candidates have taken to calling mbaMission the day after a school's Round 1 application deadline and asking whether submitting an application in Round 2 is worth the effort or whether the opportunity has passed at that point. Unfortunately, when one is being compared against a group of unknown competitors, being concerned about every perceived difference or deficiency is only natural. Some candidates grow concerned if they are a year older than the average at their target school, while others fret if they are a year younger. Many applicants worry if their GMAT score is ten points below a school's average. And of course, some worry if they submit their application in Round 2. However, the overall strength of your candidacy, which is a measure of many factors, is far more important than where you fit in relation to any single statistic—which includes whether you apply in Round 1 or 2.

So, we too would encourage candidates to apply early, if they are ready and able to do so, but we do not believe they should give up on their MBA dreams for a year if applying in Round 1 is just not practical. You may be surprised to discover that while admissions committees encourage early applications, they also concede that the difference in selectivity between the first and the second rounds is very small. To back up this statement, we offer a small selection of quotes from mbaMission's exclusive interviews with admissions officers:

> People ask, generally, is it better to apply in the first round or the second round or third round? We definitely advise people to avoid the third round if possible, because space can become an issue by the time the third round rolls around. But we do view the first two rounds as roughly equivalent.
>
> — Bruce DelMonico, admissions director, Yale School of Management

> [We] get about a third of our applications in Round 1, about 55 percent in Round 2, and the remainder in Round 3. ... We encourage people to submit their application when they feel that they offer their best possible applications. ... So, if you can get everything lined up and completed and you feel really good about it ... then I would encourage you to apply in Round 1. But if it takes you a bit longer, and you want to take the time to look at your application again and maybe have somebody else look at it, then Round 2 is fine, too.
>
> — Soojin Kwon Koh, admissions director, Michigan–Ross

> We look at statistics over the years—how many applications we got, how many we admitted, and how many we yielded—and we try to even it out so we're not being too generous in one round at the expense of another round.
>
> — Dawna Clarke, admissions director, Dartmouth–Tuck

MYTH #8: WRITING MY OWN RECOMMENDATION PUTS ME IN THE DRIVER'S SEAT

You get the courage to ask your boss for a recommendation and he not only agrees to do so, he goes even further and says, "Write it yourself and I will sign it." Writing your own recommendation letter can seem like a blessing. Suddenly, you have the power to oversee an aspect of the application process that was previously beyond your control. So, your downside risk in these letters is mitigated, and your upside is infinite, right? Well, things do not quite work that way.

Admissions committees are not seeking blustery rave reviews. Instead, they are seeking recommendations that are detailed and personal, intimate, and sincere. Can you really write about yourself with dispassionate sincerity? And even if you are a master of "dispassionate sincerity," are you able to capture the subtleties that make you stand out? For example, let's say that among the many important things you do, you also do something thoughtful that you do not even perceive to be significant—you always take new team members out to lunch. Although you may regard "closing the big deal" as significant, others may appreciate and admire this small but influential act, which helps forge team unity. Unfortunately, you may lack the objectivity necessary to ensure that this distinctive and impressive detail is included in your letter.

This is only one simple example, of course, but our point is that you probably will not know what is missing from your letter if you write it yourself. So when you approach your supervisor for a recommendation, go in ready to push back a bit if he or she asks you to write the letter yourself. Some may be busy or lazy, and others may think that they are doing you a favor by giving you control. Be prepared to impress upon your recommender that you can't help yourself but that he or she can. After all, that is why you are approaching your boss in the first place!

MYTH #9: HBS IS FOR EVERYONE

As strong a program as it offers, Harvard Business School simply is not the right fit for every single MBA candidate. We are not writing this to bash HBS—in fact, you can even replace "HBS" in our myth with the name of any other business school, because *no* program is truly appropriate for *every* candidate—but we are hoping that you will use this statement as a trigger to critically appraise your target MBA programs and determine which schools are truly best for you. Ask yourself the following questions to start:

- Would I prefer to be in a larger program, or would I be overwhelmed by a larger program's size?
- Would I prefer to be in a smaller program, or would it feel claustrophobic?
- Would I prefer to have a flexible curriculum with a consistent stream of new classmates and where I could make my own academic choices early on?
- Would I prefer to have a comprehensive core curriculum set out for me so that I am, for a period of time, learning the same material as my classmates according to a predetermined course structure?
- Am I best suited for programs that use the case method, the lecture method, or strong experiential components? (And do I really understand what each entails, such as the teamwork and public speaking that are necessary for the case method?)
- Do my target schools match my academic objectives?

- Do my target firms recruit at my target schools?
- Are alumni well placed in my target industry/post-MBA location? (Are alumni even important to my career?)
- Do my target schools have facilities and an environment that appeals to me?

Again, these questions are just a start—we could certainly pose many more. Our point is that you will get far more than a brand from your MBA studies. You will get an education and an alumni network, and you will spend two years of your life and thousands of dollars on your experience. So skip the rankings, determine what is important to you in your selection process, and then do your homework so you can pick the program that truly fits you and your needs.

MYTH #10: IF MY APPLICATION HAS A TYPO, I'M NOT GETTING IN

You have worked painstakingly on your application. You have checked and rechecked your work. You finally press "submit" and then discover—to your horror!—that you are missing a comma and in one place inadvertently used "too" instead of "to." The admissions committee is just going to throw your application out, right? Wrong.

There is a fine line between an isolated typo and pervasive sloppiness. If you have typos and grammatical errors throughout your application, you will send a negative message about your sense of professionalism and your ability to represent yourself—and in turn your target school—in a positive way. However, if you have just a minor mistake or two in your text, then you have an unfortunate situation, but not a devastating one. And let us note that there is no magic number of acceptable errors; three small mistakes will not necessarily disqualify you, either. Admissions committees understand that you are only human; if you are a strong candidate, the entirety of your professional, community, personal, and academic endeavors will outweigh these blips.

In short, don't dwell on the mistakes. Don't send new essays. Just accept your fallibility and move on.

So, there you have it—ten pervasive admissions myths destroyed. Now the key is to avoid the noise that is out there and not fall prey to other such myths. At **mbaMission.com**, we have an extensive blog with admissions tips, essay writing advice, admissions officer interviews, and much more. In addition, every Kaplan GMAT Advantage course or tutoring student is welcome to a free copy of our book *The Complete Start-to-Finish MBA Admissions Guide*. If you have further questions, we are always delighted to answer them via our free 30-minute consultation: Learn more at **www.mbamission.com/consult.php**.